The Other Emptiness

The Other Emptiness

Rethinking the Zhentong Buddhist Discourse in Tibet

Edited by

MICHAEL R. SHEEHY *and* KLAUS-DIETER MATHES

SUNY PRESS

Cover photograph by Michael R. Sheehy

Published by
State University of New York Press, Albany

For information, contact State University of New York Press, Albany, NY
www.sunypress.edu

Library of Congress Cataloging-in-Publication Data

Names: Sheehy, Michael R, [date–] editor. | Mathes, Klaus-Dieter, editor.
Title: The other emptiness : rethinking the Zhentong Buddhist discourse in Tibet / edited by Michael R. Sheehy and Klaus-Dieter Mathes.
Description: First edition. | Albany : State University of New York Press, 2020. | Includes bibliographical references and index.
Identifiers: LCCN 2019037744 (print) | LCCN 2019037745 (ebook) | ISBN 9781438477572 (hardcover) | ISBN 9781438477589 (pbk. : alk. paper) | ISBN 9781438477596 (ebook)
Subjects: LCSH: Sunyata | Buddhism—China—Tibet Autonomous Region—Doctrines.
Classification: LCC BQ4275 .O58 2020 (print) | LCC BQ4275 (ebook) | DDC 294.3/420423—dc23
LC record available at https://lccn.loc.gov/2019037744
LC ebook record available at https://lccn.loc.gov/2019037745

10 9 8 7 6 5 4 3 2 1

Contents

Acknowledgments vii

Introduction 1
The Philosophical Grounds and Literary History of Zhentong
Klaus-Dieter Mathes and Michael R. Sheehy

CHAPTER 1
**Bodhigarbha*: Preliminary Notes on an Early Dzokchen Family of Buddha-Nature Concepts 29
David Higgins

CHAPTER 2
On the Inclusion of Chomden Rikpai Raldri in Transmission Lineages of Zhentong 53
Tsering Wangchuk

CHAPTER 3
The Dharma of the Perfect Eon: Dolpopa Sherab Gyaltsen's Hermeneutics of Time and the Jonang Doxography of Zhentong Madhyamaka 65
Michael R. Sheehy

CHAPTER 4
Buddha-Nature in Garungpa Lhai Gyaltsen's *Lamp That Illuminates the Expanse of Reality* and among Tibetan Intellectuals 95
Dorje Nyingcha

CHAPTER 5
Zhentong Views in the Karma Kagyu Order 115
Klaus-Dieter Mathes

CHAPTER 6
Buddha-Nature: "Natural Awareness Endowed with Buddha Qualities" as Expounded by Zhamar Kacho Wangpo 145
Martina Draszczyk

CHAPTER 7
"There Are No Dharmas Apart from the Dharma-Sphere": Shakya Chokden's Interpretation of the Dharma-Sphere 171
Yaroslav Komarovski

CHAPTER 8
Tāranātha's *Twenty-One Differences with Regard to the Profound Meaning*: Comparing the Views of the Two Zhentong Masters Dolpopa and Shakya Chokden 197
Klaus-Dieter Mathes

CHAPTER 9
Zhentong Traces in the Nyingma Tradition: Two Texts from Mindroling 235
Matthew T. Kapstein

CHAPTER 10
Zhentong as Yogācāra: Mipam's Madhyamaka Synthesis 257
Douglas Duckworth

CHAPTER 11
Where Buddhas and Siddhas Meet: Mipam's Yuganaddhavāda Philosophy 273
Dorji Wangchuk

CHAPTER 12
Along the Middle Path in the Quest for Wisdom: The Great Madhyamaka in Rimé Discourses 323
Marc-Henri Deroche

CHAPTER 13
The Zhentong Lion Roars: Dzamtang Khenpo Lodro Drakpa and the Jonang Scholastic Renaissance 351
Michael R. Sheehy

Contributors 379

Index 383

Acknowledgments

This anthology on zhentong was several years in the making. The concept for this book first emerged with a conversation between Michele Martin and Michael Sheehy, and Michele kindly made the connection with State University of New York Press. The coeditors discussed the book in 2010 during the twenty-second congress of the International Association for Tibetan Studies in Vancouver. During that conference, Klaus-Dieter Mathes convened a panel on "The History of the *Rang-stong / Gzhan-stong* Distinction from Its Beginning through the *Ris-med* Movement," which included many of the authors contributing to the present volume. The proceedings of this panel were published in the *Journal of Buddhist Philosophy* 2 (2016): 4–131. The following year, Michael Sheehy convened a similar panel on "*Rang stong / Gzhan stong*: Perspectives on the Discourse in India and Tibet" at the sixteenth congress of the International Association of Buddhist Studies at Dharma Drum Buddhist College in Taipei, Taiwan. Though not all of the presenters in this panel are authors in this volume, and not all of the chapters by the authors in this volume were presented at the conference, it considerably helped to further organize the current authors into a cohort that catalyzed the contributions published in this book.

The editors would like to acknowledge and express their gratitude to the late Nancy Ellegate at State University of New York Press for taking an interest in publishing this volume, and for whimsically suggesting the title, *The Other Emptiness*, based on the literal translation ("being empty of other") of the topic that was mentioned offhand in an early conversation about the project. We would also like to thank James Peltz, codirector at State University of New York Press, for keeping the project alive after Nancy's untimely passing. And finally, we thank Christopher Ahn, senior acquisitions editor at the press, for his commitment to publishing this volume as quickly as possible. Last but not least, we would also like to express our gratitude to Michele Martin for critically reading the introduction.

Introduction

The Philosophical Grounds and Literary History of Zhentong

Klaus-Dieter Mathes and Michael R. Sheehy

Though the subject of emptiness (*śūnyatā*, *stong pa nyid*) is relatively well established in English-language texts on Buddhism, it is usually presented only as the emptiness of lacking independent existence or, more literally, the emptiness of an own nature (*svabhāva*, *rang bzhin*). However, the general reader of English literature on Buddhism may not be aware that such an understanding of emptiness reflects a particular interpretation of it, advanced predominantly by the Sakya, Kadam, and Geluk orders, which has exercised a particularly strong influence on the dissemination of Buddhist studies and philosophy in the West. In Tibetan discourse, this position is referred to as *rangtong* (*rang stong*), which means that everything, including the omniscience of a Buddha, is taken to be empty of an own nature. It is this lack of independent, locally determined building blocks of the world that allows in Madhyamaka the Buddhist axiom of dependent origination. In other words, rangtong emptiness is the a priori condition for a universe full of open, dynamic systems. The union of dependent origination and emptiness—the inseparability of appearance and emptiness—sets the ground for philosophical models of interrelatedness that are increasingly used in attempts to accommodate astonishing observations being made in the natural sciences, such as wave-particle duality or quantum entanglement.

Throughout the long intellectual history of Indian and Tibetan Buddhism, one of the major questions that remains unresolved is whether a systematic presentation of the Buddha's doctrine requires challenging rangtong as the exclusive mode of emptiness, which has led some to distinguish between two modes of emptiness: (1) *Rangtong (rang stong)*, that is, being empty of an own nature on the one hand, and (2) *Zhentong (gzhan stong)*, that is, being empty of everything other than luminous awareness or buddha-nature (*tathāgatagarbha, de bzhin gshegs pa'i snying po*). In later Indian and Tibetan Buddhism, when such tensions emerged, the issue was not so much about a possible justification for this distinction on the basis of certain philosophical scriptures, but rather competing hermeneutical schemes that consistently interpret the entire corpus of what was accepted to be the words of the Buddha.

While proponents of zhentong (*zhentongpas*) underline the necessity of this "empty of other emptiness," the followers of rangtong (*rangtongpas*) oppose it. Rangtongpas insist that one must follow the seventh-century Indian Buddhist scholar Candrakīrti's lead in taking the second turning cycle of teachings, which he defines as exclusively emphasizing rangtong emptiness, to be the underlying intention of any positive statement about the ultimate. Zhentongpas do not consider themselves in direct opposition to Candrakīrti but follow a strategy of inclusivism. Within their system, rangtong is understood to be a necessary basis for a correct realization of zhentong. Even though they repeatedly describe ultimate truth or reality as possessing qualities that are not empty of their own nature, it is critical to realize that these are beyond mental fabrications or reifications that are empty of an own nature as in the rangtong system.

Zhentongpas thus argue that Candrakīrti must have tacitly admitted something more than the mere nominal existence of everything (rangtong). In fact, MacDonald observes that for the Mādhyamika as a yogin, the final goal and state is not nothingness but transcendent knowing or wisdom (*jñāna*).[1] Moreover, one can discern in the *Lokātītastava* that Nāgārjuna (fl. 200 CE) indirectly accepts something more real behind the seeming, when he says in verse 7ab: "If a name and its object were not different, one's mouth would be burned by [the word] fire."[2] It should also be noted that the *Samādhirāja Sūtra*, which lends support to Madhyamaka, recognizes the ordinary factors of existence (*dharmas*) as buddha-qualities (*buddhadharmas*) for those who are trained in the "true nature of dharmas" (*dharmatā*).[3] In other words, all factors of existence, inasmuch as they are a mentally created misperception, need to be established as rangtong. This leads to a nonconceptual realization of their inconceivable and ineffable true reality that is zhentong in the sense of being empty of any reification that would be "other" to it.

ZHENTONG SOURCE LITERATURE

Literary sources for zhentong are cited by Tibetan authors in their multifaceted exegetics as coming from the canon of certain Indian Mahāyāna sūtras, that is, the so-called *Essence Sūtras* or *Sūtras on the Definitive Meaning*, along with their *śāstras* or scholastic commentarial treatises, and Tibetan authors also cite Buddhist tantra. By the time Tibetans began to receive Indic Buddhist textual traditions, two major doctrinal shifts had occurred in Indian Mahāyāna Buddhism: (1) the Madhyamaka teaching that all factors of existence (*dharma*)—which according to Abhidharma consist of an own nature (*svabhāva*)—are devoid of any such thing,[4] and (2) the Yogācāra[5] interpretation of emptiness as being based on the three natures (*trisvabhāva, rang bzhin gsum*),[6] that is, the imagined (*parikalpitasvabhāva*), dependent (*paratantrasvabhāva*), and perfect natures (*pariniṣpannasvabhāva*). The current state of research still does not allow precise dates for these two phases of development, but the *Akṣayamatinirdeśa Sūtra*, which lends doctrinal support for the Madhyamaka shift, must have already been in circulation at the time of Nāgārjuna (fl. 200 CE). The *Sandhinirmocana Sūtra*, which contains the Yogācāra interpretation of emptiness, has been dated to about 300 CE by Schmithausen.[7]

Parallel to this development, there emerged a group of sūtras, known as the Tathāgatagarbha sūtras. Again, it is difficult to provide dates, but according to Mitrikeski, the *Śrīmālādevī Sūtra* must have been already around at the beginning of the third century CE, while the compilation period of the *Mahāparinirvāṇa Sūtra* is estimated to be even earlier than that.[8] Zimmermann takes the *Tathāgatagarbha Sūtra*[9] to be the earliest exposition of the buddha-nature teaching in India.[10]

The Sanskrit term *tathāgatagarbha* is mainly taken as a *bahuvrīhi* compound referring to all sentient beings, whose nature (*garbha*) is a *tathāgata*, that is, a buddha. That means that everybody has already a fully grown buddha within.[11] Even though this doctrine shares with Yogācāra a positive description of the ultimate that lends support to zhentong, the two systems differ considerably in their respective presentations of fundamental transformation (*āśrayaparivṛtti, gnas yongs su gyur pa*). The majority of Tathāgatagarbha sūtras describe a primordially complete buddha within that will be disclosed; however, in Yogācāra, one's buddhahood must be generated from the two potentials: the *dharmakāya* from the naturally present potential (*prakṛtisthagotra, rang bzhin gnas pa'i rigs*), and the form *kāyas* from the acquired potential (*samudānītagotra, yang dag pa blang ba'i rigs*).[12]

The two doctrines of original Yogācāra and Tathāgatagarba were merged in the Maitreya works.[13] While the *Ratnagotravibhāga*[14] underwent a systematic Yogācāra-reinterpretation of the buddha-nature doctrine,[15] the *Mahāyānasūtrālaṃkāra, Madhyāntavibhāga*, and *Dharmadharmatāvibhāga* show influences of buddha-nature thought.[16] The resulting variety of Indian doctrines that attribute positive qualities to the basis of negation, which is mostly equivalent with the ultimate, lends support to various forms of zhentong.

The differences between the Jonangpas and Shakya Chokden (1428–1507) can be mainly understood by comparing the original buddha-nature doctrine to its Yogācāra interpretation.[17] In the former the basis of emptiness is something permanently (in the sense of transcending time) ultimate and primordially endowed with all buddha qualities. In the latter, it is the dynamic principle of a naturally present potential that causes a buddha's *svābhāvikakāya* or dharmakāya. This is most clearly elaborated in Tāranātha's (1575–1635) *Twenty-One Differences with Regard to the Profound Meaning* (*Zab don nyer gcig pa*), a short text that compares the views of Dolpopa Sherab Gyaltsen (1292–1361) and Shakya Chokden in twenty-one points. It was translated and discussed by Mathes in 2004.[18]

Notwithstanding these differences, Yogācāra and buddha-nature theories were eventually subsumed under the Buddha's third turning of the Wheel of Dharma as described within the Yogācāra doxography of the *Sandhinirmocana Sūtra*.[19] The relevant sūtra passage utilizes the metaphor of the Buddha's dharma wheel, which turns without effort like the wheel in front of the emperor (*cakravartin*). The Madhyamaka and Yogācāra / buddha-nature interpretations of the Prajñāpāramitā sūtras are assigned to the second and third dharma wheels, respectively.

The initial turning comprises the teaching of the Four Noble Truths for those who were genuinely engaged on the *śrāvaka* path.[20] The second turning refers to the emptiness of the Prajñāpāramitā sūtras, as commented in the analytical Madhyamaka works of Nāgārjuna.[21] It is described as follows: "Then the Illustrious One turned a second wheel of dharma for those who were genuinely engaged in the Mahāyāna. It is more wonderous still, because of the aspect of teaching emptiness, beginning with the lack of an own nature of phenomena, and beginning with their absence of production, absence of cessation, quiescence from the start, and being naturally in a state of *nirvāṇa*."[22] The third turning is defined by the same formula as that of the second turning, with two exceptions: it is meant for followers of all *yāna*s and offers, in addition to the second turning, fine distinctions (*rnam par phye ba dang ldan pa*). The context of this sūtra passage makes it clear that they refer to the Yogācāra interpretation of Prajñāpāramitā emptiness in terms of the three natures (imagined, dependent, and perfect natures). In view of this distinction the third turning has definitive meaning (*nītārtha*, *nges don*) (as opposed to the first two) for it helps, in the eyes of the Yogācāras, to avoid a nihilistic interpretation of the Prajñāpāramitā sūtras.[23]

These three Wheels of Dharma categorize the entire Buddhist canon of the sūtras. Most Tibetans, however, did not follow the *Sandhinirmocana Sūtra*'s attribution, or at least exclusive attribution, of definitive meaning to the third turning. As is discussed and explored by contributors in this volume, the Tibetan hermeneutic enterprise sought to decipher which set of sūtras represented the definitive view of the Buddha and then reconcile the doctrinal paradoxes and tensions therein. In so doing, second turning sūtras are equated with rangtong, while third turning sūtras are equated with zhentong, giving rise to the textual foundations of the rangtong / zhentong distinction, and the discourse that ensued in Tibet.

Within the Tibetan commentarial tradition, there are three, to some extent, overlapping sets of sūtras that are cited as background for the zhentong literary tradition.[24] They share in common positive descriptions of the ultimate, such as the natural luminosity of mind or buddha-nature. In addition to these core Mahāyāna sūtras, the Indic śāstra commentarial literature that is most frequently cited within zhentong exegetical works is the *Five Maitreya Works* (*Byams chos lde lnga*). Attributed to the future Buddha Maitreya, these five treatises comprise a systematic summary and interpretation of the three sets of sūtras mentioned earlier that are relevant to zhentong. The first text, the *Ornament of Realization* (*Abhisamayālaṃkāra*) summarizes the Prajñāpāramitā sūtras in a way compatible with Yogācāra and buddha-nature thought. It is followed by the *Ornament of Great Vehicle Discourses* (*Mahāyānasūtrālaṃkāra*), which groups mainly Yogācāra topics into twenty-one chapters. The three remaining *vibhāga*s are an analysis (*vibhāga*) of different subject matters. The *Analysis of the Jewel Family* (*Ratnagotravibhāga*) is the standard Indian treatise on buddha-nature and buddhahood. The *Analysis of the Middle and Extremes* (*Madhyāntavibhāga*) defines a "Yogācāra middle way" on the basis of the Prajñāpāramitā sūtras. Finally, the *Analysis of Phenomena and Their True Nature* (*Dharmadharmatāvibhāga*) is a Yogācāra work, which distinguishes between the ordinary phenomenal world (*dharmas*) and the true nature of these phenomena (dharmatā).

In all Maitreya works except the *Abhisamayālaṃkāra*, whose topic is Prajñāpāramitā, we find a synthesis of Yogācāra and Tathāgatagarbha models of reality. As this synthesis avoids the flaws common to Yogācāra tenets, namely, that a considerable group of sentient beings is completely cut off from liberation or that a dependently arising mind exists on the level of ultimate truth,[25] zhentongpas could defend this synthesis as a teaching that asserts definitive meaning. Embracing buddha-nature doctrine helps to explain away the notion of a completely cut-off potential in the *Mahāyānasūtrālaṃkāra*, since it can be pointed out that everybody is a buddha within, or at least has the potential to become a buddha. The problem of an ultimately existing mind can be solved by restricting the existence of the dependent nature, which is the mind in Yogācāra, to the level of relative truth. This move also allows for including the dependent within the *Ratnagotravibhāga*'s adventitious stains that cover buddha-nature, which is then identified with the mind's perfect nature, or suchness, an equation supported by *Mahāyānasūtrālaṃkāra* IX.37.[26] This finds further support from Asaṅga, who explains buddha-nature in his commentary on *Ratnagotravibhāga* I.148 in terms of the Yogācāra concept of luminosity, a quality of the perfect nature.[27] In the final analysis[28] of the *Ratnagotravibhāga* and the closely related *Dharmadharmatāvibhāga*, the luminous perfect nature is taken to be empty of adventitious stains. In other words, it is empty of the imagined and dependent, inasmuch as the latter is false imagining (*abhūtaparikalpa*), the term used instead of the dependent nature in the *Dharmadharmatāvibhāga*.

The final version of the *Ratnagotravibhāga*—Takasaki and Schmithausen identified older layers of this text[29]—was translated by Ratnamati into Chinese in 508 CE.[30] Schmithausen[31] dates the oldest strand with its original buddha-nature doctrine to the beginning of the fourth-century CE, namely, the time when the doctrinally close ninth chapter of the *Mahāyānasūtrālaṃkāra* was composed. The later strands of the *Ratnagotravibhāga* are mostly commentaries exhibiting a systematic Yogācāra interpretation, that is, taking buddha-nature only as a dynamic potential from which the dharmakāya of a buddha emerges. They are doctrinally and probably also chronologically close to the *Madhyāntavibhāga* and *Dharmadharmatāvibhāga*.[32]

Both the *Dharmadharmatāvibhāga* and *Ratnagotravibhāga* were ignored in India up to the eleventh-century CE. Things changed, however, when Maitrīpa (986–1063) brought tantric Mahāmudrā teachings from his teacher Śavaripa into mainstream Mahāyāna. The aforementioned synthesis of Yogācāra and buddha-nature theory provided good doctrinal support for Maitrīpa's enterprise. He used the experiential terms of Yogācāra to describe the nonconceptual realization of a Madhyamaka emptiness that radically transcends all forms of reification.[33] Traditional accounts further underline the important role Maitrīpa played in the transmission of *Dharmadharmatāvibhāga* and the *Ratnagotravibhāga*. Maitrīpa rediscovered and taught these two texts to *Ānandakīrti and Sajjana. In cooperation with Sajjana, the Tibetan scholar Ngok Loden Sherab (1059–1109) translated the *Ratnagotravibhāga* and its *vyākhyā* into Tibetan.

Loden Sherab explained buddha-nature in terms of nonaffirming negations (*prasajyapratiṣedha, med par dgag pa*), that is, as the rangtong emptiness of mind. That means that anything that appears as inherently existent during the investigation of one's mind is simply negated, without implying the existence of anything else, or another mode of existence. With such an understanding, Loden Sherab founded what is known as the "analytical tradition" (*mtshan nyid lugs*) of interpreting the Maitreya works. The corresponding "contemplative tradition" (*sgom lugs*) was founded by a disciple of Drapa Ngonshe Kawoche, known as Tsen Kawoche (b. 1021). He requested Sajjana teach him the Maitreya works as pith instructions since he wanted to make these works his "practice [of preparing] for death" (*'chi chos*). Sajjana taught him all five works of Maitreya with Lotsāwa Zu Gawe Dorje acting as the translator,[34] and gave special pith instructions on the *Ratnagotravibhāga*. This is the popular account given in Go Lotsāwa Zhonnu Pel's *Blue Annals*.[35]

Maitrīpa's teacher at Vikramaśīla, Jñānaśrīmitra (ca. 980–1040),[36] however, already knew the *Dharmadharmatāvibhāga* and *Ratnagotravibhāga* when he composed his *Sākārasiddhiśāstra*[37] and *Sākārasaṃgraha*.[38] A commentary on the *Ratnagotravibhāga*, transmitted by the Nartang abbot Kyoton Monlam Tsultrim (1219–1299), the *Instructions on the Supreme Continuum* further suggests that the *Ratnagotravibhāga* had not been lost before Maitrīpa.[39]

The third turning gives numerous positive descriptions of ultimate reality in teachings on the luminosity of awareness and buddha-nature while also making a clear-cut distinction between this positive ultimate and the adventitious stains of a suffering mind. These traits are not only found in the Maitreya works. Proponents of zhentong, or proto-zhentong in early Tibetan intellectual history, had been pointing out that the commentaries on the Buddha's third turning also include Nāgārjuna's *Collection of Hymns* and all Mahāyāna exegetes accept that this collection was composed by Nāgārjuna. In his *Dharmadhātustava* or *Praise to the Source of Buddha Qualities*, Nāgārjuna thus explains that the fire of wisdom only burns the adventitious defilements, but not the luminous mind:[40]

> When one puts [a piece of cloth] tainted by various stains over a fire, the cloth is purified as the fire burns the stains away. Likewise, luminous mind is tainted by stains arisen from desire, and wisdom burns these stains away but not the luminous [mind]. Those sūtras taught by the Victorious Ones in order to reveal emptiness—all eliminate defilements but do not diminish this [*dharma*]*dhātu*.[41]

This supports a hermeneutic that takes the third turning more literally, as Nāgārjuna clearly restricts the discourses on rangtong emptiness to the spiritual defilements. Zhentong writings frequently cite Nāgārjuna's *Dharmadhātustava* as well as his other hymns of praise in contrast to Nāgārjuna's *Collection on Reasoning* where he unequivocally relays the *via negationis* of the Madhyamaka of the second turning.[42]

To sum up, the canonical sources for zhentong are the *Five Maitreya Works*, Nāgārjuna's hymns along with the sūtra discourses of the third turning referred to as *Essence Sūtras* or also *Sūtras on the Definitive Meaning*.[43]

Candrakīrti's critique of the underlying Yogācāra hermeneutic of the *Sandhinirmocana Sūtra* is opposed by explaining the three natures in a way that is compatible with Madhyamaka and buddha-nature theory. Zhentongpas also point out that their preferred mode of emptiness is not the *Laṅkāvatāra Sūtra*'s inferior "emptiness of the one from the other" (*itaretaraśūnyatā*), but the "great emptiness of ultimate meaning, which is the wisdom of the Noble Ones" (*paramārthārya-jñānamahāśūnyatā*). In line with zhentong, the latter is explained as empty of all faults inherent in views and the related mental imprints. From a zhentong point of view, Candrakīrti's strategy of ascribing "Mind-Only"[44] and buddha-nature theories provisional meaning on the basis of the *Laṅkāvātara Sūtra* could be questioned on the grounds that this sūtra's understanding of emptiness is not rangtong but based on the Yogācāra theory of three natures. This is most evident in the *Laṅkāvatāra Sūtra*'s introduction to the list of seven types of emptiness, "The illustrious one said this: 'Emptiness—what is called emptiness—Mahāmati, is a word for the imagined nature. Again, Mahāmati, since [you people] obstinately cling to the imagined nature, we [must] talk about emptiness, nonarising, nonduality, and the nature of essencelessness.' "[45]

Zhentong Philosophy in Tibet

The most prominent proponent of zhentong, Dolpopa Sherab Gyaltsen opposes an exclusive rangtong interpretation of emptiness. In his eyes, this common mode of emptiness does not account for the emptiness of the *unchanging* perfect nature (*nirvikāra-pariniṣpanna, 'gyur ba med pa'i yongs grub*),[46] which is not empty of its own nature. Emptiness in terms of the unchanging perfect nature refers to the absence of the momentary, unmistaken (*aviparyāsa, phyin ci ma log pa'i*) perfect nature as well as the imagined and dependent natures, the underlying relationship between the basis of negation and that which is negated being zhentong.[47] Dolpopa's basis of negation is the ultimate, which must be realized as being free from mental fabrications.[48] This means that the object of negation also includes the extreme of ontological existence. Ultimate or true existence means for Dolpopa that the realization of the dharmakāya or ultimate body of reality is genuine (*don dam du bden*).[49] Relative truth is taken to be empty of a true own nature, while the ultimate is not empty of such an own nature. For instance, in his *Sun That Clarifies the Two Truths*, Dolpopa writes:

> Any object of consciousness, that which is, from its own side, empty of a true own nature, is the defining characteristic of relative truth. Any object of the genuine wisdom of the Noble Ones, that which is, from

its own side, not empty of its respective own nature, is the defining characteristic of the ultimate.[50]

In other words, for Dolpopa relative truth is rangtong and ultimate truth zhentong. This zhentong definition is similar to the *Laṅkāvatāra Sūtra*'s great emptiness that is the ultimate meaning, which is the wisdom of the Noble Ones, and mainly profits from a particular understanding of the central Yogācāra concept of the three natures as found in Vasubandhu's *Extensive Commentary*, the *Bṛhaṭṭīkā*.[51] The more traditional Yogācāra formula of the dependent nature being empty of the imagined nature, as found in the *Madhyāntavibhāga*, must then be taken only as a distinction between the real and imputed on the level of relative truth. The *Madhyāntavibhāga* thus retains a central value for Dolpopa, as he adduces from this important Maitreya work the Yogācāra explanation of sixteen forms of emptiness. The second-to-last emptiness summarizes the first fourteen as the nonexistence of the personal self and phenomena, and thus differs from the last one, which is the true existence of this nonexistence.[52] According to Dolpopa, this establishes a separate mode of emptiness, namely, zhentong.

In all fairness to Dolpopa's reasoning, it should be noted that in the second part of the first chapter of the *Madhyāntavibhāga* a positively understood emptiness takes the central role that dependent nature enjoys in the common model of the three natures.[53] This replaces or rather extends the traditional Yogācāra formula of three natures so that the imagined and dependent natures now fall into the category of adventitious stains, which fits Dolpopa's zhentong definition.[54] For Dolpopa, as Michael Sheehy explains in his chapter, zhentong emptiness was framed not only as the perfect philosophical teaching but as dharma for the Perfect Eon that is reflective of a cosmological vision of Buddhist time.

Though Dolpopa was probably the most influential proponent of zhentong, the forebearers of a rangtong / zhentong distinction can be identified in a variety of Indian texts and early Kadam manuscripts.[55] Positive descriptions of the ultimate are mainly justified by a master's direct access to the luminous nature of mind, as taught in the various traditions of Mahāmudrā or Dzokchen. As David Higgins shows in his chapter in this volume, from the eighth through the eleventh centuries, Nyingma authors employed the concept of **bodhigarbha* (*byang chub snying po*), as opposed to the term buddha-nature, in the early exegesis of Dzokchen. Dolpopa gained his decisive zhentong understanding through his practice of the sixfold yoga (*ṣaḍaṅgayoga*) during a meditation retreat on Kālacakra. Thus, it was his practice that allowed him to speak of the real and the true nature. Systems that include descriptions of realization found doctrinal support in the third turning cycle of teaching, which is not only based on the doctrine of emptiness but also distinguishes, as we have seen, between the imputed and the real—that is, phenomena and their true nature or adventitious stains and buddha-nature.

Of particular interest for the history of zhentong are the prototypes of it that can be identified in texts written and/or transmitted by Kadam masters at

Nartang Monastery in south central Tibet. As explored by Tsering Wangchuk in this volume, writings by the Kadam master Chomden Rikpai Raldri (1227–1305) cast a positive interpretation of buddha-nature, citing sources from both sūtras and tantras. Inheritance of the zhentong lineage is further complexed by one of Rikdrel's root teachers, the Eighth Abbot of Nartang Monastery, Kyoton Monlam Tsultrim. In two works by Kyoton, the *Instructions on the Supreme Continuum on the Great Way* and the *Guidance Based on the Analysis of Phenomena and Their True Nature*, textual transmission lineages record a succession of masters that include the translator Lotsāwa Zu Gawai Dorje and Tsen Kawoche.[56] Both of these masters studied with the ever-elusive eleventh-century Paṇḍita Sajjana in Kashmir. Sajjana figured prominently in the transmission of the Maitreya works by interpreting the third turning to be a teaching of definitive meaning, precisely because the distinctions between the real and imputed, and so forth, are necessary for upholding zhentong. As expressed by the Jonang scholar Kunga Drolchok (1507–1566) in his *Lineage History of the One-Hundred-and-Eight Instructions*:

> Sajjana, the paṇḍita from Kashmir, made the very significant statement that the Victorious One turned the Wheel of Dharma three times. The first turning concerned the Four Noble Truths; the middle turning the lack of defining characteristics; and the final turning careful distinctions. The first two did not distinguish between the real and the imputed. During the ultimate ascertainment of the final turning, [the Buddha] taught by distinguishing between the middle and the extremes (*madhyāntavibhāga*) and by distinguishing between phenomena and their true nature (*dharmadharmatāvibhāga*).[57]

The particular transmission linked to Sajjana via Tsen Kawoche interprets the *Five Maitreya Works* positively, emphasizing the effulgence of luminosity and the buddha-nature they reveal. This became the touchstone hermeneutic for the zhentong philosophical and contemplative tradition. Though Tsen Kawoche's writings are no longer available, fortunately, Kunga Drolchok preserved one pith instruction on zhentong by this master in his anthology, *The One-Hundred-and-Eight Instructions of the Jonang*. As Kunga Drolchok notes in his brief preface, this instruction is based on an old notebook by Tsen Kawoche called the *Iron-Hook of the Lotus*, giving us a reference to an early literary source for zhentong.[58] This short pith instruction on zhentong brings together the three natures in a manner that was later identified as being in harmony with zhentong as made explicit within the writings of Dolpopa and later Jonangpa authors. Here is the latter part of this concise text, the only surviving work by Tsen Kawoche, the *Instructions on the Zhentong View*:

> Although classified as three natures without an own nature, if you analyze—since there are no fixations and there is nothing to fixate on besides the mind—only the phenomenal quality of the dependent

> nature and the phenomenal actuality of the perfect nature are free from defilements. They are the identical ultimate actuality of phenomena that is spontaneously present.
>
> In this way, the imagined nature is devoid of an own nature, like a hare's horns. The dependent nature is devoid of the imagined nature, like an illusion. The perfect nature is devoid of both the imagined nature and the dependent nature, like space. Distinctions between the imagined and the dependent are relative, not ultimate. The perfect, the true nature of phenomena is the ultimate. This is the Great Madhyamaka: free from extremes without being in any way either identical or different in essence from the phenomenal quality of relative reality.[59]

Tsen Kawoche's instruction combines here the traditional Yogācāra emptiness—the dependent being devoid of the imagined, with the *Bṛhaṭṭīkā* emptiness—the perfect being devoid of the imagined and dependent. For the Jonangpas, however, a further step was still needed, namely, the restriction of the ultimate to the invariable perfect nature that is devoid not only of any imagined or relational elaborations but also the unmistaken perfect nature. In any case, Tsen Kawoche had set the course for subsequent zhentong interpretations of the three natures.

Apart from minor discrepancies in the lineages between Tsen Kawoche and Kyoton, the lineage records match with Tāranātha's *Supplication to the Profound Zhentong Madhyamaka Lineage*.[60] This links zhentong thought to an important master of the mainstream thirteenth-century Kadam tradition. Kyoton's *Instructions on the Supreme Continuum* equate buddha-nature with self-arisen wisdom and the dharmakāya, while presenting the four perfections of the dharmakāya as a teaching of definitive meaning.[61] In his *Repository of Wisdom* (*Ye shes kyi 'jog sa*) as well, Kyoton claims that the nature of mind is self-arisen wisdom, a buddha. Of particular interest in this text is Kyoton's explanation that self-arisen wisdom is nothing other than thoughts when their luminous nature is realized; this should be understood in contrast to the self-awareness of the Mind-Only tenet that one realizes appearances are appearances of thought.[62] In other words, this zhentong prototype is clearly distinguished from the tenet of Mind-Only.

Moreover, in Kyoton's *Instructions on Madhyamaka*, which are said to be meditation instructions by Atiśa, the final state of nirvāṇa is not only described negatively as the nonappearance of all phenomena but also taken to be luminosity that is free from all mental fabrications.[63] If such teachings were transmitted by Kadampas at Nartang, it is possible that such prototypes of zhentong were transmitted from Sajjana to Dolpopa or other masters associated with zhentong.

With Dolpopa and his immediate disciples in the early to mid-fourteenth century, zhentong became a source of controversy and polemic in Tibet. As Dolpopa's teachings attracted a wide audience among intellectuals, many of the philosophical giants of the day, including Buton Rinchen Drub (1290–1364), Remdawa Zhonnu Lodro (1349–1412), and their disciples, composed polemical works to counter

Dolpopa's view. Dorje Nyingcha's contribution elaborates a text, *The Lamp That Illuminates the Expanse of Reality*, by one of Dolpopa's fourteen main disciples, Garungpa Lhai Gyaltsen (1319–1402/03), which is a response to critiques of the Jonang philosophical presentation of zhentong. Garungpa sets his hermeneutic to resolve which of the Buddha's teachings are definitive. Relying on the logic that the Buddha himself answered this question in the *Sandhinirmocana Sūtra*, he argues that this sūtra is the basis for solving such a problem. In applying the maxim that teachings delivered by the Buddha in his third turning are definitive, Garungpa treats buddha-nature and statements made in tantras to be definitive as well. Garungpa's text is of interest not only because it preserves an early Jonang defense, but also because it preserves arguments made against the Jonang presentation of zhentong by others, most notably Tsongkhapa's (1357–1419) mentor Remdawa.[64]

Some zhentong masters, such as Shakya Chokden, diverge considerably from Dolpopa. In his chapter, Yaroslav Komarovski details Shakya Chokden's zhentong perspective that except for the *dharmadhātu* (*chos dbyings*) or source of buddha qualities, no conventional phenomena are established by valid cognition, which amounts to saying that none of them exist. Shakya Chokden's position, therefore, is that whether they accept the actual dharmadhātu or not, all Madhyamaka systems share the same view that no other phenomena exist apart from it. In the case of Shakya Chokden's zhentong, this position entails that whatever is subsumed under the category of the dharmadhātu is automatically accepted as existent in reality. In the case of rangtong systems, however, this position entails that even that which is subsumed under the category of the dharmadhātu does not exist. While Dolpopa's basis of negation is an independent ultimate beyond space and time, Shakya Chokden defines his basis of negation as the dependent nature that exists on a relative level. Subsequently, the ultimate truth is taken to be nondual wisdom that does not transcend momentariness. For Tāranātha this constitutes the main difference between Shakya Chokden and Dolpopa.[65] These two presentations of zhentong must be distinguished from more moderate presentations, such as the ones of the Seventh and the Eighth Karmapas, which admit a rangtong mode of emptiness for both the adventitious stains of relative truth as well as the ultimate nature of mind. Nonetheless, zhentong is made explicit when a contemplative practitioner with an immediate experience of the ultimate nature must distinguish the latter from the adventitious stains of mind, which do not reflect how the nature of mind truly is.

In alignment with Shakya Chokden's view of emptiness are several hierarchs of the Kagyu tradition of Tibetan Buddhism. As Klaus-Dieter Mathes makes evident in his chapter, the Kagyu presentation of zhentong is sparse and differs considerably from the Jonang presentation of zhentong. A critical difference is that for Kagyu exegetes both the basis of emptiness (*stong gzhi*) and its object of negation (*dgag bya*) are taken to be empty of an own nature, that is, rangtong. An exception is Mikyo Dorje's (1507–1554) *Abhisamayālaṃkāra* commentary, where the young Eighth Karmapa claims with reference to *Ratnagotravibhāga* I.155c that the qualities of dharmatā are not empty of an own nature (*rang gi ngo bo*), which means in this context that these qualities are inseparably connected with buddha-nature. This does not require an inherent existence of either buddha-nature or its qualities, though. Apart from this instance, Mikyo Dorje endorses zhentong only as the absence of adventitious stains from natural luminosity or buddha-nature, while everything, including buddha-nature is rangtong only. The First Karma Trinle (1456–1539) likely had such a moderate zhentong view in mind when he described the Third Karmapa Rangjung Dorje (1284–1339) and the Seventh Karmapa Chodrak Gyatso (1454–1506) to be zhentongpas. Other Kagyu hierarchs, perhaps most notably the Second Zhamarpa Kacho Wangpo (1350-1405), endorsed zhentong in terms of conventional reality. Explained by Martina Draszczyk in her contribution, the Second Zhamarpa's text, *A Dharma Discourse Clarifying Emptiness from the Perspective of Those Who Have Entered the Supremely Profound*, provides a comparison of rangtong / zhentong. Pointing out that the mind is not merely essenceless, but coemergent with wisdom, Kacho Wangpo emphasizes the ever-present luminous nature of mind. In fact, when referring to the ultimate, he is careful not to reify the nature of the mind and its qualities stating, "when one is not supposed to hold on to phenomena as emptiness, what need is there to mention clinging to them as having characteristics such as permanence, etc." Following this, the Eighth Karmapa Mikyo Dorje explicitly took issue with what he framed to be a Jonang substantialist view of buddha-nature as an ultimate permanent entity.

Throughout the sixteenth-century, more than a generation after the height of the rangtong / zhentong polemics of the late fourteenth and fifteenth centuries, new writings on zhentong continued to be created while views were modified and reinterpreted, including by authors already mentioned—Shakya Chokden, the First Karma Trinle, and the Seventh and Eighth Karmapas. Besides these authors, modern scholars have thought that this was a blackout period for writings on zhentong and that Jonangpa authors did not compose works on zhentong after Dolpopa's disciples up to Tāranātha. Though there is certainly a scarcity of zhentong literature that survives from the sixteenth century, we know from a recent discovery inside Tibet that Kunga Drolchok—the Sakya and Shangpa Kagyu master who was the twenty-fourth throne-holder at Jonang—did, in fact, compose at least one work on zhentong, which was a concise instruction text titled *Profound Points of the Zhentong View*.[66] This finding not only fills a lacuna at this critical juncture in the literary history of zhentong but also serves as a reminder of how much of the Tibetan literary archive remains inaccessible or is forever lost.

After Dolpopa, the most prolific author on zhentong was Tāranātha, who spent much of his early career reviving the arts and literature of the Jonang tradition and constructing its citadel monastic seat at Takten Puntsok Ling. When these efforts were threatened by local political conflict, Tāranātha began to write extensively on zhentong in order to preserve the Jonang tradition. Tāranātha knew that Dolpopa's zhentong view was not only controversial in the mainstream scholastic circuits, but that it had been publicly denounced from the throne at Jonang by Orgyen Dzongpa, a previous holder of the monastic seat.[67] After a decade of tireless revival efforts, by 1604 Tāranātha was faced not only with preserving the reputation of Jonang but with protecting its monastic seat from the imminent danger of being attacked by the armies who were fighting in the political wars between the regions of Jang and Tsang in southern Tibet. As Tāranātha recorded in his autobiography, during a moment of utter despondence, he went to meditate at the Great Stūpa of Jonang. Disheartened by the warfare and troubles all around him, Tāranātha prayed to Dolpopa for reassurance and clarity. Dolpopa appeared to him in a vision and encouraged Tāranātha to persevere. This led to a succession of visions and dreams of Dolpopa, during which Tāranātha recorded in his autobiography that he gained the realization of Dolpopa's true intent and vision of zhentong. To express his understanding and explicate zhentong, he composed the versified text, *Ornament of Zhentong Madhyamaka*.[68]

Tāranātha also composed numerous concise works on zhentong that continue to be studied within the contemporary Jonang scholastic curriculum. In addition to these short seminal works, including *Essence of Zhentong* and *Ascertaining the Two Systems: An Entrance into the Definitive Meaning*, there was his multivolume masterpiece, the *Supreme Vehicle of Zhentong Madhyamaka*, which was compiled by his students up to his death in order to record his commentary on the central points of zhentong philosophical thinking. After Tāranātha's passing in 1635, however, his project to revive the Jonang and preserve Dolpopa's zhentong philosophy of emptiness fell into disarray. By 1650, fifteen years after Tāranātha's death, Takten Puntsok Ling Monastery was confiscated by the Ganden Potrang central government of the Fifth Dalai Lama Ngawang Lozang Gyatso (1617–1682), and the Jonang philosophical studies curriculum was converted to Geluk. However, as is evident from the Fifth Dalai Lama's account, Jonang monks continued to teach zhentong in the mountain hermitages above Takten Puntsok Ling Monastery and in its vicinity until the monastery was officially converted in the year 1658.[69] This persistence to study and transmit zhentong after the monastery was confiscated became a further reason for the Gandenpa authorities to target zhentong. In his autobiographical reflections on this historical moment, and why the curriculum required conversion, the Fifth Dalai Lama writes:

> As is clear, not only is the curriculum enormously important for the monastic community, but the most worthwhile scholastic curriculum is extremely rare. According to the tulku of Takten, there was a naïve conviction [at Takten Puntsok Ling Monastery] that was the reason for a partiality to zhentong. By completely denigrating the followers of the protector Nāgārjuna, many beings blinded themselves and were led to the lower realms where they are prevented from being saved.[70]

With the conversion of the Jonang scholastic curriculum, the printing press at Takten Puntsok Ling Monastery was closed, and zhentong books were banned.[71]

Though the later seventeenth and early eighteenth centuries were a dark period for authorship on zhentong, particularly under the Ganden Potrang's sphere of influence in central Tibet, the transmission of zhentong continued in Kham and

Amdo. Having established a presence in the Amdo region of eastern Tibet since the Jonangpa master Ratnaśrī (1350–1435) had established Choje Monastery in the Dzamtang valley, the Jonangpa sought refuge in that region.

Tāranātha's disciple Lodro Namgyel (1618–1683) traveled from Takten Puntsok Ling Monastery to Dzamtang where in the year 1658 he established Tsangwa Monastery adjacent to Choje Monastery, creating a monastic enclave for the Jonangpas in Dzamtang.[72] While disciples of Tāranātha were sequestered to the far eastern frontier of the Tibetan plateau, the Jonangpas began to rebuild their monasteries in the Dzamtang valley and adjacent areas in Amdo. Xylographs were recarved to print the collected writings of Dolpopa and Tāranātha, and the scholastic curriculum with a focus on Zhentong Madhyamaka was reinstituted in their newly established monasteries.

Perhaps the greatest influence, however, in the history of zhentong during this period was the eighteenth-century Nyingma polymath Rikzin Tsewang Norbu (1698–1755) from Katok Monastery in Kham. His efforts were motivated by his considerable interest in the Jonang and allied traditions as distinct lines of Buddhist tantric teaching in Tibet. Tsewang Norbu sought out zhentong transmissions all across Tibet in an effort to preserve these teachings, which included his failed attempt to unlock the library at Takten Puntsok Ling Monastery in 1727. His efforts, coupled with those of his colleague and close friend, Situ Paṇchen Chokyi Jungne (1699–1774), sparked a revival of interest in zhentong literature among Tibetan intellectual circles in Kham.[73]

Contemporaneously, several authors continued to expound on zhentong in central Tibet. Among these authors was the unconventional Geluk tulku and Nyingma yogin Lelung Zhepai Dorje (1697–1740), who wrote several brief treatises on zhentong. As Matthew Kapstein points out in his chapter, also concerned about zhentong was Lochen Dharmaśrī (1654–1718), who, along with his elder brother Terdak Lingpa (1646–1714), was the cofounder of the premier Mindroling branch of the Nyingma. In response to the entreaties of his contemporary, Dorje Drak Rikzin who was the head of the Jangter lineage and of the important Nyingma monastery at Dorje Drak, Lochen Dharmaśrī composed in 1708 what appears to be the first commentary on the preeminent Nyingma synthesis of the system of the Buddhist vows, the *Ascertainment of the Three Vows* by Ngari Paṇchen Pema Wangyel. In this context, and given, in particular, Mindroling's close association with the Fifth Dalai Lama and the Ganden Potrang government, it is surprising to find that Lochen Dharmaśrī did not quietly ignore the whole matter of zhentong because it was so contested and condemned by the Great Fifth and his court. Nevertheless, in the section of the text dealing with the vows of the bodhisattva, and the progression along the path of the six perfections that this entails, there is a relatively detailed amplification of the single line of the root text that reads, "One practices the profound wisdom of audition, reflection, and contemplation."[74] Remarkably, it is here that Lochen Dharmaśrī inserts a brief but lucid account of the rangtong / zhentong distinction, elaborating a synopsis of the path that allows us to see just how he believed this distinction to operate within the Nyingma system.[75]

By the late nineteenth century, a revivification of zhentong thought had emerged from the circles of Tsewang Norbu's influence. The prolific Nyingma scholar affiliated with the tradition of Tsewang Norbu's home, Katok Monastery, the First Katok Getse Tsewang Chokdrub (1761–1829) famously advocated the Zhentong Great Madhyamaka in the context of explaining Nyingma expositions of Mahāyāna doctrine.[76] Other inheritors of Tsewang Norbu's as well as Situ Paṇ chen's vision to revive zhentong were Jamgon Kongtrul Lodro Taye (1813–1899) and Jamyang Khyentse Wangpo (1820–1892). As Marc-Henri Deroche so rightly notes in his chapter about the Rimé discourses on emptiness, throughout the course of Tibetan intellectual history, zhentong constituted both a major sectarian marker as well as a crucial point for eclecticism. In the case of Kongtrul and Khyentse's Rimé project, zhentong was assimilated as a unifying concept to emphasize the shared identity of the various religious traditions of Tibet.[77] Considering how the history of zhentong thought had caused such fervent debate and sectarian discord among the orders of Tibetan Buddhism, and how it had been persecuted under the rule of the Ganden Potrang government, their interpretation of zhentong was meant to be exceptionally inclusive. Purposing zhentong as a unifying philosophical platform suggested both a counterstance to the normative Geluk-dominated discourse as well as an invitation to impartiality. In addition to Deroche's discussion, Klaus-Dieter Mathes elaborates on differences in Kongtrul's presentation of zhentong in comparison with exemplary Jonang and Kagyu exegetes.

However, discords in the rangtong / zhentong discourse continued through the turn of the twentieth century when the Nyingma luminary Mipam Namgyel Gyatso (1846–1912) sought to synthesize and reconcile these seemingly disparate visions of emptiness. Mipam's preferred stance was an anti-standpoint, an absence of elaborations with regard to the four extremes (*mtha' bzhi spros bral*)—a position that resonates with Nāgārjuna as well as Longchen Rabjam's (1308–1363) elucidations of the absolute. Douglas Duckworth clarifies in his chapter here that, appropriating claims of zhentong discourse, Mipam posits emptiness to appear as it exists—that is, to appear in accord with reality. Based on the fact that an appearance of emptiness undermines the Madhyamaka model of two truths that distinguishes a conventional appearance from ultimate emptiness, Mipam adopted a Yogācāra model. In so doing, he asserted that nondual unity is ultimate truth while dualistic appearances are relative truth. Within this restrained context, Mipam aligns with zhentong.[78] Dorji Wangchuk suggests in his chapter that Mipam's philosophical approach of indivisible union (*yuganaddha, zung 'jug*) is a key to understanding his interpretation and reconciliation of Indian Mahāyāna doctrines in confluence with Dolpopa's zhentong view and Tsongkhapa's rangtong view. This unifying philosophy seems to be based on the fundamental assumption that a discord of philosophical views among various persons and factions would only give way to a concord of insight when they mutually envision ultimate reality. It is only then that ideological differences, and the conflicts that arise therein, come to be naturally resolved. It is at this point that awakened buddha-beings and siddha adepts meet and are of a single mind.

An inheritor of Mipam's thought and an author who was concerned with presenting the philosophical nuances of zhentong was the influential Nyingma master and scholar from Zhechen Monastery in Kham, Khenchen Gangshar Wangpo (1925–1959). Unlike Dolpopa or Shakya Chokden, Khenpo Gangshar does not present zhentong against the backdrop of the three nature theory but rather situates the rangtong / zhentong distinction within a Prāsaṅgika-Mādhyamika framework. In similar fashion to Longchen Rabjam, Khenpo Gangshar insists that everything from material form up to omniscience is rangtong. He presents the two truths as appearance and emptiness in terms of a valid cognition that analyzes for the ultimate abiding nature. In the context of a conventional valid cognition, however, which looks into the mode of an appearance, the two truths are defined in terms of the way things appear versus the way things truly are. When the abiding nature is perceived as it truly is, awareness continues, albeit in a mode that is beyond the duality of ordinary perception. That is, for Khenpo Gangshar, it is only phenomenologically that the rangtong of *saṃsāra* and zhentong of nirvāṇa need to be distinguished.[79]

At the same time that Jamgon Kongtrul and Jamyang Khyentse Wangpo were writing about zhentong and Mipam was composing his *Ketaka Gem*, *Beacon of Certainty*, and the *Lion's Roar of Zhentong*, Jonang scholarship on zhentong was reemerging in Amdo. In the chapter by Michael Sheehy, pivotal figures in the revival of Jonang scholarship on zhentong during this period are brought forth, including Dzago Geshe Lozang Chokdrub Gyatso, Ngawang Tsoknyi Gyatso (1880–1940), and Khenpo Lodro Drakpa (1920–1975). Inspired by the Rimé movement, as Sheehy demonstrates in his chapter, these figures sought to reclaim the intellectual heritage of the Jonang. Lozang Chokdrub Gyatso's life gives us a window into the historical influences of Geluk scholasticism on the revival of zhentong, at least through the lens of one scholar. Assimilating his Geluk training at Drepung Monastery, he creatively presents a distinct doxography of Zhentong Madhyamaka based on what had become a standardized textbook framework for studying Buddhist and non-Buddhist tenet systems within a Geluk curriculum.[80]

With Ngawang Tsoknyi Gyatso, a master from Dzamtang, his lenient, if not somewhat compromised rendering for the Jonang of the essence (*ngo bo*) of buddha-nature has an exegetical style that is influenced by Geluk presentations. For Khenpo Lodro Drakpa, in alignment with the mainstream Jonang proponents Dolpopa and Tāranātha, the essence of buddha-nature is not dependent arising, while Ngawang Tsoknyi Gyatso compromises this position by asserting that even the essence of buddha-nature is dependent arising. In his *Great Exposition on Zhentong*, Khenpo Lodro Drakpa looks to realign zhentong philosophical thinking with mainstream Jonang presentations. He does so by systematically explaining the vital points for understanding the zhentong view as articulated by Dolpopa in his *Mountain Dharma*. Unlike Dolpopa's synthetic presentation, however, he deciphers salient differences between sūtra zhentong and tantra zhentong. In so doing, Khenpo Lodro Drakpa and the contemporary Jonang scholastic tradition that follows him both reclaim Dolpopa's vision while creatively reimagining the myriad formulations of zhentong.

NOTES

1. MacDonald, "Knowing Nothing" 165.

2. *Lokātītastava* 7ab, see Lindtner, *Nagarjuniana* 130: *saṃjñārthayor ananyatve mukhaṃ dahyeta vahninā* /.

3. See *Samādhirājasūtra* XXXII.8ab (SRS 195), where phenomena (*dharmas*) are in reality buddha-qualities (*buddhadharmas*): "All dharmas are buddha-dharmas [for those] who are trained in dharmatā" (*sarvadharmā buddhadharmā dharmatāyāṃ ya śikṣitāḥ*).

4. While Ābhidharmikas attribute *svabhāva* to conditioned *dharmas* on the grounds that they do not depend on parts for their existence, Nāgārjuna claims that the dependent origination of *dharmas* is incompatible with their possession of *svabhāva*. See Burton, *Emptiness Appraised* 90.

5. Yogācāra is the name of a Mahāyāna system, literally, the "One Whose Conduct Is Yoga." Maintaining an idealist position, it is also known as Vijñaptimātravāda ("the position that [everything] is mental representation only"), or *sems tsam* in Tibetan ("mind only").

6. Sometimes also referred to as the three characteristics (*trilakṣaṇa*, *mtshan nyid gsum*).

7. Schmithausen, "Yogācāra" 819.

8. Mitrikeski, "Nāgārjuna and the *Tathāgatagarbha*" 158–159.

9. The *Tathāgatagarbha Sūtra* belongs to the set of sūtras on buddha-nature, called Tathāgatagarbha sūtras (not in italics and in the plural).

10. Zimmermann, *Buddha Within*.

11. Zimmermann 43–45.

12. Mathes, *Direct Path* 12–13.

13. Mathes, "*gzhan stong* Model."

14. Better known under its ornamental title *Mahāyānottaratantra*, *Theg chen rgyud bla ma*, or simply *Rgyud bla ma*.

15. The *Ratnagotravibhāga* consists of different layers, of which only the later ones show Yogācāra influence (see the discussion later in this chapter).

16. See also Mathes, *Dharmadharmatāvibhāga*.

17. It should be noted that the Nyingma master Lochen Dharmashri (1654–1717) also distinguishes a buddha-nature-based zhentong from a Yogācāra-based zhentong. See Mathes, "Presenting a Controversial Doctrine" 115.

18. Mathes, "Twenty-One Differences." We thank the editors of the *Journal of the International Association of Buddhist Studies* for permission to reprint this essay in the present volume.

19. In his commentary on the *Ratnagotravibhāga*, Asaṅga adduces the *Dhāraṇīśvararāja Sūtra*, in which a similar set of three teaching cycles is compared to a threefold cleansing process of a *vaiḍūrya* stone. This establishes, in the eyes of Go Lotsāwa Zhonnu Pel (1392–1481), the superiority of the third turning, consisting in this case of the buddha-nature doctrine (Mathes, *Direct Path* 216–234).

20. SNS VII.30 (85_{11-13}): . . . *nyan thos kyi theg pa la yang dag par zhugs pa rnams la 'phags pa'i bden pa zhi'i rnam par bstan pas chos kyi 'khor lo* . . .

21. It should be noted that both the *Chapter Requested by Maitreya in the Twenty-Five-Thousand Stanza Prajñāpāramitā Sūtra* and the *Five-Hundred Stanza Prajñāpāramitā Sūtra* are both considered zhentong textual sources, and that not all the content in the Prajñāpāramitā sūtras is considered to describe rangtong, at least by some Tibetan exponents of zhentong.

22. SNS VII.30 (85_{17-23}): *bcom ldan 'das kyis chos rnams kyi ngo bo nyid ma mchis pa nyid las brtsams / skye ba ma mchis pa dang / 'gag pa ma mchis pa dang / gzod ma nas zhi ba dang / rang bzhin gyis yongs su mya ngan las 'das pa nyid las brtsams nas theg pa chen po la yang dag par zhugs pa rnams la stong pa nyid smos pa'i rnam pas ches ngo mtshar rmad du byung ba'i chos kyi 'khor lo gnyis pa bskor te / . . .* The translation mainly follows Powers, *Wisdom of the Buddha* 139–141.

23. This is clear from the context of the seventh chapter of the *Sandhinirmocana Sūtra*. See Mathes, "Ontological Status" 327–331.

24. Ngakwang Lodro Drakpa (1920–1975) identifies the primary texts that comprise this scriptural tradition as follows: (1) *Maitreyaparipṛcchā Sūtra in the Pañcaviṃśatisāhasrikā Prajñāpāramitā Sūtra* (contained in Tohoku catalogue [hereafter, Toh.] no. 9); (2) *Pañcaśatikā Prajñāpāramitā Sūtra* (Toh. 15); (3) *Sandhinirmocana Sūtra* (Toh. 106); (4) *Laṅkāvatāra Sūtra* (Toh. 107); (5) *Gaṇḍavyūha Sūtra* (Toh. 44, text no. 45); (6) *Avataṃsaka Sūtra*, common and concordant discussions (Toh. 44); (7) *Tathāgatagarbha Sūtra* (Toh. 258); (8) Sections within the *Ratnakūṭa Sūtra*, including the *Śrīmālādevīsiṃhanāda Sūtra* (Toh. 45–93); (9) *Avikalpapraveśadhāraṇī* (Toh. 142); (10) *Suvarṇaprabhā Sūtra* (Toh. 556); (11) *Dhāraṇīśvararājapripṛcchā Sūtra* (Toh. 147, listed under *Tathāgatamahākaruṇānirdeśanāmamahāyāna Sūtra*); (12) *Tathāgataguṇajñānācintyaviṣayāvatāra Sūtra* (Toh. 185); *Aṅgulimālīya Sūtra* (Toh. 213); (13) *Mahāmegha Sūtra* (Toh. 232); (14) *Ratnamegha Sūtra* (Toh. 231); (15) *Mahābherīhārakaparivarta Sūtra* (Toh. 222); (16) *Mahāparinirvāṇa Sūtra* (Toh. 121–122); (17) *Praśantaviniścayasamādhi Sūtra* (Toh. 129). Ngag dbang, 79. In addition to these core sūtras, two sets of ten sūtras are regularly cited within zhentong writings and are regarded to be the canonical source literature for Zhentong Madhyamaka. This first set of ten sūtras is the *Essence Sūtras* according to Dolpopa's *Zhu don gnang ba* (Stearns, *Buddha from Dolpo* 178): (1) *Tathāgatagarbha Sūtra* (Toh. 258); (2) *Avikalpapraveśadhāraṇī* (Toh. 142); (3) *Śrīmālādevī-siṃhanāda Sūtra* (Toh. 92); (4) *Mahābherīhārakaparivarta Sūtra* (Toh. 222); (5) *Aṅgulimālīya Sūtra* (Toh. 213); (6) *Mahāśūnyatā Sūtra* (Toh. 291); (7) *Tathāgatamahākaruṇānirdeśa Sūtra* (Toh. 147); (8) *Tathāgataguṇajñānācintyaviṣayāvatāra Sūtra* (Toh. 185); (9) *Mahāmegha Sūtra* (Toh. 232); (10) *Mahāparinirvāṇa Sūtra* (Toh. 121–122). The second set of ten sūtras is called *Sūtras on the Definitive Meaning*: (1) *Five Hundred Stanza Prajñāpāramitā Sūtra* (Toh. 15); (2) *Chapter Requested by Maitreya* (contained in Toh. 9); (3) *Gaṇḍavyūha Sūtra* (Toh. 44, text no. 45); (4) *Praśantaviniścayasamādhi Sūtra* (Toh. 129); (5) *Ratnamegha Sūtra* (Toh. 231); (6) *Suvarṇaprabhā Sūtra* (Toh. 556); (7) *Sandhinirmocana Sūtra* (Toh. 106); (8) *Laṅkāvatāra Sūtra* (Toh. 107); (9) *Jñānālokālaṃkāra Sūtra* (Toh. 100); (10) *Buddhavataṃsaka Sūtra* (Toh. 44).

25. According to Common Madhyamaka reasoning, anything arising in dependence cannot exist ultimately. See Mathes, *Dharmadharmatāvibhāga* 168–171.

26. MSA IX.37 (40_{13-14}): "Even though suchness is undifferentiated in all [living beings], in its purified form it is the state of the Tathāgata. Therefore all living beings have the 'nature' (*garbha*) of the [Tathāgata]" (*sarveṣām aviśiṣṭāpi tathatā śuddhim āgatā / tathāgatatvaṃ tasmāc ca tadgarbhāḥ sarvadehinaḥ //*).

27. RGV I.148 (71_{5-6}): "Its nature being unchangeable, sublime, and pure, suchness is illustrated by a piece of gold" (*prakṛter avikāritvāt kalyāṇatvād viśuddhitaḥ /*

hemamaṇḍalakaupamyaṃ tathatāyām udāhṛtam //). The commentary on this verse is as follows (RGVV 71_{7-8}): "Although the mind is accompanied by limitless phenomena that are defilements or suffering, it itself does not undergo change on account of its natural luminosity. This is why it is called suchness, for it will never become something else, any more than sublime gold will" (*yac cittam [tad?] aparyantakleśaduḥkhadharmānugatam api prakṛtiprabhāsvaratayā vikāraṃ na bhajate [?]*[a] *kalyāṇasuvarṇavad ananyathī*[b]*bhāvārthena tathatety ucyate /*), *Ratnagotravibhāgavyākhyā*.

[a]Johnston edition: *-vikārānudāṛter ataḥ*; [b]Johnston edition: *ananyathā-*. As for the corrections, see Schmithausen, "Ratnagotravibhāga" 156.

28. It should be noted that neither the *Ratnagotravibhāga* nor the *Dharmadharmatāvibhāga* make direct use of three-nature terminology.

29. See Takasaki, *Study on the Ratnagotravibhāga*, and Schmithausen, "Ratnagotravibhāga."

30. See Mathes, *Direct Path* 1–2.

31. Personal communication.

32. There is also a commentary on the *Dharmadharmatāvibhāga* by Vasubandhu, of which a Sanskrit fragment has survived. For an edition, translation, and analysis of this commentary, see Mathes, *Dharmadharmatāvibhāga*.

33. See Mathes, *A Fine Blend*.

34. See Mathes, *Direct Path* 25–33.

35. Roerich, *Blue Annals* 347.

36. See Tatz, "Maitrīgupta" 698.

37. The *Dharmadharmatāvibhāgakārikā* (ll. 18–19 of the Tibetan translation) is quoted in *Jñānaśrīmitranibandhāvali*, 432.10–13, while *Ratnagotravibhāga* I.9 is summarized in *Jñānaśrīmitranibandhāvali* 478.11.

38. The verses II.95c–II.97b (*Jñānaśrīmitranibandhāvali*, 537.4–7) are nearly identical with *Ratnagotravibhāga* I.151–52.

39. See Mathes, "Pith Instructions" 304–306.

40. In contextualizing Nāgārjuna's *Chos dbyings bstod pa* within the corpus of Jonang literature, Seyfort Ruegg writes in "Le *Dharmadhātustava*" 463: "Et l'école tibétaine des Jo naṅ pa est effectivement allée jusqu'à opposer la *svabhāvaśūnyatā* (*raṅ stoṅ*), qui est enseignée par les traités scolastiques (*rigs tshogs*) de Nāgārjuna et qu'ils considèrent comme une Vacuité de destruction (*chad stoṅ*), à la *śūnyatā* «veritable»—c'est-à-dire la Vacuité des seuls facteurs relatifs et hétérogènes à l'Absolu (*gžan stoṅ*)—enseignée dans les hymnes (*bstod tshogs*) de Nāgārjuna. Ainsi, selon les Jo naṅ pa, l'enseignement des Prajñāpāramitā-Sūtra et du *rigs tshogs* relative au *raṅ stoṅ* «nihiliste» est intentionnel (*ābhiprāyika*) et de sens indirect (*neyārtha*), et c'est la théorie du *gžan stoṅ* des Sūtra du troisième Cycle enseignant le *garbha* (*sñiṅ poi mdo*) et du *bstod tshogs* qui est de sens direct et certain (*nītārtha*)."

41. The attribution of the *Dharmadhātustava* to Nāgārjuna has been uncontested throughout Tibetan intellectual history. DhS 20–22: *agniśaucaṃ*[a] *yathā vastraṃ malinaṃ vividhair malaiḥ / agnimadhye yathākṣiptaṃ malaṃ dagdhaṃ na vastratā // evaṃ prabhāsvaraṃ cittaṃ malinaṃ rāgajair malaiḥ / jñānāgninā malaṃ dagdhaṃ na dagdhaṃ tat prabhāsvaraṃ // śūnyatāhārakāḥ sūtrā ye kecid bhāṣitā jinaiḥ / sarvais taiḥ kleśavyāvṛttir naiva dhātuvināśanam //*.

[a]Seyfort Ruegg, *Dharmadhātustava* 466, has *agniḥ śaucaṃ* and translates: "Le feu étant pureté . . . ," which is syntactically problematic.

42. Nāgārjuna's *Collection on Reasoning* (*Rigs tshogs*) includes six logical works on Madhyamaka: (1) "A Precious Garland of Advice for a King" (*Rājaparikathāratnā-*

valī, Rgyal po la gtam bya bar in po che'i phreng ba); (2) "Reversing Objections" (*Vigrahavyāvartanīkārikā, Rtsod pa bzlog pa'i tshig le'ur byas pa*); (3) "Seventy Verses on Emptiness" (*Śūnyatāsaptatikārikā, Stong pa nyid bdun cu pa'i tshig le'ur byas pa*); (4) "Sixty Stanzas on Reasoning" (*Yuktiṣaṣṭikākārikā, Rigs pa drug cu pa'i tshig le'ur byas pa*); (5) "The Elegantly Woven Scripture" (*Vaidalyasūtranāma, Zhib mo rnam par 'thag zhes bya ba'i mdo*); (6) "The Root Verses on the Madhyamaka" (*Mūlamadhyamakakārikā, Dbu ma rtsa ba'i tshig le'u*). These six works on logic are contrasted to Nāgārjuna's *Collection of Hymns* (*Btsod tshogs*) that includes the *Dharmadhātustava*. On these two collections, Seyfort Ruegg, *Dharmadhātustava* 448–449, and Seyfort Ruegg, *Madhyamaka School* 34–35. For Dolpopa's writings on unraveling Nāgārjuna's intent, see Dolpopa ('Dzam thang), *Ri chos* 252–261.

43. In later zhentong literature, this is commonly referred to as sūtra zhentong (*mdo'i gzhan stong*). See the chapter on Khenpo Lodro Drakpa by Sheehy in the current volume for further discussion.

44. In his attempt to discredit the Mind-Only teaching and in the process also the *Sandhinirmocanasūtra*, Candrakīrti refers in his auto commentary to the *Madhyamakāvatāra* (MA VI.95) to a verse in the second chapter of the *Laṅkāvatārasūtra* (LAS II.123), which demonstrates for him the intentional character of "mind-only": "Just as a physician provides medicine for the sick, so the Buddhas teach mind-only to sentient beings" (LAS, $49_{2\text{-}3}$: *āture āture yadvad bhiṣag dravyaṃ prayacchati / buddhā hi tadvat sattvānāṃ cittamātraṃ vadanti vai //*). This verse indeed suggests that the mind-only teaching is being given with a purpose. But according to Yogācāra hermeneutics, the ability to discern a purpose does not entail that a statement has provisional meaning. Moreover, the following verse (LAS II.124), which has not been quoted by Candrakīrti, sheds a different light on the issue: "[This mind-only teaching] is an object neither of philosophers nor of the Śrāvakas. / The masters (i.e., the Buddhas) teach [it] by drawing on their own experience" (LAS, $49_{4\text{-}5}$: *tārkikāṇām aviṣayaṃ śrāvakāṇāṃ na caiva hi / yaṃ deśayanti vai nāthāḥ pratyātmagatigocaram //*). In other words, the *Laṅkāvatārasūtra* takes mind-only as something that can only be experienced by the Buddhas.

45. LAS, $75_{1\text{-}5}$: *bhagavān etad avocat / śūnyatā śūnyateti mahāmate parikalpitasvabhāva-padam etat / parikalpitasvabhāvābhiniveśena punar mahāmate śūnyatānutpādābhāvādvaya-niḥsvabhāvabhāvavādino bhavanti /*. For a detailed discussion, see Mathes, "*Gzhan stong* Model" 195–198.

46. The Jonangpas exclude from the perfect nature the unmistaken (*aviparyāsa*) wisdom cultivated on the path. The perfect nature thus is restricted to its unchangeable aspect (*nirvikāra*), since in an absolutely permanent and atemporal buddhahood or buddha-nature (both are ontologically the same for the Jonangpas) there is no room for it (see Mathes, "Twenty-One Differences" 288).

47. Dolpopa, *Jo nang ri chos* 150: "Since it has been said that the dharmatā [or] perfect [nature], which is empty of the imagined and dependent, ultimately exists, the ultimate is well established as being *gzhan stong* only" (*kun btags dang gzhan dbang gis stong pa'i chos nyid yongs grub don dam du yod par gsungs pa'i phyir don dam gzhan stong nyid du legs par grub po /*).

48. Dolpopa, *Jo nang ri chos* 446–447: "The dharmakāya is free from mental fabrications throughout beginningless time. Because of recognizing it as being free from mental fabrications, it is truly established" (*chos sku de ni gdod nas spros dang bral / spros dang bral ngo shes pas bden par grub /*).

49. Dolpopa's definition of ultimate truth in *Jo nang ri chos* 258: "Ultimate truth means that it is true ultimately, and not on the level of apparent [truth]" (*don dam bden pa gang yin pa de don dam du bden gyi kun rdzob tu bden pa ma yin*).

50. Dolpopa, *Bden gnyis gsal ba'i nyi ma* 4, 1–3: *rnam shes kyi yul gang zhig / gshis la rang gi ngo bo bden pas stong pa ni / kun rdzob bden pa'i mtshan nyid . . . 'phags pa'i ye shes dam pa'i yul gang zhig / gzhis la rang rang gi ngo bo bden pas mi stong pa ni / don dam pa'i mtshan nyid de /*. Mathes, "Vordergründige und höchste Wahrheit" 459.

51. This is the *Bṛhaṭṭīkā*, known in Tibetan as *Yum gsum gnod 'joms*, *The Extensive Commentary on the Perfection of Wisdom* in 18,000, 25,000, and 100,000 lines (*Śatasāhasrikāpañcaviṃśatisāhasrikāṣṭasāhasrikā-prajñāpāramitā-bṛhaṭṭīkā*). The *Bṛhaṭṭīkā* is attributed to Vasubandhu. For Tsongkhapa its author is Daṃṣṭrāsena (see Brunnhölzl, *Prajñāpāramitā* 9–14). For its explanation of the three-nature theory, see Derge Tengyur 3808, fol. 287a, 4–5: "The imagined nature [of phenomena] is that aspect [of these that leads to] form and the other [modes of] phenomena being called "form" and so forth. The dependent nature is that aspect [of them that], under the sway of ignorance and so forth, appear to consciousness as phenomena in a mistaken way. [Their] ultimate—perfect—nature is that ineffable aspect beyond characteristic signs, which is free from the [said] aspects of names and mistaken appearances" (*De la gzugs la sogs pa chos rnams la gzugs zhes bya ba la sogs par mngon par brjod pa'i rnam pa gang yin pa de ni kun brtags pa'i ngo bo nyid do / ma rig pa la sogs pa'i dbang gis rnam par shes pa la chos rnams su phyin ci log tu snang ba'i rnam pa gang yin pa de ni gzhan dbang gi ngo bo nyid do / gang ming dang / phyin ci log tu snang ba'i rnam pa de dang bral ba brjod du med pa / mtshan ma med pa'i rnam pa gang yin pa de ni don dam pa yongs su grub pa'i ngo bo nyid de /*). First quoted in translation in Mathes, "Twenty-One Differences" 317. For more on the "Maitreya Chapter" in the works of Dolpopa, see Stearns, *Buddha from Dolpo* 89–93.

52. MAV I.20 (MAVBh 26, 9–10): "The nonexistence of a person[al self] and phenomena is one emptiness here. The true existence of this nonexistence is another one" (*pudgalasyātha dharmāṇām abhāvaḥ śūnyatā 'tra hi / tadabhāvasya sadbhāvas taasmin sā śūnyatā 'para //*).

53. Emptiness as the existence of duality's nonexistence is not only an endorsement of the nonexistence of duality but also positively understood as the natural luminosity of mind. See MAVBh 27, "[Emptiness is] neither defiled nor undefiled, neither pure nor impure. How is it that it is neither defiled nor impure? It is because mind is luminous by nature. How is it that it is neither undefiled nor pure? It is because defilements are adventitious by nature" (*na kliṣṭā nāpi vākliṣṭā śuddhā 'śuddhā na caiva sā / kathaṃ na kliṣṭā nāpi cāśuddhā / prakṛtyaiva / prabhāsvaratvāc cittasya / kathaṃ nākliṣṭā na śuddhā / kleśasyāgantukatvataḥ /*).

54. See Mathes, "*Gzhan stong* Model" 190–193.

55. See Brunnhölzl; and Mathes, "Twenty-One Differences" and "*Gzhan stong* Model."

56. See Mathes, "Pith Instructions" 306.

57. Kunga Drolchok, *Khrid brgya'i brgyud pa'i lo rgyus* 83–84: *kha che paṇḍita sajjana'i gsung gis rgyal bas 'khor lo dang po bden bzhi / bar pa mtshan nyid med pa / mthar legs par rnam par phye ba'i chos kyi 'khor lo bzlas pa lan gsum bskor ba las snga ma gnyis dngos btags ma phye ba / phyi ma don dam par nges pa'i tshe / dbus dang mtha' phye / chos dang chos nyid phye nas gsungs zhing*. See also Stearns, *Buddha from Dolpo* 42–43.

58. Kunga Drolchok cites: *pad + ma lcags kyu'i ming bzhag pa'i btsan kha bo che rang gi zin tho rnying pa zhig snang ba 'di*. Kunga Drolchok, *Khrid brgya'i brgyud pa'i lo rgyus* 84 and Sheehy, "Gzhan stong Chen mo" 268–269.

59. The colophon reads, *chos kun mtshan nyid gsum pa bsdus nas / gnyis snang g.ya yis mgos pa'i / dga' ba rang grol mchog gi khrid / 'dir ni yi ger gsal bar byas* ("From a condensation of the threefold nature of reality. This is a teaching that removes the rust of dualistic perceptions. It is a lucid writing and a supreme instruction on joyful natural freedom").

Kunga Drolchok, *Zab khrid* 171. For the full translation, see Sheehy, "Gzhan stong Chen mo" 268–269.

60. Tāranātha, *Gzhan stong dbu ma'i brgyud 'debs*. The *Theg chen rgyud bla ma'i gdams pa*, 155–156, lists Drime Sherab (Tsen Kawoche), "somebody from southern Lato (*la stod lho pa gcig*)," Dopa Nyen, Nartang Kyoton Monlam Tsultrim. The *Chos nyid kyi khrid*, 316, has Phurangpa Chenpo (Tsen Kawoche), Dolpa Drelhepa (uncle and nephew), Shangpa, Lobpon Nartangpa *brgyad pa*. Tāranātha, "gZhon stong brgyud 'debs" 485–486, Tsen Kawoche Drime Sherab, Darma Tsondru, Yeshe Jungne, Jeton Kuche, Kyoton Monlam Tsultrim. See Mathes, "Pith Instructions" 306.

61. Mathes, "*Gzhan stong* Model" 202–212 (i.e., the perfections of permanence, the self [*ātman*], bliss, and purity).

62. Brunnhölzl, *Prajñāpāramitā* 187.

63. Kyoton Monlam Tsultrim, *Theg chen dbu ma'i gdams pa* 190–191: "Just as the fire kindled by two rubbing sticks burns the pieces of wood themselves, so the insight burns the very faculty it has arisen from. Just as the fire kindled by the two rubbing sticks goes out, once both of them are consumed, so it is not only that both the entities of object and subject are not established, the analyzing insight itself is not established either and disappears. The no-appearance of all phenomena, luminosity free from all mental fabrication is called nirvāṇa" (*Shing gnyis drud pa las me byung ste / byung pa de yis de nyid sreg pa ltar / de bzhin shes rab dbang po skyes nas kyang / skyes pa de yis de nyid sreg par byed ces pas / dper na shing gnyis drud pa la brten nas me 'byung ste / gnyis po zad pa'i tshe me de yang rang zhi 'gro ba bzhin du / de ltar yul dang yul can gnyis po'i ngo bo ma grub tsam na / de dpyod byed kyi shes rab de mi 'grub par rang zhi nas chos thams cad snang pa med pa 'od gsal ba spros pa thams cad dang bral ba de nyid la mya ngan las 'das pa zhes bya ste /*). First quoted and translated in Mathes, "Pith Instructions" 309.

64. On the polemics of emptiness, and particularly the fifteenth-century Sakya scholar Gorampa Sonam Sengge's (1429–1489) response to Dolpopa, see "The Refutation of Dol po pa" in Cabezón and Dargyay, *Freedom from Extremes* 97–113.

65. According to Tāranātha's *Zab don nyer gcig pa*. See Mathes, "Twenty-One Differences" 310–311 and Mathes's chapter in the present volume.

66. This is a reference to a text that was recovered by Tulku Kunga Zangpo and Michael Sheehy from a previously unknown private archive in Dzamtang. The text is titled *Gzhan stong lta ba'i zab gnad* and is slated to be published by the Mi rigs dpe skrun khang in Beijing as part of a new *gsung 'bum* of Kunga Drolchok's writings that is being compiled.

67. Stearns, *Buddha from Dolpo* 71.

68. Stearns 71–72.

69. Sheehy, "Gzhan stong Chen mo" 20.

70. Ngawang Lozang Gyatso, 2, 22. This passage reads: *gong gsal gyi par tsho mkho che bar ma zad rin cen tog gi yig cha rnams shin tu dkon pa dang rtag brtan sprul skus gzhan stong gi phyogs 'dzin rgyu'i rmongs zhen gyis mgon po klu sgrub rjes 'brang la skur ba chen po btab nas rang gi zhar la skye rgu mang po ngan song du 'khrid pa'i sgo 'gog pa la phan nam snyam.* The tulku of Takten is a reference to Jamyang Tulku, Lozang Tenpai Gyaltsen (1635–1723), the First Khalka Jetsun Dampa. See Sheehy, "Gzhan stong Chen mo" 17–21.

77. Smith, "First Paṇ chen Lama" 95.

72. Sheehy, "Lineage History of Vajrayoga" 227–228, and Ngag dbang 61–62.

73. Smith 2001, 91, and "Autobiography of the Rnying ma pa" 20–21.

74. In Tibetan: *thos bsam sgom pa'i shes rab zab mo spyad.*

75. See the Kapstein chapter in the present volume.

76. As Kapstein notes in his chapter, "The doctrinal writings of the best-known twentieth-century successor to Getse Tulku's line of thought, Dudjom Rinpoche Jigdrel Yeshe Dorje, have contributed to a general impression that the Nyingmapa are to be placed firmly in the zhentong camp" (235–36).

77. Smith, "'Jam mgon Kong sprul" 265.

78. For discussion on Mipam's zhentong view from his *Beacon of Certainty*, see Botrul Dongak Tenpai Nyima's (1846–1912) commentary. Duckworth, *Jamgon Mipam* 208–211.

79. See Mathes, "Presenting a Controversial Doctrine" 120–121.

80. See Sheehy's chapter on Khenpo Lodro Drakpa in the present volume.

BIBLIOGRAPHY

Abbreviations for Sanskrit Sources

DhS: *Dharmadhātustava* (Tibetan translation). Derge Bstan 'gyur, no. 1118.

LAS: *Laṅkāvatārasūtra*. Edited by Bunyiu Nanjio. Bibliotheca Otaniensis 1. Kyoto: 1923.

LS: *Lokātītastava*. Edited by Christian Lindtner. See Lindtner, *Nagarjuniana* 128–138.

MAVBh: *Madhyāntavibhāgabhāṣya*. Edited by Gadjin M. Nagao. Tokyo: Suzuki Research Foundation, 1964.

MSA: *Mahāyānasūtrālaṃkāra*. Edited by Sylvain Lévi. Bibliothèque de l'École des Hautes Études. Sciences historiques et philologiques 159. Paris: Librairie Honoré Champion, 1907.

RGV: *Ratnagotravibhāga Mahāyānottaratantraśāstra*. Edited by Edward H. Johnston. Patna: The Bihar Research Society, 1950. (Includes the *Ratnagotravibhāgavyākhyā*.)

RGVV: *Ratnagotravibhāgavyākhyā*. See RGV. [The manuscripts A and B on which Johnston's edition is based are described in Johnston, *Ratnagotravibhāga* vi–vii. See also Bandurski et al., *Untersuchungen zur buddhistischen Literatur* 12–13.]

SNS: *Sandhinirmocanasūtra* (Tibetan translation from the Kanjur). Edited by Étienne Lamotte. Louvain: Bureaux du Recueil, 1935.

SRS: *Samādhirājasūtra*. Edited by P. L. Vaidya. Darbhanga: The Mithila Institute of Post-Graduate Studies and Research in Learning, 1961.

Tibetan Sources

Bka' gdams gsung 'bum phyogs bsgrigs. Chengdu: dPal brtsegs bod yig dpe rnying zhib 'jug khang, 2006–2009.

Bṛhaṭṭīkā: *Śatasāhasrikāpañcaviṃśatisāhasrikāṣṭasāhasrikāprajñāpāramitābṛhaṭṭīkā* (Tibetan translation). Derge Bstan 'gyur, no. 3808.

Dol po pa Shes rab rgyal mtshan. *Jo nang ri chos nges don rgya mtsho*. Beijing: Mi rigs dpe skrun khang, 1998.

———. "Ri chos nges don rgya mtsho zhes bya ba mthar thug mong ma yin pa'i man ngag." In *Kun mkhyen Dol po pa Shes rab Rgyal mtshan Gsung 'bum*, vol. 3, 189–741. 'Dzam thang.

———. "Bden gnyis gsal ba'i nyi ma." In *Kun mkhyen dol po pa'i gsung 'bum*, published by Jamyang Khyentse, vol. 1, 1–45. Kathmandu: Shechen.

Kun dga' grol mchog. "Khrid brgya'i brgyud pa'i lo rgyus." In *Gdams ngag rin po che'i mdzod*, vol. 18, 67–98. Kathmandu: Shechen, 1998.

———. "Zab khrid brgya dang brgyad kyi yi ge." In *Gdams ngag mdzod*, vol. 18, 127–353. Kathmandu: Shechen, 1998.

Ngag dbang Blos gros Grags pa. "Rgyu dang 'bras bu'i theg pa mchog gi gnas lugs zab mo'i don rnam par nges pa rje jo nang pa chen po'i ring lugs 'jigs med dgong lnga'i nga ro." In *Blo gros grags pa'i Gsung 'bum*, vol. 1, 35–516. 'Dzam thang.

———. *Jo nang chos 'byung zla ba'i sgron me*. Qinghai: Nationalities Press (*krung go'i bod kyi shes rig dpe skrun khang*), 1992.

Skyo ston Smon lam tshul khrims. "Chos nyid kyi khrid ces bya ba ldeb." In *Bka' gdams pa'i bka' 'bum*, vol. 50, 311–317. Chengdu: Si khron mi rigs dpe skrun khang, 2007.

———. "Theg chen dbu ma'i gdams pa." In *Bka' gdams pa'i bka' 'bum*, vol. 50, 187–193. Chengdu: Si khron mi rigs dpe skrun khang, 2007.

———. "Theg chen rgyud bla ma'i gdams pa." In *Bka' gdams pa'i bka' 'bum*, vol. 50, 147–156. Chengdu: Si khron mi rigs dpe skrun khang, 2007.

Tāranātha. "gZhon stong brgyud 'debs." In *Rje btsun Tāranātha'i gsung 'bum bzhugs so*, vol. 4, 483–490. Leh: Namgyal & Tsewang Taru, 1985.

Secondary Sources

Bandurski, Frank, Bikkhu Pāsādika, Michael Schmidt, and Bangwei Wang. *Untersuchungen zur buddhistischen Literatur*. Sanskrit-Wörterbuch der buddhistischen Texte aus den Turfan-Funden. Beiheft 5. Göttingen: Vandenhoeck & Ruprecht in Göttingen, 1994.

Bötrül. *Distinguishing the Views and Philosophies: Illuminating Emptiness in a Twentieth-Century Tibetan Buddhist Classic*. Translated by Douglas Duckworth. Albany: State University of New York Press, 2011.

Brunnhölzl, Karl. *Prajñāpāramitā, Indian* "gzhan stong pas," *and the Beginning of Tibetan* gzhan stong. WSTB 74. Vienna: Arbeitskreis für tibetische und buddhistische Studien der Universität Wien, 2011.

Burton, David. *Emptiness Appraised: A Critical Study of Nāgārjuna's Philosophy*. Richmond: Curzon Press, 1999.

Cabezón, José Ignacio, and Geshe Lobsang Dargyay. *Freedom from Extremes: Gorampa's "Distinguishing the Views" and the Polemics of Emptiness*. Boston: Wisdom, 2007.

Duckworth, Douglas. *Jamgon Mipam: His Life and Teachings*. Boston: Shambala, 2011.

Fuchs, Rosemarie, translator. *Buddhanature: The Mahayana Uttara Tantra Shastra* [with commentary by Arya Maitreya; written down by Arya Asanga; and commentary by Jamgon Kongtrul Lodro Thaye]. Ithaca: Snow Lion, 2000.

Griffiths, Paul. J. "Painting Space with Colors: Tathāgatagarbha in the *Mahāyānasūtrālankāra*-Corpus IX.22–37." In *Buddha-Nature: A Festschrift in Honor of Minoru Kiyota*, edited by P. J. Griffiths and J. P. Keenan, 22–37. Tokyo: Buddhist Books International, 1990.

Grosnick, William H., translator. "The Tathāgatagarbha Sūtra." In *Buddhism in Practice*, edited by Donald S. Lopez, 92–106. Princeton: Princeton University Press, 1995.

Hakamaya, Noriaki. "Some Doubts about the Evaluation of the Ten Snying po'i mdos and Tathāgatagarbha Thought." In *Tibetan Studies: Proceedings of the Fifth Seminar of the IATS*, edited by S. Ihara and Z. Yamaguchi. Tokyo: Naritasan Shinshoji, 1992.

Iida, Shōtarō, and Edward Conze. 1968. "Maitreya's Questions in the Prajñāpāramitā." In *Mélanges d'indianisme à la memoire de Louis Renou*, 229–237. Paris: Editions E. de Boccard, 1968.

Kapstein, Matthew. "We Are All Gzhan stong pas: Reflections on the *The Reflexive Nature of Awareness: A Tibetan Madhyamaka Defence* by Paul Williams." *Journal of Buddhist Ethics* 7 (2000): 105–125.

Lamotte, Étienne. *Sandhinirmocana Sūtra: L'explication des Mystères*. Louvain: Bibliothèque de l'Université, 1935.

Lindtner, Christian. *Nagarjuniana: Studies in the Writings and Philosophy of Nāgārjuna*. Delhi: Motilal Banarsidass, 1990.

Liu, Ming-Wood. "The Doctrine of the Buddha-Nature in the Mahāyāna Mahāparinirvāṇa Sūtra." *Journal of the International Association of Buddhist Studies* 5, no. 2 (1982): 63–94.

MacDonald, Anne. "Knowing Nothing: Candrakīrti and Yogic Perception." In *Yogic Perception, Meditation and Altered States of Consciousness*, edited by Eli Franco in collaboration with Dagmar Eigner, 133–168. Vienna: Austrian Academy of Sciences, 2009.

Mathes, Klaus-Dieter. *Unterscheidung der Gegebenheiten von ihrem wahren Wesen (Dharmadharmatāvibhāga)*. Swisttal-Odendorf: Indica et Tibetica, 1996.

———. "Vordergründige und höchste Wahrheit im *zhentong*-Madhyamaka." In *Annäherung an das Fremde: XXVI. Deutscher Orientalistentag vom 25. bis 29.9. in Leipzig*, edited by Holger Preissler and H. Stein. Special issue of *Zeitschrift der Deutschen Morgenländischen Gesellschaft* 11 (1998): 457–468.

———. "Tāranātha's 'Twenty-One Differences with Regard to the Profound Meaning': Comparing the Views of the Two *gŹan stoṅ* Masters Dol po pa and Śākya mchog ldan." *Journal of the International Association of Buddhist Studies* 27, no. 2 (2004): 285–328.

———. "The Ontological Status of the Dependent (*paratantra*) in the *Sandhinirmocanasūtra* and the *Vyākhyāyukti*." In *Indica et Tibetica: Festschrift für Michael Hahn zum 65. Geburtstag von Freunden und Schülern überreicht*, edited by Konrad Klaus and Jens-Uwe Hartmann, 323–339. Vienna: Arbeitskreis für tibetische und buddhistische Studien, 2007.

———. *A Direct Path to the Buddha Within: Gö Lotsāwa's Mahāmudrā Interpretation of the Ratnagotravibhāga*. Boston: Wisdom, 2008.

———. "The *gzhan stong* Model of Reality. Some More Material on Its Origin, Transmission, and Interpretation." *Journal of the International Association of Buddhist Studies* 34 (2012): 187–226.

———. "The Pith Instructions on the Mahāyāna Uttaratantra (Theg chen rgyud bla'i gdams pa): A Missing Link in the Meditation Tradition of the Maitreya Works." In *The Illuminating Mirror: Tibetan Studies in Honour of Per Sørensen on the Occasion of his 65th Birthday*, edited by Olaf Czaja and Guntram Hazod, 303–320. Wiesbaden: Reichert, 2015.

———. *A Fine Blend of Mahāmudrā and Madhyamaka: Maitrīpa's Collection of Texts on Non-conceptual Realization (Amanasikāra)*. Vienna: Austrian Academy of Sciences, 2015.

———. "Presenting a Controversial Doctrine in a Conciliatory Way: Mkhan chen Gang shar dbang po's (1925–1958/59?) Inclusion of Gzhan Stong ('Emptiness of Other') within Prāsaṅgika." *Journal of Buddhist Philosophy* 2 (2016): 114–131.

Mitrikeski, Drasko. "Nāgārjuna and the *Tathāgatagarbha*: A Closer Look at Some Peculiar Features in the *Niraupamyastava*." *Journal of Religious History* 33, no. 2 (2009): 149–164.

Paul, Diana. "The Concept of Tathāgatagarbha in the *Śrīmālādevi Sūtra* (Sheng-man Ching)." *Journal of the American Oriental Society* 99, no. 2 (1979): 191–203.

Pettit, John. W. *Mipham's Beacon of Certainty: Illuminating the View of Dzogchen, the Great Perfection*. Boston: Wisdom, 1999.

Powers, John, translator. *Wisdom of the Buddha: The* Sandhinirmocana Sūtra. Berkeley: Dharma, 1994.

Roerich, George. N., translator. *The Blue Annals.* Parts I–II. Delhi: Motilal Banarsidass, 1996.

Schmithausen, Lambert. "Zur Literaturgeschichte der älteren Yogācāra-Schule." In *XVII. Deutscher Orientalistentag, vom 21. bis 27. Juli 1968 in Würzburg, Vorträge*, edited by Wolfgang Voigt (ZDMG, Supplementa. I.3.), 811–821. Wiesbaden: 1969.

———. "Philologische Bemerkungen zum Ratnagotravibhāga." *Wiener Zeitschrift für die Kunde Südasiens* 15 (1971): 123–177.

Seyfort Ruegg, David. "Le *Dharmadhātustava* de Nāgārjuna." In *Études Tibetaines: Dediées à la Mémoire de Marcelle Lalou (1890–1967)*, 448–471. Paris: Librairie d'Amérique et d'Orient, 1971.

———. "On the Dge lugs pa Theory of the Tathāgatagarbha." In *Pratidānam: Indian, Iranian and Indo-European Studies Presented to Francicsus Bernardus Jacobus Kuiper on His Sixtieth Birthday*, edited by J. C. Heesterman, G. H. Schokker, and V. I. Subramonium, 500–509. Paris: Mouton, 1968.

———. *The Literature of the Madhyamaka School of Philosophy in India.* Wiesbaden: Otto Harrassowitz, 1981.

Sheehy, Michael R. "The Gzhan stong Chen mo: A Study of Emptiness According to the Modern Tibetan Buddhist Jo nang Scholar 'Dzam thang Mkhan po Ngag dbang Blo gros grags pa (1920–1975)." PhD dissertation, San Francisco, California Institute of Integral Studies, 2007.

———. "The Jonangpa after Tāranātha: Auto/biographical Writings on the Transmission of Esoteric Buddhist Knowledge in Seventeenth Century Tibet." *Bulletin of Tibetology* 45, no. 01 (2009): 9–24.

———. "A Lineage History of Vajrayoga and Tantric Zhentong from the Jonang Kalachakra Practice Tradition." In *As Long as Space Endures: Essays on the Kalachakra Tantra in Honor of the Dalai Lama*, edited by Edward Carleton Arnold, 219–235. Ithaca: Snow Lion, 2009.

Smith, E. Gene. "The Autobiography of the First Paṇ chen Lama." In *Among Tibetan Texts: History and Literature of the Himalayan Plateau*, edited by Kurtis Schaeffer, 87–96. Boston: Wisdom, 2001.

———. " 'Jam mgon Kong sprul and the Nonsectarian Movement." In *Among Tibetan Texts: History and Literature of the Himalayan Plateau*, edited by Kurtis Schaeffer, 235–272. Boston: Wisdom, 2001.

———. "The Autobiography of the Rnying ma pa Visionary Mkhan po Ngag dbang dpal bzang and his Spiritual Heritage." In *Among Tibetan Texts: History and Literature of the Himalayan Plateau*, edited by Kurtis Schaeffer, 13–31. Boston: Wisdom, 2001.

Stearns, Cyrus. *The Buddha from Dolpo: A Study of the Life and Thought of the Tibetan Master Dolpopa Sherab Gyaltsen.* Albany: State University of New York Press, 1999.

Sutton, Florin Giripescu. *Existence and Enlightenment in the Laṅkāvatāra Sūtra: A Study in the Ontology and Epistemology of the Yogacara School of Mahayana Buddhism.* Albany: State University of New York Press, 1991.

Suzuki, Daisetz T., translator. *The Laṅkāvatāra Sūtra: A Mahāyāna Text.* London: Routledge and Kegan Paul, 1959.

Takasaki, Jikido. *A Study on the Ratnagotravibhāga (Uttaratantra) Being a Treatise on the Tathāgatagarbha Theory of Mahāyāna Buddhism.* Rome: Istituto Italiano per il Medio ed Estremo Oriente, 1966.

Tatz, Mark. "The Life of the Siddha-Philosopher Maitrīgupta." *Journal of the American Oriental Society* 107, no. 4 (1987): 695–711.
Williams, Paul. *Mahāyāna Buddhism: The Doctrinal Foundations*. London: Routledge, 1989.
Zimmermann, Michael. *A Buddha Within: The Tathāgatagarbhasūtra. The Earliest Exposition of the Buddha-Nature Teaching in India*. Tokyo: The International Research Institute for Advanced Buddhology, 2002.

1

*Bodhigarbha

Preliminary Notes on an Early Dzokchen Family of Buddha-Nature Concepts

David Higgins

Buddha-Nature Ideas during the Early Dissemination Period (8th–9th c.)

It has recently been alleged by scholars of the Tibetan "Ancient" (*rnying ma*) tradition that although buddha-nature theory was well known in Tibet from as early as the eighth century, it played quite an insignificant role in early Nyingma exegesis.[1] I intend in this chapter to challenge this assertion by demonstrating that buddha-nature concepts played a highly significant part in Dzokchen thought during the so-called early diffusion (*snga dar*) period, albeit mostly in the form of autochthonous **bodhigarbha* (*byang chub snying po*) or bodhi-nature concepts rather than their well-known Indian counterpart *tathāgatagarbha*[2] (*de bzhin gshegs pa'i snying po*), as well as the as yet unattested but virtually synonymous **sugatagarbha*[3] (*bde bar gshegs pa'i snying po*), which are both usually translated as buddha-nature. Although this family of terms is widespread in preclassical Dzokchen exegesis and therefore of inestimable importance for understanding the early development of buddha-nature theories in Tibet, it has hitherto received no attention in contemporary Buddhist studies. In determining the reasons for the obvious predilection for this indigenous family of buddha-nature concepts from the eighth to eleventh centuries, my aim is to clarify how bodhi-nature was understood by early Dzokchen authors, why it was distinguished from mainstream Mahāyāna-based buddha-nature concepts, and how it eventually became overshadowed by these latter during the classical period (13th–14th c.) as Indian non-tantric buddha-nature theories and controversies took center stage.[4] It is hoped that this short survey of Dzokchen bodhi-nature ideas and their cultural milieu will fill some gaps in our still fragmentary understanding of the origins of Tathāgatagarbha theory in Tibet. At the very least, it will show that a decidedly affirmative indigenous current of buddha-nature teachings flourished in Tibet several centuries prior to the ascendancy of the New (*gsar ma*) traditions and their polemically heated debates over rangtong (*rang stong*) and zhentong (*gzhan stong*) interpretations of buddha-nature.

It is important to bear in mind that the early Dzokchen (8th–11th c.) treatments of buddha-nature examined in this chapter predate the period of intensive exegesis and debate on this subject that followed the rise of new Tibetan religious schools from the late eleventh century onward. This later diffusion (*phyi dar*) period witnessed the translation of important buddha-nature texts, by far the most influential being the *Ratnagotravibhāga*,[5] which spawned a large number of Tibetan commentaries and a great deal of intersectarian debate. It is nonetheless well established that Mahāyāna buddha-nature concepts were well known in eighth-century Tibet since they are found in early translations of many important sūtras and in a few independent Tibetan treatises.[6] One of these latter was the eighth-century treatise by the renowned scholar-translator Yeshe De, titled *Distinctions of Views* (*Lta ba'i khyad par*),[7] which is probably the first independent Tibetan treatise on Mahāyāna Buddhist philosophy. In this work, with its blend of Yogācāra and Tathāgatagarbha influences, buddha-nature is explicitly identified with the embodiment of reality (dharmakāya, *chos sku*) and distinguished from the substratum consciousness (*ālayavijñāna, kun gzhi rnam par shes pa*).[8] In underscoring the distinctiveness of Mahāyāna, Yeshe De notes that "amongst the many sūtras such as the *Āryasamādhirāja* are found statements such as 'all sentient beings are endowed with buddha-nature'[9] and 'all sentient beings will become buddhas because none among them is not a [suitable] vessel.' "[10] When this buddha-nature is not clearly evident, it is called the "substratum [consciousness]" (*kun gzhi [rnam par shes pa]*), and when it is clearly evident, it is called the "embodiment of reality."[11] Each of these technical terms is carefully defined in his text. The "substratum consciousness," Yeshe De explains, is specified as a "substratum"—or, following the Tibetan translation, an "all-ground" (*ālaya, kun gzhi*)—because it is the ground of the seeds of all phenomena virtuous, nonvirtuous, and neutral.[12] And "since this is of the nature of cognition, it is also called 'consciousness.' "[13] "Substratum" is another word for the dichotomous mind (*citta, sems*), explains Yeshe De, because it builds up latent tendencies that are virtuous, nonvirtuous, and neutral.[14]

As for the term "embodiment of reality" (*chos sku*), "reality" (*chos*) here refers to the buddha-nature that is one's beginningless spiritual potential (*rigs*) because it is the very nature of all sentient beings. On account of becoming obscured by what is unreal (*yang dag pa ma yin pa*), it constitutes something defiled. But at the time of becoming free from error, through former reliance on correct application, it is present as one's very nature. This being present as one's nature is known as "embodiment of reality."[15]

Another early Tibetan treatise that discusses the buddha-nature is the *Lamp of Means and Insight* (*Thabs shes sgron ma*)[16] by the Mahāyoga proponent Lotsāwa

Bande Pelyang (8th c.)—one of the original seven monks ordained by Śāntarakṣita and the second Tibetan abbot of Samye Monastery. In this short text covering the essentials of Mahāyāna Buddhism from the standpoint of realizing the nature of mind, Pelyang explicitly identifies buddha-nature with the nature of mind. According to Pelyang, "for sentient beings who have long been deluded with regard to this buddha-nature, that is, the nature of mind, it appears individually in the mindstreams that cling to [the belief in] a self, while its very nature remains one with the dharmakāya of the victorious ones."[17] The term buddha-nature also occurs in many tantras of the period.[18] Dorji Wangchuk has also drawn attention to occurrences, albeit relatively small in number, of these standard buddha-nature concepts in Nyingma tantras of the Mahāyoga, Anuyoga, and Atiyoga classes, some dating to the Royal Dynastic period.[19]

In these sources, buddha-nature is identified with the nature of mind and nature of reality and is declared to transcend all representation by thought and language. The term buddha-nature—in its variant Tibetan reading *bde bar gshegs pa'i snying po*—is found in many early Dzokchen texts, such as the *Wheel of Existence* (*Srog gi 'khor lo*),[20] *Sprout of the Blissful Bodhicitta* (*Byang sems bde ba'i myu gu*),[21] *Guhyagarbha Tantra*,[22] and *Compendium of Intentions Sūtra* (*Dgongs 'dus pa'i mdo*).[23] All belong to the formative Mahāyoga and Mind Genre (*sems sde*), otherwise known as Mind Orientation (*sems phyogs*), traditions of Dzokchen. The first two mentioned are found among the corpus of eighteen tantras belonging to the Mind Genre that are said to have been transmitted in Tibet by Vairocana (8th c.). The *Guhyagarbha* is the root tantra (*mūlatantra*) within the *Māyājāla* (*Sgyu 'phrul drwa ba*) cycle and is generally classified as Mahāyoga. The *Compendium of Intentions* (*Dgongs 'dus*) was eventually by the fourteenth century considered to be the root tantra of the Anuyoga class[24] though nowhere is this identification made in the tantra itself or in the three works I have consulted that are attributed to Nubchen Sangye Yeshe (9th–10th c.), the remarkable scholar credited with assisting in its translation and authoring its first commentary. Rather, the scope of the tantra is the Secret Mantra tradition as a whole, inclusive of Mahā, Anu, and Ati[25] as these were known and practiced in mid-ninth to mid-tenth-century Tibet.[26]

Barking Up the Wrong Bodhi Tree?

It is thus indisputable that Indian buddha-nature doctrines and terminology were well known to Tibetans by as early as the eighth century, not only through translations of Indian sūtras and tantras but also through Tibetan-authored treatises. There is also broad consensus that buddha-nature theory was accepted as an important and valid Buddhist doctrine that, during this early period, generated little controversy. What is less conspicuous is the extent of its influence on preclassical Nyingma exegesis. Some contemporary scholars have claimed that this influence was negligible. This conclusion is understandable in light of the fairly small number of occurrences, and rather limited treatment, of the standard terms for buddha-nature[27] in the preclassical Nyingma sources. Yet the need to revisit this assessment becomes apparent when one takes account not only of the standard Indic terms for buddha-nature but also of the relative abundance of apparently indigenous buddha-nature concepts that were not only more prevalent than, but at times given explicit preference over, their Indic counterparts in these sources. These lead one to draw different conclusions: not only that buddha-nature, or more accurately "bodhi-nature" ideas occupied an important place in early Nyingma exegesis, but also that they should properly be seen as forming one of three overlapping constellations of core soteriological ideas—the other two pertaining to the nature of Mind (*sems nyid, byang chub kyi sems, ye shes, rig pa*) and the nature of reality (*de kho na nyid, de bzhin nyid, don dam pa*)—that dominate and define Dzokchen thought in this early period. These are all associated, often in the form of syntactic compounds, with the Dzokchen "ground" or "substratum" (*gzhi, kun gzhi*) in order to emphasize their common reference to human reality in its most ontologically primitive condition. In light of these associations it is also possible to confirm with corroborating statements by the eleventh-century Nyingma scholar Rongzom Chokyi Zangpo that the relative importance accorded to ideas concerning this bodhi-nature has much to do with their semantic affiliations with the all-important concept of innate bodhicitta as the fundamental basis or *conditio sine qua non* of Buddhist soteriology.

What intrigues us about the scattered references to buddha-nature in early Dzokchen scripture is that these terms, the focus of so much theorizing in later times, are here passed over with little notice. Conversely, **bodhigarbha* and its variants are distributed widely over the Mind Genre works and often treated in detail. There is substantial textual evidence to suggest that the authors of the Mahāyoga and Mind Genre scriptures, as well as their early Tibetan commentators, Nubchen and Rongzom in particular, preferred to employ the term, "quintessence of awakening" (*byang chub [kyi] snying po, snying po byang chub*) and occasionally "quintessence of the awakened mind" (*byang chub kyi sems snying po, snying po byang chub kyi sems*), over their standard Indic counterparts. The Tibetan term *byang chub snying po* or its equivalent *byang chub kyi snying po* are widely attested in early Dzokchen sources[28] while the less felicitous *snying po byang chub* comes a close second.[29]

Let us consider a few examples of terms belonging to this family and their relative importance. In the *Compendium of Intentions* (*Dgongs 'dus*), *bde gshegs snying po* occurs as but one in a series of terms for buddha-nature that includes primordial quintessence (*ye nas snying po*),[30] awakening-quintessence (*snying po byang chub*), quintessence of all (*kun gyi snying po*),[31] adamantine quintessence (*rdo rje snying po*),[32] and authentic arcane quintessence (*gsang ba dam pa snying po*).[33] These terms commonly describe an implicit, unconditioned mode of being and awareness that eludes the appropriations of reifying cognition. Significantly, Nubchen's commentary[34] on the relevant section of chapter 19 does not so much as mention the term *bde gshegs snying po* or even quote the line in which it occurs, though he does elaborate each of the other terms (except *ye nas snying po*) listed.[35] In his *Lamp for the Eye of Meditation* (*Bsam gtan mig sgron*), we are told that the quintessence of awakening is the true purport (*dgongs pa dam pa*) of all the buddhas, where "true purport" here signifies ineffable suchness, the nature of everything.[36]

Even this small sampling of bodhi-nature terminology leads one inescapably to the conclusion that buddha-nature ideas broadly defined were of considerable interest to the early Dzokchen authors, though less as a matter of defining or defending a particular line of interpretation based on Mahāyāna buddha-nature discourses, as was later increasingly the case, than as a way of conveying by means of terminology specific to the Dzokchen system the nature of mind or the awakened state itself.

*Bodhigarbha or Bodhimaṇḍa?

This brings us to the question of whether there is any Indian precedent for bodhi-nature, *byang chub snying po*. The Eighth Karmapa Mikyo Dorje (1507–1554) offers an intriguing indication that bodhi-nature indeed had an Indian Buddhist antecedent when he identifies it as one of the buddha-nature terms emphasizing the result or fruition aspect of buddhahood that the Bhagavān occasionally employed as a kind of heuristic fiction. More specifically, it is said to be a provisional locution, in need of further interpretation, that was coined in order to persuade those accustomed to thinking (erroneously) about buddha-nature in causal-teleological terms, the reality being that buddha-nature remains unchanging and beyond cause and effect.[37] Now, if bodhi-nature has yet to be attested in Indic sources, it is worth noting that the Tibetan equivalent was widely used in Tibetan translations of Indian Buddhist texts to render the Sanskrit *bodhimaṇḍa*, a term signifying both the "essence" (cream) and, by extension, the supreme place or seat of spiritual awakening. It refers, in other words, to the metaphorical and literal supreme place of awakening—the state of *bodhi* itself as well as the actual setting of the bodhi tree in Bodhgayā where a buddha attains awakening.[38] There is little doubt that the Eighth Karmapa had this Indian Buddhist idea of *bodhimaṇḍa* in mind when he presented bodhi-nature as an Indian buddha-nature concept referring to the fruition aspect of buddhahood, the result of emancipation (*bral 'bras*).[39] More specifically, he may well have had in mind the only occurrence of the term *bodhimaṇḍa* in the *Bodhicaryāvatāra* (II.26) where it indeed figures as the ultimate destination, both literal and metaphorical, of an aspiring bodhisattva. The text reads, "I go to the buddha for refuge until [reaching] the seat of awakening."[40]

In any event, this understanding of *bodhimaṇḍa* as the seat of awakening or supreme place where a buddha realizes spiritual awakening as well as the ultimate destination of an aspiring bodhisattva figures in a wide range of Mahāyāna sūtras.[41] There is also an interesting instance, in Aśvagoṣa and Śūra's *Saṃvṛttibodhicittabhāvana*, where *bodhimaṇḍa* is interpreted in the sense of a seed (*bīja*, *sa bon*) or germinal potential for awakening.[42] This calls to mind Mikyo Dorje's mention of the Buddha's other provisional explanation of buddha-nature, namely, as a cause of emancipation.[43]

It seems unavoidable to ask, at this juncture, whether the two principal employments of the Tibetan term for bodhi-nature—namely, as a Dzokchen term for buddha-nature and as a Tibetan rendering of the Sanskrit *bodhimaṇḍa*—have any genetic connection. Unfortunately, we do not yet have any textual evidence to confirm or disconfirm such an association. But the tantric and Dzokchen orientation of the Mind Genre corpus as a whole renders such an identification far from unproblematic.[44] In this regard, it must also be noted that Dzokchen interpretations of bodhi-nature explicitly eschew any attempt to frame it in terms of causes and results to the extent that Rongzom considered it a deviation (*gol sa*) from bodhi-nature to consider it as being produced by causes and conditions.[45] In short, to regard the essence of awakening as a result has at best a provisional meaning that stands in need of further interpretation. The Eighth Karmapa intimated this in his view of buddha-nature as transcending the provisional construal of it as a destination, the supreme point of awakening.

As for the provenance of the remaining early buddha-nature terms such as "awakening quintessence" and various related descriptors such as "primordial quintessence," among others—these would appear to belong to the pool of indigenous bodhi-nature terms sharing as a common reference the idea of innate awakened consciousness, the use of which are widespread in preclassical Dzokchen scriptures, though it must be noted that we have much yet to learn about the cultural transfers of ideas between Tibet and its neighboring Central Asian and Western Himalayan civilizations at this time.[46]

Bodhi-Nature versus Buddha-Nature

It is time now to return to the question of why these bodhi-nature terms were favored by early Nyingma exegetes over their well-established Indic counterparts. The predilection for these terms undoubtedly has much to do with the early Nyingma view—reflected in doxographies of the period—that tantric and Dzokchen paths are superior to sūtric both in doctrine and praxis.[47] This view reflects the ascendancy and widespread influence of Indian Buddhist tantric and Dzokchen models and teachings at the time of the Tibetan assimilation of Indian Buddhism. Dzokchen texts consecrate considerable attention to the idea of innate bodhicitta (*byang chub kyi sems*)—the ever-present awakened or wakeful consciousness within each sentient being—that the Buddhist path is said to progressively reveal. It is therefore not surprising that early Dzokchen scholars noted the strong family resemblance between its ideas of innate bodhicitta and those buddha-nature theories claiming that beings are already fully awakened buddhas even if they do not recognize this natural condition on account of adventitious obscurations. There are good reasons, then, to suppose that these bodhi-nature terms were favored primarily because of their close associations with the all-important concept bodhicitta and because of the tantric / Dzokchen identification of buddha-nature with this bodhicitta.[48]

To gain a clearer understanding of the prevalence of, and obvious preference for, bodhi-nature concepts in preclassical Dzokchen exegesis, we are assisted by Rongzom who sheds light on this issue in his commentary on *Guhyagarbha Tantra* (2.15), the only passage containing any standard term for buddha-nature in the tantra. There Rongzom distinguishes with characteristic perspicuity two contrasting ways of interpreting buddha-nature and the terminology involved:

> In this context, the term buddha-nature (*bde bar gshegs pa'i snying po*) is widely known in ordinary [scriptures] that claim that all sentient beings possess the cause of awakening and are endowed with the seed of incorruptibility. According to the profound [scriptures], it is called the "bodhi-nature" (*byang chub kyi snying po*) given that the very nature of mind is awakening. Therefore, it may appear as bondage in contrast to this state of affairs and it may appear as freedom by virtue of it[s presence]. Therefore, it is taught because one has not yet seen the reality (*don*) beyond bondage and freedom.[49]

In other words, the so-called "profound scriptures"—a category that, for Rongzom, included sūtric and tantric scriptures that discuss subjects deemed to be of definitive meaning (*nges don*)—view buddha-nature not as a germinal potential that is made to mature through appropriate causes and conditions of the causal-developmental model. Rather he suggests they are as ultimate bodhicitta itself, which is beyond the causal complex, being already fully present though temporarily shrouded by adventitious obscurations that need to be cleared away, which is the goal-disclosive model. It may be noted that although Rongzom lived during the period when the first Tibetan translations of the *Ratnagotravibhāga* were being made,[50] the text is not cited in any way in his extant writings. Certainly, the *Ratnagotravibhāga* had not yet attracted the kind of extensive scholarly attention that it soon would and it seems likely that it was unavailable and perhaps was unknown to Rongzom. Were a Sanskrit or Tibetan version of the *Ratnagotravibhāga* known to him, he would undoubtedly have found its disclosive model of buddha-nature to be congenial with, and perhaps a vindication of, the disclosive view of bodhi-nature that was advocated in early Dzokchen exegesis. At any rate, in his assessment of the buddha-nature theories known to him, bodhi-nature concepts are given explicit priority over their buddha-nature counterparts on the grounds that the former articulate a disclosive model of awakening in contrast to the developmental model of the latter. Table 2.1 serves to clarify Rongzom's distinction between these models.

Table 2.1. Rongzom's comparison of ordinary and profound buddha-nature ideas

Buddha-Nature Scriptures	Ordinary Scriptures	Profound Scriptures
buddha-nature concepts (Skt.)	*tathāgatagarbha*, **sugatagarbha*	*bodhigarbha*, **garbhabodhi*(?)
buddha-nature concepts (Tib.)	*de bzhin gshegs pa'i snying po*, *bde bar gshegs pa'i snying po*	*byang chub [kyi] snying po*, *snying po byang chub*
buddha-nature model	Developmental model	Disclosive model
Interpretation of awakening	Awakening is germinally present as "seed" that ripens through appropriate causes and conditions (path factors)	Awakening already fully present as nature of mind but obscured by adventitious defilements

At issue, then, in Rongzom's distinction between so-called ordinary (*thun mong*) and profound (*zab mo*) scriptures and their interpretations of buddha-nature is a fundamental and long-standing tension between two aforementioned Buddhist views concerning the nature of goal realization. One construes it as a developmental process of accumulating merits and knowledge that serve as causes and conditions leading to awakening, whereas the other views it as a disclosive process of directly recognizing and then becoming increasingly familiar with a primordial mode of knowing as the mind's reifications and their obscuring effects subside. These were sometimes distinguished as the cause-oriented and goal-oriented approaches (in reference to their sūtric versus tantric variants), but Rongzom, like many Tibetan scholars, includes sūtras and śāstras deemed to be of definitive meaning in the category of the profound, though he unfortunately does not specify which buddha-nature texts belong to this category.

In general terms, the developmental paradigm is represented by many currents of Indian Buddhist scholasticism. The most influential being the Madhyamaka and epistemological Pramāṇa traditions. It holds a graded course analytical investigation and ethical refinement to be indispensable to spiritual awakening. The disclosive paradigm is emphasized in Buddhist tantric and siddha traditions and in buddha-nature discourses. It accords a great deal of autonomy to the enlightened condition itself, viewing intellectual and moral refinement as only part of what makes this condition evident in the life of the aspirant. While the developmental model is concerned primarily with what is to be refuted—the superimpositions of thought—the disclosive model gives primacy to what is thereby revealed or actualized—the ever-present though strangely elusive buddha-nature or nature of mind. The difference between the developmental and disclosive paradigms, then, comes down to their comparatively thin and thick descriptions of the nonconceptual state of awakening that is regarded by both systems to be the goal of the Buddhist path.

Bodhi-Nature as the Primordial Ground

Let us now turn our attention to some relevant explanations of bodhinature in early Dzokchen works. Because this bodhi-nature reveals itself during the process of disclosure known as the path, it is characterized as the ever-present ground (*ye / gdod ma'i gzhi*) or the condition of possibility of spiritual awakening, and is therefore identified with bodhicitta. In early Dzokchen sources, the locutions ground and substratum (or "ground of all") are used synonymously with and frequently in combination with bodhicitta, arguably the most important and influential idea or ideal in early Dzokchen discourses. The conjunction awakened mind qua substratum (*kun gzhi byang chub [kyi] sems*) is attested in several of the early Nyingma tantras[51] assigned to the Mind Genre and invites comparison with the appositional compound awakened mind as awareness (*rig pa byang chub kyi sems*) that is encountered frequently. Fairly typical in this regard is the statement from the *Wheel of Existence*, one of the early texts included in the corpus of eighteen Mind Genre tantras:[52]

> The uncontrived awakened mind, the ground of all [in which appearances] are nonexistent, is luminous by nature. Since the environing world and its inhabitants without exception are fully awakened, there have never been any to train. Since everything without exception is buddhahood, it is the great way of the Tathāgatas.[53]

Other related synonyms of the ground include well-known Dzokchen technical terms mind itself (*sems nyid*), the nature of mind (*sems kyi rang bzhin, sems kyi chos nyid*), self-occurring primordial knowing (*rang byung ye shes*), awareness (*rig pa*), as well as an early neologism of Nubchen's, the self-aware awakened mind (*rang rig pa'i byang chub kyi sems*).

In his groundbreaking work on early Dzokchen, Samten Karmay made the comment that in early Dzokchen texts "no reference is made to in connection with the Primordial Basis."[54] However, two commentaries of Nubchen that have since become available explicitly identify this ground with bodhi-nature, which we have established, with corroboration from Rongzom as the early Dzokchen counterpart of buddha-nature. Commenting on a passage from the *Spontaneously Arisen Peak* (*Rtse mo byung rgyal*) that declares that bodhi-nature, which is nondual and selfless, is not found as any reality other than the unity of primordial knowing and its expanse, Nubchen explains that since the ground that is the quintessence of awakening (*snying po byang chub kyi gzhi*) is simply one's self-awareness (*rang rig pa*)—the phenomena of goal-realization are not to be discovered elsewhere.[55]

In chapter 55 of his lengthy commentary on the *Compendium of Intentions* (*Dgongs 'dus*), a chapter largely devoted to the concept of the substratum, Nubchen explicitly identifies this invariant substratum with buddha-nature. In several instances, such as the following, he describes the quintessence of awakening that is the substratum (*kun gzhi byang chub kyi snying po*), using examples and characterizations redolent of buddha-nature discourses:

> The ground and root of all qualities belonging to the dharmakāya of the perfectly realized buddha—that is, the bodhi-nature that is the substratum—is that very nature that is associated with ignorance. Thus, just as the root of a lotus flower is planted firmly in a swamp, so the root of great awakening is present in this cyclical existence itself. So too the errancy of the substratum stems from the two aspects of coemergent ignorance.[56]

Nubchen goes on to specify that the very source of buddha qualities is at the same time the source of spiritual darkness: "The nature of spiritual darkness is the awakened mind as self-awareness because its essence is difficult to realize given that it lies very deep and is difficult to fathom."[57] Nonetheless, he adds, one cannot ascertain this quintessence of awakening by means of arduous procedures of rational inference (*blos dpag*). Since bodhi-nature is realized very swiftly, it is also not arrived at through arduous progression (*brtsol bgrod*).[58] Beings remain blind to their own fundamental nature because of deeply rooted ignorance that persists up to the tenth spiritual level.

> Since coemergent ignorance without afflictions still exists even in bodhisattvas on the tenth spiritual level, the great root (*rtsa ba chen po*) remains unseen. It thus remains obscured up to the tenth level, and the obscurations are present in greater and lesser, subtler and coarser, degrees in each and every person so long as their minds arise in the states associated with dwelling on these levels.[59]

Nubchen proceeds to explain that the nature of reality that is the ground or bodhi-nature remains unseen because it is empty and therefore beyond the range of reifying thinking. In language again reminiscent of Indian buddha-nature classics, he concludes that this self-awareness is fully disclosed only at the time of spiritual awakening, though it has been present all along as an implicit knowing that, paradoxically, makes possible all explicit acts of knowing while itself remaining unknown. It is, in Nubchen's words, like the eye that cannot see itself.

Concluding Reflections

The classical Nyingma polymath Longchen Rabjam (1308–1364) will later trace this relationship between the ground and buddha-nature to the *Net of Illusion* (*Māyājāla*) tantric cycle where buddha-nature is characterized as the ground of possibility of errancy as well as freedom. One early source of such an interpretation is the previously noted passage from the *Sprout of the Blissful Bodhicitta* (*Byang sems bde ba'i myu gu*) that reads: "From the buddha-nature [present in] all sentient beings, One goes astray due to conceptualizing and karma." Now, these lines closely resemble and suggest a different reading of the two oft-quoted lines on buddha-nature from the *Guhyagarbha Tantra* (2.15): "E ma ho! From the buddha-nature, individual conceptualizing manifests due to karma."[60] Longchenpa's numerous quotations of this *Guhyagarbha Tantra* passage render *sprul* (manifest, emanate) as its near-homophone *'khrul* (err, go astray), though not in his commentary the *Dispelling Darkness in the Ten Directions* (*Phyogs bcu mun sel*), which retains *sprul*. His commentary on the passage in question, however, accommodates both readings, suggesting that errancy (*'khrul*) and the ensuing phenomenal manifestation (*sprul*) derive from a common ground, buddha-nature:

> 'E ma ho!' expresses the very nature of kindness. Errancy has derived from the dimension of the buddha-nature, one's primordial abiding condition, luminous mind itself. Here, buddha-nature refers to radiantly clear mind itself, which abides as the very essence of the three *kāyas* that are inseparably united. . . . In the *Sgyu 'phrul rgyas pa*[61] its meaning is the actual substratum that is unconditioned (*'dus ma byas don gyi kun gzhi*):

It is not the substratum of conceptualizing,
But the genuine ground that is without intrinsic nature.
That is called the expanse of phenomena,
Primordial knowing of suchness.

When errancy occurs due to any given conditions, the conceptual thinking of individual sentient beings naturally arises. Thus, the great city of saṃsāra manifests like a self-appearing dream due the amplifying [effect of] karma.[62]

The passage is also cited in the author's autocommentary to his *Wish-Granting Treasury* (*Yid bzhin mdzod 'grel*) where buddha-nature is identified as the ground, more specifically the genuine substratum as one's abiding condition (*gnas lugs don gyi kun gzhi*) from which saṃsāra and nirvāṇa emerge[63] and to which the aspirant seeks to return. The substratum in question is here qualified as the genuine or actual substratum (*don gyi kun gzhi*) to distinguish it from the conditioned substratum, or the substratum of myriad latent tendencies (*rkyen gyi kun gzhi, bag chags sna tshogs kyi kun gzhi*), the Yogācāra *ālayavijñāna*. As I have indicated elsewhere, this important distinction was introduced in early Nyingma tantras and given its first extended philosophical treatment by Nubchen in his *Armor Against Darkness* (*Mun pa'i go cha*).[64]

To conclude, it would appear that tantric bodhi-nature concepts remained in vogue in Dzokchen traditions well into the eleventh century after which time they were steadily eclipsed by the standard Indian non-tantric terminology. This gradual displacement undoubtedly had much to do with the growing influence of the *Ratnagotravibhāga* and related works within the ascendant classical Tibetan Buddhist schools and the perceived relevance of this śāstra's disclosive path model to the important Nyingma hermeneutical problem of bridging the divergent sūtric, tantric, and Dzokchen discourses concerning the Buddhist path.

NOTES

1. Wangchuk, "rÑiṅ-ma Interpretations" 179. "Yet even though the [buddha-nature] theory has certainly been present from early times in the rÑiṅ-ma literature, it seems to have played quite an insignificant role and never gained prominence or an independent status, in the way it was conceived, for instance, in the *Tathāgatagarbhasūtra*." This conclusion is repeated by Almogi, *Rong-zom-pa's Discourse on Buddhology* 160.

2. For a detailed discussion of the term buddha-nature, see Zimmermann 2002, 39–40.

3. Although **sugatagarbha* is not attested in Sanskrit (see Seyfort Ruegg, *Traité du tathāgatagarbha* 68), Wangchuk, "rÑiṅ-ma Interpretations" 178 and n. 21, points out (on the basis of references provided to him by Kazuo Kano) that "the term *bde gśegs sñiṅ po* does occur in the Tibetan translations of the *Aṅgulimālīyasūtra* (P fol. 174a5; D fol. 166b2: *bde gśegs sñiṅ po theg pa che las skyes*) and *Ghanavyūhasūtra* (P fol. 62b1; D fol. 55b1: *bde gśegs sñiṅ po dge ba'aṅ de*; cf., however, Taishō 747a7) for which the Sanskrit is not extant." We

may add that the term *bde [bar] gshegs [pa'i] snying po* occurs in a large number of Tibetan translations of Indian works. A search of the Derge Bka' 'gyur and Bstan 'gyur canons using the contraction *bde gshegs snying po* turned up occurrences in the following sūtras in addition to those mentioned earlier: *Bhadrakalpika* (D 94), *Sūtrasammucayabhāṣtaratnālokālaṃkāra* (D 3935), *Laṅkāvatāravṛttitathāgatahṛdayālaṃkāra* (D 4031), and *Sūtrālaṃkārapaṇḍārtha* (D 4031). It is also found in twenty-two tantric works: D 453, 829, 832, 833, 834, 837 (these last four belong to the *Māyājāla-Guhyagarbha* cycle), 1202, 1401, 1407, 1414, 1613, 1630, 1644, 2128, 2304, 2626, 2816, 2834, 2837, 3713, 3723, and 4449. The unabbreviated *bde bar gshegs pa'i snying po* occurs in the following tantric works: Kaṇha's *Hevajranāmamahātantrarājadvikalpamāyapañjikāsmṛtinipāda* (*Rgyud kyi rgyal po dgyes pa'i rdo rje zhes bya ba sgyu ma brtag pa gnyis pa'i dka' 'grel dran pa'i 'byung gnas*), which, however, does not contain the term buddha-nature, D 1187; *Mañjuśrīnāmasaṃgītiṭīkāvimalaprabhā* (*'Jam dpal gyi mtshan yang dag par brjod pa'i grel pa dri ma med pa'i 'od*), D 1398; *Bhagavatsarvadurgatipariśodhanatejorajatathāgatāhatsamyaksaṃbuddhamahātantrarājavyākhyāsundarālaṃkāra (Bcom ldan 'das de bzhin gshegs pa dgra bcom pa yang dag par rdzogs pa'i sangs rgyas ngan song thams cad yongs su sbyong ba gzi brjid kyi rgyal po chen po'i rnam par bshad pa mdzes pa'i rgyan)*, D 2626; *Vajravidāraṇānāmadhāraṇīpaṭalakramabhāṣyavṛttipradīpa* (*Rdo rje rnam par 'joms pa'i gzung zhes bya ba'i rim par phye ba'i rgya cher 'grel ba gsal ba'i sgron ma*), D 2687; *Tantrārthāvatāravyākhyāna* (*Rgyud kyi don la 'jug pa'i 'grel bshad*), D 2502; *Mahābalikarmakramavṛtti* (*Gtor ma chen po'i las kyi rim pa'i 'grel pa*), D 3773. This is not the place for an analysis of these occurrences. It is hoped that future research may determine whether any of them can be traced to an extant Indian work containing the term **sugatagarbha*.

4. On problems of Tibetan historical periodization and a useful variant based on existing schemes, see Cuevas, "Some Reflections." For a useful doctrinal-historical periodization scheme based on developments in Tibetan Buddhist epistemology, see van der Kuijp 1989. Loosely following van der Kuijp's proposed periodization, we can distinguish (1) the Ancient (*rnying ma*) period (8th–9th c.) corresponding to the Early Dissemination (*snga dar*) and Early Translation (*snga 'gyur*) period, which witnessed a massive program of translating Indian works into Tibetan and the growth of early Tibetan monastic communities under the sponsorship of the Tibetan Empire; (2) the Preclassical period (late 10th–12th c.) corresponding to the Late Dissemination (*phyi dar*) and New Translation (*gsar 'gyur*) periods following the collapse of the Tibetan Imperium (and ensuing Period of Fragmentation, ca. 910–1056), which witnessed a campaign of new reformed translations of Indian Buddhist texts and the ascendency of the so-called New (*gsar ma*) Tibetan Buddhist schools (and their scholastic traditions) that were henceforth distinguished from the Ancients (*rnying ma*); (3) the Classical period (13th–14th c.), which was characterized by the expansion of the major Tibetan Buddhist schools and the consolidation and systematization of their representative doctrines and practices; and (4) the Postclassical period (15th c. onward) characterized by the intensification of intersectarian dialogue and polemicism fueled by the increasingly fractious sectarian politics as Tibetan orders vied for patronage by foreign powers (Mongols and Chinese) and domestic aristocratic clans.

5. On the history of transmission of the *Ratnagotravibhāga* in India, Tibet, and China, see Kano, *Buddha Nature and Emptiness*.

6. For an illuminating overview of Nyingma views on buddha-nature, see Wangchuk, "rÑiṅ-ma Interpretations."

7. D 4360: 426.1–455.7. A different redaction of the work was retrieved from the caves at Dunhuang (ms. Pelliot Tibétain 814), on which see Seyfort Ruegg, "Autour du lTa ba'i khyad."

8. Wangchuk, "rÑiṅ-ma Interpretations," has noted that almost all of the Indian sources on buddha-nature noted by Seyfort Ruegg, *Le Traité du tathāgatagarbha*, are contained in the early *Ldan dkar ma* catalogue. Ye shes sde (8th c.) is thus able to quote or cite many of these in his *Lta ba'i khyad par*.

9. The earliest textual sources of the doctrine that "all sentient beings have buddha-nature" are the *Mahāparinirvāṇa Mahāsūtra* and *Tathāgatagarbha Sūtra*. See Zimmermann, *Buddha Within* 112–113, and Radich, *The* Mahāparinirvāṇamahāsūtra. The doctrine is subsequently taken up and developed in various sūtras such as the *Anūnatvāpūrṇatvanirdeśaparivarta*, *Śrīmālādevīsiṃhanādanirdeśa Sūtra*, and *Samādhirāja Sūtra*, and further systematized in the *Ratnagotravibhāga*. For an overview of these developments, see Kano, *Buddha Nature and Emptiness* 1 and n. 1.

10. *Lta ba'i khyad par* 434.4: . . . *'phags pa ting nge 'dzin rgyal po la sogs pa mdo sde mang po las sems can thams cad ni de bzhin gshegs pa'i snying po can yin no zhes 'byung ba dang / sems can thams cad sangs rgyas su 'gyur te / snod ma yin pa gang yang med do / zhes 'byung ba la sogs pa* . . .

11. A supporting quotation from an unidentified sūtra entitled *'Phags pa dung phreng gi mdo* reads (436.4): *de bzhin gshegs pa'i snying po gsal bar ma gyur pa'i tshe ni kun gzhi zhes bya'o / gsal bar gyur pa de'i tshe ni chos sku zhes bya'o*. The same passage and attribution are found in the early treatise *Gsung rab rin po che'i gtam rgyud dang shākya'i rabs rgyud* (D 4357: vol. 205, 273a.4) ascribed to Ska ba Dpal brtsegs, another renowned translator of the Royal Dynastic period who is counted as one of the first seven monks ordained by Śāntarakṣita.

12. *Lta ba'i khyad par* 446.3: *kun gzhi rnam par shes pa ni dge ba dang / mi dge ba dang lung du ma bstan pa'i chos thams cad kyi sa bon gyi gzhi yin pas kun gzhi'o*. Compare with the observation of Rang byung rdo rje that the term *kun gzhi* (*ālaya*) when it is used independently of *rnam par shes pa* (*vijñāna*) is not necessarily a shorthand for *kun gzhi rnam par shes pa* (*ālayavijñāna*) but "can also refer to suchness" (*tathatā, de bzhin nyid*). *Zab mo nang don gyi 'grel pa, Rang byung rdo rje gsung 'bum* vol. 7: 383.2: *'di yang kun gzhi zhes bya ba la rnam par shes pa'i sgra ma smos na de bzhin nyid la yang kun gzhis brjod du rung ba'i phyir rnam par shes pa smos so*. See Mathes, *Direct Path* 57 and n. 297. Klong chen pa also made a point of distinguishing *ālaya* from the *ālayavijñāna*. See Higgins, *Philosophical Foundations*.

13. *Lta ba'i khyad par* 446.4: *shes pa'i rang bzhin yin pas rnam par shes pa'o*.

14. *Lta ba'i khyad par* 446.4: *kun gzhi ni ming gcig tu sems zhes kyang bya ste / dge ba dang mi dge ba dang lung du ma bstan pa'i bag chags sogs pa'i phyir ro*.

15. *Lta ba'i khyad par* 436.5: *chos ni thog ma med pa nas rigs su gyur ba de bzhin gshegs pa'i snying po la bya ste / sems can thams cad kyi rang bzhin no / de ni yang dag pa ma yin pas bsgribs pas dri ma can du gyur te / gang gi tshe sbyor ba sngon du btad nas 'khrul pa dang bral ba de'i tshe rang bzhin du 'gyur ro / rang bzhin du gyur ba de ni chos kyi sku zhes bshad do*.

16. D 4449, vol. nos., 768.6–769.6. This is one of the *Six Lamps* (*Sgron ma drug*) attributed to Gnyan dpal dbyangs (8th c.), an important figure in the early history and transmission of Mahāyoga in Tibet. On the *Six Lamps*, see Tucci, *Minor Buddhist Texts II* 141–154 (includes text summaries); Ueyama, "Peruyan Cho No Daiyuga Bunken"; Karmay, *Great Perfection* 66–69; and Takahashi, "Lamps for the Mind" 100–143 (translations and critical editions: 318–429). Dpal dbyangs was also author of the *Rdo rje sems pa'i zhus lan* (*Vajrasattva Questions and Answers*) (P 5082 and Dunhuang ms. PT 837), on which see Eastman, "Mahāyoga Texts at Tun-huang"; Karmay, *Great Perfection* 67; and Takahashi, "Ritual and Philosophical Speculation" and "Lamps for the Mind" 84–99 (translation and

critical edition: 277–317). Another work entitled *Gces pa bsdus pa'i 'phrin yig bod rje 'bangs la brdzangs pa* (*Letter Summarizing the Essentials Dispatched to the Tibetan Emperor*) is attributed to Dpal dbyangs, but questions of authorship raised by Tucci and Yamaguchi remain unresolved. For the most recent discussion, see Takahashi, "Ritual and Philosophical Speculation" 143–149. I am grateful to Carmen Meinert for drawing my attention to contemporary research on Dpal dbyangs.

17. D fol. 769.1 (also *Bka' ma shin tu rgyas pa* vol. 82, 1052.2): *bde gshegs snying po sems kyi rang bzhin la / yun ring dus nas rmongs pa'i sems can rnams / bdag tu 'dzin pa'i sems rgyud so sor snang / rang bzhin nyid ni rgyal ba'i chos skur gcig.*

18. See Wangchuk, "rÑiṅ-ma Interpretations" 178–180.

19. See Karmay, *Great Perfection* 184; and Wangchuk, "rÑiṅ-ma Interpretations" 179.

20. *Srog gi 'khor lo*, Tk vol. 1, 446.3: *khams gsum brtags na 'khor ba mya ngan med / phyogs char brtses na bde gshegs snying po yin / kun gyi rang bzhin 'ja' tshon snang bzhin med.* In Tb vol. 1, the second line reads: *phyogs char 'char ba rtses na bde gshegs snying po yin.* The passage as found quoted in the *Bsam gtan mig sgron* of Gnubs Sangs rgyas ye shes is: *khams gsum brtags na 'khor ba mya ngan med / phyogs char gtsen na bde gshegs snying po min.* This reading (*min* not *yin*) is corroborated by a commentary on this tantra found in the *Bka' ma shin tu rgyas pa*, vol. 103, 248.3: *phyogs char gces na bde gshegs snying po min / kun gyi rang bzhin 'ja' tshon snang bzhin med.* "If evaluated in a partial manner [commentary: that is, by way of valid sources of knowledge], it is not the buddha-nature. The nature of all is rainbow[-like], apparent yet nothing." It is noteworthy that the term *bde gshegs snying po* is not found in the version of *Srog gi 'khor lo* contained in Bg vol. 1, 305.5, which appears to be an altogether different work, but the indigenous alternative *snying po byang chub* occurs twice. See 307.3 and also 310.5, which states: "Because the naturally occurring Bhagavān has always been the essence of ultimate reality, it is also called the awakening-quintessence which is nothing conceivable" (*rang byung gi bcom ldan 'das don dam pa'i ngo bo ye nas yin pas / snying po byang chub dgongs su med pa zhes kyang bya*).

21. Tk vol. 1, 449.7: *lhun gyis grub pas che ba la / thams cad bde gshegs snying po las / rnam rtog las kyis 'khrul pa la.* For the same passage in Tb, see vol. 1, 630.6.

22. See note 3 in this chapter for a listing of four works belonging to the *Māyājāla-Guhyagarbha* cycle that contain the contraction *bde gshegs snying po.*

23. Tb vol. 16, 31.1–2, 146.1–2.

24. Rog Bande Shes rab 'od identified it in this way in his thirteenth-century *Bstan pa'i sgron me.*

25. The *Dgongs 'dus* became the locus classicus for the well-known Nyingma classification of nine vehicles. While earlier ninefold systems had been attempted in Dunhuang texts and elsewhere, the *Dgongs 'dus* "may have been the first source to present them as they appear in the later tradition." See Dalton, "Uses of the *Dgongs pa 'dus pa'i mdo*" 85.

26. See Dalton, 318–319. Dalton notes the *rtsa rlung* (channels and winds) practices, which became a hallmark of later Dzokchen characterizations of *Anuyoga*, are given only passing reference in the *Dgongs 'dus.*

27. Tib. *de bzhin gshegs pa'i snying po* and *bde bzhin gshegs pa'i snying po*, Skt. *tathāgatagarbha* and **sugatagarbha.*

28. The term occurs frequently in the *Rtse mo byung rgyal*, Tk vol. 1, 434.4, 435.5 (*ye nas lhun grub byang chub snying po*), 437.7, 439.6, 440.4, 440.6. Among the very numerous occurrences of the term in *Sems sde* works, see *Khyung chen ldings pa*, Tk vol. 1, 422.5; *Khyung che ldings pa'i 'grel pa, Bka' ma shin tu rgyas pa* vol. 103, 19.4–5, where it is described as the true reality of all entities present in self-awareness, which due to its self-manifesting as

anything whatsoever, is difficult to apprehend as characteristics and therefore is irreducible to an epistemic object (*shes yul du rgya ma chad pa*); *Dgongs 'dus pa'i mdo*, Tb vol. 16, 415.1; *Byang chub sems 'khor lo rdo rje*, Tk vol. 2, 309.4, 310.4, *Nam mkha'i mtha' dang mnyam pa'i rgyud chen po*, Bg vol. 1, 182.1, 197.4, 237.3, 261.1. Occurrences of the term in Gnubs chen's works include *Rtse mo byung rgyal 'grel pa*, 205.5, 207; *Mun pa'i go cha*, pt. 2, 50.6, 55.1; *Bsam gtan mig sgron*, 394.4. The term is discussed by Rong zom pa in his *Theg chen tshul 'jug*, *Rong zong gsung 'bum* vol. 1, 503.9–10 where, in the context of specifying deviations (*gol sa*) from **bodhigarbha*, he characterizes it as (1) free from all characteristics of appearance (503.18ff.), (2) unmodified by extraneous influences (503.24–25), and (3) unproduced by causes and conditions (504.14–15). See also his *Rgyud rgyal gsang ba snying po dkon cog 'grel*, 127.13 (discussed later in this chapter). The term is also found in the seventeen Atiyoga tantras of the Snying thig system, as for example in *Kun tu bzang po thugs kyi me long*, Ati vol. 1, 258.1 and 260.5, where this **bodhigarbha* is said to be without obscurations or deviations: *byang chub snying po gol dang sgrib pa med pa la*. The six occurrences of the term in this tantra include the formulations *byang chub don gyi snying po* (Ati vol. 1, 250.2) and *byang chub snying po'i sku* (Ati vol. 1, 263.1). See also *Rig pa rang shar*, Ati vol. 1, 472.5, where **bodhigarbha* is held to be equal to all buddhas and linked with unchanging and unerring bodhicitta, which totally pervades living beings: *'gyur med byang chub sems la 'khrul pa ga la yod / 'khrul med byang chub sems ni 'gro ba yongs la khyab / byang chub snying po sangs rgyas kun dang mnyam*.

29. See for examples: *Srog gi 'khor lo*, Bg vol. 1, 305.5, 307.3, 310.5; *Mi nub rgyal mtshan*, Tk vol. 1, 425.3; *Bcom ldan 'das lung thams cad kyi rang bzhin*, Bg vol. 2, 232.3; *Nam mkha'i mtha' dang mnyam pa'i rgyud chen po*, Bg vol. 1, 241.4, 276.5. See also *Khyung che ldings pa'i 'grel pa*, *Bka' ma shin tu rgyas pa* vol. 103, 22.5, where *snying po byang chub* is claimed to be none other than dharmakāya that, being a naturally present great fruition (*'bras bu chen po*), eludes any attempts to strive for its attainment; and 26.5 where *ye snying po byang chub pa* is explained according to the *Nam mkha' che* (i.e., *Mi nub rgyal mtshan*). An interlinear note on the *Sbas pa'i rgum chung*. IOL 594 chap. 73-11-21 fol. 1a.1 uses the abbreviated form *nying byang chub*, which Namkai Norbu glosses as *ye gzhi snying po byang chub kyi sems* in his commentary. See Norbu 1984, 116. Gnubs chen often employs *snying po byang chub* as, for example, in *Rtse mo byung rgyal 'grel pa*, 186.6, 207.6, *Bsam gtan mig sgron*, 395.3. The term *snying po byang chub (kyi sems)* occurs frequently in Gnubs chen's *Mun pa'i go cha*, as for example pt. 1: 244.5, 245.6; pt. 2: 50.3. Rong zom pa also uses the term interchangeably with *byang chub snying po*, as in *Theg chen tshul 'jug*, 503.15, 509.14.

30. Tb vol. 16, 145.4.

31. Tb vol. 16, 146.2.

32. Tb vol. 16, 146.6.

33. Tb vol. 16, 146.7.

34. This is Gnubs chen Sangs rgyas ye shes's most extensive extant work, the *Mun pa'i go cha*, a massive commentary that fills two volumes of the recently discovered *Bka' ma shin tu rgyas pa*. This work is discussed at length in Dalton, "Uses of the *Dgongs pa 'dus pa'i mdo*. Other works attributed to Gnubs chen but no longer extant are noted by Takahashi, "Lamps for the Mind" 254–256.

35. See *Mun pa'i go cha*, pt. 1: 244.5.

36. *Bsam gtan mig sgron* 394.4: *byang chub kyi snying po ni / sangs rgyas kun gyi dgongs pa dam pa la bya'o . . . dgongs pa dam pa zhes gang la bya . . . thams cad kyi rang bzhin rang lags pa de kho na nyid do . . . thams cad kyi rang bzhin gsang sngags bya bya . . . thams cad* [text: *thad*] *kyi rang bzhin gang lags pa de ni / gang gis kyang ma mthong / mi rtog*[a]

spyod yul du ma gyur / smrar med pa / brjod pa las 'das pa / bsam du med pa / bsam gyis mi khyab pa . . .

[a]text has *rtogs*.

37. *Dpyad pa bdud rtsi'i dri mchog*: 984.4–5: "As for the name of this abiding inseparably as **buddhagarbha* and *dharmadhātujñāna*, the Bhagavān designated it with the terms 'result of buddhahood' [and] 'the supreme point of awakening' (*byang chub kyi snying po, bodhimaṇḍa*). In some cases, he referred to that [factor] by means of the locution 'cause of buddhahood.' But labeling this **buddhagarbha* in terms of cause and result is nothing but a metaphor. It is not tenable to say this buddha-nature is the result of anything because there is nothing in this buddha-nature whereby such a distinction can be made between efficient causes (*rgyu'i nyer len*) and cooperating conditions (*lhan cig byed pa'i rkyen*) that [together] produce (*skyed byed*) [the result]." Mi bskyod rdo rje goes on to explain that "the point of speaking in some cases of a cause of buddhahood and in others of a result [namely, effect] of buddhahood is this. On the part of those trainees who are under the influence of [ordinary] consciousness, the [buddha] nature at the time when it seemed to become separated from the chaff, appeared as though it were a result of emancipation (*bral 'bras*). Bearing this in mind, [the buddha] spoke of it as a 'result.' And the quintessence at the time when it appeared to be together with the chaff, appeared as though it were a cause, namely, the cause leading to the result of emancipation from that [chaff]. With this in mind, [the buddha] spoke of it as a cause, a potential, and an element. From the perspective of [ordinary] consciousness, because the mind is mistaken concerning a quintessence that is unchanging and unwavering, it cannot deeply penetrate these concepts, so sometimes [the quintessence] is mistaken for a cause, and sometimes it is mistaken for a result. However, the quintessence is not established in any way as a cause and result. With this in mind, it was stated [in RGV 27c] that "[b]ecause 'result' was metaphorically ascribed to that [buddha-nature] . . ." See RGVV, 26_3: *bauddhe gotre tatphalasyopacārād /*. This passage from the *Ratnagotravibhāgavyākhyā* is quoted by Mi bskyod rdo rje in order to defend the claim that buddha-nature is only provisionally and metaphorically (*nye [bar] btags [pa] = upacāra*) posited as a result or effect [lit., "fruit"] for the benefit of those habituated to causal-teleological modes of thought and explanation, buddha-nature being itself beyond causes and results.

38. See *Mahāvyutpatti* no. 4114. In Classical Sanskrit, *maṇḍa* (lit., "cream") properly means the "scum" that forms on top of a liquid or boiled liquid, and thus also the cream that forms on the top of milk. From this derive the cognate senses of "essence" as well as "best," "best part," "highest point," "supreme point" (compare with English expressions "the cream of the crop," "the cream of society"). See Edgerton, *Sanskrit Grammar* s.v. *maṇḍa*. Edgerton notes that "in bodhimaṇḍa the literal meaning of *maṇḍa* is clearly the best, supreme point (*snying po*, heart, essence). It is used alone, or with other qualifiers to refer to *bodhimaṇḍa*: *gacchitva maṇḍam varapādapendram*, 'Having gone to the supreme place, the excellent king of trees (i.e., the bodhi-tree).'" In this last example, one notes the convergence of literal and metaphorical senses of the "supreme place," bodhi and the bodhi tree.

39. "Result of emancipation" (*visaṃyogaphala, bral 'bras*) is included as the third of five types of fruition or result (*phala*) outlined in *Abhidharmakośa* chap. 2, 55cd–58cd. Mi bskyod rdo rje here refers to a standard sūtric paradigm of the Buddhist path comprising (1) the ground of emancipation (*bral gzhi*), (2) causes of emancipation (*bral rgyu*), (3) result of emancipation (*bral 'bras*), and (4) objects to be emancipated from (*bral bya*). In the context of Mantrayāna, they are described in terms of a clearing process rather than emancipation process. The relationship between these paradigms has been noted by the Nyingma polymath Klong chen rab 'byams pa: "In this context, one should understand there are four [phases]:

[1] the ground where emancipation occurs, [2] the causes of emancipation, [3] the result of emancipation, and [4] the objects to be emancipated from. [1] The emancipation ground is the spiritual potential, the buddha-nature; [2] the causes of emancipation are the facets that comprise the path, those virtuous actions conducive to liberation that clear away the defilements accreted on this [quintessence]; [3] the result of emancipation is the disclosure of qualities once the buddha-nature has been freed from the plethora of defilements; and [4] the objects to emancipated from comprise the eightfold ensemble [of cognitions] that are founded on the substratum of myriad latent tendencies (*bag chags sna tshogs kyi kun gzhi*) as well as the latent tendencies [themselves]. In the Mantrayāna, these phases are declared to be [1] the ground where clearing occurs, [2] the clearing process itself, [3] the goal where obscurations have been cleared away, and [4] the objects to be cleared way. Although the names used are different, their meaning is the same." *Sems nyid ngal gso 'grel* vol. 1: 273.1–2: *skabs 'dir bral gzhi / bral rgyu / bral 'bras / bral bya dang bzhir shes par bya'o / de la bral gzhi ni khams sam snying po'o / bral rgyu ni de'i steng gi dri ma sbyong byed thar pa cha mthun dge ba lam ldan gyi rnam pa'o / bral 'bras ni bde bar gshegs pa'i snying po dri ma mtha' dag dang bral nas yon tan mngon du gyur pa'o / bral bya ni bag chags sna tshogs pa'i kun gzhi la brten pa'i tshogs brgyad bag chags dang bcas pa'o / 'di dag gsang sngags ltar na / sbyang gzhi / sbyong byed / sbyangs 'bras / sbyang bya dang bzhir grags pas ming la tha dad kyang don la gcig go.*

40. *Bodhicaryāvatāra* II.26a: *buddhaṃ gacchāmi śaraṇaṃ yāvad ā bodhimaṇḍataḥ*. I am most thankful to David Karma Choepel of Thrangu Monastery, Namo Buddha, for drawing my attention to this passage. According to Prajñākaramati's *Bodhicaryāvatārapañjikā* on *Bodhicaryāvatāra* II.26: "As for *maṇḍataḥ*: The word *maṇḍa* means 'essence,' as [in the phrase] 'essence of clarified butter (*ghee*).' This being so, [one continues] until the chief goal (*pradhānaṃ*) of [or which is] awakening [is reached]. The meaning is, 'until I have realized perfect awakening.' " *maṇḍata iti / maṇḍaśabdo 'yaṃ sāravacanam / ghṛtamaṇḍa iti yathā / tathā ca sati bodhipradhānaṃ yāvat / yāvat samyaksaṃbodhiṃ nādhigacchāmi ity arthaḥ*. Prajñākaramati's gloss of bodhimaṇḍa as *bodhipradhānaṃ*, "the main aim / object that is awakening," would suggest reading bodhimaṇḍa as a karmadhāraya compound *bodhiḥ eva maṇḍaḥ*: "The supreme point / place that is awakening."

41. For examples, see Wangchuk, *Resolve to Become a Buddha* 48, 93, 130, 335.

42. In the Sautrāntika school, the seed (*bīja*) or germinal capacity (*śakti*) was closely linked with the idea of a spiritual potential or affiliation (*gotra*) that exists in all beings. It also came to be associated with the idea of a spiritual element (*dhātu*) and various other buddha-nature ideas. In the *Abhidharmasamuccaya*, for example, *dhātu* is characterized as the seed of all phenomena (*sarvadharmabīja*), an identification that connects Sautrāntika bīja theory with tathāgatagarbha *dhātu* / *gotra* conceptions. The *Bodhisattvabhūmi* establishes semantic equivalences between dhātu and the concepts *bīja*, *gotra*, *ādhāra*, *niśraya*, *hetu*, and so forth. For these and other developments of bīja theory in relation to tathāgatagarbha doctrine, see Seyfort Ruegg, *Théorie du tathāgatagarbha* 472ff.

43. In this work, Aśvagoṣa counsels that a beginner should dwell in secluded places away from worldly concerns until he or she is able to seek seclusion within, that is, in the primordial unborn nature of mind. This inner place of seclusion is described as a "seed" that is the "seat" of awakening (*byang chub snying po'i sa bon*). See Wangchuk, *Resolve to Become a Buddha* 287.

44. The distinctive Dzokchen interpretations of terms such as *rang rig*, *kun gzhi*, and *byang chub snying po* and the conspicuous attempts to distinguish them from nontantric Mahāyāna uses reveal how little is yet known about the assimilation and transformation of such ideas within early Tibetan Mahāyoga and Dzokchen traditions.

45. See note 28 in this chapter.

46. Prior to the collapse of the Imperium (late 9th c.) and well into the tenth century, Tibet was still exposed to various cultural influences in addition to India, not least of all those of the Central Asian and Western Himalayan regions. It is noteworthy that Gnubs chen claims in the colophon of his *Bsam gtan mig sgron* to have studied in the presence of various scholars in India and Nepal and to have also studied with the translator Lotsāwa Che btsan skyes of Bru sha (Gilgit-Baltistan region of Northern Pakistan). Karmay has noted that the translation colophon of the *Dgongs 'dus pa'i mdo* names Che btsan skyes as translator of the work from the language of Bru sha (a language today known as Burushaski that is still spoken in the Gilgit-Baltistan region of Northern Pakistan). This accords with the historical sources that maintain that Gnubs chen received the transmission of the *Dgongs 'dus pa'i mdo* from this teacher during his stay in Bru sha (Gilgit-Baltistan). See Karmay, *Great Perfection* 99. See also Dalton, "Uses of the *Dgongs pa 'dus pa'i mdo*" 278–279, for an account of the teachers Gnubs chen is said to have studied with during his trans-Himalayan journeys.

47. In the Nyingma ninefold doxography of vehicles as it is first systematically presented in the *Dgongs 'dus pa'i mdo*, the highest six vehicles are all Mantrayāna. Gnubs chen discusses these at length in his *Mun pa'i go cha*. His *Bsam gtan mig sgron* presents a different doxography of Buddhist traditions still flourishing during his time that comprises, from lowest to highest, the gradualist Mahāyāna system of Kamalaśīla, the simultaneist Chan system of He shang Mohoyen, the nondual Mahāyoga (Vajrayāna), and the spontaneous Dzokchen. All are considered legitimate Buddhist vehicles, but the lowest three are considered to be deviations (*gol sa*) because they still involve intentional effort and therefore miss the point of spontaneity, which is the basis for unpremeditated altruistic activity. For details and references concerning these doxographies, see Higgins, *Philosophical Foundations*.

48. On the sense and signifance of this term in the history of Buddhism, see Wangchuk, *Resolve to Become a Buddha*.

49. *Rgyud rgyal gsang ba snying po dkon cog 'grel* 127.13: *de la bde bar gshegs pa'i snying po zhes bya ba ni / thun mong du grags pa sems can rnams byang chub kyi rgyu can zag med kyi sa bon dang ldan pa'o / zhes 'dod do / zab mo ltar na sems kyi rang bzhin nyid byang chub yin pas byang chub kyi snying po'o / de ltar yin pa las bcings par snang zhing de'i dbang gis grol bar yang snang ste / bcings grol med pa'i don ma mthong bas de bstan pa phyir.*

50. In fact, he is said to have met Atīśa, who is credited with the first translation of the RGV).

51. The occurrence of this term in two of the eighteen *sems sde* tantras, the *Rtse mo byung rgyal* and *Rmad du byung ba*, and their commentaries, is discussed in Higgins, *Philosophical Foundations*.

52. There is evidence to suggest that this corpus of eighteen tantras (*rgyud bco brgyad*) that was known to early Dzokchen adherents indeed consisted of translations from Indian originals but that different recensions of these were current in India at the time. The existence of Indian originals would also account for a similar corpus of Mahāyoga tantras in China dating to the same period. See Germano, "Seven Descents" 231, who cites an unpublished paper presented by Eastman, "Mahāyoga Texts." It is worth noting that the many Tibetan texts bearing the titles of the works that traditionally make up the *rgyud bco brgyad* found in the *Rnying ma rgyud 'bum* and *Bai ro rgyud 'bum* often vary considerably from one another in length and content. This suggests the possibilities of (a) different recensions of the Indian corpus of texts translated into Tibetan and / or (b) the later addition and interpolation of material into earlier Tibetan translations.

53. See, for example, *Srog gi 'khor lo*, Bg vol. 1, 307.1–2: *med pa kun gzhi byang chub kyi sems ma bcos rang bzhin gyi 'od gsal ba yin te / snod bcud ma lus par byang chub pas*

da gdod sbyang du gang yang med pa'o / thams cad ma lus pa sangs rgyas pas bde gshegs pa'i lam chen po.

54. Karmay, *Great Perfection* 184.

55. *Rtse mo byung rgyal gyi 'grel pa*, 207.4: *bdag med gnyis med byang chub snying po las / dbyings dang ye shes mnyam sbyor ma gtogs pa / chos nyid chos tshol chos rnam gzhan na med / zhes pa / de ltar bdag nyid chen po'i rnam pa'ang mi rnyed pas tha dad pa mi rnyed pa'i snying po byang chub kyi gzhi de / tha snyad du go mjal byed pa tsam las / ngo bos rang rig pa byang chub snying pos 'bras bu'i chos gzhan nas gnyer bas 'bras bu rnams mi thob ste / rtsa ba gnas su lung ngan 'khyams pa'i phyir ro.*

56. See *Mun pa'i go cha* vol. 2, chap. 55, 50.6: *yang dag par rdzogs pa'i sangs rgyas kyi chos kyi sku'i yon tan gyi gzhi dang rtsa ba kun gzhi byang chub kyi snying po ma rig pa dang bcas pa'i ngo de nyid yin pas / dper me tog padma'i rtsa ba 'dam la zug pa ltar / byang chub chen po'i rtsa ba'ang 'khor ba nyid la yod pa'o / des kun gzhi 'khrul pa yang lhan cig skyes pa'i ma rig pa gnyis las byung ba'o.* The two aspects of coemergent ignorance are later specified as that which has afflictive emotions and that which is without afflictive emotions (still present on the tenth bhumi).

57. *Mun pa'i go cha* vol. 2, 51.4: . . . *mun pa'i rang bzhin rang rig pa byang chub sems shin tu gting dpag dka' bas ngo bo rtogs par dka' ba'i phyir.*

58. *Mun pa'i go cha* vol. 2, 48.4: *blo dpag par dka' bas nges par ma shes / byang chub snying po shin tu myur bas rtsol bgrod kyis ma slebs pa'o.*

59. *Mun pa'i go cha* vol. 2, 51.6: *sa bcu pa'i byang chub sems dpa' la'ang kun nas nyon mongs pa med pa'i lhan cig skyes pa'i ma rig pa yod pas / rtsa ba chen po ma mthong bas sa bcu man chad la sgrib cing / sa la gnas pa'i skabs sems skyes pa yan chad du rang rang la sgrib tshab che chung phra rags yod pa'o.*

60. See critical edition in Dorje, "Guhyagarbhatantra" 188, *e ma'o bde gshegs snying po las / rang gi rnam rtog las kyi sprul.*

61. This refers to the *Sgyu 'phrul brgyad bcu pa* in eighty-two chapters, which is found in Tk vol. 14, 67.6–317. I have so far been unable to locate this quotation in it.

62. *Phyogs bcu mun sel* in *Bka' ma shin tu rgyas pa* vol. 68, 118.6: *brtse ba'i rang bzhin gyis e ma ho brjod nas / gdod ma'i gnas lugs sems nyid 'od gsal ba bde gshegs snying po'i ngang las 'khrul lo / de'ang bde gshegs snying po ni sems nyid 'od gsal ba sku gsum 'du 'bral med pa'i ngo bor gnas pa de nyid yin te . . . sgyu 'phrul rgyas pa las / rnam rtog kun gzhi ma yin pa / rang bzhin med pa don gyi gzhi / de ni chos kyi dbyings zhes bya / de bzhin nyid kyi ye shes so / zhes pa dang / 'dus ma byas don gyi kun gzhi'i don nyid . . . rkyen gang gis 'khrul na sems can rang rang gi rnam par rtog pa rang shar du byung bas rgyas byas pa'i las kyis 'khor ba'i grong khyer chen po 'di rang snang rmi lam ltar sprul so.*

63. *Yid bzhin mdzod 'grel*, 151.1, 1.3: *gang las 'khrul pa'i gzhi nyid dang por bshad pa / thog ma'i 'od gsal bde gshegs snying po nyid / don gyi kun gzhi rang bzhin 'dus ma byas / ye nas rnam dag nyi mkha' lta bu la / ma rig pa'i bag chags g.yos pas na / sems can rnams 'khrul pa nyid do.*

64. See Higgins, *Philosophical Foundations.*

BIBLIOGRAPHY

Abbreviations

Bg: *The Rgyud 'bum of Vairocana: A Collection of Ancient Tantras and Esoteric Instructions Compiled and Translated by the Eighth Century Tibetan Master.* 8 vols. Leh: S. W. Tashigangpa, 1971. Published as vols. 16–23 of the *Smanrtsis shesrig spendzod.*

D: Derge edition of Bstan 'gyur. *The Tibetan Tripiṭaka*, Taipei Edition. Taipei: SMC, 1991.

P: Peking edition of Bstan 'gyur. *The Tibetan Tripiṭaka*, Peking Edition. Tokyo: Tibetan Tripiṭaka Research Institute, 1957.

Tb: Mtshams brag edition of the Rnying ma rgyud 'bum. *The Mtshams brag Manuscript of the Rnying ma rgyud 'bum*, 46 vols. Thimphu: National Library, Royal Government of Bhutan, 1982.

Tk: Gting skyes edition of the Rnying ma'i rgyud 'bum. *Rnying ma'i rgyud 'bum: A Collection of Treasured Tantras Translated during the Period of the First Propagation of Buddhism in Tibet*. 36 vols. Thimbu: Dingo Khyentse Rimpoche, 1973–1975.

Sanskrit Sources

Bodhicaryāvatāra. Śāntideva. Edited by Vidhushekhara Bhattacharya. Bibliotheca Indica. Calcutta: The Asiatic Society, 1960.

Bodhicaryāvatārapañjikā. Edited by P. L. Vaidya. *Bodhicaryāvatāra of Śāntideva with the Commentary of Prajñākaramati*. Buddhist Sanskrit Texts 12. Darbhanga: The Mithila Institute, 1960.

Mahāvyutpatti. Edited by Sakaki Ryōzaburō. *Honyaku myōgi taishū* (*Mahāvyutpatti*). 2 vols. 1916. Reprint: Tokyo: Kokusho Kanakōkai, 1987.

Tibetan Sources

Kun tu bzang po thugs kyi me long. In *Rnying ma'i rgyud bcu bdun: Collected Nyingmapa Tantras of the Man ngag sde Class of the Atiyoga (rDzogs chen)*. 3 vols. New Delhi: Sanje Doije, 1973, vol. 1: 233–280.

Bka' ma shin tu rgyas pa. 120 vol. Edited by Mkhan po 'Jam dbyangs. Chengdu: 1999.

Byang sems bde ba'i myu gu. Tk vol. 1, 448.1–453.1.

Dgongs 'dus pa'i mdo. *Sangs rgyas thams cad kyi dgongs pa 'dus pa'i mdo chen po*. Full title: *De bzhin gshegs pa thams cad kyi thugs gsang ba'i ye shes; Don gyi snying po rdo rje bkod pa'i rgyud; Rnal 'byor grub pa'i lung; Kun 'dus rig pa'i mdo; Theg pa chen po mong par rtogs pa; Chos kyi rnam grangs rnam par bkod pa zhes bya ba'i mdo*. In Tb vol. 16, 2–617.

Dpal dbyangs. *Thabs shes sgron ma*. D 4449, vol. nos., 768.6–769.6.

Dpyad pa bdud rtsi'i dri mchog. Mi bskyod rdo rje. Full title: *Rje yid bzang rtse pa'i rgyud gsum gsang ba dang / Paṇ chen Śākya mchog ldan gyi bde mchog rnam bshad gnyis kyi mthar thug gi 'bras bu gzhi dus gnas lugs / lam dus kyi rnal 'byor rnams la Dpyad pa bdud rtsi'i dri mchog*. In *Mi bskyod rdo rje gsung 'bum*. 26 vols. Lhasa: 2006, vol. 15, 975–1024.

Gnubs chen Sangs rgyas ye shes. *Bsam gtan mig sgron*. Full title: *Sgom gyi gnad gsal bar phye ba Bsam gtan mig sgron*. Smanrtsis Shesrig Spendzod series, vol. 74. Leh: 1974.

———. *Mun pa'i go cha*. Full title: *Sangs rgyas thams cad kyi dgongs pa 'dus pa'i mdo'i dka' 'grel Mun pa'i go cha lde'u mig gsal byed rnal 'byor nyi ma*. In *Bka' ma shin tu rgyas pa*: Pt. 1 (*stod cha*), vol. 93, 7–680; Pt. 2 (*smad cha*), vol. 94, 7–666.

———. *Rtse mo byung rgyal 'grel pa*. In *Bka' ma shin tu rgyas pa*, vol. 103, 179–230.

Klong chen rab 'byams pa. *Phyogs bcu mun sel*. Full title: *Dpal gsang ba snying po de kho na nyid nges pa'i rgyud kyi 'grel pa phyogs bcu'i mun pa thams cad rnam par sel ba*. In *Bka' ma shin tu rgyas pa*, vol. 68, 5–683. See also Dorje, "Guhyagarbhatantra."

———. *Sems nyid ngal gso 'grel*. Full title: *Rdzogs pa chen po Sems nyid ngal gso'i 'grel pa*. In *Rdzogs pa chen po ngal gso skor gsum*. Reproduced from xylographic prints from A 'dzom 'brug pa chos sgar blocks. 3 vols. New Delhi: 1999, vol. 1, 113–729, and vol. 2, 1–439.

———. *Yid bzhin mdzod 'grel*. Full title: *Theg pa chen po'i bstan bcos Yid bzhin rin po che'i mdzod kyi 'grel pa Padma dkar po*. In *mDzod bdun*. 7 vols. Based on the Oddiyana Institute edition published by Tarthang Rinpoche, Khreng tu'u: ca. 1999, vol. 7, 139–1591.

Rang byung rdo rje (Karmapa III). *Zab mo nang don gyi 'grel pa*. In *Rang byung rdo rje gsung 'bum*. 16 vols. Ziling: mTshur phu mkhan po lo yag bkra shis, 2006, vol. 7, 371–664.

Rmad du byung ba. In Tk under title *Rdo rje sems dpa' Nam mkha che*. Tk vol. 1, 424.1–430.2.

Rog Bande Shes rab 'od. *Bstan pa'i sgron me*. Full title: *Grub mtha' so so'i bźed gzhung gsal bar ston pa chos 'byung grub mtha' chen po Bstan pa'i sgron me*. In *Bka' ma shin tu rgyas pa* vol. 114, 107–318. See also: Nemo Leh: Tshul krims 'jam dbyangs, 1977.

Rong zom Chos kyi bzang po. *Rgyud rgyal gsang ba snying po dkon cog 'grel*. In *Rong zom gsung 'bum*, vol. 1, 31–250.

———. *Rong zom gsung 'bum*. Full title: *Rong zom chos bzang gi gsung 'bum*. 2 vols. Sichuan: Sikhron Mi-rigs-dpe skrun-khaṅ, 1999.

———. *Theg chen tshul 'jug*. Full title: *Theg pa chen po'i tshul la 'jug pa zhes bya ba'i bstan bcos*. In *Rong zom gsung 'bum*, vol. 1, 415–555.

Rtse mo byung rgyal. Tk vol. 1, 432.4–442.5.

Srog gyi 'khor lo. Bg vol. 1, 305–316. See also Tk vol. 1, 445.3–448.1.

Ye shes sde. *Lta ba'i khyad par*. D no. 4360, vol. jo, 426.1–455.7.

Secondary Sources

Almogi, Orna. *Rong-zom-pa's Discourses on Buddhology: A Study of Various Conceptions of Buddhahood in Indian Sources with Special Reference to the Controversy Surrounding the Existence of Gnosis (jñāna : ye shes) as Presented by the Eleventh-Century Tibetan Scholar Rong-zom Chos-kyi-bzang-po*. Tokyo: The International Institute for Buddhist Studies, 2009.

Crosby, Kate, and Andrew Skilton, translators. *The Bodhicaryāvatāra*. Translated from the Sanskrit. Oxford: Oxford University Press, 1996.

Cuevas, Bryan J. "Some Reflections on the Periodization of Tibetan History." *Revue d'Etudes Tibétaines* no. 10 (2006): 44–55.

Dalton, Jacob. "Uses of the *Dgongs pa 'dus pa'i mdo* in the Development of the Rnying ma School of Tibetan Buddhism." PhD dissertation, University of Michigan, 2002.

Dorje, Gyurme. "The Guhyagarbhatantra and Its XIVth Century Tibetan Commentary, *Phyogs-bcu mun-sel*." PhD dissertation, the School of Oriental and African Studies, University of London, 1987.

Eastman, Kenneth Wheeler. "Mahāyoga Texts at Tun-huang." *Bulletin of Institute of Buddhist Cultural Studies* 22 (1983): 42–60. Kyoto: Ryūkoku University.

Edgerton, Franklin. *Buddhist Hybrid Sanskrit Grammar and Dictionary, Volume 2: Dictionary*. 1953. Reprint: Kyoto: Rinsen Book Co., 1985.

Germano, David. "The Seven Descents and the Early History of Rnying ma Transmissions." In *The Many Canons of Tibetan Buddhism*, edited by Helmut Eimer and David Germano, 225–259. Leiden: Brill, 2002.

Higgins, David. *The Philosophical Foundations of Classical rDzogs chen in Tibet: Investigating the Distinction between Dualistic Mind (sems) and Primordial Knowing (ye shes).* Wiener Studien zur Tibetologie und Buddhismuskunde, Heft 78. Wien: Arbeitskreis für Tibetische und Buddhistische Studien der Universität Wien, 2013.

Kano, Kazuo. *Buddha Nature and Emptiness: rNgog Blo-ldan-shes-rab and A Transmission of the Ratnagotravibhaga from India to Tibet.* Wiener Studien zur Tibetologie und Buddhismuskunde, Heft 91. Wien: Arbeitskreis für Tibetische und Buddhistische Studien der Universität Wien, 2016.

Karmay, Samten Gyaltsen. *The Great Perfection: A Philosophical and Meditative Teaching of Tibetan Buddhism.* Leiden: E. J. Brill, 1988.

Mathes, Klaus-Dieter. *A Direct Path to the Buddha Within: Gö Lotsāwa's Mahāmudrā Interpretation of the Ratnagotravibhāga.* Boston: Wisdom, 2008.

Norbu, Namkai. 1984. *sBas pa'i rgum-chung: The Small Collection of Hidden Precepts, a Study of an Ancient Manuscript on Dzogchen from Tun-huang.* Arcidosso, Italy: Shang-shung Edizioni.

Radich, Michael. *The* Mahāparinirvāṇamahāsūtra *and the Emergence of* Tathāgatagarbha *Doctrine.* Hamburg: Hamburg University Press, 2015.

Seyfort Ruegg, David. *La Théorie du tathāgatagarbha et du gotra: Études sur la sotériologie et la gnoséologie du bouddhisme.* Publications de l'École française d'Extrême-Orient 70. Paris: A. Maisonneuve, 1969.

———. *Le Traité du tathāgatagarbha de Bu ston rin chen grub.* Publications de l'École française d'Extrême-Orient 88. Paris: A. Maisonneuve, 1973.

———. "Autour du lTa ba'i khyad par de Ye šes sde (Version de Touen-houang, Pelliot Tibétain 814)." *Journal Asiatique* 269 (1981): 207–229.

Snellgrove, David. *Indo-Tibetan Buddhism.* 2 vols. Boston: Shambhala, 1987.

Takahashi, Kammie Morrison. "Lamps for the Mind: Illumination and Innovation in Dpal dbyangs's Mahāyoga." PhD dissertation, University of Virginia, Charlottesville, 2009.

———."Ritual and Philosophical Speculation in the *Rdo rje sems dpa'i zhus lan.*" In *Esoteric Buddhism at Dunhuang*, edited by Matthew Kapstein and Sam Van Schaik, 85–141. Leiden: Brill, 2010.

Tucci, Giuseppe. 1958. *Minor Buddhist Texts II.* Rome: Is. M. E. O.

———. *Religions of Tibet.* Trans. Geoffrey Samuels. Berkeley: University of California Press, 1980.

Ueyama, Daishun. "Peruyan Cho No Daiyuga Bunken: P. Tib. 837 *Ni Tsuite* [a Mahāyoga Document Composed by Dpal Dbyangs; P. Tib. 837]." *Bukkyō bunka kenkyūsho kiyō* 16, no. (June 1977): 1–12.

van der Kuijp, Leonard W. J. *Contributions to the Development of Tibetan Buddhist Epistemology—from the Eleventh to the Thirteenth Century.* Alt-Neu-Indische Studien 26. Wiesbaden: Franz Steiner Verlag, 1983.

———. "An Introduction to Gtsang-nag-pa's *Tshad-ma rnam-par nges pa'i ṭi-ka legs-bshad bsdus pa.* An Ancient Commentary on Dharmakīrti's *Pramāṇaviniścaya*, Otani University Collection No. 13971." Introduction to the facsimile edition of the text in Otani University Tibetan Works Series, vol. 2. Kyoto: Rinsen Book Co., 1989: 1–33.

Wangchuk, Dorji. "The rÑiṅ-ma Interpretations of the Tathāgatagarbha Theory." *Vienna Journal of South Asian Studies* 48 (2005): 171–213.

———. *The Resolve to Become a Buddha: A Study of the Bodhicitta Concept in Indo-Tibetan Buddhism.* Studia Philologica Buddhica Monograph Series 23. Tokyo: The International Institute for Buddhist Studies, 2007.

Zimmerman, Michael. *A Buddha Within: The Tathāgatagarbhasūtra (The Earliest Exposition of the Buddha Nature Teaching in India)*. Bibliotheca Philologica et Philosophica Buddhica 6. Tokyo: The International Research Institute for Advanced Buddhology, Soka University, 2002.

———. "Nyraizōkyō saikō: Busshō no kyūyu wo chūshin to shite『如来蔵経』再考: 仏性の九喩を中心として" (Reconsidering Tathāgatagarbhasūtra Focusing on the Nine Similes of Buddha Nature). In *Sirīzu daijōbukkyō 8: Nyoraizō to busshō* シリーズ大乗仏教 8: 如来蔵と仏性, edited by Masahiro Shimoda et al., 97–139. Tokyo: Shunjūsha, 2014.

2

On the Inclusion of Chomden Rikpai Raldri in Transmission Lineages of Zhentong

TSERING WANGCHUK

Chomden Rikpai Raldri (bcom ldan rig pa'i ral gri, 1227–1305),[1] also known as Rikral, a Kadam (bka' gdams) master at Nartang (snar thang) Monastery in Tsang (gtsang), studied under scholars such as Sakya Paṇḍita Kunga Gyaltsen (sa skya paṇ ḍi ta kun dga' rgyal mtshan, 1182–1251), Chak Lotsāwa Choje Pel (chag lo tsā ba chos rje dpal, 1197–1264), and Kyoton Monlam Tsultrim (skyo ston smon lam tshul khrims, 1219–1299). In his long career as a thirteenth century Tibetan thinker, he penned many volumes of texts on various topics ranging from praise to the Pure Land to commentaries on Mahāyāna classics. His commentary on the *Uttaratantra* (i.e., *Ratnagotravibhāga*),[2] an early Indic treatise on buddha-nature, and his works on Madhyamaka philosophy and the Tibetan Buddhist tenet system are the main sources for this chapter that attempts to address three questions: Are Jonang (jo nang) scholars such as Sazang Mati Paṇchen (sa bzang ma ti paṇ chen, 1294–1376) and Tāranātha (rje btsun tā ra nā tha, 1575–1635) justified for including Rikral in the transmission lineages that focus on zhentong?[3] How does Rikral explain buddha-nature or ultimate truth in these texts? Finally, was Rikral included in any *Uttaratantra* lineage before Sazang incorporated him in his *Uttaratantra* transmission line?

Sazang, a student of Dolpopa Sherab Gyaltsen (dol po pa shes rab rgyal mtshan, 1292–1361), mentions Rikral in the lineage of the *Uttaratantra* masters in his exhaustive commentary on the Indic treatise. The commentary offers a long transmission lineage (*ring brgyud*) that includes Indian masters such as Asaṅga (ca. 4th c. CE), Vasubandhu (ca. 4th / 5th c. CE), and others, and Tibetan luminaries such as Rikral, Dolpopa, and so forth.[4]

While Sazang claims that he follows his teacher Dolpopa in his explication of the Indic treatise, he never uses the term zhentong in the commentary. Nonetheless, his commentary could still be construed as a zhentong interpretation of the

Uttaratantra because of how he discusses buddha-nature. Therefore, it is worth noting that Sazang includes Rikral along with Dolpopa in the lineage of the *Uttaratantra* in his commentary on the *Uttaratantra* that is a central text for the zhentong philosophy of the Jonang tradition.

Fast-forward two centuries later, and we find Tāranātha, the second most important figure after Dolpopa in the Jonang tradition, includes Rikral in the zhentong lineage of the Jonang in his *Supplication to the Lineage Holders of the Profound Middle Way of Zhentong* (*zab mo gzhan stong dbu ma'i brgyud 'debs*). In the supplication prayer, Rikral is mentioned along with Kyoton Monlam Tsultrim, Dolpopa, and other gurus.[5] Tāranātha thus takes this a step further by including Rikral and other Kadam masters in the transmission lineage of the zhentong masters. So, what in Rikral's works might have prompted the two Jonang scholars to include him in their illustrious transmission lines?

RIKRAL'S UTTARATANTRA COMMENTARY

Rikral studied under Sakya Paṇḍita[6] who criticized the interpretation of the buddha-nature as found in the *Uttaratantra* and other Tathāgatagarbha scriptures. Sakya Paṇḍita's view on Tathāgatagarbha literature will be discussed briefly to give some context for the divergent views on buddha-nature in thirteenth century Tibet. Sakya Paṇḍita's polemical writing, *Distinguishing the Three Vows* (*sdom gsum rab dbye*), does not particularly discuss the *Uttaratantra*, but it examines fifteen major issues,[7] including the topic of buddha-nature. In verses 59–63[8] of his work, Sakya Paṇḍita criticizes those who assert that the buddha-nature that is endowed with enlightened qualities exists in sentient beings. Such a claim, according to Sakya Paṇḍita, is similar to the non-Buddhist Sāṃkhya school's view that the effect preexists in its cause.

In verses 138–142[9] of the same text, Sakya Paṇḍita further contends that the buddha-nature as taught in the *Uttaratantra* and other Tathāgatagarbha literature is provisional,[10] as it meets the three criteria for being provisional.[11] Sakya Paṇḍita essentially argues that buddha-nature that is endowed with enlightened qualities cannot be accepted literally because unenlightened beings do not have it.

In his work, *Illuminating the Thoughts of the Buddha* (*thub pa'i dgongs pa rab tu gsal ba*), Sakya Paṇḍita mentions that buddha-nature exists in all sentient beings, but he does not explicitly make any reference to potential (*rigs*). He writes, "The natural potential exists in all sentient beings. The developmental potential exists [from the time that] one has cultivated bodhicitta. [The latter] does not exist in those who have not generated [bodhicitta]."[12] Furthermore he states in the same text, "Cittamātra asserts the completely cut-off potential. Madhyamaka does not accept [the completely cut-off potential]."[13]

As a scholar who wholeheartedly follows Candrakīrti's Madhyamaka treatises, Sakya Paṇḍita critiques the view that buddha-nature exists in sentient beings and interprets the Tathāgatagarbha teachings to be provisional. Based on these it seems plausible that Sakya Paṇḍita draws a distinction between a potential that exists in all sentient beings and buddha-nature that does not exist in sentient beings.[14]

With Sakya Paṇḍita's criticism of buddha-nature as explicated in the *Uttaratantra*, no formidable Kadam scholar could remain silent in thirteenth-century Tibet because the *Uttaratantra* was an authoritative source for their philosophical view. Thirteenth-century Kadam thinkers such as Gelong Choshe (dge slong chos bshes), Kyoton Monlam Tsultrim, and Rikral each wrote *The Words of Inconceivable Instruction on the Uttaratantra Treatise* (*bstan bcos rgyud bla ma'i gdams ngag bsam mi khyab kyi yi ge*),[15] *Instructions on the Uttaratantra* (*then chen rgyud bla'i gdams pa*),[16] and *The Flowers of Ornaments: An Uttaratantra Commentary* (*rgyud bla ma'i ṭi ka rgyan gyi me tog*), respectively. These commentaries offer a positive interpretation of buddha-nature that differs greatly from the readings offered by Sakya Paṇḍita and the early Kadam commentators on the *Uttaratantra* such as Ngok Loden Sherab (rngog blo ldan shes rab, 1055–1109) and Chapa Chokyi Sengge (phywa pa chos kyi seng ge, 1109–1169), who explain the buddha-nature of the *Uttaratantra* through the language of potentiality and emptiness of inherent existence.[17]

Rikral's commentary is the earliest Tibetan work available on the *Uttaratantra* that quotes from both tantric and sūtric sources such as *Hevajra Tantra*, *Guhyasamāja Tantra*, *Mañjuśrīnāmasaṃgīti*, *Laṅkāvatāra Sūtra*, and others. For instance, he cites the following verse from the *Hevajra Tantra* to demonstrate that all sentient beings have enlightened qualities from beginningless time:

> Sentient beings are solely buddhas,
> But [they] are covered by temporary defilements.
> Once [the defilements] are eliminated,
> They are solely buddhas.[18]

Similarly, Rikral paraphrases a quote from the *Laṅkāvatāra Sūtra* that says, "The buddha-nature—that is naturally luminous, that is characteristic of being completely pure from the beginning, and that is endowed with marks and signs [of a buddha]—exists within the corporeal body of all sentient beings."[19] Unlike Sakya Paṇḍita, Ngok, and Chapa, who claim that sentient beings have only the potential to achieve buddhahood in the future, Rikral here asserts that sentient beings have a complete buddha endowed with enlightened qualities.

Furthermore, Rikral says, "Buddha-element is the naturally arisen ultimate that is not produced by causes and conditions. It is merely [an object of] faith for ordinary people, but those who have achieved [bodhisattva] levels see it. However, there is nothing that needs to be eliminated, nor is there anything that needs to be achieved in the buddha-element."[20] Rikral again shows that all beings have a fully enlightened buddha-nature that does not require any purification.

Furthermore, he argues that buddha-element, potential, and all-basis are synonyms.[21] Therefore, his commentary makes it clear that his interpretation of buddha-nature as found in the *Uttaratantra* does not align with the readings offered by Sakya Paṇḍita and the two early Kadam commentators on the Indic treatise. Rather, his reading aligns with the cataphatic interpretation of the *Uttaratantra* as found in the thirteenth-century commentaries by Gelong Choshe and Kyoton Monlam Tsultrim as well as with the later zhentong interpretation of the Indic treatise.

Rikral in His Other Works

While Rikral's *Uttaratantra* commentary shares much with the Jonang order's zhentong interpretation of the *Uttaratantra*, his other works portray him to be a follower of rangtong. In his *Flowers of Ornaments for the Madhyamakakārikā* (*dbu ma rtsa ba shes rab rgyan gyi me tog*), he claims that everything exists conventionally and nothing exists ultimately.[22] Furthermore, as he argues in his *Flowers of Ornaments for the Tenet Schools* (*grub mtha' rgyan gyi me tog*), "[If someone asks,] 'does not the naturally generated gnosis exist?' The assertion that even the gnosis itself is empty [of inherent existence] is the Madhyamaka view. The claim that the nondual gnosis is truly existent is the view of Cittamātra."[23] According to the Kadam master, because gnosis does not inherently exist in his Madhyamaka system, the buddha-nature that is inherently endowed with enlightened qualities does not fit well with his Madhyamaka view.

Furthermore, in his *Flowers of Ornaments for the Tenet Schools*, Rikral proclaims, "Those who teach sentient beings as enlightened since beginningless time have a potential as the basis of intention."[24] As a traditional Kadam master, Rikral again shows that sentient beings do not have a potential endowed with enlightened qualities. Rather they have a potential that is a seed for achieving enlightenment. His presentation of the Madhyamaka view as delineated in his *Flowers of Ornaments for the Tenet Schools* demonstrates that the potential is not endowed with enlightened qualities as explained in his *Uttaratantra* commentary.[25]

While he follows Madhyamaka in his explication of ultimate truth and the potential, he is not a proponent of Candrakīrti's Madhyamaka; rather, he follows the Yogācāra Madhyamaka. As a scholar of the Yogācāra Madhyamaka, Rikral argues in *The Flower That Illuminates the Words and Meaning of the Madhyamakālaṃkāra* (*dbu ma rgyan gyi rnam par bshad pa tshig don gsal ba'i me tog*) that the *Sandhinirmocana Sūtra*, *Gaṇḍavyūha Sūtra*, *Laṅkāvatāra Sūtra*, and others are the sūtric sources for his Madhyamaka system.[26] He distinguishes his Madhyamaka from other Madhyamaka views in the text as follows: "Those who assert phenomena to have three natures (dependent nature, imputed nature, and complete nature) are proponents of Madhyamaka. Those who claim that all phenomena are unreal are the false followers of Madhyamaka."[27] Furthermore, he argues in his *Flowers of Ornaments for the Madhyamakakārika* that "all-basis-[consciousness] and others are still [asserted to] exist even in our [Madhyamaka] system, but everything is ultimately empty."[28] As Ngok argues in his *Uttaratantra* commentary, Rikral further argues that all-basis-consciousness is equivalent to buddha-element in his *Flowers of Ornaments for the Madhyamakakārika*.[29] Moreover, he claims in the same work that because everything including all-basis-consciousness exists conventionally and nothing exists ultimately, the notion that Nāgārjuna does not accept anything as conventionally existent is not correct.[30]

Moreover, true to his Kadam spirit, he claims in his *Ornaments for the Tenet Schools* that a Mahāyāna school follows either Cittamātra or Madhyamaka.[31] He also claims that Asaṅga, Vasubandhu, Dignāga, and Dharmakīrti are proponents of Cittamātra.[32] Furthermore, he includes both *Sutrālaṃkāra* and *Madhyāntavibhāga* into a group of Cittamātra texts.[33]

As a Kadam master of the Yogācāra Madhyamaka school, Rikral claims Candrakīrti to be a proponent of the Madhyamaka of the worldly convention (*'jig rten grags sde spyod pa'i dbu ma*) or the Madhyamaka that does not analyze appearances (*snang ba la mi dpyod pa'i dbu ma*), while he lists Nāgārjuna, Āryadeva, and Śāntarakṣita as the advocates of his Yogācāra Madhyamaka school.[34]

In summary, Rikral does not assert the interpretation of the potential as inherently endowed with enlightened qualities in these works. Moreover, he does not assert Asaṅga, Vasubandhu, and others to be important figures for his Madhyamaka school, nor does he include treatises such as *Sutrālaṃkāra* and *Madhyāntavibhāga* into his Madhyamaka. These Indian masters and their treatises are significantly important in the zhentong tradition of the Jonang.

Conclusion

It is clear that Rikral's *Uttaratantra* commentary provides a positive interpretation of buddha-nature using both tantric and sūtric sources that speak of buddha-nature as fully endowed with enlightened qualities. Furthermore, as a thirteenth-century Kadam scholar from Nartang, he asserts that the *Uttaratantra* explains the ultimate view of Mahāyāna. Thus, philosophically speaking, Rikral's explanation of buddha-nature in his *Uttaratantra* commentary shares much with the zhentong interpretation of buddha-nature as found in the Jonang order. Therefore, for both Sazang and Tāranātha, it appears that Rikral's interpretation of the *Uttaratantra* was one of the main reasons for including him in their illustrious transmission lineages.

However, it is important to underscore that Rikral had other philosophical affiliations in his long career, as his texts such as the *Flowers of Ornaments for the Madhyamakakārika*, *The Flower That Illuminates the Words and Meaning of the Madhyamakālaṃkāra*, and the *Flowers of Ornaments for the Tenet Schools* demonstrate. These works portray him to be another traditional Kadam scholar who accepts every phenomenon to be empty of inherent existence and who interprets the existence of buddha-nature endowed with enlightened qualities in sentient beings to be provisional.

Although much historical analysis still needs to be conducted for Rikral's inclusion in the lineages by Sazang and Tāranātha, it appears that he was included in a transmission lineage of the *Uttaratantra* commentary even before Sazang incorporated him in his transmission lineage of the *Uttaratantra*. Kyoton Monlam Tsultrim, a teacher of Rikral, who hails from the same Nartang Monastery, provides a transmission lineage of the *Uttaratantra* that includes Tsunpa Chokyi Gyaltsen right after the author himself in his *Uttaratantra* commentary.[35]

It is very plausible that Tsunpa Chokyi Gyaltsen here is none other than Rikral. As Schaeffer and van der Kuijp state, "[H]is [Rikral's] actual name in religion was Dar ma rgyal mtshan. Tibetan word *dar ma* is a loanword from Sanskrit *dharma*, which when translated renders Tibetan *chos*. Hence, he is sometimes styled *Chos kyi rgyal mtshan* [Chokyi Gyaltsen]."[36] If this is the case, a prototype for the *Uttaratantra* lineage, as given by Sazang, or the zhentong lineage as offered by Tāranātha, tracing the transmission through Rikral had already been established prior to the two Jonang masters' transmission lineages.

NOTES

1. For Rikral's biography in Tibetan, see Samten Zangpo, *Biography of Chomden Rigpai Raldri* 41–94. For a brief life story of Rikral in English, see Roerich, *Blue Annals* 336–339 and Schaeffer and van der Kuijp, *Early Tibetan Survey of Buddhist Literature* 3–8.

2. The *Uttaratantra* is credited to Maitreya in the Tibetan tradition. It is divided into five chapters—"Buddha-Element," "Enlightenment," "Enlightened Qualities," "Enlightened Activities," and "Benefits"—that discuss seven points: the Buddha, Dharma, Saṅgha, buddha-element, enlightenment, enlightened qualities, and enlightened activities.

3. Cyrus Stearns states that "[Rikral's] inclusion in a zhentong lineage is fascinating and unexpected" (*Buddha from Dolpo* 339 n. 179).

4. Sazang, *Exposition on the Uttaratantra* 519.

5. *Supplication to the Lineage Holders of the Profound Middle Way of Zhentong* 20–25.

6. As a student, the Kadam thinker knew his teacher's views and thoughts regarding the Buddhist path and went so far as to criticize his teacher. See Schaeffer and van der Kuijp, *Early Tibetan Survey of Buddhist Literature* 4–5 and 8.

7. See Rhoton, *Clear Differentiation* 15. For the fifteen issues, see Rhoton, *Clear Differentiation* 21–22.

8. The Tibetan verses from Sakya Paṇḍita's *Distinguishing the Three Vows* are as follows: *mu stegs grangs can pa rnams ni / gshis la dge sdig yod ces zer/ rgyu la 'bras bu gnas par 'dod / bod kyang la la de rjes 'brang // rdo rje rgyal mtshan bsngo ba las / 'gro kun dge ba ji snyed yod / byas dang byed 'gyur byed pa zhes / gsungs pa'i dgongs pa 'chad pa la / kha cig grags can lugs bzhin du / yod pa'i dge ba zhes bya ba/ rangyungg du ni grub par 'dod/ de la bde gshegs snying po zer // grangs can lugs 'di mi 'thad pas / lung dang rigs pas dgag par bya // bde gshegs snying po zhes bya ba / chos dbyings 'gyur med nyid la gsungs / de skad du yang rgyud bla las / sems ni rang bzhin 'od gsal ba / nam mkha' bzhin du 'gyur med gsung //* (9). For an English translation of these verses, see Rhoton, *Clear Differentiation* 49. For information on how the verses are divided, see Rhoton, 277.

9. The Tibetan verses from Sakya Paṇḍita's *Distinguishing the Three Vows* are as follows: *'on kyang mdo sde 'ga' zhig dang / theg pa chen po rgyud bla mar / gos ngan nang na rin chen ltar / sems can rnams la sangs rgyas kyi / snying po yod par gsungs pa ni / dgongs pa yin par shes par bya // de yi dgongs gzhi stong nyid yin // dgos pa skyon lnga spang phyir gsungs // dngos la gnod byed tshad ma ni / de 'dra'i sangs rgyas khams yod na / mu stegs bdag dang mtshungs pa dang / bden pa'i dngos por 'gyur phyir dang / nges pa'i don gyi mdo sde dang / rnam pa kun tu 'gal phyir ro // 'di don de bzhin gshegs pa yi / snying po'i le'u'i mdo sder ltos // slob dpon zla ba grags pas kyang / dbu ma la ni 'jug pa las / bde gshegs snying po drang*

don du / gsungs pa de yang shes par gyis // (17). Rhoton translates the word *sangs rgyas khams* in verse 140 as "buddha-realm," which I have translated as "buddha-element" here.

10. Sakya Paṇḍita argues that the sūtras and the *Uttaratantra* that teach the buddha-nature using analogies such as the precious jewel wrapped in dirty clothes should be understood as provisional teachings. Furthermore, he demonstrates that Candrakīrti's *Madhyamakāvatāra* speaks of such texts as provisional (*Distinguishing the Three Vows* 17). However, in his *Letter to the Excellent Beings* (*skyes bu dam pa rnams la zhu ba'i 'phrin yig*), which was most likely written after *Distinguishing the Three Vows*, Sakya Paṇḍita seems to show some hesitancy on the issue of buddha-nature teachings being provisional. Sakya Paṇḍita states, "Regarding buddha-nature, I have seen it taught as an interpretable principle in the *Laṅkāvatāra[sūtra]*, the *Mahāyanottaratantra*, the *Madhyamakāvatāra*, and other sūtras and [basic Indian Buddhist] treatises. Please investigate whether what I have said concurs with that which is expounded in all sūtras and treatises" (Rhoton, *Clear Differentiation* 237–238). Rhoton states that the letter was written sometime between 1233 and 1243 in response to the criticisms directed at Sakya Paṇḍita's *Distinguishing the Three Vows* (229).

11. The three in this context are: (1) the basis of intention (*dgongs gzhi*) for the buddha-nature teachings is the emptiness of inherent existence; (2) the purpose (*dgos pa*) for teaching buddha-nature discourses is to eliminate the five faults of being discouraged (*sems zhum*), showing contempt for inferior beings (*dman la brnyas pa*), grasping at unreal things (*yang dag min 'dzin*), denigrating authentic teachings (*yang dag pa'i chos la skur ba*), and seeing oneself superior (*bdag cag lhag pa*); (3) contrary to the fact (*dngos la gnod byed*) is that buddha-nature as explained in these sūtras does not exist, since there are many definitive sūtras that teach that all phenomena do not exist inherently.

12. *rang bzhin gyi rigs sems can thams cad la yod / rgyas pa'i rigs byang chub tu sems bskyed nas yod / ma bskyed pa la med* (*Illuminating the Thoughts of the Buddha* 5).

13. *gtan rigs chad pa sems tsam pa 'dod / dbu ma pa mi 'dod . . .* (*Illuminating the Thoughts of the Buddha* 6). However, Sakya scholars such as Grags pa rgyal mtshan (1147–1216) and Rong ston Smra ba'i seng ge (1367–1449) conflate the two. Grags pa rgyal mtshan argues: "In that way, if all sentient beings have a potential, would not that contradict the *Sūtrālaṃkāra*, which teaches that there are sentient beings with no potential? There is no contradiction, since this is a provisional statement from the viewpoint of Cittamātra. However, here [in Madhyamaka] a cut-off buddha-nature is not possible, as the *Uttaratantra* also states, 'Because the buddha-body pervades [all beings] . . .'" (*Precious Trees* 2). Similarly, Rongton argues, "Since the *Sūtrālaṃkāra* teaches that buddha-nature and potential are different because buddha-nature exists in all sentient beings, [whereas] there are sentient beings who are cut off from the buddha-nature the assertion that buddha-nature and potential are not the same is a position held in the Cittamātra" (*Exposition on the Uttaratantra* 95).

14. Even a century or so later, in his criticism against Dolpopa, Sgra tshad pa rin chen rnam rgyal (1318–1388) also points out that Sakya Paṇḍita did not claim buddha-essence and buddha-nature to be synonyms. See Wangchuk, "In Defense of His Guru" 155–157.

15. Dge slong chos bshes's commentary is one of the two earliest *Uttaratantra* commentaries available that offer a transmission lineage of the treatise through figures such as Sajjana (ca. 11th c.), Gzu Dga' ba'i rdo rje (ca. 11th c.), Bstan Kha wo che (b. 1021), and others (*Words of Inconceivable Instruction on the Uttaratantra Treatise* 440). Although the editors of the Collected Works of Kadam list Dge slong chos bshes's commentary under "unidentified authorship" (*mdzad byang mi gsal ba*), the colophon of the commentary identifies the author as Dge slong chos bshes. The word *she* in his name might have been a scribal error for *shes* meaning "to know" or *bshes* for "friend." I have opted for the latter in this chapter.

Unfortunately, I have not been able to find any biographical information about the author. I presented a paper entitled "An Early Contemplative Interpretation of Buddha-Nature from a Kadam's Perspective" drawing from Dge slong chos bshes's commentary at the International Association for Tibetan Studies in Ulaanbaatar, Mongolia, in 2013.

16. For a recent English translation of the commentary, see Brunnhölzl, *When the Clouds Part* 777–788. See also, Mathes, "*gzhan stong* Model of Reality" 203–204.

17. See Wangchuk, *Uttaratantra* chap. 1, which examines the two commentaries, and Kano's dissertation, which examines Ngok's commentary in detail.

18. *sems can rnams ni sangs rgyas nyid / 'on kyang glo bur dri mas bsgribs / de bsal na ni sangs rgyas nyid* (*Flowers of Ornaments* 761). For the tantra, see *Hevajra Tantra*, H 378b: vol. 79, 366b.4.

19. *de bzhin gshegs pa'i snying po de rang bzhin gyi 'od gsal ba thog ma nas rnam par dag pa'i mtshan nyid mtshan dang dpe byad dang ldan pa sems can thams cad kyi lus kyi nang na mchis pa'o* (*Flowers of Ornaments* 756). See *Laṅkāvatāra Sūtra*, H 110: vol. 51, 135b.4–6.

20. *rkyen gyis ma byas par ye nas rang byung gi don dam ni khams te / de so so skye bos dad par bya ba tsam yin gyi / sa thob pas ni mthong ngo / khams de la skyon yon bsal bsnan bya ryu ni med kyi* (*Flowers of Ornaments* 763).

21. Rikral states, "The synonyms are as follows: buddha-element, buddha-nature, basis, seed, buddha-essence, all-basis" (*ming gi rnam grangs ni khams dang rigs dang rten dang sa bon dang sangs rgyas kyi snying po dang kun gzhi la sogs pa yin te . . .*) (*Flowers of Ornaments* 749). However, Rikral does not make a distinction between basis-of-all consciousness (*ālāyavijñāna, kun gzhi rnam shes*) and basis-of-all gnosis (**ālāyajñāna, kun gzhi ye shes*), in the same way that Dolpopa does, in that the former is the basis for samsaric experiences and the latter is the enlightened entity.

22. Rikral also argues that *Madhyamakakārikā* describes the two selflessnesses as explained in the first two Wheels of Dharma, but it does not explicate the ultimate definitive meaning of the last wheel of Dharma.

23. *lhan cig skyes pa'i ye shes yod pa ma yin nam zhe na / ye shes de'ang stong par 'dod na ni dbu ma'i lta ba yin la / gnyis med kyi shes pa bden par 'dod na ni sems tsam gyi lta ba yin no* (*Flowers of Ornaments for the Tenet Schools* 153).

24. See Rikral, *Flowers of Ornaments for the Tenet Schools*: *sems can ye nas sangs rgyas su ston pa la sogs pa ni rigs la dgongs pa yin la* (153).

25. Nevertheless, Rikral's *History of Maitreya's Teachings* asserts the *Uttaratantra* to explain the ultimate view of Mahāyāna. He states, "The *Uttaratantra* explicates the ultimate view of Mahāyāna that is found in sutras such as *Tathāgatagarbha Sūtra* and others" (*History of Maitreya's Teachings* 158–159).

26. *Flower That Illuminates the Words and Meaning of the Madhyamakālaṃkāra* 510.

27. *shes bya'i gnas tshul rang bzhin gsum du smra ba ni dbu ma pa'o / shes bya thams cad brdzun par smra ba ni dbu ma ltar snang ba yin no* (*Flower That Illuminates the Words and Meaning of the Madhyamakālaṃkāra* 514–515).

28. *kun gzhi la sogs pa rnams ni rang lugs la'ang ma chad par yod la / don dam par ni thams cad stong par bzhed* (*Flowers of Ornaments for the Madhyamakakārikā* 218). Moreover, Rikral explains the basis-of-all consciousness in this way in this text: "How karmic causality in Mahāyāna comes out of basis-of-all-consciousness is the correct conventional truth. The master Nāgārjuna explains it as such in his *Bodhicittavivaraṇa*, *Ratnāvalī*, *Dharmadhātustotra*, and others" (*Flowers of Ornaments for the Madhyamakakārikā* 130); *theg chen pa'i las 'bras sems kun gzhi'i rnam shes las ji ltar 'byung ba'i tshul ni yang dag gi kun*

rdzob yin te / de'ang slob dpon gyis byang chub sems 'grel dang rin chen phreng pa dang chos kyi dbyings su bstod pa la sogs par gsal bar bshad cing.

29. *Flowers of Ornaments for the Madhyamakakārika* 208.

30. *de'i phyir slob dpon ni kun rdzob du'ang ci yang mi 'dod do zhes zer ba ni blun po rnams kyi rang dga' yin no* (*Flowers of Ornaments for the Madhyamakakārikā* 219).

31. After criticizing the divisions of nine paths (*theg pa dgu*), Rikral claims that there is no Mahāyāna school that does not fit into either Cittamātra or Madhyamaka (*Ornaments for the Tenet Schools* 130–131).

32. *Ornaments for the Tenet Schools* 108.

33. Schaeffer and van der Kuijp, *Early Tibetan Survey of Buddhist Literature* 169–170.

34. Rikral asserts that both Candrakīrti and Jñānagarbha are proponents of the Madhyamaka of the Worldly Convention (*'jig rten grags sde spyod pa'i dbu ma*) or proponents of the Madhyamaka that does not analyze appearances (*snang ba la mi dpyod pa'i dbu ma*) and that Bhāvya is a proponent of Sautrāntika Madhyamaka, but not a follower of Yogācāra Madhyamaka, which is the school that Rikral follows (*Ornaments for the Tenet Schools* 130–131).

35. Along with Rikral he also includes masters such as Sajjana, Zugawai Dorje, Tsen Kawoche, and others. The word *ze'u* in Chokyi Gyaltsen's name seems to be added later. While Kyonton Monlam Tsultrim seems to suggest that he conferred the transmission of the *Uttaratantra* onto Chokyi Gyaltsen, Samten Zangpo, Rikral's biographer, does not mention that Rikral received the transmission from Kyoton Monlam Tsultrim. Rather, it states that he received it from *Mkhan chen Mchims nam mkha grags* (1210–1285) (*Biography of Rikral* 57–58). It is certainly possible that he received the transmission from multiple masters.

36. Schaeffer and van der Kuijp, *Early Tibetan Survey of Buddhist Literature* 3–4.

Bibliography

Tibetan Sources

Chapa Choekyi Senge (phywa pa chos kyi seng ge). *Theg pa chen po rgyud bla ma'i bstan bcos kyi tshig dang don gyi cha rgya cher bsnyad pa phra ba'i don gsal ba*. In *The Collected Works of Kadam Masters* (*bka' gdams gsung 'bum*), vol. 7. Chengdu: Si khron mi rigs dpe skrun khang, 2006.

Chomden Rigpai Raldri (bcom ldan rig pa'i ral gri). *Byams pa dang 'brel ba'i chos kyi byung tshul*. In *The Collected Works of Kadam Masters*, vol. 53. Chengdu: Si khron mi rigs dpe skrun khang, 2006.

———. *Dbu ma rgyan gyi rnam par bshad pa tshig don gsal ba'i me tog*. In *The Collected Works of Kadam Masters*, vol. 61. Chengdu: Si khron mi rigs dpe skrun khang, 2009.

———. *Dbu ma rtsa ba shes rab rgyan gyi me tog*. In *The Collected Works of Kadam Masters*, vol. 62. Chengdu: Si khron mi rigs dpe skrun khang, 2009.

———. *Grub mtha' rgyan gyi me tog*. In *The Collected Works of Kadam Masters*, vol. 52. Chengdu: Si khron mi rigs dpe skrun khang, 2009.

———. *Rgyud bla ma'i ṭik ka rgyan gyi me tog*. In *The Collected Works of Kadam Masters*, vol. 62. Chengdu: Si khron mi rigs dpe skrun khang, 2009.

Drakpa Gyaltsen (grags pa rgyal mtshan). *Mngon par rtogs pa rin po che'i ljon shing*. In *The Collected Works of Drakpa Gyaltsen*, vol. 3. Sarnath: Shantarakshita Library, 1987.

Gelong Choeshe (dge slong chos bshes). *Bstan bcos rgyud bla ma'ai gdams ngag bsam mi khyab kyi yi ge*. In *The Collected Works of Kadam Masters*, vol. 76. Chengdu: Si khron mi rigs dpe skrun khang, 2009.

Kye'i rdo rje zhes bya ba rgyud kyi rgyal po (*Hevarja Tantra*), H 378b: vol. 79.

Kyoton Monlam Tsultrim (skyo ston smon lam tshul khrims). *Then chen rgyud bla'i gdams pa*. In *The Collected Works of Kadam Masters*, vol. 50. Chengdu: Si khron mi rigs dpe skrun khang, 2007.

Ngog Loden Sherab (rngog blo ldan shes rab). *Theg chen rgyud bla ma'i bsdus don*. Dharamsala: Library of Tibetan Works and Archives, 1993.

'Phags pa lang kar gshegs pa'i theg pa chen po'i mdo (*Laṅkāvatāra Sūtra*), H 110: vol. 51.

Rongton Mawai Singge (rong ston smra ba'i seng ge). *Theg pa chen po rgyud bla ma'i bstan bcos legs par bshad pa*. New Delhi: Yashodhara, 1998.

Sakya Paṇḍita Kunga Gyaltsen (sa skya paṇ ḍi ta kun dga' rgyal mtshan). *Sdom gsum rab dbye*. In *The Collected Works of the Founding Masters of Sa-skya*, vol. 12. Dehradun: Sakya Center, 1993.

———. *Thub pa'i dgongs pa rab tu gsal ba*. In *The Collected Works of the Founding Masters of Sa-skya*, vol. 10. Dehradun: Sakya Center, 1993.

Samten Zangpo (bsam gtan bzang po). *Bcom ldan rigs pa'i ral gri'i rnam thar dad pa'i ljon shing*. In *The Collected Works of Chomden Rigpai Raldri*, vol. 1. Lhasa: 2006.

Sazang Mati Paṇchen (sa bzang ma ti paṇ chen). *Rgyud bla ma'i bstan bcos kyi rnam par bshad pa nges don rab gsal snang ba*. Khreng tu'u: 2000.

Tāranātha. *Zab mo gzhan stong dbu ma'i brgyud 'debs*. In *Rdzogs ldan chos mchog dbu ma gzhan stong gi chos skor*, vol. 7. Shang kang then ma dpe skrun khang, 2005.

Secondary Sources

Brunnhölzl, Karl. *When the Clouds Part: The Uttaratantra and Its Meditative Tradition as a Bridge between Sūtra and Tantra*. Ithaca: Snow Lion, 2014.

Kano, Kazuo. "rNgok Blo-ldan-shes-rab's Summary of the *Ratnagotravibhāga*: The First Tibetan Commentary on a Crucial Source for the Buddha-nature Doctrine." PhD dissertation, Hamburg University, 2006.

Mathes, Klaus-Dieter. *A Direct Path to the Buddha Within: Gö Lotsāwa's Mahāmudra Interpretation of the Ratnagotravibhāga*. Somerville: Wisdom, 2008.

———. "The *gzhan stong* Model of Reality: Some More Material on Its Origin, Transmission, and Interpretation." *Journal of the International Association of Buddhist Studies* 34 (2012): 187–223.

Rhoton, Jared, translator. *A Clear Differentiation of the Three Codes: Essential Distinctions among the Individual Liberation, Great Vehicle, and Tantric Systems*. Albany: State University of New York Press, 2002.

Roerich, George, translator. *The Blue Annals*. Delhi: Motilal Banarsidass, 1976.

Schaeffer, Kurtis, and Leonard van der Kuijp. *An Early Tibetan Survey of Buddhist Literature: The Bstan pa rgyas pa rgyan gyi nyi 'od of Bcom ldan ral gri*. Cambridge: Harvard University Press, 2009.

Stearns, Cyrus. *The Buddha from Dolpo: A Study of the Life and Thought of the Tibetan Master Dolpopa Sherab Gyaltsen*. Ithaca: Snow Lion, 2010.

van der Kuijp, Leonard. *Contributions to the Development of Tibetan Epistemology: From the Eleventh to the Thirteenth Century*. Stuttgart: Franz Steiner Verlag, 1983.

Wangchuk, Tsering. "In Defense of His Guru: Dratsepa's Rebuttals to the Challenges Articulated by the Proponents of the Other-Emptiness Doctrine." *Journal of Indian Philosophy* 39 (2011): 147–165.

———. *The Uttaratantra in the Land of Snows: Tibetan Thinkers Debate the Centrality of the Buddha-Nature Treatise.* Albany: State University of New York Press, 2017.

3

The Dharma of the Perfect Eon

Dolpopa Sherab Gyaltsen's Hermeneutics of Time and the Jonang Doxography of Zhentong Madhyamaka

Michael R. Sheehy

The luminary Dolpopa Sherab Gyaltsen (1292–1361) embarked on a hermeneutic enterprise to classify, synthesize, and codify the Indian Buddhist dharma, as it was being received by scholars during the fourteenth century in central Tibet. This project culminated with the zhentong (*gzhan stong*) system of the Jonang, what Dolpopa referred to as the dharma of the "Perfect Eon." The dharma ciphered for this zhentong system was said to have passed aurally through the previous generations of Indian and Tibetan masters as concealed teachings (*lkog chos*), transmitted as both sūtra and tantra along parallel continuums, up to Dolpopa and the scholastic efflorescence of the Jonang that occurred during his lifetime. Synthesizing sūtra and tantra, Dolpopa brought these seemingly disparate streams of Indian Buddhist hermeneutical and exegetical thought into a coherent system, intersecting the Kālacakra transmission lineage with the Zhentong Madhyamaka, making secret zhentong more explicit.[1] Interpreting sūtras by means of tantras and vice versa, Dolpopa's interfusion of the technical tantric vocabulary found in the *Kālacakra Tantra* with the philosophical thinking of the Zhentong Madhyamaka consequently redefined the contemplative, intellectual, and literary heritage of the Jonang.

Dolpopa's hermeneutical schema has a twofold intent: (1) To contextualize the zhentong system within a broader cosmological and temporal vision of Buddhist historical time, and (2) To interpret the zhentong system within the doctrinal framework of the Indian Buddhist philosophical schools. As he makes evident in his writings, including *The Fourth Council* and the advice that he gives in his *Letter to My Disciples*, as well as several other works that he composed during the latter period of his life, Dolpopa was interested in identifying the canonical literary corpus of the Perfect Eon. In this chapter, we explore critical devices that Dolpopa employed to synchronize the temporal and doctrinal, and in so doing, come to understand how the core principles of the zhentong system were formulated. In particular, we examine how Dolpopa and later Jonang authors thought about and articulated time according to the *Kālacakra Tantra*, and how this concept is so central to their understanding of Buddhist thought that *we must seek to understand this concept of time* if we are to think seriously about the broader zhentong paradigm.[2]

The Buddhist Councils in India

Though the Buddhist Councils (*bka' bsdu*) in India are popularly conceived as well-documented events according to early Pāli sources, Tibetan historians have envisioned alternative scenarios for these monumental events. Buton Rinchen Drub (1290–1364) and Tāranātha (1575–1635) both record that the First Council was held by King Ajātaśatru soon after the passing of the Buddha while the Second Council was convened by the Arhat Yaśaḥ and seven hundred monks at the Kusumpurī Vihāra under the patronage of King Nandin approximately a century later.[3] While these accounts accord with Theravāda and Sarvāstivāda records, Tāranātha in his *History of Buddhism in India*, suggests that the Third Council took place in Kashmir due to the directive of King Kaniṣka.[4] This differs from the normative account of the Third Council being convened by King Aśoka in Patna. Tāranātha's account is in accord with what the Sarvāstivāda tradition considers to be the Fourth Council. However, it is important to keep in mind that most Tibetan historians did not conceive of a council beyond the initial three.

In his efforts to synthesize and classify Indian Buddhism, Dolpopa went to great lengths to emphasize the historical degeneration of the Mahāyāna dharma as it was received and sustained by Tibetans. Dolpopa was concerned with framing his understanding of reality in accord with the hermeneutical schema derived from India's last monumental contribution to esoteric Buddhism, the *Kālacakra Tantra*, and the lineage from which he inherited his understanding within the framework of the temporal schema described by the tantra. In so doing, Dolpopa reinterpreted Indian Buddhist doctrines (*bstan rtsis*), juxtaposing Kālacakra astrological calculations of Indian doctrines in relation to the three earlier Buddhist councils in India. Dolpopa proposed that his recalculation and subsequent doctrinal reformulation—which has come to be known as "zhentong"—had the significance of a Fourth Council (*Bka' bsdu bzhi pa*).

Dolpopa conceived these three Buddhist councils as intentional historical events that repurposed the Buddha's dharma. These initial Buddhist councils in India were used as a wireframe on which Dolpopa built out the structure of his zhentong thinking. In so doing, Dolpopa and later Jonangpa authors posited a distinct set of calculations for thinking about and articulating time. Systematizing his teachings within the cosmological schema derived from the *Kālacakra Tantra*, Dolpopa formulated his elucidations within the history of Buddhism and emphasized how the Kālacakra and final turning teachings mark a Perfect Eon.

KĀLACAKRA COSMOLOGY

Throughout Dolpopa's writings, and those of subsequent Jonangpa authors in the zhentong literary tradition, zhentong is contextualized within the cosmological schema that is derived from the *Lokadhātupaṭala* or *Chapter on World Systems* in the extensive *Vimalaprabhā* commentary on the *Kālacakra Tantra*. This schema delineates four cosmic eons (*yuga*): (1) Perfect Eon (*kṛtayuga, rdzogs ldan*), (2) Third Eon (*tretāyuga, gsum ldan*), (3) Second Eon (*dvāparayuga, gnyis ldan*), and the (4) Degenerate Eon (*kaliyuga, rtsod ldan*). Set forth in Dolpopa's work, *The Great Calculation of the Teachings That Has the Significance of a Fourth Council* along with his explanatory commentary, this schema classifies the different sets of teachings attributed to the Buddha and later Indian commentators. As the title suggests, Dolpopa proposes that the doctrines associated with zhentong assemble a Fourth Council in addition to the three councils that were held in India to compile and arrange the Buddha's sūtra discourses. The dharma teachings of the Kṛtayuga or the "Perfect Eon" are identified with the "Great Madhyamaka" (*dbu ma chen po*) or "Zhentong Madhyamaka."[5]

In the opening verses of *The Fourth Council*, Dolpopa elucidates this calculation of cosmic eons:

> The four great eons concern the quality a cosmic age, and the lesser four eons concern the quality of the teaching.
> The first division [or great eon period] is 4,320,000 years, a quarter of which is explained to be a "foot." One "foot," two, three, and four are explained to be sequentially the Perfect Eon, Third Eon, Second Eon, and the Degenerate Eon.
> As for the lesser four eons that concern the quality of the teaching, the duration of each of these four eons is a quarter of 21,600 human years.[6]

And the modern Jonangpa master, Dzamtang Khenpo Lodro Drakpa (1920–1975), further elaborates this calculation in the introduction to his *Great Exposition on Zhentong*:

> In general, the supreme teaching of the Madhyamaka of definitive meaning, the profound essential point that is the consummate intent of the victorious ones, is the distinctive teaching of the Perfect Eon that surpasses the Third Eon and subsequent eons.[7] Moreover, in regard to the cosmic time of the Perfect Eon, this is divided into both: (1) the four great eons, and (2) the four lesser eons.
>
> The four great eons concern the quality of the time of the eon. A quarter of which is 4,320,000 years or one "foot." The total of these four "foot" units as a whole is the Perfect Eon. Similarly, one foot, two,

> and three are sequentially classified as the Third Eon, the Second Eon, and the Degenerate Eon.
>
> The four lesser eons concern the quality of the teachings. A quarter of which is 21,600 human years and is measured according to each of the four cosmic eons, respectively.
>
> The teachings of the Perfect Eon are completely flawless with enlightened qualities. Similarly, the degeneration of a quarter is the first part of the Third Eon while the degeneration of almost half is the second part of the Third Eon. Then, what remains of the degeneration of three-quarters is the Second Eon. When there is not even one quarter left, that is classified as the Degenerate Eon.[8]

The four great eons and the four lesser eons are divisions of the Perfect Eon. Taking the total of these times to be the Perfect Eon, the subsequent degenerations of this age are the Third Eon, Second Eon, and Degenerate Eon. As Dolpopa states and Khenpo Lodro Drakpa reiterates, the four great eons are divided according to the criteria of the quality of time, and the four lesser eons according to the quality of the teachings associated with that particular time. The great eons are measured in quarters of 1,080,000 years, totaling 4,320,000 years. The lesser eons are measured in quarters of 5,400 years, totaling 21,600 years. Each quarter subdivision is called a "foot" (*rkang pa*), referring to the name of the temporal unit. When one "foot" or a quarter period of the Perfect Eon—half of the total cosmic age—has degenerated, that is the Third Eon. When three-quarters of the Perfect Eon has degenerated, that is the Second Eon. When there is less than a quarter of the total cosmic age, then that is the Degenerate Eon. This final eclipsed period, referred to as the time of "black dharma," is a dark age when demigods and barbarians rule the world and the Buddha's message has become virtually extinct.[9]

Codifying the Perfect Eon Dharma

With this basic architecture of cosmic time in mind, we can identify some of the historical elements at work in unfolding this narrative as we seek to better understand how the Jonangpas further codify this temporal schema to represent the rise of specific Buddhist doctrinal trends in India. Dolpopa and later Jonangpa thinkers sought to extrapolate and explicate the pure doctrine from the golden age of the Buddha's dharma, distinguishing the teachings of the Perfect Eon in comparison to those teachings of the degenerate eons. In doing so, Zhentong Madhyamaka is paralleled with what Dolpopa calls the "Kṛtayuga Dharma" or "Dharma of the Perfect Eon" (*rdzogs ldan chos*) and the "Kṛtayuga Tradition" or "Tradition of the Perfect Eon" (*rdzogs ldan lugs*). In his *Supplication to the Tradition of the Perfect Eon*, Dolpopa asserts this parallel and aligns with other major Buddhist doctrines:

> Due to a manifold decline of view,
> The teachings have degenerated.
> This is unbearable for the natural mind.

> It's unbearable because so many of our kind mother and father sentient beings have gone astray, down a perverted path.
> I cry out with sorrow to all the victors and their heirs in the ten directions—
> Seize us with compassion!
> You who are endowed with marvelous ever-present spacious omniscience,
> Power and capacity, enlightened qualities and activities,
> Bestow your blessings!
>
> Off in the opposite direction of the profound *Prajñāpāramitā*,
> Oh! How sad it is to yearn for this profound *Prajñāpāramitā*—
> Seize us with compassion!
> Off in the opposite direction of the Great Madhyamaka,
> Oh! How sad it is to yearn for this Great Madhyamaka—
> Seize us with compassion!
> Off in the opposite direction of magnificent Nirvāṇa,
> Oh! How sad it is to yearn for this magnificent Nirvāṇa—
> Seize us with compassion!
> Off in the opposite direction of Mahāmudrā,
> Oh! How sad it is to yearn for this Mahāmudrā—
> Seize us with compassion![10]

The supplication lists a series of yoga and tantra systems, including Ati Yoga, the Cakrasaṃvara and Hevajra yogas, Guhyasamāja and the Kālacakra, that are representative of the Perfect Eon dharma. These are among the teachings that Dolpopa saw to need restoration in order to revive the Perfect Eon of the Buddha's dharma, in contrast to the degenerate Third Eon. In *The Fourth Council*, Dolpopa writes:

> The Third Eon and subsequent eons are flawed. Their treatises have been contaminated like milk in the marketplace. They are in every way unable to act as witness. The earlier [eons] displace the later, just as more advanced philosophical systems refute the lesser.
>
> The Perfect Eon dharma is the untainted expression of the victorious ones, the explanations of the sovereigns on the tenth spiritual level, and the great founders of the chariot systems. It is flawless and imbued with supreme enlightened qualities.
>
> In this [Perfect Eon] tradition, not everything is rangtong. By eloquently distinguishing rangtong from zhentong, that which is relative is taught to be rangtong while that which is ultimate is taught precisely to be zhentong.[11]

Here we see a stark contrast between the doctrine associated with the Perfect Eon and that associated with the Third Eon, and later cosmic eons. This is most clearly brought into perspective with Dolpopa's distinction between teachings about rangtong—those that stress the lack of any intrinsic essence, and those on zhentong that emphasize the perpetual absolute. Now, with such disparity magnified, we find seedlings for the further systematization of the Buddha's dharma according to this concept of cosmic time. Situating Dolpopa's teachings within the broader frame of the three turnings of the dharma wheel, Khenpo Lodro Drakpa writes:

> In the initial turning, the Buddha explained the way of existence to be that relative reality actually exists. Moreover, he explained that just like what functions infallibly is a designation in accord with how it appears, in the same way what is real is merely relative. In fact, while analyzing abiding reality, what was not taught is that things exist as truly established.
>
> In the middle turning, he explained how all phenomena of saṃsāra and nirvāṇa are inherently devoid of being real. In fact, while analyzing abiding reality, he explained that what is to be refuted—the way in which there is fixation on the attributes (*mtshan 'dzin*) of the identity of phenomena—does not exist in the way in which it is conceived. What was not taught is that mere relative illusion cannot possibly exist in general. Nevertheless, on these occasions, the profound expanse of pristine awareness that is the abiding reality of what lies beyond the sphere of activity that fixates on attributes was not the subject of this teaching, because the mental aptitudes of the disciples were taken into consideration. From what was intended, because it was not explained to either exist or to not exist, the certainty of that which resembles the perpetual profound expanse as being artificial or unreal was not discussed.
>
> The consummate intent of these three turnings is unified, regardless of it being directly or indirectly; this is the self-manifesting pristine awareness of the ultimate ground expanse that is free from all constructs, the empty ground that is the totality of radiance, buddha-nature itself. However, due to the capacities of disciples and occasions: (1) First, relativity was taught in the manner of the ordinary Four Noble Truths. (2) In the middle, the expanse that is free from all constructs of attributes was taught, this is merely half of the definitive meaning. (3) Finally, the way of the utterly complete ultimate definitive meaning was taught—the ground expanse that is free from constructs, magnificent pristine awareness. In fact, these three turnings are [cycles of] teachings that were merely distinguished as being in harmony with abilities and with what was foremost required, while in the end, their intent remained definitively singular.
>
> Accordingly, the foregoing great chariots, the beautifying ornaments of our world, venerable Nāgārjuna, Asaṅga, and Vasubandhu with their hearts and thoughts in harmony, established the three turnings as a single intent. Here, this intent of the discourses is also within

> our own tradition, as it is connected with the great majestic Jonangpa [Dolpopa Sherab Gyaltsen] and the lineage-holder, master, and gentle protector Kunga Nyingpo [Tāranātha].[12]

With this juxtaposition of cosmic time against historic time, and the introduction of the three dharma wheels of Mahāyāna discourses found within the *Sandhinirmocana Sūtra* as a means for qualifying the Perfect Eon dharma, we unveil the prevailing dissonance of this narrative: that between the doctrinal and the historical. However, as we see later in connection with the Cittamātra sūtras, it becomes evident through an examination of the three turnings that the historical timing of the Perfect Eon dharma is not chronological, giving leeway for the tension between a definitive time and definitive doctrine to be resolved.

THE IMAGE OF EMPTINESS

A critical feature in understanding Dolpopa's view is that the language of zhentong is descriptive of yogic experience. Dolpopa elicits a dharma language to capture the elusive natural manifestation of absolute emptiness—that is, emptiness as he experienced it while practicing the sixfold *vajrayoga* completion process of the Kālacakra.[13] The first of these yogic procedures, the yoga of withdrawal (*so sor sdud pa*), involves the adept severing the sense faculties from objective references in an environment of total darkness. What is emphasized throughout Dolpopa's writings, and those of later Jonangpa authors, is that there is an expression of emptiness that is experiential, and that such experiences of emptiness come about through the careful execution of the yogic procedures explicated in the vajrayoga practice of the Kālacakra to withdraw one's senses from mundane stimuli. The Kālacakra literature describes a visionary experience in which the yogin begins to perceive inconceivable and intangible yet formulated manifestations of the mind that are known to be an "image of emptiness" (*śūnyatā-bimba, stong gzugs*).[14] The Tibetan term evokes the metaphor of an image that manifests (*gzugs brnyan*), like a reflection in a mirror. These are understood to be a *reflection* or *expression of emptiness*. Withdrawn from fixations in the sensible world, such an expression refers to a yogic experience of emptiness that is visceral and somatic, not merely suspended in a split-off visible domain, nor a cerebral conjecture that occurs in a suspended abstract sphere of the intellect.

The mere absence of any inherent identity, either the identity of a fixed self (*gang zag gi bdag nyid*) and/or the identity of the phenomenal world (*chos nyid bdag nyid*) are referred to as the "emptiness that lacks identity" or the "emptiness of essencelessness" (*ngo bo med pa stong pa nyid*). Though such an intimation of absence or a lack of presence is typically implied in conceiving rangtong emptiness, in zhentong contemplative thinking, the recognition of ultimate emptiness implies an acknowledgment of presence—a constant luminous presence. A danger is to think that such expressions of emptiness are external objects (*bāhyārtha, phyi don*), or things that are seen out there. This presence is an expression of emptiness.

Defining the nature of external referents in the zhentong system, Tāranātha writes in *The Essence of Zhentong*:

> In this [zhentong] system, what is not considered to be real is: That which is immaterial, such as the three unconditioned [phenomena] and imputed unconditioned [phenomena] as asserted by the Cittamātra system . . . , material forms and so forth that are known to be external referents, the eight types of ordinary awareness, the fifty-one operations of the mind, and in brief—all phenomena of outward saṃsāra.[15]

Such expressions of emptiness are understood to be omnipresent while not contingent on perception or memory and therefore not a product of imagination.

Dolpopa's zhentong system asserts that there is a presence amid absence, a continuity that persists without duality, and that these are expressions of emptiness. In his masterpiece compilation, *Mountain Dharma*, Dolpopa explains the image of emptiness in the context of the *Mahāparinirvāṇa Sūtra*:

> Moreover, the *Mahāparinirvāṇa Sūtra* eloquently discusses the distinctions between that which is associated with an image of emptiness, and that which is associated with an image of what is not empty,
>
> > Kauṇḍinya, the image [with stains] is empty [of an inherent nature]. Due to conditions of cessation, there is also an image of emptiness. This is realized to be a completely free image [of buddha-nature] that is not empty. Similarly, fully recognize [that there are these two] intervals for sensations, perceptions, impressions, and consciousness.
>
> As it says here, there are degrees to an image with adventitious stains and so forth. This is precisely emptiness devoid of substance, [the emptiness of being empty,] and that which itself is empty of an inherent essence. There is also the image of buddha-nature, and so forth, that is the emptiness of the very nature of what is devoid of substance [and the emptiness of what is not empty]. This is ultimate zhentong![16]

Echoed in this sūtra quote, the meaning stressed in the context of the Kālacakra sixfold vajrayoga terminology is that the image of emptiness is a natural manifestation of absolute emptiness. The "conditions of cessation" that are referred to in the sūtra quote are yogic procedures that withdraw one's senses from mundane stimuli. The image of emptiness is perceived through the precise process of rescinding one's involvement with objectification through a threefold practice of isolating the body, voice, and mind (*dben pa gsum*). These techniques are special preparations for the completion stage sixfold yoga and are performed to isolate the habitual activities of one's ordinary perceptions. In Dolpopa's commentary on the quote, we read that the image of emptiness is in fact an expression of the buddha-nature. Warning the reader not to conflate expressions of the relative with those of the ultimate, Dolpopa reminds us that these are actually an expression of the indwelling buddha-nature that continually pervades all things stable and wavering, tangible and intangible. With this he points to the formless, that emptiness which is the very nature of what is devoid of substance, the key variable in the zhentong code.

Rangtong versus Zhentong

In the early 1330s, emergent from his inner yogic life of the Kālacakra sixfold vajrayoga completion stage practice, Dolpopa began to articulate his contemplative experiences through a new dharma language (*chos skad*). As his contemplative understandings coalesced and he began to systematize his elucidations, Dolpopa employed an innovative set of terminology that was devised to describe his understandings of reality. This doctrinal vocabulary was framed to discuss his vision of the Perfect Eon dharma and included terms such as rangtong, zhentong, and pristine awareness as the substratum (*kun gzhi ye shes*). Seeking to reconcile one of the great philosophical conundrums of Indian Mahāyāna Buddhism—how the doctrine of emptiness (śūnyatā, a lack of an enduring essence) and buddha-nature (*tathāgatagarbha*, an enduring buddha-nature) interrelate—Dolpopa formulated a technical language and interpretive model for distinguishing two modes of emptiness: rangtong (*rang stong*), emptiness that is devoid of an intrinsic relative nature, and zhentong, emptiness that is the ultimate intrinsic nature, buddha-nature. The term zhentong literally means "empty of other" or "extrinsically empty" and was employed by Dolpopa to describe how the expressions of emptiness that he was experiencing in meditation were empty (*stong*) of everything other (*gzhan*) than the continuous luminous nature that abides as one's own intrinsic buddha-nature. Accordingly, the technical language that Dolpopa employed in his zhentong writings conveys an interpretive model for distinguishing these two modes of emptiness. This multivalent codification of śūnyatā and buddha-nature is spliced further into (a) emptiness and (b) great emptiness (*stong pa chen po*), referring to the ultimate emptiness that is permanently continuous.

Grappling with the doxographical categories that Tibetans had inherited from India and were newly organizing in Tibet during his lifetime, Dolpopa employed his creative use of a dharma language to describe his understanding of reality in conversation with these categories. In so doing, Dolpopa's project pointed to a vision of reality that was born from articulating contemplative experience while it reconciled the philosophical systems that he viewed to be miscategorized, and increasingly corrupted. His approach to this hermeneutical project was based on a syncretic method to breakdown the boundaries and oppositions of preset Buddhist classifications, both exoteric and esoteric, emphasizing a unifying vision of reality that he saw to be the inherent expression of the Perfect Eon dharma. Explicitly describing his hermeneutical method, Dolpopa writes in his autocommentary to *The Fourth Council*:

> Tantras are to be interpreted by other Tantras;
> Sūtras are to be interpreted by other Sūtras;
> Sūtras are also to be interpreted by Tantras;
> Tantras are also to be interpreted by Sūtras;
> Both should be interpreted by each other.[17]

Continuing to explain this method of interpretation and how it gives rise to yogic attainment, he comments:

> Also, through completely perfected
> Listening, reflection, and meditation,
> As well as explanation and practice;
>
> In this way, the profundities of the teachings,
> And the profundities of ground, path, and fruition
> Are realized.
>
> The entire ground and fruit of the definitive meaning
> Is singular within buddha-nature itself.
> This is the path of yoga!
>
> The grounds, paths, and fruits of the provisional meaning
> Are encompassed by each of these.
>
> This is how the supreme Perfect Eon dharma
> And the autocommentaries by the victors
> Are to be interpreted.[18]

Working through hermeneutic strategies for analyzing and interpreting the corpus of Mahāyāna and Vajrayāna Buddhist literature that was at the fore of intellectual discussions during his lifetime, Dolpopa derived his vocabulary from a distinct set of Buddhist texts. The predominant works that Dolpopa was signifying as authoritative, and which have now come to serve as the basis for zhentong philosophical literature according to the Jonang tradition, include the set of twenty definitive sūtras, the *Five Maitreya Works*, and the *Kālacakra Tantra* along with its commentary, the *Vimalaprabhā*.[19]

Crystallizing in his magnum opus, *Mountain Dharma: An Ocean of Definitive Meaning*, Dolpopa set forth in this text how his realizations were in alignment with the Buddha's enlightened intent and definitive in their meaning (*nītārtha*, *nges don*), in contrast to teachings that remain provisional in meaning (*neyārtha*, *drang don*).

These were teachings for those who live in the mountains (*ri chos*), a specific genre of Tibetan writing that was designed to include all that was essential for retreat. Dolpopa wrote his *Mountain Dharma* for the hermits and yogins who dwelled in the meditation caves above the Jomonang hermitage where he dwelt, and within his lifetime, this work became the central work of the Jonang scholastic tradition. Arranged according to the structure of the ground (*gzhi*) of reality, the path (*lam*) of spiritual transformation, and the fruition (*'bras bu*) of buddhahood, it serves as a comprehensive presentation of zhentong. Representative of his synchronic writing style, with extensive quotes from canonical literature, the *Mountain Dharma* is an anthology of sūtras and tantras that he indicated were sources for his broader exposition, according to the crux of his hermeneutical method.

Perhaps what is most striking about Dolpopa's presentation, and most controversial, is how he diametrically opposes rangtong to zhentong. Over the course of his career as an author, he teases out the contradictions and complementarities that emerge from the inherent tensions and paradoxes between these modes of emptiness. In a series of short texts, Dolpopa lists sets of opposites that he juxtaposes against each other, deciphering critical dyads that categorically shape his view. He defines what he means by the two modes of emptiness in one such work, *Differentiating Emptiness:*[20]

> All that is said about emptiness is not exclusively rangtong.
>
> There is a division between emptiness that is the profound zhentong,
> And rangtong—emptiness that is not profound.
> So, these are the dyads.
>
> There is emptiness that is ultimate,
> And emptiness that is relative.
> So, these are the dyads.
>
> There is emptiness that is the perfect nature,
> And emptiness that is the imputed nature.
> So, these are the dyads.
>
> There is emptiness of the middle
> And there is emptiness of extremes.
> So, these are the dyads.[21]

In another such text, *Seizing the Crucial Point*, Dolpopa collocates opposites in order to further elicit this stark contrast:

> If it's ultimate, it can't be rangtong.
> If it's rangtong, it can't be ultimate.

If it's the expanse of phenomena, it can't be rangtong.
If it's rangtong, it can't be the expanse of phenomena.

If it's the nature of phenomena, it can't be rangtong.
If it's rangtong, it can't be the nature of phenomena.

If it's the ultimate dimension, it can't be rangtong.
If it's rangtong, it can't be the ultimate dimension.

If it's the perfect nature, it can't be rangtong.
If it's rangtong, it can't be the perfect nature.

If it's actuality, it isn't rangtong.
If it's rangtong, it isn't actuality.

If it's ultimate reality, it isn't rangtong.
If it's rangtong, it isn't ultimate reality.[22]

With this apophatic discourse style, Dolpopa elucidates what rangtong is not. That is, by making exclusions without affirmations, that which is intrinsically empty is defined. He continues this listing through major Buddhist categories, including the objects of the triple gem. In *Seizing the Crucial Point*, Dolpopa declares:

Rangtong is not the ultimate Buddha.
If it's rangtong, it isn't the ultimate Buddha.

Rangtong is not the ultimate Dharma.
If it's rangtong, it isn't the ultimate Dharma.

Rangtong is not the ultimate Saṇgha.
If it's rangtong, it isn't the ultimate Saṇgha.

Rangtong is not the ultimate refuge.
If it's rangtong, it isn't the ultimate refuge.[23]

Reading Dolpopa's doctrinal writings, it is important to keep in mind that although he frames his discourse in the rhetoric of the sūtras and tantras, his project sought to capture a language that describes emptiness.

Zhentong Madhyamaka and Cittamātra

In his efforts to consolidate the Zhentong Madhyamaka into a coherent system, Dolpopa went to great lengths to emphasize the historical degeneration of the

Buddhist dharma as it was received and categorized by the Tibetans. The narrative of the Perfect Eon dharma along with the other interpretative devices that Dolpopa employed are reiterated by writings of later Jonangpa scholars, most notably the seventeenth-century historian Tāranātha and Khenpo Lodro Drakpa. Perhaps one of the most intriguing developments is the Jonangpa understanding of the Cittamātra philosophical system, and how it took shape in relation to the other major systems of Indian Buddhism.[24] While the Cittamātra was generally associated with the final turning set of discourses and the Indian figures Maitreya, Asaṅ ga, and Vasubandhu, Jonangpa authors challenge this as a conflation of Cittamātra doctrines with the Zhentong Madhyamaka.[25]

Scattered throughout his historical and philosophical works, Tāranātha recounts the rise of the Mahāyāna in India, emphasized by how "two systems" (*tshul gnyis*) of Indian Mahāyāna thought were formulated by Asaṅga and Nāgārjuna—the Yogācāra and Madhyamaka, respectively. Parallel to the system associated with Nāgārjuna and Candrakīrti, the exegetical tradition of Zhentong Madhyamaka references its scriptural authority in a distinct set of canonical and postcanonical collections, including specific interpretations of the *Five Maitreya Works* according to the system of Tsen Kawoche (b. 1021) (*btsan lugs*), as received from the elusive figure Sajjana during the early eleventh century in Kashmir.[26] Seeking to clarify how Zhentong Madhyamaka relates with the classical division of Indian Buddhism into Yogācāra and Madhyamaka, Tāranātha explains this differentiation in his work, *Ascertaining the Two Systems: An Entrance into the Definitive Meaning*:

> There are two distinct systems of Mahāyāna thought that express the intended meaning within their respective contexts:
>
> (1) The intended meaning of the set of sūtras from the final turning discourses, and their definitive commentaries on the intent of this set of sūtras according to the scriptural tradition of the Yogācāra, and the philosophical systems that include the scriptural traditions of those who explicate discerning cognition such as those from the majestic Maitreya, Ārya Asaṅga and his [half-] brother Vasubandhu, Dignāga, Dharmakīrti, and similar authors.
>
> (2) The explicit teachings on the middle turning discourses as asserted by the scriptural tradition of those who explicate the Madhyamaka-Essencelessness, including the intent found within master Ārya Nāgārjuna's *Collection of Reasoning*, and by Buddhapālita, Bhāvaviveka, Candrakīrti and similar authors.[27]

Here we see a conflation of the two traditional "schools" or systems of Indian Mahāyāna Buddhism, namely, the Yogācāra and Madhyamaka, with a Mahāyāna hermeneutical device that was employed in order to categorize the different sets of sūtra discourses. Imbedded within this discussion, here and elsewhere, Tāranātha makes a distinction between those who uphold the Madhyamaka-Cognition[-Only] (*dbu ma rnam rig smra ba*) and those who uphold the Madhyamaka-Essencelessness that is devoid of an intrinsic essence (*dbu ma ngo bo nyid med par smra ba*). While Tāranātha equates the Madhyamaka of discerning cognition with the final turning of discourses and zhentong, he equates the Madhyamaka that is devoid of an intrinsic essence with the middle turning and rangtong.[28]

Tāranātha remarks how misinterpretation of these two systems by Tibetans led to confusion about the Madhyamaka and Cittamātra, and a conflation of zhentong with the Cittamātra system in Tibetan doxographical literature. One of the main veins of this narrative is Tāranātha's description of how the Cittamātra system came about from a collection of sūtras gathered and cared for by five hundred Indian scholars including a figure named Avitarka. Tāranātha strings this transmission lineage from the figure Avitarka directly to his disciple, the famous mahāsiddha Saraha, and as Tāranātha explains later in his history, to the famous scholar Nāgārjuna. With this, we have Saraha situated as the earliest exponent of the Madhyamaka, writing Nāgārjuna into the next generation of Madhyamaka history. Repeating this narrative from Tāranātha's *History of Buddhism in India*, in a passage on the diffusion of the Mahāyāna in India, Khenpo Lodro Drakpa writes in his *History of the Jonang*:[29]

> Accordingly, after these three councils on the Hīnayāna discourses had convened, it is said that five hundred teachers of the dharma including the great honorable Avitarka and others came about as adherents of the Mahāyāna. These scriptural collections of the Mahāyāna including the *Laṅkāvatāra Sūtra*, the *Gaṇḍavyūha Sūtra*, and many of the Mahāyāna sūtras were later discovered in various regions, and these teachings were then kept and diffused. From these, the Mahāyāna tradition of the Cittamātra system that asserts actual existence (*dngos smra ba'i sems tsam lugs*) arose.
>
> Later, due to the arrival of the glorious Saraha, the tradition of Madhyamaka began to flourish. After that, these teachings were sustained by the master Nāgārjuna, and the Madhyamaka then began to fully flourish. From that time onward, the teachings that gradually arrived in India have been upheld by many great beings.[30]

According to this interpretation, the Cittamātra system came about from the collection of sūtras gathered and cared for by five hundred Indian scholars, including a figure named Avitarka while the Madhyamaka was initiated by Saraha and later expanded by Nāgārjuna. Tāranātha reiterates this in his *Essence of Zhentong* where he defines the Cittamātra:

> All adherents to the Mahāyāna accept all of the Mahāyāna sūtras as the Buddha's discourses. Even so, the followers of Cittamātra uphold these

> four as those known to be definitive: (1) *Sandhinirmocana Sūtra*; (2) *Laṅkāvatāra Sūtra*; (3) *Gaṇḍavyūha Sūtra*; (4) *Avataṃsaka Sūtra*. The others are considered to be provisional in their meaning. The founders of this philosophical system were the early five hundred masters [of the Mahāyāna].[31]

Tāranātha goes on to point out that although the Zhentong Madhyamaka system arose much later, it was confused by many Tibetan scholars with the Cittamātra.

> As for the general philosophical system of zhentong, this was elaborately explained by the works of Dignāga, Sthiramati, and many of their excellent students and successors. As for the extraordinary [philosophical system of zhentong], since these are difficult for others to comprehend, these were diffused through the system of ear-to-ear transmission to the most exceptional disciples. Later, there were many in India who confused this Zhentong Madhyamaka with Cittamātra. Relying upon this, most in Tibet made this same confusion.
>
> In Tibet, though there were many scholars who translated these texts, those who purely upheld this philosophical system were Lotsāwa Zu Gawai Dorje, Tsen Kawoche, and those of the meditative tradition (*sgom lugs*) of the *Five Maitreya Works*. In particular, the one who made the lion's roar of the profound zhentong pervade throughout the land was the great omniscient Dolpopa Sherab Gyaltsen.[33]

Contextualizing the Cittamātra within Indian Buddhist thought, the works of Maitreya, Asaṅga, and Vasubandhu are not Cittamātra, but interpreted, as well as the works of Nāgārjuna, as belonging to the Perfect Eon tradition.

Keeping with the schema systematized by Dolpopa, Madhyamaka is divided into the General Madhyamaka or Rangtong Madhyamaka, on the one hand, and the Great Madhyamaka or Zhentong Madhyamaka, on the other. Placing these within this hermeneutical frame, Tāranātha comments in this *Ascertaining the Two Systems*:

> Here in Tibet, those who uphold the scriptural tradition of the essenceless Madhyamaka are renowned as "Rangtong Madhyamakas." Accordingly, it is said that Cittamātra is the earlier system while Madhyamaka is the later system. Those who are renowned for adhering to zhentong hold the position of the consummate definitive meaning of the final turning sūtras. Moreover, even though the philosophical system of the General Madhyamaka is the later system, Madhyamaka includes both the contextual definitive meaning as well as the consummate definitive meaning.
>
> The earlier tradition is that of the contextual definitive meaning, the philosophical system that depends upon provisional circumstances, and that accepts the relational nature (*paratantra*, *gzhan dbang*) as truly

> established. Furthermore, this is the Cittamātra philosophical system of the tradition that asserts sensible phenomena to be real.
>
> The other philosophical system in Tibet that teaches the imaginary nature (*parikalpita, kun btags*) and the relational nature to be subsumed by the subject-object complex, that all phenomena are devoid of being real, and that the perfected nature (*pariniṣpanna, yongs grub*) and nondual pristine awareness are truly established is known as "the Cittamātra that asserts sensible phenomena to be artificial." This is how the Great Madhyamaka tradition of the consummate definitive meaning is expressed.[33]

Tāranātha takes it a step further, qualifying the Cittamātra as twofold: (1) the subsystem that asserts sensible phenomena to be real (*rnam bden pa*), and (2) the subsystem that asserts sensible phenomena to be artificial (*rnam rdzun pa*), equating the latter with Zhentong Madhyamaka. Further, explanations on the Mahāyāna scheme of the three natures (*trisvabhāva, rang bzhin gsum*) are found within several of the core sūtras that comprise the Zhentong Madhyamaka, including the *Chapter Requested by Maitreya* in the *Prajñāpāramitā*, the *Laṅkāvatāra Sūtra*, and the *Sandhinirmocana Sūtra*.[34] The primary doctrinal reason for this is that the Cittamātra system that asserts sensible phenomena to be real also asserts momentary awareness to be real in absolute terms. This is to truly establish the relational nature while the Jonangpa affirm the perfected nature, nondual pristine awareness to be truly established.[35] Summing up the position of the Cittamātra in relation to zhentong, Khenpo Lodro Drakpa quotes Dolpopa:

> If for instance someone were to say, "Because the middle turning is Madhyamaka and the final turning is Cittamātra, the middle turning is definitive in meaning and the final turning is provisional in meaning; this invalidates your position." This is extremely irrational because (a) there is no scripture or reasoning whatsoever that suggests that the final turning follow the core texts of the Cittamātra, and because (b) [the final turning] teaches what is beyond the Cittamātra, it teaches the meaning of the consummate Great Madhyamaka, and it teaches in accord with the meaning of the consummate Vajrayāna.[36]

Positioning Zhentong Madhyamaka distinctively on its own terms, in alignment with the final turning of the dharma and Vajrayāna, Dolpopa makes a strategic doxographical maneuver, one that has critical consequences for the history of Buddhist philosophy in Tibet.

Dolpopa's Final Testament

Though Dolpopa framed his project to be concerned with retrieving what he felt was lost from Indian Buddhism, later interpreters of his thought would depict him as establishing a radically new doctrine. As is made evident in *The Fourth Council*, as well as several other works that he composed during the latter period of his life, Dolpopa was interested in identifying the written philosophical corpus of the Perfect Eon dharma. This is nowhere more apparent than in the heartfelt advice that he addresses in *A Letter to My Disciples*, a testament of his final thoughts on doctrinal issues.[37] Having opened his letter with homage to those who are neither reductive nor exaggerative, and who have realized things as they are, Dolpopa warns his disciples:

> By relying on the distinctions within the numerous exalted sources, particularly the eloquent teachings of the Buddha, the Bhagavān, and the lucid teachings that are their autocommentaries, I have taught you much that is the cause for the profound and especially exalted. This will increase the intelligence and wisdom within each of you. Keep in mind that in the wake of the Perfect Eon dharma and the flawless persons that are endowed with infinite enlightened qualities, there are the persons and teachings of the Third Eon and subsequent eons that, though their message is renowned, they are in fact known to be untrue. It's improper to place your trust in them.[38]

As we have seen, Dolpopa utilized the terms rangtong and zhentong very specifically within a broader discourse on what he referred to as the Perfect Eon dharma. By codifying the Perfect Eon dharma and contrasting it with works of the Third Eon and later degenerate eons, Dolpopa and subsequent Jonangpa authors employed a Buddhist hermeneutic of time that sets forth a scheme for modeling a literary and intellectual history of zhentong. This model suggests an underlying cosmological narrative of increasing philosophical corruption recorded in literary works, as well as authors and proponents who deviated from the Perfect Eon dharma.

Much of Dolpopa's paramount advice is directed toward this primary concern: to reconcile the Indian Buddhist doxographical categories that he felt were being conflated and disorganized by Tibetan scholars, thereby creating philosophical puzzlements. For instance, as discussed earlier, Dolpopa and later Jonangpa authors insisted that primary canonical works that are designated to be Cittamātra are in fact the Great Madhyamaka, and that Indian figures including Asaṅga, Vasubandhu, and Dignāga who are labeled Cittamātra thinkers were in fact proponents of the Zhentong Madhyamaka. Imploring his followers not to perpetuate these mistakes, Dolpopa discusses how to engage in a discourse about the finer points of these categorizations.[39] He continues his argument on the basis of arranging the Prajñāpāramitā sūtras and reiterates how later Indian paṇḍitas and thinkers of the Third Eon, including Dharmamitra and Haribhadra, interpreted doctrines in ways that have contradicted their meaning.

Summing up his views, contextualizing rangtong and zhentong, Dolpopa records in his letter:

> In all of the sūtras and tantras, all of the teachings state that it is necessary to distinguish rangtong from zhentong. Accordingly, those who

> do not make such distinctions and claim that everything is exclusively rangtong—that zhentong does not suffice to be emptiness, but that only rangtong suffices to be emptiness—they also proclaim that all statements about things being ultimately existent, constant, identity, purity, and real are provisional in meaning, while all statements about things being nonexistent, inconstant, identityless, impurity, and painful are definitive in meaning. It is claimed that the order of the nine or twelve perfect natures, the ultimate dimension of reality, essential dimension, natural luminosity, natural connate, natural great blissful, natural authenticity, natural nirvāṇa, and the natural and spontaneously established maṇḍala, among others, as well as the multiple divisions that comprise the natural spiritual families and the ultimate buddha-nature with its many qualities and so forth—though these are asserted to be reality itself, that very reality is asserted to be rangtong. These are among the many with perverted views, wicked views, materialists, all of which are without enumeration.
>
> When utterly dispelled by the scriptures and reasoning of the Perfect Eon, this becomes clear. Though there are many who assert their observations according to the Third Eon and the flawed scriptures and reasoning of the later degenerate eons since these are not properly genuine observations as to the facts—do not chase these mistaken ways![40]

Dolpopa's final thoughts and sentiments reverberated across Tibetan intellectual discourse during the generations that followed. Dolpopa's multivalent formulation and codification of śūnyatā and buddha-nature sparked historic controversy in Tibet, leading to a so-called "rangtong" versus "zhentong" debate that infused Tibetan Buddhist philosophical discourse for centuries, even up to the present day.[41]

CONCLUDING REFLECTIONS: DOLPOPA'S HERMENEUTICS IN CONTEXT

To recapitulate, Dolpopa's hermeneutical schema sought to both situate the zhentong system within an exemplary Indic Buddhist vision of cosmic and historic time and, within this temporal framework, to interpret zhentong in relation to the major doctrinal rubrics of Indian Buddhist philosophy. Considering Dolpopa's hermeneutic, and how such an interpretation of Indian Buddhist time and thought were woven into the Tibetan religious imagination via narrative by later Jonangpa exegetes, we can begin to put into context tensions raised by Jonangpa scholars from Dolpopa onward about the Buddhist dialectics of temporality and doctrine in India and Tibet. With this in mind, the question arises, "What forces were at play in fourteenth-century Tibetan intellectual discourse that possibly contributed to Dolpopa's revision of Buddhist history?"

As we have seen, Dolpopa situated his understanding of reality, and thereby the view that has subsequently come to be known as zhentong, within the cosmological framework derived from the *Kālacakra Tantra* and its commentary. As the last great tantra to appear from the Vajrayāna scene in India, the *Kālacakra Tantra* provided Dolpopa with an authentic literary corpus to identify with. Living in the cultural milieu of fourteenth-century Tibet, in the wake of the later diffusion (*phyi dar*) period of Buddhism, each institutional order was seeking valid tantric source texts to define their autonomy. Authors were differentiating textual materials that were validly Indian and validly Buddhist, questioning the Indic sources of many of the works being circulated in Tibet.[42] Scholars in Tibet were seeking new ways to decipher and claim the authenticity of Indian Buddhist texts. Recognizing this formative moment, Dolpopa deployed a team of his disciples to translate the *Kālacakra Tantra*, and as he oversaw the project as editor-in-chief, the Jonangpas claimed the Kālacakra literature.

Let's also keep in mind that Dolpopa lived in close proximity to Zhalu Monastery where his contemporary Buton Rinchen Drub (1290–1364) was concurrently seeking to claim authority of the Kālacakra. However, Buton was undertaking another, much larger enterprise. In his scriptorium, Buton was compiling, editing, and producing a Tibetan-language edition of the Buddhist canon.[43] In doing so, he was devising and fortifying a taxonomical scheme based on Indian Buddhist doxographical categories. In effect, as he catalogued the words of the Buddha, Buton was participating in the millennial cultural event that would not only construct and concretize Buddhist literary genres in Tibet but would serve as the primary doxographical model for later Tibetans to navigate Buddhist literature. Similar classifications of Indian Buddhist literary categories were also made a generation earlier by Chomden Rigral (1227–1305) and Sanggye Bum at Nartang.

With this work hovering amid the intellectual discourse of his day, Dolpopa was left to sift through what he felt were historically imperfect doxographical categories. In fact, Dolpopa thought that such neat bundling of canonical materials created a miscategorization of Buddhist doctrines and thereby deserved the attention of a Fourth Council. In order to legitimize and organize Indian Buddhist doctrines, Dolpopa appropriated the power of historical time and utilized the *Kālacakra Tantra* as the authoritative source for interpreting Mahāyāna Buddhist history. By doing so, he suggested that the compilation of Buddhist doctrines by Tibetans needed to be reconsidered in light of Indian Buddhist doctrinal history. For Dolpopa, this amounted to nothing less than a total codification of Buddhist philosophical systems in India that challenged predominant assumptions about the writings of major Indian Buddhist authors, including Nāgārjuna, Candrakīrti, Asaṅga, Vasubandhu, Dharmakīrti, Haribhadra, Vimuktisena, Dharmamitra, Ponjangba, among others.[44]

Dolpopa appropriated an Indian frame of time—one that followed a classical Hindu cosmological schema that was incorporated into the *Kālacakra Tantra*—but in so doing, he acquired the main Vajrayāna hermeneutic for authenticating his work. With the declaration of *The Fourth Council*, and assertion that the zhentong view and literary heritage was retrieved from a pure age before the dharma was contaminated and intoxicated by later interlocutors, Dolpopa was reimagining and glorifying Buddhist India. However, he was also making an observation about the fluidity and interpenetrative nature of temporality itself, such that it can be marked by doctrine. In a sense, Dolpopa, and later Tāranātha, were not merely pushing forth a literary theory to authenticate their project but were interpreting the very historical act of cultural and intellectual reception that constructed Buddhist discourse in Tibet.[45] Through these efforts, the Jonangpas have contributed to a revision of the history concerning the development of the principle philosophical systems in India, and their transmission into Tibet.[46]

Appendix

Supplication to the Tradition of the Perfect Eon

By Dolpopa Sherab Gyaltsen

Translated by Michael R. Sheehy

Oṃ!
May all this be accomplished!

Due to a manifold decline of view,
The teachings have degenerated.
This is unbearable for the natural mind.

It's unbearable because so many of our kind mother and father sentient beings have gone astray, down a perverted path.

I cry out with sorrow to all the victors and their heirs in the ten directions—
Seize us with compassion!

You who are endowed with marvelous ever-present spacious omniscience,
Power and capacity, enlightened qualities and activities,
Bestow your blessings!

Off in the opposite direction of the profound Prajñāpāramitā,
Oh! How sad it is to yearn for this profound Prajñāpāramitā—
Seize us with compassion!

Off in the opposite direction of the Great Madhyamaka,
Oh! How sad it is to yearn for this Great Madhyamaka—
Seize us with compassion!

Off in the opposite direction of magnificent Nirvāṇa,
Oh! How sad it is to yearn for this magnificent Nirvāṇa—
Seize us with compassion!

Off in the opposite direction of Mahāmudrā,
Oh! How sad it is to yearn for this Mahāmudrā—
Seize us with compassion!

Off in the opposite direction of great luminosity,
Oh! How sad it is to yearn for this great luminosity—
Seize us with compassion!

Off in the opposite direction of great bliss,
Oh! How sad it is to yearn for this great bliss—
Seize us with compassion!

Off in the opposite direction of great bodhisattvas,
Oh! How sad it is to yearn for these great bodhisattvas—
Seize us with compassion!

Off in the opposite direction of ultimate truth,
Oh! How sad it is to yearn for this ultimate truth—
Seize us with compassion!

Off in the opposite direction of the profound nature of phenomena,
Oh! How sad it is to yearn for this profound nature of phenomena—
Seize us with compassion!

Off in the opposite direction of the expanse of phenomena,
Oh! How sad it is to yearn for this expanse of phenomena—
Seize us with compassion!

Off in the opposite direction of actuality,
Oh! How sad it is to yearn for this actuality—
Seize us with compassion!

Off in the opposite direction of the immutable,
Oh! How sad it is to yearn for this immutable—
Seize us with compassion!

Off in the opposite direction of the perfected nature,
Oh! How sad it is to yearn for this perfected nature—
Seize us with compassion!

Off in the opposite direction of the buddha-nature,
Oh! How sad it is to yearn for this buddha-nature—
Seize us with compassion!

Off in the opposite direction of the natural spiritual family,
Oh! How sad it is to yearn for this natural spiritual family—
Seize us with compassion!

Off in the opposite direction of the essential enlightened dimension,
Oh! How sad it is to yearn for this essential enlightened dimension—
Seize us with compassion!

Off in the opposite direction of the ultimate enlightened dimension,
Oh! How sad it is to yearn for this ultimate enlightened dimension—
Seize us with compassion!

Off in the opposite direction of the five dimensions of buddhahood,
Oh! How sad it is to yearn for these five dimensions of buddhahood—
Seize us with compassion!

Off in the opposite direction of the five types of pristine awareness,
Oh! How sad it is to yearn for these five types of pristine awareness—
Seize us with compassion!

Off in the opposite direction of Vajrasattva,
Oh! How sad it is to yearn for this Vajrasattva—
Seize us with compassion!

Off in the opposite direction of the genuine nature,
Oh! How sad it is to yearn for this genuine nature—
Seize us with compassion!

Off in the opposite direction of Ati Yoga,
Oh! How sad it is to yearn for this Ati Yoga—
Seize us with compassion!

Off in the opposite direction of Samantabhadra,
Oh! How sad it is to yearn for this Samantabhadra—
Seize us with compassion!

Off in the opposite direction of the Cakrasaṃvara and Hevajra yogas,
Oh! How sad it is to yearn for these Cakrasaṃvara and Hevajra yogas—
Seize us with compassion!

Off in the opposite direction of Guhyasamāja,
Oh! How sad it is to yearn for this Guhyasamāja—
Seize us with compassion!

Off in the opposite direction of Kālacakra,
Oh! How sad it is to yearn for this Kālacakra—
Seize us with compassion!

Off in the opposite direction of the adamantine expanse,
Oh! How sad it is to yearn for this adamantine expanse—
Seize us with compassion!

Off in the opposite direction of the *Vajra Pinnacle Tantra*,[47]
Oh! How sad it is to yearn for this *Vajra Pinnacle Tantra*—
Seize us with compassion!

Off in the opposite direction of the *Glorious Prime Supreme Tantra*,[48]
Oh! How sad it is to yearn for this *Glorious Prime Supreme Tantra*—
Seize us with compassion!

Off in the opposite direction of the profound truth of cessation,
Oh! How sad it is to yearn for this profound truth of cessation—
Seize us with compassion!

Off in the opposite direction of the awareness of the nature of phenomena,
Oh! How sad it is to yearn for this awareness of the nature of phenomena—
Seize us with compassion!

Off in the opposite direction of the ultimate logic,
Oh! How sad it is to yearn for this ultimate logic—
Seize us with compassion!

Though there are many who belong to different spiritual families,
May these blessings enter into each of their streams of awareness!

Without reifying what is not,
May we realize the abiding nature of what is!

With a decline of view and a decline of conduct,
Bestow your blessings so that we may tranquilize the demons of these two degenerations,
And swiftly perfect the view, meditation, and conduct of the Perfect Eon tradition!

This is a supplication to the Perfect Eon tradition,
That which is particularly superior to the Third Eon tradition.

May this benefit all sentient beings!

This was composed by the vagabond endowed with the Fourfold Reliance [Dolpopa Sherab Gyaltsen], based on genuine realization due to knowing the Perfect Eon dharma.

NOTES

1. Mkhan po Ngag dbang blo gros grags pa writes, "The cycle of the Kālacakra teachings from the time of the kalkī of Śambhala, on through the dissemination of these systems in the noble land of India, until the great Jonangpa master of these teachings [Dolpopa Sherab Gyaltsen] appeared in this world—did nothing more than repeat the sayings of the Rwa and 'Dro lineages without clarifying our own tradition. Nevertheless, during the latter period of his life, Dolpopa engaged in the intended meaning of the [Kālacakra] tantra and its commentary, the consummation of our [Jonang] tradition." Ngag dbang, *Jo nang chos 'byung* 97.

2. For discussion on Dolpopa in the historical context of tantra gzhan stong, see Sheehy "A Lineage History of Vajrayoga," 224–226.

3. Chimpa and Chattopadhyaya, *Taranatha's History* 68.

4. Chimpa and Chattopadhyaya, *Taranatha's History* 92. See also 86 where Tāranātha makes reference to the Third Council taking place at the time of King Mahāpadma.

5. Fortunately, this topic has been addressed in Stearns, *Buddha from Dolpo* 79–81 and 86–98, and Kapstein, *Tibetan Assimilation* 110–119. For a translation of the *Bka' bsdu bzhi pa*, see Stearns, *Buddha from Dolpo* 127–172. Note also that the versions published in Bhutan present variants in comparison to the 'Dzam thang publications in Dol po pa's *Collected Works*. Dol po pa also composed an autocommentary (*rang 'grel*) as well as a summary (*bsdus don*) of his work, Dol po pa, *Bka' bsdus bzhi pa'i don bstan rtsis*, *Bka' bsdus bzhi pa'i bsdus don*, *Bka' bsdus bzhi pa'i don bstan rtsis chen po*. For these three yugas in relation to gzhan stong, see also Ngag dbang, *Rgyud dang 'bras*, 80–85.

6. Dol po pa, *Bka' sdus bzhi pa'i don btsan rtsis chen po*, 166.

7. The phrase here is "*gsum ldan mar bcad.*"

8. Ngag dbang, *Rgyu dang 'bras* (Dharamsala) 91–92.

9. About the Kaliyuga, Dolpopa writes, "bzhi cha gcig kyang med na rtsod ldan na te/ lha min kla klo nag po'i chos su gsungs." Dol po pa, *Bka' bsdus bzhi pa* 166.

10. For a translation of Dolpopa's supplication, see the appendix to this chapter.

11. Dol po pa, *Bka' bsdus bzhi pa* 167.1–167.

12. Ngag dbang, *Rgyu dang 'bras* 42.

13. For further discussion on this topic, see Sheehy's chapter "The Zhentong Lion Roars" in this volume.

14. The full phrase in Tibetan is *stong pa nyid kyi gzugs brnyan* and is abbreviated *stong gzugs*. It is commonly translated as "empty form." The term *gzugs brnyan* is a reflection. Throughout the Kālacakra literature, the use of the phrase "image of emptiness" or "reflection of emptiness" draws a simile from the Indian prognostication rite wherein a young virgin girl divines prognostic images (*pratisenā*, *pra phab*) from a mirror divination (*phra 'bebs*).

These are said to be experienced only during the prognostication ritual and are a simile for the image of emptiness that is perceived to be the Kālacakra during the sixfold vajrayoga practice. Stearns, *Buddha from Dolpo* notes 430, 532, and 546.

15. Tā ra nā tha, *Gzhan stong snying po* 179–180.

16. Dol po pa, *Ri chos* 374.7–375.

17. Dol po pa, *Bka' bsdus bzhi pa'i rang 'grel* 642. See also Stearns, *Buddha from Dolpo* 268, and Hopkins, *Mountain Doctrine* 7.

18. Dol po pa, *Bka' bsdus bzhi pa'i rang 'grel* 642–643.

19. Kapstein, *Tibetan Assimilation* 106–116, and Stearns, *Buddha from Dolpo* 79–81. For discussion on the literary sources for gzhan stong, see the introduction to this volume by Mathes and Sheehy.

20. Dol po pa, *Stong nyid* 394. Clarifying his intent and reason for writing, in his preface to the *Differentiating Emptiness*, Dolpopa writes, "Those who do not understand the stainless scriptural tradition of the Perfect Eon, such as its explanations on emptiness, divisions of the two truths, and so forth, claim that the emptiness of zhentong does not suffice to be emptiness, since all emptiness is exclusively rangtong. By relying on this poisonous pit of wicked views that asserts rangtong to be exclusively the emptiness that explains the different divisions, such as the nature of things and so forth, there is an extreme proliferation of multiple extensions of various perverted views. In response, I compose this teaching for the sake of the unwise." Note how this paraphrasing resembles the quote from *Letter to My Disciples*.

21. Dol po pa, *Stong nyid* 294–295.

22. Dol po pa, *Bka' yang dag* 618. A translation of the full title is *Seizing the Crucial Point of Every Utterly Perfect Discourse*.

23. Permanence of the triple gem is also a topic in the *Uttaratantra* and is reiterated as a major rubric for discussion within gzhan stong literature. It is noteworthy that in his colophon to this work, Dolpopa reiterates the importance of this approach in distinguishing the yuga and he writes, "In this way, through realizing the distinctions between rangtong and zhentong, the teachings are clear. This is how the Perfect Eon [Kṛtayuga] tradition is arranged, that which is exceptionally superior to the Third Eon [Tretāyuga] tradition." Dol po pa, *Bka' yang dag* 621.

24. While it is important to distinguish the philosophical principles of Cittamātra from Yogācāra more generally, in this context, I am using the Tibetan compound that is typically employed by Jonangpa authors, including Tāranātha, which is Yogācāra-Cittamātra (*rnal 'byor spyod pa sems tsam*). Distinctions should also be made philosophically with the *Vijñaptimātra* and *Vijñānavāda*, though doxographically, these are often subsumed with the broad categorical reference of Yogācāra.

25. Stearns, *Buddha from Dolpo* 91–103.

26. See the introduction by Mathes and Sheehy in this volume.

27. Tā ra nā tha, *Tshul gnyis* 196.

28. Tā ra nā tha, *Tshul gnyis* 196.

29. Tāranātha's *History of Buddhism in India* lists a few of the names of these early five hundred teachers of the Mahāyāna, which include mahā-bhaṭṭāraka Avitarka, Vigatarāgadvaja, Divyākaragupta, Rāhulamitra, Jñānatala, and mahā-upāsaka Saṅgatala. Chimpa and Chattopadhyaya, *Taranatha's History* 98.

30. Ngag dbang, *Jo nang chos 'byung* 9.

31. Tā ra nā tha, *Gzhan stong snying po* 180.

32. Tā ra nā tha, *Gzhan stong snying po* 182.

33. Tā ra nā tha, *Tshul gnyis* 196–197.

34. Also referred to as the *mtshan nyid gsum*. For discussion on the three natures in the thought of Dolpopa, see Stearns, *Buddha from Dolpo* 91–103.

35. Stearns, 90. On the point that the final turning is not Cittamātra, Mkhan po Ngag dbang blo gros grags pa quotes the *Laṅkāvatāra Sūtra*: *sems tsam la ni brten nas su / phyi rol don du mi brtag go / snang ba med pa la brten nas/ sems tsam las ni 'da' par bya / yang dag dmigs pa la brten nas / snang ba med las 'da' bar bya/ rnal 'byor snang ba med gnas na / theg pa chen po mi mthong ngo*. Ngag dbang, *Rgyu dang 'bras* 59. For a fuller discussion on the three natures in the Cittamātra system, with special reference to the *Sandhinirmocana Sūtra* and *Prajñāpārmitā*, see Ngag dbang, *Rgyu dang 'bras* 55–59.

36. Ngag dbang, *Rgyu dang 'bras* 60.

37. For a full translation, Kapstein, *Collected Works*.

38. Dol po pa, *Slob ma* 278.

39. In an interesting passage, one that is repeated several times in the letter, Dolpopa describes his method for engaging with those who hold opposing views. Following a claim that something is not true, Dolpopa writes, "If one thinks that this is true, ask him whether he has authoritative scriptures or reasoning that make it known, and to present it. If the respondent can present it, then have him write it down." This phrase, *yi ger yang bris mdzod*, "then have him write it down," is repeated several times throughout the letter, requesting his opponents to record their claims and be accountable.

40. Dol po pa, *Slob ma* 283–284.

41. See Hopkins, *Reflections on Reality* 273–391, for analyses in the thought of Tsong-khapa on Dolpopa.

42. Davidson, *Tibetan Renaissance* 152.

43. Schaeffer, *Culture of the Book* 12–15.

44. Kapstein, *Collected Works* 35–43.

45. The fifteenth-century Jonangpa author Ngag dbang grags pa extends this hermeneutic in his work that he so provocatively titled *Bka' bsdu lnga pa* (*Fifth Council*).

46. Kapstein, *Tibetan Assimilation* 118.

47. This is a reference to the *Vajrasekhara-mahaguhya-yoga Tantra*.

48. This is a reference to the *Śrī-paramādi Tantra*.

BIBLIOGRAPHY

Tibetan Sources

Dngos grub Dpal. *Bka' bsdus bzhi ba'i 'grel ba lung rigs gter mdzod nges gsang kun gsal thub bstan mdzes rgyan*. Kun mkhyen dgongs rgyan. Beijing: Mi rigs dpe skrun khang, 2010.

———. *Ri chos nges don rgya mtsho'i bsdus don nges don mdzes rgyan tshangs pa'i sgra dbyangs*. Kun mkhyen dgongs rgyan. Beijing: Mi rigs dpe skrun khang, 2010.

Dol po pa Shes rab rgyal mtshan. *Bka' sdus bzhi pa'i don btsan rtsis chen po*, 6, 165–201. In *Kun mkhyen Dol po pa shes rab rgyal mtshan Gsung 'bum*. 'Dzam thang.

———. *Bka' bsdus bzhi pa'i bsdus don 'grel ba*, 6, 203–217. In *Kun mkhyen Dol po pa shes rab rgyal mtshan Gsung 'bum*. 'Dzam thang.

———. *Bka' bsdus bzhi pa'i don bstan rtsis chen po phyogs med ris med*, 6, 219–271. In *Kun mkhyen Dol po pa shes rab rgyal mtshan Gsung 'bum*. 'Dzam thang.

———. *Bka' bsdus bzhi pa'i rang 'grel*. Paro: Lama Ngodrup and Sherab Drimay, 1984.

———. *Bka' yang dag kun gyi gnad nas bzung ba*, 6, 617–622. In *Kun mkhyen Dol po pa shes rab rgyal mtshan Gsung 'bum*. 'Dzam thang.

———. *Gnas lugs zab mo stong pa nyid la bstod pa*, 8, 612–616. In *Kun mkhyen Dol po pa shes rab rgyal mtshan Gsung 'bum*. 'Dzam thang.

———. *Kun gzhi ye shes lnga'i rab tu dbye ba*, 6, 343–347. In *Kun mkhyen Dol po pa shes rab rgyal mtshan Gsung 'bum*. 'Dzam thang.

———. *Rang rig gsal gyi rab tu dbye ba*, 6, 317–35. In *Kun mkhyen Dol po pa shes rab rgyal mtshan Gsung 'bum*. 'Dzam thang.

———. *Rdzogs ldan gyi gsol 'debs*, 8, 367–370. In *Kun mkhyen Dol po pa shes rab rgyal mtshan Gsung 'bum*. 'Dzam thang.

———. *Ri chos nges don rgya mtsho zhes bya ba mthar thug mong ma yin pa'i man ngag*, 3, 189–741. In *Kun mkhyen Dol po pa shes rab rgyal mtshan Gsung 'bum*. 'Dzam thang.

———. *Slob ma la spring ba skur 'debs dang sgro 'dogs spang ba*, 6, 277–286. In *Kun mkhyen Dol po pa shes rab rgyal mtshan Gsung 'bum*. 'Dzam thang.

———. *Stong nyid kyi rab tu dbye ba khyad 'phags*, 6, 293–303. In *Kun mkhyen Dol po pa shes rab rgyal mtshan Gsung 'bum*. 'Dzam thang.

Nya dbon Kun dga' dpal. 1996. *Bstan pa spyi 'grel zhes bya ba'i gsol 'debs kyi rnam bshad dgongs pa rnam gsal yid kyi mun sel*. Rnga ba rang skyongs khul par 'debs bzo grwa pa.

Ngag dbang Blo gros grags pa. *Rgyu dang 'bras bu'i theg pa mchog gi gnas lugs zab mo'i don rnam par nges pa rje jo nang pa chen po'i ring lugs 'jigs med dgong lnga'i nga ro*, 1, 35–516. In *Blo gros grags pa'i Gsung 'bum*. 'Dzam thang.

———. *Jo nang chos 'byung zla ba'i sgron me*. Qinghai: Nationalities Press, 1992.

———. *Rgyu dang 'bras bu'i theg pa mchog gi gnas lugs zab mo'i don rnam par nges pa rje jo nang pa chen po'i ring lugs 'jigs med dgong lnga'i nga ro zhes bya ba*. In *Contributions to the Study of Jo-nang-pa History, Iconography and Doctrine: Selected Writings of 'Dzam-thang Mkhan-po Blo-gros-grags-pa*, II. Dharamsala: Library of Tibetan Works and Archives (LTWA), 1993.

Shes rab Dpal. *Bka' bsdu lnga ba mtha' bral dbu ma chen po'i grub mtha' rab gsal*. Jo nang dpe tshogs. Beijing: Mi rigs dpe skrun khang, 2008.

Tāranātha, Jo nang Rje btsun. *Dpal dus kyi 'khor lo'i chos bskor gyi byung khungs nyer mkho*, 2, 179–219. In *Rje btsun Tā ra nā tha'i gsung 'bum*. 'Dzam thang.

———. *Gzhan stong dbu ma'i rgyan*, 18, 109–129. In *Rje btsun Tā ra nā tha'i Gsung 'bum*. 'Dzam thang.

———. *Gzhan stong snying po*, 18, 131–170. In *Rje btsun Tā ra nā tha'i Gsung 'bum*. 'Dzam thang.

———. *Tshul gnyis rnam par 'byed pa nges pa'i don gyi 'jug ngos zhes bya ba nyung ngu rnam gsal dag cing tshang ba*, 18, 195–208. In *Rje btsun Tā ra nā tha'i gsung 'bum*. 'Dzam thang.

Secondary Sources

Chimpa, Lama, and Chattopadhyaya, Alaka, translator. *Taranatha's History of Buddhism in India*. Simla: Indian Institute of Advanced Study, 1970.

Davidson, Ronald. *Tibetan Renaissance: Tantric Buddhism in the Rebirth of Tibetan Culture*. New York: Columbia University Press, 2005.

Duckworth, Douglas. "Other-Emptiness in the Jonang School: The Theo-Logic of Buddhist Dualism." *Philosophy East and West* 65, no. 2 (2015): 485–497.

Hatchell, Christopher. *Naked Seeing: The Great Perfection, the Wheel of Time, and Visionary Buddhism in Renaissance Tibet*. Oxford: Oxford University Press, 2014.

Henning, Edward. "The Six Vajra-Yogas of the Kālacakra." In *As Long as Space Endures: Essays on the Kalacakra Tantra in Honor of the Dalai Lama*, edited by Edward A. Arnold, 237–258. Ithaca: Snow Lion, 2009.

Hopkins, Jeffrey. *Reflections on Reality: The Three Natures and Non-Natures in the Mind-Only School*. Berkeley: University of California Press, 2002.

———, translator. *Mountain Doctrine: Tibet's Fundamental Treatise on Other-Emptiness and the Buddha Matrix*. By Dö-bo-ba Śhay-rap-gyel-tsen. Ithaca: Snow Lion, 2006.

Kapstein, Matthew. *The 'Dzam-thang Edition of the Collected Works of Kun-khyen Dol-po-pa Shes-rab rgyal-mtshan: Introduction and Catalogue*. Delhi: Shedrup Books, 1992.

———. *The Tibetan Assimilation of Buddhism: Conversion, Contestation, and Memory*. Oxford: Oxford University Press, 2000.

———. "From Kun-mkhyen Dol-po-pa to 'Ba'-mda' dge-legs: Three Jo-nang-pa Masters on the Interpretation of the *Prajnaparamita*." In *Reason's Traces: Identity and Interpretation in Indian and Tibetan Buddhist Thought*. Boston: Wisdom, 2001.

Maraldo, John C. "Hermeneutics and Historicity in the Study of Buddhism." *The Eastern Buddhist* 19, I (1986): 17–43.

Mathes, Klaus-Dieter. "Tāranātha's Presentation of Trisvabhāva in the Gźan stoṅ sñiṅ po." *Journal of the International Association of Buddhist Studies* 23 (2004): 195–223.

———. *A Direct Path to the Buddha Within: Gö Lotsāwa's Mahāmudrā Interpretation of the Ratnagotravibhāga*. Studies in Indian and Tibetan Buddhism. Boston: Wisdom, 2008.

———. "The Gzhan stong Model of Reality—Some More Material on Its Origin, Transmission and Interpretation." *Journal of the International Association of Buddhist Studies* 34, nos. 1–2 (2011/2012): 187–223.

Pettit, John W. *Mipham's Beacon of Certainty: Illuminating the View of Dzogchen, the Great Perfection*. Boston: Wisdom, 1999.

Schaeffer, Kurtis. *The Culture of the Book in Tibet*. New York: Columbia University Press, 2009.

Sheehy, Michael R. "Rangjung Dorje's Variegations of Mind: Ordinary Awareness and Pristine Awareness in Tibetan Buddhist Literature." In *Buddhist Thought and Applied Psychological Research*, 69–92, edited by D. K. Nauriyal. Routledge Curzon's Critical Series in Buddhism. London: Routledge Curzon Press, 2005.

———. "The Gzhan stong Chen mo: A Study of Emptiness According to the Modern Tibetan Buddhist Jo nang Scholar 'Dzam thang Mkhan po Ngag dbang Blo gros grags pa (1920–1975)." PhD dissertation, California Institute of Integral Studies, San Francisco, 2007.

———. "A Lineage History of Vajrayoga and Tantric Zhentong from the Jonang Kalachakra Practice Tradition." In *As Long as Space Endures: Essays on the Kalachakra Tantra in Honor of the Dalai Lama*, 219–235. Ithaca: Snow Lion 2009.

———. "The Jonangpa After Tāranātha: Auto/biographical Writings on the Transmission of Esoteric Buddhist Knowledge in Seventeenth Century Tibet." *Bulletin of Tibetology* 45, no. 01 (2009): 9–24.

Stearns, Cyrus. "Dol-po-pa Shes-rab rgyal-mtshan and the Genesis of the Gzhan-stong Position in Tibet." *Asiatische Studien/Etudes Asiatiques* 49, no. 4 (1995): 829–852.

———. *The Buddha from Dolpo: A Study of the Life and Thought of the Tibetan Master Dolpopa Sherab Gyaltsen*. Ithaca: Snow Lion, 2010.

Tatz, Mark. "Review of *The Buddha from Dolpo: A Study of the Life and Thought of the Tibetan Master Dolpopa Sherab Gyaltsen*, by Cyrus Stearns." *Journal of the American Oriental Society* 121 (2001): 3.

Templeman, David. "Tarānātha the Historian." *Tibet Journal* 17, no. 1 (1981): 41–46.

4

Buddha-Nature in Garungpa Lhai Gyaltsen's *Lamp That Illuminates the Expanse of Reality* and among Tibetan Intellectuals

Dorje Nyingcha

In the fourteenth century, Tibetan intellectuals were extremely enthusiastic about further exploring various Buddhist philosophical concepts. Many who are now considered intellectual giants were involved in these discussions, making a huge contribution to the development of basic Buddhist philosophical issues such as the meaning of conventional and ultimate truths, the meaning of definitive and interpretative teachings, the concept of buddha-nature (*de bzhin gshegs pa'i snying po*), the ultimate message of the three turnings, the articulation of Madhyamaka and Yogācāra philosophy, and so on. Cyrus Stearns mentions that Dolpopa Sherab Gyaltsen's (1292–1361) zhentong philosophical view agreed with many Mahāyāna and Vajrayāna scriptures, but the majority of the Tibetan intellectual community during Dolpopa's lifetime didn't agree with his view.[1] This idea was mind-boggling to the mainstream Tibetan intellectual community of the time, for whom the doctrine of buddha-nature, the enlightenment matrix, needed interpretation in order to understand its true intention. This is the opinion of the mainstream Sakya order to which Dolpopa belonged before he met Jonang masters.[2]

The sources make it clear that the fourteenth century truly became a milestone for the development of Tibetan Buddhism in general and for the continuing development of Buddhist philosophy in particular. Cyrus Stearns also says that concern with these issues reached a critical point in the fourteenth century.[3] Moreover, these discussions changed the main trend of Buddhism in Tibet, contributing to a larger reordering of the Tibetan Buddhist community. The rise of the Geluk order is perhaps the most obvious example of the changes that emerged in the same context as these philosophical developments.[4]

Even before the fourteenth century, Tibetan intellectuals had argued over different understandings of the concept of emptiness, or śūnyatā, and other controversial issues in philosophy. The basis for these different views exists within the Tibetan Buddhist canon. However, individual scholars' interpretations depend on their own understanding of those teachings. My attention will focus on the fourteenth century, as this era was especially marked by an atmosphere of strong enthusiasm, strong interest, and a strong spirit of seeking the truth. These qualities were more alive and influential among intellectuals in that century than in preceding centuries.

In this era, the Sakya, Sangpu, Jonang, Zhalu, and many other monasteries became major degree-granting centers of learning. Many scholars received their academic education from those learning centers. For example, when Buton Rinchen Drub (1290–1364) joined Zhalu, it became a famous learning center. In addition to his outstanding scholarship in the field of Buddhist philosophy, his contributions to historiography and editorial work are also quite remarkable. Among the intellectual giants of the fourteenth century, Dolpopa's turn to the Jonang order was a turning point for the Jonang. His influence drastically altered the direction of Jonang history and brought this tradition into the mainstream of the philosophical community. Dolpopa's participation in the Jonang tradition and his new ideas about emptiness forced a major reinvestigation of a range of topics, dealing not only with philosophy but also with meditative practice.

Besides Buton and Dolpopa, other prominent intellectuals who appeared in the fourteenth century include Longchen Rabjam Drime Odzer (1308–1364), Karmapa Rangjung Dorje (1284–1339), Lama Dampa Sonam Gyaltsen (1312–1375), Remdawa Zhonnu Lodro (1349–1413), Tsongkapa Lozang Drakpa (1357–1419), Yakde Paṇchen (1299–1378), and Nyawon Kunga Pel (1285–1379), among others. These famous scholars advocated various major philosophical positions on the aforementioned controversial issues and made a huge contribution to how they would henceforth be understood within the Tibetan intellectual world. These philosophical issues were important not only in their own moment, but they are and will be important at the present time as well as in the future. Therefore, it is crucial for us to investigate these philosophical issues as they became hot topics in the fourteenth century.

Among many historical sources that discuss these issues in the fourteenth century, Garungpa Lhai Gyaltsen's (1319–1402/3) *Lamp That Illuminates the Expanse of Reality* is a good example from which we may glimpse many such discussions of controversial philosophical issues, most centrally the concept of buddha-nature.[5] One of the foremost students of Dolpopa, Garungpa saw it as his duty to prove that the Jonang philosophical view represented the true and ultimate message of the Buddha.

In this work, Garungpa mainly discusses the theory of buddha-nature. In the course of this discussion he also touches on definitive and interpretative teachings, the three turnings, the two truths, and Yogācāra and Madhyamaka philosophical traditions. Insofar as Garungpa aims to establish the truth of his own tradition, it is unavoidable that he also criticizes other scholars such as Buton, Sakya Paṇḍita Kunga Gyaltsen (1182–1251), Upa Losal Sanggye Bum, and Remdawa, among others. In particular, his main arguments directly take up and attempt to refute Remdawa's criticisms of the Jonang. Remdawa mounted a strong case against the Jonang philosophical view in his *Crystal Clarifying the Intention of the Ratnagotravibhāga*.[6] Garungpa's *Lamp That Illuminates the Expanse of Reality* was a direct response to Remdawa's critique.

Unfortunately, Remdawa's *Crystal Clarifying the Intention of Ratnagotravibhāga* is not available today. It is very fortunate, therefore, that another short commentary on the *Ratnagotravibhāga*, titled *The Essence of the Ratnagotravibhāga or Crystal Intention of Buddha-Nature*, is available.[7] In order to fully understand Remdawa's position we must consult not only his *Ratnagotravibhāga* commentary but also his commentary on the *Madhyamakāvatāra*. In his *Lamp That Illuminates the Expanse of Reality*, Garungpa not only quotes from Remdawa's *Crystal Intention of Buddha-Nature* but also from Remdawa's commentaries on the *Madhyamakāvatāra* and *Abhidharmakośa*.[8]

On a close reading of the *Lamp That Illuminates the Expanse of Reality* it is apparent that although Garungpa disagrees with Remdawa that buddha-nature is permanent and unchanging, by comparing and contrasting his argument against those he criticizes as well as those of his contemporaries, it becomes clear that their arguments are stronger than his because of their logical reasons, analysis, and arguments.

BUDDHA-NATURE FROM THE JONANG PERSPECTIVE

It is not entirely clear what the position of Jonang scholars prior to Dolpopa were regarding the concept of buddha-nature. There is no clear evidence that masters prior to Dolpopa, such as Yumo Mikyo Dorje (b. 1027), Choku Odzer (1214–1292), Kunpang Tukje Tsondru (1243–1313), Changsem Gyalwa Yeshe (1247–1320), or Ketsun Yontan Gyatso (1260–1327), discussed the idea of buddha-nature in their writings. However, Tukwan Lozang Chokyi Nyima (1737–1802) mentions in his *Crystal Mirror of Philosophical Systems* that the zhentong philosophical view was discovered by Yumo during meditation on the six-branch yoga.[9]

There are many different opinions among scholars regarding the origin of zhentong philosophical view. Cyrus Stearns says that Dolpopa's realization of the zhentong view occurred when he began a strict retreat on the six-branch yoga of the Kālacakra at the Ḍākinī Bliss Possessing (*mkha' spyod bde ldan*). Tāranātha has made this following statement in his *Guidebook to the ḍākinī Bliss Possessing*: "The exceptional zhentong view and meditation arose in his mind while staying at *Ḍākinī Bliss Possessing*, but he did not speak of it to others for several years."[10] Cyrus Stearns also discusses a poem wherein Dolpopa expressed his joyful feeling upon accomplishment of the great stūpa. In a key verse of this poem Dolpopa ties his construction of the great stūpa to the appearance of the new idea of zhentong philosophy. As a result of developing this new idea, Dolpopa composed his *Teaching of Mountain Hermit*—the main text in which he explains his philosophical position.[11] Go Lotsāwa Zhonnu Pel (1392–1481) also expressed the opinion that Dolpopa's development of zhentong philosophy was a result of building the great stūpa.[12] Garungpa also mentions the relationship between building the stūpa and composing the *Teaching of Mountain Hermit* in his *Biography of the Dharma Lord of Jonang*, also quoted by Cyrus Stearns:

> My intelligence has not been
> Refined in threefold wisdom,
> But I think raising Mount Meru
> caused the Ocean to gush forth.[13]

Tsen Kawoche (11th c.) played an important role in early discussions of the origin of the zhentong view. Some later Jonang masters, including Kunga Drolchok (1507–1565), claimed that the zhentong view was actually much earlier than Dolpopa. In the *Lineage History of the Hundred Guiding Instructions*, Kunga Drolchok refutes the position held by mainstream Tibetan scholars at that time that the view was discovered by Dolpopa.[14] As evidence for his position, Kunga Drolchok cites a conversation between Tsen Kawoche and his teacher, the Kashmiri paṇḍita Sajjana. Upon close inspection, the conversation is not good evidence for the existence of zhentong philosophy in India prior to the time of Dolpopa, as it is a general conversation about the three turnings of the wheel. However, Klaus-Dieter Mathes says that this conversation at least suggests the existence in Kashmir of a hermeneutic tradition that strictly followed the message of the *Saṁdhinimocana Sūtra*.[15] Here is the conversation between Tsen Kawoche and his teacher, Paṇḍita Sajjana, quoted by Cyrus Stearns:

> As for the guiding instructions on the view of an emptiness of other, Tsen Khawoché said, "Sajjana, the paṇḍita of Kaśmīr, made this very significant statement: 'The Conqueror turned the Dharma wheel three times. The first wheel taught the four truths, the middle one taught the lack of defining characteristics, and the final one made careful and thorough distinctions. Of these, the first two did not distinguish between the real and the imaginary. The final one, at the point of certainty concerning the absolute, taught by the distinguishing between the middle and the extremes, and distinguishing between phenomena and true nature. Only the original manuscripts of *Distinguishing Phenomena and True Nature* and the *Highest Continuum* were rediscovered. If these two texts had been lost, it would have indicated Maitreya's passing away into bliss.[16]

Appearing in an old notebook of Tsen Kawoche himself, bearing the title *Lotus Hook*, this is the argument against the later claim that the distinction of an "emptiness of other" was totally unknown in India and only appeared later in Tibet with the omniscient Dolpopa.[17] We should also examine the statement appearing in one of Buton's replies to questions, where he mentions the earlier existence of the philosophical tenet of Tanakpa Rinchen Yeshe (13th c.) that seems to have been later enhanced and maintained by Dolpopa.

According to Klaus-Dieter Mathes, Zhonnu Pel also mentions Tsen Kawoche and Sajjana in the introduction to his *Ratnagotravibhāga* commentary. Tsen Kawoche, who was a student of Drapa Ngonshe (11th c.), visited Kashmir and requested teachings on the *Dharmas of Maitreya*, along with special instructions. Since Tsen Kawoche requested these teachings as the basis for his practice in preparation for death, Sajjana took special care and gave him all the *Dharmas of Maitreya*, including special instructions. Lotsāwa Zu Gawai Dorje (11th c.) served as a translator between these two masters. Sajjana gave special instruction based on the *Ratnagotravibhāga* according to the meditation tradition.[18]

Mangto Ludrup Gyatso (1523–1596) presents yet another view regarding the origin of a zhentong view. He states in his *Chronology of the Doctrine* that Dolpopa developed the zhentong view upon being inspired by Rangjung Dorje's advice.[19] It is said that Dolpopa upheld the rangtong (*rang stong*) philosophical view before he had a discussion with Rangjung Dorje, and that Rangjung Dorje made a prophecy to him that he would uphold the zhentong view in the future. Actually, Rangjung Dorje himself definitely held the zhentong view before Dolpopa.[20] Cyrus Stearns quotes the following passage from Ludrup Gyatso's *Chronology of the Doctrine*:

> Moreover, this lord [Dolpopa] met with Karmapa Rangjung Dorjé and, it is said, when [Dolpopa] upheld the philosophical tenet of the emptiness of self-nature, the Karmapa prophesied that he would later become an adherent of the emptiness of other. In general, I think the tradition of the emptiness of other was first upheld by Karmapa Rangjung Dorjé. Those at Jonang became adherents to the emptiness of other after the great omniscient [Dolpopa].[21]

Regarding the question of how Dolpopa developed the zhentong view, and whether his inspiration came from Rangjung Dorje's advice, Karl Brunnhölzl has a different opinion. According to Brunnhölzl, Dolpopa considered all five *Dharmas of Maitreya* to convey the same message and view—that is, all of them follow the zhentong view and present the message of the third turning. However, Rangjung Dorje says that the *Abhisamayālaṃkāra* expresses the message of the second turning, and that the *Ratnagotravibhāga* expresses the message of the third turning. Brunnhölzl says that there are agreements between these two masters in the sense that both considered buddha-nature at the level of ground, path, and fruition to be exactly the same. They further agreed that buddhahood is not a result newly produced through practice.[22]

By the time that Dolpopa began to rise as the star of the Jonang order, he was able to clearly explain the concept of buddha-nature in line with the zhentong view in various writings. His explanation is clear and simple, and it relies mostly on scriptural quotations for proof of his position on buddha-nature. According to *Teaching of Mountain Hermit*, buddha-nature is the basis for the purification of stains, and the path to that purification is the practice of vajrayoga.[23]

For Remdawa, this explanation belongs to Yogācāra philosophy, and there in the context of conventional truth. Remdawa also addresses this point in great detail in his *Concise Meaning of Analysis of the Ratnagotravibhāga*. Yet the Jonang consider Remdawa's explanation that buddha-nature can be viewed differently from Yogācāra and Madhyamaka perspectives to be unacceptable. Nor can they accept Remdawa's assertion that those sūtras that talk about buddha-nature have both a surface and an underlying message. Thus, a major sticking point in this debate is the hermeneutical approach to the Tathāgatagarbha sūtras. For Jonang followers, the meaning of buddha-nature is definitive, the ultimate message of the third turning of Buddha's teaching, and coincides with the ultimate meaning of the profound tantric teachings as well. Jonang followers treat buddha-nature under the hermeneutic of the Great Madhyamaka. Garungpa repeatedly mentions this in his *Lamp That Illuminates the Expanse of Reality*.

Dolpopa rejects the idea that rangtong or self-emptiness is a synonym for ultimate truth, *tathatā*, *dhātu* of the signless, dharmadhātu, or absolute bodhicitta. Dolpopa's understanding of precisely what self-emptiness meant—in other words, what his precise definition of self-nature (*rang rang gi ngo bo*) was—is not clear to us. The following view found in *Teaching of Mountain Hermit* may lend some clarity to his understanding of "self-emptiness":

> *Objection*: The emptiness said to process many synonyms such as thusness is only self-emptiness—all phenomena's emptiness of their own entities.
>
> *Answer*: In that case, those with perverse attachment who are said to be subject to not at all attaining nirvāṇa would be suchness because they are empty of their own entities.[24]

It seems that to understand his position, we must first understand what he himself means by self-empty. Different scholars use the same term with quite different meanings. This is why one of the first elements of debate is the establishment of the meaning of terms. Confusion over variant uses of a single philosophical term has been a major issue for Tibetan Buddhist scholars since the fourteenth century and has produced many complications among them.

Regarding the meaning of self-emptiness, Dolpopa and his followers had a very different understanding than other schools of their time, because they considered self-emptiness to merely mean nothingness. For instance, in the *Lamp That Illuminates the Expanse of Reality* Garungpa says that it means complete emptiness, and that it is an interpretable meaning. Garungpa cites a passage from the second chapter of the *Mahāparinirvāṇa Sūtra*, which Jonang scholars consider to be definitive, regarding how to make a distinction among sūtras in terms of their contents:

> The second chapter of *Mahāparinirvāṇa Sūtra* teaches the drawbacks of not knowing the two modes of emptiness of the two truths and of viewing everything to be empty of itself without distinction. . . . This passage responds that a view that asserts that all that is knowable is empty in every way, empty of itself, is the result of clinging to the teachings of the middle turning that principally teaches that all phenomena are without essence in a literal, definitive way.[25]

Garungpa constantly emphasizes that the Jonang philosophical view is based on the ultimate message of the third turning of the teachings and on tantric teachings, which he takes to be ultimately true and of definitive meaning. By contrast, he considers the ultimate message of the first and second turnings of teaching to be relatively true and of interpretable meaning. Judging by the preceding comments, we may also assume that Garungpa makes no distinction between the concepts of existence and independent existence or between nonexistence and emptiness of independent existence. Remdawa considers self-emptiness not to mean mere nonexistence. For him, things exist but lack independent existence.

Garungpa also asserts that the buddha qualities exist permanently and independently, and they never result from dependent origination. In contrast, Remdawa asserts that even the Buddha's pure vision must be the result of dependent origination, for if they were not, the Buddhist position would mirror that of non-Buddhists schools such as Jainism.[26]

Regarding Dolpopa's position on buddha-nature, his *Commentary on the Ratnagotravibhāga* explains that buddha-nature means tathatā. So, whenever Dolpopa mentions buddha-nature, we must understand that he uses these two concepts in the exact same sense. When the dharmadhātu is fully concealed by defilements within sentient beings, it is called buddha-nature. When the dharmadhātu that had been tainted is completely purified by practice—the state of buddhahood—it is called dharmakāya. The ten powers, four fearlessnesses, eighteen unique qualities are called the fruition of separation and are related to the dharmakāya. However, the thirty-two major marks, and so forth, are called the fruition of ripening.

Ngari Choje Chokle Namgyal (1306–1386) discusses the concept of buddha-nature in detail in his *Destruction of Mistakes*, composed to refute Buton's *Ornament of Buddha-Nature That Is Extremely Profound and Difficult to Examine*.[27] Chokle Namgyal analyzed the main point of Buton by relying on both logical reasoning and scriptural authority. Buton states that the Buddha taught buddha-nature in order to clarify the idea of *ālayavijñāna*, quoting the *Laṅkāvatāra Sūtra* and *Śrīmālādevī Sūtra* in order to bolster this point.[28] Chokle Namgyal asks why, if Buddha taught buddha-nature in order to teach ālayavijñāna, do these sūtras say, "Buddha-nature is proclaimed to be ālayavijñāna," rather than, "The ālayavijñāna is proclaimed to be buddha-nature"?

According to Chokle Namgyal, the prior construction appears repeatedly in both sūtras, whereas the latter appears only once, which could well be due to a faulty translation. This leads Chokle Namgyal to conclude that the purpose for teaching buddha-nature was not to teach ālayavijñāna but to illustrate tainted tathatā.[29] Chokle Namgyal further supports this position with a quote from Asaṅga's *Commentary on the Ratnagotravibhāga*: "For which, tainted tathatā is the dharmadhātu not yet parted from the sheath of defilements; and this dhātu is called buddha-nature."[30] Another one of Dolpopa's students, Sazang Mati Paṇchen Lodro Gyaltsen (1294–1376), illustrates his position on buddha-nature with citations from various sūtras and tantras. When writing about ground, path, and fruition, he summarizes the existence of tathatā as the ground: "The ultimate suchness, which is the tathatā, is naturally pure, luminous, and dharmadhātu is the spontaneously existent, coemergent gnosis body, which [primordially exists] as the ground that pervades animate and inanimate phenomena."[31] Here, Mati Paṇchen shows that for him buddha-nature is ultimately tathatā. In order to support his position, he cites the *Ḍākinīvajrapañjara*:

> Stainless as space, the precious mind
> Is polluted by negative imputed conceptual thought;
> It becomes pure when the mind is purified.[32]

He also cites the *Ratnagotravibhāga*:

> Because the body of the perfectly awakened one permeates,
> Because suchness is undifferentiable,
> And because of being of the class,
> All who have bodies are always endowed with buddha-nature.[33]

This famous verse is cited widely by many scholars in order to prove that buddha-nature exists within all sentient beings. Mati Paṇchen also quotes a well-known verse from *Praise of the Dharmadhātu* in order to support his view of buddha-nature:

> The water that exists in the midst of earth remains pure.
> Likewise, the wisdom that exists in the midst of affliction remains pure.[34]

Lotsāwa Lodro Pel (d. 1354) says that buddha-nature is dharmadhātu, is naturally permanent, bliss, pure, conditioned, and spontaneously present. Buddha-nature is the object of self-knowing timeless awareness. Buddha-nature is profound, subtle, is difficult to understand and inconceivable. It is seen by the eye of gnosis and becomes a basis of benefiting oneself and others. Buddha-nature is one taste like space and is seen by yogins in meditative states. It is ultimate truth, the highest limit of reality, and profound tathatā. Buddha-nature is innately and spontaneously endowed with all good qualities. It is the element of Tathāgata and natural nirvāṇa—the ultimate refuge.[35] Dolpopa, Mati Paṇchen, and Ngari Choje never mention that buddha-nature is the ultimate refuge. So, even among Jonangpas, thoughts on buddha-nature vary. But all agree that it is the impure tathatā, dharmadhātu, and the ultimate truth.

GARUNGPA'S HERMENEUTIC IN THE LAMP THAT ILLUMINATES THE EXPANSE OF REALITY

One of the most commonplace rubrics under which Tibetans conceptualize the historical dissemination of the teachings delivered by the Buddha over the course of his teaching career is the three turnings of the wheel of dharma, taught in the *Sandhinirmocana Sūtra*. According to Garungpa's interpretation of this system, the teachings of the Buddha can be divided into three distinct turnings that span the course of his career based on differences in the level of critical reflection exhibited in each. Teachings that were given during the first turning of teaching were given without critical reflection—that is, the Buddha discussed things such as the aggregates, the elements, and so on, as if they existed, without reference to their final nature. Teachings given during the middle turning were given with some reflection on the final nature of the aggregates, elements, and so forth, which were declared to be ultimately nonexistent. Teachings given during the final turning of teaching differentiated well precisely in what way things exist and precisely in what way things do not exist. Thus, these three turnings of the wheel of dharma are comprised of both a temporally sequential and a philosophical aspect.[36]

Garungpa considers those teachings given during the final turning of the Buddha's teaching career—the wheel of good differentiation, as described in the *Sandhinirmocana Sūtra*—to be definitive in meaning, and this consideration fundamentally shapes the hermeneutic at work in his *Lamp That Illuminates the Expanse of Reality*:

> The first turning teaches that form and such exist. The middle turning teaches that everything is empty, and is definitive. The view of the middle turning teaches that natural reality, too, does not really exist. The final turning teaches that dharmin do not really exist, and that dharmatā really does exist, is permanent, stable, and so on, and is definitive.[37]

Furthermore, Garungpa reads the temporally sequential and philosophical aspects of the three turnings to be mutually pervasive of one another. That is, according to Garungpa's arguments, any teaching in which the Buddha differentiated well between what exists and what does not is definitive. Third turning teachings that differentiate between what exists and what does not are definitive. This being the case, all of the teachings included in the third turning, including the Tathāgatagarbha sūtras and commentaries that conform to them, such as the *Ratnagotravibhāga*, are held by Garungpa to be definitive in meaning and must be read literally, according to their surface meaning.

Garungpa's reading of the Tathāgatagarbha sūtras in particular, as definitive and literally true, is the source of much of the defensive argument contained in the *Lamp That Illuminates the Expanse of Reality*. At the very outset of the *Lamp That Illuminates the Expanse of Reality*, Garungpa quotes an unnamed scholar "devoted to the faction of self-emptiness," who claims that the underlying intention of the *Ratnagotravibhāga* refutes the literal reading of such sūtras. This unnamed scholar was in fact Garungpa's contemporary, Remdawa, who stridently attacked any reading of the Tathāgatagarbha sūtras or of the *Ratnagotravibhāga*—a systematic commentary on their doctrine—as literally true. By examining Garungpa's defense against Remdawa's critique as carried out in the *Lamp That Illuminates the Expanse of Reality*, we more clearly understand his unique hermeneutic.

If we examine Garungpa's many statements with regard to the interpretation of the word of the Buddha—and here again, specifically with regard to buddha-nature doctrine—we see that he finds such interpretation to be an offense against the Buddha himself. He likens such interpretive moves, for example, to splashing about in the waters of the sea of dharma without noticing that one has struck the fish of the Buddha. He even composes a verse in the middle of his text lamenting the shamelessness and lack of fear displayed by those who interpret the words of the Buddha, comparing such acts unfavorably to killing thousands of living beings. It is easy to imagine that scholars may disagree with one another regarding differences in interpretation, but Garungpa's indignance here rises to the level of hyperbole. Why does he take such offense at these acts of interpretation?

Garungpa draws the basic hermeneutic through which he understands the philosophical and soteriological import of the various teachings within the canon from the *Sandhinirmocana Sūtra* and its rubric of the three turnings of the wheel of dharma. But in order to fully grasp Garungpa's position, we must take a look at his adherence to the hermeneutic delivered in this sūtra to see what motivates this choice. There were, of course, among the Mahāyāna sūtras available to Tibetans of Garungpa's time, other sūtras that presented competing approaches to canonical hermeneutics. The *Akṣayamatinirdeśa Sūtra* and the *Samādhirāja Sūtra*, for example, both present hermeneutics that lend themselves to being used independent of the authority of the sūtras or their teacher, the Buddha. Garungpa was certainly aware of these sūtras, and even makes an oblique reference to the *Akṣayamati* in the course of his arguments in the *Lamp That Illuminates the Expanse of Reality*. So, what led Garungpa to champion the hermeneutic presented in the *Sandhinirmocana Sūtra* over those presented in other sūtras?

Garungpa never presents a patent, articulate rationale for his own approach to reading the canon. The general style with which he engages in discourse holds a wealth of clues as to his thoughts and feelings on such matters. First of all, it is clear that Garungpa has a profound and unshakeable faith in the person of the

Buddha and the infallibility of his word. We see his reliance on faith in the word of the Buddha over reason in statements such as the following:

> Though I am but like a blind man with regard to how to approach scripture, as well as how to come to realization via faith, and with regard to the area of profound reality, just like a mother will not give poison to her own kids since our teacher knows all knowable things without desire or obstruction and has great compassion for all sentient beings as if they were his only child, thinking that his instructions are flawless, practice them exactly as they are taught.[38]

Secondly, based on this adamant faith in the infallibility of the Buddha's word, Garungpa takes the scriptures spoken by the Buddha, rather than the flawed personal faculty of reason, as the highest source of authority on spiritual matters. His position on this front is given away many times throughout the text by his repeated disparaging remarks about those "enamored of reason" and his valorization of scriptural authority over all others.

In general, what accords with the word of the Buddha is an act of teaching because "[t]here is no one wiser than the Jina in this world."[39] So rather than attempt to defend his original thesis, Garungpa instead relies primarily on citing scriptural sources and pointing out all the negative consequences that arise from misunderstanding them. Garungpa's championing of scriptural statements over logical reasoning and his fervent belief in the infallibility of the Buddha's word is what motivates his adherence to the hermeneutic presented in the *Sandhinirmocana Sūtra* over others. For only in the *Sandhinirmocana Sūtra* does the Buddha himself clearly differentiate between his various statements regarding provisional and definitive statements in the canon. The *Akṣayamatinideśa Sūtra* and *Samādhirāja Sūtra* provide incomplete hermeneutics, in which the Buddha fails to clearly specify which teachings given on which occasions were interpretable and which were definitive. The fact that the Buddha himself is specifically attributed to identifying his own intent with regard to the teachings given in the three turnings of the *Sandhinirmocana Sūtra* makes it, for Garungpa, the authority on matters of canonical hermeneutics. In other words, Garungpa seems to be of the opinion that only the Buddha himself is capable of interpreting canonical statements. For others to take this task upon themselves, using logic rather than deference to the word of the Buddha, is to thoughtlessly molest the word of Buddha. Garungpa's adherence to this sūtra and its system is further strengthened by a prophecy made by the Buddha in the *Ārya Mañjuśrīmūlatantra*:

> A monk called Asaṅga will master the meaning of the treatise.
> He will differentiate the definitive and interpretable among
> the sūtras.[40]

The religious and philosophical consequences of Garungpa's adoption of the hermeneutic of the three turnings are manifold. Garungpa seems to wholly conflate the historical and philosophical aspects of the turnings, which leads him to the position that every teaching in the third turning of the Buddha's teaching is definitive and shares the same philosophical position as the *Sandhinirmocana Sūtra*. At the core of the *Sandhinirmocana Sūtra*'s interpretation of statements made during the middle turning of teaching, to the effect that things such as the aggregates and the elements are ultimately nonexistent, is the idea that the ultimate is a truly established entity in which conventional entities do not exist. Garungpa finds buddha-nature teachings sympathetic to this presentation and reads this positivist appreciation of the ultimate derived from the *Sandhinirmocana Sūtra* into all other scriptures delivered during the third turning of the teachings.

Garungpa's application of the *Sandhinirmocana Sūtra* hermeneutic to all teachings given during the final turning of teaching and their associated commentarial treatises leads him to classify the Tathāgatagarbha sūtras and the *Ratnagotravibhāga* as philosophically definitive works. In light of his belief in the infallibility of the word of Buddha, he understands definitive sūtras to be literally true and to be read according to their surface meaning, he consequently finds highly offensive Remdawa and the self-emptiness faction's treatment of the *Ratnagotravibhāga* and its source sūtras as interpretable. This particular offense seems to be the irritant that motivated Garungpa's composition of the *Lamp That Illuminates the Expanse of Reality*.

Having applied his understanding of the ultimate reality as a positive, truly established entity to all teachings given during the third turning of the Buddha's teaching, Garungpa interprets tantric statements regarding the dharmakāya, dharmadhātu, and Vajrasattva to be similarly positive, substantially and truly established entities. For instance, in his *Lamp That Illuminates the Expanse of Reality*, Garungpa criticized advocates of Madhyamaka who adhere to the so-called doctrine of self-emptiness as clinging to an understanding of the ultimate that is simply omnipresent with the vastness of space but lacking any positive qualities or attributes:

> They understand the reality of suchness to be simple omnipresence, they understand that thusness merely resembles the form of the sky, that is, self-empty and utterly without basis, advantage, disadvantage, or quality. They do not understand nonconceptual wisdom, ultimate bodhicitta, naturally radiant mind, the ultimate dharmakāya, perfect wisdom, nirvana, buddha-nature, Vajrasattva, Heruka, or the supreme primordial Buddha.[41]

In contrast, Garungpa sees himself as having a fuller understanding of suchness because his view accommodates its positive aspects as well as negative. A major element of Garungpa's hermeneutic defense of this position comes in the form of his reliance on synonymous terms. On various occasions and in various sūtras, the Buddha delivered lists of synonymous epithets for the ultimate truth. Among the various terms linked as synonyms include nonconceptual wisdom, ultimate bodhicitta, naturally radiant mind, the ultimate dharmakāya, perfect wisdom, nirvana, buddha-nature, Vajrasattva, Heruka, and a supreme primordial Buddha. By reading the Buddha's intended meaning when discussing the ultimate as revealed in the *Sandhinirmocana Sūtra* into tantric material and Madhyamaka material, Garungpa supposes an overarching systematic view of the ultimate as principally a positive phenomenon.

Having concluded that the ultimate is a positive phenomenon, rather than a view characterized merely by the recognition of the absence of imagined imputations, Garungpa proceeds to read statements regarding the primordial presence of the ultimate within sentient beings as statements indicating buddhahood as something that already exists but is hidden. According to Garungpa, suchness must be understood as equivalent to the buddha-nature, Vajrasattva, Heruka, and a supreme primordial Buddha. All sentient beings possess buddha-nature, which also means they possess an actually present Vajrasattva, Heruka, and a supreme primordial Buddha. Dolpopa agrees that buddha-nature is a synonym for dharmakāya and quotes the following from the *Anūnatvāpūrṇatva-nirdeśa-parivarta* in his *Teaching of Mountain Hermit* in order to prove that buddha-nature is an epithet (*tshig bla dags*) for the ultimate dharmakāya:

> Śāriputra, the ultimate truth should be understood by faith; Śāriputra, this one known as ultimate truth is an epithet of sentient being's dhātu; Śāriputra, this one known as sentient being's dhātu is an epithet of buddha-nature; Śāriputra, this one known as buddha-nature is an epithet of dharmakāya.[42]

Continuing in this vein, Garungpa reads buddha-nature back into the *Prajñāpāramitā Sūtra* by linking it with synonyms for the ultimate listed there. For Garungpa, since all of these concepts are synonyms, his available sources for supporting his idea really become quite various. For instance, the sources he quotes regarding the concept of emptiness do not explicitly relate to the concepts of buddha-nature and nirvana. He continues on at length, using lists of synonyms and epithets from many different locations within the canon to associate what had been traditionally thought of as divergent theories or views of reality, creating a single, comprehensive reading of the canon ultimately through the lens of the *Sandhinirmocana Sūtra*.

Remdawa's Antagonism against the Jonang

There are numerous and lengthy portions of the *Lamp That Illuminates the Expanse of Reality* where Garungpa quotes at length from Remdawa's work on the *Ratnagotravibhāga*, commenting on and refuting the latter's interpretations.

Remdawa criticizes the Jonang view quite directly and quite intensely in many of his works, particularly those on buddha-nature theory. According to Remdawa's biography, written by Sanggye Tsemo (14th c.), there is a discussion about the karmic consequences of criticizing the Jonang tradition. This interesting conversation took place between Kachupa Yontan (14th c.) and Remdawa when they met in Zangden.[43] Remdawa's attitude about such a warning was clear. He was doing his job in order to protect the Buddhist teaching from any kind of distortion and misunderstanding. Remdawa stressed that his motivation was pure and that he had no need to worry about the negative karmic consequences. He propagated his words to all people everywhere without the slightest doubt or hesitation.

By making such dangerous statements, consequently, Remdawa was accused by Garungpa of producing situations of conflict between followers of the Buddha. Garungpa asks, if Remdawa were to continuously carry out this wrong message, wouldn't his actions become precisely that situation which is stated in this sūtra? Wouldn't Remdawa be inconceivably slandering the dharma and religious figures?

Garungpa also points out that the scriptural authorities of definitive teachings he quoted in his text are like a mere drop of water compared to the many other sources.[44] Wouldn't Remdawa's philosophical views, he asks rhetorically, contradict all of these scriptural authorities? Garungpa beseeches other unbiased scholars to examine whether Remdawa's position contradicts these scriptural sources, or whether Remdawa's position commits the fault of disturbing and rejecting the teachings.

Furthermore, Garungpa warns Remdawa to learn how to protect himself from danger, the cause of danger, and the negative consequences of these dangerous actions. On at least two occasions Remdawa faced physical danger because of his outspoken critiques. For instance, Sanggye Tsemo records one such event in Remdawa's biography, as discussed by Carola Roloff:

> One day, when Remdawa and his students were walking, they encountered a young man with strong conviction in the Jonang school, walking in the opposite direction. As soon as he recognized Remdawa and his students, he cried, "For the Jonangpa, there is no difference whether I live or die. If I kill him, then [I] will eliminate the chief enemy of Jonang." He then ran towards Remdawa, planning to hit him on the head with a stone. Sanggye Tsemo, hardly an unbiased observer, claims that the assailant was overpowered by Remdawa's spiritual presence and ended up developing a deep faith in Remdawa as one of his disciples.[45]

Despite the suspect nature of this account, we might take it as evidence that it was a well-known and accepted fact that Remdawa was strongly disliked by the Jonang and lived under a cloud of (at least perceived) threat.

An interesting side note here is that Remdawa was in fact a follower of Jonang when he was young. He began his monastic education under Jonang masters Mati

Paṇchen and Nyawon. Later when he started to question the Jonang tradition and made public his criticisms of Jonang philosophical views, his relationship with his former teachers worsened. Finally, on one visit to Nyawon, one of his most important teachers, Nyawon rejected Remdawa's request to meet.[46] Eventually, Jonang followers came to consider Remdawa one of their biggest antagonists. Cyrus Stearns mentions that Remdawa is generally considered by scholars to be the founder of the Prāsaṅgika form of Madhyamaka philosophy in Tibet. However, Jonang followers viewed him as a vicious opponent who damaged the definitive teachings that were promoted and spread by Dolpopa.[47] According to Sanggye Tsemo, on one occasion Drikung Lotsāwa even tried to kill Remdawa by means of a religious ritual.[48]

CONCLUDING THOUGHTS

I have examined the philosophical and polemical content of the *Lamp That Illuminates the Expanse of Reality*, wherein Garungpa confronts Remdawa's criticism, inadvertently preserving a number of passages from Remdawa's works critical of Jonangpas. Garungpa's defense mainly relies on quotations from canonical scripture and contains very little philosophical analysis or rational inference. Ultimately, the variant ways in which Remdawa and Garungpa tackle the problem of understanding the scriptures on which their arguments depended comes down to the hermeneutic each employ. In addition, I have discussed the different views regarding the origin of zhentong philosophical views, with regard to which many scholars have divergent opinions.

In order to respond to Remdawa's *Ratnagotravibhāga* commentary, and to defend the Jonang philosophical tradition, Garungpa composed three texts that form his complete package for rebutting Remdawa and other rival scholars hostile to the Jonang position. The three form a complete system in which an attempt is made to reject Remdawa's criticism presented in his *Ratnagotravibhāga* commentary. Garungpa constructs his arguments mainly on the grounds of scriptural authority. The points that Garungpa discussed in his *Encouraging to Enter the Definitive Teaching of Sky Jewel* and *Scripture Authority Used in Encouraging to Enter the Definitive Teaching of Sky Jewel* more or less accord with the *Lamp That Illuminates the Expanse of Reality*, for he repeats his arguments and quotations again and again throughout these three texts.[49]

As an author, Garungpa is not a particularly skillful writer in terms of his use of language, vocabulary, grammar, sentence construction, and crafting arguments; however, he is skillful in his employment of the canonical source material. He utilizes a vast number of sūtric and tantric texts from the Buddhist cannon. It would be almost impossible for him to have memorized all of these quotations unless he had an extensive library. He clearly had good bibliographical knowledge for his time, utilizing a great number of sources skillfully.

As a researcher in Buddhist studies, I strongly feel that it is necessary to read entire texts from the Tibetan canon. This will give us a fuller picture of the entire system of Buddhist philosophy, and the structure of Buddhist thought. In this respect, it is not difficult for us to understand why there are so many different views and contradictory ideas in the development of Buddhist philosophy. Furthermore, it is also very important to construct an intellectual history of a certain period by examining sources, events, and the social networks of teacher and student relationships. Even in more obscure biographies, manuscripts, and small notes, we can find important details that can help to build an understanding of a specific moment in history.

NOTES

1. Stearns, *Buddha from Dolpo* 4.
2. Stearns, *Buddha from Dolpo* 3.
3. Stearns, *Buddha from Dolpo* 1.
4. The rise of the Dge lugs order is an obvious change as a result of this discussion.
5. Gha rung pa lha'i rgyal mtshan, *Chos dbyings* 1–35.
6. 'Jam dbyangs grags pa, *Rgyud bla'i dgongs bshad* 1, 3.
7. Red mda' ba, *Rgyud bla'i don bsdus* 3, 20–29.
8. Red mda' ba has composed at least two commentaries on the *Abhidharma*. However, the one quoted by Gha rung pa in his *Nges don la bskul ba nam mkha'i nor bu'i skabs su 'debs rgyu'i lung bsdus* is not available today. When Gha rung pa quotes this text, he refers simply to Slob dpon Gzhon blo's *Mngon pa'i Ti ka* but doesn't specify the title of the text. Red mda' ba's second work on *Abhidharma* is available to us today. See Red mda' ba, *Dam pa'i chos*.
9. Thu'u bkwan, *Crystal Mirror of Philosophical Systems* 200.
10. Stearns, *Buddha from Dolpo* 18.
11. Dol po pa, *Ri chos nges don rgya mtsho*.
12. Roerich, *Blue Annals* 776.
13. Stearns, *Buddha from Dolpo* 22. See Gha rung pa, *Biography of the Dharma Lord of Jonang* 22, where he writes: *shes rab gsum la blo gros sbyans min yang / lhun po bzhengs pas rgya mtsho rdol ba snyam*.
14. Kun dga' grol mchog, *Khrid brgya'i brgyud pa'i lo rgyus*.
15. Mathes, *Direct Path* 46.
16. Stearns, *Buddha from Dolpo* 42–43. Also see Kun dga' grol mchog, *Khrid brgya'i brgyud pa'i lo rgyus* 83–84. Also see Kun dga' grol mchog, *Lineage History of the Hundred Guiding Instructions* 83–84: *gzhan stong lta khrid yang btsan kha bo che'i gsung las / kha che pan di ta sajana'i gsung gis rgyal bas 'khor lo dang po bden bzhi / bar pa mtshan nyid med pa / mthar legs par rnam par phye ba'i chos kyi 'khor lo bzlas pa lan gsum bskor ba las snga ma gnyis dngos btags ma phye ba / phyi ma don dam par nges pa'i tshe / dbus dang mtha' phye / chos dang chos nyid nas gsungs zhing / chos nyid rnam 'byed dang rgyud bla ma'i dpe'i phyi mo tsam g.yar ba la yang dpe 'di gnyis nub na byams pa bde bar gshegs pa'i tshod tsam yin zer ba'i bka' gnad chen po byung zer la / pad ma lcags kyu'i ming bzhag pa'i btsan kha bo che rang gi zin tho rnying pa zhig snang ba 'dis / phyis gzhan stong bya ba'i tha snyad rgya gar du gtan ma grags bod du yang kun mkhyen dol bu phyin byung zhes sgrog pa la bya gtong du mtshon zhing / thams cad mkhyen pa bu ston gyi dris lan zhig na'ng / sngon rta nag pa rin chen ye shes pa'i grub mtha' zhig yod pa phyis dol bu bas rtsal du skyong bar snang gsungs pa la yang zhib dpyod mdzad 'tshal.*
17. *Pad ma'i lcags kyu*.
18. Mathes, *Direct Path* 32–33.

19. Mang thos, *Bstan rtsis*.

20. Mang thos, *Bstan rtsis* 122, writes: *des na rje 'di karma rang byung rdo rje dang mjal te / rang stong gi grub mtha' bzung bas karma pas phyis gzhan stong par 'gyur ba lung bstan zer / spyir gzhan stong pa'i lugs thog mar karma rang byung rdo rjes bzung bar nges so / jo nang du kun mkhyen chen po man chad byung.*

21. Stearns, *Buddha from Dolpo* 49.

22. Brunnhölzl, *Luminous Heart* 116–117.

23. Hopkins, *Mountain Doctrine* 49. Dol po pa, *Ri chos* 3.

24. Hopkins *Mountain Doctrine* 254 and Dol po pa, *Ri chos* 167, where it reads: *chos thams cad rang rang ngo bo stong ba'i rang stong kho na'o zhe na / de lta na ni 'o na log sred can gtan yongs su mya ngan las mi 'da' ba'i chos can zhes gsungs pa gang yin pa de yang / de bzhin nyid yin par 'gyur te rang gi ngo bos stong pa'i phyir ro.*

25. Gha rung pa, *Chos dbyings* 22. Gha rung pa writes: *myang 'das chen po'i bam po gnyis par. . . . bden gnyis kyi stong lugs 2 po ma shes te so sor ma phye bar thams cad rang stong du ltas pa'i nye dmigs gsungs shing / shes bya thams cad rnam kun stong ba rang stong du 'dod pa'i lta ba ni bka' bar pa chos thams cad ngo bo nyid med par gtso bor ston pa la nges don sgra ji bzhin par zhen pas lan no.*

26. Red mda' ba, *Dbu ma la 'jug pa'i rnam bzhad*, 60.

27. Phyogs las, *'Khrul 'joms*.

28. *Ārya-Laṅkāvatāra-mahāyāna Sūtra*. In *Bka' 'gyur* 49. *Śrīmālādevī-siṃhanāda Sūtra*. In *Bka' 'gyur* 44.

29. Phyogs las, *'Khrul 'joms* 12.

30. Zuiryū, *Asaṅga's Commentary* I: 39. It reads: *de la dri ma dang bcas pa'i de bzhin nyid ni nyon mongs pa'i sbubs las ma grol ba'i khams la de bzhin gshegs pa'i snying po zhes brjod pa gang yin pa'o.*

31. Ma ti Paṇ chen, *Blang dor rab gsal* 36. Ma ti Paṇ chen writes: *gzhi la don dam chos nyid de bzhin nyid // rang bzhin rnam dag 'od gsal chos kyi dbyings // rang byung lhan cig skyes pa'i ye shes sku // brtan g.yo kun la gdod nas khyab par bzhugs.*

32. *Ārya-ḍākinīvajrapañjara-nāma-mahātantrarājakalpamukhabandha*, in *Bka' 'gyur* 80, 128. It reads: *nam mkha' lta bur dri ma med // ngan par brtags pa'i rnam rtog gis // rin chen sems ni dri can byas // sems dag pas ni dag par 'gyur.*

33. Zuiryū, *Asaṅga's Commentary* I: 27, 49. It reads: *rdzogs sangs sku ni 'phro phyir dang // de bzhin nyid dbyer med phyir dang // rigs yod phyir na lus can kun // rtag tu sangs rgyas snying po can.*

34. Brunnhölzl, *Luminous Heart* 119.

35. 'Jam dpal Grags pa, *Bka' bsdu lnga ba* 334.

36. Gha rung pa, *Nges don la bskul ba nam mkha'i nor bu*.

37. Gha rung pa, *Chos dbyings* 25. Gha rung pa writes: *gzugs sogs yod par ston pa bka' dang po la ltos nas thams cad stong par ston pa bar pa nges don yin pa chos nyid gnyug ma yang don la med par ston pa bka' bar pa la ltos nas chos can rnams don la med pa dang / chos nyid don la yod pa rtag brtan sogs su ston pa tha ma nges don yin te.*

38. Gha rung pa, *Chos dbyings* 19. Gha rung pa writes: *dad pas rtogs par byed tshul yang ma yis bu la dug mi ldud zer ba'i tshul du chos nyid zab mo'i phyogs la bdag ni dmus long dang 'tra zhing / ston pa ni shes bya thams cad chags thogs med par mkhyen pa dang sems can thams cad la bu gcig pa bzhin brtse ba chen po can yin pas des gsungs pa'i gdams ngag la nor pa med snyam nas ji ltar gsungs pa bzhin spyod pa'o.*

39. Gha rung pa, *Chos dbyings* 28. Gha rung pa writes: *spyir ston pa'i bka' dang mthun pa nyid bstan pa'i bya ba ste / gang phyir rgyal las ches mkhas 'ga' yang 'jig rten 'di*

na yod min te. Zuiryū, 19, 215. It reads: *gang phyir rgyal las ches mkhas 'ga' yang 'jig rten 'di na yod min te.*

40. *Ārya-mañjuśrīmūlatantra.* In *Bka' 'gyur* 88, 880. It reads: *thogs med ces bya'i dge slong ni // bstan bcos de ni don la mkhas // mdo sde nges don drang ba'i don // rnam pa mang po'ang rab tu 'byed.*

41. Gha rung pa, *Chos dbyings* 2, writes: *chos nyid de bzhin nyid de kun khyab yin pa tsam cig go yang de nyid rang stong gzhi rtsa dang phan gnod yon tan gang yang med pa nam mkhas gzugs kyi go 'byed pa lta bu dang 'dra ba tsam cig tu go zhing mi rtog ye shes dang don dam byang chub kyi sems dang rang bzhin 'od gsal gyi sems dang / don dam chos sku dang / sher phyin dang / myang 'das dang / bde gshegs snying po dang / rdor sems dang / he ru ka dang / dang po'i sangs rgyas sogs su ma go ba dang.*

42. Zuiryū, *Asaṅga's Commentary* 3. It reads: *shā ri'i bu don dam pa ni dad pas rtogs par bya ba yin no // shā ri'i bu don dam pa zhes bya ba 'di ni sems can gyi khams kyi tshig bla dags so // shā ri'i bu sems can gyi khams zhes bya ba 'di ni / de bzhin gshegs pa'i snying po'i tshig bla dags so // shā ri'i bu de bzhin gshegs pa'i snying po zhes bya 'di ni chos kyi sku'i tshig bla dags so.*

43. Roloff, *Red mda' ba* 112.

44. Gha rung pa, *Chos dbyings* 20.

45. Roloff, *Red mda' ba* 110.

46. Rigs ldan, *Yab sras bco lnga'i rnam thar* 182.

47. Stearns, *Buddha from Dolpo* 56.

48. Roloff, *Red mda' ba* 111.

49. Gha rung pa, *Nges don la bskul ba nam mkha'i nor bu* and *Nges don la bskul ba nam mkha'i nor bu'i skabs su 'debs.*

Bibliography

Tibetan Sources

Bka' 'gyur Dpe bsdur ma. Krung go'i bod rig pa zhib 'jug lte gnas kyi bka' bstan dpe sdur khang gis rtsom sgrig byas, 1–108. Beijing: Krung go'i bod rig pa dpe skrun khang, 2006–2009.

Dol po pa Shes rab rgyal mtshan. *Ri chos nges don rgya mtsho.* In *Jo nang dpe tshogs*, 1. Beijing: Mi rigs dpe skrun khang, 2007.

Gha rung pa Lha'i rgyal mtshan. *Bstan pa spyi 'grel gyi 'grel bshad dang theg pa chen po rgyud bla ma'i bstan bcos kyi rnam par bshad pa.* In *Jo nang dpe tshogs*, 30. Beijing: Mi rigs dpe skrun khang, 2010.

———. *Nges don la bskul ba nam mkha'i nor bu.* In *Gsung thor bu*, 1–7. Unpublished manuscript. BDRC #: W1CZ996.

———. *Nges don la bskul ba nam mkha'i nor bu'i skabs su 'debs rgyu'i lung bsdus.* In *Gsung thor bu*, 7–27. Unpublished manuscript. BDRC #: W1CZ996.

———. *Chos dbyings gsal sgron.* In *Gsung thor bu*, 1–35. Unpublished manuscript. BDRC #: W1CZ996.

———. *Chos rje jo nang pa kun mkhyen chen po'i rnam thar*, 1–57. Unpublished manuscript.

'Jam dbyangs Grags pa. *Rje btsun red mda' ba gzhon nu blo gros kyi gsung 'bum dkar chags.* Unpublished manuscript.

'Jam dpal Grags pa. *Bka' bsdu lnga ba mtha' bral dbu ma chen po'i grub mtha' rab gsal.* In *Jo nang dpe tshogs*, 16, 307–381. Beijing: Mi rigs dpe skrun khang, 2007.

Kun dga' Grol mchog. *Khrid brgya'i brgyud pa'i lo rgyus*. In *Gdams ngag mdzod*. Dpal spungs dgon pa'i par khang. Paro: Lama Ngodrup and Sherab Drimey, 1981. BDRC #: W20877.

Mang thos Klu sgrub rgya mtsho. *Bstan rtsis gsal ba'i nyin byed lhag bsam rab dkar*. Unpublished manuscript. BDRC #: W2CZ7896.

Ma ti Paṇ chen Blo gros rgyal mtshan. *Blang dor rab gsal*. *Jo nang dpe tshogs*, 8. Beijing: Mi rigs dpe skrun khang, 2007.

Mnga' ris Chos rje phyogs las rnam rgyal. *Shin tu zab cing brtag par dka' ba de bzhin gshegs pa'i snying po'i rgyan gyi 'khrul 'joms*. In *Jo nang dpe tshogs*, 22. Beijing: Mi rigs dpe skrun khang, 2010.

Red mda' ba Gzhon nu blo gros. *Dbu ma la 'jug pa'i rnam bshad de kho na nyid gsal ba'i sgron ma*. In *Rje btsun red mda' ba gzhon nu blo gros kyi gsung 'bum*, 5. Lhasa: Sa skya'i dpe rnying bsdu sgrig khang, 2009.

———. *Rgyud bla'i don bsdus sam bde gshegs snying po'i don gsal*. In *Rje btsun red mda' ba gzhon nu blo gros zhabs kyi gsung 'bum*, 3, 20–29. Lhasa: Sa skya'i dpe rnying bsdu sgrig khang, 2009.

———. *Dam pa'i chos mngon pa kun las btus pa'i snying po legs bshad nor bu'i phreng ba*. In *Rje btsun red mda' ba gzhon nu blo gros zhabs kyi gsung 'bum*, 6, 251–325. Lhasa: Sa skya'i dpe rnying bsdu sgrig khang, 2009.

Rigs ldan Rgyal ba jo nang dpal bzang po. *Chos rje kun mkhyen chen po yab sras bco lnga'i rnam thar nye bar bsdus pa ngo mtshar rab gsal*. In *Dpal ldan dus kyi 'khor lo jo nang pa'i lugs kyi bla ma brgyud pa'i rnam thar*, 142–209. Beijing: Mi rigs dpe skrun khang, 2004.

Thu'u bkwan Blo bzang chos kyi nyi ma. *Thu'u bkwan grub mtha'*. Lan kru'u: Kan su'u mi rigs dpe skrun khang, 1991.

Zuiryū, Nakamura 中村瑞隆. *Asaṅga's Commentary on the Ratnagotravibhāga*. Kukyō ichijō hōshōron kenkyū 究竟一乘宝性论研究. Tokyo: Suzuki Gakujutsu Zaidan, 1967.

Secondary Sources

Brunnhölzl, Karl. *In Praise of Dharmadhātu: Nāgārjuna and the Third Karmapa, Rangjung Dorje*. Ithaca: Snow Lion, 2007.

———. *Luminous Heart: The Third Karmapa on Consciousness, Wisdom, and Buddha Nature*. Ithaca: Snow Lion, 2009.

Hopkins, Jeffrey. *Mountain Doctrine: Tibet's Fundamental Treatise on Other-Emptiness and the Buddha Matrix*. Ithaca: Snow Lion, 2006.

Mathes, Klaus-Dieter. *A Direct Path to the Buddha Within: 'Gos Lotsāwa's Mahāmudrā Interpretation of the Ratnagotravibhāga*. Boston: Wisdom, 2008.

Roerich, George. *The Blue Annals*. Delhi: Motilal Banarsidass, 2007.

Roloff, Carola. *Red mda' ba, Buddhist Yogi-Scholar of the Fourteenth Century: The Forgotten Reviver of Madhyamaka Philosophy in Tibet*. Wiesbaden: Dr. Ludwig Reichert Verlag, 2009.

Stearns, Cyrus. *The Buddha from Dolpo: A Study of the Life and Thought of the Tibetan Master Dolpopa Sherab Gyaltsen*. Ithaca: Snow Lion, 2010.

5

Zhentong Views in the Karma Kagyu Order

Klaus-Dieter Mathes

In this chapter I argue that in the Karma Kagyu order there is, with slight variations, a distinct zhentong view that considerably differs from that of the Jonang. For most zhentongpas (followers of zhentong) within the Karma Kagyu order, both the object of negation (*dgag bya*) and the basis of emptiness (*stong gzhi*) belong to dependent arising and are thus empty of an own nature (*rang stong*) like anything else including ultimate truth. It is only the absence of adventitious stains in natural luminosity or buddha-nature that is referred to as "being empty of other," that is, zhentong. The first Karma Trinlepa (1456–1539) must have had such a moderate zhentong view in mind when he described the third Karmapa Rangjung Dorje (1284–1339)[1] and the seventh Karmapa Chodrak Gyatso (1454–1506) as zhentongpas. Such a view is in stark contrast to the well-known zhentong position of the Jonang, who advocate an ultimate permanent entity (*rtag dngos*).[2] This is made clear in a text of questions and answers (*dris lan*) in which Karma Trinlepa criticizes an eternalist zhentong perspective. In the same text, this disciple of Chodrak Gyatso also takes issue with a zhentong position, according to which buddha-nature wanders in the six realms of saṃsāra.[3] Karma Trinlepa thus distinguishes the third and seventh Karmapas' zhentong from the views of the Jonang and the view of Go Lotsāwa Zhonnu Pel (1392–1481). The Jonang maintained a clear-cut distinction between buddha-nature and the adventitious stains of afflictive emotions,[4] as for example indicated by the fourth simile in the *Tathāgatagarbha Sūtra*, namely, a gold nugget that is immersed in excrement.[5] Zhonnu Pel, on the other hand, took the two as not essentially different, any more than is the ocean water and its waves, to use his example taken from the *Laṅkāvatāra Sūtra*.[6] The Eighth Karmapa Mikyo Dorje (1507–1554), too, takes issue with the Jonangpas' substantialist view of buddha-nature as an ultimate permanent entity as well as with Zhonnu Pel's full equation of buddha-nature with the nature of an individual mind stream. The views on buddha-nature[7] found in

Rangjung Dorje, Chodrak Gyatso, and Mikyo Dorje have more in common and align more easily with Asaṅga's and Vasubandhu's description of the ultimate in terms of the Yogācāra theory of three natures.

This requires including the dependent nature within the relative truth. I suggested[8] that in the *Madhyāntavibhāga* two three-nature models, similar to Sponberg's pivotal model and progressive model, existed side-by-side in an unbalanced way.[9] Without questioning my original analysis, it could be argued in line with Shakya Chokden (1428–1507) and Karmapas three, seven, and eight that the two models in the *Madhyāntavibhāga* are less unbalanced if one accepts that a common final author of the *Madhyāntavibhāga* and the *Ratnagotravibhāga* attempted a synthesis of Yogācāra and Tathāgatagarbha thought, a synthesis that can also be found in the *Dharmadharmatāvibhāga*. This requires a shift from the original Yogācāra model of an ultimately existing dependent to an emptiness that is positively understood as luminosity (as in the emptiness passage of the *Madhyāntavibhāga*). The initial distinction between an existent false imagining (*abhūtaparikalpa*) and a nonexistent duality then describes what is true and false on the level of relative truth only, just as in Vasubandhu's *Vyākhyāyukti*.[10]

Although different Kagyu masters present this view with slight variations, what I am going to identify is a continuous Kagyu zhentong interpretation, which is best defined in Mikyo Dorje's *Hundred Thousand Words of Mahāmudrā*:

> Thus, in the sūtras and tantras of the Illustrious One it is taught that one's own mind in the mode of arising nakedly as stainless awareness is zhentong with regard to [its adventitious] phenomena (*dharmin*), and rangtong with regard to [its] true nature (dharmatā).[11] Thus, its emptiness is of two kinds.[12]

That means that everything, including one's own naked awareness, is rangtong, but as the basis of negation one's stainless awareness is also "empty of the other" (zhentong), that is, the adventitious stains that do not reflect its true nature. In other words, Mikyo Dorje accepts a relational zhentong that skillfully avoids any ontological commitment of inherent existence.

The Third Karmapa Rangjung Dorje's Proto-Zhentong

The following analysis is based on Rangjung Dorje's *Profound Inner Principles* along with its autocommentary. The same results can be shown, however, from an investigation of other texts by Rangjung Dorje, such as his commentary on the *Dharmadhātustava* or his *Presentation of Buddha-Nature*.[13] The strongest argument for Rangjung Dorje being a follower of the Kagyu zhentong view (even though he does not use the term zhentong to describe his system) is that he advocates a robust Yogācāra-based distinction between an impure ālayavijñāna and a pure mind. The latter even does not arise from the ālayavijñāna but from the mental imprint of studying, which is an expression ("outflow," *rgyu mthun pa*) of the pure dharmadhātu. Even though the two occur together like milk and water,[14] they remain separate and cannot mix. This distinction between the impure and pure is based on Asaṅga's *Mahāyānasaṃgraha* I.45–48, a passage that Rangjung Dorje quotes in his autocommentary to the *Profound Inner Principles*.[15] It should be noted that Mikyo Dorje includes the same passage in his commentary on the *Abhisamayālaṃkāra*, namely, in the second paragraph of the first chapter, where he introduces the essential part of his zhentong presentation.[16] The same distinction is also found in Mikyo Dorje's *Introducing the Tenet of Madhyamaka Zhentong* and is thus, to go by the title of the work, considered to be zhentong. In the autocommentary to his *Profound Inner Principles*, Rangjung Dorje elaborates on his distinction between an impure and pure mind by distinguishing between *kun gzhi rnam shes* (*ālayavijñāna*) and *kun gzhi* (*ālaya*), which is understood as suchness (i.e., the pure mind): "In this regard, if 'ground' (*kun gzhi*) is not mentioned [together with] the term 'consciousness,' 'ground' may refer to suchness. Therefore, consciousness is mentioned [together with it]."[17] Mikyo Dorje follows Rangjung Dorje's distinction between a *kun gzhi rnam shes* and a *kun gzhi*, but with the important difference that he uses the term *kun gzhi ye shes* instead of *kun gzhi* when referring to suchness.[18] The latter is also equated with the transformation of the basis in the *Dharmadharmatāvibhāga*,[19] and with the synonyms for emptiness (including suchness) in the *Madhyāntavibhāga*.[20] In other words, Rangjung Dorje already has made the crucial distinction between an impure and pure mind, and to call the latter only *kun gzhi* instead of the controversial *kun gzhi ye shes* does not make such a big difference.

The question that arises, however, is whether this pure mind or *kun gzhi* is taken to be a permanent entity (*rtag dngos*) as the Jonangpas do. For both Rangjung Dorje and Mikyo Dorje, this is not the case. In his commentary on the first line of the first chapter in the *Profound Inner Principles* ("As to the cause, it is the beginningless true nature of the mind"[21]) Rangjung Dorje explains:

> As to "beginningless," since a beginning and end of time is a [mere] conceptual superimposition, it refers here to the true nature of both the stainless [mind] and the [mind] mingled with stains. [This true nature] is dependent arising, [the stainless mind and mind mingled with stains] being free from identity and difference. Since there is no other beginning than it, one speaks of beginningless time.[22]

In other words, the nature of the stainless mind (suchness or *kun gzhi*) is also part of dependent arising, which excludes a too substantialist version of zhentong (if one chooses to call it that at all).[23] Just as are the relative and ultimate truths, the impure and pure mind are taken as neither identical nor different and understood in terms of the Yogācāra relation between dharmin and dharmatā. This must be seen against the backdrop of the Yogācāra presentation of emptiness found in the Maitreya texts that advocate the absence of the duality of a perceived and perceiver (the imagined nature) in false imagining (the dependent nature).[24] Thus, it is stated in *Madhyāntavibhāgabhāṣya* I.1: "Emptiness refers to the fact that this false imagining is free from the [false] relationship between a perceived [object] and a perceiver."[25] Immediately after he quotes the *Mahāyānasaṃgraha*'s distinction between the impure and pure mind, Rangjung Dorje includes a description of the eight consciousnesses, and thus false imagining (which belongs to the ālayavijñāna), within the scope of impure mind, while the pure mind is the true nature of these eight consciousnesses in the form of the four types of wisdom.[26] This points to the emptiness presented in the *Ratnagotravibhāga*, in which buddha-nature is described as being empty of adventitious stains (i.e., the impure mind) that includes false imagining in the negandum (*dgag bya*). The following passage from the *Profound Inner Principles* autocommentary makes this clear:

> As for the element of sentient beings, it is the stainless buddha-nature endowed with the two truths. In this statement, buddha-nature is simply the non-existence of the stains [or] delusion of the above-mentioned eight accumulations of consciousness. However, those who have not actualized the meaning of the two truths, are deluded with regard to the mode of dependent arising, and through clinging to two separate views (with respect to the two truths), they fall into saṃsāra.[27]

As I have already shown in a previous publication,[28] the apparent truth that is contained in buddha-nature and thus part of the basis of negation (*dgag gzhi*) is only the appearance as such;[29] otherwise the basis of negation is considered to be the expressible ultimate truth or the perfect nature in terms of being unmistaken wisdom.[30] While the unchangeable perfect is the ultimate truth, the unmistaken perfect (the "pure dependent") is taken by Rangjung Dorje as a restricted form of apparent truth, in that it does not include acceptance by common consent or what is accepted as conventional truth, and the like.

To sum up Rangjung Dorje's position, the basis of negation (*dgag gzhi*) is the perfect nature in both its unchangeable and unmistaken aspects, the two truths contained in buddha-nature. The negandum (*dgag bya*) is the imagined nature but not the entire dependent nature, as the latter also belongs to the basis of negation in the form of the unmistaken perfect nature. The difference with the Jonang zhentong is that the basis of emptiness or negation is not only the unchangeable perfect (the ultimate) but also the perfect nature of unmistaken wisdom, which the Jonang take as the pure dependent. For Rangjung Dorje, the ultimate truth and a restricted form of the relative truth (i.e., the unmistaken perfect) are both contained in buddha-nature, and thus of one essence (*ngo bo gcig*).

As we will see, Mikyo Dorje may have thought of this restricted form of relative truth when he maintains as a final tenet the indivisible union (*zung 'jug*) of the two truths. This, at least, would be one meaningful way of accounting for his robust distinction between buddha-nature and its adventitious stains. At the time of perfect realization, no impure part of the relative truth is left in one's mind stream, so that indivisible union fully applies. Another possible explanation is that one eventually transcends said distinction by considering that everything—both the pure and impure mind in particular—is by nature dependent arising and as such empty of an own nature (rangtong), the standard Madhyamaka understanding of dependent arising.

Rangjung Dorje's *Mahāyānasaṃgraha*-based distinction between the pure and impure mind, which could be interpreted as a form of zhentong, would then be a bridge to the Mahāmudrā perspective of the indivisibility of appearance and emptiness.[31] In other words, we have here something similar to Mikyo Dorje's naked (*gcer bur*) awareness that is zhentong with regard to the adventitious stains and rangtong under the aspect of its true nature (dharmatā).

The Seventh Karmapa Chodrak Gyatso's Zhentong Presentation

In the aforementioned *Questions and Answers* on zhentong, the first Karma Trinlepa refers to the Maitreya texts as well as Rangjung Dorje and Chodrak Gyatso as authoritative sources for his zhentong view. The first Karma Trinlepa thus follows his teacher Chodrak Gyatso and criticizes zhentong proponents of a truly existent permanent, stable, steadfast, unchangeable ultimate. For him, however, buddha-nature is beyond the ordinary mind stream. This is clear from his *Questions and Answers*, where it is said that a buddha-nature with all sixty-four qualities of a Buddha does not circulate together with the mind stream of sentient beings in the six realms of saṃsāra.

As for the Maitreya texts, I have already elaborated elsewhere[32] that the final version of the *Ratnagotravibhāga* (whose different layers display a complex history of composition) reflects a Yogācāra interpretation of the buddha-nature theory, which retains the Yogācāra-Abhidharma doctrine of momentariness and thus avoids the eternalist interpretation of buddha-nature in the Tathāgatagarbha sūtras. This is particularly clear in the commentary on the four perfections of qualities (*guṇapāramitā*), where the perfection of permanence is taken as follows: "Attaining the perfection of permanence should be seen as the fruit of a [form of] meditation based on great compassion, inasmuch as [bodhisattvas] are possessed of the desire to continuously benefit people as long as saṃsāra lasts."[33] The problematic notion "perfection of self" (*ātmapāramitā*) is also hollowed out by taking "self" (*ātman*) as the "lack of a self" (*nairātmya*).[35] In other words, buddha-nature or the subsequent state of enlightenment, the dharmakāya, is only permanent in the sense of being a never-ending continuous dynamic principle that provides the ground for spontaneous buddha activity as long as there are sentient beings in saṃsāra (which will be never-ending). In an interlinear note on verse 28 in Sajjana's[35] *Mahāyānottaratantraśāstropadeśa*, it is claimed:

> [T]he luminous mind (*prabhāsvaraṃ cittaṃ*) is not conditioned. This is because [in the luminous mind] there is nothing to be done through

> cause and conditions coming together, based on the fact that the origination of the [luminous] mind in the succeeding moment depends on [the mind] that was generated by its (the mind's) own kind (*sajāti*) in the previous moment.[36]

Sajjana, or a later scribe, thus exempts, without any further explanation, luminous mind from the rule that only something conditioned is momentary. In other words, an unconditioned luminous mind is considered to continue in a series of moments. This position reflects a compromise between a positive description of the ultimate on the one hand and the Buddhist axiom of momentariness on the other. In support of such a strategy, Go Lotsāwa Zhonnu Pel explains that "unconditioned" means not to be artificially (*'phral du*) conditioned by adventitious causes and conditions. For him such an "unconditioned," yet momentary luminosity or buddha-nature remains as long as space exists.[37] It should be noted, as I have shown already elsewhere, that for Zhonnu Pel even dharmatā and space possess the nature of momentariness.[38]

To sum up, both the basis of negation and the negandum are presented in such a way that they relate to dependent arising in the same way as Rangjung Dorje's pure and impure mind. The luminous mind or buddha-nature is zhentong with regard to its adventitious stains but rangtong like anything else in terms of its ontological status.

Chodrak Gyatso himself uses the term zhentong only once, namely, in his *Ocean of Treatises on Valid Cognition and Reasoning*, after his presentation of the result of valid cognition (*tshad 'bras*) in his chapter on direct valid cognition. The result of valid cognition is discussed in relation to what must be cognized (*gzhal bya*) and valid cognition (*tshad ma*) on each of the following three levels: when there is no analysis, slight analysis, and thorough analysis. In the first case, the cognized object is the outer (material) object; in the second case, it is the mental aspect of the perceived, and in the last case, it is lucid and aware cognition empty of duality. While the result of valid cognition is the realization of the outer material object in the first case (when not analyzed), it is self-awareness (*rang rig*) in the latter two cases (slightly and thoroughly analyzed). As for valid cognition, in the first case it is the mental aspect of the perceived, and in the latter two cases it is the mental aspect of the perceiver.[39]

It is interesting to look at how Chodrak Gyatso summarizes the presentations of what must be cognized, valid cognition, and the result of cognition before he turns to the topic of Zhentong Great Madhyamaka:

> In the absence of external objects, how can there be the aspects of the cognized object, valid cognition, and the result? For one, the perceived aspect that appears as matter (*gzugs*), and so forth, is taken as what must be cognized; the aspect of the perceiver is taken as valid cognition; and self-awareness is taken as the result. [Moreover,] through the power of being superimposed by the intellect, caught in dualistic appearances and impaired by beginningless ignorance, this perceived

> aspect is not established as a [true] abiding nature [either]. Therefore, in reality [the perceived aspect] is not what must be cognized. Rather, at this point, the lucid and aware part [of consciousness]—the cognition free from the duality of the perceived and perceiver—is taken as the cognized object; the aspect of the perceiver is taken as valid cognition; and self-awareness is taken as the result. This is established as the ultimate presentation of the result of valid cognition.[40]

But even this latter thorough analysis does not yield the final result, which is considered to be Zhentong Great Madhyamaka:

> Even in the case of this [analysis], the proponents of Zhentong Great Madhyamaka [maintain that] it is only a presentation that accords with how [the cognized object] appears for the confused intellect. However, this is not true reality, because it is only a presentation of the triad of the cognized object, valid cognition, and its result without analyzing how the cognized object, valid cognition, and its result [only] appear to be different. They are merely a conceptual imputation.[41]

This move from the third level of presenting the triad of cognized object, valid cognition, and its result up to the final level of Zhentong Madhyamaka must be seen against the background of a threefold distinction of self-awareness in the Karma Kagyu order. Besides rejecting a form of self-awareness that serves as a straw man for the Madhyamaka refutation of a mind that is able to see itself as an object that is other to itself, two types of self-awareness are acknowledged: the self-awareness of the Pramāṇa tradition, that is, the simple capacity of any cognition to experience itself in the most basic sense, and the self-aware wisdom of Mahāmudrā (or Zhentong Madhyamaka for that matter). In this later system, self-awareness is wisdom's capacity to experience its own nature (emptiness) while simultaneously experiencing its lucidity as inseparable from this nature. Thrangu Rinpoche explains:

> This freedom from existence is not a nothingness or a voidness, because cognitive lucidity is present at the same time. Since mind's nature has this inherent wisdom, it can cognize, and therefore it can cognize itself. In that this nature knows itself, it is without the duality of viewer and viewed.[42]

Chodrak Gyatso does not turn against the Pramāṇa system of Dignāga and Dharmakīrti with his move from the third presentation of the triad of cognized object, valid cognition, and its result to zhentong but precisely refers to the *Pramāṇavārttika*[43] and the *Pramāṇaviniścaya*[44] in support of his final analysis:

> Although the nature[45] of mind is indivisible,
> It is seen by those whose view is mistaken,

As if it was divided into
A perceived, perceiver, and self[46]-awareness.[47] (PV II.354)

It is as in the case of lumps of clay and the like
Appearing as something else
To eyes under the influence of mantras, and so forth,
Even though [these lumps] are without the forms of these [appearances].[48] (PV II.355)

Because those whose eyes are not under the influence [of mantras]
Do not see these [pieces of clay] in this way.[49] (PV II.356ab)

This position that involves a cognized object, valid cognition, and result,
Is maintained in accordance with how [things] are looked at,
Even though the awareness of a perceived [object] and perceiving [subject]
Does not exist.[50] (PV II.357)

Having thus determined the underlying intention of the Pramāṇa system as being anchored in the negation of a perceived object and perceiving subject in accordance with Yogācāra, Chodrak Gyatso moves on to *Mahāyānasūtrālaṃkāra* VI.8, in which even the notion of an existing mind is negated:

Having understood with intelligence that there is nothing apart from the mind,
One realizes that even the mind does not exist.
Thus the wise understand that duality does not exist
And abide in the dharmadhātu, in which this [duality] is not contained.[51]

This accords with the sequence of meditation in *Laṅkāvatāra Sūtra* X.256c–257d and also the four exercises (*prayoga*) as explained in the *Dharmadharmatāvibhāga*.[52] It should be noted, however, that "mind" in the preceding verse only refers to its aspect of being a perceiving subject and not the mind as the underlying process of false imagining.[53] In any case, false imagining must be finally abandoned,[54] so that also this aspect of mind is left behind at the time of realization. The point is that the notion of "mind-only" (*cittamātra*) is only a preliminary step on the path to the realization of the dharmadhātu, a goal that accords with the Madhyamaka texts of Nāgārjuna, for once the ultimate existence of mind is overcome, Yogācāra and Madhyamaka become compatible. For Chodrak Gyatso as well this is the final intention of Dignāga and Dharmakīrti:

> The final intention of [Dharmakīrti's] seven treatises including [Dignāga's *Pramāṇa*]*samuccaya* is based on the Madhyamaka that has come down to us from venerable Maitreya through Asaṅga and his brother. [The final intention] also accords with the Madhyamaka texts of Nāgārjuna and his followers.[55]

In support of this, Chodrak Gyatso refers to *Madhyamakāvatāra* VI.92 and VI.96:

> If form does not exist, do not cling to the existence of mind;
> And if mind exists, do not cling to the nonexistence of form.
> In the sūtras of supreme knowledge, the Buddha[56]
> Has equally rejected both, while teaching them in the Abhidharma.[57]
> (MA VI.92)
>
> Without an object to be known the refutation of the knowing [mind]
> Can be easily obtained as the Buddha taught.
> Since in the absence of an object to be known the knowing [mind
> can] be negated,
> He negated the object to be known first.[58] (MA VI.96)

From this Chodrak Gyatso concludes:

> Therefore, the freedom from [a perceived and a perceiver]—and this includes the consciousness that functions as the support of the duality of the perceived and perceiver—is emptiness, the dharmadhātu. It is pure of both the supporting consciousness and the supported, that is, the perceived [object] and perceiving [subject], and thus luminous. In it, the nature of mind (*sems nyid*) is suitable to appear as anything whatsoever, because it is [also] established as mirrorlike wisdom. [As] the existing remainder [in the formula] of something being absent in something [else, this nature of mind] is established as ultimate truth. Thus, no matter which aspect (*ākāra*) arises in this naturally luminous ultimate truth, it is not established as any such aspect, it does not exist as anything other than this luminous nature of mind.[59]

It should be noted that Chodrak Gyatso includes in the negandum the consciousness that functions as the support of duality. This means that mind is not only negated in terms of its imagined nature but also in terms of false imagining, that is, the dependent nature.[60] If one takes the negation of mind in the preceding verse from the *Mahāyānasūtrālaṃkāra* (VI.8) in this sense, that is, as not only negating the perceiver (*grāhaka*), Yogācāra can more easily be brought in line with Candrakīrti's Madhyamaka. There remains the objection, though, that Chodrak Gyatso's equation of emptiness with the luminous nature of mind hardly finds support in Candrakīrti's system.[61] But at this point, Chodrak Gyatso is more concerned with showing that his ultimate remainder of a luminous nature of mind accords with Dharmakīrti, and he quotes *Pramāṇavārttika* I.208cd:

> This mind is naturally luminous.
> The stains are adventitious.[62]

Chodrak Gyatso relates then the naturally luminous mind in the *Pramāṇavārttika* to that which is described in *Ratnagotravibhāga* I.63ab:

> This luminous nature of mind
> Never undergoes change, just like space.[63]

This relates the original concept of a truly permanent buddha-nature theory[64] to the momentary luminosity of mind in the Pramāṇa system,[65] something that Pecchia finds misleading.[66] The point here is not, however, that Chodrak Gyatso mistakes Dharmakīrti's luminous mind to be truly permanent like buddha-nature in the Tathāgatagarbha doctrine, but rather he takes the latter in terms of unconditioned, but still momentary, luminosity of mind in the gloss on verse 28 of the *Mahāyānottaratantropadeśa* (quoted at the beginning of the chapter). In any case, Chodrak Gyatso demonstrates that his zhentong view is clearly Yogācāra-Madhyamaka-based, its basis of emptiness being different from the Jonangpas' position of the basis of emptiness (i.e., buddha-nature) as an ultimately permanent entity. This is most clear from the following passage of the *Ocean of Treatises on Valid Cognition and Reasoning*'s zhentong explanation:

> Glorious Dignāga and Dharmakīrti, who are followers of the Great Madhyamaka going back to the noble master Asaṅga and his brother, mainly ascertained the naturally luminous nature of mind abiding in emptiness. Because of that, one is able to realize that [mind's] nature is emptiness since every aspect (*ākāra*) appears due to the play of this naturally luminous [mind]. Thinking of this, they mainly taught from the side of the mind.
>
> The followers of the Great Madhyamaka going back to the noble master Nāgārjuna mainly ascertained that this nature of mind, which appears as various aspects, is not established as it appears. Because of that, one is able to realize that the [mind's] emptiness of a perceived [object] and perceiving [subject] is precisely this [mind's] natural luminosity. Thinking of this, they ascertained [it] mainly from the side of empti[ness].[67]
>
> Here, some others object: "According to this thinking, is what you call the nature of mind (*sems nyid*) of inseparable luminosity and emptiness an entity or nonentity? In the first case, those who [mistak-

enly] take emptiness as an entity would belong to the Mādhyamikas. In case it is not an entity, there would be a contradiction to its abiding as natural luminosity."

> You are right [in the case of] those who cling to the mind in the way it appears. But if the Mādhyamikas as we define them maintain that everything—such as entity, nonentity, being [something], not being [something], existing, not existing, being permanent, being impermanent, being empty, not being empty, being pacified, not being pacified, self, non-self, being one and many—is mutually dependent and thus only an appearance posited by the mistaken mind, how could such fault occur?[68]

To sum up, according to Chodrak Gyatso, zhentong is presented in line with Dignāga and Dharmakīrti. Thus, the luminous nature of mind (the basis of emptiness) must be taken as a continuous flow rather than as permanent and unchanging, like unconditioned luminous mind that still has moments (see the gloss in Sajjana's preceding text), or Rangjung Dorje's pure mind, that still belongs to dependent arising. This puts Chodrak Gyatso's zhentong closer to the zhentong view of Shakya Chokden, whose main difference with Dolpopa—according to Tāranātha's (1575–1634) *Twenty-one Profound Points*—is that Shakya Chokden takes nondual wisdom (the basis of emptiness) to be impermanent, while for Dolpopa it is permanent. Moreover, Shakya Chokden defines the basis of negation as the dependent nature that exists on a relative level, and for Dolpopa it is the unchangeable perfect nature.[69] It should be noted in this respect, what the Eighth Situpa Chokyi Jungne (1699–1776) reports in his *Kagyu Golden Rosary Biographies*:

> The great *paṇḍita* Shakya Chokden later [in his life] met the venerable seventh [Karmapa] and received special instructions. The power of commitment had become completely perfect, and he took [the seventh Karmapa] as [his] root guru. This representative of the [Kamtsang] practice lineage, the essence of definitive meaning, accepted him alone, in whom the Mahāmudrā realization of definitive meaning had arisen, as [his] root disciple, because it is said that [Shakya Chokden's] realization is an actual transmission. Any lecture he gave was in accordance with the instructions of the venerable seventh [Karmapa]: he chose his position on the ultimate view of both Mahāyāna chariots (Madhyamaka and Yogācāra) to be zhentong only. Even the Pramāṇa Cycle he taught in the tradition of the venerable seventh [Karmapa]'s *Ocean of Treatises on Valid Cognition and Reasoning*. His enlightened mind stream became one with the Karmapa himself.[70]

In other words, Shakya Chokden is said here to have determined, in accordance with Chodrak Gyatso, the ultimate view of Madhyamaka and Yogācāra as zhentong only.

The Eighth Karmapa Mikyo Dorje's Zhentong View

It is mainly in his early works that Mikyo Dorje endorses or presupposes a zhentong view. Pawo Tsuklak Trengwa (1504–1566), a close disciple of the Eighth Karmapa, informs us that his master received zhentong teachings from Chodrub Senge. Encouraged by his early teacher, when he was twenty-four years old, Mikyo Dorje upheld a zhentong view and commented on the *Abhisamayālaṃkāra* in the tradition of Jonang and Shakya Chokden.[71] It is difficult to follow this description, however, as the zhentong views of the Jonang and Shakya Chokden differ in so many points.[72] As I have already shown in another study, Mikyo Dorje maintains in his *Abhisamayālaṃkāra* commentary the same *Mahāyānasaṃgraha*-based distinction between an impure and pure mind as Rangjung Dorje. In fact, he does so with explicit reference to the autocommentary on the *Profound Inner Principles*. Thus, he does not believe that sentient beings literally possess buddha-nature. They are only related to buddha-nature as what must be purified, namely, that which is overpowered by delusion. Ultimately, sentient beings have never existed in the first place.[73] Mikyo Dorje's zhentong in the *Abhisamayālaṃkāra* commentary is as follows:

> In the *Prajñāpāramitā Sūtra*, too, the dharmatā of the perfect [nature] has been taught to be emptiness. This is very true. But was it then taught as rangtong, and not as zhentong? This is not the case. In the [*Aṣṭasāhasrikā Prajñāpāramitā*] *sūtra* it is taught: "The mind is not mind, the nature of mind being luminous." Therefore, since the adventitious mind is rangtong (empty in and of itself), it does not exist; since natural luminosity is zhentong (empty of what is other to it), it is taught that what is called luminosity is not empty. Venerable [Maitreya] said [in *Ratnagotravibhāga* I.155c]: "[Buddha-nature] is not empty of [its] unsurpassable qualities." Thus it is taught that these qualities of the unsurpassable dharmatā are not empty of an own nature.[74] This meaning has been made clear by Mañjuśrī[yaśas in the *Pradarśanānumatoddeśaparīkṣā*]: "*Skandha*s are, upon analysis, merely empty. They are like a banana tree without essence. The emptiness endowed with the most supreme of all aspects is not like that." Therefore, the *skandha*s, and so forth, are the imagined [nature]. And if one analyzes all dependent phenomena in terms of their own nature, [they are found] to be merely empty [of] an own nature (i.e., rangtong), as for example, a banana tree, which is without essence. The perfect [nature], that is, the emptiness endowed with the most supreme of all aspects, cannot be analyzed in the usual way. However much one analyzes, it does not become empty of an own nature, because it [never] turns into something other than such a supreme wisdom. This is what is taught.[75]

The way zhentong is taught here differs a little from what we have identified up to now as "Kagyu zhentong." *Ratnagotravibhāga* I.155c, "[buddha-nature] is not empty of [its] unsurpassable qualities," seems to be interpreted in the sense that the qualities of the unsurpassable dharmatā are not empty of an own nature. To be sure, the phrase "buddha-nature not being empty of buddha qualities" must be understood in the *Ratnagotravibhāga* against the background that these buddha qualities are inseparably connected with buddha-nature; nevertheless, this does not necessarily mean that either buddha-nature or its qualities exist inherently.[76] Given this textual uncertainty, one should be cautious to read a more ontological zhentong position into Mikyo Dorje's *Abhisamayālaṃkāra* commentary. The context of this zhentong passage, which contains, for example, the *Mahāyānasaṃgraha*-based distinction between sentient beings and buddha-nature, suggests rather that Mikyo Dorje maintains here as well a zhentong position that accords with Chodrak Gyatso and Rangjung Dorje. In this context, it should be noted that even Zhonnu Pel, whose position fundamentally differs from that of the Jonang, exempts buddha-nature from Candrakīrti's emptiness of an own nature because it does not arise from contact with other things—the criterion for an own nature in the *Prasannapadā*.[77] Still, buddha-nature continues for Zhonnu Pel in a momentary stream within its own sphere not depending on external conditions.

As already mentioned (and also demonstrated previously[78]) Rangjung Dorje, too, differs from the Jonang, although in another way than Zhonnu Pel does. Similar to Shakya Chokden and Mikyo Dorje, Rangjung Dorje does not restrict the perfect nature to its unchangeable aspect, and nowhere do these three masters say that it transcends time, as for example, Sazang Mati Paṇchen (1294–1376), a heart disciple of Dolpopa, advocates. Nor do they describe the ultimate as a permanent entity. However, when Mikyo Dorje describes and criticizes the Jonang in his *Madhyamakāvatāra* commentary, he uses this controversial attribute of being a permanent entity.[79] Whether Mikyo Dorje in his *Madhyamakāvatāra* commentary turns only against the zhentong of the Jonang and Shakya Chokden or also against his own zhentong needs further investigation. In his *Hundred Thousand Words of Mahāmudrā*, he explicitly states that even dharmatā is within the scope of rangtong, and as we have seen, dharmatā is only taken to be zhentong in relation to the "phenomena" (dharmin) of adventitious stains. In his *Introducing the Tenet of Madhyamaka Zhentong*, too, Mikyo Dorje never claims that buddha-nature or the ultimate is not empty of an own nature.

Between the positions of the Jonang and Shakya Chokden, Mikyo Dorje's zhentong view falls more on the side of Shakya Chokden. In his *Abhisamayālaṃkāra* commentary, the way Mikyo Dorje describes the relation between buddha-nature and adventitious stains as clearly distinct is nearly identical with what we find in the works of Rangjung Dorje, except that the latter does not refer to this position as zhentong. The same clear-cut distinction between buddha-nature and the adventitious stains can be also identified in the *Commentary on the Pointing-Out of the Three Kāyas*, where Mikyo Dorje uses the example of milk poured into water (in which the two are understood as not inseparably mixed) to illustrate the Buddha's activity in relation to sentient beings. As we have seen, the same metaphor (milk for the pure mind and water for sentient beings) is also found in the *Mahāyānasaṃgraha*.

Whatever Mikyo Dorje's final view on zhentong was, the more moderate position of the *Introducing the Tenet of Madhyamaka Zhentong* can be brought in line with his ultimate Madhyamaka position that the two truths form an inseparable unity (*zung 'jug*).[80] Whether this also includes buddha-nature and adventitious stains is another question. The indivisible unity of the two truths and the clear distinction between buddha-nature and adventitious stains (even in its zhentong form as found in the *Abhisamayālaṃkāra* commentary) can be understood, however, by following Mikyo Dorje's *Introducing the Tenet of Madhyamaka Zhentong*, where one does not need to include the impure relative truth of the adventitious stains in this indivisible unity.[81] This, in fact, would be also in line with Rangjung Dorje's presentation of the two truths in his autocommentary on the *Profound Inner Principles*, where the relative and ultimate truths are included in buddha-nature. As we have seen, this does not refer to the ordinary relative truth, however, but only to the stainless forms of consciousness or the mere appearance as such (the unmistaken perfect nature). Both Rangjung Dorje and Mikyo Dorje thus exclude the equation of buddha-nature with ālayavijñāna (as for example found in the *Laṅkāvatāra Sūtra*).[82] The impure relative truth then is the "other" (*zhen*) in Mikyo Dorje's zhentong.

Kongtrul Lodro Taye's Zhentong Overview

Another important proponent of zhentong in the Karma Kagyu tradition is Kongtrul Lodro Taye (1813–1899). A comparison of his *Ratnagotravibhāga* commentary with the one by Dolpopa shows the same fundamental difference between the zhentong of the Karmapas and the Jonangpas. Whereas for Dolpopa buddhahood is free from moments, according to Mati Paṇchen even in the sense that it does not belong to the three times, Kongtrul takes buddhahood as being unconditioned only inasmuch as its dharmakāya does not appear to disciples as something that arises and ceases.[83] This restricted negation of being conditioned, which does not exclude, for example, the permanence of an endless continuity in moments, constitutes a remarkable difference with Dolpopa[84] and reflects Kongtrul's doctrinal proximity to Shakya Chokden, for whom nondual wisdom is certainly not permanent or beyond time. Wisdom cannot be truly permanent for him if taken as a real existent whose continuity is uninterrupted. It is only conventionally designated as being permanent, because its dynamic flow is endless (as opposed to ordinary impermanent entities).[85]

In Kongtrul's *Treasury of Knowledge* there are two extensive passages on zhentong, one in the systematic presentation on tenets in book 6,[86] and the other one in the presentation of the authentic view in book 7.[87] Since huge parts of Kongtrul's encyclopedia are mostly copied literally from other authors, it is difficult to construe Kongtrul's own position. The tenets from Vaibhāṣika up to Prāsaṅgika-Mādhyamika[88] in book 6 are copied from the *Karma [Trinle's] Chariot*, a work similar to the *Treasury of Knowledge* in structure and scope by the second Karma Trinle Pelkang Lotsāwa Ngawang Chokyi Gyatso (1543–?). This second Karma Trinle was a disciple of the Eighth Karmapa Mikyo Dorje.

It is interesting to note that in the aforementioned presentation of tenets, Kongtrul did not copy Karma Trinle's concluding remark, which includes the statement that the Buddha taught in the tantras the four tenets of *Vaibhāṣika, Sautrāntika, Yogācāra, and Madhyamaka.*[89] Kongtrul lists instead Tsongkhapa's (1357–1419) eight great, uncommon theses, with which Shakya Chokden and the Eighth Karmapa, so Kongtrul, disagree (with the exception that the śrāvakas and pratyekabuddhas realize the nonself of phenomena).[90] Instead of Karma Trinle's conclusion on the topic of these tenets, we thus have a disagreement with the Gelukpa's interpretation of Madhyamaka, interestingly with reference to Shakya Chokden and Mikyo Dorje but not Tāranātha. This nicely leads then to the presentation of Zhentong Madhyamaka.

The extent to which Kongtrul goes against the author he had faithfully copied over the course of pages becomes clear from the fact that the second Karma Trinle not only has nothing to say about zhentong, but also that he argues at length that the final Madhyamaka view of the four tenets is established on the basis of the *Samādhirāja Sūtra*'s distinction of provisional and definitive meaning.[91] He thus follows the rangtong hermeneutics of the turning of the second dharma wheel (*dharmacakra*), which presents Prajñāpāramitā in the sense that everything, including the omniscience of a buddha, is empty of an own nature. This is opposed to the hermeneutics of the *Sandhinirmocana Sūtra*, whose fine distinctions between the real and merely imputed as well as the positive descriptions of the ultimate as definitive meaning, is followed by zhentongpas. The second Karma Trinle concludes with the remark that he presented the tenets in accordance with Mikyo Dorje's *Treatise Illucidating the Karmapa's Intent: Chariot for Progressing on the Great Path of Liberation*.[92]

Kongtrul's philosophical presentation of zhentong in book 6 is mainly based on passages from Tāranātha's Great Madhyamaka chapter of the *Essence of Zhentong*, which, after a general introduction, starts with a quotation from *Madhyāntavibhāga* I.1–2. Based on these initial verses, Tāranātha presents his understanding of the three-nature theory, whose distinguishing mark is that false imagining, or the dependent nature, only exists on the relative level of truth.[93] This first part of the Great Madhyamaka in the *Essence of Zhentong* contains an interesting part that Kongtrul did not copy:

> To maintain therefore that dharmatā is emptiness and that dharmatā is not emptiness is the zhentong tradition. But in the tradition known as rangtong there are internal contradictions. Therefore, as for the correct rangtong taught by the Buddha, it is that [only] the relative is empty of an own nature. [Correct rangtong] is also the three types of essencelessness. Those who maintain rangtong without mistake and those who maintain essencelessness are proponents of zhentong. That Bhāviveka and Buddhapālita are known as proponents of rangtong and essencelessness is mainly due to their reputation in the ordinary world.[94]

The reason for this omission must be doctrinal differences with Tāranātha, namely, reservations about the restriction of rangtong to the relative truth, and probably also the polemical overtones against Bhāviveka and Buddhapālita.[95] Kongtrul also stops copying Tāranātha when the latter turns to the buddha-nature doctrine in a new chapter called "Uncommon Meaning of Zhentong."[96] The point here is that Kongtrul does not follow Tāranātha, when the latter moves from Yogācāra to a buddha-nature-centered zhentong, in which the three-nature theory is deconstructed. Here, Tāranātha restricts the perfect nature to its unchangeable aspect, while the perfect nature of unmistaken wisdom is included under the pure dependent. Moreover, he includes the dependent nature under the imagined nature, so that all phenomena are included only under the imagined and perfect natures.[97] Instead of copying Tāranātha's move away from Yogācāra, Kongtrul explains that his zhentong view is free from the mistakes of the mind-only perspective:

> In this tradition, the nature of wisdom that is beyond consciousness and free from all mental fabrication is taken to be truly established. Since this wisdom, which is free from mental fabrication, is not conditioned, it is [nevertheless] taught to be without the slightest mistake of taking ultimate truth as an entity.[98]

So, we have again a Kagyu zhentong position that differs from the Jonangpas' ultimate, permanent entity. It must be admitted, however, that Kongtrul quotes a short passage from Tāranātha's "Uncommon Meaning of Zhentong" about the discussion in the *Laṅkāvatāra Sūtra* of whether the teaching of a buddha-nature is Buddhist at all. In this context, the permanence of buddha-nature is taken to be permanent in the strict sense:

> To say that the position of a permanent buddha-nature is non-Buddhist definitely goes against the Tathāgatagarbha sūtras, and it is not acceptable to take permanence [only] in the sense of a permanent continuum, because the latter also applies to saṃsāra and all [pairs] of perceived [objects] and perceiving [subjects].[99]

It should be noted that this quotation is from a passage that is clearly marked by Kongtrul to be authored by Tāranātha (instead of silently copying him). This could indicate that the view of the unconditional permanence of buddha-nature does not reflect his own opinion, as can be seen from Kongtrul's *Ratnagotravibhāga* commentary, where he deviates from Dolpopa's and Mati Paṇchen's commentaries on the issue of unconditioned buddhahood by restricting the meaning of conditioned to the context of the dharmakāya not appearing to disciples. The overall picture of the zhentong passage in the presentation of tenets is, as we have seen, that zhentong is presented more in line with Yogācāra and Shakya Chokden. This is also clear from the zhentong passage in book 7, which is dedicated to a presentation of the authentic view. After a short, more or less encyclopedic presenation of the

Jonang interpretation of zhentong as the perfect nature empty of the imagined and depedent natures, Kongtrul directs us to Shakya Chokden's view of this matter, namely, his more traditional Yogācāra interpretation of the three natures as the perfect being the dependent empty of the imagined.[100] Kongtrul also quotes and discusses the sixteen types of emptiness in the *Madhyāntavibhāga*, a more traditional Yogācāra text that lends doctrinal support to Shakya Chokden's restriction of the negandum to the imagined nature.[101]

CONCLUSION

From the time of the seventh Karmapa Chodrak Gyatso, Kagyupas in the Kamtsang or Karma tradition upheld a zhentong view that differed from the interpretation of the Jonang. In the works of Chodrak Gyatso, the word "zhentong" is found only once; nevertheless, zhentong plays an important role in the *Ocean of Treatises on Valid Cognition and Reasoning* in determining that Dharmakīrti's final intention is based on a Yogācāra-Madhyamaka perspective. A similar zhentong position (without using the word "zhentong" itself) can also be found in the works of the third Karmapa Rangjung Dorje, where a type of zhentong can be read into the clear-cut distinction between the impure and pure mind found in the *Mahāyānasaṃgraha*. To be sure, the basis of negation is not a permanent or transtemporal ultimate but an unconditioned luminous mind that continues in a series of moments. The luminous mind or buddha-nature is zhentong with regard to its adventitious stains but rangtong like anything else in terms of its ontological status.

What we find in the works of the Eighth Karmapa Mikyo Dorje is more complex, but elements of Rangjung Dorje's and Chodrak Gyatso's views can be also found in the *Hundred Thousand Words of Mahāmudrā*. In it, everything (including the dharmatā) is rangtong, while zhentong only stands for a relational absence of the dharmin in the dharmatā, or the adventitious stains in buddha-nature. It is also noteworthy that Mikyo Dorje not only endorses this moderate form of zhentong but also criticizes Jonang zhentong views in the very same text.

As has been demonstrated, Kagyu zhentong, as I provisionally suggest calling it, is more in line with the zhentong position of Shakya Chokden. This also finds support from Situ Chokyi Jungne's and Belo Tsewang Kunkyab's *Kagyu Golden Rosary Biographies* and is further supported by my analysis of the zhentong passages in Kongtrul's *Treasury of Knowledge*. The common ground of Kagyu zhentong is that its basis of negation is an unconditioned but dynamic and luminous buddha-nature that is neither an ultimate entity transcending time nor the luminous mind that wanders in the six realms of saṃsāra.

To sum up, what Kongtrul, as well as the three Karmapas (the third, seventh, and eighth) share in common with Shakya Chokden is that the basis of negation still consists of moments, like the unconditioned luminous mind that continues in a series of moments mentioned in the gloss in Sajjana's text. The basis of negation, therefore, is not separate from dependent origination. This translates into a more moderate zhentong, in which the borderline between the basis of negation and the negandum is not drawn between a transcendent and transtemporal ultimate and everything else as relative truth, but between a dependent nature and imagined nature, both of which belong to the relative truth.[102] False imagining as the underlying process that produces the imagined nature may be at times included in the negandum by our three Karmapas (to be sure it has to be abandoned anyway), but the "pure dependent," the unmistaken perfect nature in proper Yogācāra terminology, consistently belongs to the basis of negation for the three Karmapas and Shakya Chokden alike. This then constitutes the common difference to Jonang zhentong.

Notes

Improvements to my English by Michele Martin (Buddhist Digital Resource Center) and Casey Kemp (Shambhala Publications) are gratefully acknowledged. In this chapter I present first results from my FWF (Förderung der wissenschaftlichen Forschung) project "Buddha Nature Reconsidered: Mi bskyod rdo rje and the Post-Classical Tibetan *Tathāgatagarbha* Debates" (project no. P 28003-G24). I thank Dr. Martina Draszczyk, Dr. David Higgins, and Mag. Khenpo Tamphel for their collaboration on this project.

1. In the texts known to us, Rangjung Dorje does not himself use the term "zhentong." As will be shown in this chapter, his position on buddha-nature was adopted and called zhentong in some of the Eighth Karmapa Mikyo Dorje's texts.

2. For a good overview over different zhentong positions, see Burchardi, "Diversity of the Gzhan stong." The Jonang take the basis of negation as an eternal ultimate, one that is not subject to the three times of past, present, and future. This is clear from a study of Dolpopa Sherab Gyaltsen and Sazang Mati Paṇchen's *Ratnagotravibhāga* commentaries. Mathes, *Direct Path* 75–91.

3. Karma Trinle I, "Dris lan yid kyi mun sel zhes bya ba lcags mo'i dris lan bzhugs," 91_{1-4}: "My lama, the omniscient [seventh Karmapa Chodrak Gyatso,] says: 'Nowadays, some who are proud of being proponents of zhentong [claim that] a permanent, stable, steadfast, unchangeable ultimate truly exists. Further, since it is empty of the adventitious [stains resulting from] clinging to an object and a subject, [they claim that] it is profound zhentong. Being fond of such an eternalist view, they [put forth] deceiving words, claiming profundity for this emptiness, which is [actually] clinging to an extreme. This is not the pure zhentong taught in the sūtras. Being confused about Jina Maitreya's teaching [according to which] the true nature of the mind (*sems nyid*) is not empty of unsurpassable qualities, they say that the sixty-four qualities, which are [already] present at [the level of the] ground, are empty of adventitious stains and call this zhentong. [Thus] they demean the Victorious One by saying that he wanders in saṃsāra, inasmuch as a perfect Buddha whose hindrances are exhausted and whose wisdom is fully blossomed [would then] experience the suffering of the six realms—hell and so forth. What has been taught in accordance with the tantras, the *Bodhisattva Trilogy* (*sems 'grel* [*skor gsum*]), many sūtras, and the Maitreya texts is the zhentong professed by Rangjung Dorje.' Thus I have heard in the discourses of the Jinendra (i.e., the seventh Karmapa)." *bdag gi bla ma thams cad mkhyen pa gsung / ding sang gzhan stong smra bar rlom pa 'ga' / don dam rtag brtan ther zug mi 'gyur ba / bden par grub 'di gzung 'dzin glo (text: blo) bur bas / stong phyir gzhan stong zab mo 'di yin lo / 'di 'dra rtag pa'i lta ba la dga' bas / mthar 'dzin stong nyid zab mor smra byed pa'I / brdzun gyi zol tshig yin gyi mdo sde las / gsungs pa'i gzhan stong rnam dag de ma yin/ bla med chos kyis sems nyid mi stong zhes / rgyal ba byams pas gsungs pa la 'khrul nas / gzhi la bzhugs pa'i yon tan*

drug bcu bzhi / glo (text: blo) bur dri mas stong la gzhan stong zhes / sgrib pa kun zad ye shes rab rgyas pa'i / rdzogs pa'i sangs rgyas dmyal ba la sogs pa / 'gro ba drug gi sdug bsngal myong ba'i phyir / 'khor bar 'khor zhes rgyal la skur btab bo / rgyud dang sems 'grel mdo sde du ma dang / byams chos rjes 'brang bcas las gsungs pa'i don / rang byung rdo rje bzhed pa'i gzhan stong ni / rgyal ba'i dbang po'i gsung las 'di skad thos. First translated in Mathes, *Direct Path* 55. Also Burchardi, "Role of Rang rig" 319–323. For a full translation of this *dris lan*, Higgins and Draszczyk, *Mahāmudrā and the Middle Way* II.89–91.

4. Stearns, *Buddha from Dolpo* 162.

5. Takasaki, *Study on the Ratnagotravibhāga* 272.

6. Mathes, *Direct Path* 241 and 366.

7. Which Mikyo Dorje at times calls a zhentong view. It should be noted that in his *Madhyamakāvatāra* commentary, Mikyo Dorje turns against zhentong, and it can be ruled out that he does so only when commenting on Candrakīrti's main Madhyamaka work, for in his *Sku gsum ngo sprod rnam bshad*, Mikyo Dorje clearly endorses Candrakīrti's *Madhyamaka* approach of merely accepting on a relative level what is established in the world. Mikyo Dorje, *Sku gsum ngo sprod rnam bshad* vol. 1, 68_{10-19}.

8. Mathes, "Tāranātha's Presentation."

9. Sponberg, "Trisvabhāva Doctrine." The pivotal model starts from an ultimately existing or all-inclusive dependent nature. The imagined and perfect natures are just the way the dependent nature appears to be and really is. The dependent nature thus is the receptacle of the perfect nature, which is understood as something abstract, like the state of suffering or impermanence. When the dependent nature is purified it stops being false imagining and manifests in itself, and thus in everything, the perfect nature. At this stage, the latter is constituted by a really existing dependent nature that then is nonconceptual wisdom. In the progressive model, the focus lies more on a perfect nature that is an all-pervading emptiness possessing positive qualities. The latter is not only an abstract quality of the dependent but exists independent of it. Mathes, "Tāranātha's Presentation" 211–212. Some followers of the progressive model (mainly the Jonang) entirely exclude the dependent nature from the perfect nature—even to the extent that its aspect of being perfect in terms of being unmistaken (*aviparyāsaparinispattyā parinispanna*), that is, the nonconceptual wisdom of the path, is not accepted as the perfect nature but described as the "pure dependent" (*dag pa gzhan dbang*).[a]

[a]Sometimes we find also the form *dag pa'i gzhan dbang*. In the electronic version of the *Dol po pa'i gsum 'bum*, *dag pa gzhan dbang* occurs twelve times and *dag pa'i gzhan dbang* only once. According to Khenpo Tamphel (Vienna, Oct. 25, 2017) the meaning is the same.

10. Mathes, "Ontological Status" 335–336.

11. That is, taking the second *rig pa dri med gcer bur thon tshul* as an abbreviation of *rang sems rig pa dri med gcer bur thon tshul*. In the English translation it is thus not repeated.

12. Mikyo Dorje, *Phyag rgya chen po'i sgros 'bum* 54_{3-6}: *des na bcom ldan 'das kyi mdo rgyud rnams las / chos can gyi cha nas rang sems rig pa dri med gcer bur thon tshul la gzhan stong dang / chos nyid kyi cha nas rig pa dri med gcer bur thon tshul la rang stong ste de'i stong pa nyid gnyis pa'o.*

13. Mathes, *Direct Path* 51–75.

14. It should be noted that according to *Dharmadhātustava* 62, milk and water remain separate even in the same vessel, so that geese just sip the milk and not the water. Brunnhölzl, *Praise of Dharmadhātu* 89.

15. The *Mahāyānasaṃgraha* passage (MS $I.19_1$–20_9) is as follows: "If that which contains all seeds, [namely] the consciousness of maturation (i.e., the ālayavijñāna), is the cause of all defilements, how can it be the seed of the supramundane mind, which is the remedy

for this [ālayavijñāna]? The supramundane mind is "unfamiliar" (*ma 'dris pa*, "not mixed with") [with the ālayavijñāna]; thus there is no [mental] imprint from it [in the ālayavijñāna]. Question: 'If a mental imprint [of it] does not exist [there], from which seed must it be said to arise?' Answer: 'It arises from the seed [or] mental imprint of studying, which is the outflow of the very pure dharmadhātu.' Objection: 'Is the mental imprint of studying "identical with" (*ngo bo nyid*) the ālayavijñāna or not? If it were identical with the ālayavijñāna, how would it be suitable as the seed of the remedy for it? If you say that it is not identical with it, you [must] see what the basis for this seed of the mental imprint of studying is.' [Answer:] 'The mental imprint of studying occurs based on the enlightenment of the Buddhas. Occuring together with the basis into which it enters, it enters into the consciousness of maturation (i.e., the ālayavijñāna) in the same way as milk [into] water. It is not the ālayavijñāna, given that it is the seed of the remedy for [the ālayavijñāna]. From a small mental imprint, it [gradually] turns into an average one and then a big one, since you will [eventually] be endowed with [the fruits of] having studied, reflected, and meditated many times. The small, average, and big mental imprints of studying [must be] regarded as the seed of the dharmakāya. Being the remedy for the ālayavijñāna, it is not identical with the ālayavijñāna. Even though [this seed] belongs to this world, it is the outflow of the very pure supramundane dharmadhātu and thus the seed of the supramundane mind. [And] even though the supramundane mind may not have arisen [yet], it is [still] the remedy for entanglement in all defilements and migration to lower realms, and the remedy that suppresses all faults. It supports the connection with buddhas and bodhisattvas. Although it (this seed) is [still] of a mundane nature for beginner bodhisattvas, it is regarded as being included in the dharmakāya, and for śrāvakas and pratyekabuddhas as being included in the "body of liberation." It is not the ālayavijñāna but included in the dharmakāya and the "body of liberation." *sa bon thams cad pa rnam par smin pa'i rnam par shes pa ni kun nas nyon mongs pa'i rgyu yin na / de'i gnyen po 'jig rten las 'das pa'i sems kyi sa bon ji ltar rung / 'jig rten las 'das pa'i sems ni ma 'dris pa ste / de bas na de'i bag chags ni med pa nyid do / bag chags de med na sa bon gang las 'byung ba brjod dgos so zhe na / chos kyi dbyings shin tu rnam par dag pa'i rgyu mthun pa thos pa'i bag chags sa bon las de 'byung ngo / thos pa'i bag chags gang yin pa de yang ci kun gzhi rnam par shes pa'i ngo bo nyid yin nam / 'on te ma yin / gal te kun gzhi rnam par shes pa'i ngo bo yin na ni ji ltar de'i gnyen po'i sa bon du rung / ci ste de'i ngo bo nyid ma yin na ni thos pa'i bag chags de yi sa bon gyi gnas ci zhig yin par blta zhe na / sangs rgyas kyi byang chub la brten nas thos pa'i bag chags 'jug par gyur gang yin pa gnas gang la 'jug pa de lhan cig 'jug pa'i tshul gyis rnam par smin pa'i rnam par shes pa la 'jug pa ste / 'o ma dang chu bzhin no / de ni kun gzhi'i rnam par shes pa ma yin te / de'i gnyen po'i sa bon nyid yin pa'i phyir ro / bag chags chung ngu la brten nas bag chags 'bring por 'gyur ro / bags chags 'bring po la brten nas bag chags chen po 'gyur ste / thos pa dang bsam pa dang / bsgom pa lan mang du bya ba dang ldan pa'i phyir ro / de la thos pa'i bag chags kyi sa bon chung ngu dang 'bring dang chen po yang chos kyi sku'i sa bon du blta ste / kun gzhi'i rnam shes kyi gnyen po yin pas kun gzhi'i rnam shes kyi ngo bo nyid ma yin pa dang / 'jig rten pa yin yang 'jig rten las 'das pa yi chos kyi dbyings shin tu rnam par dag pa'i rgyu mthun pa yin pas 'jig rten las 'das pa'i sems kyi sa bon du gyur pa'o / de ni 'jig rten las 'das pa'i sems ma byung du zin kyang / nyon mongs pa'i kun nas dkris pa'i gnyen po dang / ngan song du 'gro ba'i gnyen po dang / nyes par byas pa thams cad dengs par byed pa'i gnyen po yin no / sangs rgyas dang byang chub sems dpa' dang phrad pa'i rjes su mthun pa'o / byang chub sems dpa' las dang po pa rnams kyi 'jig rten pa yin yang chos kyi skur bsdus pa dang / nyan thos dang rang sangs rgyas rnams kyi rnam par grol ba'i lus su bsdus par yang blta'o / de ni kun gzhi'i rnam par shes pa ma yin gyi / chos kyi sku dang rnam par grol ba'i lus su bsdus pa ste.*

16. Mikyo Dorje, *Shes rab kyi pha rol tu phyin pa'i lung* . . . 234–259. I am indebted to Karl Brunnhölzl for drawing my attention to this passage.

17. Rangjung Dorje, *Zab mo nang gi don gsal bar byed pa'i 'grel pa bzhugs so* 8a6–7: *'di la kun gzhi zhes bya ba rnam par shes pa'i sgra ma smos na de bzhin nyid la yang kun gzhi brjod du rung ba'i phyir rnam par shes pa smos so.* First quoted and translated in Mathes, *Direct Path* 57.

18. Mikyo Dorje, *Shes rab kyi pha rol tu phyin pa'i lung* . . . 238_3.

19. Mikyo Dorje, *Shes rab kyi pha rol tu phyin pa'i lung* . . . 235_6.

20. In MAV I.14, the following synonyms for emptiness are given: suchness, the extreme limit of reality, signlessness, ultimate truth, and the dharmadhātu (MAVBh 23). In his *Abhisamayālaṃkāra* commentary (238_{3-4}), Mikyo Dorje uses the term *kun gzhi'i ye shes* in reference to suchness.

21. Rangjung Dorje, *Zab mo nang gi don zhes bya ba'i gzhung bzhugs* $2b_4$: *rgyu ni sems nyid thog med la.*

22. Rangjung Dorje, *Rang 'grel* $10b_{3-4}$: *thog med la zhes bya ba ni / dus kyi thog ma dang tha ma ni rtog pas sgro btags pa yin pas 'dir ni dri ma med pa dang dri ma dang bcas pa'i rang gi ngo bo ni rten cing 'brel bar 'byung ba de nyid dang gzhan las rnam par grol ba ste / de las thog ma gzhan med pa'i phyir thog ma med pa'i dus zhes bya ste.*

23. At this point, I will take the opportunity to correct my translation of the previously quoted passage from Rangjung Dorje's autocommentary. Having taken *de nyid* together with *rten cing 'brel bar 'byung ba*, I translated "it [i.e., the true nature] is precisely this dependent arising" and took the following *gzhan las rnam par grol ba* as "completely liberated (i.e., free) from [all] else" (Mathes, *Direct Path* 62). But *de nyid* should be construed together with *gzhan las rnam par grol ba* and taken as a technical term that translates *tattvānyatvavinirmuktaṃ* (as in *Madhyāntavibhāgabhāṣya* I.13 [MAVBh 23_{10}], for example). In line with this interpretation, the *de bzhin nyid* in *de bzhin nyid dang gzhan las rnam par grol ba* at the beginning of the ninth chapter of the autocommentary should be corrected to *de nyid* and translated as follows: "The two truths, which have been explained in such a way, are free from identity (*de nyid*) and difference just as in the case of phenomena (dharma) and their true nature (dharmatā). They can be expressed as being neither identical nor different" (Rangjung Dorje, *Rang 'grel*, $63b_1$: *de ltar bshad pa'i bden pa gnyis po 'di yang chos rnams dang chos nyid ji lta ba bzhin du de bzhin nyid dang gzhan las rnam par grol ba yin pa gcig pa dang tha dad gang du'ang brjod du med do*). Thus *gzhan las grol ba* here means "free from difference" and is not understood in the zhentong sense of being "liberated from other" (as suggested in Mathes, *Direct Path* 62ff.).

24. In MAVBh I.5, false imagining is related to the dependent nature (MAVBh 19_{19-20}: *abhūtaparikalpaḥ paratantraḥ svabhāvaḥ*). In his subcommentary, Sthiramati explains: "'False imagining is the dependent nature' means that [false imagining] is other-dependent (*paratantraḥ*, otherwise translated as dependent) because it is ruled (*tantryate*) or produced by other (*parair*) causes and conditions, and hence does not exist in its own right" (MAVṬ 23_{5-7}: *abhūtaparikalpaḥ paratantraḥ svabhāva iti / parair hetupratyayais tantryate janyate na tu svayaṃ bhavatīti paratantraḥ*). To be sure, this does not exclude that correct types of cognition, such as nonconceptual wisdom, belong to the dependent nature. Dolpopa thus distinguishes the dependent nature in terms of false imagining from a "pure dependent," a term admittedly unattested in Indian Yogācāra. Still, Dolpopa uses this term to refer to the

unmistaken perfect (*aviparyāsaparinispattyā parinispanna*, i.e., the nonconceptual wisdom of the path), which he prefers not to include under the perfect nature. Mathes, "Twenty-One Differences" 304–305.

25. MAVBh 18_{2-3}: *śūnyatā tasyābhūtaparikalpasya grāhyagrāhakabhāvena virahitatā.*

26. Mathes, *Direct Path* 60. The four wisdoms are the mirrorlike wisdom, the wisdom of equality, the discriminating wisdom, and the all-accomplishing wisdom, which manifest as a result of transforming the eight consciousnesses.

27. Rangjung Dorje, *Rang 'grel*, $62b_{1-3}$: *sems can khams ni sangs rgyas kyi / snying po dri med bden gnyis ldan zhes smos so / de la sangs rgyas kyi snying po ni sngar smos pa'i tshogs brgyad kyi 'khrul pa dri ma med pa kho na yin mod kyi 'on kyang bden pa gnyis kyi don mngon sum du ma byas pa dag rten cing 'brel bar 'byung ba'i tshul la rmongs nas / lta ba tha dad pa dag 'dzin pas 'khor bar gyur to.* First quoted and translated in Mathes, *Direct Path* 66.

28. Mathes, *Direct Path* 66–68.

29. That is, what appears to mind, once it has stopped being false imagining and started operating as nonconceptual wisdom.

30. The unmistaken perfect nature is called by some Tibetan masters "pure dependent nature."

31. See also Shakya Chokden (whose zhentong position is close to the views of the Karmapas as discussed in this chapter), for advocating zhentong as a philosophical orientation that helps to approach indivisible unity. Higgins and Draszczyk, *Mahāmudrā and the Middle Way* I.60–61, II.51, and II.68).

32. Mathes, "Original *Ratnagotravibhāga*" 129–136.

33. RGVV, 32_{3-5}: *mahākaruṇābhāvanāyāḥ satatasamitam ā saṃsārāt sattvārthagodhapaliguddhatvān*[a] *nityapāramitādhigamaḥ phalaṃ draṣṭavyam.*

[a]Johnston: *-godhapariśuddhatvān*. Schmithausen, "Philologische Bemerkungen" 143.

34. RGVV, 31_{13-16}: "The Tathāgata, however, has attained through his genuine wisdom the highest perfection, namely, the lack of a self in all phenomena. This lack of a self, as seen by him, namely, as having the defining characteristic of a nonself, is not false. Therefore, [only this much] is accepted as a self at any time: a self that is nothing but the lack of a self" (*tathāgataḥ punar yathābhūtajñānena sarvadharmanairātmyaparapāram abhiprāptaḥ / tac cāsya nairātmyam anātmalakṣaṇena yathādarśanam avisaṃvāditvāt sarvakālam ātmābhipreto nairātmyam evātmeti*[a] *kṛtvā*).

[a]Johnston: *evātmani*. Schmithausen, "Philologische Bemerkungen" 143.

35. A Kashmiri *paṇḍita* from the eleventh century, who figures prominently in the transmission of the Maitreya texts in India and thus indirectly influenced later Kagyu masters.

36. Kano, *Buddha-Nature and Emptiness* 227.

37. Mathes, *Direct Path* 333.

38. Mathes, " 'Gos Lo tsā ba" 4.

39. Burchardi, "Role of Rang rig" 331–333.

40. *Tshad ma rigs gzhung rgya mtsho, Mngon sum le'u*, 405_{9-16}: *phyi rol gyi don med na / 'o na ji ltar gzhal bya dang tshad ma dang 'bras bu'i rnam par gnas she na / gzugs sogs su snang ba'i gzung ba'i rnam pa gzhal bya / 'dzin pa'i rnam pa tshad ma / rang rig 'bras bur byas pa gcig dang / gzung ba'i rnam pa de yang thog ma med pa'i ma rig pas bslad pa can gyi gnyis snang gi blos sgro btags pa'i dbang gis gnas tshul la ma grub pa' i phyir / yang dag par na gzhal bya ma yin la / de'i tshe gzung 'dzin gnyis bral gyi shes pa gsal rig gi cha gzhal bya / 'dzin rnam tshad ma / rang rig 'bras bur byas pa 'di tshad 'bras kyi rnam par bzhag pa mthar thug par grub pa yin no.*

41. *Tshad ma rigs gzhung rgya mtsho, Mngon sum le'u*, 405_{17-21}: *'dir yang dbu ma chen po gzhan stong smra ba rnams kyis ji ltar blo 'khrul pa la snang ba de ltar rnam par bzhag pa tsam yin gyi / yang dag par grub pa ni ma yin te / gzhal bya dang tshad ma dang 'bras bu tha dad par ji ltar snang ba la ma dpyad par tshad 'bras gzhal gsum gyi rnam par bzhag pa tsam yin la / de yang rtog pas btags pa tsam yin pa'i phyir te.*

42. Thrangu, *Song for the King* 88; also 86–87. Thanks to Michele Martin for drawing my attention to this passage.

43. Namely, verses II.354–356b and II.357.

44. Namely, verses I.44–46b and II.47.

43. That is, taking *-ātmā* in the sense of "nature."

44. For translating *-saṃvitti-* with self-awareness, see Vetter, *Dharmakīrti's Pramāṇa-viniścayaḥ* 91.

45. *Tshad ma rigs gzhung rgya mtsho, Mngon sum le'u*, 406_{2-5}: *blo bdag rnam par dbyer med kyang / mthong ba phyin ci log rnams kyi / gzung dang 'dzin pa myong ba dag / tha dad ldan bzhin rtog par 'gyur /* (PV 88_{15-16}: *avibhāgo 'pi buddhy*([a]*ātmā vi*[a])*paryāsitadarśanaiḥ / grāhyagrāhakasaṃvittibhedavān*[b] *iva lakṣyate*).

[a]E_M *-ātmavi-*. My reading is supported by PVin 38_5 (I.44). [b]E_M *-vām*. See also PVin 38_6 (I.44).

46. *Tshad ma rigs gzhung rgya mtsho, Mngon sum le'u* 406_{6-9}: *dper na dbang po sngags sogs kyis / bslad pa rnams la 'jim dum sogs / de yi gzugs dang bral ba yang / rnam pa gzhan du snang ba bzhin /* (PV 88_{17-18}: *mantrādyupaplutākṣāṇāṃ yathā mṛcchalādayaḥ / anyathaivāvabhāsante tadrūparahitā api*).

47. *Tshad ma rigs gzhung rgya mtsho, Mngon sum le'u*, 406_{10-11}: *de dag ma bslad mig can gyis / de ltar mthong ba med phyir ro / zhes dang /* (PV 88_{19}: *tathaivādarśanāt teṣām anupaplutacakṣuṣāṃ*).

48. *Tshad ma rigs gzhung rgya mtsho, Mngon sum le'u*, 406_{12-15}: *gzung ba 'dzin pa rig pa dag / yod pa min kyang gzhal bya dang / 'jal byed 'bras bur gnas pa 'di / ji ltar rjes su snang bzhin byas /* (PV 88_{21-22}: *yathānudarśanaṃ*[a] *ceyam meyamānaphalasthitiḥ / kriyate 'vidyamānāpi grāhyagrāhakasaṃvidām.* [a]E_M *-āñ*. PVin 38_{11} [PVin I. 47a]). The Sanskrit of PV 357cd reads: "even though it [i.e., the position] does not exist in the case of the awareness of a perceived [object] and perceiving [subject]."

49. *Tshad ma rigs gzhung rgya mtsho, Mngon sum le'u*, 406_{17-20}: *sems las gzhan med par ni blo rig nas / de nas sems kyang med pa nyid du mthong / blo dang ldan pas gnyis po med rig nas / de mi ldan pa'i chos kyi dbyings la gnas /* (MSABh 24_{3-4}: *nāstīti cittāt param etya buddhyā cittasya nāstitvam upaiti tasmāt / dvayasya nāstitvam upetya dhīmān saṃtiṣṭhate 'tadva* (text: *-ga-*)*ti dharmadhātu*).

50. Mathes, "'Gos Lo tsā ba" 16–17.

51. MSABh 24_{13-15}: "Having understood that there is no referential object (*grāhya*) apart from the mind, the nonexistence of even this mind alone (*cittamātra*) is realized by the wise. This is because in the absence of a perceived object there is also no perceiving subject" (*cittād anyad ālambanaṃ grāhyaṃ nāstīty avagamya buddhyā tasyāpi cittamātrasya nāstitvāvagamanaṃ grāhyābhāve*[a] *grāhakābhāvāt /*). [a]Lévi: *grāhyabhāve.*

52. *Madhyāntavibhāga* III.9c. Mathes, "Tāranātha's Presentation" 210.

53. *Tshad ma rigs gzhung rgya mtsho, Mngon sum le'u*, 406_{21}–407_1: *sde bdun mdo dang bcas pa'i mthar thug gi dgongs pa ni rje btsun byams pa nas thogs med sku mched las brgyud pa'i dbu mar gnas la / klu sgrub yab sras kyi dbu ma'i gzhung rnams dang yang mthun te.*

54. Taking *buddhair* as a *pluralis majestatis.*

55. *Tshad ma rigs gzhung rgya mtsho, Mngon sum le'u*, 407$_{3-6}$: *gzugs med na ni [*text: *gzugs yod nyid na] sems yod ma 'dzin cig / sems yod nyid na gzugs med ma 'dzin cig / de dag shes rab tshul mdor sangs rgyas kyis / mtshungs par spangs shing mngon pa'i chos las gsungs*. (MA 14$_{7-11}$: *rūpābhāve mā grahīś cittasattāṃ rūpābhāvaṃ cittasattve ca mā gāḥ / prajñānītau sutra ete samānaṃ buddhair kṣiptā varṇitāś cābhidharme //*). The English translation is from Brunnhölzl, *Sunlit Sky* 498.

56. *Tshad ma rigs gzhung rgya mtsho, Mngon sum le'u*, 407$_{8-11}$: *shes bya med na shes pa bsal ba ni / bde blag nyid ces sangs rgyas rnams kyis gsungs / shes bya med na shes pa bkag 'grub pa / dang por shes bya bkag par mdzad pa yin*. MA 14$_{23-26}$ (verse 96): *jñeyaṃ vinā jñānanirākṛtiś ca labhyā sukheneti vadanti buddhāḥ / jñeyasya pūrvaṃ pratiṣedham eva jñeye 'sati jñānaniṣedhasiddheḥ*.

57. *Tshad ma rigs gzhung rgya mtsho, Mngon sum le'u*, 407$_{12-19}$: *de'i phyir yang dag par na gzung 'dzin gnyis kyi rten byed pa'i shes par bcas pa bral ba'i ngo bo stong pa nyid chos thams cad kyi dbyings gzung 'dzin brten pa dang rten shes pa gnyis ka'i rnam par dag cing 'od gsal ba de la me long lta bu'i ye shes kyi ngo bor grub pas rnam pa cir yang 'char rung gi sems nyid gang na gang med pa'i lhag ma yod pa de don dam pa'i bden par grub pa yin no / des na rang bzhin gyis 'od gsal ba'i don dam pa'i bden pa 'di la gang dang gang gi rnam par shar yang de dang der ma grub cing / sems nyid 'od gsal ba de nyid las gzhan du med do*.

58. That is, the dependent nature, which is, as false imagining (*abhūtaparikalpa*), the basis of the imagined nature.

59. It should be noted, though, that in her analysis of Candrakīrti's system, Anne MacDonald, "Knowing Nothing" 156, claims that at the time of perceiving the ultimate, which is the emptiness of things that were never really there in the first place, consciousness will simply not come into being in the absence of an object to be perceived. Still, in the eyes of Candrakīrti, the Buddhas abide in objectless wisdom.

60. *Tshad ma rigs gzhung rgya mtsho, Mngon sum le'u*, 408$_{1-2}$: *sems kyi rang bzhin 'od gsal ba / dri ma rnams ni glo bur ba /* (PV 30$_{13}$: *prabhāsvaram idaṃ cittaṃ prakṛtyāgantavo malāḥ*).

61. *Tshad ma rigs gzhung rgya mtsho, Mngon sum le'u*, 408$_{5-6}$: *sems kyi rang bzhin 'od gsal gang yin pa / de ni nam mkha' bzhin du 'gyur med de /* (RGVV 43$_{9-10}$: *cittasya yāsau prakṛtiḥ prabhāsvarā na jātu sā dyaur iva yāti vikriyām*).

62. Schmithausen, "D. Seyfort Rueggs Buch" 140–141, and Zimmermann, *Buddha Within* 81.

63. See also Seyfort Ruegg, *La théorie du tathāgatagarbha* 423 and 437, and Franco, *Dharmakīrti on Compassion and Rebirth* 87–90.

64. Pecchia, *Dharmakīrti on the Cessation of Suffering* 235–236.

65. *Tshad ma rigs gzhung rgya mtsho, Mngon sum le'u*, 413$_{6-16}$: *slob dpon 'phags pa thos med sku mched nas nye bar brgyud pa'i dbu ma chen po dpal phyogs kyi glang po dang / chos kyi grags pa rnams kyis stong pa nyid du gnas pa'i sems nyid rang bzhin kyis 'od gsal ba gtso bor gtan la phab pas rang bzhin gsal ba'i rol pa las rnam pa ci dang cir snang yang de dang der ma grub par ngo bo stong pa nyid du rtogs par nus pa la dgongs nas gtso bor sems phyogs gtan la 'bebs par mdzad la / slob dpon 'phags pa klu sgrub nas nye bar brgyud pa'i dbu ma pa chen po rnams kyis ni / sems nyid rnam pa sna tshogs su snang ba 'di snang ba ltar du ma grub par gtso bor gtan la phab pas gzung ba dang 'dzin pas stong pa de nyid rang bzhin gyis 'od gsal ba de nyid rtogs nus la dgongs nas gtso bor stong pa'i phyogs nas gtan la 'bebs par mdzad pa yin no*.

66. *Tshad ma rigs gzhung rgya mtsho, Mngon sum le'u*, 413$_{17}$–414$_{4}$: *'di la gzhan dag gis bsam pa de ltar na gsal stong dbyer med kyi sems nyid ces brjod pa 'di dngos po'am / ' on*

te dngos por med pa gang yin / dang po ltar na stong nyid dngos por smra bas dbu ma pa'i nang nas bzhengs la / dngos po med na yang rang bzhin gyis gsal bar gnas pa 'gal lo zhe na / blo'i snang tshul la zhen pa khyed cag bden te / kho bo cag 'dod pa'i dbu ma pa rnams ni dngos po dang / dngos med pa dang / yin pa dang / ma yin pa dang / yod pa dang / med pa dang / rtag pa dang / mi rtag pa dang / stong pa dang / mi stong pa dang / zhi ba dang / ma shi ba dang / bdag ces bya ba dang / bdag med ces bya ba dang / gcig dang / du ma la sogs pa 'di dag thams cad ni phan tshun gcig la gcig bltos nas blo 'khrul pas bkod pa'i snang ba tsam du smra yin na / ji ltar de lta bu'i klan kar 'gyur.

67. Mathes, "Twenty-One Differences" 310–311; see also Komarovski, *Visions of Unity* 128–129 and 351 n. 57.

68. Situ Chokyi Jungne and Belo Tsewang Kunkyab, II, 250_{6-18}: *pa ṇḍi ta chen po shā kya mchog ldan ni . . . phyis rje btsun bdun pa dang mjal te gdams ngag gsan / thugs dam gyi rtsal yongs su rdzogs te rje 'di rtsa ba'i bla mar 'dzin la / sgrub brgyud nges don snying po pa 'di ni gang der nges don phyag rgya chen po'i rtogs pa skyes pa de kho na rtsa ba'i slob mar 'jog ste / rtogs pa don brgyud du gsungs pa'i phyir ro / gsung bshad gnang ba kun kyang rje bdun pa'i bzhed pa ltar theg chen shing rta gnyis ka'i mthar thug lta ba'i 'jog mtshams gzhan stong kho nar mdzad cing tshad ma'i skor yang rje bdun pa'i rig gzhung rgya mtsho'i lugs su gnang zhing // karma pa nyid dang thugs rgyud gcig par gsungs.*

69. Rheingans, *Eighth Karmapa's Life* 96–97.

70. Later, in his *Madhyamakāvatāra* commentary, Mikyo Dorje therefore criticized the zhentong views of the Jonang and Shakya Chokden separately.

71. Mathes, "Eighth Karma pa" 69–70.

72. That requires emending *rang gi ngo bo* to *rang gi ngo bos.*

73. Mikyo Dorje, *Sher phyin mngon rtogs rgyan kyi bstan bcos rgyas 'grel* $173a_6$–b_5: *yum gyi mdor yang yongs grub kyi chos nyid stong nyid du gsungs pa shin tu yang bden pa 'thad de / de ltar gyi tshe de rang stong du gsungs kyi / gzhan stong du ma gsungs so zhe na / de ni ma yin te / mdor / sems ni sems ma mchis pa ste / sems kyi rang bzhin ni 'od gsal ba'o / zhes bstan pas / glo bur ba'i sems rang stong yin pas ma mchis pa dang / rang bzhin 'od gsal gzhan stong yin pas 'od gsal ba'o zhes mi stong par bstan pa dang / rje btsun gyis / bla med chos kyis stong ma yin / ces chos nyid bla na med pa gang yin pa'i chos de rang gi ngo bo mi stong par gsungs la / don de gsal bar / 'phags pa 'jam pa'i dpal gyis / phung po rnam dpyad stong pa nyid / chu shing bzhin du snying po med / rnam pa kun gyi mchog ldan pa'i / stong nyid de ltar 'gyur ma yin / ces phung po sogs kun btags pa dang / gzhan dbang gi chos thams cad rang gi ngo bo la rnam par dpyad pa na / rang gi ngo bo stong pa nyid de / dper na chu shing snying po med pa bzhin yin la / yongs grub rnam pa kun gyi mchog dang ldan pa'i stong nyid de ni spyir dpyad mi nus pa dang / ji ltar dpyad kyang rang gi ngo bos stong pa de ltar 'gyur ba ma yin te / de lta bu'i ye shes mchog de nyid las gzhan du mi 'gyur ba'i phyir zhes gsung ngo.* Also quoted and translated in Mathes, "Eighth Karma pa" 91–92.

74. Mathes, *Direct Path* 318–320.

75. Mathes, *Direct Path* 354.

76. Mathes, "Twenty-One Differences" and *Direct Path.*

77. Mathes, "Eighth Karma pa" 92.

78. For Higgins, zhentong is here a philosophical orientation that helps to approach indivisible union. Higgins and Draszczyk, *Mahāmudrā and the Middle Way* I.60–61, II.51, and II.68.

79. Mikyo Dorje, *Phyag rgya chen po'i sgros 'bum* 152_{1-4}: "Given that one's mind—[buddha] nature, luminosity, and natural awareness—is established as pure in terms of cause, path, and fruition, the relative truth is the innate nature of mind free of the hindrances of

dharmin (phenomena), and the ultimate truth is the innate nature free of elaboration, the dharmatā free of hindrances. The two [truths] are one, and just like water poured into water, one does not block the other" (*des na rang sems snying po 'od gsal ba tha mal gyi shes pa rgyu lam 'bras bur rnam dag sgrub pas gnyug ma sems nyid chos can sgrib bral kun rdzob kyi bden pa dang gnyug ma spros bral chos nyid sgrib bral don dam gyi bden pa gnyis gcig go gcig gis mi 'gegs par chu la chu bzhag pa ltar . . .*). Also quoted and translation in Mathes, "Eighth Karma pa" 88.

80. Mathes, *Direct Path* 66–67.

81. Kongtrul refers here to Rong ston's (1367–1449) fourfold division of being unconditioned, namely, in terms of not arising and ceasing due to (1) causes and conditions, (2) karma and defilements, (3) a mental body, and (4) whether the subject in question appears to disciples as something that arises and ceases. Tsultrim Gyamtsho and Fuchs, *Buddhanature* 103–104.

82. Kongtrul otherwise nearly copies Dolpopa's *Ratnagotravibhāga* literally. For the deviation, Kongtrul Lodro Taye, R*gyud bla ma'i bshad srol* 32b$_{1-5}$.

83. Komarovski, *Visions of Unity* 231 and 380 n. 38.

84. *Shes bya kun khyab mdzod* vol. 2, 543$_{13}$–557$_{8}$.

85. Kongtrul Lodro Taye, *Shes bya kun khyab mdzod* vol. 3, 61$_{17}$–64$_{19}$.

86. Personal conversation with Pönlop Rinpoche (Kathmandu, Feb. 2013). Limited time allowed me to verify this only for the paragraphs immediately preceding the zhentong presentation, that is, the ones on "Resultant Madhyamaka" and the "Synopsis of the Main Points of the Prāsaṅgika Philosophical Tenet System." See the second Karma Trinle: *Karma'i shing rta* vol. 1, 386$_{5}$–388$_{11}$; and Kongtrul Lodro Taye, *Shes bya kun mkhyab mzdod* vol. 2, 540$_{9}$–542$_{23}$.

87. Karma Trinle II, *Karma'i shing rta* vol. 1, 388$_{15-17}$: *bcom ldan 'das kyis gsang sngags bla na med pa'i rgyud du yang / de la bye brag smra ba bstan / mdo sde pa yang de bzhin no / de nas rnal 'byor spyod pa nyid / de yi rjes su dbu ma bstan / zhes gsungs pa ltar ro.*

88. Callahan, *Treasury of Knowledge* 247.

89. Karma Trinlepa II, *Karma'i shing rta* vol. 1, 388$_{17-21}$.

90. Karma Trinlepa II, *Karma shing rta* vol. 1, 390$_{22}$–391$_{1}$.

91. Mathes, "Tāranātha's Presentation" 197–198. For the copied part, see Tāranātha, *Gzhan stong snying po* 503$_{1}$–506$_{6}$; and Kongtrul: *Shes bya kun khyab mdzod* vol. 2, 546$_{17}$–549$_{17}$.

92. Tāranātha, *Gzhan stong snying po* 505$_{7}$–506$_{3}$: *des na [[a]chos thams cad[a]] stong pa nyid dang / [[a]chos thams cad[a]] stong nyid med par khas len pa gzhan stong lugs yin gyi / rang stong par grags pa'i lugs la nang 'gal yod do / des na sangs rgyas kyis gsungs pa'i rang stong rnam dag ni kun rdzob rang stong du gnas pa 'di yin cing / ngo bo nyid med pa yang gsum po 'di yin pas rang stong ma nor bar smra ba dang / ngo bo nyid med smra ba yin des ni gzhan stong smra ba rnams yin la / legs ldan dang / sangs rgyas skyangs sogs rang stong smra ba dang / ngo bo nyid med smra bar grags pa ni 'jig rten phal pa la grags pa gtso bor byas pa yin no.*

[a]The 'Dzam thang edition reads *chos nyid* instead of *chos thams cad.* Draszczyk, *Anwendung der* Tathāgatagarbha-*Lehre* 183.

93. Draszczyk, 183.

94. Tāranātha, *Gzhan stong snying po* 506$_{7}$–511$_{7}$, is not copied by Kongtrul.

95. Mathes, "Tāranātha's Presentation" 219–20.

96. Kongtrul Lodro Taye, *Shes bya kun khyab mdzod* vol. 2, 550$_{1-4}$: *lugs 'dir rnam shes las 'das pa spros pa thams cad dang bral ba'i ye shes kyi ngo bo nyid bden grub tu bzhed*

kyang / spros bral gyi ye shes de 'dus ma byas yin pa'i phyir don dam gyi bden pa dngos por smra ba'i skyon thams cad las grol bar gsungs so.

97. Kongtrul Lodro Taye, *Shes bya kun khyab mdzod* vol. 2, 551_{14-17}: *yang snying po rtag par 'dod pa mu stegs kyi lugs so zer ba yang snying po'i mdo rnams la dgag pa byed par zad la / rtag pa'i don rgyun gyis rtag pa la 'dod pa'ang mi 'thad de rgyun gyis rtag pa tsam ni 'khor ba dang gzung 'dzin kun yang yin pa'i phyir . . .*

98. Mathes, "Twenty-One Differences" 293.

99. Kongtrul Lodro Taye, *Shes bya kun khyab mdzod* vol. 3, 61_{17}–64_{19}; for an English translation, Barron, *Treasury of Knowledge* 139–143.

100. Mathes, "Twenty-One Differences" 315.

Bibliography

Abbreviations for Sanskrit Sources

MA: *Madhyamakāvatāra*, edited by Li Xue Zhu. *China Tibetology* 1 (2012): 1–16.

MAVBh: *Madhyāntavibhāgabhāṣya*. Edited by Gadjin M. Nagao. Tokyo: Suzuki Research Foundation, 1964.

MAVṬ: *Madhyāntavibhāgaṭīkā*. Edited by S. Yamaguchi. Nagoya: Librairie Hajinkaku, 1934.

MSA: *Mahāyānasūtrālaṃkāra*. Edited by Sylvain Lévi. Paris: Librairie Honoré Champion, 1907.

MSABh: *Mahāyānasūtrālaṃkārabhāṣya*. MSA.

PV: *Pramāṇavārttika*. Edited by Yūsho Miyasaka. *Acta Indologica* 2 (1972): 1–206.

PVin: *Pramāṇaviniścaya*. Edited by Ernst Steinkellner. Vienna /Beijing: Austrian Academy of Sciences Press /China Tibetology Publishing House, 2007.

RGV: *Ratnagotravibhāga Mahāyānottaratantraśāstra*. Edited by Edward H. Johnston. Patna: The Bihar Research Society, 1950. (Includes the *Ratnagotravibhāgavyākhyā*.)

RGVV: *Ratnagotravibhāgavyākhyā*. RGV.

Tibetan Sources

Karma pa III Rang byung rdo rje. *Zab mo nang gi don zhes bya ba'i gzhung bzhugs* (block print). Published together with the *rNam shes ye shes 'byed pa* and the *bDe bar bshegs pa'i snying po bstan pa*. Rumtek Monastery, 1970.

———. *Rang 'grel: Zab mo nang gi don gsal bar byed pa 'i 'grel pa bzhugs so* (block print). N.p., n.d. (The work was composed at the O rgyan kyi mkhan po padma 'byung gnas kyi sgrub gnas in 1325 [$92b_6$]).

Karma pa VII Chos grags rgya mtsho. *Tshad ma rigs gzhung rgya mtsho*. Vol. 2, *Mngon sum le'u*. Seattle: Nitartha, 2009.

Karma pa VIII Mi bskyod rdo rje. *Sku gsum ngo sprod rnam bshad: Sku gsum ngo sprod kyi rnam par bshad pa mdo rgyud bstan pa mtha' dag gi e vaṃ phyag rgya*. Sarnath: Vajra Vidya, 2013. 3 vols.

———. "Phyag rgya chen po'i sgros 'bum," edited by sKyo brag dpa' brtan. *Nges don phyag rgya chen po'i bang mdzod*. sKyo brag bshad grwa legs bshad chos gling, Thos pa dga' rtsom sgrig khang, n.d.

———. "dBu ma gzhan stong smra ba'i srol 'byed." In *dBu ma gzhan stong skor bstan bcos phyogs bsdus deb dang po*, 13–48. Rumtek: Karma Shri Nalanda Institute, 1990.

———. *Shes rab kyi pha rol tu phyin pa'i lung chos mtha' dag gi bdud rtsi'i snying por gyur pa gang la ldan pa'i gzhi rje btsun mchog ti dgyes par ngal gso ba'i yongs 'dus brtol gyi ljon pa rgyas pa zhes bya ba bzhugs so.* A reproduction of the dPal spungs (?) block prints by Zhwa dmar Chos kyi blo gros. Rumtek: Rumtek Monastery, n.d.

Karma Phrin las pa I. "Dris lan yid kyi mun sel zhes bya ba lcags mo'i dris lan bzhugs." In *The Songs of Esoteric Practice (mGur) and Replies to Doctrinal Questions (Dris lan) of Karma Phrin las pa*, 88–92. Reproduced from prints of the 1539 Rin chen ri bo blocks. New Delhi: Ngawang Topgay, 1975.

Karma Phrin las pa II. *Karma shing rta.* Zhin hwa, Bod ljongs bod yig dpe skrun khang, 2011. 2 vols.

Kong sprul Blo gros mtha' yas. *rGyud bla ma'i bshad srol: Theg pa chen po rgyud bla ma'i bstan bcos snying po'i don mngon sum lam gyi bshad srol dang sbyar ba'i rnam par 'grel pa phyir mi ldog pa seng ge'i nga ro zhes bya ba bzhugs so.* Rumtek: Rumtek Monastery, n.d.

———. *Shes bya kun khyab mdzod.* Beijing: Mi rigs dpe skrun khang, 1982. 3 vols.

Si tu pa Chos kyi byung gnas and 'Be lo tshe dbang kun khyab. *Bka' brgyud gser phreng rnam thar zla ba chu shel gyi phreng ba.* Sarnath: Vajra Vidya, 2005. 2 vols.

Tāranātha. "gZhan stong snying po ces bya ba bzhugs so." In *rJe btsun Tāranātha'i gsung 'bum bzhugs so* vol. 4, 491–514. Leh: Namgyal & Tsewang Taru, 1982–1985.

Secondary Sources

Barron, Richard, translator. *The Treasury of Knowledge, Book Seven and Book Eight, Parts One and Two: Foundations of Buddhist Study and Practice*, by Kongtrul Lodro Taye. Boston: Snow Lion, 2012.

Brunnhölzl, Karl. *The Center of the Sunlit Sky: Madhyamaka in the Kagyü Tradition.* Ithaca: Snow Lion, 2004.

———, translator. *In Praise of Dharmadhātu: Nāgārjuna and the Third Karmapa, Rangjung Dorje*, by Nāgārjuna and Rangjung Dorje. Ithaca: Snow Lion, 2007.

Burchardi, Anne. "A Look at the Diversity of the Gzhan stong Tradition." *Journal of the International Association of Tibetan Studies* 3 (2007): 1–24.

———. "The Role of Rang rig in the Pramāṇa-Based Gzhan stong of the Seventh Karmapa." In *Mahāmudrā and the Bka'-brgyud Tradition. PIATS 2006: Proceedings of the Eleventh Seminar of the International Association for Tibetan Studies, Königswinter 2006*, edited by Roger Jackson and Matthew Kapstein, 314–344. Andiast: International Institute for Tibetan and Buddhist Studies, 2011.

Callahan, Elizabeth M., translator. *The Treasury of Knowledge, Book Six, Part Three: Frameworks of Buddhist Philosophy*, by Kongtrul Lodro Taye. Ithaca: Snow Lion, 2007.

Draszczyk, Martina. *Die Anwendung der* Tathāgatagarbha-*Lehre in Kong spruls Anleitung zur* Gzhan stong-*Sichtweise.* Vienna: WSTB, 2015.

Franco, Eli. *Dharmakīrti on Compassion and Rebirth.* Vienna: WSTB, 1997.

Higgins, David, and Martina Draszczyk. *Mahāmudrā and the Middle Way: Post-Classical Kagyü Discourses on Mind, Emptiness and Buddha-Nature.* Vienna: WSTB, 2016.

Kano, Kazuo. *Buddha-Nature and Emptiness: rNgog Blo-ldan-shes-rab and the Transmission of the "Ratnagotravibhāga" from India to Tibet.* Vienna: WSTB, 2016.

Komarovski, Yaroslav. *Visions of Unity: The Golden Paṇḍita Shakya Chogden's New Interpretation of Yogācāra and Madhyamaka.* Albany: State University of New York Press, 2011.

MacDonald, Anne. "Knowing Nothing: Candrakīrti and Yogic Perception." In *Yogic Perception, Meditation and Altered States of Consciousness*, edited by Eli Franco in collaboration with Dagmar Eigner, 133–168. Vienna: Austrian Academy of Sciences, 2009.

Mathes, Klaus-Dieter. "Tāranātha's Presentation of *trisvabhāva* in the *gZhan stong snying po*." *Journal of the International Association of Buddhist Studies* 23, no. 2 (2000): 195–223.

———. "Tāranātha's 'Twenty-One Differences with Regard to the Profound Meaning': Comparing the Views of the Two *gŹan stoṅ* Masters Dol po pa and Śākya mchog ldan." *Journal of the International Association of Buddhist Studies* 27, no. 2 (2004): 285–328.

———. "'Gos Lo tsā ba gZhon nu dpal's Commentary on the *Dharmatā* Chapter of the *Dharmadharmatāvibhāgakārikās*." *Studies in Indian Philosophy and Buddhism, University of Tokyo* 12 (2005): 3–39.

———. "The Ontological Status of the Dependent (*paratantra*) in the *Sandhinirmocanasūtra* and the *Vyākhyāyukti*." In *Indica et Tibetica: Festschrift für Michael Hahn zum 65. Geburtstag von Freunden und Schülern überreicht*, edited by by Konrad Klaus and Jens-Uwe Hartmann, 323–339. Vienna: Arbeitskreis für tibetische und buddhistische Studien, 2007.

———. *A Direct Path to the Buddha Within: Gö Lotsāwa's Mahāmudrā Interpretation of the Ratnagotravibhāga*. Boston: Wisdom, 2008.

———. "The Original *Ratnagotravibhāga* and Its Yogācāra Interpretation as Possible Indian Precedents of *Gzhan stong* ('Empti[ness] of Other')." *Hōrin* 18 (2015/2017): 119–140.

———. "The Eighth Karma pa Mi bskyod rdo rje (1507–1554) on the Relation between Buddhanature and Its Adventitious Stains." *Critical Review for Buddhist Studies* 22 (2017): 63–104.

Pecchia, Cristina. *Dharmakīrti on the Cessation of Suffering: Critical Edition with Translation and Comments of Manorathanandin's Vṛtti and Vibhūticandra's Glosses on Pramāṇavārttika II.190–216*. Leiden: Brill, 2015.

Rheingans, Jim. *The Eighth Karmapa's Life and His Interpretation of the Great Seal: A Religious Life and Instructional Texts in Historical and Doctrinal Contexts*. Bochum: Projekt Verlag, 2017.

Schmithausen, Lambert. "Philologische Bemerkungen zum Ratnagotravibhāga." *Wiener Zeitschrift für die Kunde Südasiens* 15 (1971): 123–177.

———. "Zu D. Seyfort Rueggs Buch 'La Théorie du Tathāgatagarbha et du Gotra.'" *Wiener Zeitschrift für die Kunde Südasiens* 17 (1973): 123–160.

Seyfort Ruegg, David. *La théorie du tathāgatagarbha et du gotra: Études sur la sotériologie et la gnoséologie du Bouddhisme*. Paris: École française d'Extrême-Orient, 1969.

Sponberg, Alan. "The Trisvabhāva Doctrine in India and China: A Study of Three Exegetical Models." *Bukkyō bunka kenkyūjo kiyō* 21 (1981): 97–119.

Stearns, Cyrus. *The Buddha from Dolpo: A Study of the Life and Thought of the Tibetan Master Dolpopa Sherab Gyaltsen*. Albany: State University of New York Press, 1999.

Takasaki, Jikido. *A Study on the Ratnagotravibhāga (Uttaratantra) Being a Treatise on the Tathāgatagarbha Theory of Mahāyāna Buddhism*. Rome: Istituto Italiano per il Medio ed Estremo Oriente, 1966.

Thrangu Rinpoche. *A Song for the King: Saraha on Mahāmudrā Meditation*. Commentary: Khenchen Thrangu Rinpoche. Translator of the Song and Editor: Michele Martin. Translator of the Oral Commentary: Peter O'Hearn. Boston: Wisdom, 2006.

Tsultrim Gyamtsho Rinpoche and Rosemarie Fuchs. *Buddhanature: The Mahayana Uttaratantra Shastra with Commentary*. Ithaca: Snow Lion, 2000.

Vetter, Tilmann. *Dharmakīrti's Pramāṇaviniścayaḥ*. Vienna: Austrian Academy of Sciences, 1966.

Zimmermann, Michael. *A Buddha Within: The Tathāgatagarbhasūtra—The Earliest Exposition of the Buddha-Nature Teaching in India*. Tokyo: The International Research Institute for Advanced Buddhology, 2002.

6

Buddha-Nature

"Natural Awareness Endowed with Buddha Qualities" as Expounded by Zhamar Kacho Wangpo

Martina Draszczyk

Kacho Wangpo, the Second Zhamarpa (1350-1405), received the *upāsaka* and bodhicitta vows at the age of seven from the Fourth Karmapa Rolpai Dorje (1340-1383) at Tsonang in Central Tibet. At the age of eighteen he took his final monastic ordination from Dondrub Pel. According to the hagiography written by the Fourth Zhamarpa (1453–1524), he studied extensively all fields of Buddhist philosophy and meditative training, both on the basis of the sūtras and tantras, with teachers from various traditions. Moreover, he spent much time in various hermitages.[1] He is considered an adept whose teachings had a major impact on the Mahāmudrā transmission of the Kagyu order.[2] As the main lineage-holder of Karmapa Rolpai Dorje's teachings, he passed on the esoteric instructions of the Karma Kagyu tradition to the Fifth Karmapa Dezhin Shekpa (1384-1415). His *Collected Works* comprise seven volumes, in which he covers a broad range of subjects relating to philosophical and meditative training as transmitted in the Kagyu tradition. Even though at present just half of these works are extant, they already allow some insight into his teaching system.

Here priority will be given to selected passages regarding his views on ultimate reality and buddha-nature (*tathāgatagarbha*) by posing the question whether—in a way similar to the Third Karmapa Rangjung Dorje (1284–1339)—he can be considered an exponent of that type of Mahāmudrā view that includes zhentong-associated elements and that has been cultivated in the Karma Kagyu tradition up to today.

Some Views of Karmapa Rangjung Dorje and Gampopa

It was only retrospectively, starting approximately a century after his death, that Karmapa Rangjung Dorje came to be repeatedly labeled an exponent of the zhentong view. He himself never employed this term and did not contrast a rangtong ("being empty of self") with a zhentong ("being empty of other") view. He is referred to as a zhentong exponent, for example, by the First Karma Trinlepa Chokle Namgyal (1456-1539) in his *Discussion to Dispel Mind's Darkness*[3] and by Kongtrul Lodro Taye (1813-1899) in his *Immaculate Vajra Moonrays*[4] and his *Treasury of Knowledge*.[5] What made later authors depict him as such seems to be his remarkable way of integrating the Yogācāra and the Madhyamaka doctrines with the teachings on buddha-nature and his strong emphasis that buddha-nature is primordially endowed with sublime buddha qualities.[6]

Even though Rangjung Dorje does not refer to buddha-nature as being logically equivalent to zhentong, he explicitly teaches, in tune with *Ratnagotravibhāga* I.155,[7] that while the mind as such is merely obscured by fleeting adventitious defilements, it is not empty of unsurpassable qualities. Moreover, with reference to the *Hevajra Tantra* he affirms that all sentient beings are indeed buddhas, a fact merely obscured by the adventitious stains.[8]

In making use of these source texts, Rangjung Dorje is following the lead of Gampopa (1079-1153), the founding father of what is referred to as Dakpo Mahāmudrā. As is well known, Gampopa combined two lineages, the Kadampa order, tracing back to Atiśa's (982-1054) teaching activities in Tibet, and the Mahāmudrā tradition, in which he was instructed by his guru Milarepa (1040-1123), and which goes back to Marpa (1012-1097), who in turn had been led into it by his main Indian teachers, Nāropa (1016-1100) and Maitrīpa (986–1063). Gampopa was the one who—in his instructions for the practice of Mahāmudrā—made frequent use of the expression "natural awareness" (*tha mal gyi shes pa*), identifying it with coemergent wisdom (**sahajajñāna*),[9] a term going back to the Indian siddha tradition. He points out that cyclic existence and the nature of buddhahood share the same ground, given that both are subsumed within the genuine mind.[10] And he specifies that sentient beings and buddhas do, in fact, have the same nature. Whether a given individual is a sentient being or a buddha depends, therefore, only on whether the adventitious defilements have been removed, that is, whether realization of the genuine mind is actualized or not. In his *Elegant Public Teachings* Gampopa states: "If one wonders whether there is a connection between both sentient beings and buddhas, [the answer is:] It is not the case that there is no connection; thus there is a connection. . . . It is the connection of having the same nature."[11] Consequently, with respect to the two truths, Gampopa points out that appearances and emptiness are inseparable from each other, in that appearances as such are empty and the dynamic energy of emptiness manifests as appearances. Therefore, appearances and emptiness are not a duality.[12] Again, as is stated in his *Elegant Public Teachings*:

> Appearances as such are empty, and the creative energy of emptiness manifests as appearances. Therefore, appearances and emptiness are not a duality. Saṃsāra as such is nirvāṇa. Nirvāṇa as such appears as

> saṃsāra. Therefore, saṃsāra and nirvāṇa are not a duality. The essence of happiness is emptiness. The essence of suffering also is emptiness. Thus happiness and suffering are not a duality. Flaws and qualities, in not being a duality, are of one flavor. What is to be relinquished and the remedy, in not being a duality, are of one flavor.

Moreover, Gampopa emphasizes that the mind is not essencelessness but coemergent wisdom,[13] which pertains to both the mind's emptiness and luminosity.[14] He maintains that the characteristic of the mind's essence is that realization has always been spontaneously present in it as the four buddhakāyas[15] or, in other words, that all qualities of enlightenment inherently and primordially exist within it as such.

As previously mentioned, Rangjung Dorje in this regard follows in the footsteps of Gampopa. Yet he is more explicit in his explanations regarding buddha-nature. In one of his short treatises, which obviously is to be understood from a tantric perspective, he plainly equates natural awareness with buddha-nature,[16] pointing out that the sixty-four qualities of buddhahood are the inherent qualities of this nature: "The sixty-four qualities are a coarse [description]; each one of the unhindered manifestations of this [buddha element] is said to comprise tens of millions [of qualities]."[17] Moreover, he incorporates the presentation of the three natures as taught in the Yogācāra system.[18] And, in addition to the already mentioned *Ratnagotravibhāga* I.155, which describes buddha-nature as empty of the adventitious but not empty of unsurpassable qualities,[19] he also refers to *Ratnagotravibhāga* I.51cd, in which buddha-nature is said to be unchanging: "As before, so it is afterward: it is of an unchangeable nature."[20]

Moreover, Rangjung Dorje draws a clear distinction between "mind as such" (*sems nyid*) in the sense of suchness as the ground of all pure aspects of the mind (i.e., the various *buddhajñāna*s) and the "all-ground consciousness" (ālayavijñāna) as the ground of impure (i.e., dualistic) mental activities.[21]

It was because of these features in Rangjung Dorje's works that later generations of Kagyu scholars called him a zhentongpa. Yet, for various reasons, his position cannot be identified with the zhentong expounded in the Jonang tradition, whose masters, such as Dolpopa Sherab Gyaltsen (1292–1361) and Tāranātha (1575–1634), are usually considered as the main representatives of the orthodox zhentong view. In fact, in comparing Rangjung Dorje's teachings with the zhentong expositions of these two Jonang masters, one is struck by a number of decisive differences.

First of all, Rangjung Dorje does not use Dolpopa's famous term "all-ground wisdom" (**ālayajñāna*), which the latter contrasts with the "all-ground consciousness." Likewise, Rangjung Dorje does not stress a permanent dharmakāya in the way the Jonang tradition does. His emphasis, rather, reflects the Indian siddha tradition of speaking about the "mind as such," which is inherently pure regardless of whether the mind is temporarily covered by adventitious defilements or not. This true nature, whether called dharmatā, buddha-nature, or dharmakāya, is the ground of everything that manifests as dependent arising and thus as simultaneous arising and disintegrating.[22]

Even more striking is the difference regarding the two truths. According to Jonang doctrine, the two truths cannot be considered inseparable, given that the conventional truth is rangtong and nonexistent, whereas the ultimate truth (buddha-nature) is zhentong and truly existent. The relationship between the two truths is thus explained by Dolpopa as "a difference that negates an identity" (*gcig pa bkag pa'i tha dad pa*). Thereby he points out that a relationship of the conventional to the absolute truth cannot be defined, for given the nonexistence of conventional truth it cannot be related to the ultimately existing absolute truth. Dolpopa therefore compares the two truths to two separate kingdoms or to darkness and light.[23] This Jonang view is incompatible with the essential view of the Kagyu Mahāmudrā tradition outlined earlier—that is, the inseparability of the two truths—a view maintained by virtually all Kagyu masters regardless of their positions on zhentong. Consequently they do not consider the self-empty conventional as something categorically different from the ultimate, inasmuch as both share the same nature, namely, emptiness. The only difference between buddhas and sentient beings, again, is that the latter have not realized emptiness and appearances for what they are, a position that reflects the teachings of Indian siddhas such as Saraha.[24]

From Rangjung Dorje's point of view, the two truths cannot be said to be either the same or different from each other. In his eyes, the perfect nature (i.e., the unchanging) is free from false imagining, that is, the dependent nature and the imagined nature. Still, the perfect nature is not essentially different from the pure aspect of the conventional truth—that is, mere appearances, the unmistaken[25]—thus explicitly underlining his view of the inseparability of appearances and emptiness, or of the two truths. He thereby emphasizes that buddha-nature is the unity of the two truths.

From the period of the fifteenth century until the present day, Kagyu masters do not hesitate to label Karmapa Rangjung Dorje as a zhentong proponent, even though they were fully aware of the differences he had with Jonang doctrine. Examples in this regard are Karma Trinle and Kongtrul Lodro Taye, both of whom pointed out such differences between the two teachings. Karma Trinle explains the following decisive difference between Rangjung Dorje's views and those of Jonang scholars. According to him, the Jonang zhentong masters understand ultimate truth or "nondual wisdom" (i.e., buddha-nature together with its qualities) as an ultimate and permanent metaphysical entity, whereas Rangjung Dorje avoids attributing such ontological status to buddha-nature. Karma Trinle points this out when explaining Rangjung Dorje's understanding in terms of "ultimate truth being *truly* established":

> From the *Ocean of Treatises on Valid Cognition and Reasoning*: "While the statement that 'nondual wisdom is established as ultimate truth' means '. . . established as what is ultimate truth,' it does not assert that it is 'truly established,' that is, permanent, stable and enduring.'[26] Some

> think that if something is established as ultimate truth, then it must be truly established. These people have not investigated [the matter]; they are just confused about the term 'truth.' It is, for example, as follows: Even though [something is] established as conventional truth, it need not therefore be truly established. Hence the general run of zhentong proponents these days and the writings of the glorious Rangjung differ. Also, the statement of my teacher, the All-knowing One [Karmapa Chodrak Gyatso], that rangtong and zhentong are not mutually contradictory is well taught, so that this meaning can be understood. Thus buddha-nature is to be explained in this way, as existing as the great freedom from extremes, the inseparability of appearance and emptiness, and the unity of the two truths.[27]

And Kongtrul Lodro Taye, who even considers Rangjung Dorje as one of the three great system-founding charioteers[28] for zhentong, acknowledges the varieties of zhentong positions:

> Based on the twenty sūtras on the essence of the definitive meaning in the last wheel of the dharma, on the five works of Maitreya and on the teaching traditions of Nāgārjuna, Asaṅga and their successors, here in Tibet too—from the two translators Zu and Tsen (11th c.) up till the present day—the teaching and study tradition known as Zhentong Madhyamaka arose according to circumstances.[29]

One can only speculate what he meant by "according to circumstances." Presumably, in the context of Kagyu Mahāmudrā, which, as well known, is the heart of the Kagyu tradition, this pertains to the view of the inseparability of the two truths and the understanding that what is established as ultimate truth is not asserted to be "truly" established and thus not as a permanent and enduring ontological entity, but simply as "true" in that it is nondelusive.[30] Thus, in the Kagyu tradition, this core view of the inseparability of conventional and ultimate truth is essential. In this regard one should also be aware of the fact that for Rangjung Dorje the actual conventional is "mere appearances"—which must be understood against the background of the mind's clear aspect not being distinct from its empty aspect. This position provides room for maintaining the mind as such, an immanent buddha-nature endowed with the qualities of enlightenment, without reifying either buddha-nature or its qualities.

THE COMMON GROUND OF ZHENTONG-ASSOCIATED POSITIONS

It might be helpful, at this point, to sum up a few features that serve as common ground on which masters have, justifiably or not, been labeled as exponents of a zhentong view:

The teachings on buddha-nature are considered an essential part in the distinctive teaching systems, being taken as they are in a definitive (*nītārtha*) and not just in a provisional sense (*neyārtha*).

Sūtras associated with the third dharmacakra and corresponding śāstras are explicitly referred to.

Buddha qualities (dharma / *guṇa*) are taken to be inseparable from the mind; thus the mind is considered to be primordially and inherently endowed with these qualities.

The ultimate truth is described in an affirmative way and considered to be beyond the reach of the conceptual mind.

Adventitious defilements are considered to be illusory and empty.

Moreover, it appears that these masters lay strong emphasis on the soteriological basis for the path of meditation: the focus lies on the view that the ultimate, the fruit of buddhahood, is already present in the ground and that qualities are not something that has to be newly developed. Thus, the confidence that buddha-nature with its inherent qualities can be actualized by following a suitable path places the spiritual endeavor, in both the sūtric and tantric contexts, within a framework that adepts in their striving for enlightenment can relate to. This is independent of the fact that for actually attaining this goal any conceptual notion about ultimate reality needs to be relinquished.

The following analysis of some views of the Second Zhamarpa Kacho Wangpo looks into the question of how he—in underpinning Kagyu Mahāmudrā—affirms buddha-nature with its inherent qualities without reifying it into something truly existent.

ZHAMAR KACHO WANGPO'S TEACHING SYSTEM

To judge by a number of texts contained in his *Collected Works*, Kacho Wangpo appears to have followed rather closely the views of Gampopa.

In the following section, selected excerpts from his writings will show his stance toward (1) rangtong and zhentong; (2) sentient beings, the buddhakāyas, and inherent buddha qualities; (3) the second and third cycles of the Buddha's teachings; (d) the naturally present and unfolded potentials; (4) the dharmakāya, natural awareness, and buddha-nature; and (5) the mind's luminosity at the present moment. Unfortunately, Kacho Wangpo's commentary on the *Ratnagotravibhāga*, *The Key Clarifying the Definitive Essence: A Summary of the Mahāyānottaratantra*,[31] and his *Praise of Buddha Qualities*[32] are not extant. Both would have certainly provided more details in this regard.

Rangtong and Zhentong

Kacho Wangpo's short text *A Dharma-Discourse Clarifying Emptiness [from the Perspective] of Those Who Have Entered the Supremely Profound*[33] provides a short comparison of rangtong and zhentong. Here, in terms of conventional truth, Kacho Wangpo endorses zhentong as phrased in *Ratnagotravibhāga* I.155.[34] In ultimate terms, however, he states that "what is empty of what and how" is not something that can be observed. He bolsters this view with a quote from the *Kāśyapaparivarta Sūtra*. In doing so, he is clearly ruling out the notion of buddha-nature as a permanent metaphysical ontological entity, and he focuses on the point that any given phenomenon is illusory. From his perspective, this holds true for both adventitious saṃsāric features, of which buddha-nature is empty, and pure phenomena nirvāṇic features, of which buddha-nature is not empty. In this way—as will become evident also in other works quoted later—he speaks in positive terms of buddha-nature endowed with qualities, yet without attributing any reifying characteristics to either buddha-nature or its qualities:

> I pay homage to the supremely profound emptiness, emptiness endowed with the most supreme of all features. According to the [zhentongpas], that which undergoes change [i.e., the adventitious] discontinues and comes to an end; likewise that which is without mistakenness [i.e., buddha-nature] is the perfect end and abides [timelessly] without reversal. Thus, [the zhentongpas consider] rangtong and zhentong [respectively] nonultimate and ultimate. They describe [zhentong] in definitive terms as supreme, and [rangtong] as different from it, and hold that [the former] is real, is the ultimate. They posit [it alone] as definitive, as that which penetrates the supremely profound, the freedom from extremes, and so on, and which differs from [all] else. Yet the conducting of detailed tenet-related discussions on topics such as impermanence is not unreasonable, given that in the *Laṅkāvatāra Sūtra* it is said:
>
>> Mahāmati, the emptiness of one thing of another (*itaretaraśūnyatā*) is the lowest of all types of emptiness. Therefore you should abandon it.[35]
>
> That being so, in other sūtras the point that is clearly taught is:
>
>> The [buddha] element is empty of the adventitious, which has the characteristic of being separate from it. It is not empty of unsurpassable qualities, which cannot be separated from it.[36]

> [I shall] explain how one should look at this: It presents [what] conventional fruition and the [buddha] potential are not empty and empty of: [the former] is [not empty] of the endless confusion [posed by] illusory phenomena and other illusory states [and] phenomena, while the [buddha] potential is empty of [them]. Ultimately, however, emptiness [in terms of] what is [empty] of what and how is by its very nature not [something that can be] observed, being the supreme emptiness, as taught in detail in the *Ārya Ratnakūṭa Sūtra*:
>
>> Emptiness does not make phenomena empty. Phenomena as such are empty. The lack of characteristics does not make phenomena devoid of characteristics. Phenomena as such are devoid of characteristics. Wishlessness does not turn phenomena into something that is not desirable. Phenomena as such are wishless. Those who distinguish thus, Kāśyapa, distinguish among the teachings of the Middle Way. Kāśyapa, those who [attempt to] understand emptiness by observing emptiness [in terms of what is empty of what] totally fail with respect to what I taught.[37]
>
> Therefore, when one should not cling to emptiness [conceptually], what need to speak of clinging to [it in terms of] characteristics such as permanence, and so on.[38]

Keeping this position of Kacho Wangpo regarding zhentong in mind, the following excerpts of a number of his writings will show in what sense he considers the mind as such to be primordial buddhahood with inconceivable illusory qualities.

Sentient Being, Buddhakāyas, and Inherent Buddha Qualities

In his *Miscellaneous Sayings*, Kacho Wangpo speaks about his "heartfelt" view regarding sentient beings. Primordially they *are* the three buddhakāyas, in that their essence is emptiness, their nature is clarity (i.e., awareness), and their characteristics are appearances:

> The excellent instructions of the tradition that stems from them:[39]
> The inseparability of appearance and emptiness;
> The meaning of freedom from extremes;
> The great freedom from action, the genuine state, non-arising,
> nonceasing;
> The unconditioned, the expanse, the state free from elaboration;
> Personally experienced self-awareness, prajñāpāramitā;
> Non-elaboration, the medicine that heals the plague of elaboration;

The essence of the dharmakāya, which abides primordially;
This abode [is] inseparable from all the three worlds.
This is the highest of views—immaculate [and] glorious.
With regard to it, various specific yānas have taught
An endless number of specific terms:
In the sūtras, it pertains to the sūtras of definitive meaning;
In empowerments, to the *samaya* of the *ratna* empowerment;
In the tantras, to the tantras [that teach] the inseparability of means and wisdom;
In the key instructions, to Mahāmudrā without elaborations.
The buddha-nature is primordially pure, without boundaries,
And indicated by an endless number of terms such as these:
Non-observable emptiness and prajñāpāramitā.
These and the like are employed to name the essence of the mind.
All terms such as the inseparability of clarity and emptiness, or of awareness and emptiness, are used
To name the nature of the mind.
Vast appearances, great compassion, and the like are [employed]
To name the characteristics of the mind.
Accordingly, it is certain that even if the buddhas of the three times
Searched for eons, they would not find anything
Beyond the three modes of the mind's abiding.
In short, what is the point in being long-winded?
The host of phenomena other than the three [types]—appearances, awareness, and emptiness—
Do not in the least exist; these are words from my heart.
That the three aspects [of the mind]—essence, nature, and characteristics—
Are the three buddhakāyas, was taught in all sūtras and tantras.
This is why it is certain that all sentient beings of the three realms
Primordially are the three buddhakāyas as such.[40]

In the same text, when he goes into the details of an individual's spiritual progress on the path, he homes in on emptiness or the essential, all-pervading ground of suchness, the dharmadhātu. In this context, the dharmadhātu is identified as that which is endowed with sixty-two qualities, which is likely a mistaken way of naming the sixty-four qualities associated with perfect buddhahood, that is to say, the thirty-two qualities of freedom and the thirty-two qualities of maturation.

Kacho Wangpo emphasizes that these qualities primordially abide in the mind-stream of sentient beings, and that therefore at the time of actualizing the fruit of enlightenment no new attainments are won. In other words, the fruit of enlightenment is attained when all adventitious phenomena—which, as pointed out in the last quotation, are empty—are cleared away, thus allowing for the unfolding of the buddhakāyas' qualities. His point is thus that the mind is empty of features that are different from its nature (i.e., the adventitious stains), but not empty of the buddha qualities embodied in the buddhakāyas. In his *Miscellaneous Sayings* he does not employ the term "buddha-nature," though he does give a series of synonyms of dharmadhātu that, according to him, is not mere emptiness but something more, namely, as previously specified, primordially endowed with inherent qualities. Yet, as we saw earlier in his *A Dharma-Discourse Clarifying Emptiness [from the Perspective] of Those Who Have Entered the Supremely Profound*, he cautions the reader not to reify emptiness as something and so not to attribute the nature of permanence, and so forth, to buddha-nature. In his *Miscellaneous Sayings* he says:

> Here, in terms of an individual's practice, it is to be done in five [successive] forms, namely, the ground, the path, the clearing away of hindrances, the enhancement, and the fruition. In this regard, the all-pervading ground is the dharmadhātu, suchness. The latter, moreover, abides primordially in the mind-stream of all sentient beings. Due to the confusion caused by the conceptualization of mentation, they wander in the cyclic existence of the three realms and are tormented by various sufferings. Nevertheless, as to the dharmadhātu, there is never any change to it, because it is beyond the extremes of good and bad. Also, as primordially it is something that is endowed with sixty-two qualities, it is certain that at the time of the fruit these are not newly attained.
>
> In this regard, the dharmadhātu is the utterly supreme, that which is not transformed by anything, the kāya of spontaneous presence. It is unconditioned [and] paramount beyond comparison. It pervades all sentient beings, is unchanging throughout beginningless time [and] free from all defilements. It is the genuine nature, free from all extremes. Its nature is explained as primordial purity. For some it is known as prajñāpāramitā, [for others] as the unchanging ground, as dharmakāya, as ultimate truth, and as definitive meaning. The manifold [expression of] thought in the different sūtras and tantras [when it comes to] this teaching are one in their essential meaning.[41]

The Second and Third Cycles of the Buddha's Teaching

In his *Buddha-Nature Explained with Reference to the Sūtras*,[42] Kacho Wangpo emphasizes the harmony between the middle and the third cycles of the Buddha's teachings, equating emptiness, or dharmatā, as presented in the Prajñāpāramitā sūtras with the naturally present potential (*prakṛtisthagotra*) of buddha-nature as taught in the sūtras associated with the third cycle of teachings. One should keep in mind that, for him, as pointed out earlier, this is not to be understood as a mere negation, but as suchness endowed with buddha qualities.

> In short, what in the middle [cycle of] teachings is taught as so-called suchness—dharmatā, the expanse that is free from elaboration—is buddha-nature, that is, the naturally present potential, which is taught in the last [cycle of] teachings. This is to be understood in detail from the basket of Mahāyāna sūtras.[43]

He also specifies that some make the mistake of taking the term "buddha-nature" as an equivalent for mere emptiness and thus cling to the extreme view of annihilationism. Therefore, he quotes the *Mahāparinirvāṇa Sūtra*, in which it is said that when buddha-nature is described as being empty, immature beings take this as meaning nonexistence, whereas wise people understand that the permanent and enduring buddha-nature resembles a magical illusion.[44] This is reminiscent of a description by the First Karma Trinle in his commentary on the *Abhisamayālaṃkāra* V.20, where he characterizes the wisdom of the nonduality of object and subject as not existing as an ultimately true own-being, inasmuch as it arises dependently.[45] Kacho Wangpo says elsewhere: "Ultimately, a Victor's kāyas are the equal flavor [of] appearance and emptiness. Just like reflections in a mirror and the color of Indra, they (i.e., the kāyas) are said to be precisely of a nature that cannot be grasped and that is unobstructed."[46] This is in line with Karmapa Rangjung Dorje's explanations of "mere appearances" (*snang tsam*) and the care he takes when affirming buddha qualities not to reify buddha-nature and its qualities.

The Naturally Present and Unfolded Potentials

Kacho Wangpo mentions that there are some who consider the unfolded potential (*paripuṣṭagotra*) as the cause that brings about the qualities of awakening. He himself, however, emphasizes that according to the Kagyu tradition these qualities abide throughout beginningless time in the naturally present potential as the quintessential nature of the four buddhakāyas and the five wisdoms. Thus the unfolded potential is nothing but the manifestation of the naturally present potential once what is not part of the essential nature of the mind (i.e., adventitious defilements caused by conceptualizations) is cleared away:

> In short, the intention of all [cycles of] teachings is not contradictory, but one [in meaning]. There are various ways of desiring the actualization of such [buddha] qualities as the powers, depending on [which approach to] the unfolded potential—studying and so forth—[one cultivates]. However, according to the words of the venerable masters of the past, they abide primordially wholly pure as the very nature of the four embodiments and the five wisdoms and, awakening from ignorance, one's boundless qualities, [present] from the beginning, unfold. Therefore, this is called the Ādibuddha (i.e., the original Buddha). As one practices in this way, when precisely the reality of the naturally

> present [potential] has become manifest and its unsurpassable reality has become perfect—referred to as having become unobstructed—this is explained as the naturally present [potential] having become self-illuminating. In general, by practicing without there being anything whatsoever to relinquish or to adopt, to refute or to establish, the mode of being of all phenomena, the original ground, will quickly be realized.[47]

The Dharmakāya, Natural Awareness, and Buddha-Nature

Kacho Wangpo, in his *A Clear Mirror of Pointing-Out Instructions Regarding One's Mind*,[48] deals with the mind's true nature in line with Gampopa's pointing-out instructions. He offers synonyms for the realization of the mind as such, for ultimate reality, and equates the dharmakāya with the typical Mahāmudrā terms "natural awareness" and "buddha-nature":

> . . . this very essence of the mind is called "uncontrived natural awareness," the "genuine essence of one's own mind," the "essential nature of being," the "way of abiding of the ultimate dharmakāya," the "wisdom of emptiness, of essencelessness," the "prajñāpāramitā as the basic reality," the "immaculate heart of the Victors" [i.e., buddha-nature], and the "coemergent wisdom of great bliss."[49]

In the same text he gives some explanation of the buddhakāyas and the five aspects of buddha wisdom. The underlying theme is the inseparability of appearance and emptiness:

> Is it not so that while the present natural awareness is non-arisen, it appears as if it were something arisen? This is a buddha's so-called svabhāvikakāya. Is it not so that what is without abiding and ceasing presents itself as if it were? This is the so-called form-kāya [comprising] the sambhoga- and nirmāṇa[kāyas]. Is it not so that these three are of equal flavor, being inseparable from each other? This is the so-called beginningless, uncontaminated dharmakāya. As for an explanation of the five wisdoms: The indivisibility of both clarity and emptiness of the essence of natural awareness—this is the so-called mirrorlike wisdom. That within this suchness everything of equal flavor is the so-called wisdom of equality. Liberating all conceptualizations [each] in their own place is called the discriminating wisdom. By virtue of an undiluted total clarity there is the task-accomplishing wisdom. The primordial nature of all these as being inseparable from each other is to be understood as the so-called dharmadhātu wisdom, is it not?[50]

The Mind's Luminosity at the Present Moment

Finally, Kacho Wangpo brings everything together in "just this"—in the mind's luminosity at the present moment—expressed by such terms as "natural awareness," "the ultimate," "the coemergent" and mahāmudrā, leading on to his statement that saṃsāra and nirvāṇa merely appear to be different, but are one in nature:

> The true nature of the mind in the present is luminosity, immaculate throughout beginningless time. This very nature is called the "genuine nature." Even though it is labeled with hundreds of names, "natural awareness," "the ultimate," "the coemergent, mahāmudrā, "the Ādibuddha," or the dharmakāya, it is "just this." It is not established in terms of any objective existence, being by nature the expanse of great emptiness, the actuality of everything, clarity, awareness, and unobstructedness. It is the appearance of everything, great wisdom, the equal flavor of the dharmadhātu and wisdom. It is the *mudrā* of unity, the victory [in virtue] of the equality of saṃsāra and self-liberation. These [represent] the great unity. Truly in this regard, saṃsāra and nirvāṇa, while appearing to be different, are one in nature.[51]

In proclaiming, on the one hand, the naturally present potential as the core nature of the four kāyas and five wisdoms, and the dharmakāya, and so forth, as not established with any real existence, on the other, Kacho Wangpo avoids the extremes of nonexistence and reified existence. He does not go into further details. However, in this regard and by way of comparison, it might be worthwhile to look into an extract from a song by one of his successors, the Sixth Zhamarpa Chokyi Wangchuk (1584-1630), who relates back to the "melodious lion's roar of the Kagyu forefathers." Chokyi Wangchuk, too, was retrospectively said to have maintained the zhentong view and, more specifically, the zhentong view of the expanse:[52]

> "Darkness being empty of light" and "light being empty of darkness"—as illustrated by these examples, how can there be any clinging to the extremes of permanent real existence? To get to the core of these examples: Since darkness does not inherently exist, it can very well be called rangtong. At that point [of realization], a self-luminous [mind] arises—free from conceptualizations that involve clinging to darkness—that may indeed be called, "zhentong." This self-luminosity is not established as self-luminosity either, which is why it may well be called rangtong. Still, that arising of self-luminosity free from the stains of clinging to mere luminosity can be given a name too; it can very well be called, "zhentong." Once wisdom is without elaboration, and when it is evaluated from within the expanse of wisdom, the one

> limit, that of the extreme of existence, is self-empty, as is the other limit, that of the extreme of nonexistence. The illusory appearance of wisdom—dependent arising that appears unobstructedly—is without the superimposition and depreciation on the part of either extreme and therefore said to be zhentong, that is, freed from both extreme limits. Thus all phenomena of saṃsāra and nirvāṇa, as mere appearances, are not simply nonexistent, nor do they truly exist of their own nature: As mere appearances, they are like illusions, not observed to be existent. In terms of the ultimate, however, it is not the case that they become nonexistent due to being empty of merely what is something else or the like. When discussed as a mere philosophical system, it does not matter how [doctrine] is phrased. The object of the view is to be free from elaboration. "Free" does not refer to the view of annihilationism but to the unity of appearance and emptiness. Thus the melodious lion's roar of the Kagyu forefathers resounds.[53]

Kacho Wangpo, at the end of his *A Clear Mirror of Pointing-Out Instructions Regarding One's Mind*, specifies that such unity, or buddha-nature for that matter, is precisely the mind at present:

> In short, this your present mind—uncontrived, undefiled, unaltered—is itself the heart of all the Victors. From the beginning there is nothing to remove and nothing to add. In this regard you should not have the slightest—not the slightest—hope or fear about anything whatsoever. While everything is equal, abide unwavering in the ground of your own mind.[54]

In emphasizing the mind of the present moment, Kacho Wangpo is indirectly referring to the continuous flow of natural awareness moment by moment, where there is nothing to remove and nothing to add, and one cannot but be reminded of the corresponding verse from the *Ratnagotravibhāga*:

> There is nothing to be removed from it and nothing to be added.
> The real should be seen as real, and seeing the real, you become liberated.[55]

This is also very much in line with quotes one finds in some of Kacho Wangpo's other texts. One example is his *Five Topics of Conversation*, where he quotes extensively from the *Anavataptanāgarājaparipṛcchā*:

> In this regard, what is the perfect purity of the mind? The nature of mind cannot become afflicted, because the nature of mind is luminosity; that is, it is not obscured by painful adventitious kleśas. In this regard,

> a bodhisattva does not open up any chance for adventitious upakleśas [to arise], because his very nature is utterly pure.[56]

Here Kacho Wangpo emphasizes his recurring theme: the perfect purity or in other words, mind's emptiness is equivalent with luminosity. Mind as such is not obscured by afflictions, and so is free from the adventitious.

Conclusion

Zhamarpa Kacho Wangpo's extant texts are mainly concerned with meditation. He does not elaborate much on philosophical theories or debated issues. It is therefore of no surprise that one does not find long discussions regarding the views of rangtong versus zhentong for all that—as his *Dharma-Discourse* translated earlier in this chapter shows—this topic was a burning issue during his time.

As is evident from that text, Kacho Wangpo restricts his endorsement of zhentong to conventional truth. Buddhahood and buddha-nature are "empty of the endless confusion that consists in illusory phenomena," but they are "not empty of the illusory other phenomena [i.e., buddha qualities]." In ultimate terms, however, he states that "what is [empty] of what and how is by its very nature not [something that can be] observed."[57]

Kacho Wangpo explicitly confirms that the unconditioned dharmadhātu is the unsurpassable supreme, that which is not transformed by anything. He states that it is endowed with the sixty-two qualities, meaning that the fruit of buddhahood is immanent and not something that is newly acquired. Thus, he emphasizes that according to the Kagyu tradition the buddha qualities abide as the mind's true nature primordially, as the naturally present potential, as the very nature of the four embodiments and the five wisdoms.[58] Yet, in doing so, he avoids reifying buddha-nature and its qualities into something permanent and enduring, and so does not attribute any ontological status to them.

In his *Necklace of the Immaculate Vajra Moon*,[59] a collection of quotes from sūtras, śāstras,[60] and tantras meant to illustrate the ultimate meaning, Kacho Wangpo quotes forty-three sūtras, predominantly ones said to be associated with the third cycle of teachings, and emphasizes the harmony between the middle and the third cycles of the Buddha's teachings. He equates dharmatā, emptiness as presented in the Prajñāpāramitā sūtras, with the naturally present potential of buddha-nature endowed with buddha qualities as taught in the third cycle. And he stresses the inseparability of saṃsāra and nirvāṇa, along with the identity of natural awareness with buddha-nature and its qualities. All of these points belong to the core teachings of Kagyu Mahāmudrā as set forth by Gampopa and further elucidated by the Third Karmapa Rangjung Dorje.

Furthermore, he makes use of classical dzogchen categories: distinguishing the mind's essence as emptiness, its nature as clarity or awareness, and its characteristics as appearances and compassion, among other things. In doing so, he is fully in line with Karmapa Rangjung Dorje, for example, in the latter's *Profound Inner Principles*.[61]

The main focus in Kacho Wangpo's writings appears to be the inseparability of appearance and emptiness—certainly a feature that is entirely different from the Jonang zhentong approach—and to equate the mind's true nature, natural awareness, with buddha-nature, which is inherently and primordially endowed with buddha qualities. Yet, just as adventitious defilements are illusory, so too, from the perspective of Kacho Wangpo, are buddha qualities. In short, his positive appraisal of reality, of buddha-nature, which is natural awareness endowed with buddha qualities—and thus his endorsement of other-emptiness—is restricted to conventional truth.

Notes

This research was made possible thanks to generous funding from the Austrian Science Fund (FWF) for the project entitled "Buddha Nature Reconsidered: Mi bskyod rdo rje and the Post-Classical Tibetan *Tathāgatagarbha* Debates" (Project number P28003-G24) supervised by Klaus-Dieter Mathes and hosted by the Department of South Asian, Tibetan, and Buddhist Studies at the University of Vienna. I would also like to gratefully acknowledge improvements to my English by Philip H. Pierce.

1. *Chos kyi rje mkha' spyod dbang po'i dus gsum gyi rnam par thar pa rin po che dbang gi rgyal po'i phreng ba*, in ZCsb vol. 1, 365.

2. Personal communication with the Fourteenth Zhamarpa Mipam Chokyi Lodro (1951-2014).

3. *Dri lan yid kyi mun sel*, in KPsb vol. ca. 88-92. For a complete translation of this text, see Higgins and Draszczyk, *Mahāmudrā and the Middle Way* vol. 2, 88-91, *Discussion to Dispel Mind's Darkness: A Reply to Queries of [Bsod nams lhun grub, the Governor of] Lcags mo*.

4. *Gzhan stong dbu ma chen po'i lta khrid rdo rje zla ba dri ma med pa'i 'od zer*, in *Bka' mdzod* vol. 58 (vol. ca.), 738ff. See an English translation by Draszczyk, "Putting Buddha Nature into Practice" 259-282; a German translation by Draszczyk, *Anwendung der Tathāgatagarbha-Lehre* 323-352; and another English translation by Brunnhölzl, *When the Clouds Part* 831-853.

5. *Shes bya kun khyab mdzod* vol. 1, $460_{2\text{-}13}$. The ten books of the *Shes bya kun khyab mdzod* are by now published in English under the title *The Treasury of Knowledge* (10 vols.).

6. For a study of Rang byung rdo rje's view and the question whether he teaches zhentong, see Mathes, *Direct Path* 51-75, and Brunnhölzl, *Luminous Heart* 95-109.

7. RGV I.155: "The [buddha] element is empty of the adventitious, which has the characteristic of being separate from it. It is not empty of unsurpassable qualities, which cannot be separated from it" (*śūnya āgantukair dhātuḥ savinirbhāgalakṣaṇaiḥ / aśūnyo 'nuttarair dharmair avinirbhāgalakṣaṇaiḥ*). Compare the translation in Takasaki, *Study on the Ratnagotravibhāga* 301. For Rangjung Dorje's explanation of this, see *De bzhin gshegs pa'i snying po bstan pa'i bstan bcos*, $58_{2\text{-}4}$.

8. *Hevajra* II, iv, 69: "Sentient beings are actually buddhas, though they are covered by adventitious stains. Once these [defilements] are removed, no doubt [remains] that they are buddhas." See Snellgrove, *Hevajra Tantra* p. 2, (tr.) 107, (Skt.) 70, (Tib.) 71. *sattvā buddhā eva*

kiṃ tu āgantukamalāvṛtāḥ // tasyāpakarṣanāt sattvā buddhā eva na saṃśayaḥ. For Rangjung Dorje's explanation of this, see *De bzhin gshegs pa'i snying po bstan pa'i bstan bcos* 55_{8-9}.

9. *Chos rje dwags po lha rje'i gsung / gnas lugs gnyis kyi man nag dang go cha gnyis kyi man nag la ldeb*, in Gsb vol. 3, 494_1: "[Gampopa] said, '*Sahaja* wisdom is this very presence of natural awareness [right here and] now'" (*saha dza'i ye shes ni / da lta tha mal gyi shes pa yod pa 'di nyid yin gsung*).

10. *Chos rje dwags po lha rje'i gsung / bka' tshoms dang phyag rgya chen po lnga ldan*, in Gsb vol. 3, 509_{1-2}: "Cyclic existence and the nature of buddhahood are one within the genuine mind" (*'khor ba dang / sangs rgyas kyi rang bzhin gnyug ma'i sems su gcig*).

11. *Mgon po zla 'od gzhon nus mdzad pa'i tshogs chos legs mdzes ma*, in Gsb vol. 1, 451_3-452_2: *sems can dang sangs rgyas gnyis la 'brel ba yod dam med snyam na / 'brel ba med pa ma yin te 'brel ba yod / . . . bdag nyid gcig pa'i 'brel ba yod.*

12. *Mgon po zla 'od gzhon nus mdzad pa'i tshogs chos legs mdzes ma*, in Gsb vol. 1, 441_5-442_2: *snang ba nyid stong pa yin la / stong pa nyid kyi rtsal snang bar shar ba yin pas na snang ba dang stong pa gnyis su med pa'o / 'khor ba nyid mya ngan las 'das pa / mya ngan las 'das pa nyid 'khor bar snang bas na 'khor 'das gnyis su med pa'o / bde ba'i ngo bo yang stong pa / sdug bsngal gyi ngo bo yang stong par 'dug pas na bde sdug gnyis su med / skyon dang yon tan gnyis su med de ro gcig / spang bya dang gnyen po gnyis su med de ro gcig pa'o.*

13. *Chos rje dwags po lha rje'i gsungs / tshogs chos yon tan phun tshogs*, in Gsb vol. 1, 511_{4-5}: "The truth is the actual fact that the nature of the mind is not nonexistent; coemergent wisdom is the truth" (*bden pa ni sems kyi ngo bo med pa ma yin pa'i don / lhan cig skyes pa'i ye shes bden pa yin*).

14. *Chos rje dwags po lha rje'i gsungs / tshogs chos yon tan phun tshogs*, in Gsb vol. 1, 554_{4-5}: "The nature of the mind is emptiness. The nature of the mind is luminosity. The nature of the mind is nonconceptual. It is referred to as natural awareness" (*sems kyi rang bzhin stong pa nyid yin / sems kyi rang bzhin ni 'od gsal ba yin / sems kyi rang bzhin rtog med yin / tha mal gyi shes pa zhes bya*).

15. *Chos rje dwags po lha rje'i gsung / gnas lugs gnyis kyi man nag dang go cha gnyis kyi man nag la ldeb*, in Gsb vol. 3, 451_{2-3}: "The characteristic of the essence [of the mind] is that, primordially, realization is spontaneously present as the four kāyas" (*ngo bo nyid kyi mtshan nyid ni / rtogs pa gdod ma nas sku bzhir lhun gyi grub pa yin*).

16. *De bzhin gshegs pa'i snying po bstan pa'i bstan bcos*, 56_{14-18}: "It is precisely this natural awareness that is called the dharmadhātu, the nature of the Victorious Ones (i.e., buddhas). It is not enhanced by the Noble Ones, it is not devalued by sentient beings. Although it is expressed by many terms, its meaning is not understood through expressions" (*tha mal shes pa de nyid la / chos dbyings rgyal ba'i snying po zer / bzang du 'phags pas btang ba med / ngan du sems can gyis ma btang / tha snyad du ma brjod mod kyang / brjod pas de yi don mi shes*).

17. *De bzhin gshegs pa'i snying po bstan pa'i bstan bcos*, 56_{18-19}: *de nyid ma 'gag rol pa la / yon tan drug cu rtsa bzhi po / rag pa yin te re re la'ang / bye ba phrag rer gsungs pa yin.*

18. *De bzhin gshegs pa'i snying po bstan pa'i bstan bcos*, 57_{12-15}: "At present, the opposite of these [buddha qualities] comes about. By virtue of the fact that that which is has not been determined the way it is, the nonexistent is thought to exist, which creates the imagined [nature]. The conceptualizations produced thereby are the dependent [nature]. Unaware of the perfect [nature], we are entangled in our own doings" (*de lta de la 'gal bar byed / yin la yin bzhin ma nges pas / med la yod rtog kun brtags byas / des bskyed rtogs de gzhan dbang yin / yongs su grub pa ma shes pas / rang gi byas pas gzings pa ste*). See also Draszczyk, *Anwendung der Tathāgatagarbha-Lehre* 124–125.

19. See n. 7.

20. RGV I.51cd: *yathā pūrvaṃ tathā paścād avikāritvadharmatā //*.

21. Mathes, *Direct Path* 57–58, and Draszczyk, *Anwendung der Tathāgatagarbha-Lehre* 125. It is obvious that this view is based on *Mahāyānasaṃgraha* I.45–49. Regarding this passage, Higgins and Draszczyk, *Mahāmudrā and the Middle Way* 192 and n. 557.

22. Draszczyk, *Anwendung der Tathāgatagarbha-Lehre* 131.

23. Stearns, *Buddha from Dolpo* 106–110.

24. There is no certainty about Saraha's dates. Modern historians place him around the eight or ninth century, largely based on dates assigned to some of the texts on which he commented. Traditional Tibetan sources place him within a period encompassing several hundred years, anywhere from two generations after the life of the Buddha (as a disciple of the Buddha's son Rāhula) to the second century (as Nāgārjuna's guru). See Braitstein *Adamantine Songs*.

25. *Chos dbyings bstod pa'i rnam bshad*, 169_{13-14}: "The two [aspects of the perfect], the unchangeable and unmistaken, are taken [respectively] as the defining characteristics of the two truths. Acceptance by common consent (*lokaprasiddha*) and acceptance by reason (*yuktiprasiddha*) are varieties of the apparent truth" (translated by Mathes, *Direct Path* 68; *bden pa gnyis kyi rang gi mtshan nyid kyis 'gyur ba med pa dang phyin ci ma log pa gnyis so / 'jig rten pa dang rigs pa'i grags pa ni / kun rdzob bden pa'i bye brag ste*).

26. Quote not identified.

27. *Zab mo nang don gyi rnam bshad snying po*, in RDsb vol. 14, 396_4–397_3: *rig[s] gzhung rgya mtsho las / gnyis med kyi ye shes don dam pa'i bden par grub par gsungs pa yang / de don dam bden pa yin par grub ces pa'i don yin gyi / de bden grub rtag brtan ther zug tu bzhed pa ma yin no / kha cig / don dam pa'i bden par grub na bden par grub dgos so snyam pa de dag ni ma brtags pa ste / bden pa zhes pa'i ming tsam la 'khrul par zad pas so / dper na / kun rdzob pa'i bden par grub kyang bden par grub mi dgos pa bzhin no / de'i phyir / ding sang gi gzhan stong smra ba phal dang / dpal rang byung gi bzhed pa la khyad par yod pa ste / bdag gi bla ma thams cad mkhyen pa'i zhal snga nas / rang stong gzhan stong mi 'gal zhes gsung pa'ang don 'di thugs su byon pa'i legs par bshad pa'o / de ltar na mtha' bral chen po snang stong dbyer med bden gnyis zung 'jug tu yod pa'i sangs rgyas kyi snying po de'i tshul brjod par bya'o*. Likewise he explains in his commentary on *Abhisamayālaṃkāra* V.20: *Mngon rtogs rgyan rtsa 'grel gyi sbyor ṭīka 'jig rten gsum sgron la 'jug pa* 614_{5-7}: "The wisdom of the nonduality of object and subject, moreover, is of such a nature that it does not exist as an ultimately true own-being, inasmuch as it is dependently arisen, as if, for example, it were a magical illusion" (*gzung 'dzin gnyis med kyi ye shes de yang chos can / don dam par bden pa'i ngo bo nyid du med pa yin te / rten cing 'brel bar 'byung ba yin pa'i phyir / dper na sgyu ma bzhin du'o*).

28. See Draszczyk, *Anwendung der Tathāgatagarbha-Lehre* 324. See also Brunnhölzl, *When the Clouds Part* 832.

29. *Gzhan stong dbu ma chen po'i lta khrid rdo rje zla ba dri ma med pa'i 'od zer*, in *Bka' mdzod* vol. 5, 738–739: *de la 'khor lo tha ma nges don snying po'i mdo sde nyi shu / byams chos sde lnga / klu thogs yab sras kyi gzhung lugs la brten / lo tsā ba gzu btsan rnam gnyis nas bzung da lta'i bar du bod kyi yul 'dir yang gzhan stong dbu mar grags pa'i 'chad nyan srol ka ci rigs par byung ba las . . .*

30. See above and n. 27.

31. *Theg pa chen po rgyud bla ma'i bsdus don nges pa'i snying po gsal byed pa'i lde mig*.

32. *Bde bar gshegs pa'i yon tan stod pa'i tshig bcad rnam par dbye ba*.

33. *Mchog tu zab mo la zhugs pa'i stong pa nyid gsal bar byed pa'i chos kyi rnam grangs*, in ZKsb vol. 2, 605_1-606_4.

34. See n. 7.

35. LAS, 75_{19}: *mahāmate itaretaraśūnyatā sarvajaghanyā sā ca tvayā parivarjayitavyā //.*

36. See n. 7.

37. *Kāśyapaparivartasūtra* H87, vol. 40, $230b_5$-$321a_4$: the text translated here in this chapter gives an abbreviated version of the original wording in the sūtra.

38. *Mchog tu zab mo la zhugs pa'i stong pa nyid gsal bar byed pa'i chos kyi rnam grangs*, in ZKsb vol. 2, 605_1-606_4: *stong pa nyid mchog tu zab mo stong pa nyid rnam par kun gyis mchog dang ldan pa de la phyag 'tshal lo /'di na gang dag ldog rnam par chad pa mur thug pa ltar / phyin ci log rnam par spangs pa yang dag pa'i mtha' ma log ma min par zhugs pas / stong pa nyid rang dang gzhan gyis dam pa dang dam pa ma yin pa'i don zhes mchog dang / de las gzhan du nges par smra zhing yang dag par 'dzin pa don dam pa dang / mtha' las 'das pa la sogs pa mchog tu zab mo la nye bar zhugs pa gzhan las gzhan dang nges pa kho nar gzhag mi rtag pa la sogs pas / shes shin tu gleng pa'i grub pa'i mtha' rnam par 'god pa de dag mi rigs pa ma yin te / 'phags pa lan kar gshegs pa las ci skad du / blo gros chen po cig gis cig stong pa nyid 'di ni stong pa nyid thams cad kyi tha chad yin pas de ni khyod kyis spang par bya'o zhes gsungs so / de ltar na mdo gzhan dag la rab tu bstan pa'i don / rnam dbyer bcas pa'i mtshan nyid can / blo bur dag gis khams stong gis / rnam dbyer med pa'i mtshan nyid can / bla med chos kyis stong ma yin / zhes pa 'di ci ltar lta bshad pa / zad mi shes pa'i rnam par 'khrul pa sgyu ma lta bu'i chos kyis ngang / sgyu ma lta bu'i chos gzhan gyis tha snyad kyi 'bras bu dang / rigs mi stong pa dang stong pa rnam par gzhag gi don dam par ni nam gang gis gang ji ltar stong pa nyid rang gi ngo bos ma dmigs pa stong pa nyid mchog ste 'phags pa dkon mchog rtsegs pa las / gang stong pa nyid kyis chos rnams stong par mi byed de / chos rnams nyid stong pa gang mtshan ma med pa / chos rnams mtshan ma med par mi byed de / chos rnams nyid mtshan ma med pa gang smon pa med pas chos rnams smon pa med par mi byed de / chos rnams nyid smon pa med pa gang dag de ltar so so rtog pa de ni 'od srungs / dbu ma'i chos rnams la so sor rtog pa zhes bya'o / 'od srungs gang dag stong pa nyid du dmigs pas stong pa nyid du rtogs pa de dag ni ngas gsung rab 'di las nyams rab tu nyams par bshad do zhes rgya cher 'byung ngo / de lta bas na stong pa nyid du'ang gzung bar mi bya na rtag sogs mtshan mar 'dzin pa lta smos kyang ci dgos.* I am indebted to Khenpo Konchok Tamphel for his help with this translation. For comparison's sake, see also Gshong chen Mkhas btsun bstan pa'i rgyal mtshan (16th–17th c.), in *Gsung 'bum thang stong rgyal po*, vol. 3, 411–415, quote: $413_{4\text{-}5}$: "If rangtong were not [also] zhentong, then such rangtong would be a limited emptiness. If zhentong were not [also] rangtong, what would freedom from the discursive elaborations [as to a] self-nature refer to?" (*rang gi stong pa gzhan gyis mi stong na / de 'dra'i rang stong nyi tshe'i stong pa yin / gzhan gyi stong pa rang gis mi stong na / rang gi rang bzhin spros bral gang la zer*).

39. Referring to Saraha, Maitrīpa, Marpa, Milarepa, Gampopa, et al.

40. *Gsung sgros thor bu sna tshogs*, in ZKsb vol. 4, 260_5-261_6: *de las brgyud pa'i gdams pa phun tshogs pa / snang stong dbyer med mtha' dang bral ba'i don / bya bral chen po gnyug ma skye 'gag med / 'dus ma byas dbyings spros dang bral ba'i ngang / so so rang rig shes rab pha rol phyin / spros med spros pa'i rim nad sel ba'i sman / gdod nas bzhugs pa chos kyi sku yi ngang / srid gsum kun la dbyer med gnas pa 'di / dri med dpal ldan lta ba'i yang rtse yin / 'di la sna tshogs theg pa'i bye brag gis / ming gi bye brag dpag med rab tu gsungs / mdo yi nang nas nges pa don gyi mdo / dbang gi nang nas dam tshig rin chen dbang / rgyud kyi nang nas thabs shes dbye med rgyud / man ngag nang nas spros med phyag rgya che / bde*

gshegs snying po ka dag mtha' dang bral / de sogs ming gi dbye ba dpag med bstan / dmigs mid (med) stong nyid shes rab pha rol phyin / de sogs sems kyi ngo bo'i ming du btags / gsal stong rig stong la sogs ji snyed pa / sems kyi rang bzhin sgo nas ming du btags / snang ba che dang thugs rje che la sogs / sems kyi mtshan nyid (s)go nas ming du btags / de ltar sems kyi gnas lugs rnams gsum las / 'das pa'i chos ni dus gsum sangs rgyas kyis / bskal par btsal kyang rnyed par mi 'gyur nges / mdor na mang du smras pas ci zhig bya / snang rig stong gsum las gzhan chos kyi tshogs / rdul tsam med pa kho bo'i snying gtam yin / ngo bo rang bzhin mtshan nyid rnam pa gsum / sku gsum yin par mdo rgyud kun las gsungs / de bas khams gsum sems can thams cad kun / gdod nas sangs rgyas sku gsum nyid du nges.

41. *Gsung sgros thor bu sna tshogs*, in ZKsb vol. 4, 277_3-278_2: *'dir gang zag gcig gis nyams su len pa'i dbang du byas te / gzhi dang lam dang gegs sel dang / bogs 'don 'bras bu ste / rnam pa lngas nyams su blang bar bya ste / de la kun khyab kyi gzhi / chos kyi dbyings de bzhin nyid do / 'di yang sems can thams cad kyi rgyud la gdod ma nas bzhugs pa ste / 'di yang yid byed kyi rtogs pas kun tu dkrugs pa la brten nas / khams gsum gyi 'khor bar 'khyams shing / sdug bsngal sna tshogs kyis rab tu gzir bar gyur to / 'on kyang chos kyi dbyings la ni nam du 'ang 'gyur ba med de / bzang ba dang ngan pa'i mtha' las 'das pa'i phyir ro / 'di yang gdod ma nas yon tan drug bcu rtsa gnyis dang ldan pa zhig ste / 'bras bu'i skabs su gsar du thob pa ma yin par nges so / de yang 'dir ni chos dbyings dam pa mchog / gang gis bsgyur du med pa lhun grub sku / 'dus ma byas pa dpe dang bral ba'i mchog / 'di ni sems can kun la khyab pa ste / gdod mas 'gyur med dri ma bral ba yin / 'di ni mtha' bral gnyug ma'i rang bzhin ste / ngo bo ka nas dag pa zhes su bstan / la lar shes rab pha rol phyin zhes grags / 'gyur med gshis dang chos kyi sku zhes dang / don dam bden par nges pa'i don zhes par / mdo rgyud tha dad dgongs pa sna tshogs kyis / bstan pa 'di yang don gyi ngo bor gcig.*

42. *De bzhin gshegs pa'i snying po bstan pa'i mdo sbyar*, in ZKsb vol. 3, 55-61. In this text, Mkha' spyod dbang po quotes sūtras such as the *Tathāgatācintyaguhyanirdeśa*, the *Avataṃsaka*, the *Upālipariprcchā*, the *Anūnatvāpūrṇatvanirdeśa*, and śāstras such as Nāgārjuna's *Mahāyānaviṃśikā* and Maitreya / Asaṅga's *Ratnagotravibhāga*.

43. *De bzhin gshegs pa'i snying po bstan pa'i mdo sbyar*, in ZKsb vol. 3, $57_{1\text{-}2}$: *mdor na bka' bar pa rnams chos nyid spros pa thams cad dang bral ba'i dbyings de bzhin nyid ces gang bstan pa de ni / bka' tha ma rnams su gsungs pa'i de bzhin gshegs pa'i snying po rang bzhin du gnas pa'i rigs nyid de / zhib par theg pa chen po'i sde snod rnams las rtogs par bya ba'o.*

44. *De bzhin gshegs pa'i snying po bstan pa'i mdo sbyar*, in ZKsb vol. 3, 57_6-58_1: "In the *Mahāparinirvāṇa Sūtra*: When one teaches that buddha-nature is empty, all who are immature are induced to cultivate [the practice] faultily. The wise understand that [its] permanent and enduring [nature] is merely an illusion" (*mya ngan las 'das pa'i mdor / de bzhin gshegs pa'i snying po ni stong pa yin no zhes bstan na byis pa rnams cad pa rnams su lhung ba'i yon po bsgom par byed / shes rab can rnams kyis ni / rtag pa ther zug pa ni sgyu ma tsam du yod par shes so*).

45. See n. 27.

46. *De bzhin gshegs pa'i snying po bstan pa'i mdo sbyar*, in ZKsb vol. 3, $59_{3\text{-}4}$: *don dam par rgyal ba'i sku ni snang ba dang stong pa ro mnyam pa me long gi gzugs brnyan dang / brgya byin gyi tshon ltar gzung du med cing thogs pa med pa'i bdag nyid la brjod de . . .*

47. *De bzhin gshegs pa'i snying po bstan pa'i mdo sbyar*, in ZKsb vol. 3, $58_{1\text{-}4}$: *mdor na bka' thams cad dgongs pa mi 'gal zhing gcig pa nyid do / thos sogs rgyas 'gyur gyi rigs la bsten nas / stobs sogs kyi yon tan mngon du byed pa la 'dod tshul du ma yod kyi / rje btsun gong ma rnams kyi gsung sgros rnams las / gdod nas rang bzhin gyi rnam par dag pa / sku bzhi ye shes lnga'i bdag nyid du gnas la ma rig pa sangs zhing yon tan mtha' dag gdod nas*

rgyas pas dang po'i sangs rgyas zhes bya ste / de lta bu'i tshul gyis nyams su blangs la / rang bzhin gyis gnas pa'i don de nyid mngon du gyur pa na / bla na med pa'i don mthar son pa sgrib med du 'gyur ro zhes rang bzhin du gnas pa rang gsal du 'gyur bar gsungs so / spyir gang la'ang spang blang dgag sgrub med par nyams su blangs pas / chos thams cad kyi gnas don gdod ma'i gshis myur du rtogs par 'gyur ro.

48. *Rang sems ngo sprod gsal ba'i me long.* This text is contained not in his *Collected Works* but in the *'Bri gung bka' brgyud chos mdzod chen mo* vol. 95, 183–198.

49. *Rang sems ngo sprod gsal ba'i me long* vol. 95, 187_6–188_2: *de lta bu'i sems kyi ngo bo nyid la ma bcos tha mal gyi shes pa zhes / rang sems gnyug ma'i ngo bo zhes bya'o / dngos po gshis kyi gnas lugs zhes bya'o / don dam chos sku'i bzhugs tshul zhes bya'o / bdag med stong pa'i ye shes zhes bya'o / gzhi don shes rab phar phyin zhes bya'o / dri* [text: *tri*] *bral rgyal ba'i snying po zhes bya'o / lhan skyes bde chen ye shes zhes bya'o.*

50. *Rang sems ngo sprod gsal ba'i me long* vol. 95, $189_{3\text{-}6}$: *da lta'i tha mal gyi shes pa skye ba med bzhin du skye ba ltar snang ba zhig mi 'dug gam / de la sangs rgyas ngo bo nyid sku zhes bya ba yin no / gnas 'gag med de la de ltar song pa zhig mi 'dug gam / de la longs sprul gzugs kyi sku zhes bya'o / de gsum dbyer med ro mnyam pa zhig mi 'dug gam / de la zag med gdod ma'i chos sku zhes bya ba yin no / ye shes lnga sprod pa ni / tha mal shes pa'i ngo bo gsal stong dbyer med pa 'di nyid la me long lta bu'i ye shes zhes bya'o / de nyid du thams cad ro mnyam pa mnyam nyid ye shes zhes bya'o / rnam rtog thams cad rang sar grol bas sor rtog ye shes zhes bya'o / ma 'dres kun tu gsal bas bya grub ye shes zhes bya thams cad dbyer med gdod ma'i gshis la chos dbyings ye shes zhes bya ba yin go'am.*

51. *Rang sems ngo sprod gsal ba'i me long*, $194_{3\text{-}6}$: *da lta'i sems nyid 'od gsal ba / gdod nas dri bral 'di nyid la / gnyug ma'i snying po nyid ces bya ba / tha mal shes pa don dam pa / lhan cig skyes pa phyag rgya chen / dang po'i sangs rgyas chos kyi sku / ming brgyar btags kyang 'di kho na / 'di don cir yang ma grub pa / rang bzhin stong nyid chen po'i dbyings / gsal rig 'gag med kun gyi dngos / 'di ni kun snang ye shes che / chos dbyings ye shes ro mnyam pa / 'di ni zung du 'jug pa phyag / 'khor ba rang grol mnyam pa'i rgyal / de dag zung 'jug chen po nyid / e ma 'di la 'khor dang 'das / tha dad ltar snang rang bzhin gcig.*

52. Brunnhölzl, *Gone Beyond* 130.

53. *Rtogs brjod lta sgom spyod 'bras kyi glu*, 358_6–360_2: *snang bas stong pa'i mun pa dang / mun pas stong pa'i snang ba zhes / dpe de 'dras mtshon nas yod bden gyi / rtag pa mtha' bzung ga la yin / dper na rtsa ba hril gril na / mun pa rang bzhin med tsa na / de la rang stong los rang zer / de tshe mun par bden 'dzin gyi / kun rtog bral ba'i rang gsal zhig / shar la gzhan stong los kyang zer / rang gsal yang rang gsal du ma grub pas / de la rang stong los rang zer / gsal tsam du 'dzin pa'i dri bral ba'i / rang gsal zhig shar ba de la yang / ming 'dogs la gzhan stong los kyang zer / ye shes la spros pa med tsa na / ye shes kyi dbyings nas gzhal ba'i tshe / yod mtha'i phyogs kyang rang gis stong / med mtha'i phyogs kyang rang gis stong / ye shes sgyu ma'i snang ba ni / 'gag med du snang ba'i rten 'brel la / mtha' gnyis ka'i sgro skur med pa'i phyir / mtha' gnyis ka'i phyogs nas gzhan stong zer / des na 'khor 'das kyi chos rnams kun / snang tsam du med pa ma yin zhing / rang ngo nas bden par yod min la / snang tsam du'ang sgyu ma lta bu la / yod pa yang yin par ma dmigs shing / de don dam du gzhan gis stong lta bus / med par song pa'ang ma yin pas / grub mtha' tsam du smra ba'i tshe / brjod tshul ji ltar byas kyang rung / lta yul spros pa dang bral ba yin / bral zhes chad par blta ba'ang min / snang stong zung 'jug yin no zhes / pha bka' brgyud seng ge'i sgra dbyangs bsgrags.* The translation is my own. The text has also been translated under the title "A Pronouncement of Realization: A Song on View, Meditation, Conduct, and Fruition" in Brunnhölzl, *Straight from the Heart* 343–357.

54. *Rang sems ngo sprod gsal ba'i me long*, 195_6-196_2: *mdor na khyod kyi da lta'i sems / ma bcos ma bslad ma bsgyur ba / 'di nyid rgyal ba kun gyi thugs / gdod nas bsal [*text: *gsal] gzhag med pa la / 'dir khyod gang la 'ang re dang dogs / cung zad cung zad mi bya ste / mtha' dag mnyam yang rang sems kyi / gzhi la g.yo med bzhag par bya.*

55. RGV I.157 (J I.154): "There is nothing to be removed from it and nothing to be added. The real should be seen as real, and seeing the real, you become liberated." *nāpaneyam ataḥ kiṃcid upaneyaṃ na kiṃcana / draṣṭavyaṃ bhūtato bhūtaṃ bhūtadarśī vimucyate //* (trans. Mathes, *Direct Path* 8). See also *Abhisamayālaṃkāra* V.21 (with a slight variation in b. *prakṣeptavyaṃ na kiṃcana*); Takasaki, *Study on the Ratnagotravibhāga* 300 n. 53.

56. *Gtam gyi gzhi lnga bshad pa*, ZKsb vol. 2, 545_{3-5}: *de la sems yongs su dag pa gang zhe na / sems kyi rang bzhin ni kun nas nyon mongs par bya mi nus so / de ci'i phyir zhe na / sems ni rang bzhin kyis 'od gsal ba ste / blo bur gyis nyon mongs pa rnams kyis nyen par nyon ni mi mongs so / de la byang chub sems dpa' ni / blo bur gyi nye ba'i nyon mongs pa rnams kyi skabs mi 'byed de / de rang bzhin gyis shin tu rnam par dag pa ce . . .*

57. See n. 38 and the translation provided in the text.

58. See n. 40 and 41 and translations provided in the text.

59. *Yang dag pa'i don gyi nges pa rab tu gsal bar byed pa rdo rje zla ba dri ma med pa'i phreng pa* ZKsb, vol. 2, 501–542.

60. The authors quoted are Nāgārjuna, Asaṅga, Candrakīrti, Sahajavajra, Nāropa, Vāgīśvarakīrti, Advayavajra, and Atiśa.

61. *Zab mo nang don*. Mathes, *Direct Path* 632–664.

Bibliography

Sanskrit Abbreviations and Sources

HT: Hevajra Tantra. Edited (together with the Hevajrapañjikā Muktāvalī) by Ram Shankar Tripathi and Thakur Sain Negi. Bibliotheca Indo-Tibetica 48. Sarnath: Central Institute of Higher Tibetan Studies, 2001.

LAS: Laṅkāvatāra Sūtra. Bunyiu Nanjio (Bibliotheca Otaniensis 1). Kyoto: Otani University Press, 1923.

RGV: Ratnagotravibhāga Mahāyānottaratantraśāstra. Maitreya (ascribed). Edited by Edward H. Johnston. Patna: Bihar Research Society, 1950. (Includes the Ratnagotravibhāgavyākhyā).

Kāśyapaparivarta Sūtra, H87, vol. 40.

Tibetan Sources

Dol po pa Shes rab rgyal mtshan. "Mdo'i don bde blag tu rtogs pa." Full title: "Shes rab kyi pha rol tu phyin pa'i man ngag gi bstan bco mngon bar rtog pa'i rgyan gyi rnam bshad mdo'i don bde blag tu rtogs pa," vol. 5, 245–620. In *'Dzam-thang Edition of the Collected Works of Kun mkhyen Dol-po-pa Shes rab rgyal-mtshan*, vol. 5, 245–620. 'Dzam thang bsam 'grub nor bu'i gling gi par khang, ca. 1990.

Gshong chen Mkhas btsun bstan pa'i rgyal mtshan (16th–17th c.). *Gsung 'bum thang stong rgyal po*, vol. 3, 411–415. Thimphu: National Library Bhutan, 1984–1985.

Karma pa Mi bskyod rdo rje. *Shes rab kyi pha rol tu phyin pa'i lung chos mtha' dag gi bdud rtsi'i snying por gyur pa gang la ldan pa'i gzhi rje btsun mchog ti dgyes par ngal gso ba'i yongs 'dus brtol gyi ljon pa rgyas pa shes bya ba bzhugs so*. A reproduction of the Dpal spungs (?) block prints by Zhwa dmar Chos kyi blo gros. Sikkim: Rumtek Monastery, n.d.

———. *Dbu ma gzhan stong smra ba'i srol legs par phye ba'i sgron me*. Sikkim: Rumtek Monastery, 1972. Also: "Dbu ma gzhan stong smra ba'i srol 'byed." In *dBu ma gzhan stong skor bstan bcos phyogs bsdus deb dang po*, 13–48. Rumtek: Karma Shri Nalanda Institute, 1990.

Karma Phrin las pa phyogs las rnam rgyal. "Dri lan yid kyi mun sel." In *Chos rjes karma phrin las pa'i gsung 'bum las thun mong ba'i dri lan gyi phreng ba rnams. The Songs of Esoteric Practice (Mgur) and Replies to Doctrinal Questions (Dris-lan) of Karma-'phrin-las-pa* (KPsb). New Delhi: Ngawang Topgay, 1975 (vol. ca. 88–92). Reproduced from prints of the 1539 Rin chen ri bo blocks.

———. *Mngon rtogs rgyan rtsa 'grel gyi sbyor ṭīkā 'jig rten gsum sgron la 'jug pa*, 287–708. Seattle: Nitartha International Publications, 2006.

Karma pa Rang byung rdo rje. "De bzhin gshegs pa'i snying po bstan pa'i bstan bcos." In *dBu ma gzhan stong skor bstan bcos phyogs bsdus deb dang po*, 55–62. Rumtek: Karma Shri Nalanda Institute, 1990.

———. *Phyag chen smon lam*. Full title: *Nges don phyag rgya chen po'i bod gzhung*, vol. 11, 262–289. Che'eng-tu: Si khron dpe skrun tshogs pa, 2009.

———. "Zab mo nang don gyi rnam bshad snying po." In *Karma pa rang byung rdo rje gsung 'bum* (RDsb), vol. 14, 396_4–397_3. Ziling: mTshur phu mkhan po lo yag bkra shis, 2006.

———. "Chos dbyings bstod pa'i rnam bshad." Full title: "Dbu ma chos dbyings bstod pa'i rnam bshad." In *The Illuminating Lamp and Other Works by Karma pa rang byung rdo rje*, 157–312. Varanasi: Vajra Vidya Institute Library, 2004.

Kong sprul Blo gros mtha' yas. "Gzhan stong dbu ma chen po'i lta khrid rdo rje zla ba dri ma med pa'i 'od zer." In *'Jam mgon Kong sprul blo gros mtha' yas kyi gsung 'bum rgya chen bka' mdzod. The Expanded Edition of the Writings of 'Jam mgon Kong sprul Blo gros mtha' yas (Bka' mdzod)*, vol. 5 735–765. Reproduced from the Dpal spungs xylographs from Eastern Tibet. Delhi: Shechen, 2002.

———. *Shes bya kun khyab*. Full title: *Theg pa'i sgo kun las bdus pa gsung rab rin po che'i mdzod bslab pa gsum leg par ston pa'i bstan bcos shes bya kun khyab*, 3 vols. Beijing: Mi rigs dpe skrun khang, 1982.

Sgam po pa Bsod nams rin chen. "Chos rje dwags po lha rje'i gsungs / tshogs chos yon tan phun tshogs." In *Khams gsum chos kyi rgyal po dpal mnyam med sgam po pa 'gro mgon bsod nams rin chen mchog gi gsung 'bum yid bzhin nor bu* (Gsb), vol. 1, 505–576. Kathmandu: 2000.

———."Mgon po zla 'od gzhon nus mdzad pa'i tshogs chos legs mdzes ma." In *Khams gsum chos kyi rgyal po dpal mnyam med sgam po pa 'gro mgon bsod nams rin chen mchog gi gsung 'bum yid bzhin nor bu*, vol. 1, 333–504. Kathmandu: 2000.

———. "Chos rje dwags po lha rje'i gsung / bka' tshoms dang phyag rgya chen po lnga ldan." In *Khams gsum chos kyi rgyal po dpal mnyam med sgam po pa 'gro mgon bsod nams rin chen mchog gi gsung 'bum yid bzhin nor bu*, vol. 3, 503–608. Kathmandu: 2000.

———. "Chos rje dwags po lha rje'i gsung / gnas lugs gnyis kyi man nag dang go cha gnyis kyi man nag la ldeb." In *Khams gsum chos kyi rgyal po dpal mnyam med sgam po pa 'gro mgon bsod nams rin chen mchog gi gsung 'bum yid bzhin nor bu*, vol. 3, 403–502. Kathmandu: 2000.

Tāranātha, Jo nang rje btsun. "Gzhan stong snying po." In *Jo nang rje btsun tāranātha'i gsung 'bum*, vol. 18, 171–193. 'Dzam thang dgon, ca. 1990.

Zhwa dmar pa Mkha' spyod dbang po. "De bzhin gshegs pa'i snying po bstan pa'i mdo sbyar." In *Zhwa dmar pa mkha' spyod dbang po'i gsung 'bum* (ZKsb), vol. 3, edited by Gonpo Tseten, 55-61. Gangtok: 1978.

———. "Rang sems ngo sprod gsal ba'i me long bzhugs pa'i dbu phyogs." In *'Bri gung bka' brgyud chos mdzod chen mo*, vol. 95, edited by A mgon rin po che, 183-198. Lhasa: 2004.

———. "Gtam gyi gzhi lnga bshad pa." In *Zhwa dmar pa mkha' spyod dbang po'i gsung 'bum* (ZKsb), vol. 2, edited by Gonpo Tseten, 542-558. Gangtok: 1978.

———. "Nges don rin chen sgron me chos kyi sprin phung." *Zhwa dmar pa mkha' spyod dbang po'i gsung 'bum* (ZKsb), vol. 4, edited by Gonpo Tseten, 240-244. Gangtok: 1978.

———. "Mchog tu zab mo la zhugs pa'i stong pa nyid gsal bar byed pa'i chos kyi rnam grangs." In *Zhwa dmar pa mkha' spyod dbang po'i gsung 'bum* (ZKsb), vol. 2, edited by Gonpo Tseten, 605_1-606_4. Gangtok: 1978.

Zhwa dmar pa Chos grags ye shes. "Chos kyi rje mkha' spyod dbang po'i dus gsum gyi rnam par thar pa rin po che dbang gi rgyal po'i phreng ba." In *Thams cad mkhyen pa zhwa dmar bzhi pa spyan snga chos kyi grags pa'i gsung 'bum bzhugs so* (ZCsb), vol. 1, 378-417. Beijing: Krung go'i bod rig pa dpe skrun khang, 2009.

Zhwa dmar pa Chos kyi dbang phyug. "Rtogs brjod lta sgom spyod 'bras kyi glu." In *Nges don phyag rgya chen po'i khrid mdzod*, vol. 7, 363-378. New Delhi: Rnam par rgyal ba dpal Zhwa dmar ba'i chos sde, 1997.

Secondary Sources

Braitstein, Lara. *The Adamantine Songs (Vajragīti) by Saraha: Study, Translation and Tibetan Critical Edition*. New York: American Institute of Buddhist Studies and Columbia University Center for Buddhist Studies, 2014.

Brunnhölzl, Karl. *Straight from the Heart: Buddhist Pith Instructions*. Ithaca: Snow Lion, 2007.

———. *Luminous Heart: The Third Karmapa on Consciousness, Wisdom, and Buddha Nature*. Ithaca: Snow Lion, 2009.

———. *Gone Beyond: The Prajñāpāramitā Sūtras: The Ornament of Clear Realization, and Its Commentaries in the Tibetan Kagyü Tradition*, vol. 1. Ithaca: Snow Lion, 2010.

———. *When the Clouds Part: The Uttaratantra and Its Meditative Tradition as a Bridge between Sūtra and Tantra*. Ithaca: Snow Lion, 2014.

Draszczyk, Martina. *Die Anwendung der Tathāgatagarbha-Lehre in der bKa' brgyud-Tradition gemäß einer von 'Jam mgon Kong sprul Blo gros mtha' yas verfassten Anleitung zur* Gzhan stong-*Sichtweise*. Wiener Studien zur Tibetologie und Buddhismuskunde, Heft 87. Wien: Arbeitskreis für Tibetische und Buddhistische Studien Universität Wien, 2015.

———. "Putting Buddha Nature into Practice." In *A Gathering of Brilliant Moons: Practice Advice from the Rime Masters of Tibet*, edited by Holly Gayley and Joshua Schapiro, 251-284. Sommerville: Wisdom, 2017.

Guenther, Herbert, translator. *The Jewel Ornament of Liberation*. London: Rider and Company, 1959.

Higgins, David, and Martina Draszczyk. *Mahāmudrā and the Middle Way: Post-Classical Kagyü Discourses on Mind, Emptiness and Buddha-Nature*. Wiener Studien zur Tibetologie und Buddhismuskunde, Heft 90.1-2. Wien: Arbeitskreis für Tibetische und Buddhistische Studien Universität Wien, 2016.

Mathes, Klaus-Dieter. "Blending the Sūtras with the Tantras: The Influence of Maitrīpa and His Circle on the Formation of Sūtra Mahāmudrā in the Kagyu Schools." In *Tibetan Buddhist Literature and Practice: Studies in Its Formative Period 900–1400*, edited by Ronald M. Davidson and Christian K. Wedemeyer. Proceedings of the Tenth Seminar of the IATS, Oxford 2006, vol. 10/4, 201-227. Leiden: Brill, 2006.

———. "Tāranātha's 'Twenty-One Differences with Regard to the Profound Meaning'—Comparing the Views of the Two gŹan stoṅ Masters Dol po pa and Śākya mchog ldan." *Journal of the International Association of Buddhist Studies* 27, no. 2 (2004): 285-328.

———. *A Direct Path to the Buddha Within: Gö Lotsāwa's Mahāmudrā Interpretation of the Ratnagotravibhāga*. Boston: Wisdom, 2008.

Roerich, George N., translator. *The Blue Annals*. Reprint of the 2nd ed. (1st ed. Calcutta 1949). Delhi: Motilal Banarsidass, 1979.

Snellgrove, David L. 1959. *The Hevajra Tantra: A Critical Study*. 2 vols. London Oriental Series 6, 1-2. London: Oxford University Press, 1959.

Stearns, Cyrus. *The Buddha from Dolpo: A Study of the Life and Thought of the Tibetan Master Dolpopa Sherab Gyaltsen*, 2nd ed. (1st ed., SUNY, 1999). Ithaca: Snow Lion, 2010.

Takasaki, Jikido. *A Study on the Ratnagotravibhāga (Uttaratantra) Being a Treatise on the Tathāgatagarbha Theory of Mahāyāna Buddhism*. Serie Oriental Roma XXXIII. Rome: Istituto Italiano per il Medio ed Estremo Oriente, 1966.

7

"There Are No Dharmas Apart from the Dharma-Sphere"

Shakya Chokden's Interpretation of the Dharma-Sphere

Yaroslav Komarovski

As is well known to contemporary scholarship and demonstrated by the works contained in the present volume, the Tibetan term zhentong (*gzhan stong*, being empty of other) refers not to any one unanimous view or system of thought but to a wide variety of philosophical theories formed primarily in India and Tibet. Those theories are often contrasted with rival rangtong (*rang stong*, being empty of self)[1] theories in their interpretations of reality, buddhahood, path, and other elements of the Buddhist worldiew. While many of those elements are equally open to the zhentong and rangtong interpretations, some suit one better than the other. According to the important but largely forgotten Tibetan thinker Shakya Chokden (1428–1507) whose views will be discussed in this chapter, the dharma-sphere (*chos dbyings*)—ultimate reality and source of all dharmas—is a concept that, similar to such related concepts as the buddha-nature (*de bzhin gshegs pa'i snying po*), tends to better fit the zhentong interpretations.

The dharma-sphere figures prominently in Shakya Chokden's works, where its analysis is not limited to only those texts, such as Nāgārjuna's *Praise of the Dharma-Sphere*,[2] that explicitly explore this concept but extended to multiple writings, teachings, and traditions that do not necessarily address the dharma-sphere directly, but which in his opinion refer to it via cognate ideas and categories. Although Shakya Chokden also provides accounts of the rangtong interpretations of the dharma-sphere, it is in the zhentong context that he delves into this topic in minute detail. His interpretation of the dharma-sphere, therefore, can serve as a window for exploring details of his broader position on zhentong.[3]

The dharma-sphere is given particular attention in texts written by Shakya Chokden during the period when he openly articulated and voiced support of the zhentong philosophy—a philosophy that he presented as an authentic Madhyamaka view shared by leading thinkers of the Yogācāra, Tantra, and even Niḥsvabhāvavāda systems.[4] Providing complementary arguments and targeting diverse but related ideas, these texts present a broad, multifaceted, and shared vision of the dharma-sphere.[5]

An exhaustive study of Shakya Chokden's position on the dharma-sphere would exceed the limitations of a single book chapter, even a long one. I will therefore limit myself to discussing only those elements essential to understanding his approach. First, I will briefly discuss the place Shakya Chokden assigns to the dharma-sphere in the Mahāyāna teachings. Second, I will address his claim that nothing exists apart from the dharma-sphere. Third, I will explain his approach to the nature and function of the dharma-sphere and its relationship to other dharmas. Fourth, I will outline his position on how the dharma-sphere is utilized and manifested on the path. Fifth, and finally, I will focus on his perspective on differences and similarities between the dharma-sphere and other closely related categories.

THE DHARMA-SPHERE IN THE MAHĀYĀNA TEACHINGS

Shakya Chokden attaches great significance to the correct understanding of the dharma-sphere, arguing in *Opening a Hundred Doors* that it allows us to easily comprehend such seminal topics of Buddhist teachings as the ultimate and conventional realities, clarity and emptiness, appearance and emptiness, bliss and emptiness, among others.[6] In his opinion, numerous Mahāyāna traditions share the same basic vision of the dharma-sphere and make it the main focus of their teachings. His basic strategy, exhibited in a number of writings, is to interpret the dharma-sphere as primordial mind (*ye shes*), treat it as ultimate reality, and present that reality as the focus of multiple Mahāyāna texts and traditions that refer to it by different names but share similar understanding of its nature. In *Reply to Lodrö Zangpo*, for example, he identifies the dharma-sphere as primordial mind, also calling it "primordial mind of the dharma-sphere" (*chos dbyings ye shes*), and then argues that this primordial mind is the focal point of Mahāyāna teachings, both tantric and nontantric, where it is referred to by such names as "all-creating king" (*kun byed rgyal po*), "unmixed complete perfection" (*ma 'dres yongs rdzogs*), "spontaneity" (*lhun grub*), "revelation of the hidden" (*gab pa mngon du phyung pa*), "great perfection" (*rdzogs pa chen po*), "great seal" (*phyag rgya chen po*), and "pacifier of sufferings" (*sdug bsngal zhi byed*).[7] In *Appearance of the Sun*,[8] he argues that this primordial mind is presented as ultimate reality in the teachings of the third dharmacakra, Tantra, and Yogācāra, including Dharmakīrti's *Seven Works* (*sde bdun*), as well as Asaṅga's *Summary of Mahāyāna*[9] and *Explanation of [Maitreya's] "Sublime Continuum of the Mahāyāna."*[10]

He does acknowledge important differences in the philosophical positions of such texts as Maitreya's *Sublime Continuum*[11] and Nāgārjuna's *Praise of the Dharma-*

Sphere. According to him, the former follows the zhentong approach while the latter follows a mixed rangtong / zhentong approach. Nevertheless, he insists that the main elements of their approach to the dharma-sphere are the same, since, he argues, whenever the genuine ultimate reality is taught, it is either explicitly or implicitly conceived as primordial mind. Because the dharma-sphere is ultimate reality, it has to be primordial mind too. This allows him to freely cross-fertilize its interpretation in *Ascertainment of the Dharma-Sphere* with passages and ideas from *Sublime Continuum* and other works of Maitreya.

Overall, Shakya Chokden identifies two groups of Mahāyāna thinkers: the majority, who teach the dharma-sphere and agree among themselves in its identification; and the minority, who do not accept the actual dharma-sphere at all. In *Opening a Hundred Doors*, he posits three major types of Madhyamaka—Niḥsvabhāvavāda, Alīkākāravāda Yogācāra,[12] and Tantric Madhyamaka. In his opinion, the "mainstream" Niḥsvabhāvavāda—that approaches reality in terms of rangtong—does not accept the existence of anything apart from the emptiness as nonaffirming negation (*med par dgag pa'i stong nyid*) and simply calls that emptiness "dharma-sphere." Because all nonaffirming negations are exclusively conventional realities, this type of the dharma-sphere too is a conventional reality. Because conventional dharmas do not exist, it does not exist either.[13] In effect, he argues that the mainstream Niḥsvabhāvavāda—advocated by such thinkers as Candrakīrti and Bhāviveka—posits neither the efficient ultimate reality nor the actual dharma-sphere. Alīkākāravāda and Tantra, on the other hand, approach reality in terms of zhentong and agree in their identification of the dharma-sphere as primordial mind—the continuum that persists through all the levels of the basis, path, and result (*gzhi lam 'bras bu*).[14] This primordial mind is ultimate reality; it—and only it—exists.[15]

According to Shakya Chokden, not all Mahāyāna thinkers interpret the dharma-sphere exclusively in terms of rangtong or zhentong. This is demonstrated by his interpretation of the two collections of Nāgārjuna in *Rain of Ambrosia*, where he argues that as its final position, *Collection of Reasonings* (*rigs tshogs*) accepts neither an illustration of ultimate reality nor its direct realization, treating everything that is suitable to be an object of sounds and concepts—be it called "emptiness," "natural nirvāṇa," or "dharma-sphere"—as exclusively a conventional reality because nothing can withstand analysis inquiring into the ultimate.[16] *Collection of Praises* (*bstod tshogs*), in contrast, accepts the primordial mind of the dharma-sphere and posits it as the basis of purification on the impure level of sentient beings, as the purifier on the level of the *ārya* path, and as the fundamentally transformed primordial mind (*gnas gyur gyi ye shes*) on the level of pure nirvāṇa.[17] This ultimate primordial mind of reality (*chos nyid don dam pa'i ye shes*) is the basis of all dharmas of saṃsāra and nirvāṇa. It is experienced by the individually self-cognizing primordial mind (*so sor rang gis rig pa'i ye shes*), and it becomes the primordial mind of a buddha upon the fundamental transformation (*gnas yongs su gyur pa*). On the conventional level, this primordial mind has to be accepted as the actual ultimate reality because it is experienced by the yogic direct perception of āryas, and also because it is identified as the dharma-sphere, disposition of the *sugata*-essence (*khams bde bar gshegs pa'i snying po*), and mind-*vajra* (*sems kyi rdo rje*).[18]

Because Shakya Chokden claims that the mainstream Niḥsvabhāvavāda rangtong system does not posit the actual dharma-sphere, in his works on the topic he focuses primarily on the zhentong interpretation of the dharma-sphere shared by Alīkākāravāda, Tantra, and those writings of Niḥsvabhāvavādins—such as Nāgārjuna's *Praise of the Dharma-Sphere*—that agree with it. He refers to the mainstream Niḥsvabhāvavāda position mostly for contrast, and I am following his lead in this chapter.

Why and How Only the Dharma-Sphere Exists

In *Opening a Hundred Doors*, alluding to such statements from the *Dharmas of Maitreya* as

> There are no dharmas
> Except for the dharma-sphere.[19]

Shakya Chokden writes that all three types of Madhyamaka agree that no other dharmas exist apart from the dharma-sphere. Realization of this fact is vital, he says, because it "opens hundreds of doors of the wondrous Dharma treasury."[20] In other words, it leads to understanding numerous seminal points of Buddhist teachings.

What is the logic behind his claim of the exclusive existence of the dharma-sphere? In the same text, he writes that not only the three types of Madhyamaka but in fact *all* Buddhist tenets—including Vaibhāṣika, Sautrāntika, and Cittamātra—are in consensus that conventional or relative reality does not exist.[21] To exist, he insists, means to exist truly and really, and the only dharma that exists in such a way—according to the zhentong systems that, in contrast to the systems of rangtong, do accept true existence—is the dharma-sphere, ultimate reality itself.[22] Outlining the zhentong perspective on the dharma-sphere, in *Reply to Lodrö Zangpo* he also writes that from its final perspective, except for the dharma-sphere, no conventional dharmas at all are established by valid cognition[23]—which amounts to saying that none of them exist. Shakya Chokden's position, therefore, is that whether they accept the actual dharma-sphere or not, all Madhyamaka systems share the same view that no other dharmas exist apart from it. In the case of the zhentong systems, this entails that whatever is subsumed under the category of the dharma-sphere is automatically accepted as existent in reality; in the case of the rangtong systems, this entails that even that which is subsumed under the category of the dharma-sphere does not exist. Note that the claim of the exclusive existence of the dharma-sphere does not imply that this category includes no other dharmas at all. As we will see later, for example, Shakya Chokden argues that according to the zhentong systems, this category can encompass positive qualities of a buddha as well.[24]

The exclusive existence of the dharma-sphere can also be understood in terms of what appears to a buddha's awakened mind and therefore exists in reality, in contrast to what does not really exist and is only believed to exist by deluded minds. In *Opening a Hundred Doors*, Shakya Chokden writes that the definitive meaning expressed by all such teachings as the Great Seal (*phyag rgya chen po*), Thorough Pacifier of Sufferings (*sdug bsngal rab tu zhi byed*), Revelation of the Hidden (*gab pa mngon du phyung ba*), Severance (*gcod*), and the *Dohās* is that nothing exists apart from that which appears to the mind of a perfect buddha.[25] All that buddhas see is exclusively the dharma-sphere, and what appears to a buddha's mind is none other than that mind itself. In other words, a buddha's mind is the dharma-sphere, which in turn is all that buddhas perceive. Because buddhas are omniscient and know all existents, it follows that only the dharma-sphere exists.

In the same text, he also argues that while all Mādhyamikas accept that the buddhas' mode of seeing (*gzigs tshul*) is free from the subject-object division, Alīkākāravāda in particular understands the nondual primordial mind as self-experiencing and calls it "individual self-cognition" (*so so rang rig*).[26] In a buddha's case, there is nothing that does not appear to this mirrorlike primordial mind (*me long lta bu'i ye shes*), and thus it is said that the mind of a perfect buddha knows all multiplicity (*ji snyed pa kun*). What appears to it is exclusively the dharma-sphere and perfect buddhahood, because whatever appears to it is subsumed under (*bsdus*) the buddha mind itself.[27] Only endless purity (*dag pa rab 'byams*) exists in buddhas' own appearance (*rang snang*), and only buddhas—not sentient beings—exist from buddhas' perspective (*gzigs ngo*).[28] In other words, because a buddha's mind is both omniscient and self-experiencing, because appearances of the buddha mind are none other than the buddha mind itself, and because that mind is none other than the dharma-sphere, the dharma-sphere is all that exists.[29]

Shakya Chokden does not feel uncomfortable about claiming the exclusive existence of the dharma-sphere, on the one hand, and on the other—often in the same text and even on the same page—discussing afflictions and other stains covering it, elaborating on the processes of purification of those stains, and addressing other conventional dharmas. This is because he stresses the varying modes or perspectives from which respective observers see things. As an example, we can look at *Opening a Hundred Doors* where he addresses the following question: If all dharma-spheres (*chos dbyings ji snyed pa*, i.e., dharma-spheres of all beings) are primordially free from all stains, will it not follow that they primordially possess all buddha-qualities, such as powers and so forth? He rejects this position, arguing that such statements found in sūtric and tantric traditions as "There is nothing at all to eliminate or establish here"[30]—statements indicating that one side (of positive qualities) is primordially established while the other (of stains) is primordially nonexistent—are made in terms of the perspective of a perfect buddha. Only a buddha sees the buddha-nature fully[31]—as stainless and possessing all buddha-qualities. From the perspective of a person who is still on the path to buddhahood, there are things to eliminate and establish, because that person experiences through his own self-cognition (*rang rig*) that he has stains covering the dharma-sphere, while the positive qualities of a buddha are still hidden (*lkog gyur*) from him.[32]

Based on that reasoning, Shakya Chokden argues that the view (*lta ba*, i.e., the view of ultimate reality) has to be presented in accordance with the perspective of buddhas, while action (*spyod pa*, i.e., Buddhist practice) has to be presented in accordance with the perspective of sentient beings, distinguishing thereby between those contexts where the elimination and establishment are made and where they are not. Distinguishing between these two perspectives is similar to distinguishing between the two realities, he writes.[33] He also characterizes these two contexts as that of the view on the one hand and action and meditation (*spyod [pa] dang sgom pa*) on the other. Warning against confusing them, he argues that whenever one encounters scriptural statements about all sentient beings being possessors of the buddha-essence (*sangs rgyas kyi snying po can*), it should be understood that they are made in terms of the primordial buddhahood—not in terms of grounds and paths (*sa lam*). Ultimately (*don dam par*), no sentient beings, among others, exist, and thus no stains have to be eliminated, while buddha-powers and other positive qualities exist primordially as the dharma-sphere itself and do not have to be newly established in it. Yet, in terms of the sentient beings' perspective, the dharmas of saṃsāra, no matter how much we are accustomed to them, cannot become inseparable from the dharma-sphere and therefore have to be eliminated. Emptiness whose nature is compassion (*stong nyid snying rje'i snying po [can]*) and the other dharmas of nirvāṇa, when accustomed to, become inseparable from the primordial mind of the dharma-sphere (*chos dbyings ye shes*), and therefore have to be established.[34]

The emphasis on modes or perspectives allows Shakya Chokden not only to exclude from existence any dharma that is not subsumed under the dharma-sphere but, paradoxically, to include into this category even conventional dharmas and claim that they all are the dharma-sphere. In *Ascertainment of the Dharma-Sphere*, he articulates this position with the help of the categories of the modes of being (*gnas tshul*) and appearance (*snang tshul*). When the mode of being is emphasized, he writes, all knowables, including such conventional dharmas as eyes, for example, are posited exclusively as the dharma-sphere, primordial mind. Nevertheless, this entails neither that all knowables exist nor that they all are ultimate reality. Dharmas' conventional "parts" (*kun rdzob kyi cha*) and mode of appearance do not become ultimate reality merely because their mode of being is ultimate reality. Because provisionally the two realities are ascertained in separate ways, their individual illustrations too have to be explained separately.[35]

Shakya Chokden clearly assigns more weight to the ultimate perspective than the conventional, to the mode of being than the mode of appearance, and to the perspective of buddhas than that of sentient beings. Nevertheless, he takes into account both perspectives and stresses the need of paying due attention to contexts in which different textual statements are made. This emphasis on perspectives plays an important role in his approach to the "intersection" of the ultimate and conventional dharmas, when the dharma-sphere and other dharmas are put side-by-side and the arising of the latter from the former, as well as transformation of mind, elimination of afflictions, and so forth, are addressed. The next section explores further the nature and function of the dharma-sphere, focusing on this issue in more detail.

The Dharma-Sphere versus Other Dharmas

Shakya Chokden interprets the etymology of "dharma-sphere" in several ways, depending on what text or tradition he is commenting on. Usually, he unpacks it as a cause or source of dharmas. In *Ascertainment of the Dharma-Sphere,* for example, commenting on the opening verse of *Praise of the Dharma-Sphere,* he writes that "dharma" refers to the nonabiding nirvāṇa of a buddha, and "sphere" to its cause—primordial mind that pervades all levels of the basis, path, and result.[36] A slightly different interpretation is given in *Golden Lancet* where he writes that in *Dharmas of Maitreya,* the nondual primordial mind (*gnyis med kyi ye shes*) is called the dharma-sphere because it serves as the cause of all ārya dharmas. Thus, "dharma" there is expanded to ārya dharmas and "sphere" to their cause.[37] This being said, we should note that interpretations of a term—especially contextually bound ones—do not exhaust all meanings that the term might bear. This is particularly true in the case of the dharma-sphere that, as we will see later, is treated by Shakya Chokden as the source of all dharmas of saṃsāra and nirvāṇa.

Shakya Chokden views the dharma-sphere—the only existent dharma, primordial mind—as becoming enmeshed in, coexistent with, and eventually disentangled from conventional, nonexistent, dharmas. While the dharma-sphere does not change its nature, it can be referred to by different names when addressed together with other dharmas. In *Ascertainment of the Dharma-Sphere* he writes that the dharma-sphere of a mind bound by conceptualization is called "saṃsāra" because it serves as the basis of the imputation "sentient being." The dharma-sphere at the time of liberation from all conceptualization is called "liberation from saṃsāra" because it serves as the basis of the imputation "buddha."[38] Commenting on verses 74–76 of *Praise of the Dharma-Sphere,* he further specifies that according to that treatise, the primordial mind of the dharma-sphere on the level where it has not been purified of any afflictions is called "sentient being"; on the level of being partially purified of afflictions, yet without the aspiring bodhicitta (*smon pa byang chub kyi sems*) being produced, it is called śrāvaka or pratyekabuddha;[39] on the level where aspiring bodhicitta has been produced and the dharma-sphere realized by mere faith, not directly, it is called "person aspiring for the supreme vehicle" (*theg pa mchog la mos pa'i gang zag*). Starting from the level of partial elimination of the obscurations of knowables (*shes bya'i sgrib pa*) obscuring the dharma-sphere and until its final purification of all obscurations, it is called "bodhisattva"; on the level of elimination of all stains it is called "truly perfect Buddha."[40]

In a similar manner, in *Reply to Lodrö Zangpo* he writes that on the level of the basis the primordial mind of the dharma-sphere is called "ultimate sentient being"; on the level of the path "ultimate bodhisattva"; and on the level of the result "ultimate buddha."[41] He proceeds to clarify the nature and function of the dharma-sphere in terms of the aforementioned modes of being and appearance, arguing that on the level of buddhahood the two are the same, while on the level of sentient beings they are discordant. On the latter level, the dharma-sphere's mode of appearance is saṃsāra, which is comprised of adventitious stains and is the object of abandonment. Its mode of being is nirvāṇa, which is accompanied—but not damaged—by stains, because stains are not inherent in its entity or nature. Only the positive qualities of a Buddha can inseparably be born in it on the level of Mahāyāna āryas, starting from the first bodhisattva ground.[42] As we have just seen, in his view all that appears to a buddha's mind is that mind itself, and that mind is none other than the dharma-sphere. This is one of the reasons why the mode of appearance and the mode of being on the level of buddhahood are the same. Below that level the two are different, and what appears to deluded minds is not the really existent dharma-sphere but the nonexistent stains of saṃsāra, while the dharma-sphere itself manifests only from the first bodhisattva ground, which is characterized by an initial direct realization of ultimate reality.

Approaching the topic from a slightly different angle, Shakya Chokden argues that the dharma-sphere has two "parts" (*cha*): consciousness (*rnam shes*) and primordial mind (*ye shes*). The former is called so from the perspective of saṃsāra, the latter from the perspective of nirvāṇa. The former is abandoned at the fundamental transformation, while the latter cannot be abandoned and is posited in terms of different levels as the basis, path, and result.[43] Shakya Chokden clearly treats the two parts of the dharma-sphere as the two aforementioned modes on the level prior to buddhahood. It has the saṃsāric part of consciousness only in terms of its mode of appearance on the level prior to buddhahood, when the modes of being and appearance are different. This part is not inherent in the dharma-sphere and is abandoned at the fundamental transformation, while the dharma-sphere—identified as primordial mind—is not. This interpretation is supported by other passages in his works, such as *Ascertainment of the Dharma-Sphere*'s comment on verse 59 of *Praise of the Dharma-Spere* that the dharma-sphere is the life or life-force of all afflicted and purified dharmas, but while the latter are possessed by the dharma-sphere in terms of being inseparable from it, the former dwell in it in the way of being separable.[44]

Although the modes of being and appearance remain discordant until one achieves final awakening, they are far from being unrelated: the mode of being serves as the very foundation for the emergence of pure and impure appearances as well as purification of the latter and cultivation of the former on the path to buddhahood. As Shakya Chokden puts it in *Reply to Lodrö Zangpo*, the dharma-sphere is the basis for planting seeds of all afflicted and purified dharmas, that is, all dharmas of saṃsāra and nirvāṇa arise from it, and thus it is also called "universal basis" (*kun gzhi*).[45] In *Appearance of the Sun*, he provides details of this process of arising, emphasizing the dichotomy between such categories as consciousness and primordial mind, the universal basis and consciousness of the universal basis (*kun gzhi'i rnam par shes pa*), and so forth. He writes that consciousness of the universal basis emerges from the complete ripening of predispositions of the afflicted side (*kun nas nyon mongs phyogs kyi bag chags*) smeared on the primordial mind of the dharma-sphere. That consciousness has no beginning but has an end. It gives rise to grasping at itself as "I," and that grasping leads to the emergence of all dharmas of saṃsāra. Predispositions of the purified side (*rnam par byang ba'i phyogs kyi bag chags*)—also called "stainless seeds" (*zag pa med pa'i sa bon*)—are accumulated on that primordial mind of the dharma-sphere but have neither beginning nor end. Their nourishment (*gsos btab pa*)—by hearing discourses of a buddha, meeting buddhas, and so on—leads to the emergence of all dharmas of the purified side. That root primordial mind (*rtsa ba'i ye shes*) which is the primordial mind of the dharma-sphere, is also called "disposition of buddha-essence" "buddha of natural purity" (*rang bzhin rnam dag gi sangs rgyas*), "causal continuum" (*rgyu yi rgyud*), and "universal basis." It is not called "consciousness of the universal basis," one of the reasons being that primordial mind and consciousness are contradictory. Primordial mind and consciousness have coexisted since beginningless time because neither saṃsāra nor primordial mind have a beginning, and because there can exist no consciousness that is not connected to primordial mind. However, the two are not destined to coexist forever, because consciousness is suitable for separation from primordial mind and will eventually undergo the fundamental transformation (*gnas yongs su gyur pa*).[46]

This line of reasoning demonstrates the dynamic connection between the dharma-sphere and other dharmas. The dharma-sphere is the basis, foundation, and support of everything, because all purified and afflicted dharmas depend on, arise from, and coexist with it. The very foundation of saṃsāra—the consciousness of the universal basis together with its seeds—has continuously coexisted with, and on, this basis since beginningless time. This is also true for the seeds of liberation from saṃsāra, as well as other positive dharmas related to nirvāṇa. Yet, the afflicted and purified dharmas are connected to the dharma-sphere in very different ways: while the former can be said to develop *on* it, the latter develop *within* it. The former are not subsumed under the category of primordial mind and are destined to eventually disappear. The latter, being the primordial mind of the dharma-sphere itself, will never cease to exist.[47] Shakya Chokden's interpretation of the nature and function of the dharma-sphere is summarized in table 7.1 on page 180.

Note that the parts and modes outlined in the left column are none other than the nature or entity of the dharma-sphere—primordial mind. Those in the right column refer to mistaken appearances of sentient beings. Thus, the two parts, similar to the two modes, refer not to different parts of a whole but to real, existent dharmas on the one hand and unreal, nonexistent dharmas on the other. I should also reiterate that according to Shakya Chokden the very division into such bipolar categories as saṃsāra and nirvāṇa, afflicted and purified dharmas, and so on, is possible only from the perspective of those for whom the modes of appearance and being are different. There is no planting of seeds within the primordial mind of the dharma-sphere, no arising of saṃsāra from it, no purification of stains, no development of primordial mind, and not even any fundamental transformation from the

Table 7.1. Nature and function of the dharma-sphere

dharma-sphere, universal basis, primordial mind, primordial mind of the dharma-sphere, inseparability of saṃsāra and nirvāṇa, all-creating king, unmixed complete perfection, spontaneity, revelation of the hidden, great perfection, great seal, pacifier of sufferings, disposition of the buddha-nature, buddha of natural purity, causal continuum, universal basis		terms by which the dharma-sphere is addressed in different teachings
truly perfect buddha (all obscurations are eliminated) bodhisattva (obscurations of knowables are eliminated only partially) person aspiring for the supreme path (aspiring bodhicitta is produced, the dharma-sphere is realized by mere faith) śrāvaka or pratyekabuddha (afflictions are partly purified, aspiring bodhicitta is not produced) sentient being (no afflictions are purified)		how the dharma-sphere is posited on five levels
ultimate buddha, result continuum ultimate bodhisattva, path continuum ultimate sentient being, basis continuum		how it is posited on three levels
nirvāṇa saṃsāra		how it is posited on two levels
nirvāṇa part—primordial mind (impossible to eliminate)	saṃsāra part—consciousness (eliminated at the fundamental transformation)	parts
mode of being—nirvāṇa (on the ārya level all positive qualities are inseparably born in it)	mode of appearance—saṃsāra (consists of adventitious stains, object of abandonment)	two modes when in continua of sentient beings

perspective of a buddha whose two modes are the same. Only the dharma-sphere in all its perfection and completeness exists from that perspective—nothing else.

But if for a person who is still on the path to buddhahood there are stains to purify and positive qualities to acquire, then what does this process consist of? In other words, how is the dharma-sphere purified and manifested on the path? We will explore this topic in the next section.

How the Dharma-Sphere Is Utilized on the Path

In *Great Path of Ambrosia of Emptiness*, Shakya Chokden addresses several approaches to the path that purifies stains of the dharma-sphere, characterizing them as those of zhentong and rangtong. He subdivides the former into two: those of Mantrayāna and Pāramitāyāna. He explains that according to Mantrayāna, the primordial mind of the dharma-sphere with stains (*dri ma dang bcas pa'i chos dbyings ye shes*) is taken as the basis of purification that is purified by the path of the two stages (*rim pa gnyis*); as a result, one manifests the body of union (*zung 'jug gi sku*).[48] Outlining the Pāramitāyāna approach, he refers to two texts of Maitreya: *Sublime Continuum* and *Differentiation of the Middle and Extremes*. The former posits the suchness with stains (*dri ma dang bcas pa'i de bzhin nyid*) as the basis of purification that occurs by the aspiration toward Mahāyāna teachings, great compassion, contemplation, and wisdom realizing selflessness. This results in directly seeing buddha-essence, gradually accustoming oneself to that vision—thereby purifying stains of the seven impure and three pure grounds—and eventually attaining the final result of purification—transcendence to the other shore of genuine purity, bliss, permanence, and self (*gtsang ba dang / bde ba dang / rtag pa dang / bdag dam pa*).[49] In his opinion, *Differentiation of the Middle and Extremes* shares the same basic position, but presents it from a slightly different angle: the basis of purification is the dharma-sphere with stains, which is purified of afflictive obscurations and obscurations of knowables by the purifier, identified as primordial mind directly seeing the two types of selflessness (*bdag med pa gnyis mngon sum du mthong ba'i ye shes*).[50]

Outlining the rangtong approach, Shakya Chokden addresses three positions: those of Śāntarakṣita and Kamalaśīla, Candrakīrti, and *Praise of the Dharma-Sphere*. He argues that Śāntarakṣita and Kamalaśīla's identification of the dharma-sphere accords with the basic Yogācāra position—outlined in such texts as the intermediate *Dharmas of Maitreya*—that only the dharma-sphere exists, while Candrakīrti's approach best represents the final Niḥsvabhāvavāda position that nothing exists, even the dharma-sphere.[51] *Praise of the Dharma-Sphere* follows a mixed rangtong / zhentong approach,[52] explaining the dharma-sphere first in terms of zhentong and then in terms of rangtong. More specifically, it interprets the entity (*ngo bo*) or nature of buddhahood as purity, bliss, permanence, and self (*gtsang bde rtag bdag*), but afterward it negates the existence of any dharma whatsoever.[53]

Aside from this major difference in the final interpretation of the ultimate status of the dharma-sphere, Shakya Chokden presents *Praise of the Dharma-*

Sphere's approach to the dharma-sphere in the context of the path as being in agreement with the zhentong approach. The entity of the dharma-sphere is posited in that text as primordial mind free from the duality of apprehended and apprehender. What obscures it is explained primarily as afflictive obscurations. What purifies it is presented as wisdom realizing the selflessness of persons (*gang zag gi bdag med rtogs pa'i shes rab*) and primordial mind realizing the selflessness of dharmas (*chos kyi bdag med rtogs pa'i ye shes*). The results of purification are the awakenings of śrāvakas and pratyekabuddhas, as well as dharma-bodies from the first bodhisattva ground, up to and including buddhahood.[54] Śrāvakas and pratyekabuddhas can directly see only one part (*phyogs gcig*)[55] of the dharma-sphere, and their nirvāṇas are explained as having the entity of the primordial mind of the dharma-sphere.[56]

Shakya Chokden's perspective on different approaches to the purification of the dharma-sphere demonstrates that while admitting differences in the methods or paths of purification advocated by tantric and nontantric zhentong systems, he believes that the basis—the dharma-sphere itself—is approached by them similarly. When they accept the existence of the dharma-sphere—as do Śāntarakṣita, Kamalaśīla, and provisionally Nāgārjuna in his *Praise of the Dharma-Sphere*—followers of rangtong also agree about its identification and the major points of the method of its purification. When they, like Candrakīrti, do not assert the existence of any dharmas, followers of rangtong do not accept the dharma-sphere and its identification as primordial mind.

Let us look closer at *Ascertainment of the Dharma-Sphere*, which provides further details of the purification of the dharma-sphere on the Mahāyāna path by the practice of the ten perfections (generosity, morality, patience, etc.). Here we read that due to the practice of the first three perfections, the collection of positive qualities (*bsod nams kyi tshogs*) develops (*rgyas pa*) within the disposition of the primordial mind of the dharma-sphere (*khams chos kyi dbyings kyi ye shes*). In the process, one temporarily sees the form-body (*gzugs kyi sku*) and eventally accomplishes it. Due to the practice of the next three perfections, the disposition of awakening (*byang chub kyi khams*) develops through the collection of primordial mind (*ye shes kyi tshogs*). This results in temporarily seeing in one's mental continuum the dharma-body purified of adventitious stains (*glo bur rnam dag gi chos sku*) and eventally accomplishing the ultimate body (*don dam pa'i sku*). Due to the practice of the last four perfections, the primordial mind of the dharma-sphere develops through the collection of powers (*nus pa'i tshogs*). As a result, temporarily one is not discouraged from benefiting others and eventally accomplishes perfect awakened activities (*phrin las phun sum tshogs pa*). These ten perfections are called "developmental potential" (*rgyas 'gyur gyi rigs*) because they develop the naturally abiding potential (*rang bzhin du gnas pa'i rigs*).[57]

Note that here "disposition of the primordial mind of the dharma-sphere," "disposition of awakening," and "primordial mind of the dharma-sphere" refer to the same dharma-sphere, addressing it from different angles. It indicates that to those who have not yet reached the end of the path to buddhahood—and whose modes of appearance and being are therefore different—the dharma-sphere itself appears to undergo developmental changes.[58] The dharma-body too is perceived in a similar manner. Shakya Chokden writes that prior to reaching the bodhisattva levels, as a result of faith in the positive qualities of a buddha one can see the dharma-body via a generic image (*don spyi*). Having attained the grounds, one sees it directly, as gradually evolving (*rim gyis rim gyis 'phel bar mthong*). On the eleventh ground, the state of buddhahood, one sees it as perfect and clear, like the full moon.[59]

When discussing the dharma-sphere in the context of the path, Shakya Chokden also resorts to the familiar strategy of separating the perspectives of sentient being and buddhas, as demonstrated by his elaborations in *Ascertainment of the Dharma-Sphere* on how form-bodies of a buddha appear to different types of beings. When the emanation-body (*sprul sku*) appears to a śrāvaka, pratyekabuddha, or an ordinary being, the part of the appearance of a buddha's physical body and speech belongs to their minds' dharma-sphere[60] that has developed (*rgyas pa*) due to their positive qualities (*bsod nams*) and is therefore subsumed under their own mind. A buddha's dharma-sphere merely serves as the empowering condition (*bdag po'i rkyen*) for displaying such appearance. The part of the appearance of the enjoyment-body (*longs sku*), together with the pure land in which it dwells, is subsumed under the nature of the primordial mind of a person with that appearance. It appears as increasing and decreasing (*rgya chad*) because that primordial mind has not yet been purified of predispositions (*bag chags*) to dualistic appearances. Although the causal condition (*rgyu'i rkyen*) of that appearance is the person's primordial mind, its empowering condition (*bdag po'i rkyen*) is the primordial mind of a buddha. While various manifestations of form-bodies can appear to sentient beings due to their aspirational prayers, the ultimate body (*don dam pa'i sku*) on the level of buddhahood does not have any divisions; on the eleventh ground, a person's primordial mind and primordial minds of all buddhas are "blended into one" (*gcig tu 'dres pa*).[61]

Shakya Chokden's interpretation of the dharma-sphere in the context of the path should be understood similarly to his interpretation of the dharma-sphere in relation to other dharmas outlined in the previous section: whether he addresses the dharma-sphere as the basis of emergence of pure and impure phenomena, as the focus of the Mahāyāna path nourishing the former and purifying the latter, or as the conduit by which appearances of nirvāṇa spill into the world of saṃsāra—in all those cases he either explicitly or implicitly maintains emphasis on different perspectives. From the perspective of a buddha whose modes of being and appearance are not different, the dharma-sphere undergoes no such changes as purification, development, and so forth; no buddha-bodies appear except for the dharma-body, which is none other than the dharma-sphere itself. Not even distinctions between one's own primordial mind and other buddhas' primordial minds or dharma-spheres exist—they all are "blended into one."[62] In contrast to that, from the perspective of those below the level of buddhahood, for whom the two modes are different, the dharma-sphere is seen as evolving, becoming increasingly purified of adventitious stains and imbued with more and more positive qualities. The two form-bodies appear and disappear as well, but those appearances belong only to the practitioner's own mind—not to the mental continuum of a buddha. Manifestations of buddha-bodies and the development of the dharma-sphere are caused by the practices of the ten perfections. Yet, those practices too do not transcend the mode of appearance and do not belong to the entity of the dharma-sphere—its mode of being. This being said, the dharma-spheres of both buddhas and sentient beings are what ultimately allows practices of the path to take place and bear fruits of visions of buddha-bodies; while buddhas' dharma-spheres serve as mere conditions for such processes, sentient beings' dharma-spheres contain their seeds and provide their foundation.

Differences between the Dharma-Sphere, the Dharma-Body, the Buddha-Nature, and the Disposition

In his writings on the dharma-sphere, Shakya Chokden often refers to several concepts—most notably "disposition" (*khams*), "buddha-nature," and "dharma-body" (*chos sku*)—that are closely related to the dharma-sphere but are not necessarily synonymous or interchangeable with it. These categories have already been mentioned in this chapter, and their descussion here will serve as a foil for clarifying his position on the dharma-sphere.[63]

Shakya Chokden interprets the disposition as the source or cause of buddhas and sentient beings, as the following passage from *Ascertainment of the Dharma-Sphere* demonstrates: "Explanation of the dharma-sphere as the disposition of both buddhas and sentient beings also intends that it is the cause of both."[64] This passage further demonstrates that he essentially equates the disposition with the dharma-sphere. The major difference, perhaps, being that he tends to use the former category more narrowly as a source of awakened and unawakened states and beings, and the latter more broadly, as a source of all dharmas in general. By extension, he equates the disposition with the primordial mind of the dharma-sphere, also using such elaborate terms as "disposition of the primordial mind of the dharma-sphere."[65] Little wonder—after all, both *khams* and *dbyings* are two Tibetan words used for translating the same Sanskrit word *dhātu*, a fact that Shakya Chokden, as a Sanskrit specialist,[66] was no doubt aware of.

Similar to the dharma-sphere, he interprets the disposition as the source and cause of buddhahood, and he argues that it persists in the state of buddhahood, too. He makes it clear in *Ascertainment of the Dharma-Sphere* when answering the question about whether the disposition is eliminated by antidotes as a means of achieving buddhahood. Commenting on verses 18–22 of *Praise of the Dharma-Sphere*, he writes that antidotes eliminate stains (*dri ma*) of the disposition but do not destroy the disposition itself.[67] Commenting on the next verse, he writes that the entity of the dharma-sphere is primordial mind, and because that entity is not the object of abandonment, it does not have to be eliminated.[68] It is safe to argue, then, that for Shakya Chokden the following equation holds true: disposition = dharma-sphere = primordial mind.

In contrast to this relatively straightforward take on the disposition, his interpretation of the buddha-nature, which he also calls "buddha-essence" (*sangs rgyas kyi snying po*) and "*sugata*-essence" (*bde bar gshegs pa'i snying po*) is more complex. His trademark claim regarding the buddha-nature—articulated in several texts including *Ascertainment of the Dharma-Sphere*—is that nobody but Mahāyāna āryas have it.[69] As he succinctly puts it in *Essence of Sūtras and Tantras: Explanation of the Buddha-Essence* when addressing the interpretation of the buddha-nature by *Sublime Continuum*:

> In brief, all Mahāyāna āryas
> Possess buddha-essence.
> Because sentient beings other than them
> Do have the suchness (*de bzhin nyid*) and the potential (*rigs*),
> They possess buddha-essence metaphorically.[70]

In other words, he accepts that buddhas and bodhisattvas on the ten grounds, starting from the path of seeing, possess the buddha-nature, but he does not believe that anyone else below the frist level does.

In *Ascertainment of the Dharma-Sphere*, commenting on verses 14–17 of *Praise of the Dharma-Sphere*, he also argues against all beings having buddha-essence. Supporting his position with the example of a banana tree given in the root text, he writes that although a banana tree does not have a pith or essence (*snying po*), it produces a sweet fruit because it has its disposition; likewise, although sentient beings[71] do not have buddha-essence, they have its disposition—primordial mind—that allows the fruit of buddhahood to be produced. In his opinion, this example shows a sweet fruit not as the essence of the banana tree but as its result. Likewise, buddhahood is not the essence of saṃsāra but its result. Saṃsāra has no essence. Although a banana tree has no essence, the existence in it of the disposition of the sweet fruit can be regarded as its essence. Likewise, although saṃsāra has no essence, existence in it of the disposition of a buddha is explained as its essence. Juxtaposing the categories of the disposition and the essence, he writes that although it is taught that sentient beings have the buddha-disposition (*sangs rgyas kyi khams*), buddhahood itself is not explained as the essence of sentient beings.[72]

As I have mentioned, Shakya Chokden argues that from the perspective of those whose modes of being and appearance are different, positive qualities of a buddha can inseparably be born in the dharma-sphere on the level of Mahāyāna āryas, starting from the first bodhisattva ground. He also argues that one can be posited as a possessor of the essence (*snying po can*) only when he sees the essence directly, that is, starting from the first ground. This is because from that moment on, the reality (*chos nyid*) of his mind can be posited as tathāgata and the dharma-body.[73] In other words, the dharma-sphere becomes buddha-essence only starting from the Mahāyāna path of seeing. Shakya Chokden also insists that the direct realization of the dharma-sphere is necessarily accompanied by the removal or purification of obscurations or "stains" that cover it. Nevertheless, in his opinion it is not enough to merely remove some obscurations to become a possessor of buddha-essence. Otherwise, non-Mahāyāna āryas would possess it too. Together with the partial freedom from afflictions, one also has to develop qualities unique to the Mahāyāna path, such as bodhicitta.[74]

To put it differently, the direct realization of the dharma-sphere necessarily involves its vision as pure of at least some obscurations and imbued with at least some buddha-qualities. Only when this vision has been achieved can the dharma-sphere be treated as the buddha-nature. Because this is impossible for anyone before the first ground, only Mahāyāna āryas have buddha-essence. Thus, in contrast to the dharma-sphere—which is the basis of all pure and impure visions and does not have to be seen for a person to possess it—the buddha-nature has to be directly realized or seen for that to happen. We can say that according to Shakya Chokden the equation buddha-nature = dharma-sphere holds true starting only from the first bodhisattva ground.

Shakya Chokden's position on the dharma-body is even more complex. In *Ascertainment of the Dharma-Sphere* he writes that one is called "bodhisattva" when one has obtained one part of the dharma-body (*chos kyi sku'i cha shes gcig thob pa*).[75] Similar to being posited as buddha-essence, to be posited as a part of the dharma-body, it is not enough to be merely purified of one part of afflictions; one needs *both* partial freedom from afflictions and also generation of bodhicitta. Without these two conditions being fulfilled, the disposition cannot be posited as the buddha-nature, and, by extension, a part of the dharma-body.[76] One also has to be at least partially purified of the obscurations of knowables. Although saṃsāra is destroyed through the abandonment of afflictions, without at least partial removal of the obscurations of knowables one will not be able to see the dharma-sphere, and without it being seen, the dharma-sphere cannot be posited as the dharma-body.[77] In other words, he argues that similar to obtaining the buddha-nature only starting from the first ground, one obtains one part of the dharma-body also starting from that level only.

This being said, in *Ascertainment of the Dharma-Sphere*, commenting on verses 89 and 90 of the root text, Shakya Chokden writes that the dharma-sphere is not realized by any consciousness, including mental consciousness. Prior to the first ground it is realized or seen by faith, and starting from the first ground it is directly seen by the individual self-cognition. Referring to verse 74, he also adds that both ways of seeing the dharma-sphere apply to the dharma-body as well.[78] Thus, we are led to think that in his opinion, one has the dharma-body both prior to and after the first ground. This could be further supported by his reference to the following *Ornament of Mahāyāna Sūtras* passage: "Without the body, having the body, having obtained the body,"[79] that he explains as meaning that one has (*bcas*) the dharma-body on the paths of accumulation and preparation.[80] But here he makes a subtle distinction between having (*bcas*) the dharma-body and having obtained (*thob*) it, indicating that while one has the dharma-body starting from the path of accumulation, only from the first bodhisattva ground does one obtain—and thus come into possession of—the dharma-body. This distinction between having and possessing is applied neither to the dharma-sphere nor to the disposition or the buddha-nature: one always has the dharma-sphere and the disposition, and one obtains (i.e., has) the buddha-nature starting from the first bodhisattva ground.

If we take these differences into account, can we at least say that according to Shakya Chokden, starting from the first ground one equally has the dharma-body and the buddha-nature together with the dharma-sphere? After all, one cannot stop *having* the dharma-body after having *obtained* it! While it is tempting to answer this question affirmatively, the matter is complicated by the fact that according to Shakya Chokden, having parts of the dharma-body does not qualify as having the actual dharma-body. In *Ascertainment of the Dharma-Sphere*, elaborating on the meaning of verses 75–76 of the root text, he writes that although on each of the ten grounds there exist parts of the dharma-body, tathāgata and buddha, because they are not fully complete (*yongs su ma rdzogs pa*), it is difficult to posit them as the actual (*mtshan nyid pa*) dharma-body, and so on. For example, he says, although on the first day of the month there exists one part of the moon, because not all fifteen parts are complete it cannot be posited as the moon disc.[81] This makes it clear that for Shakya Chokden, the dharma-body that one obtains on the first ground and continues to have on the next nine grounds is not the actual dharma-body.[82] Because this logic does not apply to the buddha-nature, we can conclude that according to him the actual dharma-body only overlaps with the buddha-nature and the dharma-sphere on the eleventh ground—the state of buddhahood. Similarities and differences between the dharma-sphere, disposition, buddha-nature, and dharma-body are summarized in table 7.2.

Table 7.2. Similarities and differences between the dharma-sphere, disposition, buddha-nature, and dharma-body

Levels	**Dharma-Sphere**	**Disposition**	**Buddha-Nature**	**Dharma-Body**
ordinary beings, śrāvakas, pratyekabuddhas	yes	yes	no	no; have it but do not posess it
ārya bodhisattvas	yes	yes	yes	no; have / possess only its parts
buddhas	yes	yes	yes	yes

CONCLUSION

Shakya Chokden's later works demonstrate that in general he is supportive of both rangtong and zhentong systems, tending not to take sides with either one.[83] Nevertheless, when targeting such specific categories as the dharma-sphere, he clearly gives preference to the zhentong interpretation where the dharma-sphere is treated as the only dharma existent in reality, while the existence of all other dharmas that do not belong to that category is negated. He believes that this approach is accepted wholesale by Alīkākāravāda thinkers, while Niḥsvabhāvavādins either entirely reject the actual dharma-sphere or accept its zhentong interpretation to various degrees.

The claim of the exclusive existence of the dharma-sphere makes problematic its interpretation side by side with other dharmas, such as the Buddhist path with attendant categories of afflictions, antidotes, and so forth. Shakya Chokden's response to this challenge is to emphasize the specific contexts in which different dharmas are addressed. He likens this approach to utilizing the categories of the two truths but goes further than simply claiming that dharmas exist on the conventional level, while on the ultimate level nothing exists except for the ultimate itself. He emphasizes the importance of separating the perspectives of buddhas and sentient beings, the contexts of view and action, and the modes of being and appearance. Linking what exists with what is perceived, he argues that relative dharmas exist only for deluded minds, while all that an awakened mind of a buddha perceives is exclusively the dharma-sphere—ultimate reality itself. Arguing that for buddhas the modes of being and appearance are the same, but for sentient beings different, he relegates the analysis of the dharma-sphere alongside other dharmas to the latter context. Only on the level where the two modes are different can one develop positive qualities, remove obscurations, purify the dharma-sphere, see its development, and so forth. And only on that level can one articulate differences between the dharma-sphere and other related dharmas, such as buddha-essence.

Shakya Chokden equates the dharma-sphere with ultimate reality, primordial mind, and treats it as the source and underlying reality of all dharmas. When discussing it in the context of the path, he utilizes the standard model of the ten stages and five paths according to which the ultimate is directly realized starting from the first bodhisattva ground. Following Nāgārjuna, he argues that similar to seeing the waxing moon, one sees the dharma-sphere only partially within the ten grounds and fully in the state of buddhahood. But he does not deny that it or its cognate category of the disposition exist on the level of ordinary beings and non-Mahāyāna āryas. In contrast to that, he argues that the buddha-nature has to be directly realized for one to have it. As for the dharma-body, even that alone is not sufficient—to obtain it one has to see it completely, and this happens only in the state of buddhahood.

These distinctions notwithstanding, it bears repeating that they pertain only to the perspective of sentient beings for whom the modes of being and appearance of the dharma-sphere are different. From the perspective of a buddha, who sees things as they really are, free from any differences in the two modes, none of these distinctions apply. From that perspective, there is nothing at all to eliminate or establish—there are no dharmas apart from the dharma-sphere.

Notes

1. Unless otherwise specified, all italicized terms in parentheses are Tibetan.

2. *Dharmadhātustotra*, *Chos kyi dbyings su bstod pa*, D1118, bstod tshogs, ka, 63b–67b. Translated in Brunnhölzl, "*In Praise of Dharmadhātu*" 117–129.

3. For a detailed study of Shakya Chokden's views, see my *Visions of Unity*.

4. For details of this period—that started around 1477 and continued until the end of Shakya Chokden's life, see Komarovski, *Visions of Unity* 38ff.

5. Among those texts, of particular notice is *Opening a Hundred Doors*, a work that focuses on the dharma-sphere but is not tied to any one treatise on the topic. *Ascertainment of the Dharma-Sphere*, on the other hand, is Shakya Chokden's major commentary on Nāgārjuna's *Praise of the Dharma-Sphere*, although it is far from being tied to that text only. The position of *Praise of the Dharma-Sphere* is also analyzed in a short nameless text that I will be referring to as *Reply to Lodrö Zangpo*. This short text was written in response to an inquiry by a tantric adept, Lodrö Zangpo (*blo gros bzang po*). *Great Path of Ambrosia of Emptiness*, which focuses on varying interpretations of ultimate reality and related topics by rangtong and zhentong systems, also discusses different perspectives on the dharma-sphere in significant detail. The dharma-sphere is addressed in *Appearance of the Sun*, whose main focus is the historical and philosophical analysis of the works on Buddhist logic and epistemology. Helpful information on the dharma-sphere is provided in *Ocean of Scriptural Statements and Reasoning*, which explores major themes of Mahāyāna philosophy according to different systems of Madhyamaka. Important questions regarding the dharma-sphere are addressed in *Golden Lancet*, which analyzes a panoply of problematic issues in Sakya Paṇḍita Künga Gyaltsen's (1182–1251) *Thorough Differentiation of the Three Types of Vows*. The dharma-sphere is likewise discussed in *Rain of Ambrosia*, whose main objective is to demonstrate compatibility and shared vision of the rival Alīkākāravāda and Niḥsvabhāvavāda systems. For details, Komarovski, *Visions of Unity*, which explores that perspective on Alīkākāravāda and Niḥsvabhāvavāda as its main topic.

6. Shakya Chokden, *Opening a Hundred Doors* 157.

7. Shakya Chokden, *Reply to Lodrö Zangpo* 36–37.

8. Shakya Chokden, *Appearance of the Sun* 114–116.

9. *Mahāyānasaṃgraha*, *Theg pa chen po bsdus pa*, D4048, sems tsam, ri, 1a–43a.

10. *Mahāyānottaratantraśāstravyākhyā*, *Theg pa chen po'i rgyud bla ma'i bstan bcos kyi rnam par bshad pa*, D4025, sems tsam, phi, 74b–129a.

11. *Mahāyānottaratantraśāstra*, *Theg pa chen po rgyud bla ma*, D4024, sems tsam, phi, 54b–73a. Sanskrit of this text with Asaṅga's commentary is edited in Johnston, *Ratnagotravibhāga*.

12. In contrast to the widespread interpretation of Madhyamaka as synonymous with Niḥsvabhāvavāda, and Yogācāra as synonymous with Cittamātra, Shakya Chokden treats only one of the two types of Yogācāra—Satyākāravāda—as synonymous with Cittamātra, and he treats the other type—Alīkākāravāda—as a subdivision of Madhyamaka. He applies the term

"Yogācāra Madhyamaka" (*rnal 'byor spyod (pa) pa'i dbu ma*) to both Alīkākāravāda and the Niḥsvabhāvavāda system advocated by Śāntarakṣita and Kamalaśīla. To avoid confusion, I refer to the former system only as Alīkākāravāda or Alīkākāravāda Yogācāra. For details of Shakya Chokden's approach to divisions of Madhyamaka and Yogācāra, see Komarovski, *Visions of Unity*, chapters 3 and 4.

13. Shakya Chokden, *Opening a Hundred Doors* 147. The claim of the nonexistence of the dharma-sphere does not entail the extreme of nihilism; according to Niḥsvabhāvavāda, as Shakya Chokden understands it, although it does not exist, it does not *not exist* either (Shakya Chokden, *Opening a Hundred Doors* 148).

14. Shakya Chokden, *Opening a Hundred Doors* 147.

15. This approach is found in many of Shakya Chokden's works, such as *Rain of Ambrosia* 326ff. For more details of different perspectives on existence and nonexistence, acceptance and nonacceptance of ultimate reality, and related issues, see Komarovski, *Visions of Unity* 214ff.

16. Shakya Chokden, *Rain of Ambrosia* 328.

17. Shakya Chokden, *Rain of Ambrosia* 329.

18. Shakya Chokden, *Rain of Ambrosia* 330. The term "disposition of the sugata-essence" refers to the disposition (*khams*), not sugata-essence (*bde bar gshegs pa'i snying po*). For the differences between these two categories, see the last section of this chapter.

19. *chos kyi dbyings las ma gtogs pa'i / chos gzhan med*, Shakya Chokden, *Opening a Hundred Doors* 147. Compare: "Because there are no dharmas, Except for the dharma-sphere" (*chos kyi dbyings las ma gtogs pa / gang phyir chos med de yi phyir*) from Maitreya, *Ornament of Mahāyāna Sūtras* (*Mahāyānasūtrālaṃkāra, Theg pa chen po mdo sde'i rgyan*), D4020, sems tsam, phi, 18a. Skt.: *dharmadhātu vinirmukto yasmād dharmo na vidyate*. Levi, *Exposé* 87. Also, "Thus, except for the dharma-sphere; There are no dharmas" (*chos kyi dbyings ni ma gtogs par / 'di ltar chos yod ma yin te*) from Maitreya, *Differentiation of the Middle and Extremes* (*Madhyāntavibhāga, Dbus dang mtha' rnam par 'byed pa*), D4021, sems tsam, phi, 44b. The Sanskrit version of this passage, provided in Nagao's *Madhyāntavibhāga-Bhāṣya* 67, is virtually identical to the one from *Ornament of Mahāyāna Sūtras*.

20. Shakya Chokden, *Opening a Hundred Doors* 147.

21. Shakya Chokden, *Opening a Hundred Doors* 149.

22. Komarovski, *Visions of Unity* 94, 241, 249.

23. Shakya Chokden, *Reply to Lodrö Zangpo* 36.

24. This can be viewed in a way similar to such statements as "only mind exists"—an expression that negates those phenomena that are not mind, but not those that are subsumed under the category of mind.

25. Shakya Chokden, *Opening a Hundred Doors* 157.

26. For details of experiencing versus cognizing, and so forth, see Komarovski, *Visions of Unity* chapter 5, section 3.

27. Shakya Chokden, *Opening a Hundred Doors* 153. Because according to Shakya Chokden only ultimate—not conventional—reality appears to a buddha's mind, *ji snyed pa* in this context does not refer to and is not synonymous with conventional reality, as it is often understood (its counterpart *ji lta ba* or "discerned" usually being taken as synonymous with ultimate reality). Here, *ji snyed pa* too refers to ultimate reality because it refers to primordial mind, the dharma-sphere.

28. Shakya Chokden, *Opening a Hundred Doors* 154. Shakya Chokden argues that Mādhyamikas disagree on whether buddhas have appearances, writing that according to such thinkers as Śāntideva they do, while according to Candrakīrti they do not. Shakya Chokden, *Opening a Hundred Doors* 153.

29. See Shakya Chokden, *Ascertainment of the Dharma-Sphere* 344, where he writes that in the state of buddhahood, the entity of the primordial mind of the dharma-sphere free from all obscurations is the object of functioning of primordial mind itself. Thus, it is the object of experience (*myong bya*) of only the individually self-cognizing primordial mind and entirely transcends all objects of sounds and concepts.

30. *'di la bsal dang bzhag bya ba / cung zad med*, Shakya Chokden, *Opening a Hundred Doors* 155. Compare, for example, Maitreya's *Ornament of Clear Realizations* (*Abhisamayālaṃkāranāmaprajñāpāramitopadeśaśāstrakārikā, Shes rab kyi pha rol tu phyin pa'i man ngag gi bstan bcos mngon par rtogs pa'i rgyan zhes bya ba'i tshig le'ur byas pa*), D3786, shes phyin, ka 10a: *'di las bsal bya ci yang med / gzhag par bya ba cung zad med / yang dag nyid la yang dag lta / yang dag mthong na rnam par grol.*

31. On the differences between the dharma-sphere and buddha-nature, see the last section of this chapter.

32. In the same text (*Opening a Hundred Doors* 156) Shakya Chokden also specifies that while Niḥsvabhāvavāda reasons that stains cannot be eliminated and positive qualities cannot be established because the two are established in dependence (*ltos nas grub pa*), this reasoning does not apply here, in the zhentong context, where conventional, relative dharmas are not accepted as established or existent but ultimate reality is. As for a buddha's positive qualities, they manifest only partially on the ten bodhisattva grounds and become fully manifest only in the state of buddhahood.

33. Shakya Chokden, *Opening a Hundred Doors* 154–155.

34. Shakya Chokden, *Opening a Hundred Doors* 155–156.

35. Shakya Chokden, *Ascertainment of the Dharma-Sphere* 319–321.

36. Shakya Chokden, *Ascertainment of the Dharma-Sphere* 306. Hereafter, verse numbering is based on Brunnhölzl's "*In Praise of Dharmadhātu.*" To save space, I am not providing translation of *Praise of the Dharma-Sphere*'s verses in this chapter.

37. Shakya Chokden, *Golden Lancet* 517. This position is contrasted with the interpretation of the dharma-sphere in terms of rangtong, where "dharma" refers to all knowables and "sphere" to their emptiness of reality (517).

38. Shakya Chokden, *Ascertainment of the Dharma-Sphere* 322.

39. Here, śrāvaka and pratyekabuddha refer not only to those who have attained the śrāvaka or pratyekabuddha arhatship, and thus are completely free from afflictions, but also to those āryas who are still on the path to arhatship and thus only partially free from afflictions.

40. Shakya Chokden, *Ascertainment of the Dharma-Sphere* 333–334.

41. Shakya Chokden, *Reply to Lodrö Zangpo* 36.

42. Shakya Chokden, *Reply to Lodrö Zangpo* 36.

43. Shakya Chokden, *Reply to Lodrö Zangpo* 36. An alternative, but less literal, translation of *cha* here can be "dimensions." For more details of Shakya Chokden's distinction between consciousness and primordial mind, see Komarovski, *Visions of Unity* 158ff. and 239ff.

44. Shakya Chokden, *Ascertainment of the Dharma-Sphere* 328.

45. Shakya Chokden, *Reply to Lodrö Zangpo* 36.

46. Shakya Chokden, *Appearance of the Sun* 116–117. For more details on the relationship between primordial mind and consciousness, see Komarovski, *Visions of Unity* chapter 5, section 3.

47. Note that predispositions of the purified side are none other than the dharma-sphere itself—not something merely existent in or placed on it. See *Golden Lancet* 517, where

Shakya Chokden describes stainless predispositions (*zag med kyi bag chags*) as stainless knowing (*zag med kyi shes pa*), also treating them as stainless seeds, using the nondual primordial mind as their illustration (*mtshan gzhi*) and identifyhing it with the dharma-sphere.

48. Shakya Chokden, *Great Path of Ambrosia of Emptiness* 180.

49. Shakya Chokden, *Great Path of Ambrosia of Emptiness* 181.

50. Shakya Chokden, *Great Path of Ambrosia of Emptiness* 185.

51. Shakya Chokden, *Great Path of Ambrosia of Emptiness* 196.

52. It should be noted that in *Great Path of Ambrosia of Emptiness*, Shakya Chokden outlines *Praise of the Dharma-Sphere*'s position in the section on the rangtong approach, and in general treats Nāgārjuna as a Niḥsvabhāvavādin. For further details, see Komarovski, *Visions of Unity* chapter 4, section 3, in particular 197.

53. Shakya Chokden, *Great Path of Ambrosia of Emptiness* 194. It is interesting to note that in support of this claim Shakya Chokden first (*Great Path of Ambrosia of Emptiness* 194–195) refers to the following passage: *gang phyir sangs rgyas mya ngan 'das / gtsang ba rtag pa bde ba'i gzhi* (*Praise of the Dharma-Sphere*, D1118, bstod tshogs, ka, 66a; the root text reads *dge ba* instead of *bde ba* and is read accordingly in *Ascertainment of the Dharma-Sphere*, 330), which is in fact the first two lines of verse 65, and thus follows after—rather than precedes—the passages he cites next. Then (*Great Path of Ambrosia of Emptiness* 195) he cites *sangs rgyas rtag pa'i chos nyid can / ji ltar ri bong mgo yi rwa / btags pa nyid de med pa ltar / de bzhin chos rnams thams cad kyang / btags pa nyid de yod ma yin / phra rab rdul gyi ngo bo yis / glang gi rwa yang dmigs ma yin* (*Praise of the Dharma-Sphere*, 64b, the root text giving *brtags pa* instead of *btags pa*), which are the last line of verse 29, the whole verse 30, and the first two lines of verse 31. Finally (*Great Path of Ambrosia of Emptiness* 195), he cites verse 32: *rten nas 'byung bar 'gyur ba dang / rten nas 'gag par 'gyur bas na / gcig kyang yod pa ma yin na / byis pa ji ltar rtogs par byed* (*Praise of the Dharma-Sphere*, 65a, the root text reading *brten nas 'byung bar gyur ba dang / brten nas 'gag par 'gyur bas na / gcig kyang yod pa ma yin na / byis pa ji ltar rtog par byed*). See *Ascertainment of the Dharma-Sphere* 313–315, for Shakya Chokden's commentary on these passages.

54. For details of Shakya Chokden's approach to the dharma-body, see the last section of this chapter.

55. *phyogs gcig* here expresses the same idea as *nyi tshe ba* in n. 77 in this chapter.

56. Shakya Chokden, *Great Path of Ambrosia of Emptiness* 193–194. Note that in contrast to this position, in Shakya Chokden's opinion Hīnayāna arhats have neither the dharma-body nor the buddha-nature (see the last section).

57. Shakya Chokden, *Ascertainment of the Dharma-Sphere* 330–331.

58. Note that Nāgārjuna's root text on which Shakya Chokden comments (*Praise of the Dharma-Sphere*, D1118, bstod tshogs, ka, 66a) also uses such terms as "development of the disposition" (*khams rgyas 'gyur*, verse 66), "making awakening develop" (*byang chub rgyas byed*, verse 67), and "four dharmas that develop the disposition" (*khams rgyas byed pa'i chos bzhi*, verse 68).

59. Shakya Chokden, *Ascertainment of the Dharma-Sphere* 332–333.

60. I take it as meaning that it belongs to their dharma-spheres only in terms of the mode of appearance—not the mode of being.

61. Shakya Chokden, *Ascertainment of the Dharma-Sphere* 326–327. In the same text (313) he likewise argues that buddhas' aspirational prayers and form-bodies, together with various buddha-fields (*zhing khams*) that emerge through the power of those prayers, do not manifest within buddhas' own appearances (*sangs rgyas rang snang la snang ba med*).

62. To better understand this "blending into one," we should recall Shakya Chokden's

position on the perception of a buddha: all that a buddha's mind perceives, and all that buddhahood consists of, is the buddha's mind, which is a type of primordial mind and ultimate reality. In the state of buddhahood, the perceived, perceiver, and process of perception comprise one and the same indivisible entity that transcends all differences. Thus, the "blending into one" can be understood as referring not to the blending of several things into one but to the final disappearance of dualistic, manifold visions, accompanied by the full manifestation of ultimate reality that transcends them. It can also be taken as indicating that no differences exist anymore between one's own and all buddhas' primordial minds: they all are now the same in terms of being completely free from obscurations and fully realizing the state of buddhahood.

63. Details of Shakya Chokden's position on the disposition and the dharma-body have to await further research. As for his position on the buddha-nature, I have explored it in my "Reburying the Treasure" and "Shakya Chokden's Interpretation of the *Ratnagotravibhāga*."

64. Shakya Chokden, *Ascertainment of the Dharma-Sphere* 323.

65. Compare the discussion of the dharma-sphere in the previous section, where the disposition was treated as the primordial mind of the dharma-sphere itself. But note that as has been mentioned in n. 18, when using the term "disposition of the sugata-essence," Shakya Chokden does not equate the disposition with the sugata-essence.

66. Komarovski, *Visions of Unity*, 29.

67. Shakya Chokden, *Ascertainment of the Dharma-Sphere* 310–311.

68. Shakya Chokden, *Ascertainment of the Dharma-Sphere* 311.

69. See also Komarovski, "Reburying the Treasure" for a detailed discussion of this complex topic.

70. *mdor na theg chen 'phags pa kun / bde bar gshegs pa'i snying po can / de las gzhan pa'i sems can la / de bzhin nyid dang rigs yod phyir / bde gshegs snying po can du btags. Essence of Sūtras and Tantras* 127. For the complete translation of *Essence of Sūtras and Tantras*, see Komarovski, "Reburying the Treasure."

71. Here, Shakya Chokden refers to sentient beings other than Mahāyāna āryas.

72. Shakya Chokden, *Ascertainment of the Dharma-Sphere* 309–310.

73. As will soon become apparent, this does not mean that it becomes an actual dharma-body.

74. Shakya Chokden, *Ascertainment of the Dharma-Sphere* 334.

75. Here, Shakya Chokden is referring to an ārya bodhisattva—a bodhisattva who, as in Candrakīrti's *Engaging in the Middle* (*Madhyamakāvatāra*), is posited starting from the first bodhisattva ground, when the ultimate bodhicitta is initially generated, in contrast to Śāntideva's *Engaging in Bodhisattva Deeds* (*Bodhisattvacaryāvatāra*), where a bodhisattva is posited starting from the first of the five paths (the path of accumulation) when the conventional bodhicitta is initially generated.

76. Shakya Chokden, *Ascertainment of the Dharma-Sphere* 334.

77. Shakya Chokden, *Ascertainment of the Dharma-Sphere* 344. Similarly, in *Great Path of Ambrosia of Emptiness* (181) he writes that one sees the partial (*nyi tshe ba*) dharma-sphere when afflictive obscurations have been abandoned. Nevertheless, this does not imply that ārya śrāvakas and pratyekabuddhas directly see the buddha-nature, he adds, because the dharma-sphere they see is not suitable as the dharma-body.

78. Shakya Chokden, *Ascertainment of the Dharma-Sphere* 341.

79. *sku med pa dang bcas dang sku thob dang.* See *Mahāyānasūtrālaṃkāra*, *Theg pa chen po mdo sde'i rgyan*, D4020, sems tsam, phi, 16a that provides a slightly different version: *sku med pa dang sku bcas sku thob dang.* The passage continues: "Body being fully com-

plete . . ." (*sku yongs rdzogs*). *asakāyā labdhakāyā prapūrṇakāyā ca*. Levi, *Exposé* 75, with the emendation of *laghukāyā* as *labdhakāyā* in Nagao, *Index to the Mahāyāna-Sūtrālāṃkāra* xvi. I want to thank Dr. Alberto Todeschini for drawing my attention to differences between the Tibetan and Sanskrit versions of the passage, as well as Nagao's attempt to bring both versions into agreement.

80. Shakya Chokden, *Ascertainment of the Dharma-Sphere* 341.

81. Shakya Chokden, *Ascertainment of the Dharma-Sphere* 336. See *Great Path of Ambrosia of Emptiness* 181–185, for further details.

82. We should not be misled by such passages found in *Ascertainment of the Dharma-Sphere* as: "In brief, the entity of the ten grounds is the dharma-body pure of partial adventitious stains. The entity of that [dharma-body] is the dharma-sphere" (*mdor bsdu na sa bcu'i ngo bo ni / blo bur gyi dri ma phyogs res dag pa'i chos kyi sku yin la / de'i ngo bo yang chos kyi dbyings kyi ye shes so*, 340), or in *Essence of Sūtras and Tantras* where he argues that in *Praise of the Dharma-Sphere* "[w]ith the example of gradually increasing // Parts of the new moon, [Nāgārjuna] explained that // The dharma-body exists from the ground of Utmost Joy [i.e., the first ground] // Through to the buddha-ground (*chos sku rab dga'i sa nas ni / sangs rgyas sa yi bar dag la / tshes kyi zla ba'i cha shas rnams / rims par 'phel ba'i dpe yis bsnyad* 129). Based on what has been said previously, it is safe to argue that according to Shakya Chokden the dharma-body pure of partial adventitious stains mentioned in the former passage is not the actual dharma-body, while Nāgārjuna's statement mentioned in the latter passage was made without distinguishing between the partial—and thus only imputed—dharma-body and the actual dharma-body that exists only in the buddha-ground. This applies to other passages as well. For example, commenting on *Praise of the Dharma-Sphere*'s passages related to each of the ten grounds, Shakya Chokden uses such expressions as "identifying the dharma-body of the first ground" (*sa dang po'i chos sku ngos bzung ba*), and so on. He likewise writes that on the first ground the dharma-sphere is realized as the dharma-body pure of one part of stains (*dri ma phyogs gcig gis dag pa'i chos sku*), and one thereby generates uncommon joy from being close to the dharma-body (*chos kyi sku dang nye ba*), and so on. When discussing the fourth ground he writes about its dharma-sphere having become the dharma-body (*sa 'di'i chos dbyings chos kyi skur gyur pa*), and so forth (*Ascertainment of the Dharma-Sphere* 337). Such passages do indicate that he interprets the grounds in terms of both the dharma-sphere and the dharma-body, but when he addresses these two concepts in more detail, it becomes clear that while having no issues with the former, he has issues with identifying the latter as the actual dharma-body unless it is the dharma-body of the eleventh ground—buddhahood.

83. For details see Komarovski, *Visions of Unity*, especially chapter 4, section 4.

Bibliography

Sanskrit Sources

Asaṅga. *Explanation of [Maitreya's] "Sublime Continuum of Mahāyāna"* (*Mahāyānottaratantraśāstravyākhyā, Theg pa chen po'i rgyud bla ma'i bstan bcos kyi rnam par bshad pa*). D4025, sems tsam, phi, 74b–129a. Edited Sanskrit text in Edward H. Johnston, editor, *Ratnagotravibhāga Mahāyānottaratantraśāstra*. Patna: The Bihar Research Society, 1950.

———. *Summary of Mahāyāna* (*Mahāyānasaṃgraha, Theg pa chen po bsdus pa*). D4048, sems tsam, ri, 1a–43a.

Maitreya. *Differentiation of the Middle and Extremes* (*Madhyāntavibhāga, Dbus dang mtha' rnam par 'byed pa*). D4021, sems tsam, phi, 44b. Edited Sanskrit text in Gadjin M. Nagao, *Madhyāntavibhāga-Bhāṣya: A Buddhist Philosophical Treatise Edited for the First Time from a Sanskrit Manuscript*. Tokyo: Suzuki Research Foundation, 1964.

———. *Ornament of Clear Realizations* (*Abhisamayālaṃkāranāmaprajñāpāramitopadeśaśāstrakārikā, Shes rab kyi pha rol tu phyin pa'i man ngag gi bstan bcos mngon par rtogs pa'i rgyan zhes bya ba'i tshig le'ur byas pa*). D3786, shes phyin, ka, 10a.

———. *Ornament of Mahāyāna Sūtras* (*Mahāyānasūtrālaṃkāra, Theg pa chen po mdo sde'i rgyan*). D4020, sems tsam, phi, 18a. Edited Sanskrit text in Sylvain Levi, *Mahāyānasūtrālaṃkāra: exposé de la doctrine du grand véhicule selon le systéme Yogācāra*. 2 vols. Paris: Bibliothéque de l'École des Hautes Études, 1907, 1911.

———. *Sublime Continuum* (*Mahāyānottaratantraśāstra, Theg pa chen po rgyud bla ma*). D4024, sems tsam, phi, 54b–73a. Edited Sanskrit text in Edward H. Johnston, editor, *Ratnagotravibhāga Mahāyānottaratantraśāstra*. Patna: The Bihar Research Society, 1950.

Tibetan Sources

Sa skya Paṇḍita kun dga' rgyal mtshan. *Sdom pa gsum gyi rab tu dbye ba* (*Thorough Differentiation of the Three Types of Vows*). In *Sa skya bka' 'bum*, vol. 12 (na), 1a–48b.

Shākya mchog ldan. *[Bo gros bzang po'i dris lan]* (*Reply to Lodrö Zangpo*). In *Collected Writings of Gser-mdog paṇ-chen Śākya-mchog-ldan*, vol. 23, 35–38. Thimphu, Bhutan: Kunzang Tobgey, 1975.

———. *Chos kyi dbyings rnam par nges pa'i gter sgo brgya 'byed* (*Opening a Hundred Doors of the Treasury of Ascertainment of the Dharma-Sphere*). In *Collected Writings of Gser-mdog paṇ-chen Śākya-mchog-ldan*, vol. 13, 147–157. Thimphu, Bhutan: Kunzang Tobgey, 1975.

———. *Chos kyi dbyings su bstod pa zhes bya ba'i bstan bcos kyi rnam par bshad pa chos kyi dbyings rnam par nges pa* (*Ascertainment of the Dharma-Sphere: Explanation of [Nāgārjuna's] Treatise "Praise of the Dharma-Sphere"*). In *Collected Writings of Gser-mdog paṇ-chen Śākya-mchog-ldan*, vol. 7, 303–346. Thimphu, Bhutan: Kunzang Tobgey, 1975.

———. *Nges don rgya mtsho sprin gyi 'brug sgra zab mo'i rgyas 'grel bdud rtsi'i char 'bebs* (*Rain of Ambrosia: Extensive [Auto]Commentary on the "Profound Thunder Amidst the Clouds of the Ocean of Definitive Meaning"*). In *Two Controversial Mādhyamika Treatises*, 319–499. Bir, India: Yashodhara, 1996.

———. *Sangs rgyas kyi snying po'i rnam bshad mdo rgyud snying po* (*Essence of Sūtras and Tantras: Explanation of the Buddha-Essence*). In *Collected Writings of Gser-mdog paṇ-chen Śākya-mchog-ldan*, vol. 13, 124–136. Thimphu, Bhutan: Kunzang Tobgey, 1975. Translated in Yaroslav Komarovski, Yaroslav, "Reburying the Treasure—Maintaining the Continuity: Two Texts by Shakya Chokden on the Buddha-Essence," *Journal of Indian Philosophy* 34, no. 6 (2006): 521–570.

———. *Sdom gsum gyi rab tu dbye ba'i bstan bcos kyi 'bel gtam rnam par nges pa legs bshad gser gyi thur ma* (*Golden Lancet: Resolved Abundant Discourse on the 'Thorough Differentiation of the Three Types of Vows' Treatise*). In *Collected Writings of Gser-mdog paṇ-chen Śākya-mchog-ldan*, vol. 6, 439–vol. 7, 229. Thimphu, Bhutan: Kunzang Tobgey, 1975.

———. *Theg pa chen po dbu ma rnam par nges pa'i bang mdzod lung dang rigs pa'i rgya mtsho* (*Ocean of Scriptural Statements and Reasoning: Treasury of Ascertainment of Mahāyāna Madhyamaka*). In *Collected Writings of Gser-mdog paṇ-chen Śākya-mchog-ldan*, vol. 14, 1–vol. 15, 695. Thimphu, Bhutan: Kunzang Tobgey, 1975.

———. *Tshad ma'i bstan bcos kyi shing rta'i srol rnams ji ltar 'byung ba'i tshul gtam du bya ba nyin mor byed pa'i snang bas dpyod ldan mtha' dag dga' bar byed pa* (*Appearance of the Sun Pleasing All Thinkers: Discussion of the History of the Chariot Ways of [Dignāga's] "Sūtra on Valid Cognition" and [Its] Treatises*). In *Collected Writings of Gser-mdog paṇ-chen Śākya-mchog-ldan*, vol. 19, 1–137. Thimphu, Bhutan: Kunzang Tobgey, 1975.

———. *Zab zhi spros bral gyi bshad pa stong nyid bdud rtsi'i lam po che* (*Great Path of Ambrosia of Emptiness: Explanation of Profound Pacification Free from Proliferations*). In *Collected Writings of Gser-mdog paṇ-chen Śākya-mchog-ldan*, vol. 4, 107–207. Thimphu, Bhutan: Kunzang Tobgey, 1975.

Secondary Sources

Brunnhölzl, Karl. *"In Praise of Dharmadhātu" by Nāgārjuna, Commentary by the Third Karmapa*. Ithaca: Snow Lion, 2007.

Johnston, Edward H., editor. *Ratnagotravibhāga Mahāyānottaratantraśāstra*. Patna: The Bihar Research Society, 1950.

Komarovski, Yaroslav. "Reburying the Treasure—Maintaining the Continuity: Two Texts by Shakya Chokden on the Buddha-Essence." *Journal of Indian Philosophy* 34, no. 6 (2006): 521–570.

———. "Shakya Chokden's Interpretation of the *Ratnagotravibhāga*: 'Contemplative' or 'Dialectical'?" *Journal of Indian Philosophy* 38, no. 4 (2010): 441–452.

———. *Visions of Unity: The Golden Paṇḍita Shakya Chokden's New Interpretation of Yogācāra and Madhyamaka*. Albany: State University of New York Press, 2011.

Levi, Sylvain. *Mahāyāna-sūtrālaṃkāra: exposé de la doctrine du grand véhicule selon le systéme Yogācāra*. 2 vols. Paris: Bibliothéque de l'École des Hautes Études, 1907, 1911.

Nagao, Gadjin M. *Index to the Mahāyāna-Sūtrālāṃkāra (Sylvain Lévi Edition): Part One: Sanskrit-Tibetan-Chinese*. Tokyo: Nippon Gakujutsu Shinkō-kai, 1958.

———. *Madhyāntavibhāga-Bhāṣya: A Buddhist Philosophical Treatise Edited for the First Time from a Sanskrit Manuscript*. Tokyo: Suzuki Research Foundation, 1964.

Nāgārjuna. *Praise of the Dharma-Sphere* (*Dharmadhātustotra, Chos kyi dbyings su bstod pa*). D1118, bstod tshogs, ka, 63b–67b. Translated in Karl Brunnhölzl, *"In Praise of Dharmadhātu" by Nāgārjuna, Commentary by the Third Karmapa*. Ithaca: Snow Lion, 2007.

8

Tāranātha's *Twenty-One Differences with Regard to the Profound Meaning*

Comparing the Views of the Two Zhentong Masters Dolpopa and Shakya Chokden

Klaus-Dieter Mathes

Historical Background

The distinguishing feature of zhentong Madhyamaka in the Jonang order, to which Tāranātha (1575–1634) belongs, is the fact that it normally restricts the validity of the Common Madhyamaka assertion "all phenomena are empty of an own-being" to phenomena on the level of apparent truth. The ultimate, which is inseparably endowed with innumerable buddha qualities, is considered to be not "empty of an own-being" (rangtong) but "empty of other" (zhentong), namely, accidental stains and so forth.[1] It was the famous Jonangpa Dolpopa Sherab Gyaltsen (1292–1361) who is said to have gained such an insight during a Kālacakra retreat.[2] From the *Mountain Dharma: An Ocean of Definitive Meaning*, which is one of the first works in which Dolpopa expressed his new zhentong understanding, it becomes clear that the latter's full-fledged zhentong theory requires including even an ultimate *sambhogakāya* and *nirmāṇakāya* within an ultimate realm of truth, which is equated with dharmatā, or the unchangeable perfect nature. This, we are told, is in line with extraordinary Mantrayāna.[3] But as a commentator of non-tantric texts, such as the *Ratnagotravibhāga*, Dolpopa explains that the sambhogakāya and nirmāṇakāya are brought forth by a fortified potential that arises from virtuous deeds being newly adopted with effort,[4] and it is only in texts such as the *Mountain Dharma* that we are informed that the created kāyas are merely the ones pertaining to apparent truth. In view of this hermeneutic strategy,[5] the differences between the *Mountain*

Dharma and the *Ratnagotravibhāga* commentary appear to be so fundamental that Hookham wonders if the latter is by Dolpopa at all and not rather by the Third Karmapa Rangjung Dorje (1284–1339).[6]

Still, Dolpopa to some extent reads his originally Kālacakra-based zhentong into the sūtras and such non-tantric treatises as the Tathāgatagarbha sūtras and the Maitreya works. The hermeneutic principles according to which he interprets the Buddhist teachings are laid out in his own "fourth council" (*bka' bsdu bzhi pa*),[7] in which the whole of Buddhist doctrine is reckoned by dividing the teaching into four epochs. Alongside the four epochs of varying quality that make up a cosmic age, Dolpopa uses a lesser set of four epochs to refer to the qualitatively different periods of the teaching. He thus allocates philosophical doctrines to epochs (*yuga*) according to purely dogmatic criteria.[8] The teachings transmitted by Śākyamuni and also the Maitreya works, for example, belong to the Kṛtayuga of doctrine, while other works, such as the ones by Ārya Vimuktisena and Haribhadra, represent the teachings of the inferior Tretāyuga. The common interpretation of the Yogācāra works of Maitreya, Asaṅga, and Vasubandhu as mere *cittamātra* itself reflects for Dolpopa the historical degeneration of the Dharma. The Maitreya works are only Kṛtayuga Dharma when they are explained to be Great Madhyamaka (*dbu ma chen po*).[9]

The theories of buddha-nature and *trisvabhāva* (three natures: the imagined, dependent, and perfect natures) in the Maitreya works offer good canonical support for a distinction between rangtong and zhentong, and it is thus no surprise that an interpretation that supports such a distinction is a major concern for the Jonang. Dolpopa takes the ultimate to be absolutely unconditioned, and it is the *Ratnagotravibhāga* among the Maitreya works that is adduced as the best support for this stance. Thus Dolpopa comments on RGV I.5a in his *Mountain Dharma* in the following way: "Even though [the verse RGV I.5a]: '[Buddhahood] is unconditioned and spontaneously present,'[10] and other [passages] teach that the ultimate Buddha is not conditioned, the underlying intention is that he is [also] free from moments."[11] For Dolpopa's disciple Sazang Mati Paṇchen (1294–1376), the ultimate or buddhahood is thus permanent in the sense of being beyond the three times (i.e., past, present, and future), as becomes clear in Mati Paṇchen's *Ratnagotravibhāga* commentary on RGV I.6cd:

> Buddhahood is unconditioned, since in the beginning, middle, and end it has the nature of being free from conditioned phenonema that arise, abide, and pass out of existence, as has been said in the *[Mahāpari-]nirvāṇa Sūtra*: "A phenomenon that abides in permanence does not belong to the three times. Likewise, the Tathāgata does not belong to the three times, and is therefore permanent."[12]

It is obvious that in this case the perfect nature of the Yogācāra must be restricted, as Tāranātha has done in his final summary of the trisvabhāva theory,[13] to its unchangeable aspect (*avikāra*), since in an absolutely permanent and atemporal buddhahood or buddha-nature (both are ontologically the same for the Jonang) there is no room for an unmistaken (*aviparyāsa*) wisdom cultivated on the path, namely—according to MAV III.11cd—the perfect in terms of being unmistaken.

Already at the time of Dolpopa, the Third Karmapa Rangjung Dorje was propounding a different "zhentong position," or rather a position that was eventually called zhentong by a few later Kagyu[14] such as Karma Trinle (1456–1539).[15] Rangjung Dorje bases his distinction between the true nature of mind or buddha-nature and that from which it is free on *Mahāyānasaṃgraha* I.45–49, in which an impure "ground-consciousness" (*ālayavijnyāna, kun gzhi rnam shes*) is strictly distinguished from a "transmudane mind."[16] In this context Rangjung Dorje stresses the need to distinguish "ground-consciousness" from the "ground" (*kun gzhi*) in terms of suchness.[17] Referring to this passage, Kongtrul Lodro Taye (1813–1899) proceeds in his commentary on the *Profound Inner Principles* to use the zhentong term *kun gzhi ye shes* for the transmundane mind of the *Mahāyānasaṃgraha*.[18] Kongtrul's use of the term *kun gzhi ye shes*[19] does not imply, though, that he took Rangjung Dorje's position to be the same as Dolpopa's. It rather suggests that Kongtrul himself maintains a zhentong whose "basis of emptiness" (*stong gzhi*) is defined in accordance with Rangjung Dorje's *Autocommentary on the Profound Inner Principles*, which in this crucial point follows not the *Ratnagotravibhāga* but the *Mahāyānasaṃgraha*. Rangjung Dorje is a zhentongpa for Kongtrul, but one who explains that which remains in emptiness in a way different from Dolpopa. And indeed, in the ninth chapter of his *Profound Inner Principles* Rangjung Dorje takes the stainless buddha-nature (i.e., the basis of emptiness) as being endowed with the two truths.[20] From the autocommentary it is clear, however, that it is not the normal apparent truth that is included in buddha-nature here, but only a pure aspect of the latter, namely, the "nonexistence of the stains [or] delusions in the eight consciousnesses."[21] What this latter term exactly refers to is explained a little further down in the *Autocommentary on the Profound Inner Principles*, where the use of the word "truth" in the term "apparent truth" is justified on the grounds that one cannot deny mere appearance as such, even though its interpretation as a perceived object and perceiving subject is not true:

> What has been imagined as the duality of a perceived and a perceiver does not exist at all, given the pronouncement [in MAV I.3] by the Venerable Maitreya: "A consciousness arises that has the appearances of objects, sentient beings, a self, and perceptions. It does not have a [corresponding outer] object, and since [such] an object does not exist, it (i.e., a perceiving subject) does not exist either."[22] Thus it has been said that no perceived [objects] or perceiving [subjects] of the imagined [nature] exist at all. Well then, how can it be presented as a truth? [The answer is:] Even though it does not exist, [something] appears. This is what is called apparent truth, for it has the nature (*rang gi ngo bo nyid*) of not being deceptive.[23]

In response to the objection that these mere appearances would then be the ultimate truth, since the latter is defined as not being deceptive in the treatises on logic, Rangjung Dorje further clarifies his understanding of the ultimate truth as follows:

> These [mere appearances] are presented as the expressible ultimate (*paryāyaparamārtha*), while the ultimate truth [here] is that which[24] is related to the reasoning of dharmatā, [namely,] the natural emptiness previously mentioned during the presentation of the eighteen [types of] great emptiness.[25]

In other words, the buddha-nature or the pure mind includes "mere appearances" in the form of the expressible ultimate truth, and it is only the latter that is taken as apparent truth here. That it is different from what is ordinarily included in apparent truth is clear from Rangjung Dorje's *Dharmadhātustava* commentary, where the two aspects (*nirvikāra* and *aviparyāsa*) of the perfect nature in MAV III.11cd are explained in the following way: "The two [aspects of the perfect], the unchangeable and unmistaken, are taken [respectively] as the defining characteristics of the two truths. Acceptance by common consent (*lokaprasiddha*) and by reason (*yuktiprasiddha*) are varieties of the apparent truth."[26] In other words, the unchangeable perfect is taken as the ultimate, and the perfect in terms of being unmistaken as a restricted form of apparent truth, which does not include acceptance by common consent and the like.

It should have become clear by now that Rangjung Dorje, in contrast to the Jonang, fully accepts the Yogācāra theory of trisvabhāva, that is, two aspects of the perfect nature. This entails that the latter possesses moments. In the *Profound Inner Principles* the true nature of mind is consequently equated with dependent arising.[27] In this context, it is of interest that Kongtrul Lodro Taye, who otherwise strictly follows Dolpopa's *Ratnagotravibhāga* commentary, deviates from the latter's zhentong understanding of the term "unconditioned" (*asaṃskṛta*) in his commentary on RGV I.6. Referring to Rongton Sheja Kunrik's (1367–1449) explanation of four ways of understanding "unconditioned," Kongtrul states that the dharmakāya only shares this quality of being unconditioned to a certain extent, inasmuch as it does not appear to disciples. If one claimed that it is completely unconditioned, this would contradict the fact that it possesses knowledge, compassion, and power.[28]

To sum up, whether one wants to call Rangjung Dorje's doctrine zhentong or not, there is an alternative way of defining how the pure mind or buddha-nature is free from or empty of other (i.e., adventitious stains), and some Kagyupas decided to call this zhentong, too. It should be noted that with an ultimate that still possesses moments, a "zhentong" distinction can be better brought into line with Mahāmudrā teachings,[29] and this is exactly what Rangjung Dorje did. It is thus no longer so puzzling how Situ Paṇchen Chokyi Jungne (1699/1700–1774) "blended the seemingly irreconcilable zhentong and mahāmudrā positions."[30]

Another famous scholar whose zhentong differs from the Jonang position is Serdok Paṇchen Shakya Chokden (1428–1507). In *Recognizing Reality*, Georges Dreyfus has observed that Shakya Chokden fully endorses a zhentong view only in works written after his first meeting with the Seventh Karmapa (1454–1506) in 1484,[31] and it is thus interesting that Shakya Chokden's zhentong differs from the Jonang position in a way similar to Rangjung Dorje's "zhentong." Kongtrul Lodro Taye notices in his *Treasury of Knowledge* (*Shes bya kun khyab mdzod*) that Shakya Chokden has his own views on what is exactly empty of what, or, to use the technical terms, how the negandum (*dgag bya*), the basis of negation (*dgag gzhi*), and the mode of being empty (*stong tshul*) are defined.

Kongtrul says that zhentongpas take the perfect nature as the basis of negation, the imagined and the dependent natures as the negandum, and the mode of being empty as the absence of these two neganda in the basis of negation.[32] He adds, however, that Shakya Chokden holds a view different from this and illustrates this by quoting from Shakya Chokden's *Explanation of Profound Peace Free from Mental Fabrication*:

> As to the basis that is empty, it is the dependent, the entire "mind" (*shes pa*), that takes on various forms of a perceived object and perceiving subject. The negandum is the imagined. According to the division into perceived and perceiver, it is twofold. With regard to each of them there are two, so that we have two pairs of a perceived and perceiver, one for the person and one for phenomena.[33]
>
> As to in what sense it is empty, the basis of negation is empty of the negandum by virtue of being "empty of other," not by virtue of being "empty of self," for the following reason: The negandum, namely, the duality of a perceived and a perceiver, is an "other-being" with regard to the basis of negation, [namely,] the mind" (*shes pa*), which appears as two, [duality] not being taken as its own-being. What is then the own-being of this mind that appears as two? It is the so-called nondual wisdom, namely, mere awareness and luminosity.[34]

Kongtrul continues his presentation of zhentong along this (namely, Shakya Chokden's) line of thought, elaborating it on the basis of the sixteen forms of emptiness in the *Madhyāntavibhāga*. Kongtrul's position on zhentong still needs further clarification, but it is at least noteworthy that while in the sixth chapter of his *Treasury of Knowledge* he quotes nearly the entire *dbu ma chen po* paragraph of Tāranātha's *Essence of Zhentong*, he skips the last part, where—against the purport of the Yogācāra works—the trisvabhāva theory is brought into line with that of buddha-nature by restricting the perfect nature to its unchangeable aspect.[35]

To sum up, from the time of Dolpopa it is possible to trace, parallel to the Jonang position, another zhentong that distinguishes the basis of negation from the negandum in a different way. Whereas for the Jonangpas the basis of negation is a perfect nature that is restricted to its unchangeable aspect and thus transcendent and doctrinally mainly based on the buddha-nature theory, Shakya Chokden, as well as Rangjung Dorje and some other Kagyupas, adheres to a distinction based on Yogācāra, that is, mainly the *Mahāyānasaṃgraha* and the *Madhyāntavibhāga*.

TĀRANĀTHA'S TWENTY-ONE DIFFERENCES WITH REGARD TO THE PROFOUND MEANING

For a short but brilliant analysis of the positions of Dolpopa and Shakya Chokden we are very much indebted to the Jonang master Tāranātha, who is considered to be a follower and proponent of Dolpopa's doctrine. In each point of the *Twenty-One Differences with Regard to the Profound Meaning*[36] a fictive initial statement of Shakya Chokden is followed by a similarly fictive reply of Dolpopa, Tāranātha being, of course, well aware of the fact that this is all ahistorical.[37] To be sure, it is not possible to establish Shakya Chokden's or Dolpopa's views on the basis of this short text alone, but it does sharpen our awareness of the subtle aspects of zhentong when studying the bulky and often not very systematic works of these masters. Furthermore, critically evaluating these doctrinal differences against the background of pertinent Indian texts in such traditions as the Madhyamaka, Yogācāra, and Tathāgatagarbha promises to be a second interesting task. Both are, however, beyond the scope of this chapter. Such an evaluation will, however, be undertaken with regard to the different presentations of trisvabhāva as an example of how one might proceed.

Tāranātha begins his somewhat delicate task of comparing the two masters Dolpopa and Shakya Chokden in a conciliating manner, by explaining that both supposedly see what profound reality is and hence should not have different thoughts about it. It is only to accommodate the different needs of their disciples that they enunciate variant views. Even though the essential zhentong view and meditation practices of both masters are the same, there are a lot of minor differences regarding tenets (*grub mtha'*) that arise when formulating the view on the level of apparent truth.[38]

The first four of the twenty-one points address differences in the exegesis of the Madhyamaka and Maitreya texts that are considered to be commentaries on the Buddha's intention underlying the second and third turnings of the "Wheel of the Dharma" (dharmacakra).[39] Points 5–8 embody Shakya Chokden's and Dolpopa's different understanding of nondual wisdom. In points 9–16, their views on the trisvabhāva theory are distinguished. In a related topic, Tāranātha also elaborates the different understandings of self-awareness (point 11), entities and nonentities, and conditioned and unconditioned phenonema (all in point 13). Next, our attention is drawn to different ways of relating the four noble truths with the apparent and ultimate (point 17). The last four points deal with the two masters' views on buddha-nature.

Translation: The Twenty-One Differences

DIFFERENCE NO. 1

Shakya Chokden:[40] All the views of the Prāsaṅgika- and Svātantrika-[Madhyamaka] are logically correct [and accurately represent] the Buddha's intention in the middle turning and the corpus of analytical works.[41] The explicit teaching of the middle [turning], in addition, [has to] be taken literally, and the corpus of analytical works is not in accordance with the explicit teaching of the last turning.[42]

Dolpopa:[43] Even though [the rangtongpas] are proud that these Prāsaṅgika and Svātantrika views [represent] the intention of the middle turning and the corpus of analytical works, [their interpretation of this] intention is not free from mistakes. Although the explicit teaching of the analytical works generally appears to be consistent, it is not so in a great number of cases. Since many passages[44] of the treatises of the middle turning clearly teach zhentong, the explicit teaching of the middle turning and the analytical works [should] not be [taken] literally. The explicit teaching of most passages of the middle turning and the analytical works contradicts neither the Prāsaṅgika and Svātantrika nor the zhentong. Nevertheless, for those appealing to the extraordinary tenet known as rangtong, it has become a cause of confusion. On the other hand, given that [these texts] do not teach different tenets, that they contradict other traditions, and that there are [in fact] many extraordinary passages that only teach zhentong, even the middle turning and the analytical works [can be said to] teach Zhentong Madhyamaka. From these texts [of the middle turning], however, the extraordinary points of zhentong—namely, [those reached by] following only the lines of commentary on the intention of the last turning—have not clearly or extensively emerged. They are the extraordinary tenets of the Prāsaṅgika and Svātantrika. What is nowadays known as the rangtong view was not taught [in the middle turning]; nevertheless, this rangtong [interpretation of] the intention of the Buddha and his sons is taught in detail [nowadays].[45]

DIFFERENCE NO. 2

Shakya Chokden:[46] With regard to the fact that the *Abhisamayālaṃkāra* teaches both the tenets of rangtong and zhentong, [Maitreya] considered the necessity of zhentong in terms of a meditation practice, and that of Prāsaṅgika and Svātantrika, [which are at the same time] the rangtong of the subsequent three works,[47] when it comes to cutting through mental fabrications with the help of the view. The remaining four Maitreya works[48] teach only zhentong.[49] With regard to these [latter four] there are two types: In the *Ratnagotravibhāga* ultimately only one single path is taught and the possibility of a cut-off potential refuted. In the other three [Maitreya] works[50] ultimately three paths and a cut-off potential[51] are explained.[52]

Dolpopa: There are no different tenets in the five Maitreya works at all. The tenet of the so-called rangtong is not explained even in the *Abhisamayālaṃkāra*. A real cut-off potential and three ultimate paths are not explained in the *[Mahāyāna-]sūtrālaṃkāra* and so forth.[53]

DIFFERENCE NO. 3

Shakya Chokden: Rangtong is considered to be more profound when it comes to cutting through mental fabrications with the help of the view. When it comes to the practice of meditation, however, it is said that zhentong is more profound. The rangtong[54] of the latter in turn, namely, Prāsaṅgika and Svātantrika, is acknowledged in the tradition of the subsequent three works (*Mahāyānasūtrālaṃkāra* etc.).[55]

Dolpopa: The view of rangtong as taught by the Buddha and his sons is superior in cutting through mental fabrications. Nevertheless, it is contained in zhentong, and therefore view and practice are not opposed to each other.[56] To maintain that the rangtong, [namely,] the Prāsaṅgika and Svātantrika—as it is known nowadays—is the view of the subsequent three works, [thinking that according to the latter] nothing exists ultimately, is wrong. [Such a rangtong] is therefore not better in cutting through mental fabrications with the help of the view, for this would be a false denial.[57]

Difference No. 4

Shakya Chokden: Even though zhentong goes beyond Cittamātra and is thus acceptable to Madhyamaka, rangtong is superior to it with regard to the view. Still, the former (zhentong) is not wrong, for it accords with the experiential object of meditation.[58]

Dolpopa: Rangtong, too, goes beyond Cittamātra, and thus falls under Madhyamaka within the system of the four tenets. It is not the pure ultimate, however, the highest view being zhentong alone.[59]

Difference No. 5

Shakya Chokden: For this reason, nondual wisdom is not analyzed when following the Maitreya works. When critically analyzing it, after having excluded [its] opposite, [wisdom] cannot withstand such analysis. Therefore, since it cannot withstand a critical analysis [aimed at] ascertaining the ultimate, rangtong is more profound in terms of the view. Even though it does not withstand analysis, this wisdom is experienced uninterruptedly. Therefore it abides like the experiential object of meditation, namely, zhentong.[60]

Dolpopa: Nondual wisdom does withstand critical analysis.[61] Therefore, this very analysis itself is self-delusion.[62]

Difference No. 6

Shakya Chokden: Nondual wisdom is momentary awareness (*rig pa*), not permanent, and has no chance to abide.[63]

Dolpopa: This [wisdom] is not momentary but permanent and stable, in that it is beyond the three times (i.e., past, present, and future).[64]

Difference No. 7

Shakya Chokden: Likewise, given that it is knowledge (*shes pa*), wisdom [can be] taken to be an entity / existence (*dngos po*).[65]

Dolpopa: And it [can be] taken to be beyond both [the state of] an entity/existence and a nonentity / nonexistence.[66]

DIFFERENCE NO. 8

Shakya Chokden: Likewise it [can be] taken to be conditioned.[67]

Dolpopa: It [can be] taken to be unconditioned, too.[68]

DIFFERENCE NO. 9

Shakya Chokden: If one isolates its specific aspects (*rang ldog*), all knowledge is—as generally accepted in Tibet—only clarity and awareness, and here an entity of the dependent [nature]. The isolation of the specific aspects of mere dualistic appearances that arise in this [clarity and awareness] results in the imagined nature. When viewed under its aspect of being accompanied by these dualistic appearances, clarity and awareness constitute the dependent nature. From the perspective, however, that it is unstained by these dualistic phenomena throughout beginningless time, this clarity and awareness constitute the perfect nature. Based on that, dependent entities as such are by nature the same as the perfect nature, even though they are different as isolates (*ldog cha*) and different in terms of their respective defining characteristics.[69]

Dolpopa: The imagined aspect, which is imputed by the mind's multitude of thoughts, and its appearances in the form of external objects, is the perceived. The isolation of its specific aspects is the imagined nature. The isolation of the specific aspects of the mind and mental factors results in the dependent nature, namely, knowledge constituted by knowledge or consciousness of apparent truth. Clarity and awareness, by nature free from mental fabrication, is the perfect nature. Thus the imagined and the dependent are substantially the same; their defining characteristics are very different, however. Not only are the perfect and the dependent different as isolates and in terms of their defining characteristics, but they are also not the same by nature (*ngo bo gcig pa*).[70] The previous presentations of this [trisvabhāva-theory] were mainly in line with Cittamātra, but [Dolpopa] thinks that the tradition of Madhyamaka is only this [trisvabhāva].[71]

DIFFERENCE NO. 10

Shakya Chokden: The imagined nature fully pertains to what is not true, the perfect to what is true, and the dependent to both.[72]

Dolpopa: The imagined and the dependent both fully pertain—that is to say, through and through—to what is not true.[73]

Difference No. 11

Shakya Chokden: All self-awareness—understood as the isolation of its specific aspects—[belongs] exclusively to the ultimate [truth].[74]

Dolpopa: Given that the self-awareness[75] of consciousness [belongs] exclusively to the apparent [truth], self-awareness, too, has both an apparent and an ultimate aspect.[76]

Difference No. 12

Shakya Chokden: The perfect [nature] is emptiness. The imagined [nature] is not emptiness, even though it is purely empty.[77] Emptiness fully pertains to the ultimate [truth].[78]

Dolpopa: Everything, phenomena and their true nature, can only be called emptiness. Emptiness does not pertain to (lit., "is not pervaded by") the ultimate truth. It is not counted unambiguously among the synonyms [of the ultimate]: [emptiness] is related to [the ultimate only] in a general sense.[79]

Difference No. 13

Shakya Chokden: The works on valid cognition, the Abhidharma, among others, are mostly [written] in accordance with general Dharma terminology. This being the case, the attainment of pacification fully pertains to both categories, those of entities/existence and nonentities/nonexistence;[80] knowledge (*shes pa*)[81] [only] to that of entities.[82] The ultimate is not an entity. Since it is not conditioned, it is a nonentity, [like] the sky and so forth. There are different aspects of the unconditioned—suchness not being conditioned by causal defilements, or mere clarity and awareness not being newly produced, and so forth. Therefore, when one enumerates categories, these are designated as unconditioned. They are, however, not the [real] unconditioned as opposed to the conditioned (*'du byed*) and the defining characteristics (*mtshan nyid*); therefore, they are unconditioned only in a metaphorical sense.[83]

Dolpopa: Explanations along the lines of Pramāṇa or Abhidharma belong to traditions that mainly ascertain the apparent truth. With regard here to definitive meaning, when it is mainly the ultimate truth that is being ascertained, entities and nonentities fully pertain to the apparent [truth] and vice versa.[84] The ultimate truth is neither an entity nor a nonentity; therefore, the attainment of pacification[85] certainly does not pertain to the ultimate. [If it did,] wisdom would not be an entity, while being knowledge at the same time. Therefore, knowledge would not pertain to [the category of] entities, while to maintain that the ultimate truth is a nonentity would be improper Dharma.[86] To maintain that the ultimate is an entity [is in accordance with] the tradition of maintaining the [ultimate existence of] entities. All nonentities like the sky, among others, which the Ābhidharmikas take to be unconditioned, are there considered to be conditioned, and for this reason, both entities and nonentities fully pertain to the conditioned. The ultimate is the real unconditioned. The sky, among others, are thus unconditioned [entities] only in a metaphorical sense.[87]

DIFFERENCE NO. 14

Shakya Chokden: The "very face" (*rang ngo*) of the dependent, being empty of the imagined, that is, the negandum, is the basis of emptiness. It may be taken as the ultimate being empty of the apparent.[88]

Dolpopa: The perfect is the basis of emptiness. It is empty of the two neganda, the dependent and the imagined, in that the ultimate is empty of the apparent. [The explanation of] the dependent as being empty of the imagined applies only when ascertaining mere apparent truth.[89]

DIFFERENCE NO. 15

Shakya Chokden: Even though the "pure dependent" is widely known in Tibet, it is in reality not the dependent but rather what is "perfect in terms of being unmistaken." The latter is the actual perfect nature. Since the origin and usage of the conventional [term] "pure dependent" is not clear, it is not good to use it.[90]

Dolpopa: Even though the usage of the conventional [term] "pure dependent" is not clear—the term is not found in the treatises—its meaning is fully established [in them], and therefore it is proper to use it. This follows from the fact that the Buddha's teaching is based on meaning [rather than words proper], and that in olden times in Tibet all agreed on such a convention. Therefore, it is appropriate not to find any fault in the transmitted pith-instructions deriving from Maitreya. Even though some [parts of the] wisdom of the noble [path of] learning are [called] "perfect in terms of being unmistaken" in [certain] passages of the [Maitreya works], the presentation of its conventional [term] (i.e., the term "pure dependent") is good. This is because of [instances] where some [phrases] such as "for those who have attained the [bodhisattva]-levels the ground appears as gold" are also [taken as denoting] "perfect in terms of being unmistaken."[91]

DIFFERENCE NO. 16

Shakya Chokden: The perfect in terms of being unmistaken fully pertains to the actual perfect nature.[92]

Dolpopa: This [being unmistaken] is only taught as being the expressible perfect, in the same way as the twelve limbs of the Buddha's speech have been also said to be the perfect [in terms of being unmistaken]. Thus the latter, in contrast to the unchangeable perfect nature, is in reality something that belongs to the pure dependent and is the perfect only in a metaphorical sense. The unmistaken perfect that is the same as the unchangeable [perfect] is called the "ultimate perfect in terms of being unmistaken." It is purely unchangeable.[93] Therefore, when one ascertains the true state of being, it is only this "[ultimate] perfect." When one explains in detail [its] synonyms, both types [of the perfect] (i.e., the unchangeable and the perfect in terms of being unmistaken) are presented.[94]

Difference No. 17

Shakya Chokden: The [noble] truth of the path also [belongs to] the ultimate truth.[95]

Dolpopa: Among the four noble truths the truth of cessation is the ultimate, and the other three are the apparent truth. To be more precise, only the actual cessation, which exists throughout beginningless time, [is called] ultimate [truth]. The other three [noble] truths and the analytical cessation fully pertain, in reality, to the apparent truth. Hence the actual [noble] truth of the path fully pertains to the apparent [truth], and the actual truth of cessation to the ultimate [truth]. This follows from the fact that the [noble] truth of the path in its ultimate aspect is one with the beginningless [ultimate truth]. Because it is [in reality] the [noble] truth of cessation, [this ultimate aspect] is the [noble] truth of the path [only] in a metaphorical sense.[96]

Difference No. 18

Shakya Chokden: There is no buddha-nature in the mind-stream of sentient beings. The natural luminosity of the mind of sentient beings is merely the cause of the buddha-nature and [its] "basic element" (*khams*). Therefore, there is a buddha-nature or basic element as a cause in all ordinary sentient beings, but it is not like the actual [buddha-nature], which is rather the [same as] buddha wisdom.[97]

Dolpopa: The actual buddha-nature is nothing else than [the buddha-nature] of the mind-stream of sentient beings, and if it is the actual [buddha-nature] of a buddha, then it is established that sentient beings possess it, precisely because it is the dharmatā of sentient beings. This is proven, in particular, by a number of canonical passages. The explanation [of the buddha-nature] as the basic element and cause [refers to] a cause different from the sphere / element (*dbyings*),[98] given that the latter is neither an efficient cause nor an efficient sphere.[99]

Difference No. 19

Shakya Chokden: [Passages that] state that buddha-nature is endowed with essentially inseparable qualities refer only to the fruit [of the path]. On the level of the cause, the qualities still have to be developed. Having this capability, buddha-nature exists only as seeds [in ordinary sentient beings].[100]

Dolpopa: The essentially inseparable qualities are naturally present. They exist even in the buddha-nature of the basis, since [first] something that arises, [in the sense of being] newly [acquired], may possibly be not naturally present; [second], the division of basis, path, and fruit applies only to the level of "phenomena" (dharmin)[101] [or] apparent truth; and [third], there is, [in terms of] the nature [of phenomena], only one buddha-nature. It must henceforth be the buddha-nature, adorned with all the qualities of the ultimate.[102]

Difference No. 20

Shakya Chokden: The major and minor marks and the like [of a Buddha do not belong] to the qualities of the dharmakāya.[103, 104]

Dolpopa: With regard to all types of buddha qualities, there is an aspect of them that pertains to the ultimate qualities of the dharmakāya, and appears only to the Buddha himself, and another aspect that pertains to the apparent qualities of the form kāyas, and appears to others, namely, the disciples [of the Buddha]. As for the explicit teaching of the *Ratnadārikā Sūtra*[105] and the *Uttaratantra* [*Ratnagotravibhāga*], in general it is necessary to explain them in terms of the qualities of the two kāyas.[106] On the whole, with respect to the major and minor [marks of a Buddha], [Dolpopa] only makes analogies in accordance with what is generally accepted. When taken as taught in other sūtras and the tantras, both [the dharmakāya and the form-kāyas] share aspects common to all of them.[107] What is different [from the *Ratnagotravibhāga*] when Mantra[yāna is taught] with regard to zhentong is precisely this [inclusion of all qualities in the ultimate].[108, 109]

Difference No. 21

Shakya Chokden: Only the seeds of the fruit are inherently present in the form of the natural luminosity of mind. [Their] improvement is achieved by meditating on the path, until the fruit is finally actualized.[110]

Dolpopa: Throughout beginningless time, wisdom is effortlessly perfect in the form of the ultimate maṇḍala. On the path, stains are removed by meditating on it, and [this ever-present wisdom] is actualized.[111]

Tāranātha's Conclusion

Having elaborated Shakya Chokden's and Dolpopa's twenty-one differences with regard to the profound meaning, Tāranātha concludes by pointing out one fundamental difference, to which all the other ones basically refer:

> Paṇchen Shakya Chokden takes nondual wisdom to be nonabiding and impermanent in every moment, in that it is not something single but multiple. [For the] omniscient Jonangpa (Dolpopa) it is in reality neither one nor many; provisionally he accepts it as reasonable when [wisdom] is presented as being single, and takes it as being permanent, impartible, all-pervading, free from mental fabrication and ineffable. In view of this, the [main] difference is, in short, that [the former] takes [wisdom] as being impermanent, and [the latter] takes it as being permanent.[112]

We are further informed that Dolpopa infers from the omnipresence of nondual wisdom that all qualities of a Buddha are already present in ordinary beings. For the same reason, nondual wisdom cannot be impaired by reasoning, such as that to the effect that it is neither one nor many, and hence withstands analysis. On these grounds the tenets of the Prāsaṅgika and Svātantrika, which assert the destruction of nondual wisdom by analysis, is wrong, and hence these Prāsaṅgika and Svātantrika views are impure. One comes to know this by way of analysis that makes use of reasoning without distorting the original intention of the middle turning. Dolpopa and Shakya Chokden agree, however, that ultimately the buddha-nature is beyond words and thoughts, and the unmistaken object of nonconceptual wisdom. Tāranātha concludes by explaining at length that Dolpopa's "permanent" is not the ordinary opposite of impermanent: "This ['permanent'] is free from mental fabrications. It is the unchangeable sphere that is free from both the impermanence of an established entity and the permanence of a negated nonentity. It is free from the characteristic signs of permanence."[113]

Tāranātha's Presentation of Dolpopa's and Shakya Chokden's Positions

A comparison of Tāranātha's summary of Dolpopa's position with what we find in the latter's pertinent works, such as the *Mountain Dharma*, shows that the subject matter is correctly presented. Of particular interest are Tāranātha's elaborations on difference no. 20, where he confirms my own observation that Dolpopa explains buddha-nature more in line with general Mahāyāna when commenting on the *Ratnagotravibhāga*.[114] Also, the presentation of the trisvabhāva theory is in accordance with the *Mountain Dharma*, in which Dolpopa explains: "The basis that is empty of the imagined is the dependent, and the basis which is empty of even the dependent is the true nature of phenomena, the perfect."[115] A little further down Dolpopa further explains: "It has been taught that phenomena that [belong to] the imagined [and] the dependent do not really exist, and that the true nature of phenomena, [namely,] the perfect really does. The meaning of rangtong and zhentong is taught in these two statements."[116]

These two quotes clearly show that it is only the perfect that really exists as the basis that is empty of the dependent (and thus also the imagined). Moreover, the following passage from the *Mountain Dharma* confirms Tāranātha's observation in difference no. 14 that "[the explanation of] the dependent as being empty of the imagined applies only when ascertaining mere apparent truth":

> As to the lack of an own-being in the imagined, the [imagined] does not exist in terms of its own defining characteristics. Being established as the mere apparent, [or rather as] the mere mistaken apparent, it is established neither as apparent truth nor as the correct apparent. As to the lack of an own-being in the dependent, even though [the dependent] exists on the level of apparent [truth] as an own-being that arises from something else, it does not exist as an own-being that arises from itself and is not in the least established in reality. In this way, the two lack an own-being, because they are rangtong. As to the true nature of phenomena, the perfect, or the basis of the nonexistence of these two (i.e., the imagined and dependent), even though it is not the case that it lacks an own-being, it is the basis for the lack of an own-being in the phenomena of apparent [truth], which are different from [this basis]. Therefore it is the own-being of the ultimate truth, or the "body belonging to the own-being" (*svābhāvikakāya*).[117]

That the ultimate basis of emptiness is restricted to the unchangeable perfect becomes clear in the following passage where the perfect in terms of being unmistaken is equated with the form-kāyas of the apparent truth:

> Thus the ultimate Buddha is the kāya of the five self-arisen wisdoms. He abides permanently in the form of these five wisdoms, which are suchness and the unchangeable perfect. The form-kāyas of the apparent [truth] possess correct wisdom, namely, the perfect in terms of being unmistaken, and thus the wisdom of the Mahāyāna[-path] of no more learning that is not beyond moments.[118]

For Dolpopa, the ultimate is beyond moments and the three times. The permanence of the ultimate wisdom is thus not an ordinary permanence as opposed to impermanence but one that is, as Tāranātha puts it, beyond these latter two categories. To be sure, for Dolpopa all kāyas have an ultimate aspect that is beyond the three times:

> That the permanent Buddha and the liberation of the Buddha are form, that even space is the form of the Buddha, and so forth—the meaning of such statements must be understood in the context of forms, and so forth, being explained [on the level] of suchness or as forms, and so on, which are beyond the three times and the threefold world.[119]

Such an extreme form of transcendence explains Dolpopa's sharp distinction between the ultimate and apparent truths—which he defines with the phrase: "a difference in terms of a negation of an identity" (*gcig pa bkag pa'i tha dad pa*). From this it does not follow, though, that the two truths are different entities,[120] but simply that the ultimate exists and the apparent does not (negation of identity). To be sure, since there is only one essence for Dolpopa, namely, that of the ultimate, it does not make sense to speak of an essential difference, since this would require the existence of another essence from which it differs. This also means that Dolpopa's distinction between ultimate and apparent kāyas does not entail the absurd ontological view that there really are two different sets of kāyas.[121] It is rather that only the ultimate kāyas exist ontologically. The kāyas of apparent truth, which are equated with the perfect in terms of being unmistaken, do not really exist, any more than the apparent world does. Still, on the level of apparent truth they are produced to the same extent that the accidental stains of the apparent truth are removed (which enables the ultimate to manifest on the level of apparent truth), and in this sense there are accumulations of merit and wisdom. Tāranātha's restriction of the perfect to its unchangeable aspect is thus perfectly in line with the position of Dolpopa.

Things become a bit more complicated in the case of Shakya Chokden. Even later Tibetan thinkers had difficulties in pinning down his position.[122] To give an example, in his short presentation of buddha-nature, which was written in 1474,[123] Shakya Chokden endorses Buton Rinchen Drub's (1290–1364) and Sakya Paṇḍita's (1182–1251) Madhyamaka hermeneutics[124] of ascribing a provisional meaning (*neyārtha*) to buddha-nature theory. But in difference no. 21 Shakya Chokden is said to hold that the seeds of the fruit (buddhahood) are naturally present in the form of the natural luminosity of mind. This is strikingly similar to the position of Go Lotsāwa Zhonnu Pel (1392–1481), who speaks of "subtle qualities" or "seeds of qualities" in the mind-stream of sentient beings. By explaining a natural growth of qualities, Zhonnu Pel is able to read the *Ratnagotravibhāga* as a teaching with definitive meaning (*nītārtha*), without being forced to accept the ontological consequences of buddha-nature theory.[125] It is likely that Shakya Chokden later adopted such a stance, Tāranātha being right in this point, but only a careful study of Shakya Chokden's works written after 1484 will tell.

The notion in points 1–4 that rangtong is more profound when mental fabrications are cut through with the help of the view finds support in Shakya Chokden's *Dharmadharmatāvibhāga* commentary, in which the commentator shows that the teaching of a transformation of the basis (*āśrayaparivṛtti*) does not contradict the Svātantrika and Prāsaṅgika views.[126]

A comparison with the *Explanation of Profound Peace Free from Mental Fabrication*[127] shows that Tāranātha also got the main points of Shakya Chokden's definition of the basis of emptiness and the negandum right. Tāranātha's difference no. 14, though, which has Shakya Chokden equating the emptiness of the dependent from the imagined with the ultimate, which is empty of the apparent, is problematic. In fact, Shakya Chokden takes the dependent to exist ultimately only when describing Cittamātra. Thus he says in his *Distinguishing the Two Chariot Traditions*:[128]

> Outside objects and what is explained as general characteristics are the imagined, and empty of an own-being. What appears as [the imagined] through mental imprints is the dependent and truly established. Emptiness that [is taken as] the basis of negation (the dependent), empty of the negandum (the imagined), is the perfect. Therefore it is the ultimate truth.[129]

The Yogācāras, on the other hand, who according to Shakya Chokden[130] belong to the Madhyamaka, are not said to claim the ultimate existence of the dependent nature. Ultimate truth is equated rather with the unchangeable perfect nature:

> The Yogācāras explain: "The imagined is empty of an own-being, and the dependent empty of an other-being. The remainder left over as something that does not lack an own-being is precisely the nature of the dependent or the so-called perfect. [. . .] When both Mādhyamikas (i.e., the Yogācāras and the Asvabhāvavādins) postulate what must be meditated upon or experienced in the meditative equipoise of the Noble Ones, their perception is in mutual accordance: both explain it as the wisdom of dharmadhātu. When labeling it after rising from meditative equipoise, they differ: The Yogācāras label it [the experiential] wisdom of dharmadhātu or nondual wisdom, which goes by the name "unchangeable perfect"—the actual ultimate truth, the supreme self, the permanent, stable, quiescent, steady, and truly established.[131]

In other words, Shakya Chokden restricts the ultimate truth in the same way as the Jonang to the unchangeable perfect nature, which is also equated with wisdom. Against the background of this passage, the quintessence of Tāranātha's comparison of Dolpopa with Shakya Chokden, namely, that they take wisdom to be resepectively permanent and impermanent, appears questionable. The main difference is rather that Shakya Chokden does not define zhentong as the ultimate being empty of the apparent but includes the dependent nature within the basis of negation. This is also clear in the following passage from the *Explanation of Profound Peace Free from Mental Fabrication*, where Shakya Chokden disagrees with a popular zhentong position:

> The apparent [truth], [comprising] all conditioned entities, is empty of an own-being (rangtong), while the ultimate, everything[132] unconditioned,

> is empty of other (zhentong). This explanation is the assertion of the great Mādhyamika Vasubandhu, for this is how it is explained in the *Bṛhaṭṭīkā*. Such an explanation does not hold true, since it is not in accordance with the basic Maitreya works and contradicts the clear zhentong teachings of the indisputable works of Asaṅga and his brother, as well as the text tradition of Dignāga and his disciple.[133]

Shakya Chokden continues by presenting his own definition of zhentong based on the *Madhyāntavibhāga*, namely, that the dependent is empty of the imagined, and he explains:

> Just as in the lines: "False imagining [equated with the dependent nature] exists. Duality is not found in it"[134] the dependent is "phenomena" (dharmin), or the basis of emptiness, and both [aspects of the] imagined, the perceived object and the perceiving subject, are the neganda, or that of which [the dependent] is empty. There is an explanation of the wisdom beyond the duality of a perceived object and the perceiving subject as an entity that is empty, but [the latter] is not taken as the subject, or the basis of emptiness.[135]

It should be noted that for Shakya Chokden the dependent nature, or false imagining, exists in terms of its own-being, specific marks, and its own nature, but not truly, on the level of ultimate truth, or in reality. It is like an illusion.[136] This presentation is based on the reasonable interpretation of the Yogācāra works as implying that the dependent nature only exists on the level of apparent truth. Shakya Chokden is, of course, well aware that in the *Ratnagotravibhāga* and the *Bṛhaṭṭīkā* the perfect nature is taken to be empty of the imagined.[137]

From what has been said till now, it is clear that the way Tāranātha summarizes Shakya Chokden's view on trisvabhāva is not strictly accurate. Even though the dependent nature is undoubtedly taken to be the basis of negation, Shakya Chokden describes it as existing ultimately only in the Cittamātra, but not in the Yogācāra. And it is the presentation of the trisvabhāva in the Yogācāra that reflects his own zhentong view. It is also questionable whether wisdom is really only a conditioned entity for him; as we have seen earlier, Shakya Chokden explains the unchangeable perfect nature as being nondual wisdom.

The Theory of Trisvabhāva in the Madhyāntavibhāga and Its Commentaries

The trisvabhāva theory of the *Madhyāntavibhāga* plays an important role not only for those zhentongpas who define the basis of emptiness in line with Yogācāra, but also the Jonangpas, whose main doctrinal support otherwise is buddha-nature theory. How is it possible, though, that such different positions on emptiness can be doctrinally supported by one and the same text?

The main focus for the proponents of both "Yogācāra zhentong" and "Tathāgatagarbha zhentong" lies on the initial two stanzas of the first chapter of the *Madhyāntavibhāga*, in which the Middle Path is defined by three philosophical propositions: (a) false imagining exists; (b) subject-object duality, though created by false imagining, is not found in the latter itself; (c) false imagining is found in relation to emptiness in the sense that emptiness is found in false imagining as its true nature.[138] One has to bear in mind that the root text, which does not make much use of trisvabhāva terms in the initial stanzas, equates the perceived object with the imagined nature, false imagining with the dependent nature, and the absence of duality, or emptiness, with the perfect nature in MAV I.5.

As I have already noted in my article on Tāranātha's *Essence of Zhentong*,[139] the relationship between false imagining and emptiness can be variously defined along the lines of two different trisvabhāva models, in the *Madhyāntavibhāga* and its Indian commentaries. The central focus of the first model, which is mainly based on the first section of the first chapter (MAV I.1–11), lies on a false imagining or dependent nature that at times is taken to exist ultimately, though not by Maitreya and Vasubandhu. Duality and emptiness are just two different aspects of false imagining, namely, the way it appears and the way it really is. In the second section (MAV I.12–22) a positively understood emptiness (comparable to suchness or the buddha element in the RGV) replaces false imagining at the center of the old equation. It is now emptiness, defined as natural luminosity, that can appear in two modes, either as being accompanied by adventitious stains (under which false imagining is included) or free from these stains (see the end of this section). This results in two trisvabhāva models that come close to what Sponberg, in his article "The Trisvabhāva Doctrine in India and China," calls the pivotal and progressive exegetical model of trisvabhāva.[140] The first model is centered on the dependent nature as a bearer of the perfect, which latter is understood as something abstract, like the state of suffering or impermanence. In the progressive model the focus lies more on an emptiness that pervades or transcends all phenomena of the dependent nature. This all-pervading emptiness possesses positive qualities and can exist, contrary to the first model, in its own right. The three natures represent three levels, each revealing a progressively deeper degree of reality.[141]

This leads to the question whether the *Madhyāntavibhāga* takes the dependent nature as existing on the level of ultimate truth.[142] One might argue that the Yogācāra does not distinguish existence on two levels of truths, its trisvabhāva theory being rather an alternative to the apparent and ultimate truths of the Madhyamaka.[143] Many passages in the *Madhyāntavibhāga* support this. This becomes particularly evident in the third chapter (on reality), where older concepts relating to truth / reality, such as the four noble truths of early Buddhism or the apparent and ultimate truth of the Madhyamaka, are explained in terms of the new trisvabhāva. Even the noble truth of cessation is subsumed under the scheme of the imagined, dependent, and perfect natures. A continuity between mainstream Buddhist thought and Yogācāra is thereby established. It is noteworthy, however, that in the case of the ultimate truth of the Madhyamaka, only the perfect nature is accepted as a fit candidate for it, the dependent nature, or false imagining, being dismissed as something to be ultimately given up. If one applies this to the definition of the *madhyamā pratipat* in MAV I.1–2, it would be safe to say that the propositions "the existence of false imagining" (MAV I.1a) and "the nonexistence of duality" (MAV I.1b) refer to the level of apparent truth, while "the mutual existence of false imagining and emptiness" (MAV I.1cd) defines the relation between apparent and ultimate truth. Resorting to two levels of truth not only explains the initial stanzas in a meaningful way, but also resolves some of the tensions between the two parallel trisvabhāva models mentioned earlier. And this is exactly what Śāntarakṣita did when he explained the theory of trisvabhāva in terms of his favored Yogācāra-Svātantrika-Madhyamaka.[144]

The first chapter of the *Madhyāntavibhāga* is divided into two sections, one on false imagining and the other on emptiness. While the latter is in perfect harmony with the *Ratnagotravibhāga*, the former seems to draw on older strands of more conservative Yogācāra material. Vasubandhu (and to some extent also the author of the root text) nevertheless managed to harmonize the originally unbalanced strands. In MAV I.1 false imagining and emptiness are said to mutually exist in each other, and based on this Vasubandhu defines emptiness in his *bhāṣya* as "the state of this false imagining being free from the relation of a perceived object and perceiving subject."[145] Whereas emptiness is simply taken here as a property of the dominant "false imagining," the latter hardly matters in the definition of emptiness in the second part of the first chapter, where emptiness is not only the absence of something in false imagining, but something more positive, the own-being of nonduality, which is associated with positive attributes such as the natural luminosity of the mind. In fact, in MAV I.22 emptiness is defined in the same way as in the *Ratnagotravibhāga*:

> [Emptiness is] neither defiled nor undefiled, neither pure nor impure (MAV I.22ab). How is it that it is neither defiled nor impure? It is because it is by its very nature the luminosity of mind (MAV I.22c). How is it that it is neither undefiled nor pure? It is because of the adventitious nature of defilements (MAV I.22d).[146]

It is obvious that the natural luminosity of the mind has taken the place of false imagining here.[147] That the latter cannot truly partake of the luminous nature is clear from a passage in the *Sāgaramatiparipṛcchā* quoted in RGVV I.68, in which the example of an ever-pure *vaiḍūrya* stone drawn out from mud is taken to illustrate the relation between the luminous mind and accidental stains:

> In the same way, O Sāgaramati, the Bodhisattva knows the natural luminosity of the mind of sentient beings. He also perceives that it is defiled by adventitious defilements. Then the Bodhisattva thinks as follows: These defilements would never penetrate into the natural luminosity

> of the mind of sentient beings. These adventitious defilements have sprung from false imagining.[148]

It is now luminosity that is centered on and occurs in two modes, one of which is being stainless and thus even free from the false imagining that causes these adventitious stains. That the natural luminosity of the mind refers to an originally pure nature of the mind in the *Madhyāntavibhāga*, too, becomes clear in stanza I.16, on the differentiation of emptiness:

> How should the differentiation of emptiness be known? As being defiled as well as pure (MAV I.16a). Thus is its differentiation. In which state is it defiled and in which is it pure? It is accompanied as well as not accompanied by stains (MAV I.16b). When it occurs together with stains it is defiled, and when its stains are abandoned it is pure. If, after being accompanied by stains it becomes stainless, how is it then not impermanent, given that it has the property of change? This is because its purity is considered to be like the one of water, gold, and space (MAV I.16cd). [A change is admitted] in view of the removal of adventitious stains, but there is no change in terms of its own-being.[149]

It should be noted how the terms "defiled" and "pure" of the first section are explicitly equated with the imported terminology "accompanied by stains" and "stainless." The latter doubtlessly stem from the *Ratnagotravibhāga*, where buddha-nature is defined as suchness accompanied by stains (*samalā tathatā*) and the transformation of the basis as stainless suchness (*nirmalā tathatā*).

To sum up, the *Madhyāntavibhāga* combines the traditional Yogācāra formula "the perfect is the dependent empty of the imagined" with strands from buddha-nature theory, according to which an unconditioned[150] buddha element is empty of adventitious stains, but not of the inseparable buddha qualities.[151]

However one wishes to combine these two formulas, a consistent reading of the *Madhyāntavibhāga* requires, as I already pointed out in my article on Tāranātha's *Essence of Zhentong*, operating with the Madhyamaka distinction of two truths, and following MAV III.10 in accepting only the perfect nature as the ultimate truth. In doing so, one should not overlook the fact of two models of trisvabhāva that reflect varied, not yet completely harmonized strands of thought. In this respect, the *Madhyāntavibhāga* does not differ from other texts of the early Yogācāra school in not only drawing on early Mahāyāna thought but also featuring a rich background of Abhidharma analysis. Sthiramati's uncertainty about the ontological status of false imagining may thus reflect the Abhidharmic background of this early Yogācāra material. Thus, it is generally asserted in the Hīnayāna schools that conditioned, dependently arising entities really exist.[152] On the other hand, such a stance would of course be incompatible with a Madhyamaka understanding of the Yogācāra, which is at least attempted in some passages.

CONCLUSION

Both Shakya Chokden and Dolpopa profit from the tensions between different trisvabhāva models in the pertinent passages of the *Madhyāntavibhāga* and its commentaries, and they follow the exegetical solution by restricting the ontological status of false imagining to the level of apparent truth. But from this point onward the two masters depart from each other. Shakya Chokden remains more faithful to the Yogācāra, in taking the dependent nature as being empty of the imagined. What remains in emptiness is thus not only an unchangeable perfect nature but also perfect in terms of being unmistaken. This is similar to Rangjung Dorje's "mere appearance," which corresponds to the apparent truth included in buddha-nature. Following the Yogācāra definition of emptiness in such a way, the *Ratnagotravibhāga* must be interpreted in terms of a buddha-nature that is inside time and thus consists of moments. This allows for a theory of seeds that naturally grow into the qualities of a buddha. For Shakya Chokden, the basis of emptiness is thus not the ultimate truth alone. In other words, his Yogācāra-based zhentong is not defined along the lines of an ultimate being empty of the apparent.

Dolpopa, on the other hand, follows more the *Ratnagotravibhāga* when defining his zhentong: an unconditioned buddha element interpreted as being completely transcendent (beyond the world and time)[153] is taken to be empty of adventitious stains. Such a buddha-nature-based zhentong requires reinterpreting the trisvabhāva theory by taking a perfect nature restricted to its unchangeable aspect as the basis of negation. Given the *Ratnagotravibhāga* elements in the *Madhyāntavibhāga*, such an interpretation is not completely out of question. One could argue in support of Dolpopa that Shakya Chokden's zhentong interpretation of the first part of the first chapter in the *Madhyāntavibhāga*, which is centered on false imagining or the dependent nature, defines in a first step the emptiness of the correct apparent from the false apparent. From that one still has to go one step further, though, and explain the emptiness of the ultimate from the correct (and false) apparent in line with the *Ratnagotravibhāga*.

NOTES

This essay was first published under the same title in the *Journal of the International Association of Buddhist Studies* 27, no. 2 (2004): 285–328. Only a few minor stylistic changes and corrections have been made.

1. Mathes, "Tāranātha's Presentation" 195–196.

2. Dolpopa's disciple Lhai Gyaltsen (1319–1401) informs us that his master's realization was connected with the *Kālacakra Tantra* (see Stearns, "Genesis of the *zhentong*" 829–831).

3. Dol po pa Shes rab rgyal mtshan, *Ri chos nges don rgya mtsho*, 343_{19-21} and 344_{8-9}: "As to the two aspects of the form-kāyas, they are here the commonly known sambhogakāya and nirmāṇakāya of the apparent [truth]. As to the ultimate sambhogakāya and nirmāṇakāya, they are completely [contained] in the dharmatā, perfect [nature], and suchness.

[. . .] Therefore the ultimate sambhogakāya and nirmāṇakāya are known by way of the extraordinary Mantra[yāna]" (*de la gzugs sku rnam pa gnyis ni kun rdzob kyi longs spyod rdzogs pa dang sprul pa'i sku ste thun mong du rab tu grags pa'o / don dam pa'i longs spyod rdzogs pa dang sprul pa'i sku ni chos nyid yongs grub de bzhin nyid la tshang ste / [. . .] des na don dam gyi longs spyod rdzogs pa dang sprul pa'i sku ni thun mong ma yin pa sngags kyi tshul la grags pa'o*).

4. Dol po pa Shes rab rgyal mtshan, "Nyi ma'i 'od zer," 986_6–987_3: "For example, in the same way as the inexhaustible treasure underground is naturally present, not newly brought about by effort, while the tree with its fruits gradually grows in a garden by bringing about [the necessary conditions] with effort, the Buddha-potential, which has the ability to bring forth the three kāyas, should be known to be twofold as well. It is both the natural potential, [namely,] the pure dharmadhātu (which latter is intimately present as the nature of [one's] mind throughout beginningless time), and the fortified potential [which is] supreme in terms of virtues (which are conducive to liberation). [The latter potential] arises from [virtuous deeds] being newly adopted with effort, [namely by] something being done, such as focusing on [the naturally present potential] and studying" (*dper na 'bad rtsol gyis gsar du ma bsgrubs shing longs spyod zad mi shes pa dang ldan pa'i gter chen sa'i 'og na rang bzhin gyis gnas pa dang 'bad rtsol gyis bsgrubs pas 'bras bu dang bcas pa'i shing ljon sa skyed mos tshal du rim gyis skye ba ji lta ba bzhin du sku gsum 'byung du rung ba'i sangs rgyas kyi rigs de yang rnam pa gnyis su shes par bya ste / thog ma med pa'i dus nas sems kyi rang bzhin du nye bar gnas pa'i chos kyi dbyings rnam par dag pa rang bzhin gyi rigs dang / de la dmigs te thos pa la sogs pa byas pas 'bad rtsol gyis gsar du yag dag par blangs pa las byung ba'i dge ba thar pa'i cha dang mthun pas mchog tu gyur pa rgyas 'gyur gyi rigs nyid do*).

5. The possibility that Dolpopa wrote his *Ratnagotravibhāga* commentary before achieving his insight into zhentong can be ruled out, for he also refers to ultimate qualities in his "Nyi ma'i 'od zer" ($911_{3\text{-}4}$).

6. She reinforces her view with the assertion that the text was copied by Kongtrul Lodro Taye nearly verbatim (Hookham, *Buddha Within* 173–174). But such an assumption is unlikely, since the text is signed by "One Endowed with the Four Reliances" (*rton pa bzhi ldan*), which was the most common pseudonym used by Dolpopa in his works (Stearns, *Buddha from Dolpo* 201).

7. Virtually the entire Buddhist tradition accepts only three great councils in India held for the purpose of consolidating the teaching after the Buddha's nirvāṇa.

8. Kapstein, *Tibetan Assimilation* 115–116.

9. Kapstein, "Introduction" 24–25.

10. See RGVV $7_{14\text{–}15}$: *asaṃskṛtam anābhogam aparapratyayoditam / buddhatvaṃ jnyāna-kāruṇyaśaktyupetaṃ dvayārthavat.*

11. Dol po pa Shes rab rgyal mtshan, *Ri chos nges don rgya mtsho* $97_{15\text{–}17}$: *'dus ma byas shing lhun gyis grub / ces pa la sogs pas mthar thug gi sangs rgyas 'dus ma byas su gsungs pa yang skad cig dang bral ba la dgongs pa yin no.*

12. Sazang Mati Paṇchen, "Theg pa chen po rgyud bla ma'i bstan bcos kyi rnam par bshad pa nges don rab gsal snang ba" $55_{2\text{–}3}$: *sangs rgyas nyid thog ma dang dbus dang mtha' mar 'dus byas kyi chos skye ba dang gnas pa dang 'jig pa rnams med pa'i rang bzhin can yin pa'i phyir 'dus ma byas pa ste / mya ngan las 'das pa'i mdo las / rtag tu gnas pa'i chos ni dus gsum la* [text: *las*] *ma gtogs te / de bzhin gshegs pa yang de dang 'dra bar dus gsum la ma gtogs pa de bas na rtag pa'o zhes gsungs pa ltar ro.*

13. Mathes, "Tāranātha's Presentation" 219–220.

14. It should be noted that the term zhentong is found nowhere in the works of Rangjung Dorje.

15. Karma 'Phrin las pa, "Dris lan yid kyi mun sel zhes bya ba lcags mo'i dri lan bzhugs so" 91_{1-4}.

16. This is clear from Rangjung Dorje's autocommentary on the *Zab mo nang gi don* ($9b_4$–$10b_1$) and commentary on the *Dharmadhātustotra* ($12b_1$–$13b_6$).

17. Rang byung rdo rje, *Zab mo nang gi don gsal bar byed pa'i 'grel pa* fol. $8a_{6-7}$: "In this regard, if 'ground' (*kun gzhi*) is not mentioned [together with] the word 'consciousness,' 'ground' may refer to suchness. Therefore, consciousness is mentioned [together with it]" (*'di la kun gzhi zhes bya ba rnam par shes pa'i sgra ma smos na de bzhin nyid la yang kun gzhi brjod du rung ba'i phyir rnam par shes pa smos so*).

18. Kong sprul Blo gros mtha' yas, *Zab mo nang gi don gyi 'grel pa* $17b_{4-6}$.

19. A term thought to be newly coined by Dolpopa.

20. Rang byung rdo rje, *Zab mo nang gi don* $22b_6$: "The [buddha]-element in sentient beings, the stainless buddha-nature, is endowed with the two truths" (*sems can khams ni sangs rgyas kyi / snying po dri med bden gnyis ldan*).

21. Rang byung rdo rje, *Rang 'grel* $62a_7$–$62b_2$: "What exists ultimately? It is the mind beyond every net of thought, the naturally pure element of sentient beings, [and] the buddha-nature (*sangs rgyas kyi snying po*). Because these two exist, they have been expressed by way of these [terms]. Therefore it is stated: 'as for the element of sentient beings, the stainless buddha-nature is endowed with the two truths.' In this regard, the buddha-nature is simply the nonexistence of stains [or] delusion in the aforementioned eight accumulations [of consciousness]" (*don dam par gang zhig yod na / rtog pa'i drwa ba thams cad las 'das pa'i sems rang bzhin gyis dag pa'i sems can gyi khams sangs rgyas kyi snying po dag ni yod pas de'i tshul brjod pas / sems can khams ni sangs rgyas kyi / snying po dri med bden gnyis ldan zhes smos so / de la sangs rgyas kyi snying po ni sngar smos pa'i tshogs brgyad kyi 'khrul pa dri ma med pa kho na yin mod kyi . . .*).

22. MAVBh 18_{21-22}: *arthasattvātmavijñaptipratibhāsam prajāyate / vijñānaṃ nāsti cāsyārthas tadabhāvāt tad apy asat*. My additions in brackets are accordings to Vasubandhu's *bhāṣya*.

23. Rang byung rdo rje, *Rang 'grel* $63a_{3-5}$: *gzung ba dang 'dzin pa gnyis su kun btags* [text: *brtags*] *pa ni rnam pa thams cad du med pa dag yin te / 'phags pa byams pa'i zhal snga nas kyang /* [MAV I.3] */ ces kun btags* [text: *brtags*] *pa'i gzung ba dang 'dzin pa thams cad rnam pa thams cad du med pa nyid du gsungs so / 'o na bden pa ji ltar bzhag ce na / med bzhin du yang snang ba tsam de ni kun rdzob kyi bden pa zhes bya ste / bslu ba med pa'i rang gi ngo bo nyid yin pa'i phyir ro.*

24. The use of the plural particle *dag* should be noted here. It indicates that there is more than one truth related to *dharmatāyukti*.

25. Rang byung rdo rje, *Rang 'grel* $63a_{5-6}$: *'di yang rnam grangs kyi don dam par bzhag pa yod mod kyi / chos nyid kyi rigs pa'i rjes su 'brel pa dag ni stong pa nyid chen po bco brgyad kyi rnam par bshad pa'i rang bzhin stong pa nyid sngar smos pa de nyid don dam pa'i bden pa yin no.*

26. Rang byung rdo rje, *dBu ma chos dbyings bstod pa'i rnam par bshad pa* $7b_{1-2}$: *bden pa gnyis kyi rang gi mtshan nyid kyis 'gyur ba med pa dang phyin ci ma log pa gnyis so / 'jig rten pa dang rigs pa'i grags pa ni / kun rdzob bden pa'i bye brag ste.*

27. Rang byung rdo jre, *Rang 'grel* $10b_{3-4}$: "As to 'beginningless,' since a beginning and end of time is a [mere] conceptual superimposition, it refers here to the true nature of both the stainless [mind] and the [mind] mingled with stains. [This true nature] is dependent

arising, [the stainless mind and mind mingled with stains] being free from identity and difference. Since there is no other beginning than it, one speaks of beginningless time" (*thog med la zhes bya ba ni / dus kyi thog ma dang tha ma ni rtog pas sgro btags pa yin pas 'dir ni dri ma med pa dang dri ma dang bcas pa'i rang gi ngo bo ni rten cing 'brel bar 'byung ba de nyid dang gzhan las rnam par grol ba ste / de las thog ma gzhan med pa'i phyir thog ma med pa'i dus zhes bya ste*).

28. Kong sprul Blo gros mtha' yas, *Rgyud bla ma'i bshad srol* 32b$_{1-5}$; see also Tsultrim Gyamtsho and Fuchs, *Buddhanature* 103–104.

29. A dharmakāya that possesses moments is not entirely transcendent and can be experienced as the true nature of thoughts and the like.

30. Smith, "Introduction" 34.

31. Dreyfus, *Recognizing Reality* 29.

32. In the subchapter on ascertaining the view (7.3.), Kongtrul (*Shes bya kun khyab mdzod* vol. 3, 61$_{19-24}$) defines the tradition of the zhentong Madhyamaka as follows: "The basis of negation is the perfect, the sphere (*dhātu*), suchness, what is beyond [any] mentally fabricated object. The negandum is the two defining characteristics of the imagined and the dependent. The mode of being empty is: 'empty of these two neganda in the basis of negation.' Only the perfect, therefore, is empty of other. Thus says the Yogācāra, the proponents holding the tradition of zhentong" (*dgag gzhi yongs grub dbyings de bzhin nyid spros pa'i yul las 'das pa / dgag bya kun btags* [text: *brtags*] *dang gzhan dbang gi mtshan nyid gnyis / stong tshul dgag bya de gnyis kyis dgag gzhi la stong pas yongs grub nyid gzhan gyis stong pa yin ces rnal 'byor spyod pa ste gzhan stong gi srol 'dzin pa rnams smra'o*).

33. Kong sprul, *Shes bya kun khyab mdzod* vol. 3, 62$_{1-4}$: *gang stong pa'i gzhi ni gzhan dbang ste gzung 'dzin gnyis snang can gyi shes pa mtha' dag go / dgag bya ni kun btags* [text: *brtags*] *pa ste gzung ba dang 'dzin pa'i dbye bas gnyis yin la / de re re la'ang gang zag gi dbang du byas pa dang / chos kyi dbang du byas pa'i gzung 'dzin gnyis gnyis so.* Shakya Chokden, *Zab zhi spros bral gyi bzhad pa stong nyid bdud rtsi'i lam po che* 114$_{3-4}$.

34. Kong sprul, *Shes bya kun khyab mdzod* vol. 3, 62$_{4-10}$: *ji ltar stong pa'i tshul ni / dgag bya des dgag gzhi de gzhan stong gi tshul gyis stong pa yin gyi / rang stong gi tshul gyis ni ma yin te / dgag bya* ([a]*kun btags* [text: *brtags*] *kyi*[a]) *gzung 'dzin gnyis po de ni*[a] *dgag gzhi gnyis snang gi shes pa gnyis po de la ltos pa'i gzhan gyi ngo bo yin gyi / de'i rang gi ngo bor mi 'jog pa'i phyir / gnyis snang gi shes pa de'i rang gi ngo bo gang zhe na / gnyis med kyi ye shes zhes*[b] *bya myong ba rig cing gsal tsam de nyid do.* This corresponds to Shākya Mchog ldan, *Zab zhi spros bral gyi bzhad pa*, 114$_{7}$–115$_{2}$.

[a]Added by Kongtrul.

[b]The edition of the collected works of Shakya Chokden reads *zhes* against *shes* in the *Shes bya kun khyab mdzod*.

35. Kong sprul, *Shes bya kun khyab mdzod* vol. 2, 546–549.

36. *zab don khyad par nyer gcig pa*, which is the title according to the colophon. Tāranātha, *Zab don nyer gcig pa* 795$_{5}$.

37. Tāranātha, *Zab don nyer gcig pa* 792$_{4}$.

38. These remarks should not be taken too seriously, though. Barawa Gyaltsen Pelzang (1310–1391) launches into his *Chos rje rnam gnyis kyi dgongs bshad nyi ma'i 'od zer* (496–498) by stating, in a similar way, that Dolpopa and Buton (*sic*) are both omniscient and must see the same reality but teach it in various ways with hidden intentions.

39. The Indo-Tibetan exegetical traditions summarize the teachings of the Buddha in three circles or turnings of the Wheel of the Dharma (dharmacakra). Mathes, *Dharmadharmatāvibhāga* 155.

40. Literally, "The one named Shākya claims that . . ." Here and in the following sentence this pattern is not strictly followed but freely rendered by giving the proponent's name and a colon in bold.

41. For example, the analytical works of Nāgārjuna, such as the *Mūlamadhyamakakārikā.*

42. Tāranātha, *Zab don nyer gcig pa* 782$_{3-5}$: *de la shākya'i mtshan can ni / thal rang gi lta ba 'di kun 'khor lo bar pa dang / rig tshogs kyi dgongs don 'thad ldan yin cing / bar pa'i dngos bstan sgra ji bzhin pa yang yin / rig tshogs dang 'khor lo tha ma'i dngos bstan mi mthun par bzhed la.*

43. Literally, "the great omniscient one from Jonang."

44. Literally, "words."

45. Tāranātha, *Zab don nyer gcig pa* 782$_{5}$–783$_{6}$: *kun mkhyen jo nang pa chen po ni / thal rang gi lta ba 'di 'khor lo bar pa dang rig tshogs kyi dgongs par rlom pa yin kyang / dgongs pa rma med pa ma yin la / rig tshogs dngos bstan gyi tshig phal cher la 'byor ba ltar snang yang / mi 'byor ba yang mang du yod la / 'khor lo bar pa'i gzhung tshig mang pos gzhan stong gsal bar ston pas 'khor lo bar pa dang rig tshogs kyi dngos bstan sgra ji bzhin pa ma yin no / de la 'khor lo bar pa dang rig tshogs kyi tshig phal cher gyi dngos bstan ni thal rang dang gzhan stong gnyis ka la mi 'gal yang / rang stong par grags pa'i thun mong ma yin pa'i grub mtha'i khungs la 'dren pa rnams ni / de rnams nyid la 'khrul gzhi byung ba yin gyi / grub mtha' de dang de mi ston cing / de las gzhan de'i lugs dang 'gal zhing / gzhan stong kho na ston pa thun mongs ma yin pa'i tshig kyang du ma yod pas / bar pa dang rig tshogs kyis kyang gzhan stong dbu ma nyid ston no / 'on kyang de dag nas / 'khor lo tha ma dgongs 'grel dang bcas pa tsam du gzhan stong thun mongs ma yin pa rnams gsal zhing rgyas par 'byung ba min la / thal rang gi thun mongs ma yin pa'i grub mtha' / deng sang rang stong gi lta bar grags pa de mi ston kyang / rgyal ba sras bcas kyi dgongs pa'i rang stong de rgyas par bstan te / ces gsung so.*

46. From here on, Shakya Chokden and Dolpopa are referred to as "the former" and "the latter."

47. That is, the *Mahāyānasūtrālaṃkāra, Madhyāntavibhāga,* and *Dharmadharmatāvibhāga.*

48. That is, the *Mahāyānasūtrālaṃkāra, Madhyāntavibhāga, Dharmadharmatāvibhāga,* and *Ratnagotravibhāga.*

49. This does not obviously exclude recourse to a Prāsaṅgika view when cutting through mental fabrications in the *Mahāyānasūtrālaṃkāra,* among other works.

50. That is, *Mahāyānasūtrālaṃkāra, Madhyāntavibhāga,* and *Dharmadharmatāvibhāga.*

51. Usually, a cut-off potential and the potentials for entering on the paths of the śrāvakas and pratyekabuddhas and on the Mahāyāna are distinguished.

52. Tāranātha, *Zab don nyer gcig pa* 783$_{6}$–784$_{3}$: *mngon rtogs rgyan gyis / rang stong gzhan stong gi grub mtha' gnyis ka ston pa ni / lta bas spros pa gcod pa la thal rang gzhung phyi gsum gyi rang stong dang / sgom pas nyams len gzhan stong dgos pa la dgongs la / byams chos lhag ma bzhis gzhan stong kho na ston mod / de la'ang rigs gnyis te / rgyud blar mthar thug theg gcig bshad / rigs chad bkag gzhung gzhan gsum du mthar thug theg gsum dang / rigs chad bshad gsung.*

53. Tāranātha, *Zab don nyer gcig pa* 784$_{3-4}$: *byams chos sde lnga la grub mtha' so so ba ye med / rang stong par grags pa'i grub mtha' mngon [rtogs] rgyan nas kyang ma bshad / mdo [sde] rgyan sogs nas kyang / gtan nas rigs chad pa dang mthar thug theg gsum ma bshad / zhes gsung ngo.*

54. The zhentong view includes a rangtong that refers to the negandum but not to what is left over in emptiness.

55. Tāranātha, *Zab don nyer gcig pa* 784_{4-5}: *lta bas spros pa gcod pa la rang stong zab / sgom pas nyams su len pa la gzhan stong zab ces te / de'i rang stong yang thal rang gzhung phyi gsum gyi lugs la ngos 'dzin* [text: *'dzi]*.

56. As would be the case if the former were strictly rangtong and the latter strictly zhentong.

57. Tāranātha, *Zab don nyer gcig pa* 784_{5-7}: *rgyal ba sras bcas bzhed pa'i rang stong gi lta ba de spros pa gcod byed mchog yin kyang / gzhan stong du 'dus pas lta grub logs logs pa min la / deng sang grags pa'i rang stong thal rang gzhung phyi gsum gyi lta ba don dam bden med du 'dod pa ni nor ba yin pas / lta bas spros pa gcod pa la bzang ba min te / skur 'debs su 'gyur ba'i phyir yin zhes gsung.*

58. Tāranātha, *Zab don nyer gcig pa* 784_{7}–785_{1}: *gzhan stong sems tsam las 'das pas dbu ma go chod po yin kyang / lta ba'i ngos nas de bas kyang rang stong mtho / 'on kyang snga ma de nor bar* [text: *par] ni mi 'gyur te / sgom don dang mthun pas so gsung.*

59. Tāranātha, *Zab don nyer gcig pa* 785_{1-2}: *rang stong yang sems tsam las 'das pas / grub mtha' bzhi'i dbu mar bsdu ba tsam yin kyang / rnam dag mthar thug min la / lta ba'i mtho shos gzhan stong kho na yin no gsung.*

60. Tāranātha, *Zab don nyer gcig pa* 785_{2-4}: *de'i rgyu mtshan du / byams chos rjes 'brang dang bcas par / gnyis med kyi ye shes la dpyad pa mi byed pa yin la / spyi ldog nas de yang rig pas dpyad na dpyad mi bzod pas / don dam gcod byed kyi rig pas dpyad bzod mi srid pas lta ba rang stong zab / dpyad ma bzod kyang ye shes de nyams myong rgyun mi 'chad pas / sgom don gzhan stong ltar gnas gsung.*

61. For it is beyond one and many. Moreover, wisdom is omnipresent, in that the buddhas embrace with their nondual wisdom the all-pervading suchness of all phenomena (cf. Tāranātha's conclusion).

62. Tāranātha, *Zab don nyer gcig pa* 785_{4}: *gnyis med ye shes rigs pas dpyad bzod yin pas / de la dpyod pa de rang gi 'khrul gsung.*

63. Tāranātha, *Zab don nyer gcig pa* 785_{5}: *gnyis med ye shes de rig pa skad cig ma yin / rtag pa min / gnas pa'i go skabs med pa cig yin gsung.*

64. Tāranātha, *Zab don nyer gcig pa* 785_{5-6}: *de skad cig ma ma yin / dus gsum las grol bas rtag pa brtan pa yin gsung.*

65. Tāranātha, *Zab don nyer gcig pa* 785_{6}: *de bzhin du shes pa yin pa'i phyir dngos por bzhed pa dang.*

66. Tāranātha, *Zab don nyer gcig pa* 785_{6}: *dngos po dngos med gnyis ka las grol bar bzhed pa ste.*

67. Tāranātha, *Zab don nyer gcig pa* 785_{7}: *de bzhin du 'dus byas su bzhed pa dang.*

68. Tāranātha, *Zab don nyer gcig pa* 785_{7}: *'dus ma byas su bzhed pa yang ste.*

69. Tāranātha, *Zab don nyer gcig pa* 785_{7}–786_{3}: *bod spyi dang mthun rung du shes pa thams cad kyi rang ldog gsal rig tsam 'di ka gzhan dbang gi dngos po yin la / de nyid la shar ba'i gnyis snang kho na'i rang ldog nas kun btags* [text: *brtags] yin no / gsal rig gnyis snang de dang bcas pa'i cha nas gzhan dbang dang / gsal rig de la gnyis chos gdod nas ma gos pa'i cha nas yongs grub yin pas / gzhan dbang yongs grub ldog cha nas tha dad cing / mtshan nyid kyi cha nas tha dad kyang gzhan dbang gi dngos po de nyid dang / yongs grub ngo bo gcig par bzhed do.*

70. This negation of identity has been often misunderstood and misleadingly represented. (Cf. Newland, *Two Truths*, who writes that for Dolpopa the two truths are different entities [*ngo bo tha dad pa*]). Instead of referring directly to the Jonang material, however, he quotes Seyfort Ruegg, Hopkins, and Thurman (Newland, *Two Truths* 30 and 260). In fact, Dolpopa negates not only identity but also difference. In his "bDen gnyis gsal ba'i

nyi ma" $23_{2\text{-}3}$, he explains that "the two truths should be called neither identical (*de nyid*) in terms of their nature nor different (*gzhan*) [in terms of their nature].[a] See also Mathes, "Vordergründige und höchste Wahrheit" 465–466.

[a]For *de nyid dang gzhan*, *tattvānyatva*, see MAVBh 23_{10}.

71. Tāranātha, *Zab don nyer gcig pa* $786_{3\text{-}6}$: *blo rnam rtog sna tshogs pas brtags pa'i btags cha dang / phyi don du snang ba'i snang cha ste / gzung ba'i rang ldog kun btags* [text: *brtags*] *dang / sems sems byung shes pa'i rang ldog kun rdzob pa'i shes pa'am rnam shes kyis bsdus pa'i shes pa gzhan dbang dang / spros pa dang bral ba'i rang bzhin gsal rig yongs grub ste / des na kun btags* [text: *brtags*] *ni gzhan dbang las rdzas tha dad du med kyang / mtshan nyid kyi sgo nas ni shin tu tha dad do / yongs grub dang gzhan dbang ni / ldog cha dang mtshan nyid tha dad par ma zad / ngo bo gcig pa yang ma yin no / snga ma'i rnam gzhag ni sems tsam dang mthun shas che la / dbu ma'i lugs ni 'di kho na'o zhes dgongs so.*

72. Tāranātha, *Zab don nyer gcig pa* $786_{6\text{-}7}$: *kun btags* [text: *brtags*] *la bden med kyis khyab / yongs grub la bden yod kyis khyab / gzhan dbang la cha gnyis mdzad.*

73. Tāranātha, *Zab don nyer gcig pa* 786_{7}: *kun btags* [text: *brtags*] *gzhan dbang gnyis ka la mtha' gcig tu bden med kyis khyab par mdzad do.*

74. Tāranātha, *Zab don nyer gcig pa* 786_{7}–787_{1}: *rang rig thams cad rang rig gi rang ldog nas don dam kho na yin gsung la.*

75. The Tibetan uses the plural: "moments of self-awareness."

76. Tāranātha, *Zab don nyer gcig pa* $787_{1\text{-}2}$: *kun rdzob rnam shes kyi rang rig rnams kun rdzob kho na yin pas / rang rig yang kun rdzob don dam gnyis yod par bzhed do.*

77. That is, it is the negandum and nothing more.

78. Tāranātha, *Zab don nyer gcig pa* 787_{2}: *yongs grub stong pa nyid yin / kun btags* [text: *brtags*] *stong pa tsam yin kyang stong pa nyid min / stong pa nyid la don dam gyis khyab par bzhed.*

79. Tāranātha, *Zab don nyer gcig pa* $787_{2\text{-}3}$: *chos dang chos nyid thaṃs cad la stong nyid tsam du brjod dgos / stong nyid la don dam gyis ma khyab / ming gi rnam grangs la khyab mtha'i ma rtsi / gtso bo'i don du sbyor gsung.*

80. Pacification, or cessation, falls under this latter category by virtue of being unconditioned.

81. In the context of the Abhidharma: usually the "knowledge of the destruction [of passions and so on]" (*kṣayajñāna, zad pa shes pa*) and the "knowledge of no further occurrence [of passions and so on]" (*anutpādajñāna, mi skye ba shes pa*).

82. In the following *dngos po* is rendered as "entity," even though the Sanskrit equivalent *bhāva* also means "existence."

83. Tāranātha, *Zab don nyer gcig pa* $787_{3\text{-}6}$: *tshad ma'i gzhung dang mngon pa sogs spyi skad dang phal cher mthun par / zhi grub pa la dngos po dngos med gang rung gis khyab / shes pa la dngos pos khyab / don dam dngos po min / 'dus ma byas* [text: *om. byas*] *pas ni dngos med nam mkha' sogs yin / de bzhin nyid la las nyon gyi 'dus ma byas dang / gsal rig tsam gsar du 'dus ma byas sogs / 'dus ma byas pa'i cha re yod pas / rnam grangs kyi sgo nas 'dus ma byas su btags pa yin gyi / 'du byed dang mtshan nyid 'gal ba'i 'dus ma byas ma yin te / des na 'dus ma byas btags pa ba yin gsung.*

84. This means that the totality of entities and nonentities is exactly identical with the apparent truth.

85. Dolpopa restricts the ultimate truth to the actual cessation, which exists throughout beginningless time. The actual pacification attained thus still forms, together with suffering, a dualistic concept yet to be transcended.

86. This reductio ad absurdum presupposes the inclusion of wisdom under the ultimate truth.

87. Tāranātha, *Zab don nyer gcig pa* 787_{6}–788_{3}: *tshad mngon sogs su bshad pa de / kun rdzob gtso bor gtan la ‘bebs pa’i lugs yin / don dam gtso bor gtan la ‘bebs pa’i nges don gyi skabs ‘dir / kun rdzob la dngos po dang dngos med kyis khyab cing / dngos po dngos med la’ang kun rdzob kyis khyab / don dam dngos po yang min / dngos med* [text: *mod]* *kyang min pas zhi* [text: *gzhi]* *grub la nges ma khyab / ye shes dngos po ma yin la shes pa yin pas / shes pa la dngos pos ma khyab dngos med don dam du ‘dod pa chos mi rigs la / don dam dngos por ‘dod pa dngos smra ba’i lugs so / mngon pa ba rnams ‘dus ma byas su ‘dod pa’i nam mkha’ sogs / dngos med thams cad kyang skabs ‘dir ‘dus byas yin pas / dngos po dngos med la ‘dus byas kyis khyab / don dam ‘dus ma byas dngos yin / nam mkha’ sogs ‘dus ma byas btags pa ba yin gsung.*

88. Tāranātha, *Zab don nyer gcig pa* 788_{4}: *stong gzhi gzhan dbang gi rang ngo de dgag bya kun btags kyis stong pa ste / de nyid kun rdzob kyis stong pa’i don dam du mdzad do.*

89. Tāranātha, *Zab don nyer gcig pa* 788_{4-6}: *stong gzhi yongs grub / dgag bya gzhan dbang kun btags* [text: *brtags]* *gnyis kyis stong pa / don dam kun rdzob kyis stong pa’i don yin la / gzhan dbang kun btags* [text: *brtags]* *kyis stong pa ni / kun rdzob bden pa kho na gtan la ‘bebs pa’i skabs kho na yin par bzhed do.*

90. Tāranātha, *Zab don nyer gcig pa* 788_{6-7}: *dag pa gzhan dbang zhes bod spyi la grags kyang / don la gzhan dbang min cing phyin ci ma log pa’i yongs grub yin la / phyin ci ma log pa’i yongs grub kyang yongs grub mtshan nyid pa yin cing / dag pa gzhan dbang gi tha snyad pa’ang khungs gsal med pas / de’i brda ‘chang byed pa mi legs par dgongs so.*

91. Tāranātha, *Zab don nyer gcig pa* 788_{7}–789_{3}: *dag pa gzhan dbang zhes pa’i tha snyad gzhung las gsal po ma byung yang / don tshang bas tha snyad byar rung ste / sangs rgyas kyi bstan pa don la brton pa yin pa dang / bod snga ma thams cad tha snyad de lta bu mthun par byed pas / byams pa nas brgyud pa’i man ngag ma nor ba yin du rung bas so / de’i nang tshan ‘phags pa slob pa’i ye shes ‘ga’ zhig phyin ci ma log pa’i yongs grub yin kyang / sa thob pa rnams la sa gzhi gser du snang ba sogs ‘ga’ zhig phyin ci ma log pa’i yongs grub yin pa’ang yod pas / de’i tha snyad rnam gzhag legs par dgongs so.*

92. Tāranātha, *Zab don nyer gcig pa* 789_{4}: *phyin ci ma log pa’i yongs grub la / yongs grub mtshan nyid pas khyab par bzhed.*

93. The distinction between “perfect in terms of being unmistaken” and “ultimate perfect in terms of being unmistaken” reflects the Jonangpas’ view that wisdom,[a] like all other buddha-qualities, mainly pertains to the unchangeable ultimate truth and only to a limited extent to the apparent truth.

[a]In the Yogācāra, “the perfect in terms of being unmistaken” usually refers to nonconceptual wisdom cultivated on the path.

94. Tāranātha, *Zab don nyer gcig pa* 789_{4-7}: *de ni rnam grangs kyi yongs grub tu bstan pa tsam ste / gsung rab yan lag bcu gnyis kyang yongs grub tu gsungs pa dang ‘dra’o / des na / ‘gyur med yongs grub kyi zlas drangs pa’i phyin ci ma log pa de ni gzhan dbang dag pa pa yin cing / yongs grub btags pa ba yin / ‘gyur med nyid dang gcig pa’i yongs grub phyin ci ma log pa de la / don dam pa’i phyin ci ma log pa’i yongs su grub pa zhes bya ste / ‘gyur med kho na’o / des na / gnas tshul gtan la ‘bebs pa’i skabs su yongs grub de nyid kho na yin la / rnam grangs rgyas par bshad pa’i skabs su gnyis kyi rnam gzhag byed do gsung.*

95. Tāranātha, *Zab don nyer gcig pa* 789_{7}–790_{1}: *lam bden yang don dam par mdzad la.*

96. Tāranātha, *Zab don nyer gcig pa* 790_{1-3}: *bden pa bzhir phye ba’i ‘gog bden don dam dang / bden pa gzhan gsum kun rdzob tu bzhed / zhib mor na / ‘gog bden mtshan nyid pa*

gdod ma'i 'gog bden la don dam kho na dang / gzhan bden pa gsum dang / so sor brtags 'gog la kun rdzob kyis khyab par don la gnas pas / lam bden mtshan nyid pa la kun rdzob kyis khyab / 'gog bden mtshan nyid pa la don dam gyis khyab / don dam pa'i lam bden ni gdod ma dang gcig pa'i phyir / 'gog bden nyid yin pas / lam bden btags pa ba yin gsung.

97. Tāranātha, *Zab don nyer gcig pa* 790_{3-5}: *sems can kyi rgyud la bde gshegs snying po med sems can kyi sems rang bzhin 'od gsal de / bde gshegs snying po'i rgyu dang khams tsam yin pas / rgyu bde gshegs snying po'am khams bde gshegs snying po sems can thams cad la yod kyang / de ni de 'dra mtshan nyid pa min / sangs rgyas kyi ye shes bde gshegs snying po'o.*

98. Buddha-nature with all its qualities is already present in one's mind-stream and thus does not need to be generated. Here, buddha-nature as cause means that focusing on the true nature of mind, which is buddha-nature, causes the removal of all defilements.

99. Tāranātha, *Zab don nyer gcig pa* 790_{5-7}: *sems can gyi rgyud kyi de ka bde gshegs snying po mtshan nyid pa yin te / sangs rgyas de kyi mtshan nyid pa yin na / de nyid ka sems can gyi chos nyid yin pas / sems can bde gshegs snying po can du grub la / khyad par lung mtha' yas pas grub bo / khams dang rgyur bshad pa yang / skyed rgyu dang skyed khams min par dbyings dang bral rgyu la dgongs pa'o gsung.*

100. Tāranātha, *Zab don nyer gcig pa* 790_{7}–791_{1}: *snying po la yon tan ngo bo dbyer med rang bzhin nyid ldan du gsungs ba 'bras bu kho na'i skabs yin la / rgyu'i skabs su yon tan 'byung rung gi nus pa sa bon tsam yod par bzhed.*

101. In the context of phenomena (dharma) and their true being (dharmatā), dharmin refers to the dharmas that possess dharma[tā]. Mathes, *Dharmadharmatāvibhāga* 185.

102. Tāranātha, *Zab don nyer gcig pa* 791_{1-4}: *yon tan ngo bo dbyer med / rang bzhin nyid ldan de gzhi bde gshegs snying po la yang yod de / gsar du byung bas rang bzhin gyis ldan par mi 'gro ba'i phyir dang / gzhi lam 'bras bu gsum kun rdzob chos can gyis phye ba ma gtogs / rang bzhin bde gshegs snying po gcig kho na yin pa'i phyir / bde gshegs snying po yin phyin chad don dam pa'i yon tan thams cad kyis brgyan pa yin dgos par bzhed do.*

103. The Yogācāras use the term dharmakāya in an exclusive as well as in an inclusive sense. In its exclusive sense, the term dharmakāya is defined as the transformation of the basis that results in the nonconceptual wisdom of the purity of suchness. In its inclusive sense, it refers to the totality of buddhahood including all kāyas. The interpretation of the dharmakāya as a distinct kāya, which does not include the sambhogakāya, is also found in the particular four kāya theory of Haribhadra's commentary on the *Abhisamayālaṃkāra*. Haribhadra qualifies the dharmakāya for the first time with the compound *jñānātmaka*, "the dharmakāya consisting of wisdom," and understands it as conditioned *jñāna*s on the level of apparent truth. It is only the svābhāvikakāya that encompasses suchness, or the ultimate emptiness of all phenomena. Contrary to this, Ārya Vimuktisena takes dharmakāya as a synonym of svābhāvikakāya, and as such the totality of buddhahood comprising all kāyas (see Makransky, *Buddhahood Embodied* 9–13 and 39–41).

104. Tāranātha, *Zab don nyer gcig pa* 791_{4}: *chos sku'i yon tan la mtshan dpe sogs mi bzhed /.*

105. The explanation of the sixty-four qualities in the third chapter of the *Ratnagotravibhāga* is based on the *Ratnadārikā Sūtra* (see Takasaki, *Study on the Ratnagotravibhāga* 14).

106. That is, the thirty-two qualities of the dharmakāya and the thirty-two qualities of the form-kāyas.

107. Which means that the dharmakāya possesses aspects of the major and minor marks and the form-kāyas aspects of the thirty-two qualities of the dharmakāya.

108. This sentence is the beginning of the following paragraph, but it refers to the previous one.

109. Tāranātha, *Zab don nyer gcig pa* 791_{4-7}: *sangs rgyas kyi yon tan gyi rigs thams cad la / chos sku'i yon tan don dam pa sangs rgyas rang snang re dang / gzugs sku'i yon tan kun rdzob pa gdul bya gzhan snang gi cha re thams cad de yod pa yin la / bu mo rin chen gyis zhus pa'i mdo dang / rgyud bla ma'i dngos bstan ni spyir sku gnyis ka'i yon tan 'chad dgos pa la gtso che chung gi dbang las / grags pa spyi dang mthun pa dper brjod tsam du mdzad la / mdo gzhan rnams dang rgyud sde sogs las gsungs pa ltar na / gnyis ka la thams cad kyi char yod pa yin no gsung [. . .] de ni sngags kyi skabs su gzhan stong la mi 'dra ba ni 'di yin te.*

110. Tāranātha, *Zab don nyer gcig pa* 791_{7}–792_{1}: *sems rang bzhin 'od gsal la 'bras bu'i sa bon tsam rang chas su yod pa / lam bsgoms pas gong 'phel thob / mthar 'bras bu mngon gyur du 'byung bar bzhed.*

111. Tāranātha, *Zab don nyer gcig pa* 792_{1-2}: *gdod ma nas ye shes don dam pa'i dkyil 'khor du lhun grub tu rdzogs pa de lam bsgoms dri ma bsal te mngon du gyur pa yin par bzhed do.*

112. Tāranātha, *Zab don nyer gcig pa* 792_{5-6}: *paṇ chen shākya'i mtshan can ni / gnyis med kyi ye shes de gcig pu ma yin pa du ma'i tshul can / skad cig gis mi gnas pa mi rtag par bzhed pa dang / kun mkhyen jo nang pa ni / de dngos gnas la gcig min du ma yang min par nges mod / gnas skabs su gcig pu'i* [text: *bu'i]* *rnam gzhag 'thad ldan du mdzad cing / de rtag pa / cha med kun khyab / spros bral brjod bral yin par bzhed pa'i dbang las te / mdor na mi rtag pa dang rtag par bzhed pa'i khyad par ro.*

113. Tāranātha, *Zab don nyer gcig pa* 794_{6-7}: *'di ni spros bral te / dngos po sgrub pa mi rtag pa dang / dngos med dgag pa rtag pa gnyis ka las grol ba'i dbyings 'gyur med de yin / rtag pa'i mtshan ma las grol zhing.*

114. See my introductory remarks on Dolpopa in the first paragraph of this chapter.

115. Dol po pa Shes rab rgyal mtshan, *Ri chos nges don rgya mtsho* 148_{3-4}: . . . *kun btags [*text: *brtags] kyis stong pa'i gzhi ni gzhan dbang ngo / gzhan dbang gis kyang stong pa'i gzhi ni chos nyid yongs grub bo [*text: *po] /.*

116. Tāranātha, *Zab don nyer gcig pa* 149_{8-10}: . . . *kun btags [*text: *brtags] gzhan dbang gi chos rnams ni yang dag par med pa dang / chos nyid yongs grub ni yang dag tu yod par bstan te 'di dag gis kyang rang stong dang gzhan stong gi don bstan pa yin no.*

117. Tāranātha, *Zab don nyer gcig pa* 319_{16-24}: *kun btags ngo bo med pa ni rang gi mtshan nyid kyis med pa ste kun rdzob tsam mam log pa'i kun rdzob tu grub pa tsam las kun rdzob bden pa'am yang dag kun rdzob tu yang ma grub bo / gzhan dbang ngo bo nyid med pa ni kun rdzob tu gzhan las skye ba'i ngo bor yod kyang rang las skye ba'i ngo bor med cing yang dag par na cir yang ma grub pa ste de ltar de gnyis ni rang stong yin pa'i phyir rang gi ngo bo med pa'o / de gnyis med pa'i gzhi chos nyid yongs grub ni rang gi ngo bo med pa ma yin yang de las gzhan pa kun rdzob kyi chos rnams kyi ngo bo nyid med pa'i gzhi yin pa'i phyir don dam bden pa'i ngo bo ste ngo bo nyid kyi sku . . .*

118. Tāranātha, *Zab don nyer gcig pa* 356_{22}–357_{2}: *de ltar don dam pa'i sangs rgyas ni rang byung ye shes lnga'i sku yin la / de yang de bzhin nyid dang 'gyur med yongs grub nyid ye shes lngar rtag tu bzhugs pa'o / kun rdzob gzugs kyi sku ni yang dag ye shes phyin ci ma log pa'i yongs grub dang ldan pa ste theg chen mi slob pa'i ye shes skad cig las ma 'das pa dang ldan pa'o.*

119. Tāranātha, *Zab don nyer gcig pa* 142_{17-19}: *sangs rgyas rtag pa dang sangs rgyas kyi thar pa gzugs yin pa dang nam mkha' yang sangs rgyas kyi gzugs yin / zhes pa la sogs pa'i don ni [. . .] de bzhin nyid kyi gzugs sogs dang / khams gsum dang dus gsum las 'das pa'i gzugs sogs zhes pa la sogs pa 'chad par 'gyur pa'i skabs su rig par bya . . .*

120. See Dol po pa Shes rab rgyal mtshan, *Bden gnyis gsal ba'i nyi ma* 23_{2-3}: *bden pa gnyis ni ngo bo de nyid dang gzhan du brjod du med pa gcig pa bkag pa'i tha dad pa yin te.*

121. See also Broido, "Jo-nang-pas on Madhyamaka" 88, who has made the same observation with regard to two sets of skandhas in the *Ri chos nges don rgya mtsho.*

122. For a short description of Shakya Chokden's position, see also Tillemans and Tomabechi, "Le *dbu ma'i byung tshul*" 891–896.

123. Shakya Chokden, *Sangs rgyas gyi snying po'i rnam bshad mdo rgyud kyi snying po* 136_{3}.

124. Seyfort Ruegg, *Traité du Tathāgatagarbha* 29–33.

125. Mathes, "Gzhon nu dpal's Extensive Commentary" 88–89. In his *Ratnagotravibhāga* commentary, Gzhon nu dpal refers to these qualities in sentient beings as "seeds" (Mathes, *Rgyud bla ma'i 'grel bshad* 121_{6-7}).

126. Shakya Chokden, *Byams chos lnga'i lam gyi rim pa* 154_{1-7}. See also Mathes, *Dharmadharmatāvibhāga* 176.

127. That is, the two passages (114_{3-4} and 114_{7}–115_{1}) quoted in the first paragraph of this chapter.

128. According to Dreyfus, this work was written in 1489. Dreyfus, *Recognizing Reality* 29.

129. Shākya Mchog ldan, *Shing rta srol gnyis rnam dbye* 476_{3-5}: *[sems tsam pa'i mnyam bzhag gi lta ba ni . . . des drangs pa'i rjes thob kyi grub mtha' ni] phyi rol gyi don dang spyi mtshan du bshad pa rnams ni kun btags dang rang gi ngo bos stong pa'o / bags chags kyis der snang ba ni gzhan dbang dang bden par grub pa'o / dgag gzhi gzhan dbang de dgag bya kun btags kyis stong pa'i stong pa nyid ni yongs grub dang / des na don dam pa'i bden pa'o.*

130. The Yogācāra treatises on the Maitreya works, for example, are taken to go beyond Cittamātra and thus to be in accordance with the intention of the Madhyamaka. Shakya Chokden, *Byams chos lnga'i nges don rab tu gsal ba* 6_{3-7}; and Mathes, *Dharmadharmatāvibhāga* 174.

131. Shākya Mchog ldan, *Shing rta srol gnyis rnam dbye* 483_{7}–484_{4}: *rnal 'byor spyod pa pas ni / kun btags rang gi ngo bos stong pa dang / gzhan dbang gzhan gyi ngo bos stong pa dang / de'i shul du rang gi ngo bos mi stong par lus pa ni / gzhan dbang gi ngo bo'am yongs grub ces bya ba de nyid do / zhes 'chad [. . .] dbu ma pa de gnyis ka yang 'phags pa'i mnyam gzhag gis bsgom bya'am mnyam su myong bya zhig khas len pa'i tshe ngos 'dzin tshul ni mthun pa yin te / gnyis kas kyang chos kyi dbyings kyi ye shes la 'chad pas so / mnyam gzhag de las langs pa'i rjes thob tu tha snyad 'dogs tshul ni mi mthun pa yin te / rnal 'byor spyod pa pas ni 'gyur ba med pa'i yongs grub ces bya ba'i ming can / chos dbyings ye shes sam gnyis su med pa'i ye shes de nyid don dam pa'i bden pa dngos dang / bdag dam pa dang / rtag brtan zhi ba g.yung drung dang / bden par grub pa nyid du tha snyad 'dogs par byed la.*

132. The plural particle shows that there is more than one unconditioned element.

133. Shākya Mchog ldan, *Zab zhi spros bral gyi bzhad pa* 117_{1-3}: *kun rdzob 'dus byas kyi dngos po thams cad rang stong dang / don dam 'dus ma byas rnams gzhan stong du 'chad pa 'di ni dbu ma pa chen po dbyig gnyen gyi bzhed pa yin te / yum gyi gnod 'joms las de ltar bzhad pa'i phyir / zhes 'chad pa ni rigs pa ma yin te / rje btsun gyi gzhung rtsa ba dang mi mthun zhing / thogs med sku mched kyi gzhung rtsod med rnams dang / phyogs glang yab sras kyi gzhung lugs las gzhan stong gi 'chad tshul gsal par gsungs pa rnams dang 'gal ba'i phyir ro.*

134. MAVBh 17_{16} (MAV I.1ab): *abhūtaparikalpo 'sti dvayan tatra na vidyate.*

135. Shākya Mchog ldan, *Zab zhi spros bral gyi bzhad pa* 117_{5}: *ji skad du / yang dag ma yin kun rtog yod / de la gnyis po yod ma yin / zhes 'byung ba ltar / gzhan dbang stong gzhi'i chos can dang / gzung 'dzin kun btags [*text: *brtags] gnyis po gang gis stong pa'i dgag*

bya dang / gzung 'dzin gnyis med kyi ye shes la stong pa'i dngos por bshad pa zhes bya ba zhig yod pa yin gyi / stong gzhi'i chos can du 'jog pa ma yin te.

136. Shākya Mchog ldan, *Zab zhi spros bral gyi bzhad pa* 115_3: *de ltar na gzhan dbang yang dag pa ma yin pa'i kun tu rtog pa zhes bya ba rang bzhin kyis yod pa dang / rang gi mtshan nyid kyis dang / rang gi ngo bos yod pa ni yin la / bden pa dang / don dam par dang / de kho na nyid du yod pa ni ma yin te sgrub byed go rim bzhin du / dgag bya dag gnyis kyis stong pa'i phyir dang / don dam pa'i bden pa ma yin pa'i phyir dang / de kho na nyid ma yin pa'i phyir dang / sgyu ma bzhin no.*

137. Shākya Mchog ldan, *Shing rta chen po'i srol gnyis rnam dbye* 520_{2-3}: *rgyud bla ma dang yum gyi gnod 'joms su chos nyid yongs grub dgag bya kun btags kyis stong par bshad pa'o*. In other words, here again the dependent nature is not included in the negandum. The *Bṛhaṭṭīkā* (*Karmapa Tengyur* [Tōhoku no. 3808], *Shes phyin, pha* 572_5) supports the Jonang, however, in that the ultimate, or the perfect nature, is defined as "that which is free from these names (roughly referring to the imagined nature in the *Bṛhaṭṭīkā*) and the forms of mistaken appearances (i.e., the dependent nature),[a] and that which is ineffable and the form of signlessness" (*gang ming dang / phyin ci log tu snang ba'i rnam pa de dang bral ba brjod du med pa / mtshan ma med pa'i rnam pa gang yin pa de ni don dam pa yongs su grub pa'i ngo bo nyid de*).

[a]The expression "forms of mistaken appearances" defines the dependent nature: "The forms, which, under the sway of ignorance and so forth, appear to the consciousness in a mistaken way as phenomena, are the dependent nature" (*ma rig pa la sogs pa'i dbang gis rnam par shes pa la chos rnams su phyin ci log tu snang ba'i rnam pa gang yin pa de ni gzhan dbang gi ngo bo nyid do, Karmapa Tengyur* [Tōhoku no. 3808], *Shes phyin, pha* 572_{4-5}).

138. While (a) and (b) are the *pāda*s MAV I.1a and I.1b, proposition (c) reflects the double locative relationship between false imagining and emptiness in the second part of MAV I.1 (But emptiness is found there [i.e., in false imagining] and [false imagining] is found in relation to it [i.e., emptiness] as well). If the second locative (*tasyām*, i.e., *śūnyatāyām*) is taken literally in the sense that *x* is found in *y*, and *y* in *x*, *x* would be *y*. Total identity, however, of false imagining and emptiness can be excluded on the grounds that the first is considered to be conditioned and the latter not (cf. MAVBh on I.2). I therefore suggest the preliminary translation "in relation to" for the two locatives.

139. Mathes, "Tāranātha's Presentation" 195–223.

140. Sponberg, "The Trisvabhāva Doctrine in India and China" 99.

141. Mathes, "Tāranātha's Presentation" 204–214.

142. This is what Tsongkhapa (1357–1419), for example, claims on the basis of MAVṬ I.1, where the verse *abhūtaparikalpo 'sti* is glossed as *svabhāvataḥ*. A little further down Sthiramati does not object to an opponent's claim of its ultimate existence: "[Opp.:] If thus duality was entirely nonexistent, like a hare's horn, and false imagining existed ultimately in its own right . . ." (Sanskrit in brackets reconstructed: [*yadi evaṃ dva*]*yaṃ śaśaviṣāṇavat sarvathā nāsti / abhūtaparikalpaś ca paramārthataḥ svabhāvato 'sty* . . . , MAVṬ, 10_{17-19}). See Thurman, *Speech of Gold* 226–228.

143. Boquist, *Trisvabhāva* 17–22.

144. Lindtner, "*Cittamātra* in Indian Mahāyāna 193.

145. MAVBh 18_{2-3}: *śūnyatā tasyābhūtaparikalpasya grāhyagrāhakabhāvena virahitā.*

146. MAVBh 27_{5-9}: ***na kliṣṭā nāpi vākliṣṭā śuddhā 'śuddhā na caiva sā*** */ kathaṃ na kliṣṭā nāpi cāśuddhā / prakṛtyaiva /* ***prabhāsvaratvāc cittasya*** */ kathaṃ nākliṣṭā na śuddhā /* ***kleśasyāgantukatvataḥ***.

147. What is defined as all defilements (*saṃkleśa*) in MAV I.10–11 can here only be the adventitious defilements.

148. RGVV 49_{9-12}: *evam eva sāgaramate bodhisattvaḥ sattvānāṃ prakṛtiprabhāsvaratāṃ cittasya prajānāti / tāṃ punar āgantukopakleśopakliṣṭāṃ paśyati / tatra bodhisattvasyaivaṃ bhavati / naite kleshāḥ sattvānāṃ cittaprakṛtiprabhāsvaratāyāṃ praviṣṭāḥ / āgantukā ete kleśā abhūtaparikalpasamutthitāḥ.*

149. MAVBh 24_{4-13}: *kathaṃ śūnyatāyāḥ prabhedo jnyeyaḥ /* ***saṃkliṣṭā ca viśuddhā ca*** */ ity asyāḥ prabhedaḥ / kasyām avasthāyāṃ saṃkliṣṭā kasyāṃ viśuddhā /* ***samalā nirmalā ca sā*** */ yadā saha malena varttate tadā saṃkliṣṭā / yadā prahīṇamalā tadā viśuddhā / yadi samalā bhūtvā nirmalā bhavati kathaṃ vikāradharmiṇītvād anityā na bhavati / yasmād asyāḥ* ***abdhātukanakākāśaśuddhivac chuddir iṣyate*** *// āgantukamalāpagamān na tu tasyāḥ svabhāvānyatvaṃ bhavati.*

150. See RGV I.5–6, where buddhahood is taken to be without beginning or end and thus unconditioned. RGVV 7_{14}–8_{1}: "Buddhahood is unconditioned. [. . .] As having neither beginning, middle, nor end by nature, it is unconditioned" (*asaṃskṛtam* [. . .] *buddhatvaṃ* [. . .] // *anādimadhyanidhanaprakṛti*[a]*tvād asaṃskṛtam*).

[a]Johnston reads *-prakṛta-*.

151. RGVV 76_{3-4} (RGV I.155): "The [buddha] element is empty of adventitious [stains], which have the defining characteristic of being separable; but it is not empty of unsurpassable qualities, which have the defining characteristic of not being separable" (*śūnya āgantukair dhātuḥ savinirbhāgalakṣaṇaiḥ / aśūnyo 'nuttaraiḥ dharmair avinirbhāgalakṣaṇaiḥ*).

152. See von Rospatt, *Buddhist Doctrine of Momentariness* 69ff., who observes that in the early Yogācāra the contradiction between Abhidharma and Mahāyāna ontology was solved by more or less incorporating the doctrine of the existence of momentary caused entities into the description of the dependent nature. The Mahāyāna stance that the momentariness of the dharmas means nothing other than their mere nonexistence could then be comfortably brought into line with the imagined nature of the trisvabhāva doctrine.

153. It is not the case though, that all parts of the *Ratnagotravibhāga* explain buddha-nature or buddhahood in such a way. Thus the explanations of the three kāyas in the second chapter rather suggest that the latter constantly remain in saṃsāra—and thus in time—as long as sentient beings need help. Takasaki, *Study on the Ratnagotravibhāga* 331–335.

Bibliography

Sanskrit Abbreviations and Sources

Bṛhaṭṭīkā (Tibetan translation). Quoted from the *Karmapa Tengyur* (= Tōhoku no. 3808). Rumtek / Delhi: n.d.

MAV: *Madhyāntavibhāga*. See *Madhyāntavibhāgabhāṣya*.

MAVBh: *Madhyāntavibhāgabhāṣya*. Edited by Gadjin M. Nagao. Tokyo: Suzuki Research Foundation, 1964.

MAVṬ: *Madhyāntavibhāgaṭīkā*. Edited by S. Yamaguchi. Nagoya: Librairie Hajinkaku, 1934. See also NGMPP reel no. A 38/10.

RGV: *Ratnagotravibhāga Mahāyānottaratantraśāstra*. Edited by Edward H. Johnston. Patna: The Bihar Research Society, 1950. (Includes the *Ratnagotravibhāgavyākhyā*.)

RGVV: *Ratnagotravibhāgavyākhyā*. See *Ratnagotravibhāga*.

Tibetan Sources

'Ba' ra ba Rgyal mtshan dpal bzang. "Chos rje rnam gnyis kyi dgongs bshad nyi ma'i 'od zer." In *A Tibetan Encyclopedia of Buddhist Scholasticism: The Collected Writings of 'Ba' ra ba rgyal mtshan dpal bzang*, vol. 11, 496–557. Dehra Dun: Ngawang Gyaltsen and Ngawang Lungtok, 1970.

Dol po pa Shes rab rgyal mtshan. "Bka' bsdu bzhi pa'i don gtan tshigs chen po." In *Kun mkhyen dol po'i gsung 'bum*, vol. *ka*, 363–418. Delhi: Jamyang Khyentse, 1984.

———. *Jo nang ri chos nges don rgya mtsho*. Beijing: Mi rigs dpe skrun khang, 1998.

———. [Nyi ma'i 'od zer:] "Theg pa chen po rgyud bla ma'i bstan bcos legs bshad nyi ma'i 'od zer." In *The 'Dzam-thang Edition of the Collected Works of Kun-mkhyen Dol-po-pa Shes-rab rgyal-mtshan*, vol. 4 (*ma*), 883–1161. Delhi: Shedrup Books, 1992.

———. "Bden gnyis gsal ba'i nyi ma." In *Kun mkhyen dol po pa'i gsung 'bum*, 1–45. Published by Jamyang Khyentse. Kathmandu: Shechen, n.d.

'Gos Lo tsā ba Gzhon nu dpal. *Theg pa chen po rgyud bla ma'i bstan bcos kyi 'grel bshad de kho na nyid rab tu gsal ba'i me long*. Edited by Klaus-Dieter Mathes. Stuttgart: Franz Steiner Verlag, 2003.

Karma pa III Rang byung rdo rje. *Dbu ma chos dbyings bstod pa'i rnam par bshad pa bzhugs so*. 52 fols., *dbu med*, unpublished.

———. *Zab mo nang gi don zhes bya ba'i gzhung bzhugs so* (block print). Published together with the *Rnam shes ye shes 'byed pa* and the *Bde bzhin bshegs pa'i snying po bstan pa*. Rumtek: Rumtek Monastery, 1970.

———. *Rang 'grel: Zab mo nang gi don gsal bar byed pa'i 'grel pa bzhugs so* (block print). N.p.: n.d. (The work itself was composed at the O rgyan kyi mkhan po padma 'byung gnas kyi sgrub gnas in 1325 [fol. 92b6]).

Karma 'Phrin las pa. "Dris lan yid kyi mun sel zhes bya ba lcags mo'i dris lan bzhugs so." In *The Songs of Esoteric Practice (mGur) and Replies to Doctrinal Questions (Dris lan) of Karma 'Phrin las pa*, 88–92. Reproduced from prints of the 1539 Rin chen ri bo blocks by Ngawang Topgay. New Delhi: The Mujib Press, 1975.

Kong sprul Blo gros mtha' yas. *Rgyud bla ma'i bshad srol: Theg pa chen po rgyud bla ma'i bstan bcos snying po'i don mngon sum lam gyi bshad srol dang sbyar ba'i rnam par 'grel pa phyir mi ldog pa seng ge'i nga ro zhes bya ba bzhugs so*. Rumtek: Rumtek Monastery, n.d.

———. *Zab mo nang gi don gyi 'grel pa: Rnal 'byor bla na med pa'i rgyud sde rgya mtsho snying po bsdus pa zab mo nang gi don nyung ngu'i tshig gis rnam par 'grel ba zab don snang byed*. Rumtek: Rumtek Monastery, 1970.

———. *Shes bya kun khyab mdzod*. Beijing: Mi rigs dpe skrun khang, 1982.

Sa bzang Mati paṇ chen 'jam dbyangs blo gros rgyal mtshan. "Theg pa chen po'i rgyud bla ma'i bstan bcos kyi rnam par bshad pa nges don rab gsal snang ba." In *Sa skya pa'i mkhas pa rnams kyi gsung skor*, vol. 4, 1–520. Kathmandu: Khenpo Abbey, 1999.

Gser mdog Paṇ chen shākya mchog ldan. "Byams chos lnga'i nges don rab tu gsal ba zhes bya ba'i bstan bcos bzhugs so." In *Gser mdog pang chen shākya mchog ldan gyi gsung 'bum legs bshad gser gyi bdud rtsi glegs bam*, vol. 11, 1–38. Collected Works. Thimphu: Kunzang Topgey, 1975.

———. "Byams chos lnga'i lam gyi rim pa gsal bar byed pa'i bstan bcos rin chen sgron gyi sgo 'byed ces bya ba bzhugs so." In *Gser mdog pang chen shākya mchog ldan gyi gsung 'bum legs bshad gser gyi bdud rtsi glegs bam*, vol. 11, 39–155. Collected Works. Thimphu: Kunzang Topgey, 1975.

———. "Zab zhi spros bral gyi bzhad pa stong nyid bdud rtsi'i lam po che zhes bya ba bzhugs so." In *Gser mdog pang chen shākya mchog ldan gyi gsung 'bum legs bshad gser gyi bdud rtsi glegs bam*, vol. 4, 107–207. Collected Works. Thimphu: Kunzang Topgey, 1975.

———. "Shing rta chen po'i srol gnyis kyi rnam par dbye ba bshad nas nges don gcig tu sgrub pa'i bstan bcos kyi rgyas 'grel bzhugs so" In *Gser mdog pang chen shākya mchog ldan gyi gsung 'bum legs bshad gser gyi bdud rtsi glegs bam*, vol. 2, 471–619. Collected Works. Thimphu: Kunzang Topgey, 1975.

———. "Sangs rgyas gyi snying po'i rnam bshad mdo rgyud kyi snying po." In *Gser mdog pang chen shākya mchog ldan gyi gsung 'bum legs bshad gser gyi bdud rtsi glegs bam*, vol. 13, 124–136. Collected Works. Thimphu: Kunzang Topgey, 1975.

Tāranātha. "Gzhan stong snying po." In *rJe btsun tāranātha'i gsung 'bum bzhugs so*, Collected Works, vol. 4, 491–514. Leh: Namgyal and Tsewang Taru, 1982–1985.

———. "Zab don nyer gcig pa bzhugs so." In *rJe btsun tāranātha'i gsung 'bum bzhugs so*, Collected Works, vol. 4, 781–795. Leh: Namgyal and Tsewang Taru, 1982–1985.

Secondary Sources

Boquist, Ṛke. *Trisvabhāva: A Study of the Three-Nature-Theory in Yogācāra Buddhism*. Department of History of Religion. Lund: Lund University, 1993.

Broido, Michael M. "The Jo-nang-pas on Madhyamaka: A Sketch." *Tibet Journal* 14, no. 1 (1989): 86–91.

Dreyfus, Georges B. J. *Recognizing Reality*. Albany: State University of New York Press, 1997.

Hookham, Susan K. *The Buddha Within*. Albany: State University of New York Press, 1991.

Kapstein, Matthew T. "Introduction." *The 'Dzam-thang Edition of the Collected Works of Kun-mkhyen Dol-po-pa Shes-rab rgyal-mtshan*. Delhi: Shedrup Books, 1992.

———. *The Tibetan Assimilation of Buddhism: Conversion, Contestation and Memory*. Oxford: Oxford University Press, 2000.

Lindtner, Christian. "*Cittamātra* in Indian Mahāyāna until Kamalaśīla." *Wiener Zeitschrift für die Kunde Südasiens* 41 (1997): 159–206.

Makransky, John J. *Buddhahood Embodied*. Albany: State University of New York Press, 1997.

Mathes, Klaus-Dieter. *Unterscheidung der Gegebenheiten von ihrem wahren Wesen (Dharmadharmatāvibhāga)*. Swisttal-Odendorf: Indica et Tibetica, 1996.

———. "Vordergründige und höchste Wahrheit im *zhentong*-Madhyamaka." In *Annäherung an das Fremde: XXVI. Deutscher Orientalistentag vom 25. bis 29.9. in Leipzig*, edited by Holger Preissler and H. Stein, special issue of *Zeitschrift der Deutschen Morgenländischen Gesellschaft*, no. 11 (1998): 457–468.

———. "Tāranātha's Presentation of *Trisvabhāva* in the *gZhan stong snying po*." *Journal of the International Association of Buddhist Studies* 23, no. 2 (2000): 195–223.

———. "'Gos Lo tsā ba Gzhon nu dpal's Extensive Commentary on and Study of the *Ratnagotravibhāgavyākhyā*." In *Religion and Secular Culture in Tibet: Tibetan Studies II. Proceedings of the International Association of Tibetan Studies 2000*, edited by Henk Blezer, 79–96. Leiden: Brill, 2002.

———, editor. See 'Gos Lo tsā ba Gzhon nu dpal. *Theg pa chen po rgyud bla ma'i bstan bcos kyi 'grel bshad de kho na nyid rab tu gsal ba'i me long*.

Newland, Guy. *The Two Truths in the Mādhyamika Philosophy of the Ge-luk-ba Order of Tibetan Buddhism*. Ithaca: Snow Lion, 1992.

Seyfort Ruegg, David. *Le Traité du Tathāgatagarbha de Bu ston rin chen grub*. Paris: École française d'Extrême-Orient, 1973.

Smith, E. Gene. "Introduction." *Kongtrul's Encyclopaedia of Indo-Tibetan Culture*, edited by Lokesh Chandra, vol. 1, 1–28. New Delhi: International Academy of Indian Culture, 1970.

Sponberg, Alan. "The Trisvabhāva Doctrine in India and China: A Study of Three Exegetical Models." *Bukkyō bunka kenkyūjo kiyō* 21 (1981): 97–119.

Stearns, Cyrus. "Dol-po-pa Shes-rab rgyal-mtshan and the Genesis of the *zhentong* Position in Tibet." *Asiatische Studien* 49, no. 4 (1995): 829–852.

———. *The Buddha from Dolpo: A Study of the Life and Thought of the Tibetan Master Dolpopa Sherab Gyaltsen*. Albany: State University of New York Press, 1999.

Takasaki, Jikido. *A Study on the Ratnagotravibhāga (Uttaratantra) Being a Treatise on the Tathāgatagarbha Theory of Mahāyāna Buddhism*. Rome: Istituto Italiano per il Medio ed Estremo Oriente, 1966.

Thurman, Robert, A. F. *The Speech of Gold: Reason and Enlightenment in the Tibetan Buddhism*. Delhi: Motilal Banarsidass, 1989.

Tillemans, Tom J. F., and Toru Tomabechi. "Le *dbu ma'i byung tshul* de Shākya mchog ldan." *Asiatische Studien* 49, no. 4 (1995): 891–918.

Tsultrim Gyamtsho Rinpoche and Rosemarie Fuchs. *Buddhanature: The Mahayana Uttaratantra Shastra with Commentary*. Ithaca: Snow Lion, 2000.

von Rospatt, Alexander. *The Buddhist Doctrine of Momentariness*. Stuttgart: Franz Steiner, 1995.

Zhāng, Yísūn. *Bod rgya tshig mdzod chen mo: Záng-Hàn Dàcídian*. 3 vols. Beijing: Mi rigs dpe skrun khang, 1985.

9

Zhentong Traces in the Nyingma Tradition

Two Texts from Mindroling

MATTHEW T. KAPSTEIN

Our knowledge of the reception and assessment of Dolpopa Sherab Gyaltsen's (1292–1361) distinctive teaching of zhentong[1] among adherents of the Nyingma lineages remains spotty at best. Indeed, it is not even clear that we are entitled to speak of a discrete Nyingma "school" at any time in the past that had a definite standpoint with respect to the issue. The two figures now most often cited as fountainheads of Nyingma doctrinal thought—Rongzom Chokyi Zangpo (11th c.) and Longchen Rabjampa (1308–1364)—though aligned with trends that are now considered to be broadly harmonious with zhentong, did not engage with it directly: the former, after all, lived several centuries prior to Dolpopa;[2] and Longchenpa, though Dolpopa's contemporary, never seems to have addressed himself to the Jonang master's contributions, despite the evident affinities between them on a number of points.[3]

Over the past several centuries, however, leading Nyingma authors have sometimes made explicit their standpoint regarding zhentong, and it is now evident that there has been no uniform view among them in regard to the matter. Two of the key figures associated with the eighteenth-century renewal of Katok Monastery in Kham are known to have played cardinal roles in introducing zhentong thought into the Nyingma mainstream. Although the first of these, Katok Rikzin Tsewang Norbu (1698–1755), seems to have been moved primarily by his considerable interest in the Jonang and allied traditions as distinct lines of Buddhist tantric teaching in Tibet,[4] it was the prolific Katok Getse Paṇḍita Tsewang Chokdrub (1761–1829) who most forcefully advocated the zhentong approach to "Great Madhyamaka" in the context of properly Nyingma expositions of Mahāyāna doctrine.[5] The doctrinal writings of the best-known twentieth-century successor to Getse Paṇḍita's line of thought, Dudjom Rinpoche Jikdrel Yeshe Dorje (1904–1987), have contributed to a general impression that the Nyingma are to be placed firmly in the zhentong camp.[6]

Other voices, however, urge us to be cautious in this regard. The Nyingmapa thinker whose doctrinal and philosophical views have been perhaps the most influential in recent decades, Mipam Namgyel Gyatso (1846–1912), seems to have been reserved in his embrace of zhentong.[7] His preferred idiom was clearly that of *tazhi trödrel* (*mtha' bzhi spros bral*), "absence of elaboration with respect to the four extremes," an "anti-standpoint" that reflects the Madhyamaka thought of the Sakya master Gorampa Sonam Sengge (1429–1489) and that in any case resonates well with Longchenpa's apophaticism.[8] Although those who are partial to the zhentong teaching have sometimes sought to claim Mipam as one of their own, it seems clear, on reading Mipam's own works, that he was prepared to endorse zhentong discourse chiefly in the relatively restrained context of "conventions pertaining to pure vision" (*rnam dag gzigs snang gi tha snyad*) and not in regard to the proper characterization of the absolute.[9] Some even go so far (at least in oral teaching if not in writing) as to hold that Mipam's apparent gestures in support of zhentong represent only sketches of positions to adopt in debate, should one be challenged to defend it.[10]

Still other Nyingma thinkers remained entirely aloof to the zhentong question and, in a few cases, appear to have regarded zhentong with disapproval. One of Mipam's contemporaries, Tubten Chokyi Drakpa (a.k.a. Minyak Kunzang Sonam, 1823–ca. 1905), for instance, clearly favored a Geluk approach to Madhyamaka, from which any concession to zhentong thought was excluded.[11] He was not alone, by any means, in espousing Prāsaṅgika-Mādhyamika along the lines delineated by Tsongkhapa as marking the summit of the teaching of the sūtras, while affirming practice in the Seminal Essence tradition of the Great Perfection (*rdzogs chen snying thig*) to be the culmination of the tantras. Indeed, it is my impression that some such synthesis was closer to the norm in the eighteenth and nineteenth centuries, particularly in Kham and Amdo, than was any affirmation of Dzokchen teaching tinged by the zhentong doctrine. This harmonization of Prāsaṅgika-Mādhyamika and the teachings of the Seminal Essence is particularly well exemplified in the work of Jigme Lingpa (1730–1798) and certain of his successors and commentators.[12]

All of this gives rise to uncertainty concerning the precise relationship between zhentong and Nyingma teaching. Is it best to regard zhentong as a brother-in-arms of Nyingma instruction, a distant cousin, or a complete stranger? And if these and perhaps other options are available, might we not be warranted to conclude that the zhentong problematic is in the last analysis irrelevant when seen from the Nyingma vantage point?

This situation reflects in part the fact that, among the Nyingma, the formation of monastic colleges came relatively late. Although the old Zur lineage, during the eleventh and twelfth centuries, appears to have created a well-formed curriculum based principally on tantric exegesis, and though this tradition had some degree of continuity in the subsequent development of a distinct line of teaching at Katok monastery in Kham,[13] most Nyingma masters, if they received scholastic training at all, did so under the aegis of one or another of the new schools. Longchenpa's education at the Kadam college of Sangpu is a case in point.[14] It is perhaps not surprising, therefore, that Nyingma thought evolved without a clear "party line" formulated in respect to zhentong. In all events, Dolpopa's teaching was never thought to be integral to the distinctive Nyingma tantric doctrines, despite its apparent affinities with aspects of them,[15] and the Nyingma perhaps did not perceive themselves as having much of a stake in fully clarifying their assessment of zhentong doctrine.

This all began to change, however, during the seventeenth century, when, in tandem with, and to some degree under pressure from, the rising Ganden Potrang regime in Central Tibet, the modern Nyingma monastic system emerged and with it the formation of a system of Nyingma monastic colleges (*bshad grwa*). From this time on, and particularly during the nineteenth century, we find clear evidence of a drive to produce suitable Nyingma textbooks to guide instruction in the exoteric subjects as well as in tantra.[16]

It is in the light of these circumstances that the passages considered here seem particularly pertinent. They derive from the writings of two of the preeminent masters of Mindroling, the leading Central Tibetan Nyingma center,[17] whose intimate connections with the Fifth Dalai Lama and the Ganden Potrang government that he founded might lead us to anticipate that they would have either rejected or quietly ignored the whole matter of zhentong. For by their time that doctrine, which was closely associated with the Jonang tradition that had been condemned by the Great Fifth and his court, had come to be considered to all intents and purposes anathema.

The first author we shall consider here, Lochen Dharmaśrī (1654–1717), was one of those responsible, under the guidance of his elder brother Terdak Lingpa Gyurme Dorje (1646–1714), for the ascension of Mindroling overall.[18] This involved a sustained effort on the part of the brothers to establish the ritual protocols of the Nyingma on the basis of the surest available lines of teaching, an effort reflected above all in their contributions to the redaction of the *Nyingma Kama* (*Rnying ma bka' ma*), the "Oral Tradition of the Nyingma," embodying the lineages of tantric teaching believed to reach back to the epoch of the Tibetan monarch Tri Songdetsen (r. 755–c. 797).[19] Because the proper transmission of the vows, rules, and guidelines associated with each of the three grades of Buddhist practice—respectively, those governing adherence to the *prātimokṣa*, the lifestyle of the bodhisattva, and the practice of the tantras—provides the framework for the entire edifice, it is not surprising that the establishment of a correct understanding of these regulations became a major preoccupation for the Nyingma order. For this reason, in response to the entreaties of the contemporary Dorje Drak Rikzin, Pema Trinle (1641–1717), who was the head of the Northern Treasure (Jangter) lineage and of the important Nyingma monastery of Dorje Drak,[20] we find Lochen Dharmaśrī composing, in 1708, what appears to be the first commentary on the preeminent Nyingma synthesis of the system of the Buddhist vows, the *Ascertainment of the Three Vows*

(*Sdom gsum rnam nges*) by Ngari Paṇchen Pema Wangyel (1487–1543).[21] The perceived importance of Lochen Dharmaśrī's commentary may be gauged from the fact that, at the request once more of the Dorje Drak Rikzin, and with the additional encouragements of his brother Terdak Lingpa, the finished work was published xylographically at Mindroling within a year of its completion.[22]

There was, it must be stressed, nothing at all in Ngari Paṇchen's text that required a comment on zhentong. Nevertheless, in the section treating the vows of the bodhisattva, and the progression along the path of the Six Perfections (*pāramitā*) that this entails, we find a relatively detailed amplification of the single line of the root text that reads: "One practices the profound wisdom of audition, reflection, and contemplation" (*thos bsam sgom pa'i shes rab zab mo spyad*).[23] Remarkably, it is here that Lochen Dharmaśrī inserts a brief but lucid account of the rangtong / zhentong distinction, elaborating at the same time a synopsis of the path that allows us to see just how he believed this distinction to operate within the system of Nyingma Buddhism overall.

The second work to be discussed, intended to supplement Lochen Dharmaśrī's commentary on the three vows, was written by Lochen's brilliant nephew, Terdak Lingpa's son Terse Pema Gyurme Gyatso (1686–1717), following the teaching of the commentary in 1710 by a master he names only as Kenchen Lama-chok, the "venerable guru and great preceptor," but who was certainly his uncle, who held the title of second Kenchen ("great preceptor, abbot") of Mindroling.[24] Both of these distinguished masters, uncle and nephew, perished as victims of the Dzungar assault on the Nyingma monasteries of Central Tibet in 1717, as did the Dorje Drak Rikzin.[25] Given their authoritative status, we may take their remarks on our subject as definitive representations of the assessment of zhentong affirmed at Mindroling during the early eighteenth century and subsequently influential throughout its extensive network of branch monasteries and Nyingma centers at large.

Zhentong in Lochen Dharmaśrī's Wish-Granting Sheaf (Dpag bsam snye ma)

The context for Lochen Dharmaśrī's introduction of zhentong into the exposition of the *Ascertainment of the Three Vows* appears toward the end of the second section of the work, concerning the vows of the bodhisattva. Ngari Paṇchen's text includes here a terse summary of the manner in which the aspirant bodhisattva is to adhere to the six perfections, the excellences (*pāramitā*) of the Mahāyāna path. Concerning the sixth, the perfection of discernment, or wisdom (*prajñāpāramitā*), he says only, as we have seen, "One practices the profound wisdom of audition, reflection, and contemplation." This, of course, is the well-known threefold training in wisdom, consisting of the wisdom of receiving the teaching by hearing it from one's masters (*śrutamayī-*), of penetrating its meaning through critical investigation of it (*cintāmayī-*), and, finally, of assimilating it into the fabric of one's life by means of the discipline of meditation (*bhāvanāmayī-prajñā*). I translate here Dharmaśrī's commentary on this short passage in its entirety:

With respect to its meaning, there are three topics:

1. The essential nature of wisdom is a virtuous attentiveness, endowed with four distinctive characteristics,[26] that well analyzes phenomena and is inclusive of the seeds [for the further ripening of such virtuous attentiveness].

2. The verbal meaning: *shes rab* ("wisdom") comes from the Sanskrit word *prajñā*, in which *jñā*, "to achieve mastery, to realize," is preceded by the prefix *pra*. This root meaning thus suggests "to realize, or to achieve mastery, excellently," the object of this realization being the supreme objective (*don dam pa*, *paramārtha*). What is "supreme" in this case is the gnosis of sublime beings in balanced absorption, while the "objective" is the scope of its activity. It is *shes rab*, wisdom, due to the realization, or accomplished mastery, of just that.

3. If it be divided, there are three; for Nāgārjuna[27] has said:

> Audition serves to expand wisdom,
> As does critical reflection. If those two are present,
> Then contemplation also arises.

Accordingly:

3.1. Concerning wisdom that emerges from audition, the objects of audition are the inner sciences, consisting of the scriptures of the Conqueror together with the commentaries on their intention. One should also study the four outer sciences as facets of them, whereby disciples are gathered into the following: grammar and logic, the two sciences for eliminating others as adversaries, and the technical arts and medicine, the two sciences for gathering others into the following.[28] For it is the level of omniscience that must be attained. As it says (*Mahāyānasūtrālaṃkāra*, 11.60):

> Without immersing himself in the five sciences, the superior person cannot advance to omniscience;
> Hence, to correct and to attract others, and for the sake of his own knowledge, he thus devotes himself to them.

It is also said (*Bodhicaryāvatāra*, 5.100ab):

> Nowhere is there anything
> That the Conqueror's Sons do not learn.

In particular, in order to master to the full extent the meaning of the scriptures, one must assess them in terms of definitive and provisional significance, indirect and allusive intention, and so forth. These, however, may be known elsewhere. Here, in fact, wisdom is insight, the ultimate truth. Among the arguments that serve to establish it, there are five great axioms:[29]

i. The absence of one and many, which investigates the essence;
ii. "Diamond fragments," which investigates the cause;
iii. Negating the production of an existent or nonexistent, which investigates the result;
iv. Negating production in respect to the four alternatives, which investigates both cause and result.

These four are the arguments that exclude the extreme of exaggeratedly imputing existence.

v. Fifth is the axiom of interdependent origination that cuts through the elaborations of both existence and nonexistence, because what is not established in essence, by virtue of its dependence upon another, is not nonexistent conventionally.

Thus, the five great axioms establish all phenomena in terms of the middle without extremes.

Now, concerning the ways to cut through elaborations, there are two, the way of rangtong (*rang stong*) and that of zhentong (*gzhan stong*). Of them, the way of rangtong holds that because, except for their mere appearance, the bearers of properties (*dharmin*, *chos can*) are empty of a proper essence, it is emptiness as an existential negation (*med dgag*) that is the ultimate.[30] Although, among the proponents of Madhyamaka, who are all antiessentialists, there is no difference in respect to the ultimate, there are those who set forth the autonomous proposition (*svātantrika-pratijñā*) that what is established ostensibly is apparitional, and those who, by drawing out only the entailments [of the opponents' affirmations, *prāsaṅgika*], refute even the merely ostensible reality (*kun rdzob tsam*, *saṃvṛtimātra*) that is affirmed. Hence, two systems have appeared.

For the proponents of the Madhyamaka who establish the ultimate to be zhentong, all that can be known is held to comprise the three characteristics or to comprise the two, the imaginary and the absolute.[31] Based on this distinction, two dissimilar ways of identifying the topic of inquiry have arisen. For, according to the textual tradition of Yogācāra, the ground of emptiness is explained to be that which is dependent, which is absolute insomuch as it is empty with respect to the negandum, that which is imputed (*kun btags*); while, in the *Sublime Continuum* and elsewhere, it is said that reality is the absolute, which is empty with respect to the negandum, namely, that which is imaginary (*kun brtags*).[32]

Thus, in its essence, this absolute, which is the reality of mind, the expanse of the supreme objective, is without taints to be abandoned or unprecedented qualities to be newly achieved. Because it is primordially pure by nature, with its qualities spontaneously achieved, it surpasses fault and virtue (*skyon yon*), construction and clearing (*grub bsal*). Hence, that expanse of the supreme objective is not such as to be empty of its own essence (*rang gi ngo bos stong pa*). And because the elaborated aspects of apprehended object and apprehending subject are phenomena manifest to ephemeral bewilderment, which are not established in the subtending stratum (*gshis*), the ostensible is empty of its own essence. As such they are extrinsic with respect to the reality that is the supreme objective, so that it is explained that "the supreme objective is empty of extrinsic essence" (*don dam gzhan gyi ngo bos stong pa*). As it says in the *Sublime Continuum* (1.155):

> The elemental stratum is empty of the ephemeral
> Whose characteristic is to be separable,
> But not empty of the [buddha] qualities
> Whose characteristic is to be inseparable.

In brief, if this be pondered in respect to the ostensible, there is emptiness, whether as an existential negation or predicate negation. If it be pondered in respect to the expanse of the supreme objective, there is emptiness of the conceptual objects that are extrinsic to it.

But if you wonder, "with what intention is it said that the supreme objective is empty of its own essence?" the intention is that, in objectifying the supreme objective, it is not established as the intellect grasps it to be.

Concerning these points, because wisdom born of audition is most important on the level of ordinary individuals, we give here just an introduction to how they are to be established, for, without audition, reflection and contemplation are impossible. As is said (*Sublime Continuum*, 5.15cd):

> Wisdom is supreme and its ground
> Is audition; wherefore, audition is supreme.

3.2. As for wisdom born of reflection, not leaving what was learned as just something heard, the ascertainment of its meaning depends upon reflection, for which reason the wisdom associated with reflection must be engendered. As it says in the *Wish-Granting Treasury* (*Yid bzhin mdzod*, 13.1ab):

> Thus adorned with genuine audition, one must then
> Surely generate the wisdom of reflection in the mind.[33]

About that, by carefully investigating the literal meaning of what one has heard and turning attention to it within, without leaving it to be mere generality, but by considering with the wisdom of reflection that discerns the particulars, with respect to each and every sequence of word and meaning, whether it is erroneous or not, one must ascertain what one has heard. It says in the *Jñānasārasamuccaya*:

> Like gold that is burned, cut, and ground,
> Investigate my pronouncements
> And take them up, but not so out of respect.[34]

According to this example, one does not just enter into the words and meaning of the sūtras and tantras through faith, but they should be taken up following the investigation of these three: scriptures that inspire confidence, reasonings that proceed from the force of reality (*vastubalapravṛtta, dngos po stobs zhugs*), and the absence of internal contradiction (lit., "noncontradiction before and after"). It says in the *Catuḥśataka*:

> The meaning that is well articulated:
> According to scripture and reason,
> Without contradiction before or after,
> Should be accepted by worthy persons.[35]

Moreover, it is explained that the three knowables[36] are to be examined through both scripture and reason.

3.3. Concerning the wisdom born of contemplation, it says in the *Wish-Granting Treasury* (chap. 18, v. 1ab):

> Thus, when the objects of reflection are exhausted,
> Wisdom born of contemplation must be engendered in mind.

Hence, in general, through acceptance and rejection one attains the objectives as one has come to know them and cultivates them experientially. In particular, one penetrates the wisdom of insight, the contemplation of nonconceptual gnosis. As it says in the *Bodhicaryāvatāra* (8.4):

By insight and well-endowed with tranquility
One knows to overcome the afflictions.

Now, in respect to the view that is to be experientially cultivated through contemplation, according to the explicit teaching of the middle turn as exposed in the *Collection of Reason*,[37] it is held that it is the existential negation that is of definitive meaning. Hence, it is explained that to contemplate nothing at all is the contemplation of emptiness and to see nothing at all is the realization of just what is. But according to the intention of the final turn, the texts of the *Dharmas of Maitreya*, as exposed by Asaṅga and his brother [Vasubandhu] and in the *Collection of Hymns* of Venerable Nāgārjuna,[38] it is explained that that which is to be experientially cultivated through contemplation is precisely gnosis without duality of apprehended object and apprehending subject. And that, moreover, is in agreement in its intention with the profound tantras of secret mantra.

Hence, although you may think that there is a contradiction, because the all-knowing king of Dharma, the venerable Longchenpa Chokyi Ozer, when identifying that which is to be established through audition, in his works including the *Treasury of Philosophical Systems* (*Grub mtha' mdzod*) and the root text and commentary of the *Wish-Granting Treasury*, proves the Prāsaṅgika-Mādhyamika to be the pinnacle of the causal Mahāyāna, but when he treats the experiential establishment of contemplation, he holds that what is to be experienced is the individual, intuitive gnosis (*so so rang rig pa'i ye shes*, **pratyātma-saṃvedanīyaṃ jñānam*) without duality of apprehended object and apprehending subject, nonetheless there is no contradiction here.[39] For, on the level of the ordinary individual, when establishing the view through audition and reflection, it is difficult to undo the intellect's grasping of signs (*mtshan 'dzin*), so that it is wisdom born from audition and reflection that acts to negate [the grasping of signs] and, for that, the Prāsaṅgika reasoning that cuts through exaggerated projections is acute. But when establishing the wisdom born of contemplation, it is the Mādhyamika view taught in the final turn that is profound and most excellent. For it is just the expanse that is naturally pure, the truth of the supreme objective and self-emergent gnosis, that is the primordially abiding nature of all phenomena and accords, as well, with the experiential cultivation of the view as explained in the profound tantras of secret mantra—this thought was his intention.

For these reasons, in accord with the intention of the sūtras teaching the nucleus,[40] as taught in the *Sublime Continuum* and the Mādhyamika *Collection of Hymns*, having mastered the tenet of the nucleus of buddha-nature (*tathāgatagarbha*), one who is "of the clan,"[41] cultivating a spirit bent on enlightenment (*bodhicittotpāda*), [comprehends that] the disclosure of the final significance of the elemental stratum, the abiding nature, depends upon entering into a nonconceptual concentration (*nirvikalpasamādhi*). Therefore, sitting with legs crossed upon a comfortable seat, in accord with the words (*Sublime Continuum*, 1.154, and *Abhisamayālaṃkāra*, 5.21),

> Here nothing is to be removed,
> Nothing at all to be established.
> Really viewing the real,
> By really seeing, one is free.

one mulls over none of the signs or objects of discursive thought, and, in the face of whatever arises, acting neither to remove nor establish them, one settles in equipoise, one-pointed with regard to one's own true face, limpid and transparent, without any apprehensive assertions at all. Thus, all the proliferations of mind and mental events being arrested, one comes to behold the nonconceptual gnosis, free from the dichotomy of apprehended object and apprehending subject, the very essence of which is intuited individually. As it says in the *Sublime Continuum* (4.26cd):

> The body of reality that is the inner nature
> Is seen with the eye of gnosis.

And in the *Hymn to the Expanse of Reality* (*Dharmadhātustava*, 38ab):

> Relying on eye and form
> Taintless appearance arises.

And in Rāhula's *Hymn to the Mother*:

> Homage to the mother of the Conquerors of the Three Times,
> Perfection of Wisdom,
> not spoken, thought, or uttered,
> Unborn, unceasing, essence of space,
> in the range of individual, intuitive gnosis.

Moreover, as when clouds are dispersed so that the orb of the sun shines forth, the final significance of equipoised awareness, gnosis beyond intellect without any apprehensive assertions, resting nakedly in its self-radiance, is intuited from within as mind that is naturally luminous gnosis. It says in the *Introduction to the Conduct of a Bodhisattva* (9.35):

> When neither being nor nonbeing
> Stand before the mind,
> Then, with no further recourse,
> Without objectification, one finds peace.

> In that way, when certitude in regard to the final significance of the nucleus is obtained through wisdom born of contemplation, owing to the great force of compassion for beings who have not realized the gnosis abiding within themselves, an uncontrived courage to reach the level of unsurpassed enlightenment arises. On that basis, one's engagement in the contemplation of nonconceptual concentration is reinforced, thereby forming a cycle, like a wheel, in relation to profound causality (*zab mo'i rgyu 'bras*).
>
> In brief, one contemplates nonconceptual gnosis in equipoise and, rising from that, in the aftermath (*pṛṣṭhalabdha*, *rjes thob*), views all appearances as illusory, appearing without an established nature. Then, a dedication [of merit] should be performed on behalf of illusory beings.

There are many interesting features of this passage that seems often to be ignored, even among Nyingma scholars who have studied the *Wish-Granting Sheaf.* I have more than once had the experience of discussing zhentong with learned Nyingmapas who were not particularly well disposed to it, who were bemused to be reminded of Dharmaśrī's words on the subject. Perhaps because they occupy only a few paragraphs in a very large commentary, where the root text offers no hint that such a digression is required, it is easy to pass lightly over them; and perhaps, for the same reason, Dharmaśrī's affirmation of zhentong seems to have gone unnoticed in the pronouncedly anti-zhentong milieu of early eighteenth-century Central Tibet.

It is notable, too, that Dharmaśrī, though introducing in cursory manner the distinction between intrinsic and extrinsic emptiness, or zhentong, and mentioning the Svātantrika- and Prāsaṅgika-Mādhyamika traditions that, after all, were generally predominant in Tibetan Madhyamaka thought, has relatively little to say about these things and treats his subject almost exclusively in relation to zhentong and the question of buddha-nature. He considers Longchenpa's avowal of Prāsaṅgika to be restricted in scope to the domain of audition and reflection and affirms that master's treatment of contemplation to resemble the zhentong approach he himself espouses here. In so doing, he seems to attribute to Longchenpa something like the position that during the nineteenth century would be articulated by the great Jonang scholiast Bamda Gelek, which I have described elsewhere in writing that he held Prāsaṅgika "to be an inferior, but nevertheless legitimate, and propaedeutically valuable, approach to Madhyamaka thought, which, once mastered, opened the way for an appropriate engagement in the 'Great Madhyamaka,' that is, the teaching of extrinsic emptiness."[42]

There are, indeed, indications scattered about Longchenpa's copious writings that would support such an interpretation; we cannot imagine that Dharmaśrī would have been either inaccurate or tendentious in his citation of the "Second Samantabhadra." However, I would suggest that Longchenpa's position about this shifts somewhat according to context, so that the reading proposed by Dharmaśrī may not be the sole one available. In particular, we must note that in some of his writings on meditation, Longchenpa is strikingly apophatic in his approach; this is, for instance, quite apparent throughout his *Trilogy on Natural Liberation* (*Rang grol skor gsum*). I suspect that Longchenpa's shifting use of affirmative and negative dialectic contributed, in some respects, to the emergence of differing lines of interpretation within the Nyingma that favored one strategy or the other.[43]

THE UNMENTIONED PRESENCE OF ZHENTONG

However we assess Lochen Dharmaśrī's commitment to zhentong—and a thorough assessment must await a broader consideration of relevant themes throughout the considerable body of his writings—it is immediately striking that he is fully explicit in his embrace of it in what is certainly one of his fundamental works. That this was not quite exceptional and that the current of zhentong thought made manifest here was normative at Mindroling at the beginning of the eighteenth century may be seen in one of the texts of his nephew Pema Gyurme Gyatso, the *minling tersé* (*smin gling gter sras*), that is, the son of Mindroling's founder (and the Fifth Dalai Lama's protégé) Terdak Lingpa. In this case, however, the word "zhentong" is never used, though there can be little doubt that it is the teaching intended.

The text in question is presented as a supplement to the *Ascertainment of the Three Vows* and bears the full title *Heart of the Definitive Philosophical System, Intimate Instructions on Ground, Path, and Fruition, Following from the Ascertainment of the Three Vows.*[44] In essence, the work responds to the problem of demonstrating the background by virtue of which adherence to the course of practice embodied in the three vows is warranted. That is to say, how do the reality of things and the possibilities of actualization that this reality affords render the spiritual discipline of Nyingma Buddhism both possible and desirable?

In presenting a treatise on ground, path, and fruition as an adjunct to the teaching of the three vows in this manner, Pema Gyurme Gyatso seems to have been following the lead of the Sakya master Gorampa Sonam Senge (1429–1489), who similarly supplemented Sakya Paṇḍita's *Analysis of the Three Vows* with a work on the same three basic topics, but of course from the Sakyapa perspective.[45] If this was indeed his source of inspiration, however, Pema Gyurme Gyatso nowhere acknowledges it. He tells us only, as mentioned earlier, that the work was composed following his uncle's teaching of the *Wish-Granting Sheaf* during the summer retreat of 1710.

It must be stressed at the outset that Pema Gyurme Gyatso, unlike Lochen Dharmaśrī, does not explicitly reference the rangtong / zhentong distinction, and in fact does not use these terms at all. In introducing the three topics of ground, path, and fruition, he identifies the first, the ground (*gzhi*), precisely with buddha-nature (here **sugatagarbha, bde gshegs snying po*) and proceeds to define this briefly in relation to the teachings of the four philosophical schools—Vaibhāṣika, Sautrāntika, Yogācāra, and Madhyamaka—in turn. Much of the treatise, in fact, is then devoted to elaborating his understanding of the Madhyamaka treatment of buddha-nature, which he introduces in these words:

> Concerning the fourth school, the Madhyamaka, we present both a sketch of others' systems and the established order of our own. As for the first: though they generally agree in holding spiritual-affinity (*gotra, rigs*) to be the tainted reality (*samaladharmatā, dri bcas chos nyid*) just as it is, there appear to be many different ways of recognizing it:
>
> - The great translator Ngok Loden Sherab and his followers held it to be the expanse pervading the whole trio of ground, path, and fruition, unqualified by attributes such as the buddhas' powers (*bala, stobs*), [and identified as] naturally pure emptiness, the aspect of existential negation (*prasajyapratiṣedha, med dgag*).
> - The lord of the Dharma Sakya Paṇḍita and others recognized it as qualified by attributes such as the buddhas' powers but held that its presence within sentient beings was of heuristic significance (*neyārtha, drang don*).
> - Most of the readers / reciters[46] of Tibet, in recognizing buddha-nature, hold it to be the aspect of natural purity alone.
> - The venerable Pakmodrupa and others held the powers and other such attributes of buddha-nature to be the potential attributes of the realized body of reality (*rtogs pa chos sku*).
> - Bodong Paṇchen Jikme Drakpa[47] was among those who held them to be the attributes of the natural body of reality (*rang bzhin chos sku*).
>
> And there have been many other tenets besides.
>
> Second is the order of our own system: Here, we accord with the expositions of the uncommon system of the Mahāyāna as presented in the writings of the all-knowing king of the Dharma, Longchen Drime Ozer, the great, all-knowing Jonang Master of the Four Reliances,[48] and the venerable Rangjung Dorje,[49] among others, as well as the uncommon

> intended meaning of the supreme scholar, Buton Rinpoche, expounded in, for instance, the section on the explanation of the causal continuum (*rgyu rgyud*) in his *General Presentation of the Tantras* (*Rgyud sde spyi rnam*). . . . According to these sources, mind as such, which is primordially pure by nature, empty, limpid, incessant, and abiding without change or transformation in its all-pervading essence, is the base, buddha-nature (**sugatagarbha, bde gshegs snying po*). For as it says in the *Sūtra of the King of Samādhi*:
>
> Pure, limpid, and luminous,
> Unagitated and unconditioned,
> The buddha-nature
> Is primordially abiding reality.[50]

The text that follows these prefatory remarks provides, in essence, a thorough summary of the content of the *Sublime Continuum of the Mahāyāna*, supplemented by discussions of specifically tantric approaches to the topics at hand, where the focus is primarily upon the *Web of Illusion* (*Māyājāla, Sgyu 'phrul drwa ba*) tantras, with occasional references to the teachings of Dzokchen as well. In the context of the present chapter, it will not be necessary to enter into the details of all this, interesting though they may be. Readers of the present work, it is assumed, will already have some idea of the buddha-nature teaching of the *Sublime Continuum* and its capital significance for zhentong thought.

A question may be raised, however, concerning what, if anything, this has to tell us of Pema Gyurme Gyatso's opinion of zhentong, which, as we have mentioned, is nowhere explicitly named in his text. The buddha-nature theory of the *Sublime Continuum*, after all, formed part of the standard śāstric curriculum in all schools of Tibetan Buddhism, though interpretation of it varied considerably, some taking it to be a Yogācāra work, others holding it to represent Prāsaṅgika-Mādhyamika, and still others reading it as an expression of zhentong or allied viewpoints.[51] Just where does the teacher from Mindroling stand on this?

A response of sorts may be found by attending closely to the passage cited earlier. It is clear that Pema Gyurme Gyatso excludes reading buddha-nature as equivalent to the existential negation equated with emptiness in some Tibetan approaches to Prāsaṅgika-Mādhyamika, and it is equally clear that he rules out interpretations that would treat it and its qualities as merely metaphorical, potential, or heuristic. And as he has already made explicit that he is presenting here the Mādhyamika view of the ground, having rapidly dispensed with the three lower schools, including Yogācāra, it is evident that he will not accept a hermeneutic privileging the latter tradition. Pema Gyurme Gyatso, therefore, considers buddha-nature, as taught in the *Sublime Continuum*, to represent the Madhyamaka teaching of definitive significance as was previously taught by a number of masters he names, including Dolpopa.

But is this sufficient to demonstrate our author's embrace of zhentong? The answer, I think, is "yes and no." Yes because, given the range of positions he excludes, some variety of zhentong appears to be the last man standing. But no because, in view of the four figures he references as representative of his standpoint, he is perhaps reaching for the common ground to be found behind their approaches, without quite endorsing zhentong per se, at least in its Jonang formulation. This would suggest that he sought to defend a sort of mitigated zhentong, much as Jamgon Kongtrul would do a century and a half later. Perhaps we may even ask whether it is a mere coincidence that the monastery at which Kongtrul received his Nyingma formation, Zhechen, was the major branch of Mindroling in Kham?

Seen in this fashion, Pema Gyurme Gyatso's simultaneous endorsement of the teachings of Karmapa III Rangjung Dorje, Longchen Rabjam, and Kunkyen Dolpopa makes good sense and, indeed, appears to offer a clear precedent for the zhentong-friendly doctrinal orientations of the so-called Rimé movement. More unusual is the stress he lays upon Buton Rinchen Drub as representing a similar doctrinal lineage, for Buton, as we know, is more frequently presented as Dolpopa's arch rival in respect to the interpretation of buddha-nature thought. Interestingly, though, Pema Gyurme Gyatso pointedly emphasizes certain of Buton's tantric writings here and *not* his famed treatise on buddha-nature.[52] It remains a question for subsequent research to determine whether, indeed, Buton espoused a second doctrine of buddha-nature, more in line with the thinking of the other three masters mentioned, in his discussions of the causal continuum. If so, it would go a long way toward explaining the attempt on the part of another of the great fourteenth-century scholar-adepts, the Kagyupa Barawa Gyaltsen Pelzang (1310–1391), to demonstrate how the positions of Buton and Dolpopa might be reconciled.[53]

Conclusion

As we have seen, it was by no means incumbent upon Nyingmapa thinkers to affirm zhentong and, as a matter of fact, many did not. It may therefore seem remarkable that two of the leading figures in the Nyingma lineage most closely associated with the Fifth Dalai Lama should have steered so close to dangerous shoals. The reasons for which they did are not entirely clear. Although Terdak Lingpa's "Record of Teachings Received" establishes that he had some familiarity with works by Jonang masters Kunga Drolchok (1507–1566) and Tāranātha (1575–1634), there is little there to suggest that zhentong was a particular point of interest for him.[54] And it remains an open question whether the tantric ritual traditions of the *Nyingma Kama*, and particularly those of the cycle of the *Magical Net*, lend themselves to a harmonization with zhentong thought, perhaps more so than do the teachings of the *Seminal Essence of the Great Perfection*, which seem often to be emphasized when we find mergers of the Nyingma and Geluk traditions. The cardinal position of Longchenpa for both sides of the discussion, however, urges circumspection in this regard.

What we are left with, then, is a puzzle that one hopes to see cleared up in the course of future research. In all events, it is evident that among the closest Nyingma protégés of the Fifth Dalai Lama, who was himself celebrated as a Nyingma visionary, we find the continuing affirmation of a stream of the zhentong teaching that the Great Fifth and his followers are supposed to have banned.

Notes

1. My preference is to use the phrase "extrinsic emptiness" as an approximate English equivalent to zhentong (*gzhan stong*), but I concur with the editors that it is best to employ one standard throughout the volume as a whole.

2. Almogi's *Rong-zom-pa's Discourses* and "Writings of Rong zom Chos kyi bzang po" treat issues in Rongzompa's thought that intersect with aspects of the later zhentong controversies.

3. Mathes, *Direct Path* 98–113, usefully surveys Longchenpa's approach to buddha-nature.

4. See, for instance, Kaḥ-thog rig-'dzin, *Kaḥ thog rig 'dzin tshe dbang nor bu'i bka' 'bum* vol. 1, 662–667 (on the Jonang teaching of the *ṣaḍaṅgayoga*); vol. 2, 404–411 (on the iconography of the eighty-four *mahāsiddha*s as established by Tāranātha); and vol. 2, 447–453 (on the ritual cycle maintained at the former Jonang seat of Rtag brtan dga' ldan phun tshogs gling), among other works similarly referencing a Jonang background.

5. Makidono's "Kaḥ thog Dge rtse Mahāpaṇḍita's Doxographical Position" and *Great Middle Way of Other-Emptiness* detail Katok Getsé Paṇḍita's contributions on zhentong.

6. Dudjom, *Nyingma School* vol. 1, 169–216, precisely follows Katok Getsé Paṇḍita (usually verbatim in fact) in treating "Great Madhyamaka" as the pinnacle of the teaching of the sūtras.

7. Kapstein, "Mipam Namgyel," and Pettit, *Mipham's Beacon of Certainty*. See also Duckworth, chapter 10, and Wangchuk, chapter 11, both in the present volume; and, for Mipam's treatment of buddha-nature thought more broadly, Duckworth, *Mipam on Buddha-Nature*. For a brief, judicious assessment of Mipam's view of zhentong thought, refer to Karma Phuntsho, *Mipham's Dialectics* 17.

8. Karma Phuntsho, 93ff. and chap. 4. For background on Gorampa's approach, see Cabezón, *Freedom from Extremes*. Longchenpa's cleaving to the via negativa is perhaps best exemplified by his *Trilogy on Natural Liberation* (*Rang grol skor gsum*).

9. Mipam himself puts it this way: "The inerrant ultimate is affirmed to exist as the object of the inerrant intellect, as veridical, and as empty with respect to relative error. Conventionally, it is held to be intrinsically not empty, and to exist in the vision of those who are sublime" (Kapstein, "Mipam Namgyel" 71). It is important to note that the second sentence takes away what the first seems to offer, for the discourse of an "inerrant ultimate," and so forth, is itself only conventional.

10. I am particular grateful to the late Rahor Khenpo Thubten (1931–2010) for his comments about this.

11. Thub bstan Chos kyi grags pa, *Spyod 'jug gi 'grel bshad rgyal sras yon tan bum bzang*. A French translation of the commentary on the ninth chapter of the *Bodhicaryāvatāra* included there is available in Padmakara, *Comprendre la vacuité*.

12. In the main doctrinal work of Jigmé Lingpa, the *Yon tan rin po che's mdzod* and its two-volume autocommentary, there appears to be no hint of zhentong at all, and indeed,

as Karma Phuntsho, *Mipham's Dialectics* 250, n. 120, remarks, some contemporary Nyingma Khenpos have been troubled by its evident proximity to Tsongkhapa's thinking. Nor does one find zhentong invoked by later commentators on this work. In the English translation of the commentary by the noted recent teacher Kangyur Rinpoche (1897–1975), one brief reference to zhentong does occur, but in a note added by the translators, not in Kangyur Rinpoche's own text (Padmakara, *Treasury of Precious Qualities* 459 n. 108). And in the most substantial treatise inspired by the *Yon tan mdzod*, the five-volume *Mdo rgyud rin po che'i mdzod* of Choying Tobden Dorje (1785–1848), zhentong seems also to be ignored, though topics associated with zhentong thought, chiefly Tathāgatagarbha and the definitive status of the "third turning of the wheel," are embraced by him and treated in some detail. Moreover, reliable oral tradition reports that zhentong was alien to the college (*bshad grwa*) of the Dodrup Chode, perhaps the foremost center in Amdo of the *Longchen Nyingtik* tradition stemming from Jigme Lingpa. Finally, we may add that the scholastic curriculum favored at the Śrīsiṃha College of Dzokchen Monastery and its affiliates, that of Khenpo Zhenpen Chokyi Nangwa (Zhenga, 1871–1927), in its strict adherence to Indian textual models also steers clear of zhentong.

13. Kapstein, "*All-Encompassing Lamp*."

14. Dudjom, *Nyingma School* vol. 1, 577–579.

15. Karmay, *Great Perfection* 179 and passim.

16. Dza Patrul Rinpoche (1808–1887) is often regarded as spearheading the drive to create a distinctively Nyingma *yig-cha*. However, a precedent seems to be apparent at Mindroling, in Lochen Dharmaśrī's extensive commentary on Ngari Paṇchen's *Ascertainment of the Three Vows*, as will be discussed herein, and Terse Pema Gyurme Gyatso's commentary on the fundamental Indian treatise for Tibetan scholastic education, the *Abhisamayālaṃkāraśāstra*.

17. It should be recalled that, under the Ganden Potrang government, Mindroling was officially the primary seat of the Nyingma, the holder of its throne (the Minling Trichen) or his regent being the recognized head of the order.

18. On Lochen Dharmaśrī, see Dudjom, *Nyingma School* vol. 1, 728–732, and on Terdak Lingpa, *Nyingma School* vol. 1, 825–834.

19. In this regard it may be noted that the original Dzokchen monastery xylographic edition of the *Oral Traditions of the Nyingma* (*Rnying ma bka' ma*), compiled by Gyelse Zhenpen Taye during the first half of the nineteenth century, was nine volumes in extent. Lochen Dharmaśrī's writings on the *Oral Traditions*, by contrast, occupy a full seven volumes of his twenty-volume *Collected Works*, and much of this was in fact included in the Dzokchen edition.

20. On Pema Trinle, see Dudjom, *Nyingma School* vol. 1, 719–720.

21. Dudjom, 805–808, summarizes the life and work of this figure. Dudjom Rinpoche's own commentary on Ngari Paṇchen's *Ascertainment of the Three Vows* is summarized in Dudjom, *Perfect Conduct*, on which see the comments of Sobisch, *Three-Vow Theories* 6–8. Chapter 15 of Sobisch's book provides a fine survey of Nyingma contributions to the "three-vow" theories, with particular attention to Ngari Paṇchen and Lochen Dharmaśrī.

22. Lochen Dharmaśrī, *Dpag bsam gyi snye ma*, 358–359.

23. Lochen Dharmaśrī, *Dpag bsam gyi snye ma*, 198.

24. Padma 'Gyur med rgya mtsho, *Gzhi lam 'bras bu'i man ngag*, 406–407.

25. Dudjom, *Nyingma School* vol. 1, 957, and vol. 2, n. 1371.

26. *Khyad chos bzhi ldan*. Skyed tshal Paṇḍita, in his commentary on the *Abhisamayālaṃkāra*, explains these as (1) absence of the opposing force of stinginess and the like (*mi mthun phyogs ser sna sogs dang bral ba*), (2) possession of the allied force of nonconceptual

gnosis that directly realizes emptiness (*grogs stong nyid mngon sum du rtogs pa'i mi rtog ye shes ldan*), (3) the function of fulfilling the wishes of others (*byed las gzhan gyi 'dod don rdzogs par byed pa*), and (4) causing disciples to mature to the awakening of the three vehicles (*gdul bya rnams theg pa gsum gyi byang chub tu smin par byed pa*).

27. Though the verse that follows is often attributed to Nāgārjuna in Tibetan works that cite it, the source text in fact seems to be the *Samādhisambharaparivarta* (*Ting nge 'dzin gyi tshogs kyi le'u*), whose author, according to the colophon, is Bodhibhadra. The verse cited here will be found in the *Bstan 'gyur dpe bsdur ma*, vol. 64, 238.

28. On the treatment of the sciences here, with references to earlier scholarship, see Kapstein, "Spiritual Exercise."

29. Mipam's treatment of these arguments is summarized in Kapstein, *Reason's Traces* 325–326; for a more detailed treatment, see Karma Phuntsho, *Mipham's Dialectics* chap. 3.

30. See, by way of comparison, Karma Phuntsho 120–131.

31. The "three characteristics" are those of classical Yogācāra, as listed in n. 36 in this chapter. I am not familiar with the textual background for Dharmaśrī's reduction of these to two.

32. It is not entirely clear to me whether the spelling variation we find here—*kun btags / kun brtags*—quite warrants the distinction I am making by translating them as "imputed" and "imagined," respectively. *Bod rgya tshig mdzod chen mo*, 18, treats them as mere orthographical variants.

33. Literally, "continuum" (*santāna, rgyud*).

34. This verse is known from a number of sources, including the *Jñānasārasamuccaya*, referenced here: *Bstan 'gyur dpe bsdur ma* vol. 57, 854. The original Sanskrit is conserved in Śāntarakṣita's *Tattvasaṃgraha*, v. 3587.

35. The verse does not in fact appear in the *Catuḥśataka* but does occur in the commentary to the *Jñānasārasamuccaya*: *Bstan 'gyur dpe bsdur ma* vol. 57, 898.

36. *Shes bya gsum*. An alternative designation for the "three natures" (*trisvabhāva, rang bzhin gsum*) or "three characteristics" (*trilakṣaṇa, mtshan nyid gsum*) taught in classical Yogācāra: the imaginary (*parikalpita, kun b(r)tags*), the dependent (*paratantra, gzhan dbang*), and the absolute (*pariniṣpanna, yongs grub*).

37. That is, the six major philosophical works attributed to Nāgārjuna and enumerated in Dudjom, *Nyingma School* vol. 1, 94.

38. Dudjom vol. 1, 95, and vol. 2, 208.

39. On Longchenpa's treatment of Prāsaṅgika-Mādhyamika thought, see also Higgins, *Philosophical Foundations*.

40. An influential enumeration of these may be found in Kaḥ thog Rig 'dzin, *Bka' 'bum*, vol. 2, 412–413.

41. *rigs can*, that is, of the *bodhisattvagotra*.

42. Kapstein, *Reason's Traces* 311.

43. Refer to Higgins, *Philosophical Foundations*, for discussion of Longchenpa's dialectical strategies.

44. Padma 'Gyur med rgya mtsho, *Gzhi lam 'bras bu'i man ngag*.

45. Go rams pa, *Sdom gsum kha skong*. Refer to Sobisch, *Three-Vow Theories* 29.

46. *klog pa po*. It is not clear to me who, exactly, he has in mind in using this expression. If we take the phrase as meaning "reciters," then it is possible that he refers to "ritualists," that is, monks and lay priests trained to perform the rites (especially funerals) required for services on behalf of the laity, but not often educated in the śāstras.

47. That is, Bodong Paṇchen Chokle Namgyel (1376–1451).

48. *rton pa bzhi ldan*, one of Dolpopa's frequently used epithets, referring to the four *pratisaraṇa*, the canonical injunctions to rely upon the teaching (dharma), not the person (*pudgala*); to rely upon the meaning (*artha*), not the words (*śabda*); to rely upon the definitive significance (*nītārtha*), not heuristics (*neyārtha*); and to rely upon gnosis (*jñāna*), not consciousness (*vijñāna*).

49. Among past masters, the Third Karmapa seems to have been particularly esteemed at Mindroling. Dudjom, *Nyingma School* vol. 1, 827, refers to Terdak Lingpa's having memorized Rangjung Dorje's *Profound Inner Meaning* (*Zab mo nang don*) in the course of his studies.

50. The first half of this verse corresponds to *Samādhirāja Sūtra* 13.28bc.

51. See, by way of comparison, Mathes, *Direct Path* chaps. 1–2.

52. Buton's treatise on buddha-nature has been studied and translated into French in Seyfort Ruegg, *Traité du Tathāgatagarbha*; however, his several *Rgyud sde spyi'i rnam gzhag*, to which Pema Gyurme Gyatso alludes, have yet to receive attention.

53. 'Ba' ra ba, *Collected Writings*; Mathes, *Direct Path* 113–125.

54. Gter bdag gling pa, *Record of Teachings Received* 781–783, references several works of Tāranātha, including the zhentong treatise *Dbu ma snying po* (i.e., the *Gzhan stong snying po*), and on 596 we find an entry for the *Jo nang khrid brgya* of Rje bstun Kun dga' grol mchog.

Bibliography

Tibetan Sources

'Ba' ra ba Rgyal mtshan dpal bzang po. *Chos rje rnam gnyis kyi dgongs bshad nyi ma'i 'od zer*. In *A Tibetan Encyclopedia of Buddhist Scholasticism: The Collected Writings of 'Ba' ra ba rgyal mtshan dpal bzang*, vol. 11, 512–573. Dehra Dun: Ngawang Gyaltsen and Ngawang Lungtok, 1970.

Bstan 'gyur dpe bsdur ma. 120 vols. Beijing: Krung-go'i bod-rig-pa'i dpe-skrun-khang, 1994–2008.

Go rams pa Bsod nams seng ge. *Sdom pa gsum gyi rab tu dbye ba'i kha skong gzhi lam 'bras gsum gsal bar byed pa'i legs bshad 'od kyi snang ba*. In *Sdom gsum*, Dpal ldan sa skya pa'i gsung rab, vol. 12 (*stod cha*), 128–180. Beijing: Mi-rigs dpe-skrun-khang, 2004.

Gter bdag gling pa. *Record of Teachings Received: The Gsan yig of Gter-bdag-gliṅ-pa 'Gyur-med-rdo-rje of Smin-grol-gliṅ*. New Delhi: Sanje Dorje, 1974.

Kaḥ thog Rig 'dzin tshe dbang nor bu. *Kaḥ thog rig 'dzin tshe dbang nor bu'i bka' 'bum*. 3 vols. Beijing: Krung-go'i bod-rig-pa dpe-skrun-khang, 2006.

Lo chen Dharmaśrī. *Sdom pa gsum rnam par nges pa'i 'grel pa legs bshad ngo mtshar dpag bsam gyi snye ma*. In *Rnying ma'i sdom gsum phyogs bsgrigs*, edited by Mkhan-po 'Jam-blo, vol. 1, 19–359. Chengdu: Rgyal-khab dpe-mdzod-khang dpe-skrun-khang, 2015.

Mkhan po 'Jam blo, editor. *Rnying ma'i sdom gsum phyogs bsgrigs*. 5 vols. Chengdu: Rgyal-khab dpe-mdzod-khang dpe-skrun-khang, 2015.

Padma 'Gyur med rgya mtsho. 2015. *Sdom gsum rnam nges las 'phros pa gzhi lam 'bras bu'i man ngag nges don grub mtha'i snying po*. In *Rnying ma'i sdom gsum phyogs bsgrigs*, edited by Mkhan-po 'Jam-blo, vol. 1, 367–407. Chengdu: Rgyal-khab dpe-mdzod-khang dpe-skrun-khang, 2015.

Thub bstan Chos kyi grags pa. *Spyod 'jug gi 'grel bshad rgyal sras yon tan bum bzang*. 3 vols. Beijing: Krung-go'i bod-rig-pa dpe-skrun-khang, 1990.

Thub bstan smon lam, editor. *Skyed tshal 'Jam dbyangs-kun dga' chos bzang gi gsung 'bum*. 5 vols. Chengdu: Bod-ljongs bod-yig dpe-rnying dpe-skrun-khang, 2015.
Zhāng, Yísūn. *Bod rgya tshig mdzod chen mo*. 3 vols. Beijing: Mi rigs dpe skrun khang, 1985.

Secondary Sources

Almogi, Orna. *Rong-zom-pa's Discourses on Buddhology: A Study of Various Conceptions of Buddhahood in Indian Sources with Special Reference to the Controversy Surrounding the Existence of Gnosis (jñāna: ye shes) as Presented by the Eleventh-Century Tibetan Scholar Rong-zom Chos-kyi-bzang-po*. Studia Philologica Buddhica Monograph Series XXIV. Tokyo: The International Institute for Buddhist Studies, 2009.

———. "Yogācāra in the Writings of the Eleventh-Century Rnying ma Scholar Rong zom Chos kyi bzang po." In *The Foundation for Yoga Practitioners: The Buddhist* Yogācārabhūmi *Treatise and Its Adaptation in India, East Asia, and Tibet*, edited by Ulrich Timme Kragh, 1330–1361. Harvard Oriental Series 75. Cambridge: Department of South Asian Studies, Harvard University, 2013.

Cabezón, José Ignacio. *Freedom from Extremes: Gorampa's "Distinguishing the Views" and the Polemics of Emptiness*. Somerville: Wisdom, 2007.

Duckworth, Douglas S. *Mipam on Buddha-Nature: The Ground of the Nyingma Tradition*. Albany: State University of New York Press, 2008.

Dudjom Rinpoche, Jikdrel Yeshe Dorje. *The Nyingma School of Tibetan Buddhism: Its Fundamentals and History*, 2nd ed. Trans. Gyurme Dorje and Matthew Kapstein. Boston: Wisdom, 2002.

Dudjom Rinpoche, Jikdrel Yeshe Dorje. *Perfect Conduct: Ascertaining the Three Vows*. Trans. Khenpo Gyurme Samdrub and Sangye Khandro. Boston: Wisdom, 1996.

Higgins, David. *The Philosophical Foundations of Classical Rdzogs chen in Tibet: Investigating the Distinction between Dualistic Mind (sems) and Primordial Knowing (ye shes)*. Wiener Studien zur Tibetologie und Buddhismuskunde 78. Vienna: Arbeitskreis für Tibetische und Buddhistische Studien, 2013.

Kapstein, Matthew T. "We Are All Gzhan stong pas." *Journal of Buddhist Ethics* 7 (2000): 105–125.

———. *Reason's Traces: Identity and Interpretation in Indian and Tibetan Buddhist Thought*. Boston: Wisdom, 2001.

———. "Mipam Namgyel: The Lion's Roar Affirming Extrinsic Emptiness." In *Buddhist Philosophy: Essential Readings*, edited by William Edelglass and Jay L. Garfield, 61–71. New York: Oxford University Press, 2009.

———. " 'Spiritual Exercise' and Buddhist Epistemologists in India and Tibet." In *The Blackwell Companion to Buddhist Philosophy*, edited by Steven Emmanuel, 270–289. Oxford: Blackwell, 2013.

———. "*The All-Encompassing Lamp of Awareness*: A Forgotten Treasure of the Great Perfection, Its Authorship and Historical Significance." In *Unearthing Himalayan Treasures. Festschrift for Franz-Karl Ehrhard*, edited by Volker Caumanns, Marta Sernesi, and Nikolai Solmsdorf, 259–286. Marburg: Indica et Tibetica, 2019.

Karma Phuntsho. *Mipham's Dialectics and the Debates on Emptiness*. London: Routledge, 2005.

Karmay, Samten G. *The Great Perfection: A Philosophical and Meditative Teaching of Tibetan Buddhism*. Leiden: Brill, 1988.

Makidono, Tomoko. "Kaḥ thog Dge rtse Mahāpaṇḍita's Doxographical Position: The Great Madhyamaka of Other-Emptiness (*gzhan stong dbu ma chen po*)." *Indian International Journal of Buddhist Studies* 12 (2011): 77–119.

———. *Dge-rtse Mahāpaṇḍita's Great Middle Way of Other-Emptiness*. Bibliotheca Tibetica et Buddhica 2. Tokyo: Sankibo Busshorin, 2016.

Mathes, Klaus-Dieter. *A Direct Path to the Buddha Within: Gö Lotsāwa's Mahāmudrā Interpretation of the Ratnagotravibhāga*. Boston: Wisdom, 2008.

Padmakara Translation Group. *Comprendre la vacuité: Deux commentaires du chapitre IX de la marche vers l'éveil de Shântideva*. Plazac: Éditions Padmakara, 1997.

———. *Treasury of Precious Qualities: Commentary by Longchen Yeshe Dorje, Kangyur Rinpoche*. Book 1. Boston: Shambhala, 2010.

Pettit, John. *Mipham's Beacon of Certainty*. Boston: Wisdom, 1999.

Rhoton, Jared. *A Clear Differentiation of the Three Codes: Essential Distinctions Among the Individual Liberation, Great Vehicle, and Tantric Systems*. Albany: State University of New York Press, 2002.

Seyfort Ruegg, David. *Le Traité du Tathāgatagarbha de Bu ston rin chen grub*. Publications de l'École française d'Extrême-Orient 88. Paris: École française d'Extrême-Orient, 1973.

Sobisch, Jan-Ulrich. *Three-Vow Theories in Tibetan Buddhism: A Comparative Study of Major Traditions from the Twelfth through Nineteenth Centuries*. Wiesbaden: Ludwig Reichert Verlag, 2002.

Stearns, Cyrus. *The Buddha from Dolpo: A Study of the Life and Thought of the Tibetan Master Dolpopa Sherab Gyaltsen*. Albany: State University of New York Press, 1999.

10

Zhentong as Yogācāra

Mipam's Madhyamaka Synthesis

Douglas Duckworth

Introduction

In *Eliminating Doubts*, a short text responding to a criticism of his commentary on the *Madhyamakālaṃkāra*, Ju Mipam Gyatso (1846–1912) states as follows: "I don't have any burden of establishing the view of zhentong; I am in accord with the texts of Nāgārjuna, Longchenpa, and Rongzom."[1] Despite this claim, he also wrote a text that explicitly defends a view of zhentong, called *Lion's Roar: Affirming Zhentong*.[2] In this text, he says:

> First it is necessary to ascertain the lack of intrinsic nature of all phenomena in accordance with the scriptures of the protector Nāgārjuna; because if this is not known, one will not be able to ascertain the way that relative [phenomena] are empty from their own side and the way that the ultimate is empty of what is other. Therefore, one should first ascertain the freedom from constructs which is what is known reflexively.[3]

Mipam's relationship with zhentong is complex because he supports it in some contexts and denies it in others. In this chapter, I offer an interpretation of this bivocality by showing that Mipam's integration of the discourses of zhentong reflects his synthesis of Yogācāra and Madhyamaka. That is, I will show that his nuanced distinction between assertions pertaining to conventional and ultimate truth allows him to integrate the claims of zhentong into Madhyamaka, in a way that parallels his presentation of Yogācāra and Madhyamaka as compatible systems.

Zhentong and Yogācāra

A key to appreciating Mipam's explanations of emptiness is to understand his interpretation of the two truths. In *Shedding Light on Thusness*, a text that responds to a critique of his commentary on the ninth chapter of the *Bodhicaryāvatāra*, Mipam clearly lays out two models for understanding the two truths, and thus two meanings of the ultimate:

> In the great scriptures there are two ways in which the two truths are posited: (1) the term "ultimate" designates reality as nonarising and the term "relative" designates the conventional mode of appearance, and (2) in terms of conventional apprehension, the term "ultimate" designates both the subject and object of appearance in accord with reality and the term "relative" designates both the subject and object of appearance in discord with reality. . . . Although the terms "ultimate" and "relative" are the same in these two systems, the way of presenting the meaning is different.[4]

His first two-truth model is based on the difference between appearance and emptiness (where "relative" [*saṃvṛti*] appearance conveys what is *conventional*), while the second model is based on the distinction between what is deceptive (where "relative" [*saṃvṛti*] appearance conveys what is *concealing*) and nondeceptive. In contrast to a model of the two truths that asserts the relative truth as exclusively appearance and the ultimate truth as exclusively emptiness, the latter model allows for another way to interpret the two truths—as unity—where appearances are not necessarily deceptive nor is the ultimate necessarily a mere absence. In this way, Mipam leaves room for the presence of undistorted (relative) appearances and an ultimate not tethered to what is solely empty.

For Mipam, the meaning of emptiness is not simply the absence of one thing in another. Rather, emptiness means something more (and less). He states as follows in his *Difficult Points of Scriptures in General*:

> If a pot is not empty from its own side, but is empty of another phenomenon, this is not sufficient (*go mi chod*) as the emptiness of a pot itself. Just as a cow is absent in a horse, but this is not sufficient as the emptiness of a horse itself; or while the horn of an ox is empty of a rabbit horn, this is not sufficient as the emptiness of an ox horn. Among the seven types of emptinesses stated in the *Laṅkāvatāra Sūtra*,[5] it is inferior—such as a temple's emptiness of a spiritual community; it is to be abandoned.[6]

Mipam conveys here that the lack of one thing in another is inferior and is not sufficient as the meaning of emptiness. Emptiness must be the complete lack of intrinsic existence (and nothing more) or the nonconceptual unity of appearance and emptiness (and nothing less). Ultimate emptiness is more than a mere absence because it is the unity of appearance and emptiness; it is less than a mere absence because it is nonconceptual, so it is not conceptualized as an absence.

Ultimate emptiness for Mipam lacks intrinsic existence and it is a nondeceptive appearance. In his *Difficult Points of Scriptures in General*, he states:

> The appearances that are included in the relative also need to be distinguished as distorted or undistorted, deceptive or nondeceptive—not everything that is relative must necessarily be a distorted appearance. Nor must everything with the name ultimate be solely empty because the two ways to arrive at the distinctive names in [two] ways of assessing the relative and ultimate are widely proclaimed in the great sūtras and śāstras.[7]

Mipam again outlines two ways for emptiness to be understood: as a quality of absence and as an inconceivable unity (appearance in accord with reality).[8] The former portrays emptiness as an *absence* of ultimate existence (as in Madhyamaka), and the latter accounts for the *presence* of the ultimate that is not merely an absence (as in Yogācāra and zhentong). Mipam integrates these two claims as facets of a larger meaning—unity—within a structure that can accommodate both Madhyamaka and Yogācāra. For this reason, we can say that he can be read to both affirm and deny the claims of zhentong.

His first two-truth model lays out the two truths in a way characteristic of Madhyamaka, while his second model lays out the two truths according to Yogācāra.[9] The fact that his latter model conforms to Yogācāra (based on whether or not appearance accords with reality) can be seen in the way that Mipam glosses the consummate nature (*pariniṣpanna*, *yongs grub*) as ultimate among the "three natures" in Yogācāra exegesis. In his commentary on the *Madhyāntavibhāga*, he explicitly affirms that the consummate nature is appearance in accord with reality: "The exclusive object of pure gnosis is not the imagined or dependent natures but is said to be only the consummate nature, because when that [consummate nature] is the realm of experience, appearance accords with reality."[10] Mipam also maintains the empty quality of such an ultimate when he says that the consummate nature is not truly established: "Being 'truly established' (*yongs su grub*) is not because of an essence that is truly established (*bden grub*) but is designated with that name because of being the unerring reality."[11] Thus we see that this ultimate is still empty in the former sense, that is, it is both empty (as the absence of true establishment á la Madhyamaka) and nondeceptive (appearance in accord with reality a la Yogācāra and zhentong). As nondual experience, he affirms the consummate nature to be ultimate: "The ultimate, or the ultimate meaning, is only the consummate nature among the three natures; the other two are not: (1) because the consummate nature is of the nature of nondual experience beyond ordinary consciousness and expression, or (2) because only this is appearance in accord with reality."[12] Here Mipam delineates the consummate nature as ultimate due to it being nondeceptive experience, that is, appearance in accord with reality, which he also describes as the nature of nondual experience. He thus makes the distinction between dualistic consciousness (*rnam shes*) and nondual gnosis (*ye shes*) as this way of delineating the two truths: "The subject of appearance in accord with reality is called 'gnosis,' being free from duality; 'consciousness' is the apprehending [subject] of appearance that does not accord with reality, being dualistic."[13] In this way, we can see two distinctive ways in which he portrays the ultimate: as appearance in accord with reality and as the lack of true existence.

Significantly, in his *Difficult Points of Scriptures in General*, Mipam asserts that the ultimate of zhentong is appearance in accord with reality: "The way of establishing the ultimate of zhentong is by means of whether or not appearance accords with reality."[14] Rather than the ultimate simply being the emptiness of intrinsic nature, as it is in the first model of two truths, it is appearance in accord with reality that characterizes the ultimate in the contexts of both Yogācāra and zhentong. Thus, in Mipam's presentation of Madhyamaka, he incorporates zhentong in the way he incorporates Yogācāra by claiming that the ultimate in these discourses is based on another model of two truths, a model other than that which is enframed by a strict dichotomy of conventional appearance and ultimate emptiness.

Before discussing further how Mipam interprets the claims of zhentong, we will first consider his treatment of negation, which is a central component to understanding these two ways of representing emptiness. There are two types of negation that play into the distinction between zhentong and rangtong. An implicative negation (*paryudāsa, ma yin dgag*) is a negation that leaves something else and a nonimplicative negation (*prasajyapratiṣedha, med dgag*) is simple denial. An implicative negation, which is affirmed in the Jonang tradition to indicate the ultimate truth, is characterized as an explicit negation that implicates something else, for instance, like the classic example, "the fat Devadatta does not eat during the day." This negation implies something else, namely, that Devadatta eats at night. In contrast, a nonimplicative negation, which is affirmed to be the meaning of emptiness in the Geluk tradition, is characterized as an explicit negation that does not imply anything else, for instance, "Brahmins should not drink alcohol." In contrast to implicative negations, the connotative force of a nonimplicative negation is denial rather than an implied affirmation.

So, which kind of negation does Mipam accept? In his *Beacon of Certainty*, he poses and responds to just this question:

> It is said that the Geluk (*dge ldan*) view is a nonimplicative negation,
> Other traditions speak of an implicative negation—
> If one asks, "Which is the tradition of the early translations [of Nyingma]?"
> Considering only the manner of emptiness,
> When questioned [what is the Nyingma view], it is only a nonimplicative negation.[15]

He elaborates on this point in his *Commentary on the Wisdom Chapter [of the Bodhicaryāvatāra]*, where he outlines a context where emptiness is to be understood as a nonimplicative negation:

> In the context of indicating emptiness, the negation of form, and so on, is only a nonimplicative negation. Since an implicative negation is also in the end a fixation upon an entity, it is not suitable to be the meaning of emptiness. Therefore, while it is a nonimplicative negation, due to appearing as an unfailing interdependent arising, it is the unity of emptiness and appearance so any apprehension of negation or affirmation should deconstruct.[16]

He states that the negating language expressed to indicate emptiness is only a nonimplicative negation, not an implicative one, because an implicative negation is in the end a fixation upon an entity. Yet he emphasizes the meaning of emptiness as the unity of appearance and emptiness and states that emptiness understood as separate from appearance is in fact an implicative negation.[17] Moreover, he highlights how the meaning of the ultimate itself is beyond negation and affirmation and thus is beyond the mind:

> Although appearances are designated as lacking intrinsic nature, if this is understood to mean something empty separate from appearance, even though it may be called a "nonimplicative negation" it has become an implicative negation. Appearance itself appears while nonexistent, it is a unity—marvelous—thus, through abiding as the ineffable indivisibility of appearance and emptiness, it is beyond the mind because it is free from negation and affirmation in the consummate meaning.[18]

Mipam here represents the ultimate truth as unity beyond negation and affirmation. He further states that since gnosis transcends the mind and is not the domain of thoughts and words, there is no partiality for nonimplicative or implicative negations, emptiness or appearance in that perspective:

> Since gnosis transcends the mind,
> It is inconceivable by an extrinsic thought.
> Since it is not an object of language or thought,
> There is no partiality for
> Nonimplicative negations or implicative negations,
> Difference, appearance or emptiness, and so forth.[19]

And:

> From the perspective of the great gnosis of unity
> The elimination of the object of negation by "nonexistent"

> Implies neither a mere existential absence (*med*) nor a predicative negation (*ma yin*)—
> What other phenomenon is there to imply by negation?
> Both of these are merely mental imputations.
> I assert neither as the [consummate] meaning.[20]

We can see that neither implicative nor nonimplicative negations denote what Mipam characterizes as the consummate meaning of ultimate emptiness, which is the inconceivable unity of appearance and emptiness beyond negation and affirmation. Thus, he does not depict the meaning of the ultimate truth as simply positive; it is also empty. He does not depict the meaning of the ultimate truth as simply negative either; it is also a nonconceptual unity. That is, Mipam presents the ultimate not only as the presence of absence but as the presence of nonconceptual unity.

Significantly, ultimate emptiness within the view of gnosis is not a negation (since it is not the referent of thought or words), even though emptiness can be conceptually (or conventionally) distinguished as a nonimplicative negation when abstracted from its unified appearance. Unity is the way he expresses the nonconceptual ultimate truth, not simply its conventional representation in absence. Yet his denials are precisely what make this view also compatible with the universality of emptiness in Madhyamaka, as he states in his commentary on the *Mahāyānasūtrālaṃkāra*:

> If one understands the self-luminous, nondual consciousness, which the proponents of Mind-Only assert, to be a consummate, dualistic consciousness—merely a consciousness inexpressible in terms of what is the perceived and perceiver, truly established and not empty of its essence—then this is what is to be negated. However, if one understands that this cognition has a nature that is primordially without origination and is the self-luminous gnosis free from perceiver and perceived and directly experienced by self-awareness, then it is what is to be affirmed. This is necessarily asserted in both Tantra and Madhyamaka.[21]

We can see here how Mipam both affirms and denies gnosis here, and thereby affirms and denies the claims of zhentong.

Zhentong and Madhyamaka

In a typically Madhyamaka style, Mipam critiques the position of zhentong by depicting it as a view that does not negate enough. In his *Beacon of Certainty*, he says that the view of zhentong leaves a remainder, an "empty-ground":

> Saying, "A pillar is not empty of pillar" or
> "Suchness is empty of pillar"
> Is leaving an empty-ground, which is zhentong.

These are two: zhentong in words and zhentong in meaning.[22]

Stating that a phenomenon like a pillar is empty of true reality but not empty of itself is a statement of zhentong in that it conveys that something is empty of something else. In the same way, claiming that ultimate nature, suchness, is not empty of itself but is empty of phenomena like pillars also shares the meaning of zhentong. Both of these claims represent a zhentong view: emptiness is held as the denial of some extrinsic quality while a (nonempty) ground remains in the place of the absence.

In Dolpopa's Jonang tradition, the ultimate suchness of reality is said to be empty of all relative phenomena.[23] Mipam calls this position "ultimate zhentong" (*don dam gzhan stong*).[24] In contrast is a Geluk view, in which relative phenomena like pillars are the empty ground(s) of the ultimate quality of emptiness (that is, the lack of true establishment).[25] Mipam also enlists this view as having the meaning of zhentong by associating zhentong with the claim that a pot is not empty from its own side, but is empty of another—true establishment.[26] When a (nonempty) ground of emptiness is taken as an implication of such claims as "a pillar is not empty of pillar," in effect it becomes a zhentong view due to the fact that emptiness is understood as one thing being empty of another, with an empty-ground left behind.[27] He calls such a view "relative zhentong" (*kun rdzob gzhan stong*) and states that while the Jonang tradition accepts ultimate zhentong and relative rangtong, this view accepts relative zhentong and ultimate rangtong.[28] By affirming unity, Mipam maintains contexts for both affirming and denying the claims of relative and ultimate zhentong (and rangtong).

An important aspect of Mipam's interpretation is the fact that he maintains that appearance in accord with reality (nondeceptive experience) is called "ultimate" from the perspective of a conventional source of knowledge (*tshad ma*): "From the perspective of a conventional source of knowledge analyzing the mode of appearance, the subjects and objects of the incontrovertible accordance between the modes of appearance and reality are called 'ultimate' and the opposite are called 'relative.' "[29] And again:

> Positing (1) both the objects and subjects for which the mode of appearance is in accord with the mode of reality as ultimate and (2) both the objects and subjects for which appearance and reality are not in accord as relative, should be posited as such due to being conventionally nondeceptive or deceptive.[30]

Thus, according to his delineation, the ultimate in zhentong is ultimate from the perspective of a *conventional* source of knowledge. In effect, Mipam treats the claims of zhentong in a way that parallels his treatment of Yogācāra when he says: "The manner of Mind-Only is very much the true nature of conventional reality; however, the aspect of clinging to the nature of a self-illuminating (*rang gsal*) consciousness as truly real is what is to be negated."[31] In the same way that he positions the claims of zhentong as conventionally true but not ultimately so, he affirms the conventional reality of Mind-Only in his presentation of Yogācāra-Madhyamaka, but denies its ultimate existence.

As a proponent of Madhyamaka, Mipam denies that anything is truly real and argues that the perspective of a conventional source of knowledge cannot establish something to be not empty of its own essence. This is the domain of an ultimate source of knowledge. Attributing ultimate existence to conventional assertions is precisely the place where the traditions of Yogācāra (qua Mind-Only) reify the mind and the discourses of zhentong reify the ultimate. That is, they overstep the bounds of the domain of a conventional source of knowledge and proclaim what is simply a conventional truth to be ultimately real.

For Mipam, the perspective of a conventional source of knowledge does not discern whether something is truly real or not; rather, that status is discerned by an ultimate source of knowledge. He states that what is truly real—not empty of its own essence—cannot be established by any source of knowledge in his *Lion's Roar: Exposition of Buddha-Nature*:

> Not empty of its own essence, being truly established it is completely impossible to be the suchness of an extrinsic phenomenon, and so forth. It also cannot be the outcome of ascertainment by the source of knowledge of ultimate analysis because the presence of something truly established is not accurate as a handprint [result] of the analysis of the lack of true existence of all phenomena—like darkness [arising] from light. True establishment is not established by a conventional source of knowledge either because even though [it may appear to be] truly real from that [conventional] perspective, by merely that there is never an ability to establish phenomena to be nonempty. Without being able to be established by the two sources of knowledge, the means of establishment has gone the way of a [nonexistent] space-flower; therefore, establishing this becomes meaninglessly tiresome.[32]

He states that something truly established and not empty of its own essence cannot result from an ultimate source of knowledge, which establishes the lack of true existence. Nor can a conventional source of knowledge establish something to be not empty of its own essence, despite that it may deceptively appear that way from that perspective.

Mipam thus delineates the criterion for existence through an epistemological definition: via sources of knowledge, conventional or ultimate:

> In short, the conventional [existence] of that which is established to exist in the perspective of a conventional source of knowledge cannot be refuted by anyone at all. The conventional existence of that which is undermined by a conventional source of knowledge cannot be estab-

> lished by anyone at all. Nobody at all can affirm that something is ultimately existent which has been established to not exist by an ultimate source of knowledge.[33]

For Mipam, an ultimate source of knowledge (*don dam la dpyod pa'i tshad ma*) concerns the ultimate in a Madhyamaka model of the two truths (i.e., appearance/emptiness), for which the ultimate is an absence of true reality. The ultimate in a Yogācāra model of the two truths (i.e., appearance in accord with reality), on the other hand, is the domain of a conventional source of knowledge. It is this latter model that frames the ultimate as experience that accords with reality realized by gnosis in the context of meditative experience. This experiential realization by meditative gnosis is what advocates of zhentong, in both the Nyingma and Jonang traditions, evoke to support their claims of true establishment: it is truly established "because it is just what is experienced by the undistorted gnosis of the sublime beings (*'phags pa*)"[34] or "due to being true in the abiding reality of the basic nature as the object of ultimate reflexive awareness free from constructs."[35] Mipam, however, respects the integrity of both two-truth models and emphasizes a universal empty quality without affirming anything that exists ultimately.

In his *Difficult Points of Scriptures in General*, Mipam characterizes the tradition of zhentong as accepting that what is ultimate ultimately exists. In contrast, he says that nothing ultimately exists in the tradition of rangtong. With this distinction, he identifies himself with the tradition propounding rangtong:

> In the tradition of rangtong, since there is only the ultimately nonexistent, an ultimately existing phenomenon is impossible. In the tradition of zhentong, what is ultimately nonexistent is the relative, and what is ultimately existent is the ultimate itself. My tradition is clear in the *Rapsel Rejoinder*,[36] the tradition propounding rangtong.[37]

While Mipam states that emptiness is the ultimate truth, he does not affirm that anything, even emptiness, ultimately exists. In this way, he identifies his tradition as propounding rangtong; thus, he denies that anything ultimately exists. Here it is clear that Mipam defines himself as a proponent of rangtong—as one who propounds that there is nothing ultimately existent—in accord with his definition of the term. This is because, for Mipam *nothing is ultimately existent*—not gnosis, or even emptiness. Nevertheless, *gnosis is the ultimate truth* as appearance in accord with reality. While he affirms that the claims of zhentong—that the ultimate is empty of the relative and that the undistorted is empty of the distorted—are *conventionally* true, this does not entail that any such truth exists *ultimately*. In this way, we can see how a distinction can be made between ultimate truth and ultimate existence through his framework of sources of knowledge.

A similar distinction can also be made between conventional truth and conventional existence. For instance, Mipam shows that a pot is not empty of pot in terms of the conventional: "In terms of the conventional, I assert that a pot is not empty of pot, because if it were empty conventionally, the pot would become nonexistent."[38] And in his *Lion's Roar: Affirming Zhentong*, he states:

> If a [conventional phenomenon like a] pot, were empty of pot, then would it not be that a pot would not be a pot, and thus a pot would not exist conventionally? [Response:] So be it. Hence, in the same way, if the ultimate truth were empty of ultimate truth, then the ultimate truth would not be ultimate truth, and thus the ultimate would not exist even conventionally.[39]

Here Mipam also shows how a claim of a nonempty ultimate can be supported. He reveals that a consequence used to defend the conventional existence of phenomena also can support a defense of the (conventionally existent) ultimate truth: he shows the conventional nonexistence of the ultimate as an absurd consequence that would follow if the ultimate truth were empty of ultimate truth. Furthermore, he argues that just as someone may assert that true establishment is to be negated, but not its *absence*, in a similar way, one can assert that the distorted relative is to be negated, but not the undistorted ultimate:

> The assertion that although true establishment is negated, the absence of true existence is not negated, not to be negated, nor is appropriate to be negated, is similar to the assertion that although the relative distortions are negated, the undistorted ultimate is not negated, not to be negated, nor is suitable to be negated.[40]

He argues here that an assertion that one should not negate the absence of true existence is similar to the assertion that one should not negate the ultimate itself. In this way, he shows a similarity between the two claims that (1) the absence of true existence (the ultimate in a Madhyamaka two-truth model) is not to be negated, and (2) the undistorted ultimate as appearance in accord with reality (the ultimate in a two-truth model of Yogācāra/zhentong) is not to be negated. In this way, Mipam shows how an assertion that the ultimate truth is (conventionally) not empty of itself is supported by the same logic that is used to defend a pot's conventional nonemptiness of itself. In doing so, he depicts how affirmations of the ultimate can be conventionally true, a move on par with an assertion that emptiness conventionally exists.

According to Mipam, what is "conventional" is the realm of thought, words, and physical actions.[41] Thus, a pot can be said to be a conventionally existent phenomenon (since it can be thought, expressed, and acted upon) and a conventional truth (from the aspect of its appearance). As a conventional phenomenon, it is empty, because "the phenomena that are the realm of thought and speech, when analyzed, are absent; therefore, they are empty like an illusion and are never able to withstand analysis."[42] Consequently, the emptiness of a pot, as an empty quality that is a referent of thought and expression, can be said to be the ultimate truth and conventionally existent.[43] Although Mipam does not make this distinction explicit in this way, we can see how such a distinction is made in his treatment of existence (*yod pa*) and truth (*bden pa*). This distinction between existence and truth in Mipam's works reveals an affinity with Tsongkhapa.[44] This affinity is often overlooked due to the fact that most of Mipam's polemics target views held by followers of the Geluk tradition. Nevertheless, Mipam's appropriation of Tsongkhapa's treatment of the ultimate (as a negation) can be seen as a node in a dialectical analysis that culminates in a synthesis of appearance and emptiness, when analysis is complete. This kind of interpretation is precisely what Mipam argues when he cites Tsongkhapa's *Three Principal Aspects of the Path* in his own commentary on the *Madhyamakālaṃkāra*:

> As long as the two—the ineluctable appearance of dependent arising and
> The understanding of emptiness free from assertions—are seen to be separate,
> One has still not understood the intent of the Buddha.
> When they are seen to be in invariable, dependent relation,
> As simultaneous without alternation,
> All apprehensions of determinate objects dissolve—
> One has perfected the analysis of the view.[45]

Mipam's embrace of unity at the end of analysis—encompassing rangtong and zhentong, Madhyamaka and Yogācāra—is an important way he articulates the view of his Nyingma tradition.

Conclusion

We have seen how, for Mipam, two models of the two truths—those of Madhyamaka (conventional appearance vs. ultimate emptiness) and Yogācāra (distorted relative vs. undistorted ultimate)—play an important role in the way he positions his view of emptiness. The two models are respectively based on two sources of knowledge, conventional and ultimate. An ultimate source of knowledge is based on an analysis of the nature of appearance, where appearance is the conventional truth and emptiness (which is the nature of appearance) is the ultimate truth. In contrast, a conventional source of knowledge is based on the quality of experience as deceptive or nondeceptive. In the case of a conventional source of knowledge, the ultimate is framed in terms of what is nondeceptive (appearance in accord with reality), while the relative (or deceptive) truth is framed in terms of appearance in discord with reality.

For Mipam, emptiness appears as it exists—it is appearance in accord with reality. The fact that emptiness *appears* undermines a Madhyamaka model of two separate truths of (conventional) appearance and (ultimate) emptiness. This is where a second model, a Yogācāra model, comes into play. This is the model that collapses duality in nondeceptive experience, where appearance accords with reality. This nondual unity is the ultimate truth and dualistic appearance (deceptive experience) is the relative truth, as it is with the assertions of zhentong. Even so, such assertions (and distinctions) are always only conventional.

Mipam appropriates the claims of zhentong into a Yogācāra model of two truths, in which the ultimate is characterized as appearance in accord with reality. In doing so, he argues for the presence of the nonconceptual ultimate along with the presence of emptiness. He affirms the reality of nondual gnosis but, like a good Mādhyamika, also denies that this—or anything else—exists ultimately. Thus, in his Madhyamaka view of unity, he both affirms and denies the claims of zhentong.

Notes

1. Mipam, *Eliminating Doubts* 521.

2. Mipam, *Lion's Roar: Affirming Zhentong* (*gzhan stong khas lan seng gei' nga ro*). See an English translation of the complete text in John Pettit, *Mipham's Beacon of Certainty* 415–427.

3. Mipam, *Lion's Roar: Affirming Zhentong* 361.

4. Mipam, *Shedding Light on Thusness* 304.

5. Suzuki, *Laṅkāvatāra Sūtra* 67. Purbu Tsering, *Dictionary of Internal Knowledge* (*Nang rig pa'i tshig mdzod*) 515 delineates the seven emptinesses (*stong nyid rnam pa bdun*) as: "(1) emptiness of characteristics, (2) emptiness of the nature of entities, (3) emptiness of existence, (4) emptiness of nonexistence, (5) emptiness that is the inexpressibility of all phenomena, (6) great emptiness that is the ultimate gnosis of sublime beings, (7) emptiness of something in another."

6. Mipam, *Difficult Points of Scriptures in General* 545.

7. Mipam, *Difficult Points of Scriptures in General* 452. See also Karma Phuntsho, *Mipham's Dialectics and the Debates on Emptiness* 114–120.

8. Mipam, *Beacon of Certainty* 51: " 'Abiding reality' that is the emptiness of entities and 'abiding reality' that is the indivisible two truths, although both are the same word, the meanings are as distinct as the earth and space. Likewise, 'suchness,' 'field of reality,' 'emptiness,' 'freedom from constructs,' 'limit of cessation,' 'ultimate,' and so on, are similar expressions, yet since the distinction is vast between the consummate and the partial, having delineated the distinctive context, they should be explained without error."

9. Elsewhere, I have referred to these two models as the "ontological" and "phenomenological" models. Duckworth, "Two Models of the Two Truths."

10. Mipam, *Garland of Light Rays* 709.

11. Mipam, *Words That Delight Guru Mañjughoṣa* 59–60.

12. Mipam, *Garland of Light Rays* 706–707.

13. Mipam, *Difficult Points of Scriptures in General* 466–467.

14. Mipam, *Difficult Points of Scriptures in General* 450.

15. Mipam, *Beacon of Certainty* 5.

16. Mipam, *Commentary on the Wisdom Chapter* 10.

17. In his commentary on the *Madhyamakālaṃkara*, he claims, "An indication that entities lack intrinsic nature is a nonimplicative negation because an implicative negation

establishes the essence of another phenomenon; as such it does not have the meaning of unity." Mipam, *Words That Delight Guru Mañjughoṣa* 380–381.

18. Mipam, *Words That Delight Guru Mañjughoṣa* 380.

19. Mipam, *Beacon of Certainty* 49.

20. Mipam, *Beacon of Certainty* 5.

21. Mipam, *Feast on the Nectar of the Supreme Vehicle* 100; see Dharmacakra Translation Committee, *Ornament of the Great Vehicle Sūtras* 131.

22. Mipam, *Beacon of Certainty* 6.

23. Dolpopa, *Ocean of Definitive Meaning* 431: "Within the abiding reality, the ultimate Truth Body is not nonexistent because [within the abiding reality] thusness that is pure self, the self that is the great identity of Buddha, is not severed. Within the abiding reality, relative form bodies (*kun rdzob gzugs sku*) do not exist because [within the abiding reality] not any relative phenomena is established."

24. See Mipam, *Difficult Points of Scriptures in General* 549.

25. Tsongkhapa states: "The ultimate truth is posited as solely the negation of truth [that is, inherent existence] upon a subject that is a basis of negation . . ." Tsongkhapa, *Lesser Exposition of the Stages of the Path* 396.

26. Mipam, *Difficult Points of Scriptures in General* 548. Tsongkhapa, however, denied that this claim represents zhentong. In his commentary on the *Madhyamakāvatāra*, Tsongkhapa says: "The statement, 'That a pot is not empty of pot, but empty of true existence is zhentong; therefore, a pot empty of pot is the assertion of rangtong,' is utterly unreasonable because: if a pot were empty of pot, a pot would have to be nonexistent in itself, and if it were nonexistent in itself, it would be nonexistent everywhere else, too; therefore, a pot would [absurdly] be utterly nonexistent." Tsongkhapa, *Thoroughly Illuminating the Viewpoint* 213.

27. Mipam also argues that a view that accepts real entities as an implication of the negation of a separate true establishment is in effect an implicative negation. See Mipam, *Difficult Points of Scriptures in General* 545.

28. Mipam, *Difficult Points of Scriptures in General* 548–549.

29. Mipam, *Words That Delight Guru Mañjughoṣa* 56.

30. Mipam, *Difficult Points of Scriptures in General* 465. See also Mipam, *Words That Delight Guru Mañjughoṣa* 56; Duckworth, *Mipam on Buddha-Nature 6–13; Bötrül, Distinguishing the Views and Philosophies* 128–134.

31. Mipam, *Words That Delight Guru Mañjughoṣa* 48.

32. Mipam, *Lion's Roar: Exposition of Buddha-Nature* 591.

33. Mipam, *Words That Delight Guru Mañjughoṣa* 74–75.

34. Getse Paṇchen, *Discourse of the Four Reliances* 119: "Thus, the suchness that is the empty-ground of all phenomena is truly established because it is just what is experienced by the undistorted gnosis of the sublime beings."

35. Khenpo Lodro Drakpa, *Roar of the Fearless Lion* 63: "The gnosis that is the subject of the last teaching is truly established due to being true in the abiding reality of the basic nature as the object of ultimate reflexive awareness free from constructs."

36. *Shedding Light on Thusness* (*gzhan gyis brtsad pa'i lan mdor bsdus pa rigs lam rab gsal de nyid snang byed*). This is a text that Mipam wrote in response to the criticism of the Geluk scholar Dpa' ris Blo bzang rab gsal (1840–1910), concerning Mipam's commentary on the ninth chapter of the *Bodhicaryāvatāra (sher le'u 'grel pa nor bu ke ta ka).*

37. Mipam, *Difficult Points of Scriptures in General* 450.

38. Mipam, *Immaculate Crystal Rosary* 539. Tsongkhapa makes a similar claim: "If a pot were empty of pot, a pot would have to be nonexistent in itself, and if it were nonexistent

in itself, it would be nonexistent everywhere else, too; therefore, a pot would [absurdly] be utterly nonexistent." Tsongkhapa, *Thoroughly Illuminating the Viewpoint* 213.

39. Mipam, *Lion's Roar: Affirming Zhentong* 374.

40. Mipam, *Lion's Roar: Affirming Zhentong* 370.

41. Mipam, *Gateway to Scholarship* 129.

42. Mipam, *Commentary on the Wisdom Chapter, 11.*

43. For Mipam, such a conceptual emptiness is the "enframed ultimate" (*rnam grangs pa'i don dam*). The unenframed ultimate (*rnam grangs ma yin pa'i don dam*), or the nonconceptual ultimate in itself, is the ultimate truth not divided into two truths. He states: "One should know that the Prāsaṅgika's unique object of negation is the aspect of apprehending the two truths as distinct." Mipam, *Words That Delight Guru Mañjughoṣa* 97. Furthermore, he states that there is no distinction between the enframed and unenframed ultimates in Prāsaṅgika-Madhyamaka: "One should know that in this context of Prāsaṅgika, since the emphasis is on the great Middle Way, which is a unity and free from constructs, there is no twofold distinction between the enframed and unenframed ultimates in this tradition." Mipam, *Commentary on the Wisdom Chapter* 9. See also, Duckworth, "Mipam's Middle Way Through Yogācāra and Prāsaṅgika" 432–436.

44. For a discussion of a similar distinction between existence and truth in the works of Tsongkhapa, see Guy Newland, *Two Truths* 93–94; *Thupten Jinpa, Self, Reality and Reason in Tibetan Philosophy* 152–153.

45. Tsongkhapa, *Three Principal Aspects of the Path* 6–7; see Mipam, *Words That Delight Guru Mañjughoṣa* 107–108.

BIBLIOGRAPHY

Tibetan Sources

Dol po pa (dol po pa shes rab rgyal mtshan, 1292–1361). *The Mountain Doctrine: Ocean of Definitive Meaning* (*ri chos nges don rgya mtsho*). Gangtok: Dodrup Sangyey Lama, 1976.

Dge rtse Paṇ chen, 'Gyur med tshe dbang mchog grub. *Rgyal bstan 'khor lo gsum dgongs pa gcig tu rtogs pa ston pa bzhi ldan gyi gtam* (*Discourse of the Four Reliances: Realizing the Victorious One's Teaching of the Three Wheels as One Viewpoint*). In *Collected Works* (Sichuan ed.), vol. 1, 105–120.

Ngag dbang Blo gros grags pa. *Rgyu dang 'bras bu'i theg pa mchog gi gnas lugs zab mo'i don rnam par nges pa rje jo nang pa chen po'i ring lugs 'jigs med gdong lnga'i nga ro* (*Roar of the Fearless Lion*). Dharamsala: Library of Tibetan Works and Archives, 1993.

'Ju Mi pham rgya mtsho. *Theg pa chen po mdo sde'i rgyan gyi dgongs don rnam par bshad pa theg mchog bdud rtsi'i dga' ston* (*A Feast on the Nectar of the Supreme Vehicle: Commentary on the Ornament of the Great Vehicle Sūtras*). In Mipam's *Collected Works* (Dilgo Khyentsé's expanded redaction of *sde dge* edition), vol. 2 (*a*), 1–760. Kathmandu: Zhechen Monastery, 1987.

———. *Nges shes sgron me* (*Beacon of Certainty*). In *Nges shes sgron me rtsa 'grel*, 1–54. Sichuan: Nationalities Press, 1997.

———. *Spyod 'jug sher 'grel ke ta ka* (*Commentary on the Wisdom Chapter of the Bodhicaryāvatāra*). Sichuan: Nationalities Press, 1993.

———. *Dbu ma sogs gzhung spyi'i dka' gnad skor gyi gsung sgros sna tshogs phyogs gcig tu bsdus pa rin po che'i za ma tog* (*Difficult Points of Scriptures in General*). In Mipam's *Collected Works*, vol. 22, 427–710. Kathmandu: Zhechen Monastery, 1987.

———. *Dam chos dogs sel* (*Eliminating Doubts*). In *Dbu ma rgyan rtsa 'grel*, 498–563. Sichuan: Nationalities Press, 1990.

———. *Dbu dang mtha' rnam par 'byed pa'I bstan bcos kyi 'grel pa 'od zer phreng ba* (*Garland of Light Rays: Commentary on the Madhyāntavibhāga*). In Mipam's *Collected Works*, vol. 4 (*pa*), 659–786. Kathmandu: Zhechen Monastery, 1987.

———. *Mkhas pa'i tshul la 'jug pa'i sgo* (*Gateway to Scholarship*). In *Mkhas 'jug*. Qinghai: Nationalities Press, 1994.

———. *Dbu ma la 'jug pa'i 'grel pa zla ba'i zhal lung dri med shel phreng* (*Immaculate Crystal Rosary: Commentary on the Madhyamakāvatāra*). In Mipam's *Collected Works*, vol. 1 (*oṃ*), 497–837. Kathmandu: Zhechen Monastery, 1987.

———. *Gzhan stong khas len seng ge'i nga ro* (*Lion's Roar: Affirming Zhentong*). Mipam's *Collected Works*, vol. 12 (*ga*), 359–738. Kathmandu: Zhechen Monastery, 1987.

———. *Bde gshegs snying po'i stong thun chen mo seng ge'i nga ro* (*Lion's Roar: Exposition of Buddha-Nature*). In Mipam's *Collected Works*, vol. 4 (*pa*), 563–607. Kathmandu: Zhechen Monastery, 1987.

———. *Gzhan gyis brtsad pa'i lan mdor bsdus pa rigs lam rab gsal de nyid snang byed* (*Shedding Light on Thusness*). In *Spyod 'jug sher 'grel ke ta ka*, 133–463. Sichuan: Nationalities Press, 1993.

———. *Dbu ma rgyan gyi rnam bshad 'jam byangs bla ma dgyes pa'i zhal lung* (*Words That Delight Guru Mañjughoṣa: Commentary on the Ornament of the Middle Way*). In *Dbu ma rgyan rtsa 'grel*. Sichuan: Nationalities Press, 1990.

Phur bu Tshe ring, editor. *Nang rig pa'i tshig mdzod* (*The Dictionary of Internal Knowledge*). Beijing: Nationalities Press, 1994.

Tsong kha pa Blo bzang grags pa. *Lam rim chung ba* (*The Lesser Exposition of the Stages of the Path*). In *Collected Works*, vol. 21, 1–438. New Delhi: Ngawang Gelek Demo, 1979.

———. *Dgongs pa rab gsal* (*Thoroughly Illuminating the Viewpoint*). Sarnath: Central Institute of Higher Tibetan Studies, 1998.

———. *Lam gyi gtso bo rnam gsum* (*Three Principal Aspects of the Path*). Xining: *sku 'bum byams pa gling*, 2001.

Secondary Sources

Bötrül. *Distinguishing the Views and Philosophies: Illuminating Emptiness in a Twentieth-Century Tibetan Buddhist Classic*. Translated, annotated, and introduced by Douglas Duckworth. Albany: State University of New York Press, 2011.

Duckworth, Douglas. *Mipam on Buddha-Nature: The Ground of the Nyingma Tradition*. Albany: State University of New York Press, 2008.

———. "Mipam's Middle Way Through Yogācāra and Prāsaṅgika." *Journal of Indian Philosophy* 38, no. 4 (2010): 431–439.

———. "Two Models of the Two Truths: Ontological and Phenomenological Approaches." *Journal of Indian Philosophy* 38, no. 5 (2010): 519–527.

Kapstein, Matthew. "Mipam Namgyel: Lion's Roar Affirming Extrinsic Emptiness." In *Buddhist Philosophy: Essential Readings*, edited by Jay Garfield and William Edelglass, 61–72. Oxford: Oxford University Press, 2009.

Newland, Guy. *The Two Truths*. Ithaca: Snow Lion, 1992.
Pettit, John. *Mipham's Beacon of Certainty*. Boston: Wisdom, 1999.
Phuntsho, Karma. *Mipham's Dialectics and the Debates on Emptiness*. London: Routledge-Curzon, 2005.
Suzuki, D. T., translator. *The Laṅkāvatāra Sūtra*. London: Routledge, 1968.
Thupten Jinpa. *Self, Reality and Reason in Tibetan Philosophy*. London: RoutledgeCurzon, 2002.

11

Where Buddhas and Siddhas Meet

Mipam's Yuganaddhavāda Philosophy

Dorji Wangchuk

In a recent review article on Douglas S. Duckworth's study of Mipam Namgyel Gyatso's (1846–1912) interpretation of the buddha-nature (*tathāgatagarbha*) theory,[1] I pointed out that while Duckworth is absolutely right in his characterization of Mipam's philosophy (or philosophical approach) as "dialectical monism," there is still a need to define and refine our understanding of—as I prefer to call it—Yuganaddhavāda (*zung 'jug tu smra ba*) philosophy,[2] namely, by (a) explicating some of the tacit assumptions underlying his *yuganaddha*-related (*zung 'jug*) thought, (b) tracking down and discussing his definitions and synonyms of yuganaddha, (c) presenting his ideas relating to faulty notions of yuganaddha, (d) proposing a typology of core yuganaddha concepts defined or redefined by him, and (e) systematizing various strategies or arguments employed by him for establishing a yuganaddha relationship between any two opposed or juxtaposed poles. In this contribution, I intend therefore to explore some of these avenues, with an assumption that understanding his Yuganaddhavāda philosophy is key to understanding his interpretation, appreciation, and reconciliation of the major Mahāyāna doctrines in India and Tibet that crystallized into the form of yuganaddha doctrine—which he believed was taught by all "awakened ones" (buddhas) and "accomplished ones" (siddhas) alike—particularly of Dolpopa Sherab Gyaltsen's (1292–1361) zhentong (*gzhan stong*) philosophy and Tsongkhapa Lozang Drakpa's (1357–1419) rangtong (*rang stong*) philosophy.[3]

The Term Yuganaddha

A brief explanation of the key term *zung du 'jug pa* (or *zung 'jug*)—the Tibetan translation of the Sanskrit *yuganaddha*—which underlies Mipam's Yuganaddhavāda philosophy, may be required here. Whether specified or not, the expression *xy zung 'jug* always seems to be employed as a *bahuvrīhi* (i.e., adjectival) compound that qualifies other nouns (represented by *z*). Thus the expression *chos kun gyi gnas lugs dbyings rig zung du 'jug pa*[4] (i.e., where *x* is *dbyings*, *y* is *rig pa*, and *z* is *chos kun gyi gnas lugs*) may be translated as "the reality of all phenomena, which is characterized by the nature of unity / integrality (lit., perhaps 'state of being yoked / paired / conjoined / unified') of the sphere [of reality] and cognition." Other forms such as *zung du zhugs pa*,[5] *zung du chud pa*,[6] and *zung du 'brel ba*[7] have also been used. In all of these, what seems to be worth bearing in mind is that *'jug pa* is obviously understood in the sense of an intransitive and heteronomous verb and thus would mean something like "to occur (or co-occur) in (or as) a pair."

Mipam's Yuganaddhavāda Philosophy

Mipam, as a Mahāyāna philosopher, can be regarded as a Yuganaddhavādin par excellence, inasmuch as he was a proponent of the view that major authoritative Mahāyāna scriptures, systems, and scholars in India and Tibet had one great enterprise, namely, to elucidate the ultimate true reality, spiritual path, and spiritual goal, as all having a unitary (or monopolar / unipolar) yuganaddha nature.[8] He may philosophically be designated as a monist, inasmuch as he consistently held that any given (mostly) binary poles of entity versus reality are only apparently and relatively dual or diverse but are actually and ultimately one or unitary. In particular, as we shall see, Mipam's consistent and persistent argument that there can ultimately be only "one mode of reality" (*bden pa gcig*) as the ultimate "one object of cognition" (*gzhal bya gcig*) and thus ultimately only "one valid type of cognition" (*tshad ma gcig*)—which involves no subject-object dichotomy, and where the object of cognition (*shes bya*) and cognition (*shes pa*) become inseparably fused into one singular point, which may best be described as the "Dharmakāyaic point of singularity" (*chos sku thig le nyag gcig*)[9]—seems to be crucial for his Yuganaddhavāda philosophy. In other words, Mipam's Yuganaddhavāda philosophy seems to culminate in the idea of the "indivisibility of cognition and the object of cognition" (*shes dang shes bya dbyer med*), which is identical with the idea of the "yuganaddha of the sphere of reality and gnosis" (*dbyings ye / rig zung 'jug*) or the "indivisibility of the sphere of reality and gnosis" (*dbyings ye / rig dbyer med*),[10] as also asserted by Rongzompa.[11] Such a line of thought is also linked with the "one vehicle" (*theg pa gcig*) theory,[12] proposed by all Tibetan Buddhist traditions and scholars including again Rongzompa.[13]

Hermeneutically or methodologically, however, Mipam may be characterized as a harmonist, inasmuch as he sought to explain and interpret any given pair of (authoritative but often diametrically) opposed or juxtaposed poles of scriptures, systems, traditions, schemes, standpoints, and so forth, so as to recognize that they are actually noncontradictory and complementary (and so to be in a position to harmonize or reconcile them). His monistic and harmonistic attitude and agenda, which run like a thread through his writings dealing with Buddhist religion and philosophy,[14] seem to have played a crucial role in his lifelong philosophical and hermeneutical project. The present contribution, however, will focus on his monistic rather than his harmonistic approach.

MIPAM'S THREE THEORIES OF MAHĀYĀNIC HERMENEUTICS

In the expectation that understanding the hermeneutical schemes underlying Mipam's Yuganaddhavāda philosophy will help us enhance our understanding of his Yuganaddhavāda philosophy, I would like to briefly discuss three of his theories of exposition and interpretation, namely, his theories of (a) the two models of twofold truth (*satyadvaya*, *bden pa gnyis*), (b) the two types of valid cognition (*tshad ma gnyis*), and (c) the two soteriological models.

The Two Models of Twofold Truth

Mipam proposed his theory of "two different *satyadvaya* models" (*bden pa gnyis kyi 'jog tshul mi 'dra ba gnyis; bden gnyis 'jog tshul gnyis*) on more than one occasion,[15] without ever apparently giving them technical labels. The labels given by later Tibetan scholars, such as Botrul Dongak Tenpai Nyima (1898 / 1900–1958),[16] are (a) "twofold (objective / ontic) reality [comprising the modes of] appearance [and] emptiness," (*snang stong bden gnyis*) and (b) "twofold (subjective / epistemic) truth [comprising] the existence-perception [relation]" (*gnas snang bden gnyis*). The first is an (objective) reality model defining an ontology, and the second a subjective truth model defining an epistemology. According to the first model, two aspects or dimensions are attributed to the ontological entity or reality, namely, an appearance aspect (*snang cha*) or mode of appearance (*snang tshul*), called "conventional reality" (*saṃvṛtisatya*, *kun rdzob bden pa*), and an emptiness aspect (*stong cha*) or mode of existence (*gnas tshul*), which is called "absolute reality" (*paramārthasatya*, *don dam bden pa*). This model presupposes an objective reality independent of any perception or conception of it, or of any of its propositions that could possibly be true. The relationship between the objective satyadvaya accepted by Mipam would be one of "intrinsic identicality but aspectual separateness" (*ngo bo gcig la ldog pa tha dad*).[17] Such a position seems to have been already proposed by Rongzompa.[18] As far as I understand, according to the second model, a cognitive object and a cognitive subject between which there is no concordance—that is, between the former's objective mode of existence and the latter's subjective mode of perception (*gnas tshul dang snang tshul mi mthun pa'i yul dang yul can*)—are called the "conventional" (*kun rdzob*); a cognitive object and a cognitive subject between which there is concordance—that is, between the former's objective mode of existence and the latter's subjective mode of perception (*gnas tshul dang snang tshul mthun pa'i yul dang yul can*)—are called the "absolute" (*don dam*). The basic idea presupposed in this model is that a subjective perception, conception, or proposition can be regarded as "truth" only if it tallies with objective "reality." The relationship between the conventional and absolute according to the subjective truth model cannot be that of "intrinsic identicality but aspectual separateness" (*ngo bo gcig la ldog pa tha dad*) but rather one of "identicality-rescinding separateness" (*gcig pa bkag pa'i tha dad*).[19]

A question that poses itself is whether the theory of the "indivisibility of the *satyadvaya*" (*bden gnyis dbyer med*) or the "yuganaddha of the satyadvaya" (*bden gnyis zung 'jug*), which is certainly the bedrock of Mipam's Yuganaddhavāda philosophy, works according to the first "(ontic) reality model," the second "(epistemic) truth model," or both. There is no doubt that the yuganaddha of the satyadvaya works perfectly well according to the first model. But according to the second model, the yuganaddha of the satyadvaya, would seem actually impossible, inasmuch as the relationship between *x* and *y* that constitute the yuganaddha can hardly be one of essential identicality (*ngo bo gcig*) and may even appear to be one of mutual contradiction and exclusion, given that what is conventional is actually "false" (*rdzun pa*) and only what is absolute is actually "true" (*bden pa*). My position, however, is that the yuganaddha of the satyadvaya should work and does indeed work also according to the second model, but only on the basis of a different conceptualization. The *xy*-yuganaddha according to the first model is based on the principle of the integrity and coequality of *x* and *y*. The *xy*-yuganaddha according to the second model is based on the principle according to which *x* and *y* are considered to be indivisible and one, inasmuch as *x* does not actually exist. In other words, it is based on a principle according to which virtual *x* and actual *y* are one and the same, just as in the case of a virtual pauper (who is a citizen) and an actual prince (who is a ruler) being one and the same person.[20] The slightest suggestion of a real or actual existence of *x* would imply a relation of mutual contradiction or exclusion between *x* and *y*, and thus render the idea of *xy*-yuganaddha impossible.[21] The concepts of "indivisibility of saṃsāra and nirvāṇa" (*'khor 'das dbyer med*),[22] "coequality of saṃsāra and nirvāṇa" (*'khor 'das mnyam nyid*),[23] "coequality of existence and quiescence" (*srid zhi mnyam nyid*),[24] and so on, which are ad sensum also endorsed by Rongzompa[25] and, importantly, by the zhentong philosophy, would make sense only on the basis of the second satyadvaya model.[26] Mipam seems to have sincerely believed that a failure to recognize the second satyadvaya model led to the depreciation and even demonization of zhentong philosophy in Tibet. Rongzompa, too, appears to have proposed, albeit only implicitly, the two models of twofold truth, inasmuch as he clearly interprets the "absolute" as "true reality" and "true gnosis" (*paramajñāna*, *ye shes dam pa*) and offers both ontological and gnoseological interpretations of the *de kho na nyid*,[27] thereby implying a satyadvaya model defining an ontology and a satyadvaya model defining an epistemology.

The point of intersection or convergence between the first "(objective) reality model" and the second "(subjective) truth model" seems to be the gnoseological or Buddhological *xy*-yuganaddha (where *x* is the absolute [e.g., dharmadhatu] according to both the first and second models, whereas *y* is the absolute [e.g., jñāna] according to the second model). Interestingly, depending on whether one presupposes the "(objective) twofold-reality model" or the "(subjective) twofold-truth model," Mipam's model of *bden pa gcig* itself can be said to be of two types, namely, a "one-reality model" and a "one-truth model." The one-reality model is essentially his "one-(*pra*)*meya*" (*gzhal bya gcig*) model, while the one-truth model would be his "one-(*pra*)*māṇa* model," which we shall examine later. In sum, Buddhological yuganaddha, which is the perfection and culmination of gnoseological yuganaddha, seems to represent a case in which not only the objective reality model and subjective truth model converge and merge but also the one-reality model and one-truth model meet and merge into the "one singular dharmakāyaic point" (*chos sku thig le nyag gcig*).

Two Types of Valid Cognitions

As someone with a strong conviction in the efficacy and necessity of logic and epistemology, Mipam constructed his entire philosophical edifice—his *philosophische Gedankengebäude*, so to speak—including his Yuganaddhavāda philosophy, within the framework of Buddhist logic and epistemology.[28] A crucial point of departure here is the assumption that the Buddha taught two types of to-be-cognized (*rtogs bya*) or cognitive object (*[pra]meya*, *gzhal bya*), each in the form of two modes of reality,[29] namely, the mode of appearance of as-many-as-there-are (*yāvat*, *ji snyed pa*) phenomenal entities (dharmin, *chos can*), which is the conventional reality (*saṃvṛtisatya*, *kun rdzob kyi bden pa*), and the mode of existence of true reality (dharmatā, *chos nyid*) as-it-is (*yathāvat*, *ji lta ba*), which is the absolute true reality. He believed in the logical demonstrability and cognitive (prajñāic and jñānaic) penetrability of the two modes of reality, that is, either by means of indirect conceptual cognition or direct perceptual cognition. For him,[30] the statement according to which the sphere of true reality is the cognitive object of gnosis in the meditative state (*samāhitajñāna*, *mnyam bzhag ye shes*) and the statement according to which the absolute true reality is not a domain of cognition are reconcilable inasmuch as the former is to be understood in conventional terms (*tha snyad du*) and in terms of negative determination (*rnam gcod du*), whereas the latter is to be understood in the context of the absolute and in terms of positive determination. Because the absolute cannot be determined positively, it is said to be even beyond the cognition of a buddha. Because it can be determined negatively, the absolute is for him not only a cognitive object of a bodhisattva who is a noble being (*ārya*, *'phags pa*) but also of a bodhisattva who is still an ordinary being (*pṛthagjana*, *so so skye bo*).

Similarly, corresponding to the two kinds of cognitive objects (*[pra]meya*, *gzhal bya*) in the form of two modes of reality, there are two kinds of valid cognitions (*[pra]māṇa*, *tshad ma*), namely, "conventional valid cognition" (*vyāvahārikapramāṇa*, *tha snyad pa'i tshad ma*) and "absolute valid cognition" (*pāramārthikapramāṇa*, *don dam pa'i tshad ma*).[31] Corresponding to the two conventional modes of reality, namely, the conventional mode of appearance (*tha snyad snang tshul*) and conventional mode of existence (*tha snyad gnas tshul*), Mipam has proposed two kinds of conventional valid cognitions,[32] namely, one based on ordinary (lit., "of this-side," i.e., this-worldly) perception (*arvāgdarśana* / *aparadarśana*, *tshu rol mthong ba*) and the other based on pure perception (**śuddhadarśana, dag pa'i gzigs pa*). Also corresponding to the two absolute modes of reality, namely, quasi-absolute true reality (**saparyāyaparamārtha, rnam grangs pa'i don dam*) and actual absolute true reality (**aparyāyaparamārtha / *niṣparyāya, rnam grangs ma yin pa'i don dam*), he has proposed two kinds of absolute valid cognitions.[33]

Because there is ultimately only one mode of reality (*bden pa gcig*),[34] a concept that seems well attested in Indian sources,[35] and that is the one ultimate object of cognition, there is ultimately only one valid cognition, which Mipam, unlike Rongzompa,[36] equates with self-occurring gnosis (*svayaṃbhūjñāna, rang byung gi ye shes*).[37] His idea of a single ultimate valid cognition actually tallies with Candrakīrti's idea of "one direct valid cognition" (*mngon sum gcig*), namely, the gnosis of the Omniscient One.[38] Mipam thus occasionally also speaks of three kinds of valid cognition,[39] that is, two types of pramāṇa that culminate in one pramāṇa. In proposing this scheme, Mipam seems to have fully exploited Dharmakīrti's proposition that there must be two kinds of pramāṇa, namely, *pratyakṣa* and *anumāna*, because there are two kinds of *prameya*, namely, *svalakṣaṇa* and *sāmānyalakṣaṇa*,[40] but ultimately there can be only one pramāṇa because there is ultimately only one (*pra*)*meya*.[41]

Two Types of Soteriological Models

Various Buddhist sources and systems seem to presuppose various soteriological models including what may be called the "generation model," "transmutation model," "clearance model," "purification model,"[42] "separation / dissociation model,"[43] "revelation model," a mixed model, and so on. On the basis of the two kinds of causal mechanism presupposed for a Buddhist soteriology, one can, as I have suggested on an earlier occasion,[44] speak about two kinds of soteriological models, namely, a "nature / revelation model" and a "nurture / generation / illumination model"—based on or explained by employing the concept of the two kinds of causes (*hetu, rgyu*), namely, a "generating cause" (*utpādakahetu, skyed par byed pa'i rgyu; skyed byed kyi rgyu*) and an "illuminating cause" (*[abhi]vyañjakahetu, gsal bar byed pa'i rgyu; gsal byed kyi rgyu*).[45] Those who endorse the "nature model" would normally not reject the "nurture model" per se but interpret it "inclusivistically" as being in conformity with the phenomena's "apparitional mode" (*snang tshul*), and thus as ultimately being in conformity with the phenomena's "existential mode" (*gnas tshul*).

The implication of such an inclusivistic interpretation is that there is ultimately only one soteriological model, and this seems to have overriding significance for Mipam's Yuganaddhavāda philosophy, which is what one might call a "cognitive-penetration model" based on three related concepts, namely, (a) the concept that it is only through recognizing and cognizing the true reality as it is that one can bring about a soteriological breakthrough,[46] (b) the concept of the "indivisibility of cause and goal" (*rgyu 'bras dbyer med pa*),[47] and (c) the concept of the "indivisibility of the to-be-abandoned and antidote" (*spang gnyen dbyer med*),[48] all of which are already attested in Rongzompa's writings. That is, a kind of soteriological model that dissolves the cause-effect (*rgyu 'bras*) and abandonment-adoption (*spang blang*) relationship[49] between *x* and *y*,[50] with the argument that *x* is actually *y*, or more precisely, that *x* has never deviated from its *y* nature, just as a prince wandering unbeknownst to or incognito among his subjects (*rgyal bu dmangs su 'khyams pa*) has never deviated from his princely nature.[51] This is a model that becomes increasingly relevant and conspicuous as one ascends the staircase of doxographical hierarchy, so that the system of the Dzokchen, which, according to the Nyingma tradition, is the zenith of all Buddhist vehicles, exclusively follows the cognitive-penetration model. The cognitive-penetration model is not a "linear-gradual ladder model" but rather a "singular-point model," according to which the ontological-spiritual ground (*gzhi*), gnoseological-spiritual path (*lam*), and the buddhological goal (*'bras bu*) are conceived of as a singular point of totality or integrality,[52] an idea also proposed by Rongzompa.[53]

Propositions Related to Ontology, Epistemology, Gnoseology, and Soteriology

Some philosophical propositions underlying Mipam's Yuganaddhavāda philosophy related to ontology, epistemology, gnoseology, and soteriology may now be considered. First, with regard to ontology, it could be maintained that for Mipam all conventional cognizable objects culminate or terminate in "particulars" (*svalakṣaṇa, rang gi mtshan nyid*). This is in line with the Dharmakīrtian system that emphasizes *vyāvahārikapramāṇa*. Similarly, according to the Nāgārjunian or Candrakīrtian system that emphasizes *pāramārthikapramāṇa*, it can be said that all absolute cognizable objects culminate in the particular of true reality (*chos nyid rang mtshan*). All absolute true realities, whether quasi-absolute or genuine absolute, culminate in the yuganaddha of appearance and emptiness (*snang stong zung 'jug*). Rongzompa, too, contends that all cognizables (*shes par bya ba'i chos*) culminate in nothing other than innate nature or true reality (*rang bzhin nam chos nyid tsam*).[54]

Second, with regard to epistemology and gnoseology, it is maintained that all logical proofs (*hetu, gtan tshigs*) culminate in "proofs of innate nature" (*svabhāvahetu, rang bzhin gyi gtan tshig*),[55] and thus also all types of connection (*saṃbandha, 'brel ba*) between the proof and the to-be-proven culminate in "natural connection" (*svarūpasambandha*, rang bzhin gyi 'brel ba).[56] All types of logical reasoning (*yukti, rigs pa*) culminate in "logical reasoning of rule-boundedness" (*dharmatāyukti, chos nyid kyi rigs pa*).[57] All conceptual cognitions (*anumāna, rjes dpag*) culminate in perceptual cognitions (*pratyakṣa, mngon sum*).[58] All perceptual cognitions culminate in self-cognition (*svasaṃvedanā; svasaṃviti, rang rig*).[59] This can be maintained to be true for both a vyāvahārikapramāṇa and a pāramārthikapramāṇa. Self-cognition that is a vyāvahārikapramāṇa can be de facto a vijñānaic self-cognition (*sems rang rig pa*), whereas self-cognition that is a pāramārthikapramāṇa can only be a jñānaic self-cognition (*ye shes rang rig pa*),[60] which can be equated with self-occurring gnosis, at least for Mipam.

Third, with regard to soteriology, it may be stated that whatever is to be abandoned (*heya*, *spang bya*) culminates in nescience (*avidyā*, *ma rig pa*), or all intellectual-emotional defilements (*kleśa*, *nyon mongs pa*) culminate in mere disorientedness (*rmongs pa tsam*).[61] All gnoses culminate in insight consisting in the cognition that all phenomena are characterized by nonessentiality (*chos thams cad la bdag med par rtogs pa'i shes rab*),[62] which can also be equated with self-occurring gnosis.

Some Tacit Assumptions

Mipam's Yuganaddhavāda philosophy is obviously based on some tacit assumptions, which may require some explication. First, it presupposes bipolar tensions, which he attempts to revolve or dissolve between two entities, two qualities of one and the same entity, two modes of reality, two philosophical systems, two positions, two schemes or models, and so on. Second, the poles *x* and *y* must necessarily command equal weight inasmuch as both, each in its given context, are equally tenable or authoritative and hence cannot be dismissed as wrong. A Yuganaddhavādin thus tentatively accepts both poles as correct but ultimately transcends both in finding some kind of unity between the two. He would not dismiss one of the poles as untenable. Third, the tension between the two opposed or juxtaposed poles *x* and *y* presupposes a mutual contradiction or exclusion, or else there would be no tension between them and hence no need for resolving it. Fourth, two kinds of mutual contradiction or exclusion seem to be presupposed in Mipam's yuganaddha mode of thinking, namely, *actual* and *virtual*.

Fifth, Mipam's strategies for diffusing the tension between the two poles seem to differ according to the type of contradiction presupposed. That is, if an *actual tension* based on a *real contradiction* is presupposed between the two poles, then the tension is resolved by establishing a common pivot point that underlies them or a singular point that transcends them. If a *virtual tension* based on an *apparent contradiction* is presupposed between the two poles, then the "apparent / putative *x*" is equated with *y*, thereby establishing their unity. The basic assumption is that apparent contradiction is no contradiction. An establishment of the yuganaddha of the two is nonetheless held desirable because normal humans wrongly hold the contradiction or tension between them to be real or actual. It is said to require a bodhisattva of the eighth stage (*bhūmi*, *sa*) to correctly fathom the eight kinds of profundity involving paradoxical statements of Mahāyāna scriptures.[63] The sixth presupposition is an ethical-spiritual commitment to reverse growing religious polemics and sectarianism in Tibet.[64] That is, the driving motivational forces behind a yuganaddha mode of thinking seems to be a desire for harmony, a sense of awe for the Buddhist doctrines, and the wish to avoid running the risks of passing categorical judgments, and thereby incurring the "transgression of abandoning the Dharma" (*chos spong gi las*) by way of disparagement and denial.

Faulty Notions of Yuganaddha

Evidently, Mipam considered all notions of yuganaddha that do not meet the criteria of his own idea of the yuganaddha of nature as faulty.[65] He also evidently assumed that the faulty understanding of the yuganaddha at the level of the spiritual path and the one at the resultant level are due to a faulty understanding of the yuganaddha at the level of the ontological ground.[66] He obviously rejects any understanding or interpretation of *xy*-yuganaddha that attributes to it the nature or quality of (a) artificiality, (b) conditionality, (c) partiality (here in the sense of "fragmentariness"), (d) bipolarity or plurality, or (e) antitheticality (or contradictoriness) of *x* and *y*.[67] (a) He rejects any suggestion of an idea of yuganaddha in which *x* and *y* are intertwined, in the way white and black threads are interwoven (*srad bu sgrim pa bzhin*),[68] thereby implying that either the yuganaddha relationship between *x* and *y* is not natural but rather artificial, that is, that the understanding of the yuganaddha concept is superficial.[69] (b) For Mipam, genuine yuganaddha must necessarily be the ultimate state of reality that transcends the bipolar states of being conditioned (*saṃskṛta*, *'dus byas pa*) and unconditioned (*asaṃskṛta*, *'dus ma byas pa*), although occasionally it may be described as the "great [state of being] unconditioned" (*'dus ma byas chen po*). In other words, for him, any proposition or suggestion that the genuine yuganaddha should be a conditioned state—that is, a state subjected to the processes of origination, continuation, and disintegration—is faulty and untenable. (c) Mipam clearly rejects the notion of an ultimate reality characterized by mere absence of hypostatic existence or nonimplicative negation (*med par dgag pa*)—described by him as the "lopsided / fragmented emptiness" (*stong pa phyang chad*),[70] "lopsided / fragmented cognition" (*rig pa phyang chad*),[71] "bare emptiness" (*stong rkyang*),[72] and so on—posited by the radical Intrinsic Emptyists (*rang stong pa*). He also rejects the notion posited by the radical Extrinsic Emptyists (*gzhan stong pa*) of an ultimate reality characterized by the presence of positive qualities or implicative negation (*ma yin par dgag pa*) as partial (or fragmentary) and hence faulty. A genuine yuganaddha for him must be beyond negation and affirmation.[73] Moreover, for him there can never be a yuganaddha relationship between what he calls "absence of a rabbit's horn and presence of a yak's horn" (*ri bong rwa med dang g.yag gi rwa yod*).[74] The ontological ground, which, for him by default has a yuganaddha nature, must be free from all modes of dualities (*gnyis chos kyi tshul kun dang bral ba*) and without limitation / fragmentation and one-sidedness (*rgya chad phyogs lhung med pa*).[75] (d) A genuine yuganaddha must be one characterized by singularity and never by plurality, as his insistence on the idea of the "one truth" (*bden pa gcig*) demonstrates, and also never by one-dimensionality, as his emphasis on the indivisibility or inseparability of the twofold truth (*bden gnyis dbyer med*)[76] testifies. Finally, (e) Mipam seems to have had difficulties with any proposition or presupposition that suggests a relationship of antitheticality between *x* and *y*, that is, a relationship defined by mutual exclusion or contradiction.[77]

Traditional Typologies of Yuganaddha

Before proposing some typologies of the yuganaddha concept, five different types of clusters, or a classification of yuganaddha, may be mentioned. These seem to suggest some of the attempts made by the Tibetan tradition to classify the idea on the basis of various doctrinal systems and criteria. First, in a non-tantric Madhyamaka context, the scheme of "ground madhyamaka, which is the yuganaddha of twofold truth" (*gzhi dbu ma bden gnyis zung 'jug*); "path madhyamaka, which is the yuganaddha of two accumulations (i.e., *puṇyasaṃbhāra* and *jñānasaṃbhāra*)" (*lam dbu ma tshogs gnyis zung 'jug*); and "goal madhyamaka, which is the yuganaddha of two [*buddha*] bodies (i.e., dharmakāya and *rūpakāya*)" (*'bras bu dbu ma sku gnyis zung 'jug*) is suggestive of an attempt to classify yuganaddha according to the levels of the ground, path, and goal.[78] Second, in the tantric context, the expression "twenty-three [kinds of] yuganaddha" (*zung 'jug nyer gsum*) associated with the *Pañcakrama* has been employed,[79] which is indicative of an attempt to bring various types of yuganaddha under one roof. Third, also in the tantric context, one finds a de facto classification of yuganaddha at the level of the path into "yuganaddha of training (*śaikṣa*)" (*slob pa'i zung 'jug*) and "yuganaddha of no-longer-training (*aśaikṣa*)" (*mi slob pa'i zung 'jug*).[80] The former is divided into "yuganaddha characterized by abandonment (i.e., of *kleśa*s, etc.)" (*spangs pa zung 'jug*) or "ordinary *śaikṣa*-yuganaddha" (*slob pa'i zung 'jug phal pa*)[81] and "yuganaddha characterized by realization (i.e., of *dharmanairātmya*, etc.)" (*rtogs pa zung 'jug*) or "special *śaikṣa-yuganaddha*" (*slob pa'i zung 'jug khyad par can*).[82] Fourth, a list of "four [kinds of] yuganaddha" (*zung 'jug bzhi*) can also be found, namely,[83] "yuganaddha of appearance and emptiness" (*snang stong zung 'jug*), "yuganaddha of [gnostic] cognition and emptiness" (*rig stong zung 'jug*), "yuganaddha of bliss and emptiness" (*bde stong zung 'jug*), and "yuganaddha of clarity / luminosity and emptiness" (*gsal stong zung 'jug*), to which we shall return. Fifth, it may also be mentioned that a section from the *Maṇi Kabum* alludes to "three [kinds of] yuganaddha" (*zung 'jug gsum*), namely, "yuganaddha of *utpatti[krama*] and *utpanna[krama] / niṣpanna[krama]*" (*bskyed rdzogs zung 'jug* or *bskyed rdzogs zung du 'jug pa*), "yuganaddha of *upāya* and *prajñā*" (*thabs shes zung 'jug* or *thabs shes zung du 'jug pa*), and "yuganaddha of [dharma]dhātu and *jñāna*" (*dbyings dang ye shes zung du 'jug pa*).[84] There may be other ways of classifying the yuganaddha concept found in Tibetan sources,[85] but no attempt has been made to trace them all.

Tradition-Inspired Typology of Yuganaddha

In the following few paragraphs, a new typology of the yuganaddha concepts will be proposed by drawing inspiration from what appears to be a popular typological scheme devised for classifying major Tibetan Buddhist themes such as Madhyamaka.[86] That is, one may classify yuganaddha (partly with some neo-Tibetanisms) as either (a) "yuganaddha of the expressible referent" (*brjod bya don gyi zung 'jug*) or (b) "yuganaddha of the expressive word" (*rjod byed tshig gi zung 'jug*), consisting of scriptures or systems that posit the Yuganaddhavāda philosophy. The former type of yuganaddha would revolve around content (*inhaltlich*) and actuality, and the latter around the nominal-conceptual (*begrifflich*) and virtuality.

Yuganaddha of the Expressible Referent

Although hardly explicit in traditional Tibetan sources, I have ventured to subclassify what I call "yuganaddha of the expressible referent" (*brjod bya don gyi zung 'jug*) into "ground yuganaddha," "path yuganaddha," and "goal yuganaddha."[87] The word "ground" is employed here in the sense of the "metaphysical ground," a dimension of being or reality, which is conceived of as being totally independent of any cognition or realization. It is meant to render the Tibetan term *gzhi*, which in turn renders a number of different Sanskrit words.[88] Our context seems to demand that we understand it in the sense of a metaphysical or ontological "substratum" (*ādhāra*, *rten*), "base" or "ground" or "foundation" (*pratiṣṭhā*), or "root" or "basis" (*mūla*, *rtsa ba*), which in turn is often understood as either the ultimate true reality or the philosophical view (*lta ba*) of this reality,[89] and hence also as the soteriological "point of departure" for any given Buddhist system.[90] It should be noted that even those Buddhist systems, such as the Sarvadharmāpratiṣṭhānavāda, that deny any kind of metaphysical substratum would have their own notion of "ground," namely, so to speak, a "groundless ground" or a "substratumless substratum." The word "path" in the expression "path yuganaddha" is always to be understood as a Mahāyānic spiritual or soteriological path leading to direct meditative insight (*jñāna*, *ye shes*), which always has ground yuganaddha as its cognitive object (i.e., its underlying substrate or nature). Mipam seems to distinguish a "jñānaic" path yuganaddha from a prajñāic / vijñānaic path yuganaddha, the actual path yuganaddha being for him, of course, always jñānaic and never prajñāic or vijñānaic, insofar as a qualitative distinction is made between the two. The word "goal" in the expression "goal yuganaddha" is to be understood in the sense of the Mahāyānic spiritual or soteriological goal or result, that is, buddhahood. Hence it may also be called "resultant yuganaddha" or "buddhological yuganaddha," and it is actually nothing but a perfected form or state of path yuganaddha, that is, a completely revealed or exposed ground yuganaddha.

Ground Yuganaddha

Mipam employs multiple terms to express the concept of ground yuganaddha. Some of them are very specific to a certain system, whereas others are used generally, in all Mahāyāna systems. Although ad sensum these are said to be identical, each system comes with a unique preferred terminology of its own. Of the numerous expressions Mipam employs in different contexts and for different systems, seven terms that explicitly contain the term yuganaddha may be mentioned here: (1) Of all these, the expression "yuganaddha of appearance and emptiness" (*snang stong zung 'jug*)[91]—along with a host of synonyms, such as "yuganaddha of emptiness and dependent arising" (*stong rten 'byung zung 'jug*),[92] "indivisibility of appearance and emptiness" (*snang stong dbyer med*),[93] "inseparability of appearance and emptiness" (*snang stong 'du bral med pa*),[94] and "coequality of appearance and emptiness" (*snang stong mnyam pa nyid*)[95]—is employed mainly in the sūtric Mahāyāna context, although it is often presupposed within mantric Mahāyāna systems. (2) Another key term that expresses Mipam's Yuganaddhavāda philosophy in this context is the "yuganaddha of twofold reality" (*bden gnyis zung 'jug*),[96] which is also equatable with the "indivisibility of twofold truth"[97] and "twofold reality, which is one savor" (*bden gnyis ro gcig*).[98] (3) There is yet another key term that is employed mainly (but not exclusively) in the "Zhije and Lamdre" tradition of the Sakya tradition, namely, the "yuganaddha of clarity / luminosity and emptiness"[99] or "indivisibility of clarity / luminosity and emptiness" (*gsal stong dbyer med*),[100] an expression that Mipam, too, often employs and endorses.[101] (4) A term for ground yuganaddha that might be more appropriate for the Yoginītantric or Anuyogic systems of the Nyingma tantric tradition is the "yuganaddha of bliss and emptiness"[102] or else the "indivisibility of bliss and emptiness" (*bde stong dbyer med*).[103] Mipam evidently took for granted that the tradition of the *Kālacakra Tantra*, too, professes the "yuganaddha of bliss and emptiness." (5) Perhaps the expression "yuganaddha of E and Waṃ" (*e waṃ zung 'jug*)[104] can also be seen as denoting the same ground yuganaddha from a tantric perspective. The reason why the "yuganaddha of E and Waṃ" pertains to the ground is because it is said to be the *hetutantra* (*rgyu'i rgyud*) according to the highest system.[105] (6) Two of the typical expressions for ground yuganaddha employed in the context of the Dzokchen are "yuganaddha of (gnostic) cognition and emptiness"[106] and "indivisibility of (gnostic) cognition and emptiness" (*rig stong dbyer med*).[107] (7) Also, the expression "yuganaddha of primordial purity and the immanence [of intrinsic qualities]" (*ka dag lhun grub zung 'jug*),[108] equatable with "indivisibility of primordial purity and the immanence [of intrinsic qualities]" (*ka dag lhun grub dbyer med*),[109] is used by Mipam to designate the "ontological Dzokchen," or more literally, "Dzokchen [at the level of the] ground" (*gzhi rdzogs pa chen po*).[110]

Path Yuganaddha

What I call "path yuganaddha" will be discussed here in connection with a few relevant issues. First, it is obvious that although there are several forms of *xy*-yuganaddha pertinent to the Mahāyāna spiritual path, path yuganaddha for Mipam meant an "as yet unperfected gnoseological or jñānaic yuganaddha," and as such it excludes cognitively unpenetrated ground yuganaddha, prajñāic path yuganaddha (which is, strictly speaking, not yet bona fide path yuganaddha), and goal yuganaddha. Second, the way one conceives of the precise nature and function of path yuganaddha, and its relation to ground yuganaddha and goal yuganaddha may differ according to the soteriological model one proposes or presupposes. No Yuganaddhavādin would, however, consider the Mahāyānic spiritual path of meditative practices to be otiose,[111] although its superfluousness is often mentioned as an undesirable consequence of the soteriological model followed by a competing tradition or system. It may be restated here that at least for Mipam's tradition, the "higher" one ascends on the doxographical hierarchy, the tighter or more natural the relation between *x* and *y* that constitutes the *xy*-yuganaddha and the interrelationship among the path yuganaddha, ground yuganaddha, and goal yuganaddha become.

Third, one occasionally realizes that one cannot always neatly classify a certain *xy*-yuganaddha into the categories of ground, path, or goal yuganaddha. For instance, what about saṃsāra-nirvāṇa-yuganaddha (*'khor 'das zung 'jug*)—an expression that, though occasionally found, is apparently not employed by Mipam or his mentors—that is, "indivisibility of saṃsāra and nirvāṇa" (*'khor 'das dbyer med*)?[112] Is the indivisibility of saṃsāra and nirvāṇa ground or path yuganaddha? We do encounter the concepts of "the path, which is the indivisibility of saṃsāra and nirvāṇa" (*lam 'khor 'das dbyer med*) and "the view of the indivisibility of saṃsāra and nirvāṇa,"[113] which seem to identify saṃsāra-nirvāṇa-yuganaddha with path yuganaddha rather than with ground yuganaddha. As briefly suggested earlier, some traditions wish to identify the view of the ultimate true reality with the "ground," as is evident from the use of the expression "establishing the view, which is the ground" (*gzhi lta ba gtan la 'bebs pa*), whereas for others the view of the ultimate true reality is identified rather with prajñāic path yuganaddha. At any rate, the indivisibility of saṃsāra and nirvāṇa itself, as an expression of ultimate true reality, must be identified with ground yuganaddha, and it is only in connection with cognitive (i.e., either prajñāic or jñānaic) access to it that one properly speaks of the "the view of the indivisibility of saṃsāra and nirvāṇa" (*lta ba 'khor 'das dbyer med*) and "the path of the indivisibility of saṃsāra and nirvāṇa." I would thus contend that this is true also in the case of the "indivisibility of existence and quiescence" (*srid zhi mnyam nyid*).

This brings us to the fourth and final point, namely, a host of *xy*-yuganaddha concepts associated with path yuganaddha that seems to have primarily to do with prajñāic or jñānaic cognition of the ground yuganaddha, which is the view (*lta ba*) and its application or implementation in one's actual praxis of meditation (*sgom pa*) and in one's actions or transactions (*spyod pa*). One is thus bound to encounter expressions such as "yuganaddha of view and meditation"[114] and "yuganaddha of view and conduct."[115] Six key terms and concepts that convey the path yuganaddha may be mentioned here: (1) Clearly, the concept of "yuganaddha of *śamatha* and *vipaśyanā*" (*zhi lhag zung 'jug*)[116] is fundamental to both Mahāyāna and non-Mahāyāna soteriology. In his commentary on the *Abhisamayālaṃkāra*, Mipam explains the "path that comprises the combination / concurrence of *upāya* and *prajñā*" (*thabs dang shes rab zung du 'brel ba'i lam*) as a path that does not fall into one of the extremes of śamatha and vipaśyanā, turbulent saṃsāric existence and nirvāṇic quietude (*zhi lhag gam srid zhir mi lhung ba*).[117] (2) The concept of the "yuganaddha of upāya and prajñā" (*thabs shes zung 'jug*)[118] seems obviously important for Mahāyāna soteriology. A path devoid of the yuganaddha of *karuṇā* (i.e., upāya) and prajñā (*snying rje dang shes rab zung 'jug*) has often been considered a deficient Mahāyānic path and hence distant from the "resultant mother" (*'bras yum*) or the resultant *prajñāpāramitā*.[119] (3) Similarly, the Mahāyāna soteriological path can be said to be defined purely along the lines of the "yuganaddha of the twofold accumulations" (*tshogs gnyis zung 'jug*),[120] that is, of the accumulation of beneficial resources (*puṇyasaṃbhāra, bsod nams kyi tshogs*) and the accumulation of gnosis (*jñānasaṃbhāra, ye shes kyi tshogs*). (4) It may seem that the "yuganaddha of *utpatti[krama]* and *utpanna[krama]*,"[121] or the "nonduality of *utpatti[krama]* and *utpanna[krama]*" (*bskyed rdzogs gnyis su med pa*),[122] is a typical mantric path yuganaddha, which presupposes or includes in one way or another all preceding types of path yuganaddha. In addition to the "yuganaddha of the twofold accumulations," which for him would be a sūtric path yuganaddha, Mipam alludes to (5) the "yuganaddha of the illusory body and luminosity" (*sgyu 'od zung 'jug*), which would be a mantric path yuganaddha, and (6) the "yuganaddha of primordial purity and innate actuality" (*ka dag dang lhun grub zung 'jug*) as the ultimate path yuganaddha of Dzokchen.[123]

Goal Yuganaddha

Mipam's position on what I refer to as "goal yuganaddha" is inextricably linked with his positions on buddhology, ontology, gnoseology, and soteriology,[124] and thus it will be beyond the scope of this study to do justice to the topic. Nonetheless, a few points can be made here. First, a traditional term that would be the closest to our "goal yuganaddha" occurring in the sūtric Madhyamaka context would be "yuganaddha of the two kāyas" (*sku gnyis zung 'jug*),[125] or *aśaikṣa*-yuganaddha (*mi slob pa'i zung 'jug*), which occurs in the mantric context.[126] Second, for Mipam, both the exclusive sūtric and mantric Mahāyāna can be said to be equally suitable for establishing the same ground yuganaddha and realizing the same goal yuganaddha,[127] the difference between sūtric and mantric Mahāyāna being the different manner in which cognitive (i.e., prajñāic and jñānaic) access is gained to the ground yuganaddha and how goal yuganaddha is realized. Third, for the proponents of "special Mahāyāna" (*theg chen thun mong ma yin pa*), who follow the "nature model" or "cognitive-penetration model" of soteriology, which presupposes the "indivisibility of ground and goal" (*gzhi 'bras dbyer med*),[128] the ground and goal yuganaddha are necessarily identical in essence. In plain terms, what one gets in the end is what one already had in the beginning! This is particularly true from the standpoint of Vajrayānic soteriology, according to which one "takes the goal as the path" (*'bras bu lam byed*). One implication of a consequent application of the cognitive-penetration model is that the goal itself takes the place of the path in such a way that the "path" as commonly understood is relativized. Mipam, for instance, understands self-occurring gnosis not only as ground yuganaddha,[129] goal yuganaddha,[130] or valid cognition (as we have seen), but also as the most powerful path or antidote characterized by jñānaic cognition, inasmuch as all paths are subsumed under it and no other path turns out to be as direct an antithesis (*dngos *'gal*) of nescience as self-occurring gnosis does.[131] What he de facto maintains is that ultimately only buddhological self-occurring gnosis is in a position to fully and cognitively penetrate the ontological self-occurring gnosis and that even a bodhisattva on the tenth stage is said to barely fathom it, as if trying to perceive a visible object in the night (*mtshan mo'i gzugs mthong ba ltar*).[132] For the proponents of the cognitive-penetration model of soteriology, there is thus only one *eliminatum* (*spang bya gcig*), namely, noncognition (*ma rig pa*), and whether or not one has realized the goal yuganaddha is a mere matter of cognition or noncognition (*rig dang ma rig tsam*)[133] of the ground yuganaddha. For one who has obtained a jackal's faculty of sight (*lce spyang gi mig*), there would be neither a need to dispel darkness (*mun pa bsal mi dgos*) nor to rely on the power of light (*snang ba'i mthu la brten mi dgos*), for one would perceive objects regardless of day or night (*nyin mtshan bye brag med par*) and cognize space (*nam mkha'*) to be luminous by nature. Similarly, for one who has obtained the immaculate dharmic faculty of sight (*chos kyi mig dri ma med pa*), there would be neither noncognition to be eliminated nor a cognition to be generated,[134] since noncognition itself shines as jñānaic cognition.[135]

Yuganaddha of the Expressive Word

What we refer to as the "yuganaddha of the expressive word" may be discussed here briefly by addressing two questions, namely, which scriptures and systems can be considered to express yuganaddha and where they are said to converge and diverge. First, all those Mahāyāna scriptures and systems that expound the "indivisibility of the twofold reality"—which seems to be the most important criterion for the definiteness of the teaching[136]—would qualify as "the yuganaddha of the expressive word." Scripturally speaking, Mipam reiterated that the Buddha had in all profound sūtric—that is, Mahāyāna scriptures of the Middle (*bka' bar pa*) and Final Promulgations (*bka' tha ma*)—and Buddhist tantric scriptures (*mdo rgyud kun*) one overriding concern, namely, to teach the ultimate true reality, which is characterized by a yuganaddha nature (i.e., Yuganaddhavāda philosophy).[137] A similar position can be found in Rongzompa's writings.[138] In terms of traditions or systems, the Indian Mahāyāna traditions of Maitreya and Asaṅga, Mañjuśrī and Nāgārjuna complexes (*tshul gnyis zung* 'jug),[139] the Svātantrika-Madhyamaka and Prāsaṅgika-Madhyamaka traditions,[140] particularly, the Madhyamaka tradition described by Mipam as *bden gnyis zung 'jug gi dbu ma*, *bden gnyis zung 'jug khas len dang bral ba'i dbu ma*, or *zung 'jug rab tu mi gnas pa'i dbu ma chen po*[141]—which he clearly identified with Sarvadharmāpratiṣṭhānavāda or with Prāsaṅgika-Madhyamaka.[142] Also included are the Zhije (*zhi byed*) and Lamdre (*lam 'bras*) traditions, and the Tibetan traditions of the so-called Three Great Ones (*chen po gsum*),[143] can be regarded as the yuganaddha of the expressive word, inasmuch as all of these have ontological or gnoseological yuganaddha as their main doctrinal content.[144] Also with regard to Buddhist scholars and saints both in India and Tibet, the Yuganaddhavāda doctrine is said to have been thoroughly elucidated, directly or indirectly (*dngos dang brgyud pa'i tshul du*), by such learned persons as the Six Ornaments (*rgyan drug*) of Jambudvīpa, and put into practice by all great siddhas and *vidyādharas*. It has also been a tent unifying all leading Tibetan scholars from the Nyingma and Sarma traditions, including Intrinsic Emptyists or rangtong proponents such as Tsongkhapa and Extrinsic Emptyists or zhentong proponents such as Dolpopa.[145]

Second, expressing verbal yuganaddha is like the proverbial finger that points to the moon (i.e., the ontological yuganaddha) and once prajñāic or ideally jñānaic access has been gained to it, that is, the gnoseological yuganaddha state has been attained, all saints and scholars see with one vision and speak with one voice. It is at this stage and in such a context that the "buddhas and siddhas are said to be one in intent" (*sangs rgyas dang grub thob dgongs pa gcig*).[146] For Mipam, this was where all Mahāyāna scriptures, systems, and scholars converged.

How are we then supposed to explain the undeniable differences and divergences that we observe among various Mahāyāna scriptures, systems, and scholars? For Mipam, the answer lies in not whether the Yuganaddhavāda philosophy is at all taught but rather *how* it is taught or introduced. The difference for him is thus all about whether ground yuganaddha has been taught by way of negation (*via negationis*) or by way of affirmation (*via eminentiae*); whether and to what degree it has been taught apophatically, cataphatically; how explicitly or implicitly; how intensively or extensively; or how successively (*rim gyis*) or simultaneously (*cig char*).[147] For him, Mahāyāna scriptures of the Middle Promulgation and the Mañjuśrī-Nāgārjuna tradition elucidate the essential nature (*ngo bo gsal bar mdzad*) of yuganaddha (i.e., buddha-nature) by teaching emptiness (*stong pa nyid bstan pa'i sgo nas*), mainly as *via negationis*, whereas Mahāyāna scriptures of the Final Promulgation and of the Maitreya and Asaṅga tradition elucidate its natural texture (*rang bzhin gsal bar mdzad*), mainly as *via affirmationis*.[148] This is also true in Tibet of the writings of Intrinsic Emptyists such as Tsongkhapa and of Extrinsic Emptyists or zhentong proponents such as Dolpopa.[149] Of the Cittamātric and Madhyamic systems, the only point of objection that he sees in the former is its clinging to auto-luminous cognition devoid of subject-object) dichotomy (*gnyis stong gi shes pa rang gsal*) as hypostatically existent.[150] In the particular case of the Madhyamic systems, Svātantrika-Madhyamaka is said to establish the ontological *xy*-yuganaddha gradually or sequentially and in conformance with the prajñāic yuganaddha, whereas Prāsaṅgika-Madhyamaka to do so all at once, from the very outset (*dang po nas*), and in conformance with jñānaic yuganaddha.[151]

Similarly, sūtric Mahāyāna or Pāramitāyāna and mantric Mahāyāna are said to differ in the way yuganaddha is put into practice. According to the sūtric method, yuganaddha is put into practice through analytical acumen (*yid dpyod kyis bsgom pa*) and the four extremes constitutive of *x* and *y* are eliminated turn by turn (*res 'jog gi tshul du*), whereas according to the mantric method, it becomes manifest by compulsive means (*thabs kyis btsan thabs su shar*).[152]

Taking for granted a doxographical or systemic hierarchy, Mipam maintains that elements of defectiveness or limitation found in the "lower" systems are removed or compensated for by the "higher" systems.[153] That is, a subtle limitation of the Svātantrika-Madhyamaka system is "the elements [in it] of clinging to the separateness of the twofold truth" (*bden gnyis so sor zhen pa'i cha*), which is a negandum (*dgag bya*) for the Prāsaṅgika-Madhyamaka system.[154] A subtle limitation of the sūtric system such as Prāsaṅgika-Madhyamaka is the "elements [in it] of clinging to emptiness" (*stong par zhen pa*), which is compensated for by the doctrine of "great bliss" (*mahāsukha, bde ba chen po*) taught by the mantric Mahāyāna.[155] How about the differences among various mantric systems? For him, these systems differ in the manner in which certainty regarding the yuganaddha is gained.[156] In a similar vein, Rongzompa has stated that the indivisibility of the twofold reality (*bden pa gnyis dbyer med*)—"coequality" (*mnyam pa nyid*) or "viewing [all phenomena] as being coequal" (*mnyam par lta ba*)—has been taught in both sūtric scriptures of definitive sense (*nges pa'i don gyi mdo sde*) and in mantric scriptures. The difference between the two, however, is that the former does not teach the "means of practicing coequality" (*mnyam par sgrub pa'i thabs*). The difference among the six mantric systems lies in the quality of the view of coequality, which is inversely proportional to the degree of clinging to a substantialist view (*dngos por lta ba'i zhen pa*) or a view of inequality (*mi mnyam par lta ba*).[157] One of the differences between exoteric (*phyi pa*) and esoteric (*nang pa*) tantric systems is said to be that the practitioners of the former "grasp the two modes of reality alternately" (*bden gnyis res 'jog tu 'dzin par byed*) and are incapable of "meditating on the yuganaddha of utpattikrama and utpannakrama" without alternating (*res 'jog med par*) from one to the other. Whereas the practitioners of the latter are able to meditate on the yuganaddha of utpattikrama and utpannakrama in the form of "great self-occurring gnosis, characterized by the indivisibility of the [twofold] reality" (*bden pa dbyer med rang byung gi ye shes chen po*) and attain in one lifetime "Vajradharahood characterized by yuganaddha" (*zung 'jug rdo rje 'chang gi 'go 'phang*).[158] The distinction among the three esoteric tantric systems is said to be based on their means of accessing self-occurring gnosis,[159] as in the Sarma tantric traditions, where "yuganaddha reality" (*zung 'jug gi don*) is established by all the highest tantric systems, and yet a distinction can be made on the basis of the explicitness of, or emphasis on, the "gnosis of the fourth initiation" (*dbang bzhi pa'i ye shes*).[160] In short, the difference is not really about whether the ontological *xy*-yuganaddha is taught at all but *how x* and *y*, which together constitute both the ontological and gnoseological forms of yuganaddha, have been explicated, established, and realized, or on which pole (*x* or *y*) the accent lies.

Yuganaddha of Nature and Yuganaddha of Nurture

Another way of classifying the types of the yuganaddha concept identifiable in Mipam's writings would to be to divide it into the "yuganaddha of nature" and the "yuganaddha of nurture." That is, in the former type, the *x* and *y* that constitute the yuganaddha are innately and essentially one, and the relation between the two variables must be one defined by their identicality and simultaneity.[161] The separation of *x* and *y* in this case is always mere conceptual or conventional and never actual. All those discourses about *x* and *y* are thus mere means of gaining a cognitive access to *xy*-yuganaddha.[162] In the latter type, however, *x* and *y* may initially have different origins or be two separate entities, and hence the desired *xy*-yuganaddha may have to be acquired or nurtured through effort and practice.[163] A recognition of the two types of *xy*-yuganaddha, one based on a natural relationship and another based on an artificial relationship, may help us subsume various kinds of *xy*-yuganaddha that can be traced in Buddhist sources. Of the two types, Mipam generally seems to have held the yuganaddha of nature—which he seems to identify with the metaphysical or ontological yuganaddha at the level of the ground with which the view is linked—to be philosophically speaking the most significant. He also tends to see the buddhological yuganaddha at the level of spiritual goal as yuganaddha of nature, inasmuch as, for him, buddhahood must have an identity of totality and integrality of some kind. The yuganaddha at the level of the spiritual path seems to be considered yuganaddha of nurture—inasmuch as, for instance, the yuganaddha of the two types of accumulation, namely, of beneficial resources and of gnosis, must be acquired or cultivated through spiritual practice. Importantly, however, the preference for (or prominence of) the yuganaddha of nature and the yuganaddha of nurture seems to be determined by the type of soteriological model proposed or presupposed. Accordingly, as Mipam ascends the hierarchical staircase of Buddhist doxographies, the concept of yuganaddha of nature seems to play for him an increasingly important role, even as the concept of yuganaddha of nurture retreats into the background.

Ontological Yuganaddha and Gnoseological Yuganaddha

A careful observation of Mipam's use of the term yuganaddha in various contexts reveals that he presupposes two kinds of genuine yuganaddha, namely, ontological (or ontic) yuganaddha and gnoseological (or gnostic) yuganaddha, which together would be coextensive with the ground, path, and goal yuganaddha we have seen earlier. Ontological yuganaddha should be understood here as the ultimate true reality, which has gnoseological yuganaddha as its ultimate cognitive subject, whereas gnoseological yuganaddha as the direct meditative insight that has ontological yuganaddha as its direct cognitive object.[164] But although there is an object-subject relationship between the two, there is said to be no subject-object dichotomy involved. In other words, ontic yuganaddha is said to be cognized by gnostic yuganaddha in such a way that the two mingle into one singular point. The real fusion of the two can be said to happen at the *buddhabhūmi*, for which reason the goal yuganaddha is also characterized as "the to-be-attained indivisibility of ground and goal" (*'thob bya gzhi 'bras dbyer med*). Importantly, the yuganaddha relationship—the relationship of indivisibility between *x* and *y*—underlying gnoseological yuganaddha is to be distinguished from such a relationship between the *x* and *y* of ontological yuganaddha. That is, *x* and *y* in an ontological yuganaddha must be something like "appearance" and "emptiness" following the "twofold-reality mode" and thus must not involve a subject-object relationship, whereas the relationship between *x* and *y* in a gnoseological yuganaddha seems to be always defined as an subject-object relationship, though again never an subject-object dichotomy.

The two kinds of yuganaddha can be comparable to the one between what I elsewhere called "ontological" and "gnoseological" bodhicitta,[165] or, perhaps to the two kinds of nirvāṇa, namely, "nirvāṇa characterized by natural purity" (*rang bzhin rnam dag gyi myang 'das*) and "nirvāṇa characterized by freedom from adventitious impurities" (*glo bu dri bral gyi myang 'das*)[166]—so to speak, intrinsically pure nirvāṇa and extrinsically pure nirvāṇa—which Lambert Schmithausen once aptly described as "nirvāṇa as a metaphysical entity" (*das Nirvāṇa als metaphysische Größe*) and "nirvāṇa as a spiritual event" (*das Nirvāṇa als spirituelles Ereignis*).[167] Other classifications, such as of the Yogācāra's "perfect nature" (*pariniṣpanna, yongs grub*) into "unchanging pariniṣpanna" (*'gyur med yongs grub*) and "unerring pariniṣpanna" (*phyin ci ma log pa'i yongs grub*),[168] are also very much reminiscent of the classification of yuganaddha in ontological and gnoseological terms.

Synonyms of Yuganaddha

Synonyms (*ming gi rnam grangs*) of ontological and gnoseological yuganaddha, which for Mipam always represent the genuine yuganaddha, may be discussed here briefly. In general, when talking about the synonyms of yuganaddha, it is particularly important to bear in mind that whether or not one and the same pertinent technical term denotes the same semantic referent (*tshig gi yul*) is always to be determined contextually and never mechanically. For example, whether a term *y* only stands for the quasi-ultimate true reality—which is usually a mere absence or negation of *x*, which in turn is particularly for Mipam only on a par and forming a pair with *x*—or whether it stands for the *xy*-yuganaddha (the bona fide true reality) has to be determined carefully, on the basis of context. Although these may share the same name or represent namesakes (*ming gcig*)—let us say *y* and *Y*—there is a "sky-and-earth-like difference" (*khyad par gnam sa bzhin*) between the two.[169] Rongzompa, too, has already stated something to the same effect.[170]

In particular, given a myriad of terms and expressions employed by Mipam either as synonyms or attributes of yuganaddha, there seems to be a need to systematize and explain them according to a certain set of more or less overlapping criteria or factors. First, the manner in which yuganaddha is said to have been taught—that is, either by way of negation or by way of affirmation[171]—may be one factor that would explain the various synonyms. That is, in theory one employs both *x* (e.g., *snang tsam* "mere appearance") and *y* (e.g., *rang bzhin ma grub pa* "absence of an essential nature") as synonyms of *xy*-yuganaddha, although *xy*-yuganaddha (or often simply great *Y*) is in reality always greater than both *x* and *y*. The complementarity, coequality, and thus in the end synonymy of *x* and *y* seems to have been extremely important for Mipam.[172] Second, although ontological yuganaddha in itself can never be distinguished in terms of its nature (*ngo bo*), it can be expressed in various forms and terms on the basis of "the property bearer (i.e., entity or reality), which is the substrate of emptiness" (*stong gzhi chos can*).[173] Thus, according to Mipam, one speaks of two kinds of true reality (*tathatā*, *de bzhin nyid*), namely, "intrinsically pure true reality" (*rang bzhin rnam dag gi de bzhin nyid*) and "extrinsically pure true reality" (*glo bur bral dag gi de bzhin nyid*); or "maculate true reality" (*dri bcas kyi de bzhin nyid*) and "immaculate true reality" (*dri med kyi de bzhin nyid*); or "true reality [on the level of the] ontological ground" (*gzhi'i de bzhin nyid*) and "true reality [on the level of the] soteriological path" (*lam gyi de bzhin nyid*), and "true reality [on the level of the] soteriological goal" (*'bras bu'i de bzhin nyid*);[174] or, the "nonessentiality of person[hood]" (*gang zag gi bdag med pa*) and the "nonessentiality of phenomena" (*chos kyi bdag med pa*).[175] One also speaks of three or four means of salvific release (*rnam thar sgo gsum* or *bzhi*), corresponding to the emptiness of the cause, result, and nature (*rgyu 'bras ngo bo nyid gsum stong pas cha nas*), namely, the "signlessness of causes" (*rgyu mtshan ma med pa*), the "aspirationlessness toward [any] result" (*'bras bu smon ma med pa*), and the "emptiness of essence" (*ngo bo stong pa nyid*), and "nonconditioned luminously pure nature" (*rang bzhin 'od gsal 'dus ma byas pa*). Similarly, the sixteen, four, eighteen, or twenty kinds of emptiness are said to be distinguished not qualitatively but rather in terms of the substrate of emptiness, which is the bearer of the property that is emptiness (*stong gzhi chos can*).[176] Though not made explicit by Mipam, various forms of *xy*-yuganaddha[177] seem to be distinguished or distinguishable on the basis of the "property bearer, the substrate of emptiness" (*stong gzhi chos can*). That is, *xy*-yuganaddha is established by usually taking *x* as the "property bearer" (*chos can*) and *y* as the "property" (*chos* or *chos nyid*), but should the need be felt to "hypostatize" or attribute a real identity to true reality—to, as it were, "prapañcicize" (i.e., turning true reality into a mental fabrication [*prapañca*], which actually is always *niṣprapañca*)—any entity or reality can be made a "property bearer, the substrate of emptiness" (*stong gzhi chos can*) and its emptiness can be established. That would explain why we have the concept of the "emptiness of emptiness" (*śūnyatāśūnyatā*, *stong pa nyid stong pa nyid*). The problem of *regressus ad infinitum* can be avoided with the argument that a full conceptual or perceptual penetration of ontological or gnoseological *xy*-yuganaddha, which is characterized by niṣprapañca (an absence of prapañca), should be able to lay all prapañcas to complete rest, the result being a "cessation of [subjective / objective] manifoldness" (*prapañcopaśama*, *spros pa nye bar zhi ba*).[178] Thus both *x* and *y* as substrates of emptiness (*stong gzhir byas nas*) and *xy*-yuganaddha,[179] which can also be represented as *Y*, always transcend *x* and *y*.[180] In the case of the Mahāyoga concept of what is known as the "higher conventional truth" (*lhag pa'i kun rdzob kyi bden pa*) and "higher absolute truth" (*lhag pa'i don dam bden pa*), each of the two is said to exist inseparably as appearance and emptiness (*snang stong 'du bral med par gnas*) and thus as the yuganaddha of appearance and emptiness (*snang stong zung 'jug*).[181]

Third, though qualitatively never coequal, yuganaddha may be referred to with different terms on the basis of the sequence of a person's gaining cognitive access to (*gang zag gi blo 'jug pa'i rim pa*) yuganaddha, that is, in terms of the manner of realization (*rtogs tshul gyi dbang du byas*). The classification of the absolute into quasi-absoluteness (*rnam grangs pa'i don dam*) or quasi-emptiness (*rnam grangs pa'i stong nyid*) and actual absoluteness (*rnam grangs ma yin pa'i don dam*) or actual emptiness (*rnam grangs ma yin pa'i stong nyid*) is said to meet this criterion.[182] It is also clear that the ontological yuganaddha expressed by the notion of the "four phases of the rise [of ascertainment regarding ontological] madhyamaka" (*dbu ma'i 'char rim bzhi*)[183]—namely, śūnyatā, yuganaddha, niṣprapañca, and samatā (*mnyam pa nyid*)—has been conceived not along the line of what is established but rather *how* it is established.

Fourth, as has been previously suggested, doxographical systems (*siddhānta*, *grub mtha'*), vehicles, religious traditions (*chos lugs*), and personal predilections affect the employment of and preference for individual terms standing for yuganaddha. Some terms may be commonly used by many systems, whereas others are unique to a certain system. Naturally, older and purportedly "lower" systems do not contain terms unique to later and purportedly "higher" systems. Whereas the "higher" and later systems presuppose terms found in "lower" and older systems. For Mipam, the one true reality has been, with respect to its emptiness (*stong pa nyid kyi cha nas*), referred to in the Prajñāpāramitā scriptures as dharmadhātu, *bhūtakoṭi*, tathatā, and so on. With respect to the presence of the appearance of bodies and gnosis (*sku dang ye shes kyi snang ba dang bcas pa'i cha nas*), it has been referred to as buddha-nature in the Tathāgatagarbha scriptures; and in the tantras, it has been referred to as the "primordial (ontological) ground maṇḍala, characterized by the indivisibility of [the two modes of reality] of appearance and emptiness and having the nature of great purity and equality" (*snang stong bden pa dbyer med dag mnyam chen po'i bdag nyid gdod ma gzhi'i dkyil 'khor*).[184] One of the numerous synonyms or near-synonyms of yuganaddha, the term *svayaṃbhūjñāna* (self-occurring gnosis)[185] came to be used profusely in the Nyingma tradition. The idea, too, of "emptiness endowed with all excellent features,"[186] understood by Mipam as a synonym of ontological and gnoseological yuganaddha, plays a crucial role in his philosophy of Yuganaddhavāda.

Conclusion

In sum, what I have attempted here is to paint as accurate a picture as possible of Mipam's Yuganaddhavāda philosophy. While a diachronic or historical view of his philosophy still requires further investigation, it is hoped that our synchronic view of it has now become fairly clear. It may also be stated by way of conclusion that while Mipam's monistic thoughts are deeply rooted in the tradition that precedes him and are profoundly influenced by his predecessors Rongzompa and

Longchenpa,[187] in terms of a high degree of persistency and consistency with which he pursued his monistic agenda as his lifelong and overarching enterprise, we can indeed speak of his innovation. Mipam's philosophy of Yuganaddhavāda seems to be based on the fundamental assumption that an *Ansicht*-based discord among various persons and factions would only give way to *Einsicht*-based concord[188] when they gained insight into the ultimate true reality, namely, the ontological yuganaddha. It is only then and there that the ideological differences, and the conflicts based on them, would come to be resolved and dissolved naturally. That is why beings such as buddhas and siddhas begin to think with one intent (*dgongs pa gcig*) and speak with one voice (*dbyangs gcig*).

Notes

I would like to thank Philip Pierce who, despite having a long waiting list of editorial work, corrected my English and made valuable comments and suggestions.

1. Duckworth, *Mipam on Buddha-Nature.*

2. Wangchuk, "Was Mipam a Dialectical Monist? 35.

3. A few technical notes may be warranted here. First, although it would have been desirable to examine Indian and early Tibetan sources that underlie Mipam's monistic and harmonistic ideas—mainly in order to observe the historical development of the Yuganaddhavāda philosophy—the emphasis has been laid not so much upon tracing and explaining the history of his ideas as on determining his philosophy. In other words, the aim has been not so much to provide a diachronic as a synchronic view of his Yuganaddhavāda philosophy. Second, although I occasionally do point out similar ideas found in some Indian and early Tibetan (mainly Rongzompa's) writings, the focus has been on identifying more than one parallel source in Mipam's writings so as to consolidate our understanding of his positions. Third, with regard to the choice of sources, emphasis has been laid on primary Tibetan sources, and mainly Mipam's own writings. For want of time, references to only one version or edition of the sources have been given. A secondary source that may be mentioned here is Broido, "Padma-dkar-po on Integration," which is perhaps the only study devoted exclusively to the idea of yuganaddha. Apparently, the idea of yuganaddha also played a key role in Prajñāraśmi's alias Trengpo Terton Sherab Ozer's (1518–1584) nonsectarian (*ris med*) mode of thinking (for which see Deroche, *Prajñāraśmi*). Fourth, a general investigation of the philosophy and history of the idea of yuganaddha, taking into account various interpretations of yuganaddha by various Tibetan Buddhist traditions and scholars, though desirable, would seem to be an immensely difficult task, and hence it appears to be sensible at this point to try to determine some particular Tibetan scholar's understanding of yuganaddha—one whose position is in general regarded as authoritative and representative by his order.

4. Mipam, *'Od snying* 256.3; compare *Rgyud bla'i mchan* 73.6: *dbyings rig dbyer med kyi khams*; *Gnyug sems zur dpyad* 277.6: *dbyings rig dbyer med kyi gnas lugs.* For a discussion of the term *zung 'jug* and its various renderings in English, see Broido, "Padma-dkar-po on Integration" 5–8.

5. Mipam, *'Od snying* 164.6–165.1: *bdag gnyis kyis stong pa'i dbyings dang zung du zhugs pa'i snang ba rnams*; *Dbu ma rgyan 'grel* 371.2–3: *tha snyad dang don dam pa'i bden pa gnyis zung du zhugs pa'i lam tshul.*

6. Mipam, *Dbu ma rgyan 'grel* 362.4: *bden gnyis zung du chud tshul*; *Rgyud bla'i mchan* 27.4: *snang stong zung du chud*; *Mngon rtogs rgyan 'grel* 404.5, 417.5: *bden gnyis zung*

du chud pa'i sgo nas lam sgrub pa; *Dbu ma rgyan 'grel* 472.6: *mnyam rjes dbyer med bden gnyis zung du chud*; *Sdud 'grel* 9.4: *bden gnyis zung du chud pa*; *Sdud 'grel mdo sbyar* 220.6: *bden gnyis zung du chud pa*; compare *Stong thun seng ge* 196.5.

7. It may be noted that Rongzompa also employs the expression *zung du 'brel ba* on several occasions. See, for example, his *Rgyud spyi'i dngos po*. Almogi, *Rong-zom-pa's Discourses on Buddhology* 369: *sngags zhes bya ba ni / thabs dang shes rab zung du 'brel ba'i bdag nyid la bya ste*; *Lta 'grel* (as cited in Wangchuk, *Resolve to Become a Buddha* 132 n. 160): *byang chub kyi sems ni mdor bsdu' na shes rab dang snying rje zung du 'brel ba'o*. He does not, however, seem to employ the expression *zung 'jug* or *zung du 'jug pa* to refer to the ontological yuganaddha but instead prefers the synonymous expression *dbyer med pa*.

8. Mipam, *Nges sgron* 525.3–4: *des na snga 'gyur ring lugs 'dir / gzhi lam 'bras bu'i chos skad la / rtag dang mi rtag bden gnyis sogs / rgya chad phyogs lhung bral ba yi / zung 'jug kho na'i grub mtha' skyong*. See also his *Bstan rgyas* 699.2: *yod med phyogs rer zhen pa'i dmigs gtad zhig / mthar 'dzin lta ba'i 'dzin stang [sic] drung nas phyung / gzhi lam 'bras bus [sic] snang stong zung du 'jug / mtsho skyes rgyal ba'i bstan pa*; *Rab gsal brtsad lan* 521.6–522.1: *bdag cag gi lugs la chos kyi dbyings zhes pa med dgag phyang chad tsam min par snang stong zung 'jug gam rnam kun mchog ldan gyi stong nyid yin pas / gzhi lam 'bras bu'i skabs kun tu ya gyal med pa'i kha yar ba nam yang mi 'dod do*.

9. The expression *thig le nyag gcig* is employed by Mipam, for example, in his *'Od snying* 173.3, 265.5, 307.5; *Bka' brgyad* 602.2, 672.4; *Sdud 'grel* 60.6, 61.2, 99.6; *Stong thun seng ge* 197.6, 208.5; *Gsung sgros* 916.6; *Ye shes ral gri* 480.2; *Grub bsdus* 668.5; *Gnyug sems zur dpyad* 277.4, 325.4–6; *Lta phreng mchan 'grel* 43.5. For the idea of the object of cognition (*shes bya*) being fused with the cognition (*shes pa*), see, for instance, his *Ye grub ut pal* 496.6: *shes bya spros med de nyid dang / dbyer med ye shes rnam 'dres pa / de nyid sangs rgyas thams cad kyi / ye shes chos sku zhes byar brjod*; *Mchog grub ut pal* 487.1–2: *shes dang shes byar dbyer med par / chos kyi dbyings las ma g.yos pas / de bzhin gshegs pa mthar thug ni / ye shes rdo rje sku zhes bya*. Compare how Rongzompa explains the view of the Dzokchen in terms of the ontological bodhicitta, described as "one great point of singularity" (*thig le chen po gcig*), for example, in his *Theg tshul* 492.21–22: *chos thams cad byang chub kyi sems thig le chen po gcig gi rang bzhin du sangs rgyas par lta'o*.

10. Mipam, *bKa' brgyad* 601.6: *dbyings ye dbyer med*; compare *Bka' brgyad* 609.4–5: *snang stong thabs shes bden gnyis dbyings ye rnams gnyis su med pa*.

11. Rongzompa, *Mtshan brjod 'grel pa* 261.8–9: *dbyings dang ye shes zung du 'brel ba*; *Theg tshul* 502.15: *dbyings dang ye shes gnyis su myed pa'i rig pa*; *Dkon mchog 'grel* 143.20, 150.7–8: *dbyings dang ye shes gnyis su med pa*. Also noted in Almogi, *Rong-zom-pa's Discourses on Buddhology* 232 n. 144. Almogi also points out there that "[i]n view of Rong-zom-pa's rejection of any cognitive feature within self-occurring gnosis or the dharmadhātu, it will be worthwhile to examine how he understands the notion of the 'non-duality of the sphere and gnosis' (*dbyings dang ye shes gnyis su med pa*), which he clearly seems to profess." An attempt on my part to explain Rongzompa's idea of *dbyings dang ye shes zung du 'brel ba* or *dbyings dang ye shes gnyis su med pa* would be that for him, a gnostic (or jñānaic) cognition, whose existence as such he does not deny, would prevail, as long as it lasts free of all subject-object dichotomy. Such an explanation is supported by his use of the expression *dbyings dang ye shes gnyis su myed pa'i rig pa*.

12. Mipam, *Nges sgron* 512. 1–2: *chos kun de nyid gcig yin cing / de nyid mthong ba'i tshul gcig pas / mthar thug theg gcig sgrub pa yi / rigs pa klu sgrub yab sras smra*; *Ketaka* 90.3–5; *Gsung sgros* 770.1, 790.2; *Sdud 'grel* 6.4: *mthar thug theg gcig*; *Sdud 'grel* 29.4: *mthar thug theg pa gcig*; *'Od snying* 177.6: *mthar thug theg pa gcig*; *Stong thun seng ge* 194.3–6;

Mngon rtogs rgyan 'grel 476.5–477.6; *Rgyud bla'i mchan* 94.2, where he also alludes to the *Saddharmapuṇḍarīka Sūtra* and *Mahāparinirvāṇa Sūtra*; *Sa skya'i dri lan* 600.2: *rigs can rnam gsum sna tshogs theg pas brtul / nges pa'i don du mthar thug theg gcig bstan*. The issue of *ekayāna* is discussed often in the context of the question whether śrāvakas and pratyekabuddhas realize or cognize the nonessentiality of phenomena (*dharmanairātmya*, *chos kyi bdag med pa*). For Mipam's position on this issue, see his *Nges sgron* 507.6–50124; *Dbu ma rgyan 'grel* 685.2–689.2; *Zla ba'i zhal lung* 218.2–223.4. For a discussion of the *ekayāna* theory, see Wangchuk, *Resolve to Become a Buddha* 111–112.

13. Rongzompa, *Dkon mchog 'grel* 46.20–22: *'di ltar 'phags pa rtogs chen phyag rgya pa las / theg pa ni gcig tu bas te / gnyis dang gsum du ma mchis so / zhes gsungs pa lta bu ste / 'di ltar yang dag par rdzogs pa'i sangs rgyas gcig kho na'o*. Cited in Wangchuk, *Resolve to Become a Buddha* 112 n. 30. Compare his *Theg tshul* 473.17–474.8, where the Dzokchen system is claimed to be the "zenith of all vehicles," or rather, the "best of all ways" (*theg pa thams cad kyi yang rtse*), with the argument that the "best way is that which [needs] no walking" (*bgrod du med pa nyid lam gyi mchog*).

14. Duckworth, *Mipam on Buddha-Nature* xi. Wangchuk, "Was Mipam a Dialectical Monist?" 36.

15. The two different satyadvaya models (*bden gnyis 'jog tshul gnyis*) have been mentioned (and discussed in varying detail) by Mipam in his (1) *Dbu ma rgyan 'grel* (366.3–368.5; (2) *Rab gsal brtsad lan* 442.4–443.2; (3) *Brag dkar brgal lan* 243.6–245.1; (4) *Gzhi'i le'u'i tshig 'grol* 753.2–6; (5) *Gzhan stong seng ge* 221.2–223.5; (6) *Gsung sgros* 785.1–786.6. The discussion in the *Gzhan stong seng ge* is particularly useful, since it explains at length the practical application of the second model, which is not always clear. To my knowledge (cf. Phuntsho, *Mipham's Dialectics* 114), these two models have not been explicated by Mipam in his *Nges sgron* or *Shes rab ral gri*. Some of these sources have been provided also in Almogi, *Rong-zom-pa's Discourses on Buddhology* 199 n. 32.

16. Botrul in his *Lta grub shan 'byed* fols. 5b6–6a1 employs the terms *snang stong bden gnyis* or *snang stong chos kyi bden gnyis* and *gnas snang bden gnyis* or *gnas snang chos kyi bden gnyis*. See also Phuntsho, *Mipham's Dialectics* 174. Interestingly, even though Je Gendun Rinchen (1926–1997), adopts Botrul's expression *gnas snang chos kyi bden gnyis*, he also employs the term *snang stong rten 'byung bden gnyis*. See Schwerk, *Spiegel der Sichtweise* 95–96. Note, however, that the expressions *snang stong gi bden gnyis* (*Gzhan stong seng ge*, 223.2; *gSung sgros*, 785.6) and *gnas snang mthun mi mthun gyi dbang du byas pa'i bden gnyis* or *gnas snang gi dbang gis bden gnyis 'jog tshul* (*Gsung sgros*, 786.4, 797.2) are employed by Mipam himself. The two satyadvaya models have been briefly presented in German in Wangchuk, "Madhyamaka" 221–222.

17. See the *Zla ba'i zhal lung* 68.2–72.2, where Mipam justifies at length why the relation between *x* and *y* should be *ngo bo gcig la ldog pa tha dad*. In his *Mngon rtogs rgyan 'grel* 419.5–6, he states that on the absolute level (*don dam du*), *x* and *y* are beyond being identical or separate. On the conventional level, the *x-y* relationship is one of *ngo bo gcig la ldog pa tha dad*, and the *x-xy* relationship is one of *gcig pa bkag pa'i tha dad*. See also his *Gsung sgros* 807.5–811.5; *Mkhas 'jug* 52.2–5; and in addition his *Nges sgron* 526.2–3: *yang dag dypod pa'i shes rab ngor / snang dang stong pa 'di gnyis po des yod mnyam med mnyam ngo bo gcig / ldog pa tha dad dbye bar 'dod*. In general, Mipam's deliberations on the question "Which of the two modes of reality is the prime?" (*bden pa gnyis las gang zhig gtso*) in his *Nges sgron* 524.2–529.2 can be seen as an attempt to determine the *x-y*

relationship presupposed in a natural yuganaddha. For Mipam's allusion to the idea found in the *Sandhinirmocana Sūtra* that positing the absolute and the conventional to be either identical (*gcig*) or separate (*tha dad*) would have four undesirable consequences (*skyon bzhi bzhi dag*), see his *Ketaka* 45.4–5; *Dbu ma rgyan 'grel* 371.1–3; *Stong thun seng ge* 195.3–4; *Mngon rtogs rgyan 'grel* 419.1–420.1; *Gnyug sems zur dpyad* 239.1–4; *Gnyug sems shan 'byed* 83.6–84.1; *Mdo sde rgyan 'grel* 101.3; compare *Nges sgron* 541.5–6: *gnas snang phan tshul 'gal ba na / bden gnyis tha dad skyon bzhi 'bab / gnas snang phan tshul gzhan min na / bden gnyis gcig pa'i skyon bzhis gnod.*

18. Rongzompa has stated that of the Three Jewels (*dkon mchog gsum*), buddha and *saṃgha* are specifications (*bye brag*) of *jñāna*, while dharmas are? their / dharma is its? dharmatā. In this context, he defines the relationship between jñāna and dharmatā by stating that on the mere conventional level (*kun rdzob tsam du*), jñāna and dharmatā—as relating "property" (*chos*) to "property bearer" (*chos can*)—are essentially one (*bdag nyid gcig pa*), but on the absolute level (*don dam par*) they are without duality (*gnyis su med (pa)*), inasmuch as they are characterized by the absence of all subjective and objective manifoldness. See his *Dkon mchog 'grel* 223.16–23.

19. Mipam, *Brag dkar brgal lan* 244.4: *'di dag gi lugs la bden gnyis kyang gcig pa bkag pa'i tha dad du bzhed do*; *Gzhan stong seng ge* 223.1–3: *de lta na don dam rang ngos mi stong zer ba 'di rnam pa kun tu bden gnyis phyi ma'i 'jog tshul ltar byas te / bden pa gnyis po gcig pa bkag pa'i tha dad du khas len pa la go dgos kyi / snang stong gi bden gnyis ngo bo gcig la ldog pa tha dad kyi 'jog tshul ltar go ba de gtan min no.*

20. To explain the second satyadvaya model on the basis of the "pauper-prince" analogy: if the citizen "pauper" (object) and the "misconception / misperception" of him (subject) were the *saṃvṛtisatya*, the prince (object) and the cognition / recognition (subject) of him as such would be the *paramārthasatya*. One can still posit a yuganaddha (*zung 'jug*) or indivisibility (*dbyer med*) relationship between the saṃvṛtisatya and paramārthasatya with the argument that not only has our "(ruled) pauper" always been our "(ruling) prince," he has even been in reality perceived without being recognized as such. This understanding is secured by Mipam, who provides the "rope-snake" analogy. See his *Gzhan stong seng ge* 223.5–224.1: *tha snyad du dper bya na thag khra lta bu la don dam bden pa / sbrul lta bu kun rdzob bden par bzhag dgos te / gcig tha dad du grub pa dang / gcig ma grub pa'i khyad par phyed dgos kyi gnyis ka 'khrul pa dang / gnyis ka bden pa yin mi srid pa bzhin no.* For two references to the prince analogy, see Wangchuk, "rDzogs-chen Meditation" 175 n. 57.

21. Mipam, *Sngags kyi ral gri* 477.4: *gal te nyon mongs nyid grub na / spang dang bsgyur ba yongs mi nus / ma grub phyir na nyon mongs ni / sgyu 'dra don na ma grub cing.*

22. Mipam, *Dka' gnad ci rigs* 374.6, 675.3; *Gzhi'i le'u'i tshig 'grol* 750.4, 755.1; *Bka' brgyad* 608.1. Mipam does not seem to employ the term *'khor 'das zung 'jug*, although we do find it being used by Kunkhyen Pema Karpo (1527–1592). See Broido, "Padma-dkar-po on Integration" 32.

23. Mipam, *Sa skya'i dri lan* 603.5–6: *phar phyin theg par 'khor 'das mnyam nyid spros bral du bshad pa yod cing de dang mngon du rtogs pa ni dag sa gsum gyi khyad chos te / srid zhi mnyam nyid rtogs pa sogs dag sa gsum gyi skabs na bshad pas so /* . Compare the *Nges sgron* 519.4–5: *'khor dang mya ngan 'das pa la / don du bzang ngan yod ma yin / bzang ngan med par mnyam nyid du / rtogs pa nges shes bzang po yin.*

24. Mipam, *Gzhi'i le'u'i tshig 'grol* 756.1: *srid zhi mnyam pa nyid*; *Stong thun seng ge* 189.5; *Gzhan stong seng ge* 229.6–230.1; *Gsung sgros* 781.1, 897.6; *Sdud 'grel* 144.4: *srid zhi*

mnyam nyid; *Sdud 'grel mdo sbyar* 302.1; *Mngon rtogs rgyan 'grel* 407.1. Although we do encounter the term *srid zhi zung 'jug* being used, for example, by Pema Karpo (Broido, "Padma-dkar-po on Integration" 33), Mipam does not seem to employ it.

25. The idea of *'khor 'das dbyer med*, *'khor 'das mnyam nyid*, or *srid zhi mnyam nyid* can be also traced in Rongzompa's works. See, for example, *Dkon mchog 'grel* 49.4: *kun nas nyon mongs pa dang rnam par byang ba dbyer med pa*; *Dkon mchog 'grel* 53.13–14: *'khor ba dang mya ngan las 'das pa'i chos thams cad rdo rje ltar dbyer med pa*; compare *Dkon mchog 'grel* 61.24–62.1: *'khor ba dang mya ngan las 'das pas bsdus pa'i chos thams cad gdod ma nas dbyer med pa*; *Gsung thor bu* 39.5–6: *kun nas nyon mongs pa dang rnam par byang ba'i chos dbyer med pa*; *Grub mtha'i brjed byang* 208.14–15: *'khor ba dang mya ngan las 'das pa gnyis su med pa*; *Lta 'grel* 338.1–3: *kund nas nyon mongs pa'i chos 'khor ba rgyu dang 'bras bur bcas pa thams cad dang / rnam par byang ba'i chos mya ngan las 'das pa' rgyu dang 'bras bur bcas pa thams cad dbyer myed*.

26. See Mipam's *Gzhan stong seng ge* 229.4–223.1, where he explains the logic behind the concept of *srid zhi mnyam nyid*. The expression also occurs in the *Nges sgron* 507.1; *'Od snying* 157.1–2; *rGyud bla'i mchan* 95.6; *Dbu ma rgyan 'grel* 722.6; *Mngon rtogs rgyan 'grel* 407.1; *Mkhas 'jug* 186.6; *Sdom byang* 368.5: *srid zhi mnyam nyid zhing dag sbyor /* .

27. Rongzompa, *Lta 'grel* 326.1–9; *Dkon mchog 'grel* 57.4–8: *de kho na nyid ces pa ni / spyir don la phyin ci ma log pas de kho na nyid ces bya ste / de yang mi 'gyur ba dang / don la mi bslu ba'o / de la mi 'gyur ba'i sgo nas ni / chos thams cad kyi de bzhin nyid ni rtag tu ji ltar ba bzhin nyid de / 'di la 'gyur ba med pas de bzhin nyid ces bya'o / de rtogs pa'i ye shes kyang don dang mthun par skye ste / 'di la bslu ba med pas de kho na nyid ces bya'o*. Compare this with the use of the expressions *'bras bu don dam*, *ye shes don dam*, and *dbyings don dam* in Mipam's *'Od snying* 125.2.

28. The following verses should show that Mipam was through and through a Pramāṇavādin (*Shes rab ral gri*, 440.2–3): *tshad ma tshad min ma dpyad par / 'jig rten mthong ba tsam zhig gis / don dam nyid la 'jig ce na / de ltar bkag pa med mod kyi / 'di las 'di 'byung mthong ba ni / 'jig rten pa yi mngon sum la / de rten don dpog rjes dpag phyir / ming ma btags kyang don mi spong*. See also *Shes rab ral gri* 445.3: *tshad mar gyur pa rgyal ba'i gsung / tshad ma dag gis grub pas na / tshad ma'i lam nas nges bskyed pas / tshad ma'i gsung gis bden 'bras mthong*. See also the *Dbu ma rgyan 'grel* 614.3–615.4, where Mipam vehemently defends the necessity of *dngos po'i stobs zhugs kyi rigs pa* (*vastubalanyāya*) or *dngos po stobs zhugs* (*vastubalapravṛtta*) in general and particularly in Buddhist philosophy (*ādhyātmikavidyā*; *adhyātmavidyā*, *nang rig pa*).

29. Mipam, *Ketaka* 45.1–2. Note that here he cites the famous Sūtric verse that serves as a locus classicus of the twofold truth, which is also cited twice by Candrakīrti in his *Madhyamakāvatārabhāṣya*, once indicating the *Pitāputrasamāgama Sūtra* (*Madhyamakāvatārabhāṣya*, 70.5–9) as the source and once the *Tattvanirdeśasamādhi Sūtra* (*ibid*., 174.7–12): *'jig rten mkhyen pas gzhan la ma gsan par / bden pa 'di gnyis nyid kyis bstan par mdzad / gang zhig kun rdzob de bzhin don dam ste / bden pa gsum pa gang ma mchis so*. Likewise he cites there *Madhyamakāvatāra* 6.23: *samyagmṛṣādarśanalabdhabhāvaṃ rūpadvayaṃ bibhrati sarvabhāvāḥ / samyagdṛśāṃ yo viṣayaḥ sa tattvaṃ mṛṣādṛśāṃ saṃvṛtisatyam uktam*. See also the *Shes rab ral gri* 434.2–3: *sangs rgyas rnams kyis chos bstan pa / bden pa gnyis la yang dag brten / 'jig rten kun rdzob bden pa dang / dam pa'i don gyi bden pa'o*. This is clearly an adaptation of the Tibetan translation of the *Mūlamadhyamakakārikā* 24.8: *dve satye samupāśritya buddhānānaṃ dharmadeśanā / lokasaṃvṛtisatyaṃ ca satyaṃ ca paramārthataḥ //* . See also his *Nges sgron* 545.2–3: *des na dbu ma'i lugs thams cad / bden gnyis tshul gyis*

rnam par bzhag / bden pa gnyis la ma brten par / zung 'jug khong du chud mi 'gyur / rgyal bas ji snyed gsungs pa yang / bden pa gnyis la yang dag brten; *Nges sgron* 542.4–5: *med ces bden stong nges pa dang / yod ces snang cha nges pa gnyis / res 'jog tshad ma gnyis kyis ni gzhal tshe so sos rnyed don nam / mthong don bden pa gnyis zhes brjod*; *Mkhas 'jug* 147.1–6; *Sdom byang* 383.2: *kun rdzob dang ni don dam pa / 'di ni bden pa gnyis su 'dod.*

30. Mipam, *Ketaka* 49.5–52.1; *Dbu ma rgyan 'grel* 629.6–633.4; *Rab gsal brtsad lan* 522.6–524.3.

31. Mipam, *Shes rab ral gri* 434.3–4: *bden pa gnyis kyi rang bzhin la / ma nor nges pa'i blos 'jug na / dri med tshad ma rnams gnyis kyi / mig bzang mchog tu bsgrub par bya*; *Nges sgron* 547.1: *snang ba tha snyad tshad ma'i yul / stong pa don dam dpyod pa'i yul*; *Mkhas 'jug* 289.1–2; *Mkhas 'jug* 305.5: *bden pa gnyis kyi gnas tshul la tshad ma gnyis*; *Sdom byang* 404.3: *bden gnyis dpyod pa'i tshad ma gnyis*; *Blo'i ral gri* 481.2–3: *ji ltar snang grags chos rnams kun / ma brtags nyams dgar snang tsam pa / tha snyad kun rdzob bden pa dang / dpyad na don la ma grub pa / gnas lugs don dam bden pa ste / tshad ma gnyis kyi gzhal bya ba yi / bden gnyis ma 'dres so sor 'jog.*

32. Wangchuk, "Relativity Theory" 217–224.

33. Mipam, *Shes rab ral gri* 439.3–4: *don dam la yang rnam grangs dang / rnam grangs min pa'i tshul kyis / de 'jal don dam dpyod byed kyi / tshad ma de yang gnyis su 'gyur.*

34. The idea of *bden pa gcig* (or *de bzhin nyid gcig*) has been mentioned by Mipam on several occasions. See, for examples, his *Nges sgron* 512.1: *chos kun de nyid gcig yin cing*; *Nges sgron* 532.4: *gnas lugs bden gcig zung 'jug ste*; *Nges sgron* 532.4: *mthar thug de kho na nyid ni / gcig las med phyir*; *Nges sgron* 512.3: *de bzhin nyid gcig de yin te*; compare *Nges sgron* 535.3: *snang stong zung 'jug dbyings de ni / mthar thug de kho na nyid yin*; *Shes rab ral gri* 440.5: *mthar thug bden pa dbyer med pa'i / bden gcig myang 'das yang dag mtha'*; *Mkhas 'jug* 237.4–6; *Mkhas 'jug* 147.5–6: *bden pa dang po gnyis su phye yang mthar thug so sor mtshan nyid kyis grub pa med par bden pa gcig pu zung 'jug mnyam pa chen por bstan pa yin te / de ni don dam bden pa mthar pa chos kyi dbyings so*; *Ketaka* 90.4, 131.4–132.2; *Dbu ma rgyan 'grel* 644.4: *de kho na nyid nyag gcig* (= *chos kyi dbyings*).

35. Some of the Indian sources cited are the *Bodhisattvapiṭaka* (cited in the *Rab gsal brtsad lan*, 370.5, 448.4–5: *gzhan yang bden pa ni / gcig pu / gnyis ma yin pa ste / 'di lta ste / 'gog pa'i bden pa'o*; *Rtsa shes mchan 'grel* 312.1: (citation) *dge slong dag bden pa dam pa ni gcig kho na ste / mi bslu ba'i chos can gyi mya ngan las 'das pa'o*; *Yuktiṣaṣtikā* 35 (cited in the *Rab gsal brtsad lan*, 449.4: *mya ngan 'das pa bden gcig pur / rgyal ba rnams kyis gang gsungs pa*; *Madhyāntavibhāga* (Mipam, *'Od phreng* 341.6): *dam pa'i don ni gcig pu'o*; *Adhīśa, *Satyadyayāvatāra* (cited in the *Rab gsal brtsad lan* 384.5–6): *dam pa'i don ni gcig nyid de*; *Dbu ma rgyan 'grel* (377.4, referring to the *Madhyamakāvatārabhāṣya*). See also the *Ketaka* 132.1–2.

36. See Almogi, *Rong-zom-pa's Discourses on Buddhology* 14, 232, where a crucial difference between Mipam's understanding of *svayaṃbhūjñāna* and Rongzompa's understanding of it has been observed.

37. The view that there is ultimately only "one valid cognition" (*tshad ma gcig*) is clearly advanced by Mipam in his *Nges sgron* 532.4–5, as has been pointed out in Almogi, *Rong-zom-pa's Discourses on Buddhology* 220, and Wangchuk, "Relativity Theory" 221. See also the *Nges sgron* 512.2–3: *'dir ni zung 'jug ye shes gang / mthar thug gzigs pa de kho na / de bzhin nyid gcig de yin te / 'phags kun de la gzhol zhing 'bab.*

38. Candrakīrti, *Madhyamakāvatārabhāṣya* (de La Vallée Poussin, *Madhyamakāvatāra par Candrakīrti* 300.7–8: *'dir ni mngon sum gcig nyid kho nar zad de gang thams cad mkhyen*

pa'i ye shes so; *Madhyamakāvatāra*-Tib. 6.214 (de La Vallée Poussin, *Madhyamakāvatāra par Candrakīrti* 337.4–7): *rnam kun mkhyen nyid ye shes ni / mngon sum mtshan nyid can du 'dod // gzhan ni nyi tshe ba nyid kyis / mngon sum zhes byar mi 'dod do*. Compare Nāgārjuna, *Ratnāvalī* 4.91bc (Hahn, *Nāgārjuna's Ratnāvalī* 128–129): *buddhair anyat pramāṇaṃ ca ko 'sminn arthe jinādhikaḥ*; *don 'di la ni rgyal ba las / lhag pa'i tshad ma gzhan su yod /* (cited in the *Rab gsal brtsad lan*, 513.3, cf. 578.3).

39. Almogi, *Rong-zom-pa's Discourses on Buddhology* 232.

40. Dharmakīrti, *Pramāṇavārttika* 3.1a (as cited *Pramāṇavārttikālaṃkāra*, 169.10–11; compare Wangchuk, "Relativity Theory" 220 n. 21): *mānaṃ dvividhaṃ meyadvaividhyāt: gzhal bya gnyis phyir tshad ma gnyis /* (cf. Negi 1993–2005: s.v. *gzhal bya*).

41. Dharmakīrti, *Pramāṇavārttika* 3.53d (as cited in the *Pramāṇavārttikālaṃkāra* 212.28; Wangchuk, "Relativity Theory" 221 n. 22): *meyaṃ tv ekam svalakṣaṇam. rang gi mtshan nyid gcig gzhal bya /* (cf. Negi, *Tibetan-Sanskrit Dictionary*: s.v. *gzhal bya*). Analogous to *gzhal bya gnyis phyir tshad ma gnyis*, *gzhal bya gcig phyir tshad ma gcig* could actually also be proposed. Compare Mipam, *Mkhas 'jug* 29.3: *de'i phyir shes byed thams cad blo dang / shes bya thams cad chos su 'du'o*.

42. See Mipam, *Grub bsdus* 656.2–6, where Tantric soteriology has been implied according to which the skylike "basis to be purified" (*sbyangs gzhi*) (i.e., *tathāgatagarbha*, *rang bzhin 'od gsal ba'i snying po*), cloudlike "to-be-purified" (*sbyang bya*; i.e., *'khor ba'i rang bzhin*), windlike "purifier" (*sbyong byed*; i.e., *thabs zab mo*), and "result of being purified" (*sbyangs 'bras*; i.e., buddhahood) have been mentioned.

43. The soteriological model based on the concept of (1) "basis of separation or dissociation" (*bral gzhi*; i.e., *svayaṃbhūjñāna* or *ye nas gnas pa'i chos nyid zung 'jug spros bral chen po*), (2) "to-be-dissociated" (*sgrib gnyis*), (3) "result of dissociation" (*bral ba'i 'bras bu / bral 'bras*; i.e., *rang byung ye shes kyi sku*) is suggested in Mipam's *Dka' gnad ci rigs* 738.4–739.2 and *Gnyug sems shan 'byed* 157.3–6.

44. Wangchuk, *Resolve to Become Buddha* 36–41.

45. Wangchuk, "Was Mipam a Dialectical Monist?" 29–30; Wangchuk, *Resolve to Become Buddha* 39–41. The two soteriological models and the underlying concept of the two kinds of cause (*hetu*, *rgyu*) are mentioned by Mipam in his *Rnam bshad pad dkar* 437.6–438.2; Wangchuk, "Was Mipam a Dialectical Monist?" 30 n. 28; briefly suggested in Wangchuk, "Madhyamaka" 218) stating that these have been taught in the *Mahāparinirvāṇa Sūtra* and *Vajrajñānasamuccaya Tantra*. It is yet to be verified if he was thinking of a certain passage in the *Mahāparinirvāṇa Sūtra*. As for the second case, he must have been thinking of the passage in *Vajrajñānasamuccaya Tantra* T, fol. 269b5, containing the term "manifesting cause" (*snang ba'i rgyu*). In his *Gnyug sems zur dpyad* 239.5–241.1, Mipam suggests that the "denotational exemplifying gnosis" (*mtshon byed dpe'i ye shes*) is the "illuminating cause" (*gsal byed kyi rgyu*) of the "to-be-denoted actual gnosis / reality" (*mtshon bya don gyi ye shes / gnas lugs*) and not its "appropriating cause" (*nyer len gyi gyu*). Similarly, the to-be-denoted actual gnosis is the "effect of separation" (*bral 'bras*) rather than the "effect of maturation" (*smin 'bras*). The two models are also suggested by Rongzompa in his *Dkon mchog 'grel*. Wangchuk, *Resolve to Become Buddha* 41.

46. Rongzompa, *Bden gnyis 'jog tshul* (cited in Wangchuk, *Resolve to Become Buddha* 44 n. 103): *'di ltar nyan thos kyi theg pa nas gzhi bzung nas / rdzogs pa chen po'i mthar thug gi bar du / gang zhig yang dag pa'i don mthong na rnam par grol lo zhes thun mong du grags pa yin la*. For a discussion on the basis of some Indian sources, see Wangchuk, *Resolve to Become Buddha* 43–44.

47. Rongzompa, *Mdo rgyas* 353.22–354.6; *Gsung thor bu* 39.2: *rgyu 'bras dbyer med pa*; *Mtshan brjod 'grel pa* 282.7: *rgyu 'bras kyi sgo dbyer med pa.*

48. See Rongzompa's *Theg tshul* 520.5–21, where the expression *mi mthun pa dang gnyen po dbyer med* (from the *Lta ba yang dag sgron ma*) is explained as *spang bar bya ba'i mi mthun pa'i phyogs dang bsten par bya ba'i gnyen po gnyis rang bzhin gyis dbyer med pa.* See also *Theg tshul* 523.4: *mi mthun pa dang gnyen po dbyer myed pa*; *Dkon mchog 'grel* 93.6; *Dkon mchog 'grel* 96.9: *mi mthun pa dang gnyen po dbyer med pa*; *Lta 'grel* 340.11–12: *mi mthun pa dang gnyen po' gnyis su dbyer med pas / rang bzhin gyis mya ngan las 'das pa'o.*

49. Mipam, *Nges sgron* 541.6–542.1: *tshul des sangs rgyas sems can kyang / gnas tshul snang tshul tsam yin gyi / rgyu 'bras nyid du 'dod pa ni / theg pa chung ngur shes par bya*; *Rgyud bla'i mchan* 23.6–24.1: *des na sems dang snying po'i ye shes chos can dang chos nyid yin la sangs rgyas dang sems can kyang gnas tshul dang snang tshul gyi dbang du byas nas ston pa'i phyir rgyu la 'bras gnas sogs kyi rigs pa'i gnod pa ston pa ni phyogs ma go bar zad do*; *Stong thun seng ge* 188.1–2.

50. Such as between *samudayasatya* and *duḥkhasatya*, *mārgasatya* and *nirodhasatya*, *saṃvṛtisatya* and *paramārthasatya*, *saṃsāra* / *saṃkleśa* and *nirvāṇa* / *vyavadāna*, *sattva* and *vajrasattva*.

51. Guenther, *Teachings of Padmasambhava* 183 (*rgyal bu dmangs su 'khyams pa bzhin*). It is maintained that the system of the Dzokchen does not even distinguish between an apparitional mode (*snang tshul*) and an existential mode (*gnas tshul*), whence the expression "without color being shifted or hair being transformed" (*mdog ma rjes spu ma bsgyur*). See, for example, the *Bka' brgyad* 576.5–577.4. See also Rongzompa, *Lta 'grel* 339.21–24: *de yang 'di' skad du / sems can 'khrul pa'i dus na 'khor ba / ma 'khrul bar rtogs na byang chub ces bshad pa ni / rdzogs pa chen po'i gzhung du yang mi 'gyur te / theg pa 'og ma rnams kyang de ltar 'dod pa'i phyir ro /* (cited and translated into German in Wangchuk, "rDzogs-chen Meditation" 175).

52. See, for instance, Mipam's beautiful manifesto of aspirational wishes having Dzokchen philosophy as its theme, where he states (*Rdo rje'i rang gdangs*, 473.4): *shes bya'i gzhi dang bgrod par byed pa'i lam / 'thob bya 'bras bu'i chos su btags pa yang / rang bzhin gshis la nam mkha'i go rim 'dra.*

53. The idea that the ground (*gzhi*), path (*lam*), and goal (*'bras bu*) are indivisible is put forward by Rongzompa in his *Dkon mchog 'grel* 201.24–202.3 (cited in Wangchuk, *Resolve to Become Buddha* 41 n. 92); *Dkon mchog 'grel* 94.11–13; *Mdo rgyas* 344.16–345.6 (cited in Wangchuk, *Resolve to Become Buddha* 323 n. 166).

54. Rongzompa, *Mdo rgyas* 310.14: *de bas na shes par bya ba'i chos kyang rang bzhin nam chos nyid tsam mo.*

55. Rongzompa, *Mdo rgyas* 310.15: *de sgrub par byed pa'i gtan tshig [sic] kun kyang rang bzhin gyi gtan tshig tsam mo.*

56. Rongzompa, *Mdo rgyas* 310.15–17: *de bas na 'brel ba'ang rang bzhin gyis 'brel ba kho na tsam te / rgyu 'bras kyi 'brel ba lta bu'ang dgos pa'i skabs kyis rang bzhin nyid la rnam par brtags pa tsam du zad do.* For details, see *Mdo rgyas* 310.17–311.10.

57. Mipam, *Shes rab ral gri* 436.1–2: *bya ba byed dang ltos pa yang / dngos po'i chos nyid yin pas na / rig* [rigs] *pa'i mtha' ni chos nyid la / thug nas rgyu mtshan tshol du med*; *Dbu ma rgyan 'grel* 614.2–3: *mngon sum de'ang chos nyid 'ba' zhig la gtugs dgos te 'di ltar bya byed ltos pa gnyis kyang dngos po'i chos nyid yin pas chos nyid kyi rigs pa kho nar 'du zhing / des na rigs pa thams cad kyi gros thag gcod cing zad sar skyel ba ni chos nyid kyi rigs pa yin la / der thug nas de phan chad 'thad pa gzhan sgrub dgos pa ma yin te / me tsha ba'i rgyu

mtshan bshad du med pa bzhin no; *Mkhas 'jug* 291.5–6: *de'i phyir rigs pa'i mtha' thams cad chos nyid kyi rigs pa la thug nas rgyu mtshan gzhan 'tshol du med de / dngos po'i chos nyid me'i tsha ba lta bu la sus kyang gzhan du bsnyon mi nus pa bzhin no.*

58. Mipam, *Shes rab ral gri* 437.3: *rjes dpag mngon sum rtsa ba can*; *Mkhas 'jug* 295.1: *de yang rjes su dpag pa ni mthar mngon sum pa'i rtsa ba can yin la*; *Dbu ma rgyan 'grel* 498.6: *de'ang rjes dpag tshad ma'i mtha' mngon sum la thug cing*; *Dbu ma rgyan 'grel* 614.1–2: *rjes dpags kyang yul lkog gyur de dpogs nus kyi rgyu mtshan can gyi chos tshad mas bzung ba yin pas mthar mngon sum la gtugs shing.*

59. Mipam, *Shes rab ral gri* 437.3–4: *mngon sum rang rig nyid kyis nges / ma 'khrul blo yi nyams myong la / thug nas sgrub byed gzhan du med*; *Mkhas 'jug* 294.5–6: *de thams cad shes pas rang rang gi yul mngon sum myong ba yin zhing / myong ba thams cad kyi mtha' rang rig pa la thug pa ste / mngon sum myong ba'i don la sgrub byed gzhan mi dgos pa ni / rang blo ma 'khrul ba nyid rang gsal du nyams su myong ba las the tshom chod pa yin pas rang rig 'di ni tshad ma thams cad kyi mtha' gtug sa yin no*; *Mkhas 'jug* 295.1: *mngon sum gyi mtha' rang rig gis nges te ma 'khrul pa'i blo yi nyams myong la thug nas sgrub byed gzhan btsal mi dgos pa bde sogs nyams su myong ba bzhin no.*

60. The term *ye shes rang rig pa* is employed by Rongzompa in his *Dkon mchog 'grel* 133.5, but, though its use is justified, he does not seem to employ its counterpart *sems rang rig pa*, even if he does explain saṃsāric phenomena as being "mental self-representations" (*sems rang snang ba*) and nirvāṇic phenomena as being "gnostic self-representation" (*ye shes rang snang ba*). See *Dkon mchog 'grel* 132.16–18.

61. Mipam, *Dbu ma rgyan 'grel* 687.5: *nyon mongs pa thams cad kyi rtsa ba mthar thug ni rmongs pa tsam yin la.*

62. Rongzompa, *Lta 'grel* 316.7–9: *dngos su na ye shes thams cad kyang gcig yin te chos thams cad la bdag med par rtogs pa'i shes rab bo / nyon mongs pa thams cad kyang gcig yin te / 'di' ltar bdag tu rmongs pa'i rtog pa'o.* The entire passage containing these lines is cited by Mipam in his *Dbu ma rgyan 'grel* 685.2–687.4.

63. Mipam, *sDom byang* 395.4–5: *bden gnyis zung 'jug rtogs tshul gyi / zab mo'i chos nyid rnam pa brgyad.* For details, see his *Mkhas 'jug* 237.6–241.4; *Mngon rtogs rgyan 'grel* 579.5–582.6. See also the *Rab gsal brtsad lan* 571.3–573.2; *Nges sgron* 536.4–10: *snang stong 'di la nges shes na / bri gang bral ba'i dkyil 'khor du / srid pa stong dang mi stong sogs / chos nyid bsam gyis mi khyab la / zab mo'i bzod pa khong nas skye*; *Gnyug sems zur dpyad* 322.4–5: *zab mo brgyad ldan*; *Sdud 'grel mdo sbyar* 297.4–301.6. Compare *Shes rab ral gri* 444.2: *bden gnyis tshul la mkhas byas pa / bden gnyis zung 'jug don mthong tshe / snying po'i phyir du spun sel ltar / thabs kun de la gzhol bar shes.*

64. See, for example, Mipam's *Rab gsal brtsad lan* 504.2–505.2: *gangs can 'di na rnying ma pa'i rdzogs chen / bka' brgyud pa'i phyag chen / sa skya pa'i lam 'bras / jo nang pa'i rdo rje rnal 'byor sogs sgrub 'jug gi nyams len zab mo du ma yod pa de dag rdo rje 'chang nas 'phags yul gyi paṇ grub tshad ldan rnams dang bod kyi dam pa dag las rim par brgyud de deng sang gi bar du nyams len gyi gnad dang man ngag ma 'chugs pas lam gyi drod rtags dang nyams myong skyes pa yod la / de thams cad zhal 'chams par spros pa dang bral ba'i de kho na nyid sgom pa'i phugs su byed cing mi rtog ye shes bsgom pa sha stag yin pa la bsnyon 'ding du med bzhin / de thams cad ha shang gi lta ba dang / chad lta / sangs rgyas kyi bstan pa min pa dang / bdud kyi bstan pa'o zhes smra bar spobs pa'i snying kham can du ma zhig mthong ngo / rgya bod mkhas grub de thams cad kyis gcig du bral sogs kyi rtags la brten nas dgag bya bden grub khegs pa'i dgag rtog tsam mi mkhyen pa cang e srid na ste / 'on kyang snying kham can dag gis gong ltar smras ba na / skye bo phal mo che dag 'di snyam du /*

rtsod med kyi mkhas grub chen po de thams cad kyis mthar thug gi bsgom byar ma dgongs pa'i lta sgom gsar pa rnam rtog las ma 'das pa 'di yang ci 'dra zhig yin na zhes the tshom skye ba las / de ltar yin no snyam pa'i dad pa bla lhag tu 'phel bar mi byed pa dag kyang mthong ba rang bzhin 'phros gtam du bgyis pa'o.

65. Mipam's stance on the flawless and flawed notions of yuganaddha should become clear from his deliberation on the question: "Which [of the two] views [determined respectively by the] two types of negation is one to propose?" (*lta ba dgag gnyis gang ltar smra*). See his *Nges sgron* 504.6–507.6.

66. Mipam's discussion of *sangs rgyas kyi sa* in his *Me tog phreng ba* (Almogi, *Rong-zom-pa's Discourses on Buddhology* 383–386 [Tibetan text], 199–206 [English translation] shows this clearly).

67. A greater part of Mipam's deliberations on śūnyatā, madhyamaka, prajñāpāramitā, tathāgatagarbha, and so on—from sūtric and tantric, particularly Mahāyogic and Atiyogic perspectives—concerns difficulties that he sees in positing only pole *y* as the ultimate true reality, that is, in place of *xy*-yuganaddha. It is beyond the scope of this contribution to provide textual sources on these issues coherently and conveniently, but most of the sources that I cite here (e.g., his *Gsung sgros*) do largely give us an accurate picture of his concerns. In fact, one of the main purposes of Mipam's *Gnyug sems skor gsum* (i.e., here our *Gnyug sems 'od gsal*, *Gnyug sems shan 'byed*, and *Gnyug s rdor phreng sems*) is to identify faulty notions and positions regarding *xy*-yuganaddha (e.g., *rig stong zung 'jug. gnyug sems*) that attach the aforementioned attributes to *x* and *y* to refute them. It is very obvious that for Mipam there is much at stake, because a misunderstanding or misinterpretation of the *xy*-yuganaddha doctrine would undermine the very essence of both the tantric and non-tantric Mahāyāna teachings.

68. Mipam, *Ketaka* 74.5–75.1: *bsam gyis mi khyab pa'i chos nyid ni skal dman rnams skrag pa'i gnas rab yin pas de'i tshul ni mi shes shing / dngos med du bstan na chad stong du bzung / snang bcas su bstan na bden grub tu bzung / zung 'jug ces brjod na tha gu dkar nag bsgrol ba lta bu'i don du bzung / bsam gyis mi khyab ces brjod na cang med ci med hwa shang gi lta ba lta bu zhig las mi 'char ba yin te.* See also the *Gnyug sems zur dpyad* 1007.15: *srad bu dkar nag zung sgril lta bu'i nyi tshogs zhig; Gnyug sems zur dpyad* (1017.15: *srad bu sgril ba lta bu'i zung 'jug*); *Zla ba'i zhal lung* 171.2: *srad bu dkar nag bsgril ba ltar* (contrasted with *stong rten 'byung zung 'jug*); *Dbu ma rgyan 'grel* 666.5: *srad bu dkar nag bsgrims pa lta bu; Dam chos dogs sel* 748.4; *Lta mgur 'grel pa* 17.2–26.2; *Gsung sgros* 850.1–2; *Rab gsal brgal lan* 411.1–2.

69. Mipam, *Ketaka* 133.6: *chu la chu bzhag pa bzhin du; Rab gsal brgal lan* 411.1–4: *bdag cag gis stong rten 'byung zung 'jug ngo bo dbyer med du 'dod kyis / ri bong gi rwa med pa dang / glang gi rwa yod pa gnyis zung 'jug tu byed pa lta bur ni mi 'dod pas chos kyi dbyings rang gi ngo bo 'phel 'byi med par gnas par 'dod la . . . don du skye ba med kyang skye ba ltar snang ba 'gal med du 'dod do.*

70. Mipam, *Stong thun seng ge* 176.6: *bde bshegs snying po ngo bo mi stong pa'i bden grub rtag pa* vs. *yon tan med pa'o stong pa phyang chad; Gzhan stong seng ge* 231.2–5: *snang ba phyang chad* vs. *stong pa phyang chad; Dam chos dogs sel* 774.5. See also Mipam's *Me tog phreng ba* in Almogi, *Rong-zom-pa's Discourses on Buddhology* 384, 202.

71. Mipam, *Gnyug sems shan 'byed* 164.3.

72. Mipam, *Gnyug sems 'od gsal* 6.3, 7.4, 11.5; *Gnyug sems shan 'byed* 1162.13; *Gnyug sems zur dpyad* 194.5; *Stong thun seng ge* 177.4: *stong rkyang tsam; dKa' gnad ci rigs* 374.5, 376.4; *Rgyud bla'i mchan* 19.2–21.5. Note that *gzhi bden pa dbyer med zung 'jug gi don*

is contrasted with *stong pa med rkyang tsam* (*'Od snying* 258.6–259.1) and *chos dbyings snang stong zung 'jug* with *stong rkyang tsam* (*'Od snying* 260.6–261.2). Compare *ibid.* 112.5: . . . *mdor na bden gnyis dbyer med rang byung gi ye shes su bstan pa'o*; *Gsung sgros* 770.1: *stong rkyang tsam gnas lugs mthar thug pa min no.*

73. Mipam, *Nges sgron* 504.6–505.2; *Dbu ma rgyan 'grel* 643.2–644.4.

74. *Mkhas 'jug* 264.6: *ri bong go rwa med dang gnag gi rwa yod ltar zung 'jug*; *Gnyug sems zur dpyad* 1033.19–20: *gnag rwa yod dang ri bong rwa med zung 'jug lta bu*); *Gsung sgros* 774.3–6, 866.1–3.

75. Mipam, *'Od snying* 114.1; compare *Dbu ma rgyan 'grel* 373.5: *snang stong ris su ma chad pa'i dbyings*; *Sdud 'grel* 12.1: *snang ba dang stong pa kun rdzob dang don dam zhes pa'i gnyis chos thams cad gnyis su med par gyur pa'i chos dbyings rnam grangs min pa'i don dam.*

76. Mipam, *Mkhas 'jug* 305.3–4: *bden gnyis dbyer med mthar dpyod pa'i tshad ma*; *Mkhas 'jug* 273.3–4: *bden gnyis dbyer med zung du zhugs pa'i rnam kun mchog ldan gyi stong nyid* and *snang stong bden pa dbyer med mnyam pa nyid nam mkha'i dkyil lta bu'i don*; *Rgyud bla'i mchan* 19.3–4: *bden gnyis dbyer med pa'i gnad zab pa las shing tu zab pa*; *Rgyud bla'i mchan* 20.5; *Gzhi le'u'i tshig 'grol* 750.3; compare *Dbu ma rgyan 'grel* 412.1: *ka dag lhun grub bden pa dbyer med*; *Grub bsdus* 669.1: *ka dag lhun grub dbyer med*; *Ye shes rnam 'byed* 271.2; *Sdud 'grel* 102.1–2: *gnas lugs mthar thug pa'i sher phyin dang ldan na ye shes de'i ngor thabs shes 'du bral med de bden gnyis dbyer med pa'i yul can yin pa'i phyir ro*; *Sdud 'grel mdo sbyar* 218.5: *thabs shes zung du 'brel ba stong nyid snying rje snying po can gyi lam*; *ibid.* 305.5: *stong nyid snying rje zung du 'jug pa.*

77. *Mkhas 'jug* 458.3–7, where Mipam states that the Vastuvādins are only being disputatious when they claim that *śūnyatā* and *pratītyasamutpāda* are contradictory, the Mādhyamikas holding them to be semantically identical *don gcig*. See also *Mkhas 'jug* 454.1–11; *Nges sgron* 533.3–4: *dngos gcig steng gi bden pa gnyis / mi 'gal ye shes yul yin phyir.*

78. It would be worthwhile to trace the earliest possible source for the expressions. Gorampa in his *Lta ba'i shan 'byed* employs the terms and attributes them to "early scholars" (*sngon gyi mkhas pa rnams*). Cabezón and Dargyay, *Freedom from Extremes* 206–207. See also Mipam, *Grub bsdus* 654.2–3: *gzhi dbu ma bden gnyis / lam dbu ma tshogs gnyis / 'bras bu dbu ma sku gnyis zung 'jug tu 'dod de.* It would be quite legitimate to specify the first two expressions as *gzhi dbu ma bden gnyis zung 'jug* and *lam dbu ma tshogs gnyis zung 'jug*. See also Mipam's *Sa skya'i dri lan* 603.5–6: *lam dbu ma tshogs gnyis zung 'jug*; *Gnad kyi me long* 517.6: *gzhi bden gnyis / lam tshogs gnyis / 'bras bu sku gnyis zung 'jug gi tshul*; compare *Gzhi le'u'i tshig 'grol* 750.4: *gzhi bden pa dbyer med, lam 'khor 'das dbyer med*, and *thob bya gzhi 'bras dbyer med*; *Dbu ma rgyan 'grel* 348.6: *'bras bu sku gnyis zung 'jug.* Note that according to Broido, "Padma-dkar-po on Integration" 47, Pema Karpo, in his *Nges don grub pa'i shing rta*, employs the following terms: *gzhi dbu ma bden gnyis zung 'jug, lam dbu ma thabs shes zung 'jug*, and *'bras bu dbu ma sku gnyis zung 'jug.*

79. Mipam, *Rab gsal brtsad lan* 507.1–508.5.

80. Perhaps *śaikṣa*-yuganaddha (*slob pa'i zung 'jug*) and *aśaikṣa*-yuganaddha (*mi slob pa'i zung 'jug* should best be considered within the frame of Mantrayāna soteriology. See, for example, the *'Od snying* 142.3–144.3, where Mipam presents the five Mantric soteriological paths in terms of gnosis (*ye shes*), luminosity (*'od gsal*), and divine bodily form (*lha sku*): (1) *dag mnyam bden pa dbyer med kyi go yul tsam* (gnosis is not applicable here), *go yul tsam gyi 'od gsal*, and *mos pa'i lha sku* are attributed to the *saṃbhāramārga*; (2) *dpe'i 'od gsal*, (*mtshon byed*) *dpe'i ye shes*, and *rlung sems kyi lha sku* are associated with the *prayogamārga*; (3) (*mtshon bya*) *don gyi ye shes*, (*mtshon bya*) *don gyi 'od gsal*, and*'od gsal gyi lha sku* are

associated with the *darśanamārga*; (4) *slob pa'i 'od gsal, slob pa'i ye shes*, and *slob pa'i zung 'jug gi lha sku* are attributed to the *bhāvanāmārga*; (5) *mthar thug gi 'od gsal, mi slob pa'i zung 'jug*, and *mi slob pa'i zung 'jug gi lha sku* are associated with the *aśaikṣamārga* or *buddhabhūmi*. See also the *Nges sgron* 523.4–6.

81. *Tshig mdzod chen mo* (s.v. *spangs pa zung 'jug*): *spangs pa zung 'jug sngags lugs kyis nyon sgrib zad par spangs te dag pa'i sgyu lus dngos thob pa ste slob pa'i zung 'jug phal pa'o.*

82. *Tshig mdzod chen mo* (s.v. *rtogs pa zung 'jug*): *rtogs pa zung 'jug dag pa'i sgyu lus dang don gyi 'od gsal gnyis sku thugs su ngo bo gcig tu 'dres pa'i zung 'jug ste slob pa'i zung 'jug khyad par can no.*

83. *Tshig mdzod chen mo* (s.v. *zung 'jug bzhi*). Compare also Mipam's *'Od snying* 284.3–4, where *snang stong sku rdo rje, gsal stong gsung rdo rje, bde stong thugs rdo rje*, and *rig stong ye shes rdo rje* are linked with the four *mudras*; namely, *karmamudrā, dharmamudrā, samayamudrā*, and *mahāmudrā*, respectively.

84. The slightly abbreviated form *dbyings ye zung 'jug* is employed by Mipam in his *Gsung sgros* 799.6; *Sdud 'grel mdo sbyar* 353.2. See also the *Mngon rtogs rgyan 'grel* 659.1: *dbyings dang ye shes gnyis su med pa'i ngo bo nyid kyi sku*; *'Od snying* 124.1: *sku bzhi ye shes lnga'i bdag nyid mi slob pa'i zung 'jug drug pa rdo rje 'chang chen po.* Note that the notion of a "yuganaddha of [dharma]dhātu and *jñāna*" has also been proposed by Rongzompa. See his *Mtshan brjod 'grel pa* 261.8–9: *dbyings dang ye shes zung du 'brel ba*; *Theg tshul* 502.15: *dbyings dang ye shes gnyis su myed pa'i rig pa*; *Dkon mchog 'grel* 143.20, 150.7–8: *dbyings dang ye shes gnyis su med pa* (also noted in Almogi, *Rong-zom-pa's Discourses on Buddhology* 232 n. 144).

85. Nine explicit *xy*-yuganaddha terms used by Pema Karpo, reported in an appendix in Broido, "Padma-dkar-po on Integration" 32–39 are: (1) *'khor 'das zung 'jug*, (2) *srid zhi zung 'jug*, (3) *snang stong zung 'jug*, (4) *rnam shes dang ye shes zung du 'jug pa*, (5) *gsal stong zung 'jug*, (6) *thabs shes zung 'jug*, (7) *stong nyid snying rje zung 'jug*, (8) *bden gnyis zung 'jug*, and (9) (most probably) *bskyed rim dang rdzogs rim zung 'jug*. The reported reading *bskyed rim rdzogs rim dang zung 'jug* is problematic.

86. See, for example, Mipam's *Dbu ma rgyan 'grel* 422.5, where *madhyamaka* is subdivided into "madhyamaka of expressible content" (*brjod bya don gyi dbu ma*) and "madhyamaka of the expressive word" (*rjod byed tshig gi dbu ma*), which is also called "scripture / tractate madhyamaka" (*gzhung dbu ma*). The former is further divided into "ground madhyamaka" (*gzhi dbu ma*), "path madhyamaka" (*lam dbu ma*), and "goal madhyamaka" (*'bras bu'i dbu ma*). Discussed briefly in Wangchuk, "Madhyamaka" 215–216. See also Mipam's *Rab gsal brtsad lan* 434.5: *bdag cag gis chos thams cad snang stong zung 'jug spros mtha' brgyad bral de nyid gzhi dbu ma / de ltar rtogs pa'i blo de dbu ma'i lam la gnas pa zhes tha snyad byed*; *Rab gsal brtsad lan* 460.5–461.1: *des na chos thams cad gdod nas yod med kyi mtha' gnyis sogs spros pa'i mtha' thams cad dang bral ba bden gnyis zung 'jug ni gzhi dbu ma yin cing / de ji bzhin rtogs pa mtha' gang du'ang mi gnas pa'i ye shes dngos sam rjes mthun pa lam dbu ma / des 'bras bu'i dbu ma shin tu rnam par dag pa gnyis su med pa'i ye shes chen po rnam pa thams cad mkhyen pa sku gnyis zung 'jug gi sangs rgyas 'grub pa yin no.* The term *brjod bya don gyi dbu ma* recurs also in his *Dam chos dogs sel* 749.4. Note that Rog (1166–1244) in his *Bstan sgron* 254.5 has already employed the terms *gzhi dbu ma, lam dbu ma*, and *'bras bu dbu ma.*

87. Note that the expressions "ground yuganaddha," "path yuganaddha," and "goal yuganaddha" have been employed in Broido, *Rab gsal brtsad lan* 17–19, and also that the following corresponding Tibetan expressions occur in an outline (31): *gzhi zung 'jug rtogs tshul, lam zung 'jug bsgom tshul*, and *'bras bu zung 'jug 'char tshul.*

88. See, for example, Negi, *Tibetan-Sanskrit Dictionary*: s.v. *gzhi*.

89. For example, Anuyoga's view is called the "view of the indivisibility of bliss and emptiness" (*bde stong dbyer med kyi lta ba*) (*'Od snying*, 126.3); Atiyoga's view is called "view of the innate [indivisibility] of gnostic cognition and emptiness" (*rig stong gnyug ma'i lta ba*) (*'Od snying*, 126.6). Compare *'Od snying* 255.1: *rig stong gnyug ma spros bral rang byung gi ye shes.*

90. See, for example, the expression in the *Tshig mdzod chen mo* (s.v. *gzhi lam 'bras gsum*): "establishment of the view, which is the [soteriological] basis (or starting point)" (*gzhi lta ba gtan la phab pa*), "practicing the [soteriological] path through meditation" (*lam sgom pas nyams su blangs pa*), and the "attainment of [the state of] awakening, which is the [soteriological] goal" (*'bras bu byang chub thob pa*).

91. Some of the sources that explicitly mention the expression *snang stong zung 'jug* (or *snang stong zung du 'jug pa*) are: *Dbu ma rgyan 'grel* 620.6, 630.3, 626.4; *Nges sgron* 507.1; *Gsung sgros* 768.6, 775.5: *snang stong zung 'jug* vs. *stong pa rkyang pa'i dbyings*; *Gnyug sems zur dpyad* 231.6; *Gnyug sems shan 'byed* 108.6, 117.4; *Gnyug sems zur dpyad* 230.6; *Lta phreng mchan 'grel* 27.2, 44.4; *Shel gyi me long* 725.3; *Rab gsal brtsad lan* 521.2–6; *'Od snying* 258.1–2: *sems kyi gnas lugs snang stong zung 'jug brjod pa dang bral ba nyid yin pa'i phyir ro*; *'Od snying* 155.2: *gnas lugs snang stong zung 'jug*; *Mngon rtogs rgyan 'grel* 607.6: *snang stong zung du 'jug pa'i chos nyid*; *'Od snying* 632.6, 638.2: *snang stong zung 'jug*; *Zla ba'i zhal lung* 176.6; *Ketaka* 47.4–5, 48.6, 78.2, 133.6: *snang stong zung [du] 'jug [pa]*; *Bka' brgyad* 585.1, 601.3; *Sdud 'grel mdo sbyar* 306.4, 324.1–2, 346.2, 349.4, 350.5. For Pema Karpo's use of the term *snang stong zung 'jug*, see Broido, "Padma-dkar-po on Integration 18, 49.

92. The expression *stong rten 'byung zung 'jug* occurs, for example, in Mipam's *Dbu ma rgyan 'grel* 634.3; *Gnyug sems zur dpyad* 275.5; *Mngon rtogs rgyan 'grel* 468.2; *Zla ba'i zhal lung* 45.1; *Lta mgur 'grel pa* 13.1–2: *stong dang rten 'byung zung 'jug. stong nyid rten 'byung zung 'jug*; *Gsung sgros* 850.2, 866.3; compare *Lta mgur 'grel pa* 770.1: *stong rten 'byung ye nas zung 'jug yin la*; *Sdud 'grel* 212.6–213.1: *'di yi dge bas skye ba thams cad du / zab mo stong dang rten 'byung zung 'jug don / legs rtogs rgyal ba dgyes pa'i lam bzang las / nam yang gzhan du ldog par ma gyur cig.*

93. Mipam employs the expression *snang stong dbyer med* in his *Dbu ma rgyan 'grel* 368.5, 401.6, 626.6, 643.6; *Nges sgron* 529.2; *Gnyug sems zur dpyad* 316.5–6; *Lta phreng mchan 'grel* 44.2, 48.6; *Dka' gnad ci rigs* 733.1; *Rgyud bla'i mchan* 21.3; *Shes rab ral gri* 438.4–5: *gnas lugs don la stong gzhi dang / stong pa tha dad du med pas / snang stong dbyer med brjod dang bral / so so rang gis rig bya'o.* The expression *snang stong gnyis med* occurs, too, as in his *Sdud 'grel mdo sbyar* 322.6–323.1.

94. Mipam, *Dka' gnad ci rigs* 372.5; *Gzhi'i le'u'i tshig 'grol* 755.1; compare *Ketaka* 75.4–5: *stong dang rten 'byung ye nas 'du bral med pa'i chos nyid mnyam pa chen po.*

95. For Mipam's use of the term *snang stong mnyam pa nyid*, see his *'Od snying* 170.1; *Dka' gnad ci rigs* 733.5; *Sdud 'grel mdo sbyar* 302.2, 335.3–4; *Mngon rtogs rgyan 'grel* 468.2.

96. Mipam, *Dbu ma rgyan 'grel* 384.6: *don gyi bden gnyis zung 'jug rab tu mi gnas pa'i dbyings*; *Dbu ma rgyan 'grel* 401.6–402.1: *bden gnyis zung 'jug gi dbu ma*; *Dbu ma rgyan 'grel* 630.3–4; *Dam chos dogs sel* 749.5; *Rgyud bla'i mchan* 20.3; *Gsung sgros* 780.6–781.1; *Mkhas 'jug* 192.4: *bden gnyis zung 'jug rnam kun mchog ldan gyi stong pa nyid*; *Sdom byang* 402.6: *bden gnyis zung du 'jug pa ni / dbu ma'i lam gyis rtogs bya ste / snang stong gnyis med mnyam pa nyid / chos kyi dbyings zhes mthar thug don / bsam brjod bral ba de kho na / so so rang gis rig bya'o*; *Stong thun seng ge* 181.2; *Rab gsal brgal lan* 348.3, 448.1; *Ye shes rnam 'byed* 245.1.

97. For occurrences of the expression *bden gnyis dbyer med*, see Mipam's *Gnyug sems zur dpyad* 293.2, 296.4, 318.6; *Lta phreng mchan 'grel* 27.2; *Dka' gnad ci rigs* 731.6; *'Od snying* 151.6; *Blo'i ral gri* 481.3; *Rgyud bla'i mchan* 20.5; *Gsung sgros* 827.2, 918.1; *Sdud 'grel* 126.6; *Sdud 'grel* 127.5: *bden pa gnyis dbyer med pa*; *Sdud 'grel* 180.7: *bden gnyis dbyer med pa*; *Sdud 'grel mdo sbyar* 279.3: *bden gnyis dbyer med*.

98. The expression *bden gnyis ro gcig* occurs, for example, in Mipam's *Dka' gnad ci rigs* 731.5, and *bden gnyis ro mnyam* similarly in his *Sdud 'grel mdo sbyar* 294.5.

99. For occurrences of the expression *gsal stong zung 'jug*, see the *Mngon rtogs rgyan 'grel* 445.5; *Mdo sde rgyan 'grel* 51.4; *Gnyug sems shan 'byed* 142.4; *Gnyug sems zur dpyad* 237.3, 258.1; *Shel gyi me long* 725.5; compare *Blo'i ral gri* 481.5. As noted in Broido, "Padma-dkar-po on Integration" 19, 49, the expression *gsal stong zung 'jug* has been employed also by Pema Karpo.

100. Mipam, *Gnyug sems 'od gsal* 40.1; *Gzhi'i le'u'i tshig 'grol* 756.6; *Rgyud bla'i mchan* 19.3–4. Compare the *Gnyug sems 'od gsal* 12.2: *gsal stong gnyis med*.

101. It has already been pointed out that Mipam does not seem to criticize the Sakya view of *gsal stong zung 'jug* or *gsal stong dbyer med*; that indeed he himself endorses it. Wangchuk, "Was Mipam a Dialectical Monist?" 34. See also Mipam's *Rgyud bla'i mchan* 20.2–3; *Gzhi le'u'i tshig 'grol* 756.6.

102. Mipam, *Shel gyi me long* 725.5. Note that in his *'Od snying* 154.6–155.1, Mipam treats *bde stong zung 'jug* as if it were interchangeable with *dbyings rig zung 'jug*. See also his *Sngags kyi ral gri* 477.3–4: *ma 'gag snang ba thabs kyi sku / rang bzhin med pa shes rab yum / gnyis med zung 'jug bde ba che / 'di ni chos kun de bzhin nyid*. An annotation, obviously by the author, says that the reading must be kept as is, since these are the actual words (quoted) from a tantric scripture.

103. The term *bde stong dbyer med* is employed, for example, in Mipam's *Gnyug sems zur dpyad* 198.6. See also his *Bka' brgyad* 640.4: *bde stong gnyis su med pa*.

104. *Tshig mdzod chen mo* (s.v. *e waṃ zung 'jug*): *rnam kun mchog ldan gyi stong nyid dang / mchog tu mi 'gyur ba'i bde chen gnyis dbyer med zung du 'jug pa'o*.

105. *Tshig mdzod chen mo* (s.v. *rgyu'i rgyud*).

106. Some of the instances where the expressions *rig stong zung 'jug* occur are Mipam's *Shel gyi me long* 726.1–5; *Gnyug sems 'od gsal* 8.3, 37.1, 43.1; *Gnyug sems shan 'byed* 136.1, 140.3; *Gnyug sems zur dpyad* 209.1, 261.6, 291.1, 309.5; compare *Nges sgron* 519.1: *'bras bu bzhi pa'i dbang gi lam / rig stong rang byung ye shes nyid / kho na rtsal du bton gyur pa / 'od gsal rdo rje rtse mo'i lugs / mthar thug theg pa'i skyel so yin*; *Me tog phreng ba* in Almogi, *Rong-zom-pa's Discourses on Buddhology* 384: *rig stong zung du 'jug pa*.

107. Mipam, *Gnyug sems 'od gsal* 291.1; *Gnyug sems zur dpyad* 320.2.

108. Mipam, *Nges shes sgron me* 522.5: *ka dag lhun grub zung 'jug gi / ye shes chen po kho na yin*; *Gnyug sems shan 'byed* 1219.10–11: *mthar thug ka dag lhun grub zung 'jug rdzogs pa chen po*; compare *Lta phreng mchan 'grel* 49.1: *gzhi ka dag dang lhun grub zung du 'jug pa'i byang chub kyi sems*.

109. Mipam, *Gnyug sems shan 'byed* 91.6; *bKa' brgyad* 574.2: *ka dag dang lhun grub dbyer med pa*.

110. Mipam, *Gnyug sems 'od gsal* 956.18–19, 987.7.

111. Mipam, *Nges sgron* 542.1–3: *gnas tshul gang yin sgrib pa yis / bsgribs phyir nye bar mi snang bas / lam la 'bad par byed pa ni / rang gzhan gnyis kas 'dod pa nyid*; *Nges sgron* 535.6: *des na yul dang yul can rnams / rang bzhin gdod nas dag na yang / glo bur dri*

mas bsgribs pa'i phyir / dri ma sbyang la 'bad par bya; Padma'i zhal lung 6.6–7.1: *'o na lam gyi [gyis] ci bya na / gshis kyi ye shes de mthong phyir / ji ltar gzugs ni 'gyur min yang / mig skyon sel ba'i sman bzhin no.*

112. Mipam, *Dka' gnad ci rigs* 735.3–5; *Gnyug sems zur dpyad* 280.4; *'Od snying* 157.6: *sngags lam du dang por thos bsam gyis sgro 'dogs bcad pa'i dus nas kyang 'khor 'das dbyer med dag pa chen por lta bas na lta ba ma rmongs pa yin no.*

113. *'khor 'das dbyer med kyi lta ba; lta ba 'khor 'das dbyer med.* For the Nyingma tradition, too, as far as Rongzompa is concerned, it is the view of the Dzokchen. See his *Lta 'grel* 337.20–338.15.

114. *lta sgom zung du 'jug; sbrel; 'brel pa. lta sgom zung 'jug; sbrel; 'brel.* See, for example, Mipam's *Sa skya'i dri lan* 603.6: *lta sgom zung 'jug (thabs shes zung 'jug).*

115. *lta spyod zung du 'jug; sbrel; 'brel pa. lta spyod zung 'jug; sbrel; 'brel.* Compare Mipam, *bsTan rgyas* 689.2–3: *rmad byung za hor mkhan po'i spyod pa dang / mtshungs med dpal ldan klu yi lta ba gnyis / zung 'brel brgyud pa'i bka' srol phyag rgyas btab / mtsho skyes rgyal ba'i bstan pa.*

116. Mipam, *Mdo sde rgyan 'grel* 599.1: *zhi gnas dang lhag mthong zung du 'brel ba*; Rongzompa, *Dkon mchog 'grel* 147.12: *zhi gnas dang lhag mthong zung du 'brel ba'i ting nge 'dzin*; *Theg tshul* 537.11–12: *zhi gnas dang lhag mthong zung du 'brel ba*, a citation from the *Mahāparinirvāṇa Sūtra*; *Theg tshul* 543.24: *zhi gnas dang lhag mthong cha mnyam pa*; *Gsung thor bu* 45.7: *zhi gnas dang lhag mthong zung du 'brel par gyur pa*; *Bka' brgyad* 587.3: *zhi lhag zung du 'brel ba.*

117. Mipam, *Mngon rtogs rgyan 'grel* 456.6: *zhi lhag gam srid zhir mi lhung ba.*

118. For occurrences of the expression *thabs shes zung 'jug*, see Mipam's *Lta phreng mchan 'grel* 48.6; *Sa skya'i dri lan* 603.6: *thabs shes zung 'jug*; *Lta mgur 'grel pa* 14.5: *pha ma thabs shes zung 'jug gi lta ba rin po che.* Compare *Lta phreng mchan 'grel* 51.2: *thabs shes zung du 'brel ba*; *Mngon rtogs rgyan 'grel* 456.6: *thabs dang shes rab zung du 'brel ba'i lam*; *Mngon rtogs rgyan 'grel* 625.2: *thabs shes zung 'jug sher phyin zab mo'i sbyor ba la mkhas par bya'o*; *Mdo sde rgyan 'grel* 19.4: *thabs dang shes rab zung du 'brel ba*; *Mkhas 'jug* 151.3–4: *zab pa'i shes rab dang rgya che ba'i thabs mkhas zung du 'jug pa*; *Sdom byang* 387.3–4: *thabs shes zung 'jug thams cad kun / lam gyi grogs gyur thabs mkhas so*; *Sdom byang* 368.4: *thabs shes zung du 'jug pa yi / sher phyin gdams ngag legs nos nas / nang gi yongs 'dzin ldan par bya*; compare *Rgyud bla'i mchan* 94.2: *stong nyid snying rje zung 'jug*; *Sdud 'grel* 6.1: *stong nyid rtogs pa dang snying rje'i sems zung du 'jug pa*; *Sdud 'grel* 122.5–6, 123.3: *shes rab dang snying rje zung du 'jug pa*; compare *Sdud 'grel* 91.6: *thabs dang shes rab ya ma bral ba'i lam*; *Sdud 'grel* 114.3: *thabs shes zung du 'brel ba*; *Sdud 'grel* 127.5: *stong nyid snying rje gnyis su med pa'i sher phyin*; *Sdud 'grel* 190.1: *rang bzhin med par rtogs pa'i shes rab dang snying rje chen po zung du zhugs pa'i thabs*; *Sdud 'grel mdo sbyar* 336.6–337.1; *Padma'i zhal lung* 5.3: *ji ltar mkha' la gshog pa ni / zung med mkha' la bgrod mi nus / de bzhin thabs shes bral ba'i lam / yang dag min ces rgyal bas gsungs.* See also Rongzompa, *Dkon mchog 'grel* 49.11: *thabs dang shes rab zung du 'brel ba.* See Broido, "Padma-dkar-po on Integration" 19, where the Sanskrit terms *prajñopāyayuganaddha* and *śūnyatakaruṇayuganaddha* [*sic*] are mentioned.

119. See, for example, Mipam's *Mngon rtogs rgyan 'grel* 505.4–5.

120. Mipam, *Sdom byang* 385.3: *bsod nams dang ni ye shes tshogs gnyis po / zung 'jug lam gyis don kun yongs rdzogs byed.*

121. For the occurrence of the term *bskyed rdzogs zung 'jug*, see Mipam's *Grub bsdus* 663.2; *'Od snying* 131.4; *Bka' brgyad* 560.6.

122. Mipam, *Dbu ma rgyan 'grel* 348.6: *'bras bu sku gnyis zung 'jug gi sangs rgyas*; *'Od snying* 106.5, compare *'Od snying* 104.3: *bskyed rdzogs dbyer med*. See also the *Grub bsdus* 981.10: *rgya che ba bskyed pa'i rim pa dang zab mo rdzogs pa'i rim pa gnyis*; *Bka' brgyad* 598.2: *drang don bskyed rim* and *nges don rdzogs pa'i rim pa*.

123. Mipam, *Gnyug sems zur dpyad* 266.4–5: *bden gnyis dbyer med kyi gnas lugs gdod ma gzhi yi 'od gsal du byas nas / de la sbyor byed lam gyi rim pa la / ring lam tshogs gnyis zung 'jug rgyu yi theg pa / nye lam sgyu 'od zung 'jug sngags kyi theg pa / mthar thug ka dag dang lhun grub zung 'jug rdzogs pa chen po gsum du byas nas 'chad pa spyi'i ching bla na med pa yin no*. A similar statement can be found in his *Gnyug sems shan 'byed* 149.2–4.

124. For Mipam's deliberations on buddhology and the issues of gnoseology and ontology that are linked with it, see his *Me tog phreng ba*; his catalogue of Rongzompa's writings have already been studied in Almogi, *Rong-zom-pa's Discourses on Buddhology* 193–206 and 383–386, including a critical edition of the text. It is clear that for him, the way one perceives and conceives of Mahāyāna ontology at the metaphysical (*gzhi*) level affects the way one perceives and conceives of buddhology at the resultant (*'bras bu*) level. See, for example, his *Sdud 'grel mdo sbyar* 350.4–351.4; *Mngon rtogs rgyan 'grel* 638.2–639.1.

125. Mipam, *Nges sgron* 529.2: *lam de ji bzhin goms pa las / sku gnyis zung 'jug ye shes thob*; *Dbu ma rgyan 'grel* 348.6; compare *Dbu ma rgyan 'grel* 730.6: *sku gnyis zung du 'jug pa*.

126. See, for example, the *'Od snying* 126.4, where the soteriological goal of the Anuyoga system is described as the *mi slob pa'i zung 'jug*.

127. For Mipam, the ultimate soteriological goal of the Mahāyāna, be it sūtric or mantric, is the *buddhabhūmi*, and he, like Rongzompa and Longchenpa, but unlike the Zurpa masters, posited that there is no qualitative or hierarchical difference between the *buddhabhūmi* obtained through sūtric (i.e., non-mantric) Mahāyāna and *buddhabhūmi* obtained through mantric Mahāyāna. See his *bKa' brgyad* 555.1–5; Rongzompa, *Lta 'grel* 344.17–345.16; *Dkon mchog 'grel* 190.18–191.6, 247.11–248.8.

128. The expression *gzhi 'bras dbyer med* occurs, for example, in Mipam's *Gzhi'i le'u'i tshig 'grol* 750.4, 756.4; *'Od snying* 185.6, 210.6, 213.4; *Gnyug sems shan 'byed* 161.5: *'di la bsam na gzhi 'bras ngo bo dbyer med / tha snyad kyi dbyer yod yin no*; *Gnyug sems zur dpyad* 281.2–3; *Lta phreng mchan 'grel* 48.4. Note that the idea of *gzhi 'bras dbyer med* is also suggested by *rgyu 'bras dbyer med* found, for example, in Rongzompa's *Dkon mchog 'grel* 49.2.

129. Mipam, *Sdom byang* 388.1–2: *rigs ni bde bshegs snying po ste / sku dang ye shes dbyer med dbyings / rang byung ye shes 'dus ma byas / kun khyab 'pho 'gyur med pa'o*; *Mkhas 'jug* 184.1–6; *Nges sgron* 547.5: *e waṃ zung du zhugs pa yi / rang byung ye shes gnas med snang*; compare *Nges sgron* 518.6: *gzhi la ji ltar bzhugs pa ltar / bde stong lam gyi e waṃ gyis / bsgrubs pas tshe 'di nyid la yang / zung 'jug 'bras bu mngon du 'gyur*.

130. Mipam, *Mkhas 'jug* 206.6–207.4: *rnam pa thams cad mkhyen pa. rang byung gi ye shes kyi bdag nyid can*; *Nges sgron* 536.2: *rtogs na kun kyang ro mnyam gyi / ngang du 'bras bu'i btsan sa 'dzin / dus gsum dus med gnyug ma'i klong / rang byung ye shes rgyal bar 'gyur*.

131. Mipam, *Ye grub ut pal* 496.2–3: *rang gnas rang byung ye shes kyis / lam 'dir 'og ma'i lam kun rdzogs / ye shes rig pa dang 'gal ba'i / ma rig gnyen por 'di nyid che / lam gzhan ji ltar bsgoms byas kyang / 'di dang dgnos 'gal mi 'gyur bas / sgrub gnyis drung nas 'joms mi nu*.

132. Mipam, *Gzhi'i le'u'i tshig 'grol* 757.5–758.1; *Stong thun seng ge* 174.3, compare 207.4; *Mchog grub ut pal* 492.1: *de phyir de nyid ches zab cing / brling ba nyid kyis mthar thug pas / sems dpa' ches rnams kyis kyang ni / ji bzhin rtogs par dka' bar gsungs*; *Gnyug sems zur dpyad* 257.2: *sangs rgyas kyi yul mthar thug ni sa bcu'i sems dpas kyang mi mthong ngo*

/ de ni gzhi don gyi gnas lugs la sgrib pa phra mos med pa sangs rgyas kho na yin pas so; Padma'i zhal lung 6.4–5: *thabs shes 'du bral med pa yi / de bzhin gshegs pa'i snying po de / sa bcu'i sems dpa' chen pos kyang / mtshan ma'i* [mo'i] *gzugs ltar mi gsal zhes / gsungs phyir rtog ge'i yul min yang / thabs shes zung 'jug lam khyad kyis / dbyer med sras su grub pa yi / ye shes pra pheb [sic] lta bur snang; Rgyud bla'i mchan* 85.3–86.3.

133. Mipam, *Nges sgron* 532.4–5: *mthar thug de kho na nyid ni / gcig las med phyir do kho na / mthong ba'i tshad ma gcig yin te / tshad ma gnyis pa mi srid do / gnas lugs bden gcig zung 'jug ste / tshad ma rang byung ye shes nyid / spang bya ma rig gcig pu las / med phyir rig dang ma rig tsam*. See also his *Dbu ma rgyan 'grel* 685.2–689.2, particularly 688.1: *de lta bu'i phyir na rdo rje theg pa las / sangs rgyas dang sems can ni rig dang ma rig tsam gyi khyad par ro / zhes gsungs pa'ang zab par shes nus la; Gsung sgros* 941.5: *des na 'khor 'das rig ma rig gi khyad par yod pa tsam ste / 'di'i phu thag rdzogs chen gyi gzhung kho nas chod dgos so*. See also Rongzompa, *Theg tshul* 458.13–16: *de bas na chos thams kyi rang bzhin shes pa dang ma shes tsam la / kun nas nyon mongs pa dang rnam par byang bar tha snyad btags pa tsam ma gtogs pa / 'di la bsal bar bya ba'i rdzas sam / gzhag par bya ba'i rdzas kyi ngo bo gang yang myed de*. Cited and translated in German in Wangchuk, "rDzogs-chen Meditation" 173: *'on kyang ma shes pa'i dus na 'khrul snang gi tshul de ltar snang ba tsam yin no*.

134. Rongzompa, *Theg tshul* 493.15–496.11. See also Mipam, *Nges sgron* 535.6–536.1: *spang bya'i dri ma rnams kyang ni / rang gi ngo bos dag pa las / logs shig ma dag pa min pas / rang bzhin 'od gsal mnyam pa nyid*.

135. Rongzompa, *Dkon mchog 'grel* 93.4–7: *de yang gsang sngags kyi tshul ltar na / ma rig pa nyid ye shes gsal / nyon mong sdug bsngal byang chub mchog / ces gsungs pa lta bu ste / mi mthun pa dang gnyen po dbyer med pa'i don gyis sangs rgyas pa'o*. See the discussion of Rongzompa's "special Mahāyāna" in Wangchuk, "Relativity Theory" 226–227. In his *'Od snying* 127.6, he attributes the view that "suffering itself is awakening and intellectual-emotional defilements themselves the great gnosis through which release [occurs]" (*sdug bsngal nyid byang chub / nyon mongs nyid rnam grol gyi ye shes chen po*) exclusively to the Niruttarayoga system. See, however, *'Od snying* 157.6–158.2: *de'i phyir kun 'byung lam bden dang sdug bsngal 'gog bden gyi ngo bor shar bas nyon mongs pa ye shes dang sdug bsngal bde ba chen por grol bas na rgyu 'bras dbyer med du lta bas 'bras bu'i theg pa dang / rdo rje'i theg pa zhes bya ste / de'i dbang gis phung khams skye mched la'ang rdo rje'i ming gis bstan to; 'Od snying* 182.3–5: *yang 'jam par rnam par rol pa la sogs pa'i mdo las / nyon mongs pa rnams ni byang chub rdo rje'i gzhi lags so / zhes pa la sogs pas nyon mongs nyid ye shes su bstan pa dang / 'jam dpal rnam par 'phrul pa sogs las / 'khor ba bsal nas mya ngan las 'das pa bsgom par bya ba ma yin gyi / 'khor bar dmigs pa nyid mya ngan las 'das pa'o / zhes 'khor ba byang chub tu bstan pa dang*. See also Mipam's *Sngags kyi ral gri* 477.4–5: *nges don gnas tshul zab mo la / nyon mongs nyid kyang ye shes te / sdug bsngal rnam grol chen po yin*.

136. Importantly, Rongzompa's stance on the much vexed issue of which doctrines and scriptures are of definitive meaning (*nītārtha, nges pa'i don*) and which of provisional meaning (*neyārtha, drang ba'i don*) seems to be that for him some scriptures teach only neyārtha doctrines; some scriptures consider doctrines taught by other scriptures to be neyārtha and vice versa; some scriptures contain a mixture of neyārtha and nītārtha doctrines; some scriptures, such as, for Mipam, Dzokchen scriptures) teach nothing but nītārtha (*nges pa'i don 'ba' zhig*) doctrines. And the doctrinal criterion for the neyārtha / nītārtha distinction for him seems to be whether and to what degree the doctrine of the "indivisibility of the twofold reality," that is, our ontological yuganaddha, is being taught. In a similar note, Mipam also

maintains that various mantric systems differ in positing varying grades of certainty with regard to the mode of yuganaddha (*bden gnyis zung 'jug gi tshul*). See his *'Od snying* 124.2.

137. Mipam, *Stong thun seng ge* 174.2–3: *mdo dang sngags kyi chos kun gyi gnad gcig pu ni kun khyab bde gshegs snying po de kho na yin zhing*; *Rgyud bla'i mchan* 19.2–28.4; compare *Gzhi'i le'u'i tshig 'grol* 758.2–4; Wangchuk, "Was Mipam a Dialectical Monist?" 33. See also the *Rab gsal brtsad lan* 506.5–509.1, where Mipam explains that the yuganaddha view is shared by both sūtric and mantric Mahāyāna.

138. Rongzompa distinguished what he calls "exclusive" (*thun mong ma yin pa*) Mahāyāna, which includes both its sūtric and mantric forms, from the "common" (*thun mong*) Mahāyāna on the basis of the doctrine of the "indivisibility of the twofold reality" (*bden gnyis dbyer med*; *bden pa rnam pa gnyis dbyer med pa*). To the group of scriptures of the "exclusive Mahāyāna" belong scriptures of definitive meaning (*nītārtha*, *nges pa'i don*), such as the *Vimalakīrtinirdeśa Sūtra*, *Ratnaguṇasaṃcayagāthā*, and the **Guhyagarbha Tantra*. See Wangchuk, "Relativity Theory" 226; Almogi, *Rong-zom-pa's Discourses on Buddhology* 468–470 and 319–322. See also Rongzompa, *Lta 'grel* 336.22–23: *nges pa don gyi mdo sde dang gsang sngags kyi tshul ni / bden pa gnyis dbyer myed par lta' zhing / phung po lnga yang sangs rgyas su lta*; *Lta 'grel* 341.9–12: *de yang chos thams cad dond dam par ma skyes pas so so ma yin pa dang / kun rdzob sgyu ma'i mtshan nyid du so so yin pa gnyis ni / theg pa chen po'i thun mong ste / de phyir bden pa gnyis kyis skad kyis gzhag go / de gnyis dbyer med par rtogs pa' ni thun mong ma yin pa'o*.

139. Mipam, *Dbu ma rgyan 'grel* 350.3; *Nges sgron* 512.3–4. See also the *Stong thun seng ge* 181.5–6, 197.2, where he maintains that Nāgārjuna, and Maitreya and Asaṅga are one in their intent (*dgongs pa gcig*). See also his *Mdo sde rgyan 'grel* 104.5–6: *dbu sems kyi shing rta chen po dag mthar thug gi dgongs pa mthun par bzung bar bya'o*. For justifications, see *Mdo sde rgyan 'grel* 104.6–108.2. See also the *Ye shes rnam 'byed* 246.3: *dbu sems zung 'jug gi tshul*.

140. For Mipam, the distinction between Svātantrika-Madhyamaka and Prāsaṅgika-Madhyamaka traditions does not lie in what or whether they are both able to establish the nature of ultimate true reality (i.e., yuganaddha)—they both do so—but rather how they establish it. See his *Ketaka* 48.2–4.

141. Expressions such as *snang stong dbyer med*, *bden gnyis zung 'jug gi dbu ma*. *Dbu ma rgyan 'grel* 401.6–402.1; *Dam chos dogs sel* 749.5, or *bden gnyis zung 'jug khas len dang bral ba'i dbu ma*; *Dbu ma rgyan 'grel* 423.6, or *khas len thams cad dang bral ba'i dbu ma chen po*; *Ketaka* 148.6, or *zung 'jug rab tu mi gnas pa'i dbu ma chen po*; *Dbu ma rgyan 'grel* 425.4. *Mkhas 'jug* 261.1–2: *snang stong zung 'jug dbu ma chen po* (described as *klu sgrub kyi bzhed pa* and *rgyal ba'i dgongs pa mthar thug pa*); *zung 'jug rab tu mi gnas pa'i dbu ma*. *Dam chos dogs sel* 748.5; *zung 'jug spros pa dang bral ba'i dbu ma chen po*. *Ketaka* 48.3. For details on the various Madhyamaka traditions, see the *Bka' brgyad* 543.1–545.6 and Almogi, "Māyopamādvayavāda." Compare *sTong thun seng ge* 180.5–6: *rnam grangs min pa'i don dam bden gnyis zung 'jug chen po rab tu mi gnas pa'i dbu ma'i don*.

142. On the subclassification of Madhyamaka into Māyopamādvayavāda and Sarvadharmāpratiṣṭhānavāda, see Almogi, "Māyopamādvayavāda."

143. Namely, *dbu ma chen po*, *phyag rgya chen po*, and *rdzogs pa chen po* (designated as *zung 'jug rdzogs pa chen po'i tshul*). Mipam, *'Od snying* 178.1–4; compare *'Od snying* 112.4: *dag mnyam bden pa dbyer med rdzogs pa chen po'i tshul*; *Bka' brgyad* 575.6: *dag mnyam bden pa dbyer med*.

144. See, for example, Mipam's *Lta mgur 'grel pa* 12.6–13.1: *stong pa mtshan nyid pa'am / dbu ma chen po'am / phyag rdzogs sogs ming tha dad kyang don du gcig pa'i snang stong zung 'jug gi ye shes la gus pa'o.*

145. Wangchuk, "Was Mipam a Dialectical Monist?" 33–34; Wangchuk, "rÑiṅ-ma Interpretations" 199–201.

146. The expression *sangs rgyas dang grub thob dgongs pa gcig* is employed by Mipam in his *Nges sgron* 522.6–523.1: *rdzogs chen sems sde'i man ngag rer / mkhas grub so so'i nyams bzhes pas / phyag chen lam 'bras zhi byed dang / zung 'jug dbu ma chen po sogs / mtshan gyi rnam grangs so sor grags / don la sems las 'das pa yi / ye shes yin phyir kun kyang mnyam / sangs rgyas grub dgongs pa ni / gcig ces mkhas kun mgrin gcig smra*; *Dbu ma rgyan 'grel* 414.6–415.1. See also Wangchuk, "rÑiṅ-ma Interpretations" 201 n. 105 where Sapan's *Thub pa dgongs gsal* is referred to. Wangchuk, "Was Mipam a Dialectical Monist?" 35. See also Wangchuk, "Rongzompa's Werk dargestellt wird" 45–46, and Wangchuk, "Defence of the *Guhyagarbhatantra*" 287–288 where Rongzompa's position that the teachings of the Buddha are of a single type (*tshul gcig pa*) and single savor (*ro gcig pa*) is presented.

147. For Mipam, the crucial difference between Svātantrika-Madhyamaka and Prāsaṅgika-Madhyamaka is thus not *whether* they both establish (or are capable of establishing and realizing) yuganaddha but *how* they do so. The former approach of "allowing each of the two modes of reality to be applicable in its own right" (*bden gnyis so so rang sa na ma nyams par bzhag pa*) is for a beginner (*las dang po pa*) more convenient (*bde ba*), but the conceptual separation of the two modes of reality (*bden gnyis so sor 'dzin pa*) must ultimately dissolve. See his *Ketaka* 46.6–49.2. Wangchuk, "Madhyamaka" 223. Wangchuk, "rÑiṅ-ma Interpretations" 194 n. 83. Wangchuk, "Yogācāra School" 1321–1322.

148. For example, Mipam's *Tsong thun seng ge* 174.2–5.

149. Wangchuk, "rÑiṅ-ma Interpretations" 193–201.

150. Mipam, *Dbu ma rgyan 'grel* 360.1–2: *des na sems tsam pa'i tshul 'di kun rdzob tha snyad kyi de kho na nyid shin tu bden pa yin mod / 'on kyang 'di'i rnam shes rang gsal gyi rang bzhin la bden grub tu zhen pa'i cha de dgag bya yin no.* See also his *Mdo sde rgyan 'grel* 107.2–6; *Ye shes rnam 'byed* 360.1–3.

151. Remarkably, Mipam does not hesitate to introduce and distinguish several pairs of Madhyamaka either by way of explication or implication: (1) "Causal / Path Madhyamaka" (*rgyu'i / lam gyi dbu ma*) vs. "Resultant Madhyamaka" (*'bras bu'i dbu ma*), (2) "Mini-Madhyamaka" (*dbu ma chung ngu*) vs. Mega-Madhyamaka (*dbu ma chen po*), (3) "Gross Madhyamaka" (*dbu ma rags pa*) vs. "Subtle Madhyamaka" (*dbu ma phra ba*); (4) "Madhyamaka That Proposes Theses" (*khas len dang bcas pa'i dbu ma*) vs. "Madhyamaka That Does Not Propose Theses" (*khas len dang bral ba'i dbu ma*); (5) Prajñāic / Vijñānaic Madhyamaka (*shes rab / rnam shes kyi dbu ma*) vs. Jñānaic Madhyamaka (*ye shes kyi dbu ma*); (6) "Alternating Madhyamaka" (*res 'jog kyi dbu ma*) vs. "Simultaneous Madhyamaka" (*gcig char gyi dbu ma*); (7) "Pṛṣṭhalabdha-Madhyamaka" (*rjes thob kyi dbu ma*) vs. Samāhita-Madhyamaka (*mnyam bzhag gi dbu ma*)—see also "Samāhitajñāna-Madhyamaka" (*mnyam bzhag ye shes kyi dbu ma*) in the *Dbu ma rgyan 'grel* 627.1. That is, via expressions such as *mnyam rjes kyi dbu ma*, *Dbu ma rgyan 'grel* 424.6. And *'bras bu mnyam bzhag dbu ma*, *Dbu ma rgyan 'grel* 425.1; (8) *bden gnyis so sor 'byed pa'i dbu ma*, *Dbu ma rgyan 'grel* 425.1 vs. *snang stong dbyer med* or *bden gnyis zung 'jug gi dbu ma*, *Dbu ma rgyan 'grel* 401.6–402.1 and *Dam chos dogs sel* 749.5. Note that the opposed or juxtaposed pairs fall either under the category of "Content / Referent Madhyamaka" (i.e., either ontological or gnoseological madhyamaka) or that of "Systemic Madhyamaka" (i.e., Svātantrika-Madhyamaka or Prāsaṅgika-Madhyamaka). When a pair refers

to the Content / Referent Madhyamaka, the distinction between the pair is one of omneity and ultimacy (i.e., whether it is merely *y* or whether it is *xy*-yuganaddha). When a pair refers to Systemic Madhyamaka, the difference between the pair lies in the sequentiality or immediacy of their approach (i.e., in how sequentially or directly *xy*-yuganaddha is established). Thus only that Content / Referent Madhyamaka that is identifiable as *xy*-yuganaddha is genuine Content / Referent Madhyamaka, and only that Systemic Madhyamaka that establishes *xy*-yuganaddha directly (*thad kar*) or from the very outset (*dang po nas*), is a Mega-Madhyamaka. Genuine Madhyamaka (*dbu ma mtshan nyid pa*) must be Yuganaddha-Madhyamaka (*zung 'jug dbu ma*) or Niṣprapañca-Madhyamaka (*spros bral dbu ma*). Most of these terms can be found in the *Nges sgron* 539.3–4, 540.6, 544.6, 545.3, 546.2–5, 548.4–5. See also the *Brag dkar brgal lan* 167.6: *khas len dang bcas pa'i dbu ma* vs. *khas len thams cad bral ba'i dbu ma chen po*; *Ketaka* 48.3: *zung 'jug spros pa dang bral ba'i dbu ma chen po*.

152. Mipam, *Ketaka* 49.2–3: *kha cig 'di sngags lam gyi sgom yin gyi / mdo'i min no zer yang / mtha' bzhi dang bral ba'i zung 'jug de yid dpyod kyis bsgom pa dang / thabs kyis btsan thabs su shar ba'i khyad par tsam las chos kyi dbyings la mi 'dra ba yod pa min no*; *'Od snying* 154.1–2: *mdo yi lam gyis yid dpyod kyis sgom pa'i gnad kyang mthar gtug na bden gnyis dbyer med la 'bab kyang / las dang po pas bden gnyis zung 'jug ro mnyam du nges pa dang myang bar dka' bas / mtha' rnams so so nas bkag pa'i stong par zhen pa gtso che zhing / sngags su zung 'jug 'od gsal ba'i ye shes rang sar ston pa ste*; *'Od snying* 180.3–5, and particularly: *dang po nas zung 'jug bstan pa'i phyir gcig char ba'i bshad tshul yin la*. The sūtric approach in accessing ontological yuganaddha has been compared by Khenpo Jikme Puntsok (1933–2004) (via personal communication) to the ascertainment of the absence of an elephant in a small room somewhere, and the mantric approach to the ascertainment of the absence of an elephant on one's palm. *Nges sgron* 548.1–2: *mdo lam thabs dang shes rab gnyis / gcig la gcig gis rtsis zin par / byed kyi 'dir ni thabs shes nyid / 'du bral med par rtogs goms nyid*; *Nges sgron* 548.3–4: *'on kyang mdo las zung 'jug don / dpyad pas gtan la phab pa nyid / sngags su rang gi rig dbyings su / thad kar myongs bas grub pa yin*; *Gsung sgros* 782.1–783.1; *Gnyug sems zur dpyad* 279.4–6.

153. In the context of discussing the need to rely on *nītārtha* instead of on *neyārtha* in his *Shes rab ral gri* 442.2–443.2, Mipam states that of the four Buddhist religio-philosophical systems (*grub mtha' bzhi*) and series of sūtric and mantric vehicles (*theg pa'i rim pa*), "the uncomprehended elements of the lower systems" (*'og mas ma rtogs cha gang yin*) are seen to be "elucidated by the higher ones" (*gong mas gsal bar byas pa*).

154. Mipam, *Dbu ma rgyan 'grel* 404.2: *de ltar bden gnyis so sor zhen pa'i cha de thal 'gyur ba'i dgag bya thun mong min pa yin te*.

155. Mipam, *Nges sgron* 518.3–4: *stong par zhen pa bzlog phyir du / sngags las bde ba chen po bstan*. See also Wangchuk, *Resolve to Become a Buddha* 222–221 n. 108. Mipam also suggests that a jñānaic view is a "resultant" and Mantric view, whereas a prajñāic view is "causal" and sūtric. See his *Nges sgron* 548.4–5: *de phyir dbu ma zhes pa yang / bden gnyis so sor dpyod pa yi / shes rab lam gyi dbu ma dang / des drangs bden gnyis ro gcig pa'i / zung 'jug 'bras bu'i dbu ma gnyis // rgyu 'bras mdo sngags lta ba ste / snga ma shes rab cha yin la / phyi ma ye shes kho na yin*.

156. Mipam, *'Od snying* 128.5–6: *bden gnyis dbyer med la nges pa 'drongs tshul gyi yul can gong nas gong du 'phags pa'i khyad par*.

157. Rongzompa, *Theg tshul* 502.17–503.3. Compare his explanation of the expression *man ngag thams cad kyi snying po* as one of the attributes of the *rdzogs pa chen po'i tshul* in the *Theg tshul* 476.2–477.10.

158. Mipam, *Grub bsdus* 980.17–981.14.

159. Mipam, *Bka' brgyad* 555.1: *de lta bu'i rang byung gi ye shes nyid la rim dang cig char du 'jug pa'i thabs kyi man ngag gi cha nas bskyed rdzogs rdzogs chen gsum du rnam par bzhag pa yin no.* For Rongzompa, Mahāyoga, Anuyoga, and Atiyoga are distinguished on the basis of the mental capacity of the yogins (*rnal 'byor pa rnams kyi blo rtsal*) to assume *bodhicittavajra*, which is the *bodhicitta* par excellence (*samantabhadraṃ bodhicittam*). See the pertinent passage from the *Mdo rgyas*. Cited and translated in Wangchuk, *Resolve to Become a Buddha* 313.

160. Mipam, *Grub bsdus* 982.11–983.5. According to the *'Od snying* 100.5–101.3, of the three esoteric tantric systems (i.e., *pha rgyud*, *ma rgyud*, and *gnyis med kyi rgyud*), the third (e.g., the system of the *Kālacakra Tantra*) is considered the highest because of its emphasis on the "gnosis of yuganaddha" (*zung 'jug gi ye shes*) also described as "to be marked actual gnosis characterized by yuganaddha" (*mtshon bya don gi ye shes zung 'jug*), "gnosis consisting in the oneness of efficient strategies and insight" (*thabs shes gnyis su med pa'i ye shes*), and "gnosis of the fourth initiation" (*dbang bzhi pa'i ye shes*), which are obviously for him synonymous. See also the *Nges sgron* 521.4–522.1, where he explains why a distinction can be made between the three esoteric or Niruttarayoga systems of the Nyingma. *Nges sgron* 527.3–529.2.

161. For example, the *xy*-yuganaddha suggested in the following verse can be said to be the "yuganaddha of nature." *Nges sgron* 526.1–2: *de phyir snang dang stong pa dag / so so'i cha ni shes na yang / don du nam yang dbye ba med / de phyir zung 'jug ces brjod do.*

162. In his *Dbu ma rgyan 'grel* 425.1–426.1, Mipam discusses the "means-end relation" (*upāyopeyabhāvaḥ sambandhaḥ, thabs dang thabs las byung ba'i 'brel ba*) between conventional truth (*vyavahārasatya, tha snyad kyi bden pa*) and absolute truth (*paramārthasatya, don dam bden pa*) as expressed in *Madhyamakāvatāra* 6.80ab (*upāyabhūtaṃ vyavahārasatyam upeyabhūtaṃ paramārthasatyam*); *Mūlamadhyamakakārikā* 24.10ab (*vyavahāram anāśritya paramārtho na deśyate*). According to him, both the *x* and *y* that constitute the ontological *xy*-yuganaddha are subsumed under *vyavahārasatya* and hence *upāyabhūta*, inasmuch as *xy*-yuganaddha can only be established on the basis of *x* and *y*, whereas the actual *xy*-yuganaddha or here *paramārthasatya* is *upeyabhūta*. This explanation is key to understanding his Yuganaddhavāda philosophy.

163. It can reasonably be maintained that the kind of *xy*-yuganaddha exemplified by "yuganaddha of *śamatha* and *vipaśyanā*" (*zhi lhag zung 'jug*) is the "yuganaddha of nurture."

164. In the tantric context, Mipam often employs the term *zung 'jug gi ye shes*, *mtshon bya don gi ye shes zung 'jug*, and *thabs shes gnyis su med pa'i ye shes*, which are obviously for him synonymous. See, for example, his *'Od snying* 100.5–101.3.

165. Wangchuk, *Resolve to Become a Buddha* 195–217.

166. For the use of the expressions *rang bzhin rnam dag gyi myang 'das* and *glo bu dri bral gyi myang 'das*, Mipam's *Ketaka* 60.5; *Sdud 'grel* 114.1–5.

167. Schmithausen, "Ich und Erlösung im Buddhismus" 159, 161–162, 166, 169 *das Nirvāṇa als metaphysische Größe*; 162, 166, 168 *das Nirvāṇa als spirituelles Ereignis*.

168. Mipam, *Grub bsdus* 640.3: *yongs grub la'ang gnyis / 'gyur med yongs grub ni yul de bzhin nyid dang / phyin ci ma log pa'i yongs grub yul can gyi ye shes so.* See also Rongzompa, *Grub mtha'i brjed byang*: *yongs su grub pa la yang gnyis te / mi 'gyur bar yongs su grub pa dang {chos rnams kyi chos nyid la bya} / phyin ci ma log par yongs su grub pa'o {yang dag pa'i ye shes la bya}*. Almogi, "Yogācāra" 1355 and 1338–1339.

169. Mipam, *Nges sgron* 548.6–549.1: *dngos po stong pa'i gnas lugs dang / bden gnyis dbyer med gnas lugs gnyis / ming gcig na yang don la ni / khyad par gnam sa bzhin du mchis*

/ de bzhin chos nyid chos dbyings dang / stong nyid spros bral 'gog pa'i mtha' / don dam la sogs sgra mtshungs kyang / mthar thug dang ni nyi tshe ba'i / khyad par che phyir skabs so sor / phye nas ma nor bshad bya ste / sendha pa [saindhava] *yi sgra bzhi bzhin no.* Also, *Dbu ma rgyan 'grel* 466.1–2.

170. See Rongzompa, *Theg tshul* 476.5–9: *'di ltar chos rnams kyi don ni / stong zhing bdag med pa dang / rang bzhin myed pa dang / skye ba myed pa dang / mnyam pa nyid dang / gnyis su myed par gtan la phab bo zhes shes par bya ste / sgra 'di rnams kyang res 'ga' ni don gyi bye brag myed par ston / res 'ga' ni tshig gi sgo ji lta ba bzhin du tshig gi yul so sor yod par ston te skabs kyis sbyar ro.*

171. Mipam, *Nges sgron* 543.1: *mdo dang bstan bcos gzhung kun na / dgag sgrub rnam pa ji snyed pa / la la don dam khas len te // la la kun rdzob dbang du gsungs.*

172. See, for example, the *Dbu ma rgyan 'grel* 366.3–368.5.

173. Mipam, *Mkhas 'jug* 229.2–230.1; *Sdom byang* 394.6–395.2: *'dus ma byas pa'i rang bzhin gyi / de bzhin nyid kyi rnam grangs la / rang bzhin rnam par dag pa dang / glo bur bral dag rnam pa gnyis / de bzhin dri bcas dri med gnyis / chos dang gang zag bdag med gnyis // gzhi lam 'bras bu'i de nyid gsum / stong nyid mtshan med smon med gsum.*

174. Rongzompa in his *Dkon mchog 'grel* 57.4–21 also employs and explains terms such as "causal true reality" (*rgyu'i de kho na nyid*), "resultant true reality" (*'bras bu'i de kho na nyid*), and "true reality characterized by the one savor of cause and result" (*rgyu 'bras ro gcig pa'i de kho na nyid*). He considers the terms as "specific terminology of this scripture, the *Guhyagarbha Tantra* (*gzhung 'di nyid kyi rang skad*).

175. For Mipam *pudgalanairātmya* and *dharmanairātmya*, too, are distinguished merely on the basis of "the substrate of emptiness, which is the bearer of the property" (*stong gzhi chos can*). *Ketaka* 85.5–6.

176. That various kinds of *tathatā*, and contextually also *śūnyatā*, are differentiated in terms of *stong gzhi chos can* is made clear in Mipam's *Mkhas 'jug* 292.3; *rab gsal brtsad lan* 298.4–299.4; *Gnyug sems zur dpyad* 304.5–6. Mipam explains that the sixteen kinds of *śūnyatā* have been taught for therapeutic or didactic reasons. See his *Ketaka* 76.4: *dngos dang dngos med du zhen pa sna tshogs pa'i tshul bzlog pa'i phyir stong nyid bcu drug tu bshad pa lta bu ste.*

177. Such as *snang stong zung 'jug, gsal stong zung 'jug, bde stong zung 'jug* or *rig stong zung 'jug.* Note that it has been pointed out that for Mipam, as suggested in his *Nges sgron* 518.4–5: *snang dang gsal dang rig pa gsum / bde ba de yi rnam grangs yin; snang stong zung 'jug, gsal stong zung 'jug, bde stong zung 'jug,* and *rig stong zung 'jug* are synonymous. Wangchuk, "Was Mipam a Dialectical Monist?" 34 n. 36. In his *Shel gyi me long* 725.1–726.2, Mipam considers *stong zung 'jug* in Mahāyoga; *gsal stong zung 'jug* and *bde stong zung 'jug* in Anuyoga; and *rig stong zung* in Atiyoga; as four types of paths connected with four types of initiation.

178. The idea of *niṣprapañca* always presupposes that the "two extremes of manifoldness" (*spros pa'i mtha' gnyis*) are de facto coextensive with the "four extremes of manifoldness" (*spros pa'i mtha' bzhi*), the "eight extremes of manifoldness" (*spros pa'i mtha' brgyad*), or the "thirty-two superimpositions" (*sgro 'dogs so gnyis*). Compare the way the expression *spros mtha' brgyad bral* or *sgro 'dogs so gnyis dang bral ba* is used in the *Ketaka* 47.3 and *Dam chos dogs sel* 749.1–750.6 and *Gnyug sems zur dpyad* 304.6–305.1 and *Mngon rtogs rgyan 'grel* 407.6.

179. Mipam, *Nges sgron* 525.6–526.1: *dngos dang dngos med gnyis po yang / stong gzhir byas nas stong dgos phyir / snang kun btags pa tsam zhig la / stong pa'ang blo yis btags pa tsam.*

180. It is only in this sense that *snang stong zung 'jug*, *gsal stong zung 'jug*, *bde stong zung 'jug*, and *rig stong zung 'jug* can be said to be synonymous. One of the most important sources for this idea is *Mūlamadhyamakakārikā* 25.13cd: *asaṃskṛtaṃ hi nirvāṇaṃ bhāvābhāvau ca saṃskṛtau*. See Mipam, *Mkhas 'jug* 236.6 and *sTong thun seng ge* 185.6 and *gSung sgros* 908.3–909.3.

181. Mipam, *'Od snying* 125.2–6.

182. Mipam, *Mkhas 'jug* 234.2–237.4. *Sdom byang* 395.4: *don dam rtogs tshul rim pa las / rnam grangs rnam grangs min gnyis so*.

183. Mipam, *Dbu ma rgyan 'grel* 402.3–5. Though explained, the expression *dbu ma'i 'char rim bzhi* is not used in this instance. In his *'Od snying*, too, the idea of *dbu ma'i 'char rim bzhi* is implied, again without the collective expression, as a practice of the *kāyasmṛtyupasthāna* according to the mantric system, 138.2–3: *stong nyid spros bral mnyam pa chen po dang zung du 'jug pa'i tshul la blo bzhag pa ni sems dran pa nye bar bzhag pa*. *Dbu ma rgyan 'grel* 176.6–177.1: *de ltar stong pa dang / zung 'jug dang / spros bral dang / mnyam pa nyid de de bzhi po snga ma snga ma shes pa la brten nas phyi ma phyi ma'i tshul la 'jug gi / snga ma la nges pa ma rnyed bar du phyi ma gtan la pheb pa mi 'byung ngo*. For further discussion of Mipam's *dbu ma'i 'char rim bzhi*, see also Phuntsho, *Mipham's Dialectics* 150, 274. See also Mipam's usage of the expression *ye shes 'char tshul gsum* in the tantric context, *'Od snying* 255.6: *ye shes 'char tshul la gsum ste / snang ba'i ye shes / stong pa'i ye shes / zung 'jug gi ye shes so*. *'Od snying* 132.6: *stong pa'i ye shes 'od gsal / snang ba'i ye shes sgyu lus / de gnyis zung du 'jug pa'i ye shes te gsum yod cing*. Compare also the concept of "fourfold emptiness" (*stong nyid bzhi sbyor*) mentioned in the *Gsung sgros* 857.6–859.2 and *Rab gsal brtsad lan* 535.1–537.1 and *Zla ba'i zhal lung* 176.6.

184. Mipam, *'Od snying* 113.4–114.6: *gzhi rang bzhin lhun gyis grub pa'i dkyil 'khor / gnas lugs ngo bo nyid kyi gzhi. rgyu'i rgyud / chos kyi dbyings / yang dag pa'i mtha' / de bzhin nyid. de bzhin gshegs pa'i snying po / snang stong bden pa dbyer med dag mnyam chen po'i bdag nyid gdod ma gzhi'i dkyil 'khor*.

185. One of the scriptural sources for the term and concept of *svayaṃbhūjñāna* is the following verse from the *Buddhāvataṃsaka Sūtra*, often cited under the *Gaṇḍavyūha Sūtra*, located and discussed in Almogi, *Rong-zom-pa's Discourses on Buddhology* 245–246 n. 26: *'jig rten khams rnams la la dag / bsam gyis mi khyab tshig gyur kyang / nam mkha' 'jig par 'gyur ba med / rang byung ye shes de bzhin no*. Almogi points out that Rongzompa cites the verse on a number of occasions, namely, in his *Theg tshul*, *Sangs rgyas sa chen mo*, *Mdo rgyas*, *Mdo sngags grub bsdus*, and *Snang ba lhar sgrub*. Mipam also cites this verse in several of his works, for example, in his *'Od gsal snying po*. See Almogi, *Rong-zom-pa's Discourses on Buddhology* 245 n. 26 and *Mngon rtogs rgyan 'grel* 527.1–2 and *Gnyug sems shan 'byed* 167.5.

186. *sarvākāravaropetā śūnyatā*, *rnam pa kun gyi mchog dang ldan pa'i stong pa nyid / rnam kun mchog ldan gyi stong nyid*. The idea of *sarvākāravaropetā śūnyatā* found in the following verse from Mañjughoṣa Narendrakīrti or perhaps Mañjuśrīyaśas, *Svadarśanamatoddeśa* (N, 24b6; B, vol. 42, p. 576.4–6) seems to have greatly inspired Mipam: *phung po rnam dpyad stong pa nyid / chu shing bzhin du snying po med / rnam pa kun gyi mchog ldan pa'i / stong nyid de dang 'dra ma yin /* (nyid B, ni N; [2]'dra B, 'gyur N). It is cited in such works of his as the *Mkhas 'jug* 237.1–2 and *Gzhan stong seng ge* 233.1 and *Gnyug sems shan 'byed* 88.3. *Gnyug sems zur dpyad* 265.3, 322.6: *phung po rnam dpyad* and reflected in his *Nges sgron* 547.3–4: *snang cha thabs kyi rnam pa dang / ldan pa rnam kun mchog ldan gyi / stong nyid spros bral chen po dang / lhan skyes phyag rgya chen po sogs / mtshan gyi rnam grangs mang mnga' ba / sems 'das ye shes yin pa'i phyir / rtog pa gzhan gyis bsam mi khyab*. *Nges sgron* 545.3–4: *phung po rnam dpyad stong pa nyid / dag bya bcad pa'i med dag tsam*. For some

secondary references to the expression *sarvākāravaropetā śūnyatā*, see Wangchuk, *Resolve to Become a Buddha* 210 n. 60.

187. In this regard, I wish to make four points. First, it has been argued that Rongzompa, Longchenpa, and Mipam, whom I collectively refer to as *rong klong 'ju gsum*, have been considered the "archetypical intellectual models" of the Nyingma, and their positions on any given religio-philosophical issue the authoritative and representative (i.e., "official") positions of the tradition. Wangchuk, "rÑiṅ-ma Interpretations" 173. The trio, in short, are icons of Nyingma intellectualism and mysticism. Wangchuk, "Was Mipam a Dialectical Monist?" 32. Second, Mipam saw himself as the follower of Rongzompa and Longchenpa and as an elucidator of their positions. Wangchuk, "rÑiṅ-ma Interpretations" 173 n. 6. Third, one can question whether and to what extent Mipam's positions are in line with those of Rongzompa and Longchenpa. Khenpo Rinchen, a.k.a. Khenpo Triso Rinchen (1926–1985), who taught in the Nyingma monastic seminary at Namdroling in Bylakuppe in Mysore, South India, reportedly contended that Mipam's views did not conform with those of Longchenpa, whose views are more in line with Sakya views. An attempt has been made to clearly point out the similarities and dissimilarities between Longchenpa, Jonang, Sakya, and Geluk positions on emptiness or buddha-nature (and hence also on yuganaddha as the ultimate reality). Wangchuk, "rÑiṅ-ma Interpretations" 201–203. Fourth and finally, it will have to be conceded that no two traditions or scholars could possibly have had exactly identical views (*Ansichten*) on every single issue, and thus Mipam's concerns, priorities, and views are neither identical with nor diametrically opposed to those of Rongzompa and Longchenpa. Wangchuk, "Was Mipam a Dialectical Monist?" 32–33. Had Mipam suggested or presupposed that the views of various traditions and scholars are identical in all respects, he would have seen no need to reconcile and harmonize them. Had he seen these views as being totally antithetical to each other, he could not possibly have harmonized them even if he had wanted to. For all the differences, he saw a common pivotal point in the idea of yuganaddha, on the basis of which he attempted to reconcile seemingly diametrically opposed or juxtaposed views. Wangchuk, "rÑiṅ-ma Interpretations" and Wangchuk, "Was Mipam a Dialectical Monist?" Philosophically speaking and mutatis mutandis, as already pointed out, the most important point of convergence among Rongzompa, Longchenpa, and Mipam seems to be their understanding of the "groundless-cum-rootless" (*gzhi med rtsa bral*) ontology and the indivisibility of the two modes of reality. Wangchuk, "Was Mipam a Dialectical Monist?" 33. In particular, the ontology of "mere phantasm of nonexistence" (*med pa gsal snang tsam*) proposed by Longchenpa (the significance of which has been pointed out in Ehrhard, *"Flügelschläge des Garuḍa"* 264–265 n. 5) and that deserves to be examined closely—seems to, through and through, conform to Rongzompa's Sarvadharmāpratiṣṭhānavāda ontology and Mipam's Yuganaddhavāda philosophy.

188. The *Ansicht-Einsicht* distinction presupposed by Tibetan Buddhist scholars, in my view (*Ansicht*), can be very useful in explaining a number of doctrinal issues within Tibetan Buddhism. For an attempt to explain the Geluk position on Substantialism and soteriological exclusivism by means of this distinction, see Wangchuk, "Yogācāra" 1321–1323.

Bibliography

Sanskrit Sources

Candrakīrti. *Madhyamakāvatārakārikā*. Skt. For the Sanskrit edition of *Madhyamakāvatāra* 6.1–6.97, see Li, "Madhyamakāvatāra-kārikā" 3–14; Tib., see de La Vallée Poussin, *Madhyamakāvatāra*.

Madhyamakāvatārabhāṣya. See de La Vallée Poussin, *Madhyamakāvatāra*.
Mañjughoṣa Narendrakīrti (or perhaps Mañjuśrīyaśas). *Svadarśanamatoddeśa*. B. *bsTan 'gyur dpe bsdur ma*. 120 vols. Beijing: Krung go'i bod rig pa'i dpe skrun khang, 1994–2005, vol. 42; N. *sNar thang bstan 'gyur* [TBRC-W22704], vol. *pu*, fols. 22a–52a.
Nāgārjuna. *Mūlamadhyamakakārikā*. See de Jong, *Mūlamadhyamakakārikāḥ of Nāgārjuna*.
———. *Ratnāvalī*. See Hahn, *Nāgārjuna's Ratnāvalī*.
———. *Yuktiṣaṣṭikā*. See Lindtner, *Master of Wisdom* 72–93 (Tibetan text and English translation), 174–175 (Sanskrit fragments).
Prajñākaragupta. *Pramāṇavārttikālaṃkāra*. See Sāṅkṛtyāyana, *Pramāṇavārttikabhāshyam*.
Vajrajñānasamuccayatantra. T (*sTog bka 'gyur*) 412. Number according to Skorupski, *Catalogue of the sTog Palace Kanjur*.

Tibetan Sources

Bod sprul Mdo sngags bstan pa'i nyi ma. *Lta grub shan 'byed gnad kyi sgron me*. Xylographic print. rDzogs chen shrī siṃha, n.d. TBRC–W10198.
Go ram pa Bsod nams seng ge. *Lta ba'i shan 'byed theg mchog gnad kyi zla zer*. See Cabezón and Dargyay, *Freedom from Extremes*.
Krang dbyi sun, et al. *Bod rgya tshig mdzod chen mo*. Beijing: Mi rigs dpe skrun khang, 1993.
Mi pham Rnam rgyal rgya mtsho. *Bde bshegs snying po'i stong thun chen mo seng ge'i nga ro*. In *Mi pham gsung 'bum*, vol. 15, 173–218.
———. *Brgal lan nyin byed snang ba*. In *Mi pham gsung 'bum*, vol. 18, 161–273.
———. *Byang chub sems sgom pa'i thabs blo yi ral gri*. In *Mi pham gsung 'bum*, vol. 17, 481–483.
———. *Bya rtsol kun tu gcod pa ye shes ral gri*. In *Mi pham gsung 'bum*, vol. 17, 479–480.
———. *Chos dang chos nyid rnam par 'byed pa'i tshig le'ur byas pa'i 'grel pa ye shes snang ba rnam 'byed*. In *Mi pham gsung 'bum*, vol. 15, 241–289.
———. *Dbu dang mtha' rnam par 'byed pa'i bstan bcos kyi 'grel pa 'od zer 'phreng ba*. In *Mi pham gsung 'bum*, vol. 15, 297–413.
———. *Dbu ma la 'jug pa'i 'grel pa zla ba'i zhal lung dri med shel phreng*. In *Mi pham gsung 'bum*, vol. 13, 1–277.
———. *Dbu ma rgyan gyi rnam bshad 'jam dbyangs bla ma dgyes pa'i zhal lung*. In *Mi pham gsung 'bum*, vol. 13, 333–743.
———. *Dbu ma rtsa ba'i mchan 'grel gnas lugs rab gsal klu dbang dgongs rgyan*. In *Mi pham gsung 'bum*, vol. 12, 223–453.
———. *Dbu ma sogs gzhung spyi'i dka' gnad skor gyi gsung sgros sna tshogs phyogs gcig tu bsdus pa rin po che'i za ma tog*. In *Mi pham gsung 'bum*, vol. 17, 765–975.
———. *Don rnam par nges pa shes rab ral gri*. In *Mi pham gsung 'bum*, vol. 17, 433–446.
———. *Dpal sgrub pa chen po bka' brgyad kyi rnam par bshad pa dngos grub snying po*. In *Mi pham gsung 'bum*, vol. 23, 513–699.
———. *Gnyug sems 'od gsal gyi don rgyal ba rig 'dzin brgyud pa'i lung bzhin brjod pa rdo rje snying po*. In *Mi pham gsung 'bum*, vol. 24, 1–51.
———. *Gnyug sems 'od gsal gyi don la dpyad pa rdzogs pa chen po'i gzhi lam 'bras bu'i shan 'byed blo gros snang ba*. In *Mi pham gsung 'bum*, vol. 24, 53–179.
———. *Gnyug sems zur dpyad skor gyi gsung sgros thor bu rnams phyogs gcig tu bsdus pa rdo rje rin po che'i phreng ba*. In *Mi pham gsung 'bum*, vol. 24, 181–385.

———. *Gsang 'grel phyogs bcu mun sel gyi spyi don 'od gsal snying po*. In *Mi pham gsung 'bum*, vol. 23, 97–319.
———. *Gsung 'bum: Mi pham rgya mtsho*. 32 vols. Chengdu: [Gangs can rig gzhung dpe rnying myur skyobs lhan tshogs], 2007.
———. *Gu ru'i tshig bdun gsol 'debs kyi rnam bshad padma dkar po*. In *Mi pham gsung 'bum*, vol. 24, 386–450.
———. *Gzhan gyis brtsad pa'i lan mdor bsdus pa rigs lam rab gsal de nyid snang byed*. In *Mi pham gsung 'bum*, vol. 18, 275–586.
———. *Gzhan stong khas len seng ge'i nga ro*. In *Mi pham gsung 'bum*, vol. 15, 219–239.
———. *Gzhi lam 'bras bu'i shan 'byed sangs rgyas padma'i zhal lung*. In *Mi pham gsung 'bum*, vol. 23, 1–7.
———. *'Jam dpal rdzogs pa chen po gzhi lam 'bras bu dbyer med pa'i don la smon pa rig stong rdo rje'i rang gdangs*. In *Mi pham gsung 'bum*, vol. 24, 471–475.
———. *Kun rtog 'ching ba gcod pa sngags kyi ral gri*. In *Mi pham gsung 'bum*, vol. 17, 475–480.
———. *Lcang skya rol pa'i rdo rje'i lta ba'i mgur zab mo'i 'grel pa*. In *Mi pham gsung 'bum*, vol. 18, 7–40.
———. *Le'u bco brgyad pa'i tshig 'grol*. In *Mi pham gsung 'bum*, vol. 17, 749–763.
———. *Mchog grub pa'i utpala*. In *Mi pham gsung 'bum*, vol. 17, 486–492.
———. *Mkhas 'jug gi sdom byang*. In *Mi pham gsung 'bum*, vol. 17, 359–405.
———. *Mkhas pa'i tshul la 'jug pa'i sgo zhes bya ba'i bstan bcos*. In *Mi pham gsung 'bum*, vol. 17, 1–317.
———. *Nges shes rin po che'i sgron me*. In *Mi pham gsung 'bum*, vol. 17, 501–551.
———. *Rdo grub pa dam chos zhes pas gzhan gyi zer sgros bsdus nas mkhas su re ba'i 'khyal ngag de dag mi mkhas mtshang phud du kho rang nas bskul ba bzhin nyams mtshar du bkod pa*. In *Mi pham gsung 'bum*, vol. 13, 747–807.
———. *Rgyud lung man ngag gi tshig don cung zad bshad pa dri med shel gyi me long*. In *Mi pham gsung 'bum*, vol. 23, 723–736.
———. *Rje btsun sa skya pa'i lta grub kyi gnad 'ga' zhig la dri ba byung ba'i dogs sel*. In *Mi pham gsung 'bum*, vol. 18, 599–611.
———. *Sdud 'grel yum la 'jug pa'i legs bshad las mdo dang bstan bcos sbyar tshul ma pham zhal lung*. In *Mi pham gsung 'bum*, vol. 14, 217–560.
———. *Sher phyin mngon rtogs rgyan gyi mchan 'grel puṇḍa ri ka'i do shal*. In *Mi pham gsung 'bum*, vol. 14, 391–662.
———. *Shes rab kyi le'u'i tshig don go sla bar rnam par bshad pa nor bu ke ta ka*. In *Mi pham gsung 'bum*, vol. 18, 41–159.
———. *Slob dpon padma 'byung gnas kyis mdzad pa'i man ngag lta ba'i phreng ba'i mchan 'grel nor bu'i bang mdzod*. In *Mi pham gsung 'bum*, vol. 23, 13–61.
———. *Snga 'gyur bstan pa rgyas pa'i smon lam chos rgyal dgyes pa'i zhal lung*. In *Mi pham gsung 'bum*, vol. 32, 695–700.
———. *Theg pa chen po mdo sde rgyan gyi dgongs don rnam par bshad pa theg mchog bdud rtsi'i dga' ston*. In *Mi pham gsung 'bum*, vol. 16, 1–807.
———. *Theg pa chen po rgyud bla ma'i bstan bcos kyi mchan 'grel mi pham zhal lung*. In *Mi pham gsung 'bum*, vol. 15, 1–171.
———. *Tshogs gnyis zung 'jug gi nyams len gnad kyi me long*. In *Mi pham gsung 'bum*, vol. 32, 515–518.
———. *Ye shes grub pa'i utpala*. In *Mi pham gsung 'bum*, vol. 17, 494–497.

———. *Yid bzhin mdzod kyi grub mtha' bsdus pa*. In *Mi pham gsung 'bum*, vol. 17, 599–671.

———. *Yid bzhin rin po che'i mdzod kyi dka' gnad ci rigs gsal bar byed pa*. In *Mi pham gsung 'bum*, vol. 17, 673–747.

———. *Yon tan rin chen sdud pa'i 'grel pa rgyal ba'i yum gyi dgongs don la phyin ci ma log par 'jug pa'i legs bshad*. In *Mi pham gsung 'bum*, vol. 14, 1–215.

Rog Shes rab 'od. *Bla ma rog gi ban dhe shes rab 'od kyis mdzad pa'i grub mtha'i so so'i bzhed gzhung gsal bar ston pa chos 'byung grub mtha' chen mo bstan pa'i sgron me*. In *Bka' ma shin tu rgyas pa*, 120 vols, vol. 14, 105–315. [Chengdu: Kaḥ thog mkhan po 'Jam dbyangs, 1999].

Rong zom Chos kyi bzang po. *Dam tshig mdo rgyas chen mo*. In *Rong zom gsung 'bum*, vol. 2, 241–389.

———. *Gsung thor bu*. In *Rong zom gsung 'bum*, vol. 2, 27–130.

———. *Lta ba dang grub mtha' sna tshogs pa brjed byang du bgyis pa*. In *Rong zom gsung 'bum*, vol. 2, 197–231.

———. *Man ngag lta phreng gi 'grel pa rong zom paṇḍi ta chen po chos kyi bzang pos mdzad pa*. In *Rong zom gsung 'bum*, vol. 1, 301–351.

———. *Mtshan yang dag par brjod pa'i 'grel pa rnam gsum bshad pa*. In *Rong zom gsung 'bum*, vol. 1, 255–290.

———. *Rgyud rgyal gsang ba snying po dkon cog 'grel*. In *Rong zom gsung 'bum*, vol. 1, 31–250.

———. *Rong zom chos bzang gi gsung 'bum*. 2 vols. Chengdu: Si khron mi rigs dpe skrun khang, 1999.

———. *Theg pa chen po'i tshul la 'jug pa zhes bya ba'i bstan bcos*. In *Rong zom gsung 'bum*, vol. 2, 415–555.

Secondary Sources

Almogi, Orna. *Rong-zom-pa's Discourses on Buddhology: A Study of Various Conceptions of Buddhahood in Indian Sources with Special Reference to the Controversy Surrounding the Existence of Gnosis (jñāna: ye shes) as Presented by the Eleventh-Century Tibetan Scholar Rong-zom Chos-kyi-bzang-po*. Studia Philologica Buddhica Monograph Series 24. Tokyo: International Institute for Buddhist Studies, 2009.

———. "Māyopamādvayavāda versus Sarvadharmāpratiṣṭhānavāda: A Late Indian Subclassification of Madhyamaka and Its Reception in Tibet." *Journal of the International College for Postgraduate Buddhist Studies* 14 (2010): 135–212.

———. "Yogācāra in the Writings of the Eleventh-Century Rnying ma Scholar Rong zom Chos kyi bzang po." In *The Foundation for Yoga Practitioners: The Buddhist Yogācārabhūmi Treatise and Its Adaptation in India, East Asia, and Tibet*, edited by Ulrich Timme Kragh, 1330–1361. Harvard Oriental Series 75. Cambridge: Department of South Asian Studies, Harvard University, 2013.

Broido, Michael M. "Padma-dkar-po on Integration as Ground, Path and Goal." *The Journal of the Tibet Society* 5 (1985): 5–54.

Cabezón, José Ignacio, and Geshe Lobsang Dargyay. *Freedom from Extremes: Gorampa's "Distinguishing the Views" and the Polemics of Emptiness*. Boston: Wisdom, 2007.

de Jong, Jan William, editor. *Mūlamadhyamakakārikāḥ of Nāgārjuna*. Madras: Adyar, 1977.

de La Vallée Poussin, Louis, editor. *Madhyamakāvatāra par Candrakīrti: Traduction tibétaine*. Bibliotheca Buddhica 9. St. Petersburg: Imprimerie de l'Académie Impériale des Sciences, 1912.

Deroche, Marc-Henri. *Prajñāraśmi ('Phreng po gter ston Shes rab 'od zer, Tibet, 1518–1584): Vie, œuvre et contribution aux renaissances de l'école anciennes (rnying ma) et à la floraison de l'approche non-partisane (ris med). [=Prajñāraśmi ('Phreng po gter ston Shes rab 'od zer, Tibet, 1518–1584): Life, Works, and Contributions to the Rnying ma School and the Ris med Movement].* PhD thesis. Paris: École Pratique des Hautes Études, Section des Sciences Religieuses, 2011.

Duckworth, Douglas S. *Mipam on Buddha-Nature: The Ground of the Nyingma Tradition.* Albany: State University of New York Press, 2008.

Ehrhard, Franz-Karl. *"Flügelschläge des Garuḍa": Literar- und ideengeschichtliche Bemerkungen zu einer Liedersammlung des rDzogs-chen.* Tibetan and Indo-Tibetan Studies 3. The Institute for the Culture and History of India and Tibet, University of Hamburg. Stuttgart: Franz Steiner Verlag, 1990.

Guenther, Herbert. *The Teachings of Padmasambhava.* Leiden: E. J. Brill, 1996.

Hahn, Michael. *Nāgārjuna's Ratnāvalī. Vol. 1: The Basic Texts (Sanskrit, Tibetan, Chinese).* Indica et Tibetica 1, edited by Michael Hahn. Bonn: Indica et Tibetica Verlag, 1982.

Li, Xuezhu, editor. "Madhyamakāvatāra-kārikā." *China Tibetology* 18, no. 1 (2012): 1–16.

Lindtner, Chr., editor and translator. *Master of Wisdom: Writings of the Buddhist Master Nāgārjuna, Translation and Studies.* Revised edition. Yeshe De Project. Berkeley: Dharma, 1997.

Negi, J. S., et al. *Tibetan-Sanskrit Dictionary.* 16 vols. Sarnath: Central Institute of Higher Tibetan Studies, Dictionary Unit, 1993–2005.

Phuntsho, Karma. *Mipham's Dialectics and the Debates on Emptiness: To Be, Not to Be or Neither.* Oxford Centre for Buddhist Studies. London: Routledge Curzon, 2005.

Sāṅkṛtyāyana, Rāhula, editor. *Pramāṇavārttikabhāshyam or Vārtikālaṃkāraḥ of Prajñākaragupta (Being a Commentary on Dharmakīrti's Pramāṇavārtikam).* Patna: Kashi Prasad Jayaswal Research Institute, 1953.

Schmithausen, Lambert. "Ich und Erlösung im Buddhismus." *Zeitschrift für Missionswissenschaft und Religionswissenschaft* 53, no. 2 (1969): 157–170.

Skorupski, Tadeusz. *A Catalogue of the sTog Palace Kanjur.* Bibliographia Philologica Buddhica Series Maior 4. Tokyo: The International Institute for Buddhist Studies, 1985.

Schwerk, Dagmar. *Spiegel der Sichtweise: Die Kernpunkte [der Philosophie] des Mittleren [Weges] (dBu ma'i bsdus don lta ba'i me long): Eine kurze Abhandlung über das Madhyamaka rJe dGe-'dun-rin-chens (1926–1997), dem 69. rJe mKhan-po von Bhutan.* Magister thesis. Hamburg: University of Hamburg, 2012.

Wangchuk, Dorji. "Madhyamaka aus der Sicht der rNying-ma Tradition." In *Buddhismus in Geschichte und Gegenwart* 4, 211–233. Hamburg: University of Hamburg, 2000.

———. "Die große Vollendung wie sie in Rongzompa's Werk dargestellt wird." In *Buddhismus in Geschichte und Gegenwart* 5, 41–53. Hamburg: University of Hamburg, 2001.

———. "An Eleventh-Century Defence of the *Guhyagarbhatantra*." In *The Many Canons of Tibetan Buddhism*, edited by Helmut Eimer and David Germano, 265–291. Leiden: Brill, 2002.

———. "Einige philosophische Grundlagen der rDzogs-chen Meditation." In *Buddhismus in Geschichte und Gegenwart* 8, 165–181. Hamburg: University of Hamburg, 2003.

———. "The rÑiṅ-ma Interpretations of the *Tathāgatagarbha* Theory." *Wiener Zeitschrift für die Kunde Südasiens* 48 (2004): 171–213. [Appeared in 2005.]

———. *The Resolve to Become a Buddha: A Study of the Bodhicitta Concept in Indo-Tibetan Buddhism.* Studia Philologica Buddhica Monograph Series 23. Tokyo: The International Institute for Buddhist Studies, 2007.

———. "A Relativity Theory of the Purity and Validity of Perception in Indo-Tibetan Buddhism." In *Yogic Perception, Meditation, and Altered States of Consciousness*, edited by Eli Franco and Dagmar Eigner, 215–237. Vienna: Austrian Academy of Sciences, 2009.

———. "Was Mipam a Dialectical Monist? On a Recent Study of Mipam's Interpretation of the Buddha-Nature Theory." *Indo-Iranian Journal* 55 (2012): 15–38.

———. "On the Status of the Yogācāra School in Tibetan Buddhism." In *Foundation for Yoga Practitioners: The Buddhist Yogācārabhūmi Treatise and Its Adaptation in India, East Asia, and Tibet*, edited by Ulrich Timme Kragh, 1316–1328. Harvard Oriental Series 75. Cambridge: Department of South Asian Studies, Harvard University, 2013.

12

Along the Middle Path in the Quest for Wisdom

The Great Madhyamaka in Rimé Discourses

Marc-Henri Deroche

Introduction

Madhyamaka, as the expression of the Buddhist middle path (*madhyamā pratipad, dbu ma'i lam*) par excellence, came to be the keystone of Tibetan doxographies of Indian Buddhist philosophy. Its view thus plays a central role in organizing and interpreting the whole of Buddhist scriptures and traditions transmitted from India to Tibet. As such, in the course of Tibetan intellectual history, Madhyamaka has constituted a major sectarian marker as well as a crucial point for eclectic approaches. In this regard, the relation between discourses on emptiness and those about buddha-nature or luminosity is of decisive importance, with major implications for the exegetical and practical questions of the relation between sūtra and tantra. The purpose of this chapter is to examine the value and function of the "Great Madhyamaka" zhentong (*gzhan stong*) system in eclectic strategies that intend to give a unified presentation of Buddhist traditions in Tibet.

The late E. Gene Smith (1936–2010) noted the use of zhentong by Jamgon Kongtrul Lodro Taye (1813–1899), in his *Impartial History of Buddhism* (*Ris med chos 'byung*), as a "unifying concept" employed to emphasize the essential unity of the various religious traditions of Tibet.[1] Smith insisted on the exceptional inclusive nature of Jamgon Kongtrul's interpretation of zhentong, itself a notion that had caused much debate among the various Tibetan orders, resulting in it being severely condemned under the rule of the Geluk order. In this regard, it can be argued that the so-called Rimé (*ris med*) or "impartial" movement of nineteenth-century eastern Tibet constituted a reaction and a renaissance of the ancient earlier orders including the Nyingma, Kagyu, Sakya, Jonang, and Bon.

To bring new elements for the academic study of this historical dialectic between sectarianism and eclecticism in Tibet, I analyze significant sources of the Rimé movement, written at the very time of the crystallization of sectarian identities in sixteenth-century central Tibet. The analysis of these works, both historiographical and philosophical, by Prajñāraśmi, alias Trengpo Terton Sherab Ozer (1518–1584) will enable us to identify key elements at stake for the perspective of the unity of Buddhist teachings within the Rimé movement. Then we shall see how these elements are integrated in Jamgon Kongtrul's zhentong model within the inclusive framework of his *Impartial History of Buddhism*. In this way, we shall better identify the nature of this eclectic middle path and its soteriological implications.

The Rimé Movement in the Dialectics of Tibetan Buddhist History

To begin, I would like to remark that before being specified as nonsectarian or even as defining a nineteenth-century specific religious activity in Khams, the Tibetan term "rimé" has expressed the general virtue of impartiality, sharing common features with the early Buddhist notion of the middle path. Just as Madhyamaka transcends "extremes" (*ananta*, *mtha' med*), the expression *phyogs ris su med pa* (**apakṣapāta*), designates the negation (*med pa*) of a "bias" or "partiality" (*phyogs ris*). In a sense, following the middle path is also not to side with any position: it is to remain impartial. An impartial approach within Tibetan Buddhism also stresses the importance of completeness both in terms of Buddhist teachings and in terms of yogic realization. In the context of meditation instructions, rimé means "without bias or inclination," as related to meditation "without an object" (*anālambana*, *dmigs med*) in the pure contemplation according to Mahāmudrā or Dzokchen traditions.[2] Impartiality is indeed linked here to the Buddhist ideals of detachment and contemplation.

For heuristic purpose, and with some reservation, I will keep here the expression "Rimé movement" understood as a trans-sectarian activity of collection, revelation (*gter ma*), compilation, and transmission of Buddhist lineages and teachings, led by the spiritual trio of Jamyang Khyentse Wangpo (1820–1892), Jamgon Kongtrul, and Chogyur Dechen Lingpa (1829–1870), through the network of several monasteries in and around Derge, belonging mainly to the Kagyu, Sakya, and Nyingma orders. To designate in English the approach of the Rimé movement, I have chosen here to use the term "eclecticism" as another designation of a middle path avoiding the extremes of "sectarianism" that affirms the superiority of one's own tradition over others' and "syncretism" that mixes or confuses the different traditions.

The eclectic nature of the Rimé movement, collecting different traditions and showing their unity while maintaining the integrity of each, is particularly exemplified by Kongtrul's collection of the *Treasury of Spiritual Instructions* (*Gdams ngag mdzod*) as E. Gene Smith's remarked:

> By collecting the instructions and confirmations of an enormous number of such *gdams ngag* and passing them on to his disciples as an organized unit, Kong sprul was implicitly pointing out their ultimate identity. [. . .] The arrangement of the collection is in itself a statement of the nonsectarian movement; this compilation is a source of profound importance for understanding what Kong sprul and his colleagues were trying to do.[3]

I will examine here some major sources used by Kongtrul in his *Treasury of Spiritual Instructions*. Matthew T. Kapstein has shown that the model of the "Eight Great Chariots of the Lineages of Practice" (*sgrub brgyud shing rta chen po*) that forms the organizing structure of the *Treasury of Spiritual Instructions* was attributed to Prajñāraśmi.[4] Jamyang Khyentse wrote a commentary on them that was then expanded by Kongtrul in the catalogue (*dkar chag*) of his *Treasury of Spiritual Instructions*.[5] Elsewhere, I have studied only a small portion of Prajñāraśmi's works where he exposed the history and instructions of the eight lineages of practice. The purpose of this chapter is to analyze these works in their entirety and to present their specific strategy to unify Buddhist teachings, sūtra and tantra, scholastic exegesis (*bshad*) and contemplative practice (*sgrub*).

The other main source of the *Treasury of Spiritual Instructions*, both in terms of inspiration and content, is the *Hundred Instructions of the Jonang* (*Jo nang khrid brgya*), compiled by Kunga Drolchok (1507–1565).[6] Thus, the two main sources of the *Treasury of Instructions*—understood to exemplify the nineteenth-century Rimé movement—belong to the sixteenth century, when the earlier orders, that is, the "Reds," were strongly reasserting themselves in opposition to the newly rising Geluk order, the "Yellows."[7] This shows us how the Rimé movement activated the renaissance of the earlier Tibetan orders by making full use of these Red voices of the past, some of which had been censored for three centuries, most notably Dolpopa Sherab Gyaltsen (1292–1361) and Serdok Paṇchen Shakya Chokden (1428–1507), up to the mid-seventeenth century.

Unification of Buddhism through the Development of Wisdom: Prajñāraśmi's Ambrosia of Study, Reflection, and Meditation

Khyentse and Kongtrul's primary sources, two epistles (*spring yig*) that form a single unit, are attributed to Prajñāraśmi: (1) *The Ambrosia of Study and Reflection* (*Thos bsam 'chi med kyi bdud rtsi*) on scholastic exegesis (*bshad*) and (2) *The Ambrosia of Meditation* (*Sgom pa 'chi med kyi bdud rtsi*) on contemplative practice (*sgrub*). According to their colophons, these works were written at the fort of the Chonggye ('phyong rgyas) valley in central Tibet, at the place named Chingwa Taktse ('phying ba stag rtse) associated with the ancient Tibetan empire, and the birthplace of the Fifth Dalai Lama Ngawang Lozang Gyatso (1617–1682). I have chosen to call them "epistles" since they are said to have been sent (*bsrings*) by the author to his contemporaries from the fort of Chonggye.[8] They are in a sense "open letters" addressed to his peers.

Prajñāraśmi was initially trained as a geshe (*dge bshes*) in the Sakya and Geluk orders, and he later became a yogin and treasure-revealer (*gter ston*) in the Kagyu and Nyingma orders.[9] He was thus learned and accomplished (*mkhas grub*) within four of the main orders of Tibetan Buddhism. He also founded Pelri Tekchen Ling (dpal ri theg chen gling) Monastery in Chonggye, where the great Jigme Lingpa (1729 / 30–1798) was later born and trained.[10] Prajñāraśmi's first teacher in Tangkya Ewam (thang skya e waṃ) Monastery was the Sakya master Dorje Gyalpo (15th c.), a disciple and biographer of Shakya Chokden. His root master was Drikung Rinchen Puntsok (1509–1557), the abbot of Drikung. Rinchen Puntsok was the disciple of the Fourth Zhamarpa Chodrak Yeshe (1453–1524),[11] who had a preeminent political and religious position in Tibet from 1498 to 1517 and was himself a student of the eclectic author Go Lotsāwa Zhonnu Pel (1392–1481).[12] It could be argued that the works of Shakya Chokden and Zhonnu Pel, two precedent masters in Prajñāraśmi's lineage, represent important sources and influences of Prajñāraśmi's epistles to be studied here.

The development of wisdom (*prajñā*, *shes rab*) is traditionally described according to the three steps of study, reflection, and meditation, and it is understood to be an internalization of the Buddha's teachings. Prajñāraśmi's two epistles encompass Buddhist knowledge in Tibet according to the progression toward the full blossoming of wisdom. In the study of a major work by Prajñāraśmi's contemporary, the Eighth Karmapa Mikyo Dorje (1507–1554) on Madhyamaka, David Seyfort Ruegg made the following comment that points out the heart of the present problematic:

> And in the study of the Indo-Tibetan traditions such factors with their human, social and even psychological dimensions will have to be considered together with doctrinal and philosophical criteria on the levels of learning (*thos pa* = *śruta*), reflective analysis (*bsam pa* = *cintā*) and meditative realization (*sgom pa* = *bhāvanā*). Here we may have something comparable in part to what are known today as "knowledge traditions."[13]

In the context of sectarian rivalries, these epistles appear as an eclectic approach concerning the different Buddhist orders of Tibet, and at the same time as a manifesto of the early orders reasserting themselves in opposition to the Geluk. The fact that Tsongkhapa Lozang Drakpa (1357–1419) and his followers are surprisingly not mentioned is an important element, not to be neglected. This possible implicit message by the author may be polemics by omission. Even if unlike Shakya Chokden, Prajñāraśmi was not directly offensive, he used similar rhetorical elements in some writings of Shakya Chokden that play a central role in these epistles. Specifically, the two epistles in their entirety are structured according to the notion of Tibet's former lineages of exegesis and practice. Komarovski has shown that Shakya Chokden, several decades earlier, made use of the same notions in order to ostracize the Geluk order apart from the authoritative sources of Tibetan Buddhist orders.[14] The heart of the problematic was the competitive claim that sought possession of Tibet's Buddhist legacy and authority over its prestige. I mean that competing Buddhist orders were then claiming against each other to be the sole true holders of the main lineages that established Buddhist exegesis and practice in Tibet. We can easily see how this is intimately connected to the struggle for politico-religious hegemony between the Reds and Yellows.

While we cannot assert the true intent of Prajñāraśmi, it is certain that these epistles present a reassertion of the historicity, authenticity, and authority of the early orders through an exegesis that references the Indian origins of the Buddhist transmission to Tibet. The first epistle offers an overview of Indic materials of the Tibetan canon, sūtras, tantras, and their commentaries by Indian masters (śāstra), as well as their translation and study in Tibet. The second details the esoteric lineages originated from Indian mahāsiddhas and transmitted to Tibet. While rejecting various plausible deviations and establishing an authentic path, these texts present an ingenious strategy to show the underlying unity of Tibetan Buddhist traditions. We shall now examine the most salient content of each of these two epistles through their exegesis of study, reflection, and meditation.

The Ambrosia of Study and Reflection

After a preliminary homage to the historical Buddha Shākyamuni, the first epistle begins by stating the correct orientation and scope of traditional Buddhist exegesis:

> Those who aspire to listen and explain the holy teachings of the scriptures,
> The supports of which are like crowns on the top of genuine spiritual friends' heads,
> Must study and reflect with diligent discernment
> The Victor's speech and authentic sages' treatises.[15]

The text goes on by honoring the emperor Songtsen Gampo (617–650) and enumerating the "ten great pillars that established the lineages of exegesis in Tibet" (*bshad rgyud 'degs pa'i ka chen bcu*).[16] The author lays out the plan of his treatise: the three wheels of the Dharma and the four sections of tantra. For each, he gives his definition, and the transmission's history from India to Tibet.

The first wheel is basically identified with the *Vinaya* and the emergence of the eighteen ancient schools of Indian Buddhism. Concerning the second or intermediate wheel, a distinction is made between the "hidden meaning" (*sbas don*) and the "explicit meaning" (*dngos bstan*). The first refers to the content of the *Abhisamayālaṃkara* attributed to Maitreya and the second to the doctrine of the two truths (*satyadvaya*, *bden gnyis*) of Madhyamaka by Nāgārjuna, followed by Bhāviveka, Buddhapālita, and Candrakīrti with their Prāsaṅgika / Svātantrika distinction. Concerning the third or last wheel, Prajñāraśmi states:

> Remaining in the basis of purification that is nondual wisdom,
> Having no doubt that all apprehended phenomena are never existent,
> And that the apprehending knowledge is also illusory,
> Is the stage of the final wheel's path.[17]

Associated with this final wheel doctrine are the four works attributed by Tibetans to Maitreya,[18] Nāgārjuna's *Collections of Hymns* (*Bstod tshogs*), and Asaṅga's and Vasubandhu's works. In regard to these two latter authors, Prajñāraśmi makes clear that he considers them to be Mādhyamika and not to be disregarded at a lower position under the Cittamātra label:

> Here in the hermitages of the snowy mountains [Tibet],
> As for the excellent and marvelous works of the invincible and victorious Maitreya, Asaṅga and his brother Vasubandhu,
> Although many commentate them upon the distinction between Madhyamaka and Cittamātra,
> There is no doubt that they are treatises of the Madhyamaka.[19]

Thus the Madhyamaka as understood by Prajñāraśmi also includes the discourses on buddha-nature and the luminosity of the nature of mind as taught in the treatises of the Yogācāra. We have here a clear element in common with the zhentong system, even if Prajñāraśmi uses this word with a special care.

He describes the lineages of Abhidharma as well as the traditions of Dignāga and Dharmakīrti. At this point, Prajñāraśmi exposes his classification of the Madhyamaka subschools, while paying special reverence to the Sakyapa continuators:

> The commentaries of Niḥsvabhāvavāda-Madhyamaka (*ngo bo nyid med pa'i dbu ma pa*), Yogācāra-Madhyamaka (*rnal 'byor spyod pa'i dbu ma pa*),
> And of the Madhyamaka following worldly conventions (*'jig rten grags sde'i dbu ma pa*)
> Gave rise, here in Tibet, to three exegetical traditions.
> Distinct and noble among all is the tradition of the Sakya.[20]

This classification is similar to what the Kadam scholar Upa Losal (14th c.) explicated in *Losal's Philosophical Systems*.[21] Even if this author recognized the Prāsaṅgika / Svātantrika distinction, before Tsongkhapa it was not seen as a hierarchical distinction between the classification of Madhyamaka subtraditions. Prajñāraśmi placed an emphasis on Sanskrit and its grammar as the true mark of an authentic Buddhist scholar in Tibet, one able to study and explain the Indian originals, while dismissing Tibetans incapable of doing so:

Even if there are renowned sages well versed in the [Three] Baskets (*piṭaka*, *sde snod*),
If they do not know Sanskrit, [as for] the treatises of India,
Who could trust them,
When they shall explain bases (**prakṛti*, *rang bzhin*), suffixes (**pratyaya*, *rkyen*), and declension of cases (**vibhakti*, *rnam dbye*), and so forth?[22]

This epistle continues with a few stanzas on the secular sciences. The second main part is on the four sections of tantra according to the Sarma model, enumerating the *Kriyā tantra*, *Caryā tantra*, *Yoga tantra*, and *Yoganiruttara*. Curiously, the Nyingma system of tantras is not mentioned, though it becomes important in the next epistle that corresponds with the lineages of practice. Of much importance for the present discussion is the conclusion of the first epistle:

In India and here also in Tibet,
The great progression of sūtra and tantra without illusion,
Is the exegetical tradition explained by sages of the ancient generations;
The scriptures taught by the Victor of the three times.[23]

This authoritative statement establishes the continuity of sūtra and tantra, that is, the unity of Buddhism according to its correct interpretation, while it reassesses the authority of the early orders. The author denounces what he sees as deviations from this supposed line of consent:

The tantra of the Great Secret, the tradition of the chariots of Madhyamaka and Cittamātra,
The intention of Nāgārjuna and the incomparable exegetical tradition
Of its excellent commentary according to the two systems of Prāsaṅgika and Svātantrika
Are interpreted for the most part in a distorted way.[24]

We find here a list of the focal points of sectarian tension during this time. They include Buddhist esotericism, as well as Buddhist philosophy with the bipartition of Madhyamaka and Cittamātra. We have previously seen that for our author, Maitreya, Asaṅga, and Vasubandhu belong to the Madhyamaka, the ultimate correct view, and not to Cittamātra, the idealist view to be surpassed in ascension to the perfect insight of absolute reality. In this passage, Prajñāraśmi stresses that the real intended meaning of Nāgārjuna's works, the doctrine of emptiness, and the related exegetical traditions of Prāsaṅgika and Svātantrika are generally not interpreted correctly. All of these categories, exoteric and esoteric, Cittamātra and Madhyamaka, Prāsaṅgika and Svātantrika, are major points articulating the Tibetan doxographies of Indian Buddhism, raising questions about their hierarchical relationships. The interpretations of these categories had become the ground for hard sectarian delimitations and scholastic disputations that our author strongly criticizes in behavioral and ethical terms:

> Some are proud of holding the Buddha's doctrine through study and exegesis.
> But in order to prove others' treatises wrong and establish their own,
> [They utter] deceitful bubbles, garlands of meaningless words.
> The debates where they brandish the position of their own camp (*rang phyogs*) create troubles to the doctrine of the Buddha.[25]

The search for mundane glory or profit with a competitive attitude is seen to be a great violation of the objective of Buddhist scholarship. In the same vein, he sees the eclipse of the study of Indian exegetical traditions, and promotion of the study of systems conceived by Tibetans by their own sectarian affiliation, to be a major deviation from the scholastic curricula:

> Some having entirely abandoned the study and the exegesis of the authentic treatises
> [Written] according to the Victor's speech and its commentary,
> Study and explain a tradition composed with their individual opinions.
> How surprising is that they spend their lifetime doing so![26]

This critique of new Tibetan compositions is resonant with similar statements found in the works by Shakya Chokden.[27] Similarly, the summit of exegesis is seen to be attained in the footsteps of the forefathers who established Buddhism in Tibet according to the traditions of their natural successors, before any of the late Tibetan scholastics:

> This is why, you people with clear mind and making an effort in learning,
> Having perfectly understood the distinction between your philosophical system and others',
> With a diligent examination of the exegetical traditions explained by the ancient masters of exegesis,
> Reach the bounds of study![28]

Sectarianism is seen as a partiality that is separated from the different domains of traditional knowledge studied within the monastic colleges. In contradistinction, the author's approach is based on the example of his own root teacher:

> [Some say:] "For some people, only sūtra, and for some people, only tantra.

For others, only grammar and logic." This is a biased perspective
(*phyogs re'i mig*).
The venerable Ratna [Rinchen Puntsok], totally victorious in all
directions,
Was eloquent and virtuous in all sciences.[29]

For the author, all branches of knowledge, from grammar and logic with the other secular sciences, and all Buddhist teachings, sūtras and tantras, are to be studied. We may find here a sociological reflection on the problems arising from specialization, which tend naturally to appear within large scholastic institutions. Scholars tend to have only a partial knowledge of Buddhist scholarship and opposition emerges in reference to each other, resulting in the creation of factions. The author insists on a complete scholastic training that is finally to be followed, completed, and led to its ultimate spiritual end by means of meditation, according to the Buddhist ethos of detachment and solitary contemplation. On this topic, we shall now turn to the next epistle.

The Ambrosia of Meditation

After paying homage to the primordial ahistorical Buddha Vajradhara, the second epistle is explicitly structured in five parts. The introductory chapter presents the "eight pillars that established the lineages of practice" (*sgrub brgyud 'degs pa'i ka chen brgyad*).[30] The genius of this eclectic model is to present the genealogy of the esoteric lineages (*brgyud*) at the foundation of the various Tibetan Buddhist orders (*chos lugs*), while emphasizing their unity through the convergence of their contemplative instructions (*gdams ngag*).[31] In the next four chapters, Prajñāraśmi exposes the unity of the eight lineages of practice in terms of (1) view (*lta ba*), (2) meditation (*sgom pa*), (3) conduct (*spyod pa*), and its (4) fruit (*'bras bu*).

In the chapter about the view, the author distinguishes the Buddhist view from non-Buddhist traditions, most notably the Hindu and Bön.[32] He also does the following analysis of Buddhist philosophical systems:

[The view according to which] all manifestation is one's own mind is
common to both Sautrāntika and Cittamātra.
The cessation of the subject / object duality [is taught by]
Alīkākāravāda-Madhyamaka.
We assert as the Great Madhyamaka the presentation of the view
Through the refutation of the true establishment of nondual gnosis.[33]

We see here at work the delineation between the Satyākāra and Alīkākāra schools, which are identified as, respectively, Cittamātra and Madhyamaka in the works of Shakya Chokden.[34] Moreover, the "Great Madhyamaka" asserted in this context does not appear to be the zhentong type elucidated by Dolpopa. It has more of a Prāsaṅgika orientation, similar to some writings of Longchen Rabjam (1308–1364), or later, Mipam Namgyel Gyatso (1846–1912),[35] in the sense of eliminating any conceptual reification of nondual gnosis. With such a precaution given, this gnosis is nevertheless said to be the main teaching on the view of the eight lineages of practice. The following passage is of utmost importance for our present discussion:

> This gnosis that is knowledge, clear, vivid, and nonconceptual,
> Introduced as the primordial gnosis itself,
> Free from all the elaborations of the subject / object duality made by the mind,
> Is the main teaching of all the lineages of practice.[36]

Prajñāraśmi points out the direct presentation of nondual gnosis to be the common point, the unity, and the heart of the eight lineages of practice. Different lineages have different means for various individuals to accomplish this fundamental gnoseological recognition, direct self-knowledge. This is recognized as the liberating and transformative insight that is free from the dualistic mind and the suffering created by deluded thoughts, passions, and actions / reactions. The concept of gnosis is however to be clearly distinguished from gnosis itself, which is nonconceptual. The concept of gnosis is understood to be a convention during the postmeditative period. Its actual meaning is realized during contemplation:

> In that way it is a convention of the postmeditative period.
> But during meditative equipoise, the domain of space without limits
> Is the mode of entering into the view to be seen and the subject seeing it, expression and concept.
> In the definitive meaning, they are like water and waves.[37]

Through the images of water and waves, Prajñāraśmi expresses how subject and object dissolve during meditation. Gnosis as an object of study, and reflection is just a convention while gnosis as contemplative experience is beyond subject and object. We are confronted here with the central problem of zhentong philosophy, and of Buddhist philosophy in general, that is to say the relation between (1) philosophical discourse, (2) discursive reflection, and (3) supradiscursive contemplation, the three steps for the development of wisdom. The relation between gnosis and its postmeditative convention is pointed out by Kongtrul as key to the demarcation between rangtong and zhentong:

> Rangtong and zhentong do not differ in regard to the way that relative truth is empty or in regard to the cessation of the extremes of discursiveness during meditative equipoise. They differ over whether the nature of reality (dharmatā) exists or not as a convention during postmeditation and whether gnosis is truly established or not by ultimate analysis.[38]

According to this stance, rangtong and zhentong lead to the same realization during contemplation. They differ in that zhentong maintains realization of dharmatā, the "nature of reality," as a convention that leads to such experience, affirming that gnosis is truly existent. Nevertheless, such reification of gnosis is denied according to Prajñāraśmi's definition of the "Great Middle Path," as we have seen. Just as he does not show a preference for Prāsaṅgika or Svātantrika, Prajñāraśmi does not side with either rangtong or zhentong. Furthermore, in another passage, he expresses how tantric meditation integrates both views of zhentong and rangtong:

> Knowing that the creation phase corresponds to the tradition of zhentong,
> And that the completion phase corresponds to the tradition of rangtong,
> The yogin of the Mahāyāna who meditates their conjunction
> Is the crown ornament of all vajraholders.[39]

This corresponds to tantric Madhyamaka, important for Shakya Chokden and later adopted by Kongtrul in his *Treasury of Knowledge*. The tantric phase of creation proceeds through a visualization appearing from emptiness, showing that emptiness is not just inert but contains the power of apparition, sound, and luminosity. All the perfect qualities of enlightenment are visualized according to the symbolic attributes of a divinity. In contradistinction, the phase of perfection implies the dissolution of the visualization and all concepts into the pure contemplation of naked emptiness. From emptiness to form and clarity, and from form and clarity to emptiness—tantric practice is here interpreted as the conjunction of zhentong, the clear aspect of emptiness, and rangtong, the empty aspect of clarity. The notion of conjunction (yuganaddha, *zung 'brel*) shows how tantric inner alchemy leads to this *coincidentia oppositorum*.[40] In accord with this process, Kongtrul again points out the central importance of the experience of gnosis.[41]

In the chapter on meditation, which includes discussion of both the conceptual analysis and nonconceptual positioning of mind, meditation methods that are common to all lineages of practice, gnosis is described as follows:

> Whatever may be the methods to examine and posit the mind,
> The principal meditation of all the lineages of practice
> Is the own character, nature, clear light,
> Appearing clear and vivid, without meditation, without distraction.[42]

We notice here the clear and vivid aspect of gnosis experienced during contemplation. This seems to be a determining element for zhentong as a philosophical view that unifies these traditions in the works of Kongtrul. The transcendence of both meditative effort and mundane distraction shows how the heart of meditation is pure, nonconceptual, and nondual contemplation.

Concerning conduct, the general framework appears to be the doctrine of the three codes (*sdom pa gsum*) of personal liberation, bodhisattva, and tantra. In line with this, the author insists on Buddhist orthodoxy and orthopraxy and warns against various deviations from tantric practice.

As for the fruit, the author insists on an absence of bias between Nyingma and Sarma notions of the absolute body of the Buddha:

> We assert that Samantabhadra, the teacher of Dzokchen,
> And Vajradhara are without duality the body of reality (dharmakāya).
> With partisan (*phyogs 'dzin*) conceptions detached from scriptures or reasoning,
> How surprising it is to make a distinction of good or bad within the [ultimate] body of the Buddha![43]

He points out that the common fruit of the eight lineages is complete buddhahood, including the formal aspects displayed for the benefit of others and subsumed under the notion of the Buddha's body of enjoyment (*saṃbhogakāya*):

> The tendencies of transmigration, which are especially to be eliminated,
> Having been vanquished by the antidote of the gnosis of great bliss,
> The buddha's body of enjoyment endowed with eight qualities will appear.[44]
> This is the ultimate fruit of the eight great traditions.[45]

And in conclusion, Prajñāraśmi points out the nature and unity of the eight lineages of practice:

> The eight great traditions are the supreme quintessence of the eighty-thousand collections of the Dharma,
> Even if there are methods to progressively guide disciples according to circumstances,
> And their main practices are distinct,
> It is certain that ultimately the presentation of their view and meditation is one.[46]

As in the first epistle, he emphasizes their authority for Indian and Tibetan Buddhism:

> In India and here also in Tibet,
> These traditions followed by the mahāsiddhas of the ancient generations,
> Great progression without error of the examination and positioning [of the mind]
> Are the unique vehicle of all the Victors of the three times.[47]

Then he tackles again the problem of partiality as a disjunction of methods and wisdom, equated with view and conduct. In fact, the two epistles integrate exegesis and practice, sūtra and tantra, and can be seen as a sophisticated response to this problem:

> Nevertheless, here in the snowy hermitages of the North,
> Some disregard the method and hold the view as supreme;
> Others neglect wisdom and hold the conduct as supreme.
> Thus appeared two biased traditions falling into partiality (*phyogs re*).[48]

In parallel, he also criticizes the disjunction between sūtra and tantra. He claims that the adhesion to Mahāyāna's philosophical systems should not lead to dismissal of the profundity of Vajrayāna's revealed teachings:

> Some believe that any view and conduct other than those by the two
> chariot traditions of commentary by reason,
> Of the two noble and supreme ones [Nāgārjuna and Asaṅga],
> As well as the tradition of the glorious Candrakīrti,
> Are erroneous teachings.[49]
> You people who aspire to liberation, be vigilant:
> Do not reject the dharma of the main oral lineages
> Taught appropriately to fortunate beings
> By Vajradhara and the powerful and venerable [Vajra]yoginī.[50]

Vajrayāna leads to the authentic view of the nature of reality through its skillful means. Nevertheless, Mahāyāna philosophy is necessary to maintain the correct Buddhist view:

> This view [, which is based on] personal experience and confidence
> Through the blessing of empowerment, the coming of gnosis,
> The meditation of the perfection phase and profound devotion,
> Is the quick path to obtain buddhahood in this life.[51]
> Yet, if this view of the profound path
> Is separated from the examination of discriminative conceptual
> knowledge,
> One's own position and instructions to others
> Will not eliminate the attachment to mistaken paths.[52]

The author exhorts his contemporaries to debate these matters according to the complete perspective of the various exegetical and contemplative lineages, with suitable attitude and foundations:

> Seeing all ways of teaching exegesis and practice,
> Without inflaming others' minds with low thoughts and conduct,

> If you wish to debate according to trusted scriptures and completely correct reasoning,
> Discern the circumstances of debate![53]

Finally, in parallel with the end of the first epistle, Prajñāraśmi expresses his wishes that all will perfectly master correct study, reflection, and meditation.

Synthesis

Table 12.1 presents a synthesis of Prajñāraśmi's two epistles. We observe a clear continuity between the third dharma wheel, positively reevaluated, and the common view of the eight tantric lineages of practice through their common reference to nondual gnosis. The essence of the third dharma wheel is defined as the exposition of nondual gnosis, while the view shared by all the eight lineages of practice is said to be the direct presentation of nondual gnosis. Through the three steps of the development of wisdom—study, reflection, and meditation—this discourse uses gnosis as a postmeditative convention to point out its direct experience, what is supradiscursive, and beyond subject and object. The structure articulates exegesis and practice, sūtra and tantra, view and conduct, wisdom and means. Even if these works do not strictly side with the zhentong discourse but ingeniously conjoin it with the rangtong perspective in the course of tantric practice, they include all the essential points that define Kongtrul's use of zhentong as a unifying concept linking sūtra and tantra.[54] The emptiness taught in the sūtras is not only a nonimplicative negation or an inert emptiness. These are preliminary steps completed by the third dharma wheel that teaches emptiness to be a positive nature endowed with luminosity and the potential of enlightened qualities. This establishes the complete view that is implemented in the tantras through the skillful means that relies on the dynamic, vibrant, and vivid qualities of the energy of emptiness, the nondual gnosis of great bliss. Here, the history of Buddhist teachings and tradition is framed according to this soteriological and gnoseological path. Kongtrul proceeds through similar articulations but, in his case, with the full adoption of the "Great Middle Path" as an articulation of zhentong.

The Great Middle Way in Jamgon Kongtrul's Impartial History of Buddhism

Kongtrul's *Impartial History of Buddhism*,[55] is a short treatise without formal structure but in which we can clearly identify three main parts: (1) The history of Indian Buddhist philosophy;[56] (2) The history of Tibet's religious traditions and schools;[57] and (3) The exposition of the philosophical systems of Tibetan Buddhist orders.[58] The text first pays homage to the historical Buddha and describes his realization in terms of the "ordinary vehicle" (*theg pa thun mong*), that is, Mahāyāna, in contrast with Vajrayāna. Ultimately, Kongtrul tells us that "having realized what is the nature

Table 12.1. Synthesis of Prajñāraśmi's Two Epistles

Study and Reflection (*thos bsam*)		
Introduction		Ten Pillars that establish the lineages of exegesis in Tibet
Sūtra	1	*Vinaya*, eighteen Indian schools, and so on
	2	Hidden meaning (*sbas don*)—Maitreya's *Abhisamayālaṃkara*
Three Wheels		Explicit meaning (*dngos bstan*) • Nāgārjuna: Madhyamaka • Bhāviveka: Svātantrika • Buddhapālita: Prāsaṅgika, and so on.
	3	Nondual gnosis (*gnyis med ye shes*) • Maitreya's *Mahāyānasūtrālaṁkāra, Ratnagotravibhāga, Dharmadharmatāvibhāga, Madhyāntavibhāga* • Nāgārjuna's *Collection of Hymns* (*Bstod tshogs*) • Asaṅga and Vasubandhu: Madhyamaka
Tantra **Four Sections**		*Kriyā, Caryā, Yoga, Yoganiruttara*
Meditation (*sgom*)		
Introduction		Eight Pillars that establish the lineages of practice in Tibet
View		Main teaching: primordial gnosis
Meditation		Main meditation: clear light, without meditation or distraction
Conduct		Three codes of conduct of Hīnayāna, Mahāyāna, and Vajrayāna
Fruit		Ultimate fruit: buddhahood with the Body of Enjoyment

of buddha-nature which is the basis, [the Buddha obtained] perfect buddhahood in the sphere of all phenomena (i.e., the dharmadhātu)."[59] From this perspective, he turned the three dharma wheels:

> For the benefit of disciples of inferior faculties, as the first set of discourses, he turned the dharma wheel of the revolution of the twelve aspects, by repeating three times the four truths of suffering, origin, path, and cessation. For the benefit of disciples of intermediate faculties, as the medium set of discourses, he turned the dharma wheel establishing the absence of defining characteristic of all grasped self-character of phenomena belonging to saṃsāra and nirvāṇa, from form up to omniscience. For the benefit of disciples of higher qualities, as the final

> set of discourses, he turned the dharma wheel, excellently distinguishing existing and not existing phenomena, and which is empty or not empty, through the doctrine of the three natures: imaginary, dependent, and thoroughly established.[60]

After the Third Council, the tradition of the hearers (śrāvaka, *nyan thos*) developed into the eighteen ancient schools from which appeared the philosophical systems of the Vaibhāṣika and the Sautrāntika. Later appeared the philosophical system of the Cittamātra. Kongtrul equates, respectively, each of Nāgārjuna's collections, of advice (*gtam tshogs*), reasoning (*rigs tshogs*), and hymns (*bstod tshogs*), with each of the three dharma wheels. Then follows the description of Prāsaṅgika and Svātantrika along the diffusion of Rangtong Madhyamaka. The philosophical progression is concluded with the five works that Maitreya reportedly transmitted to Asaṅga. Vasubandhu and Candragomin are said to have brought certainty for the exegesis of these works and the twenty Tathāgatagarbha sūtras. As in Prajñāraśmi's epistles, they are not included in the Cittamātra school but said to belong to the Madhyamaka, in the way that Kongtrul presents that they were "later known as the philosophical system of the Madhyamaka of definitive meaning according to the proclamation of the great lion's roar of the unmistaken zhentong."[61] This zhentong presentation is just followed by an account of the apparition of the tantras, the eighty-four mahāsiddhas, and numerous adepts who realized the "body of nondual gnosis" (*gnyis su med pa'i ye shes kyi sku*).[62] It is interesting to note again the continuity between zhentong and tantra through this same notion of nondual gnosis. In this first section on Indian Buddhism, the report of the Buddha's enlightenment, the three dharma wheels, the progression of the philosophical systems, the evocation of tantra and corresponding realization, all point to zhentong as their ultimate intent.

For Tibet's religious history, Kongtrul does not follow any classificatory model since his account is generalized and includes Bon as well. Kongtrul begins with the historical myths of the Tibetan people's origins, the ancient rulers' genealogy, and the history of the Zhangzhung kingdom.[63] He includes a description of Bon with the model of the nine vehicles. He continues with the Nyingma[64] and the Kadam.[65] The various four great and eight small Kagyu traditions form the longest passage[66] maybe because, as the colophon says, the text was composed at Situpa's monastery of Pelpung (dpal spungs). Kongtrul also describes some streams unifying Nyingma and Kagyu teachings.[67] The text goes on with the Shangpa Kagyu,[68] the Sakya,[69] Zhije and Chod lineages.[70] Then, the history of the Jonang is presented in association with zhentong.[71] Immediately after, Kongtrul includes a developed and respectful passage on the Gandenpa.[72] This concludes the section on the history of Tibetan Buddhist orders.

The last section is an account of the philosophical systems adopted by these schools (*chos lugs de rnams kyi grub mtha'*). Kongtrul affirms that in Tibet, there was only the Mādhyamika's view and the Sarvāstivādin's conduct. According to the imperial decision of the great Dharma King Trisong Detsun, upholders of the Vaibhāṣika, Sautrāntika, and Cittamātra were not allowed. The reference to the ancient Tibetan emperor represents a source of authority for the foundational past of Tibetan Buddhism. Kongtrul presents what E. Gene Smith named "the most inclusive interpretation of the zhentong that has never been put forward by a Tibetan scholar."[73] Kongtrul writes:

> The view and realization of the followers of the great from Oḍḍiyāna [Padmasambhava], the omniscient [Longchenpa (Klong chen pa)] Drime Ozer (Dri med 'od zer), and the scholars and accomplished masters of the ancient secret mantra; from Marpa (Mar pa), Milarepa (Mi la ras pa), Dagpo (Dwags po), later the scholars and accomplished masters of the four great and eight small Kagyu traditions, which appeared, until the spiritual friend of the entire teachings, the all-seeing [Eighth Situpa] Chokyi Jungne (Chos kyi 'byung gnas, 1699 / 1700–1774); Sachen Kunga Nyingpo (Sa chen Kun dga' snying po, 1092–1152), the uncle [Sakya paṇḍita] (1092–1152) and his nephew [Phagpa Lodro Gyaltsen ('Phags pa Blo gros rgyal mtshan)] (1235–1280); Zhilung paṇchen (Zi lung paṇ chen) [Shakya Chokden]; the supreme omniscient Buddha of the three times, the great Dolpopa, and the most venerable Tāranātha (1575–1635) who clarified his intention, as well as all the great individuals of the oral lineage of Jonang who progressively appeared, were solely Zhentong Madhyamaka. But from the point of view of subdivisions, there are a few individual distinctions.[74]

This coalition of Nyingma, Kagyu, Sakya, and Jonang is to remind us of Prajñāraśmi's epistles and inspirations, even if Prajñāraśmi was not using the term zhentong in the same way. Here, the meaning of Kongtrul's zhentong is largely extended in order to designate the perceived common denominator of all these traditions in terms of view and practice, while minimizing their differences. Kongtrul considers that in Tibet there were only a few upholders of the Svātantrika system, including Rongton Sheja Kunrik (1367–1449), Tratsangpa Lochok Dorje (1595–1671), Dorje Drakpa, among others. They are said to have been true followers of Śāntarakṣita. Masters of Sakya, Ngor and Tshar, the omniscient Buton Rinchen Drub (1290–1364), the Eighth Karmapa Mikyo Dorje, Drukchen Pema Karpo (1527–1592), and Tsongkhapa together with the later Geluk followers put their emphasis on the Prāsaṅgika school, with important distinctions among them.[75] Kongtrul avoided mentioning any conflict between rangtong and zhentong but let the differences appear in the sole Prāsaṅgika sphere, in essence, the absence of discursiveness (*niṣprapañca, sprod pa med*).

In the very final section, Kongtrul relates the transmission lineage of what became known as the "instructions on the view of the Madhyamaka that are the Ganden Mahāmudrā" (*dbu ma'i lta khrid dga*['] *ldan phyag chen*) coming from Umapa Pawo Dorje (14th c.). Similarly, Kongtrul presents the transmission lineage of the "instructions on the view of Zhentong Madhyamaka" (*gzhan stong dbu ma'i lta khrid*), which concludes the whole work. It is informed by

> the collections of explicit discourses according to the twenty sūtras on buddha-nature, which are ordinary and of definitive meaning, and the teachings on the inseparability of profundity and clarity, which is the meaning of the additional instructions (*man ngag*) of the extraordinary treatises of Maitreya . . .[76]

This specific mention in the end of these two main traditions of spiritual instructions, the Mahāmudrā of Ganden and Zhentong Madhyamaka, is significant. In this specific case, the common point of these two traditions is that they are lineages of "instructions on the view," that is to say, of contemplative nature, which is the approach underlying the varied eclectic discourses studied in this chapter. Kongtrul himself has integrated some elements of this Geluk contemplative tradition within the Kadam section of his *Treasury of Instructions*.[77] Indeed, it is the zhentong contemplative tradition that ends the final section of Kongtrul's *Impartial History of Buddhism*. Like the central channel of the whole body of Buddhist traditions, Kongtrul uses zhentong to be an expression of the middle path.

Conclusion: Buddhist Philosophy in the Light of Wisdom

The eclectic works presented here are responses, and at some level, echoes of the sectarian debates that shaped the history of Tibetan Buddhism. Whether they can extract themselves entirely from sectarian preoccupations is a question that remains open. To conclude with a positive note, which corresponds to the affirmative nature of the contemplative approach followed by Prajñāraśmi and the inclusive zhentong model of Kongtrul, I would like to point out their common emphasis on nondual gnosis. This is coupled with their conjoined reference to practical instructions for contemplative practice, the "spiritual instructions" (*gdams ngag*) of the eight lineages of practice, and the "instructions on the view of Zhentong Madhyamaka."

Such "spiritual instructions" or "instructions on the view" in Buddhism are similar to what French philosopher Pierre Hadot has described as "spiritual exercises" in Western ancient philosophy.[78] This notion played a central role in Hadot's reinterpretation of ancient *philosophia* as a *quest for wisdom*, engaging the conversion of the whole person in a philosophical *way of living* and a radically new vision of the self and the world. Kapstein has shown the unique value of Hadot's contribution[79] in order to examine the very possibility of using the expression "Buddhist philosophy" and investigate further the Buddhist use of rational discourse and exercises of self-transformation, discursive or supradiscursive. In Buddhism, the continuity between these different levels appears in the three steps of study, reflection, and meditation. The unity of the whole reveals itself in the light of its perspective and ultimate goal, which is wisdom (*shes rab*, *prajñā*) or gnosis (*ye shes*, *jñāna*). It is in this sense that Prajñāraśmi (literally, in Sanskrit, the "Light of Wisdom") used this model to unify the sources of Buddhist traditions in Tibet. The strong reliance of our Tibetan authors on spiritual instructions seems analogous to Hadot's emphasis on spiritual exercises with a similar result: the emphasis on wisdom or gnosis. The similarity lies in the sense of a *way of being* and a *way of seeing* as the main goal, with the effect of minimizing differences between various philosophical traditions while showing their overall unity of ultimate intent. From this point of view, the philosophical significance of the virtue of rimé impartiality appears to be ideally the impartiality of the sage who sees everything from the perspective of totality.

Notes

1. Smith, "'Jam mgon Kong sprul" 265.

2. For the different meanings of rimé, and especially in the context of contemplation, see Deroche, "On Being 'Impartial.'"

3. Smith, "'Jam mgon Kong sprul" 264.

4. Kapstein, "*gDams ngag*."

5. Deroche, "'Phreng po gter ston Shes rab 'od zer (1518–1584) on the Eight Lineages of Attainment."

6. They are included in the DNgDz vol. 18, 127–153.

7. Tucci, *Tibetan Painted Scrolls* 39–66.

8. This statement is repeated in the introduction and in the colophon of both epistles: TS, 231.3–4, 242.2–3; G, 244.2–3, 266.6–7.

9. Deroche, "Sherab Wozer."

10. Deroche, "dPal ri Monastery."

11. See Ehrhard, "Observations on Prāsaṅgika-Madhyamaka in the rÑing-ma-pa School" 11–31. In particular, we should note that the Fourth Zhamarpa was teaching Madhyamaka on the basis of the so-called five treatises of Maitreya and following the zhentong approaches of Dolpopa and of the Seventh Karmapa Chodrak Gyatso (1454–1506). His own teacher, Zhonnu Pel, also played an important role for the interpretation of Maitreya's *Ratnagotravibhāga* from the point of view of the Mahāmudrā of the Kagyu, as studied by Mathes, *Direct Path*.

12. On the eclectic or nonsectarian attitude of Zhonnu Pel, who was able to receive instructions and empowerments from the most important masters of his time while having direct access to the Indian origins of Tibetan Buddhism, see Mathes, *Direct Path* 131–147.

13. Seyfort Ruegg, "A Karma bka' brgyud Work."

14. See in particular this passage of Shakya Chokden in his *Chos kyi 'khor lo bskor ba'i rnam gzhag ji ltar grub pa'i yi ge gzu bor gnas pa'i mdzangs pa dga' byed*, in *Śā mchog gsung 'bum*, vol. 16, 473.1–2, given and translated in Komarovski, *Visions of Unity* 92. He says that Tsongkhapa and his followers created a new system of sūtra and tantra outside of "all Tibet's former lineages of exegesis and lineages of practice" (*sngon bod kyi bshad rgyud pa dang sgrub rgyud pa mtha' dag*) and then disregarded the ancient and genuine traditions. From the perspective of the Geluk themselves, according to the *Thu'u bkwan grub mtha'*, the Geluk have absorbed all former Tibetan Buddhist teachings as profound instructions and have purified them from the errors and lack of realization of later Tibetan masters. So even if these teachings still exist in earlier orders, the Geluk are said to be superior to all of them. *Thu'u bkwan grub mtha'* 375: *man ngag zab mor byed pa ji snyed mchis pa mtha' dag ma tshang ba med pa dge ldan pa la mnga'o / de dag kyang bar skabs su ma rtogs pa dang log par rtogs pa'i skyon gyis gos pa rnams rje yab sras kyis bsregs bcad brdar ba'i gser bzhin du dag par mdzad*

pas gzhan dag la yod pa las kyang khyad par du 'phags pa 'ba' zhig go. These strong assertions from both camps problematize further the question of eclecticism, the inclusive approach toward all traditions, and paradoxically, its possible use for sectarian agenda.

15. TS 231.2–3: *lung gi dam chos nyan dang 'chad 'dod rnams / bshes gnyen dam pa spyi ba'i thod bzhin brten / rgyal ba'i bka' dang tshad ldan mkhas pa'i gzhung / rnam dpyod brtson pas thos dang bsam par bya*.

16. (1) Tonmi Sambota (Thon mi Sam bho ṭa, b. ca. 619), (2) Vajra Śrī [supposed to have dispelled obstacles, Padmasambhava?], (3) Pagor Vairocana (Pa gor Vairocana, 8th c.), (4) Kawa Peltsek (Ska ba dpal brtsegs, 8th c.), (5) Chokro Lui Gyaltsen (Cog ro klu'i rgyal mtshan, 8th c.), (6) Zhang Yeshe De (Zhang ye shes sde, 8th c.), (7) Rinchen Zangpo (Rin chen bzang po, 957–1055), (8) Ngok Loden Sherab (Rngog blo ldan shes rab, 1059–1109), (9) Sakya Paṇḍita Kunga Gyaltsen (Sa skya Paṇḍita Kun dga' rgyal mtshan, 1182–1251), (10) Buton Rinchen Drub (Bu ston rin chen grub, 1290–1364).

17. TS 234.2–3: *gzung ba'i chos kun nam yang yod min zhing / 'dzin byed shes pa 'ang 'khrul par gdon mi za / gnyis med ye shes sbyang gzhir gzhag pa ste / 'khor lo tha ma'i lam gyi rim pa'o*.

18. *Dharmadharmatāvibhāga*, *Madhyāntavibhāga*, *Mahāyānasūtrālaṁkāra*, *Ratnagotravibhāga*.

19. TS 234.4–5: *gangs ri'i khrod 'dir mi pham rgyal ba dang / thogs med mched kyi gzhung bzang ngo mtshar can / dbu sems so sor 'grel byed rnam mang yang / gang de dbu ma'i gzhung du gdon mi za*.

20. TS 235.2–3: *ngo bo nyid med rnal 'byor spyod pa dang / 'jig rten grags sde'i dbu mar 'grel ba yis / gangs ri'i khrod 'dir bshad srol rnam pa gsum / kun las khyad 'phags sa skya pa'i lugs*. This special reverence to the Sakya, quite unusual in this general and "eclectic" context, might be considered a possible indicator of the connection with Shakya Chokden.

21. Mimaki, *Blo gsal grub mtha'* 27. According to Mimaki, Upa Losel makes two different classifications. In the first, similar to the present treatise, he distinguishes the (1) Sautrāntika-Mādhyamika system of Bhāviveka, the (2) Yogācāra-Madhyamaka system of Śāntarakṣita and Haribhadra, and the (3) Jñānagarbha system of Candrakīrti (*'jigs rten grags sde spyod pa'i dbu ma pa*). Then he makes a second classification between the (1) Svātantrika of Bhāviveka, etc. and the (2) Prāsaṅgika of Buddhapālita, etc. Mimaki remarks that contrary to later Geluk scholars, Upa Losel's two classifications are not combined and do not give preeminence to the Prāsaṅgika.

22. TS 235, 3–4: *sde snod mang thos grags ldan mkhas rnams kyang / legs sbyar mi shes 'phags yul mkhas pa'i gzhung / rang bzhin rkyen dang rnam dbye'i 'jug tshul sogs / gang 'chad de la su zhig yid rton byed*. We might also add that he was signing his own works with a Sanskrit version of his Tibetan name, Prajñāraśmi. Mathes, *Direct Path* 136, also reports that Zhonnu Pel criticized some Gelukpa for being expert in Tsongkhapa's *Lam rim chen mo* without knowing Atiśa's *Bodhipathapradīpa*. It is not totally impossible that Prajñāraśmi had a similar intention here. On the grammatical terms mentioned in this passage and the importance of Sanskrit grammatical scholarship in Tibet, see Verhagen, *History of Sanskrit Grammatical Literature in Tibet*.

23. TS 238.5–239.1: *'phags pa'i yul dang gangs ri'i khrod 'dir yang / mdo sngags gnyis kyi 'gros chen ma 'khrul pa / sngon rabs mkhas pas bkral ba'i bshad srol te / dus gsum rgyal ba kun gyi[s] bzhed gzhung yin*.

24. TS 239.4–5: *gsang chen rgyud dang dbu sems shing rta'i srol / klu sgrub dgongs pa thal rang srol gnyis kyis / legs par bkral ba'i bshad srol zla med pa / de dag phal cher 'khyog po'i lam du bkral*.

25. TS 239.6–240.1: *nyan bshad thub bstan 'dzin par rlom rnams kyang / gzhan gzhung 'joms dang rang gzhung sgrub pa'i phyir / khungs med tshig phreng sbu [slu] ba'i zol gyis ni / rang phyogs 'phyar ba'i rtsod pas thub bstan dkrugs.*

26. TS 240.2–3: *la la rgyal ba'i bka' dang dgongs 'grel gyis / tshad ldan gzhung gyi nyan bshad kun dor nas / rang rang 'dod pas sbyar ba'i gzhung lugs la / nyan bshad bgyid pas tshe lo 'da' ba mtshar.*

27. Compare this passage with Shakya Chokden's *Gzi bsam 'grub gling pa'i dge 'dun spyi'i dris lan ya mtshan bcu bdun pa*. In *Sha mchog gsung 'bum*, vol. 23, 419.3–5, given and translated in Komarovski, *Visions of Unity* 93, where he vilipends the creation in Tibet of sectarian compositions in disharmony with all the ancient lineages of exegesis and practice that originally appeared in Tibet.

28. TS 240.3–4: *de phyir blo gsal klog pa lhur len rnams / rang gzhan grub mtha'i rnam dbye legs rtogs nas / sngar bshad mkhas pas bkral ba'i bshad srol la / rnam dpyod brtson pas thos pa'i pha mthar skyol.*

29. TS 241.4–5: *la lar mdo dang 'ga' zhig sngags gzhung tsam / gzhan dag sgra tshad tsam zhes phyogs re'i mig / phyogs las rnam par rgyal ba ratna'i zhabs / rig gnas kun la spobs pa dge ba can.*

30. According to this treatise, the eight pillars are: (1) Pagor Vairocana (Pa gor Vairocana, 8th c.), (2) Dromton Gyalwe Jungne ('Brom ston pa Rgyal ba'i 'byung gnas, 1005–1064), (3) Khyungpo Neljor Tsultrim Gonpo (Khyung po Rnal 'byor tshul khrims mgon po, ca. 1050–ca. 1140), (4) Drokmi Lotsāwa ('Brog mi Lo tsa ba shakya ye shes, 992 / 993–1043 / 1072), (5) Marpa Lotsāwa Chokyi Lodro (Mar pa Lo tsa ba chos kyi blo gros, 1012–1097), (6) Padampa Sanggye (Pha dam pa Sangs rgyas, d. 1117), (7) Gyicho Dawe Ozer (Gyi co Zla ba'i 'od zer), (8) Orgyen Rinchen Pel (O rgyan pa Rin chen dpal, 1230–1309). They established, respectively, the practice lineages of the (1) Nyingma (*rnying ma*), (2) Kadampa (*bka' gdams*), (3) Shangpa Kagyu (*shangs pa bka' brgyud*), (4) Lamdre (*lam 'bras*), (5) Marpa Kagyu (*mar pa bka' brgyud*), (6) Zhije (*zhi byed*), (7) Six Yogas of the *Kālacakra* (*sbyor drug*), and the (8) Dorje Sumgyi Nyendrup (*rdo rje gsum gyi bsnyen sgrub*).

31. Deroche, " 'Phreng po gter ston Shes rab 'od zer (1518–1584) on the Eight Lineages of Attainment."

32. Prajñāraśmi does not show the same attitude as Kongtrul concerning the Bon. Nevertheless, as Samten Karmay remarked, there was no major Bonpo institution in central Tibet in this time; personal communication, Kyōto University, December 2009.

33. G 253.4–5: *gang shar rang sems mdo sems thun mong ba / gzung 'dzin 'gog pa rnam brdzun dbu ma'i lugs / gnyis med ye shes bden grub 'gog pa yis / lta ba'i rnam gzhag dbu ma chen por 'dod.*

34. As studied in detail by Komarovski, *Visions of Unity*.

35. See Ehrhard, "Observations on Prāsaṅgika-Madhyamaka in the rÑing-ma-pa School." I have also presented "instructions on the view" (*lta khrid*) by Prajñāraśmi on the two truths of Madhyamaka in Deroche, "Instructions on the View (*lta khrid*) of the Two Truths." In his *Lamp Illuminating the Two Truths* (*Bden gnyis gsal ba'i sgron me*), he generally follows a Prāsaṅgika approach according to the sources of the first Kadampa.

36. G 254.2–3: *blos byas gzung 'dzin spros pa kun bral ba'i / gnyug ma'i ye shes rang ngo 'phrod pa yi / shes pa gsal d[w]angs rtog med ye shes de / sgrub rgyud kun gyi bstan pa'i gtso bo yin.*

37. G 254.3–4: *rjes thob dus kyi tha snyad de lta na'ang / mnyam gzhag dus su mtha' bral nam mkha'i dbyings / lta bya lta byed sgra rtog 'jug tshul yin / nges pa'i don tu chu dang chu rlabs bzhin.*

38. SK vol. 2, 550: *gzhan stong rang stong kun rdzob stong tshul dang / mnyam gzhag spros mtha' 'gog la khyad par med / rjes thob tha snyad chos nyid yod med dang / dpyod mthar ye shes bden grub ma grub khyad.*

39. G 255.2–3: *de yang bskyed rim gzhan stong smra ba'i lugs / rdzogs rim rang stong lugs bzhin shes nas ni / zung 'brel sgom pa'i theg chen rnal 'byor pa / rdo rje 'dzin pa yongs kyi gtsug rgyan yin.*

40. For further discussion on this topic, see Dorji Wangchuk's chapter 11 in this volume.

41. SK vol. 2, 557: *zab mo gsang sngags kyi tshul las byung ba'i dbu ma ni / gnyis med kyi ye shes gtso che bas rnal 'byor spyod pa'i dbu ma dang mthun shas che ste / 'khor lo tha mar rgyas par gsung pa'i sems kyi rang bzhin . . . de nyid gtso bor gtan la 'bebs shing nyams su len pa'i phyir ro.* "The Madhyamaka appearing from the methods of the profound secret mantra gives the greatest importance to nondual gnosis. Thus, it is very much in accord with Yogācāra-Madhyamaka [zhentong] because it ascertains and takes as its practice the nature of mind . . . taught extensively in the ultimate wheel."

42. G 257.1–2: *dpyad dang 'jog pa'i sgom tshul ci yang rungs / rang gi mtshan nyid rang bzhin 'od gsal ba / gsal d[w]angs shar la sgom med ma yengs pa / sgrub rgyud kun gyi sgom pa'i gtso bo yin.*

43. G 261.4–5: *rdzogs chen ston pa kun tu bzang po de / rdo je 'chang dang gnyis med chos skur 'dod / lung rigs bral ba'i phyogs 'dzin rtog pa yis / sangs rgyas sku la bzang ngan dbye ba mtshar.*

44. Those eight qualities have yet to be identified precisely.

45. G 262.5–6: *spang bya'i khyad par 'pho ba'i bag chags te / bde chen ye shes gnyen pos bcom pa las / yan lag brgyad ldan longs sku'i sangs rgyas 'byung / srol chen brgyad kyi 'bras bu'i mthar thug yin.*

46. G 263.1–2: *chos phung brgyad khri'i yang snying srol chen brgyad / gnas skabs gdul bya'i rim pas 'khrid tshul dang / nyams len gtso bo la sogs so so na'ang / mthar thug lta sgom rnam bzhag gcig tu nges.*

47. G 263.2–3: *'phags pa'i yul dang gangs ri'i khrod 'dir yang / dpyad dang 'jog pa'i 'grod chen ma 'khrul ba / sngon rabs grub chen gshegs pa'i lam srol de / dus gsum rgyal ba kun gyi bgrod gcig lam.* Compare this passage with Shakya Chokden's *Gzi bsam 'grub gling pa'i dge 'dun spyi'i dris lan ya mtshan bcu bdun pa*, in *Sha mchog gsung 'bum*, vol. 23, 419.2–3, given and translated in Komarovski, *Visions of Unity* 93, where he insists on the harmony between the ancient lineages of Tibetan Buddhism on the topics of the two truths, view, and meditation.

48. G 263.3–4: *'on kyang byang phyogs gangs ri'i khrod 'di ru / thabs cha khyad gsod lta ba mchog 'dzin dang / shes rab bskur 'debs spyod pa mchog 'dzin gyi / phyogs rer lhung ba'i 'khyog po'i srol gnyis byung.*

49. G 264.3–4: *'ga' zhig 'di na 'phags mchog rnam gnyis kyi / rig pas bkral ba'i shing rta'i srol gnyis dang / dpal ldan zla ba'i ring lugs las gzhan pa'i / lta sgom thams cad nor pa'i chos yin lo.*

50. G 264.4: *rdo rje 'chang dbang rje btsun rnal 'byor mas / skal ldan 'gro la tshul bzhin 'doms pa yi / snyan rgyud phal cher spong ba'i chos tshul la / thar 'dod skye bo rnams kyis bag yod mdzod.*

51. G 264.4–5: *dbang bskur byin brlabs ye shes phebs pa dang / rdzogs rim sgom dang zab mo'i mos gus kyis / rang gi nyams myong yid ches lta ba de / tshe 'dir sangs rgyas sgrub pa'i nye lam yin.*

52. G 264.5–6: *da dung zab mo'i lam gyi lta ba de / sor rtog shes pa'i dpyad pa dang bral bas / log pa'i lam du mngon zhen mi 'dor bar / rang nyid khas len gzhan la 'doms pa dag.*

53. G 264.6–265.1: *bshad dang sgrub pa'i chos tshul kun mthong zhing / bsam sbyor dman pas gzhan rgyud mi bsreg par / yid ches lung dang rnam dag rig pa yis / brtsod par 'dod na brtsod pa'i skabs phye zhig.*

54. SK vol. 2, 550: *don dam bden pa'ang rang bzhin ma grub pa'i / med dgag tsam ni bem stong yin par 'dod / gnyis stong ye shes rang rig nyid la 'jog / mdo sngag mtshams sbyor zab mo'i lta bar bzhed.* "[Zhentong] asserts that [if] absolute truth were simply a nonimplicative negation of a nonestablished nature, it would be an inert emptiness. [Zhentong] posits it to be the self-cognizing gnosis empty of duality. This is explained to be the profound view linking sūtra and mantra."

55. For a full and alternative translation of this work, see Gardner, "The Twenty-Five Great Sites of Khams" 219–243.

56. RC 5–9.

57. RC 9–42.

58. RC 42–45.

59. RC 6: *gzhi bde gshegs snying po'i rang bzhin ci yin pa mngon tu mdzad nas / chos thams cad kyi dbyings su mngon par rdzogs pa sangs rgyas.*

60. RC 6–7: *gdul bya dbang po tha ma'i don tu bka' dang po sdug bsngal kun 'byung lam 'gogs pa'i bden pa bzhi lan gsum du bzlas te rnam pa bcu gnyis su bskor ba'i chos kyi 'khor lo / dbang po 'bring gi don tu bka' bar pa gzugs nas rnam mkhyen gyi bar gyi 'khor 'das kyi chos rang mtshan 'dzin pa thams cad mtshan nyid med pa gtan la phab pa'i chos kyi 'khor lo / dbang po rab kyi don tu bka' tha ma kun brtags gzhan dbang yongs grub ste mtshan nyid gsum gyis chos yod med dang stong mi stong legs par rnam par phye ba'i chos kyi 'khor lo bskor.*

61. RC 8: *phyir mi ldog pa gzhan stong seng ge'i sgra chen po bsgrags nas nges don dbu ma'i grub mtha.*

62. RC 8–9.

63. RC 9–10.

64. RC 13–15.

65. RC 15–17.

66. RC 17–31.

67. RC 23–24.

68. RC 31–32.

69. RC 33–35.

70. RC 35–38.

71. RC 38–39.

72. RC 39–41. It is said: "This great being endowed with complete knowledge and realization, the summit Tsongkhapa Lozang Drakpa from the east, who was blessed by Mañjuśrī, established [the monastery of] Drok Riwo Ganden Namgyel Ling," and so on (*'jam dpal dbyangs kyis byin gyis rlabs pa'i shar tsong kha pa blo bzang grags pa'i dbal zhes mkhyen rtogs yongs su rdzogs pa'i bdag nyid chen po des 'brog ri bo dge ldan rnam rgyal gling btab /*).

73. Smith, "'Jam mgon Kong sprul" 265.

74. RC 42–43: *o rgyan chen po'i rjes 'brang kun mkhyen dri med 'od zer sog[s] / gsang sngags rnying ma'i mkhas grub rnams dang / mar mi dwags gsum nas bzung / phyis yongs rdzogs bstan pa'i bshes gnyen kun gzigs chos kyi 'byung gnas kyi bar du byon pa'i bka' brgyud che bzhi chung brgyad kyi mkhas grub rnams dang / zi lang [lung] paṇ chen / bo dong pa /*

khyad par kun mkhyen dus gsum sangs rgyas dol po pa chen po de'i dgongs pa gsal byed rje btsun chen po tā ra nā tha sogs jo nang bka' brgyud kyi skyes chen rim byon thams cad kyi lta grub ni gzhan stong dbu ma kho na yin la / nang gses bzhed tshul gyi khyad par mi 'dra ba cung zad yod de.

75. RC 43–44.

76. RC 44: *thun mong ba nges don snying po'i mdo sde nyi shus dngos bstan gyi tshogs bshad dang / thun mongs ma yin pa byams chos kyi phyi ma'i man ngag gi don zab gsal dbyer med gdams pa.*

77. Two texts dealing of the Geluk (*dga' ldan; dge ldan; dge lugs*) contemplative tradition are included in the DNgDz vol. 4, 489–498: *Dge ldan bka' brgyud rin po che'i phyag chen rtsa ba rgyal ba'i gzhung lam*; 499–548: *Dge ldan bka' brgyud rin po che'i bka' srol phyag rgya chen po'i rtsa ba rgyas par bshad pa yang gsal sgron me.*

78. Hadot, *What Is Ancient Philosophy?*

79. Kapstein, *Reason's Traces*. See in particular the introductory essay.

Bibliography

Abbreviations for Tibetan Sources

Deb ther sngon po: 'Gos *lo tsā ba* gZhon nu dpal (1392–1481). *Deb ther sngon po*, 2 vols. Chengdu: Si khron mi rigs dpe skrun khang, 1984.

DNgDz: 'Jam mgon Kong sprul Blo gros mtha' yas (1813–1899). *gDams nag mdzod: A Treasury of Precious Methods and Instructions of All of the Major and Minor Buddhist Traditions of Tibet, Brought Together and Structured into a Coherent System*. 18 vols. Paro: Bhutan, Ngodrup and Sherab Drimay, 1979–1981.

DNgDzK: 'Jam mgon Kong sprul Blo gros mtha' yas (1813–1899). *sGrub brgyud shing rta chen po brgyad kyi smin grol snying po phyogs gcig bsdus pa gdams ngag rin po che'i mdzod kyi dkar chag bkra shis grags pa'i rgya mtsho*. In DNgDz, vol. 18, 381–547.

G: Prajñāraśmi ('Phreng po gter ston Shes rab 'od zer, 1518–1584). *sGom pa 'chi med kyi bdud rtsi*. In *gSung 'bum*, 1 vol., 243–266. Gangtok: Gonpo Tseten, 1977.

G': 'Jam dbyangs mKhyen brtse'i dbang po (1820–1892). *Gangs ri'i khrod kyi spong ba bsam gtan pa rnams kyi snyan du bsrings pa bsgom pa 'chi med bdud rtsi*. In *Collected Works (gSung 'bum)*, 24 vols., 347–374. Gangtok: Gonpo Tseten, 1977–1980.

GKDz: 'Jam mgon Kong sprul blo gros mtha' yas (1813–1899). *rGya chen bka' mdzod: A Collection of the Writings of 'Jam mgon Kong sprul Blo gros mtha' yas*. 20 vols. Paro: Ngodrup, 1975–1976.

Jo nang khrid brgya: Kun dga' grol mchog (b. 1507). *Khrid brgya'i brgyud 'debs brjod bde brgyud pa'i mtshan sdom. Jo nang khrid brgya: A Precious Collection of Texts Containing the Explanations of the Khrid for One Hundred and Eight Special Precepts of Buddhist Practice Whose Transmissions Converged and Were Collected in the Jo-nang-pa Tradition*. Migmar tseten: Dehradun, 1984.

TS: Prajñāraśmi ('Phreng po gter ston Shes rab 'od zer, 1518–1584). *Thos bsam 'chi med kyi bdud rtsi*. In *gSung 'bum*, 1 vol., 231–242. Gangtok: Gonpo Tseten, 1977.

TS': 'Jam dbyangs mKhyen brtse'i dbang po (1820–1892). *Gangs ri'i khrod kyi klog pa nyan bshad pa rnams kyi snyan du bsrings pa thos bsam 'chi med bdud rtsi*. In *Collected Works (gSung 'bum)*, 24 vols., 327–347. Gangtok: Gonpo Tseten, 1977–1980.

RC: 'Jam mgon Kong sprul Blo gros mtha' yas (1813–1899). *Ris med chos kyi 'byung gnas mdo tsam smos pa blo gsal mgrin pa'i mdzes rgyan*. Kathmandu: Zhe chen bstan gnyis dar rgyas gling, n.d. (The pagination used in this chapter refers to this convenient edition. However, it has been necessary to verify passages according to the version of Kongtrul's *rGya chen bka' mdzod*, 20 vols., vol. 9, 69–100, dPal spungs edition [Paro: Ngodrup, 1976–1977].)

SK: 'Jam mgon Kong sprul Blo gros mtha' yas (1813–1899). *Theg pa'i sgo kun las btus pa gsung rab rin po che'i mdzod bslab pa gsum legs par ston pa'i bstan bcos shes bya kun khyab*. 3 vols. Beijing: Mi rigs dpe skrun khang, 1982.

Shā mchog gsung 'bum: gSer mdog paṇ chen Śākya mchog ldan (1428–1507). *The Complete Works (gsuṅ 'bum) of Gser-mdog Paṇ-chen Śakya-mchog-ldan*, 24 vols. Thimphu: Kunzang Tobgey, 1975.

Thu'u bkwan grub mtha': Thu'u bkwan Blo bzang chos kyi nyi ma (1737–1802). *Grub mtha' thams cad kyi khungs dang 'dod tshul ston pa legs bshad shel gyi me long*. Lan kru'u: Kan su'u mi rigs dpe skrun khang, 1984.

Sanskrit Sources

Abhisamayālaṃkara (attrib. Maitreya). Edited by Ramshankar Tripathi (with the *Abhisamayālaṁkāravṛttiḥ Sphuṭārthā*) (Bibliotheca Indo-Tibetica Series 2). Sarnath: Central Institute of Higher Tibetan Studies, 1993.

Dharmadharmatāvibhāga (attrib. Maitreya). Editing of Tibetan text and Sanskrit fragments by Klaus-Dieter Mathes, *Unterscheidung der Gegebenheiten von ihrem wahren Wesen* (*Dharmadharmatāvibhāga*) (Indica et Tibetica 26). Swittal-Odendorf: Indica et Tibetica Verlag, 1996.

Madhyāntavibhāga (attrib. Maitreya). Included in the *Madhyāntavibhāgabhāṣya* (attrib. Vasubandhu). Edited by G. Nagao. Tokyo: Suzuki Research Foundation, 1964.

Mahāyānasūtrālaṁkāra. First edition by S. Bagchi (1970), second edition by Sridhar Tripathi. Darbhanga: Mithila Institute, 1999.

Mahāyānasūtrālaṁkāra. Edited by Sylvain Lévi, Bibliothèque de l'École des Hautes Études, Sciences historiques et philologiques, 159. Paris: Librairie Honoré Champion, 1907.

Ratnagotravibhāga Mahāyānottaratantraśāstra (attrib. Sāramati or Maitreya). Included in the *Ratnagotravibhāgavyākhyā* (attrib. Sāramati or Asaṅga). Edited by E. H. Johnston. Patna: The Bihar Research Society, 1950.

Secondary Sources

Deroche, Marc-Henri. "'Phreng po gter ston Shes rab 'od zer (1518–1584) on the Eight Lineages of Attainment: Research on a *Ris med* Paradigm." In *Contemporary Visions in Tibetan Studies: Proceedings of the First International Seminar of Young Tibetologists*, edited by Brandon Dotson, Kalsang Norbu Gurung, Georgios Halkias, and Tim Myatt, 319–41. Chicago: Serindia, 2009.

———. "Prajñāraśmi ('Phreng po gter ston Shes rab 'od zer, Tibet, 1518–1584): Vie, œuvre et contribution à la tradition ancienne (*rnying ma*) et au mouvement non-partisan (*ris med*)." Doctoral thesis, École Pratique des Hautes Études, Paris, 2011.

———. "Sherab Wozer (b.1518–d.1584)." In *The Treasury of Lives: Biographies of Himalayan Religious Masters*. New York: Rubin Foundation, 2011. Electronic publication, consulted 7 May 2013, URL: http: // treasuryoflives.org / biographies / view / Sherab-Wozer / 8964.

———. "Instructions on the View (*lta khrid*) of the Two Truths: Prajñāraśmi's (1518–1584) *Bden gnyis gsal ba'i sgron me*." In *Revisiting Tibetan Religion and Philosophy:*

Proceedings of the International Seminar of Young Tibetologists, Paris, 2009, edited by Marc-Henri Deroche, Joshua Schapiro, Seiji Kumagai, and Kalsang Norbu Gurung, 139–213. Dharamsala: Amnye Machen Institute, 2012.

———. "dPal ri Monastery in the Tibetan 'Valley of the Emperors': History of the Forgotten Mother-Monastery of the rNying ma School." *Bulletin of Tibetology* 49-1 (2013): 77–112.

———. "On Being 'Impartial' (*ris med*): From Non-Sectarianism to the Great Perfection." *Revue d'Etudes Tibétaines* 44 (2018): 129–158.

Dreyfus, Georges, and Sara L. McClintock, editors. *The Svātantrika-Prāsaṅgika Distinction: What Difference Does a Difference Make?* Boston: Wisdom, 2003.

Ehrhard, Franz-Karl. "Observations on Prāsaṅgika-Madhyamaka in the rÑing-ma-pa School." In *Tibetan Studies*, 139–147. Munich: Studia Tibetica, Quellen und Studien zur tibetischen Lexikographie, 2, 1988.

———. *Life and Travels of Lo-chen bSod-nams rgya-mtsho*. Lumbini International Research Institute, Monograph Series, vol. 4. Lumbini: Lumbini International Research Institute, 2002.

Eltschinger, Vincent. "Pierre Hadot et les 'exercices spirituels': Quel modèle pour la philosophie bouddhique tardive?" *Asiatische Studien / Études Asiatiques* 62, no. 2 (2008): 485–544.

Gardner, Alexander. "The Twenty-Five Great Sites of Khams: Religious Geography, Revelation, and Nonsectarianism in Nineteenth-Century Eastern Tibet." Doctorial dissertation, University of Michigan, 2006.

Hadot, P. *What Is Ancient Philosophy?* Translated from the French by Michael Chase. Cambridge: Belknap Press, 2002. (Original version: *Qu'est-ce que la philosophie antique?* [Paris: Gallimard, 1995].)

Jamgön Kongtrul Lodrö Tayé. *The Treasury of Knowledge: Book Six, Part Three: Frameworks of Buddhist Philosophy*. Kalu Rinpoché Translation Group. Translated by Elizabeth Callahan. Ithaca: Snow Lion, 2007.

Kapstein, Matthew T. "*gDams ngag*: Tibetan Technologies of the Self." In *Tibetan Literature: Studies in Genre*, edited by José I. Cabezón and Roger R. Jackson, 275–289. Ithaca: Snow Lion, 1996.

———. *Reason's Traces: Identity and Interpretation in Indian and Tibetan Buddhist Thought*. Boston: Wisdom, 2001.

———. "Tibetan Technologies of the Self, Part II: The Teachings of the Eight Great Conveyances." In *The Pandita and the Siddha: Tibetan Studies in Honour of E. Gene Smith*, edited by Ramon N. Prats, 110–129. Dharamsala: Amnye Machen Institute, 2007.

Komarovski, Yaroslav. *Visions of Unity: The Golden Paṇḍita Shakya Chokden's New Interpretation of Yogācāra and Madhyamaka*. Albany: State University of New York Press, 2011.

Mathes, Klaus-Dieter. *A Direct Path to the Buddha Within: Gö Lotsāwa's Mahāmudrā Interpretation of the Ratnagotravibhāga*. Boston: Wisdom, 2008.

May, Jacques. "La philosophie bouddhique idéaliste." *Asiatische Studien / Études asiatiques* 25 (1971): 265–323.

May, Jacques, and Katsumi Mimaki. "Chūdō 中道." In *Hōbōgirin, Dictionnaire encyclopédique du bouddhisme d'après les sources chinoises et japonaises*, vol. 5., 456–470. Paris: Académie des Inscriptions et Belles Lettres, Institut de France, 1979.

Mimaki, Katsumi. *Blo gsal grub mtha', chapitres IX (Vaibhāṣika) et XI (Yogācāra) édités et chapitre XII (Mādhyamika) édité et traduit*. Kyoto: Zinbun Kagaku Kenkyusyo, Université de Kyōto, 1982.

Seyfort Ruegg, David. "A Karma bka' brgyud Work on the Lineages and Traditions of the Indo-Tibetan dBu ma (Madhyamaka)." In *Orientalia Iosephi Tucci memoriae dicata. Edenda curaverunt G. Gnoli et L. Lanciotti*, vol. 3, 1279–1280. Rome: Istituto italiano per il Medio ed Estremo Oriente, 1988.

Smith, Gene E. "'Jam mgon Kong sprul and the Nonsectarian Movement." In *Among Tibetan Texts: History and Literature of the Himalayan Plateau*, edited by Kurtis Schaeffer, 235–272. Boston: Wisdom, 2001. (First published as the introduction to *Kongtrul's Encyclopedia of Indo-Tibetan Culture*, edited by Lokesh Chandra [New Delhi: International Academy of Indian Culture, 1970].)

Thuken Losang Chökyi Nyima. *The Crystal Mirror of Philosophical Systems: A Tibetan Study of Asian Religious Thought*. Translated by Geshé Lhundub Sopa with E. Ann Chávez and Roger R. Jackson; special contributions by Michael Sweet and Leonard Zwilling; edited by Roger R. Jackson. Boston: Wisdom in association with the Institute of Tibetan Classics (The Library of Tibetan Classics, vol. 25), 2009.

Tucci, Guiseppe. *Tibetan Painted Scrolls*, 3 vols. Rome: La Libreria Dello Stato, 1949. (Rpt: 2 vols. Kyoto: Rinsen Books, 1980).

Verhagen, Pieter C. *A History of Sanskrit Grammatical Literature in Tibet. Volume 1: Transmission of the Canonical Literature*. Leiden: Brill, 1994.

———. *A History of Sanskrit Grammatical Literature in Tibet. Volume 2: Assimilation into Indigenous Scholarship*. Leiden: Brill, 2001.

13

The Zhentong Lion Roars

Dzamtang Khenpo Lodro Drakpa and the Jonang Scholastic Renaissance

Michael R. Sheehy

In early fourteenth-century Tibet, the scholar and tantric adept Dolpopa Sherab Gyaltsen (1292–1361) articulated a technical language and interpretive model for distinguishing two modes of emptiness: (a) emptiness that is an absence of an intrinsic nature (rangtong, *rang stong*) and (b) emptiness that is devoid of everything other than the continuous radiance that pervades all living beings (zhentong, *gzhan stong*).[1] This multivalent codification of emptiness provoked historic controversy and polemic in Tibet, leading to a so-called rangtong versus zhentong debate that has infused Tibetan Buddhist philosophical discourse for centuries. Nearly three hundred years after Dolpopa, during the mid-seventeenth century, political and sectarian forces prohibited the production and distribution of zhentong writings in central Tibet. During this period of persecution, Jonang monasteries and nunneries were confiscated and converted and books on zhentong were banned. The Jonangpas were sequestered to the northwestern region of Amdo where they setup nomadic enclaves and built monasteries. After 1959, while Tibetans fled their homeland, the Jonangpas remained largely isolated in these remote corners of the plateau. Consequently, due to historical circumstance, the body of Jonang zhentong literature has received little attention from both modern Tibetan and international scholars. With more recent access to the living Jonang tradition inside Tibet, and with greater availability of zhentong literature, we can now better evaluate these critically important contributions to Buddhist philosophy and intellectual history.

To expemplify the continuity of zhentong philosophy, this chapter is dedicated to the modern Jonangpa master Khenpo Ngawang Lodro Drakpa (1920–1975) from Tsangwa Monastery in Dzamtang. His most formidable philosophical work is his *Great Exposition on Zhentong*, the full title of which is *The Fearless Lion's Roar: Ascer-*

taining the Definitive Meaning of the Profound Abiding Reality of the Supreme Causal and Fruition Vehicles According to the Sequential Lineage of the Great Glorious Jonangpa.[2] This work is devoted to elucidating zhentong, the view that ultimate reality is effulgently full of enlightened qualities while vacuously devoid of superficial temporary phenomena. Before introducing this important work and Khenpo Lodrak's contributions to zhentong thinking, let's first consider some of the historical forces that situated his thought within the broader intellectual discourse of modern Tibet.

JONANG MASTERS AND THE RIMÉ MOVEMENT

It was largely due to the enthusiasm of the eighteenth-century Nyingma polymath Rikzin Tsewang Norbu (1698–1755) from Katok Monastery in Kham that the revival among the Jonangpas was sparked. With Tsewang Norbu's diplomatic attempt to unlock and recover books at the sealed Jonang library at Takten Puntsok Ling Monastery in central Tibet, and to seek out transmissions of the Jonang teachings in the year 1727, a broader interest in the Jonang began to emerge among the intellectual communities in Kham. This concerned interest lay not merely with Tsewang Norbu but was shared by his contemporary and close friend, Situ Paṇchen Chokyi Jungne (1699–1774), who had visited Takten Puntsok Ling in 1723. Their travels to Takten Puntsok Ling, reception of Jonang transmissions in Tsang, and authoring of works on the Jonang Kālacakra and zhentong paved the way for what would later emerge.

With this earlier spark, and the rise of the Rimé nonsectarian movement during the late nineteenth century on the eastern frontiers of Tibet, there was a confluence of newfound interest in the Jonang contemplative and philosophical articulation of zhentong and the Kālacakra sixfold vajrayoga (*rdo rje rnal 'byor ba yan lag drug*) practice tradition that amounted to nothing less than a scholastic renaissance among the Jonangpas. Though this revival eventually reached an apex with the luminary Khenpo Ngawang Lodro Drakpa, it was born from the progenitors of the Rimé movement, Jamgon Kongtrul Lodro Taye (1813–1899) and Jamyang Khyentse Wangpo (1820–1892), influences of Geluk scholasticism on the Jonang, and amid the milieu of the Buddhist philosophical writings of the period.

As a religious movement, the pluralism of Rimé sought to consolidate and preserve the diverse array of intellectual and contemplative traditions in Tibet and, in so doing, challenged the status quo scholastic curricula that had become regimented in many monastic learning institutions. Jamgon Kongtrul was particularly attentive to appropriate Jonang thought and practices into his project to both challenge existing scholastic conventions as well as to present a platform of inclusivity.[3] Kongtrul was deeply influenced by the eclecticism of Kunga Drolchok (1507–1566) and Tāranātha (1575–1635), utilizing Kunga Drolchok's anthology of *One Hundred and Eight Instructions* as the template for his *Treasury of Precious Instructions* and recompiling Tāranātha's works on the Kālacakra and other tantric systems. Under these influences, Kongtrul was considered by his contemporaries to be an inheritor of Kunga Drolchok and Tāranātha's reincarnation line. These influences are important for understanding not only the dynamics of the Rimé vision, but how the groundwork was set for the reemergence of zhentong thinking and Jonang scholasticism.

In the year 1848, on his quest for Jonang teachings, Jamgon Kongtrul traveled to Tsangwa Monastery in the valley of Dzamtang to receive transmissions from the vajramaster Ngawang Chopel (1788–1865). Among the instructions received were those for the performance of the sixfold *yoga* (*ṣaḍaṅgayoga*, *sbyor ba yan lag drug*) of the Kālacakra according to the Jonang, instructions on zhentong, and a cycle of teachings on *chod* severance practice.[4] Kongtrul also had the fortuitous occasion to forge a relationship with the master Ngawang Chopel; for it was through Ngawang Chopel's prodigy disciple, Bamda Tubten Gelek Gyatso (1844–1904), that the Jonangpas would most profoundly be linked with the Rimé movement.

Bamda Gelek traveled from his hometown in Dzamtang to the Derge region of Kham at the age of eighteen to immerse himself in the intellectual and spiritual eclecticism that was on the scene. He studied closely with Jamgon Kongtrul, Dzokchen Dza Patrul Rinpoche (1808–1887), and Purtsa Khenpo Akon (1837–1897).[5] Though Bamda Gelek's scholastic output is tremendous and many of his writings serve as core textbooks for the contemporary Jonang curricula, he did not compose a single work on Zhentong Madhyamaka. Rather, his writings on zhentong remain confined to tantra zhentong, primarily expressed within his extensive works on the sixfold vajrayoga of the Kālacakra. Yet while none of the writings in his *Collected Works* explicate a sūtra view of zhentong, there is an intriguing oral story about the zhentong text that Bamda Gelek almost wrote.[6] As the narrative was relayed to me at his monastery in Dzamtang, Bamda Gelek was at the end of his life when a small group of Jonang monks arrived to receive teachings from him. During their visit, a discussion developed about the inner meaning of zhentong, and the monks urgently pleaded that he write a text to elucidate the subject. Bamda Gelek is said to have agreed and to have started to compose this text during his final days. He even gave the text the title *The Roaring Melodious Laughter of Zhentong*.[7] During the final days of his life, however, Bamda Gelek became consumed with completing his large exegesis on the *Prajñāparamitā* and passed away before he was able to complete the composition of his work on zhentong.

However ironic, perhaps the most pivotal interlocutor in the Jonang discourse on emptiness during the latter nineteenth and early twentieth centuries was the Geluk-trained scholar Dzago Geshe Lozang Chokdrub Gyatso.[8] Born in the Dzago region of Gyarong south of the Dzamtang valley, Lozang Chokdrub traveled to Lhasa where he acquired his Geshe degree in Geluk philosophy at Drepung Monastery. Raised in a Jonang family, he was embedded within the local Jonang intellectual milieu in southern Amdo at a young age. By the time he was nineteen, he had met his root teacher, the Jonang master Kunga Ngedon (1834–1906), who was a student of Jamgon Kongtrul. Such Rimé influences seem to have sincerely affected his own life trajectory as well as his vision of Buddhist philosophy. For instance, in the late 1870s or early 1880s, he was instrumental in hosting Dzokchen Dza Patrul Rinpoche during his visit to teach the *Bodhicāryāvatāra* at Dzamtang.

In 1901, having received his Geshe degree, Lozang Chokdrub returned to his homeland where he established a hermitage high in the mountains of Gyarong. During the latter years of his life, he employed the dialectical skills and philosophical sensibilities that he had acquired through his Geluk training to compose several important works on zhentong. His most prodigious work on zhentong philosophical thinking is his commentary on the final chapter of Tāranātha's masterpiece on zhentong, the *Supreme Vehicle of Zhentong Madhyamaka*—the only chapter that Tāranātha left incomplete at the time of his death.[9] Keeping in mind that there is a long-standing practice of completing another author's works in the Tibetan literary tradition, to have written Tāranātha's unfinished chapter on his cornerstone zhentong work more than 250 years after his passing was a bold feat.

Though seemingly normative at first glance, Lozang Chokdrub's most intriguing composition is arguably his *Exposition on Inner and Outer Philosophical Systems*.[10] Replicating his writings on what had become the template for a standardized textbook on Buddhist and non-Buddhist tenets of philosophy within the Geluk curricula, Lozang Chokdrub creatively inserts a significant section on Zhentong Madhyamaka. Treating zhentong as a distinct philosophical system within the established doxography positions Zhentong Madhyamaka in contrast to Prāsaṅgika Madhyamaka—or, as it is framed in the text, the third turning of the dharma wheel in contrast to the second turning. Though there certainly are precedents for this positioning within Dolpopa's distinct doxography as well as Tāranātha's presentation in his *Essence of Zhentong* and *Ornament of Zhentong Madhyamaka*, there existed no nineteenth-century textbook within the Jonang curricula that explicitly presented zhentong as a valid philosophical system on its own terms. With this valiant gesture, Lozang Chokdrub elevated Zhentong Madhyamaka on par with Cittamātra and Prāsaṅgika-Madhyamaka, the integral systems within the Geluk organization of Buddhist tenets. In so doing, Jonang knowledge was reapproapriated into the broader philosophical discourse.

In many ways, Bamda Gelek and Lozang Chokdrub epitomized the renaissance spirit that inspired the Jonang tradition during the early twentieth century in Amdo. Their writings and influences were critical to reestablishing the rigorous scholasticism of the Jonang during this important moment in the intellectual life of the tradition. One of the primary inheritors of their intellectual legacy was Ngawang Tsoknyi Gyatso (1880–1940), a direct disciple of Bamda Gelek and mentor to Khenpo Lodrak.[11]

Tsoknyi Gyatso, a vajramaster at Dzamtang Tsangwa Monastery, is known for his expertise on the Kālacakra maṇḍala and its symbolism, but he was also the author of several intriguing works on zhentong. His writings are important because they disclose the internal workings of a major Jonang scholar during this critical period whose works present a particularly perplexing species of zhentong. Compared with mainstream presentations of zhentong by Dolpopa and Tāranātha,

Tsoknyi Gyatso's writings on zhentong present a lenient, if not compromised, rendering of the nature (*ngo bo*) of buddha-nature (tathāgatagarbha, *de bzhin gshegs pa'i snying po*).[12] Such moderate presentations reflect an exegetical style that was likely influenced by Geluk interpretations. This could be characterized as a kind of "zhentong lite." Though Tsoknyi Gyatso was not Khenpo Lodrak's main preceptor for zhentong, it is constructive to consider how Khenpo Lodrak's writings on zhentong were possibly a corrective to Tsoknyi Gyatso's presentation, reasserting the mainstream Jonang presentation. As we will see, within his masterpiece, the *Great Exposition on Zhentong*, Khenpo Lodrak deliberately makes efforts to reiterate seminal themes and core principles of classical zhentong philosophical thinking, as if seeking to realign the modern Jonang tradition with presentations by Dolpopa and Tāranātha. However, it is at least interesting to note that each of the running titles for Tsoknyi Gyatso's three works on zhentong begin with a homage to Dolpopa, explicitly situating his writings squarely within the mainstream Jonang lineage of zhentong.[13]

The Life and Influence of Khenpo Lodrak

A vajramaster at Dzamtang Tsangwa Monastery, Khenpo Lodro Drakpa—affectionately referred to simply as "Mati Rinpoche"—was undeniably the most influential teacher and leading intellectual among the Jonangpas during the twentieth century.[14] Though he lived during the height of the Cultural Revolution and died at the relatively young age of fifty-six, his disciples are beacons of their generation and his writings are studied widely across the Jonang scholastic curricula. He is regarded by the tradition to have been a miraculous manifestation (*rnam rol*) of the Tibetan masters Dolpopa Sherab Gyaltsen, Kunga Drolchok, Tāranātha, Rikzin Namnang Dorje, Terton Kacho Lingpa (b. 1858), and the Nyingma luminary Mipam Jamyang Gyatso (1846–1912).[15] Filling ten large volumes, his *Collected Works* exhibit an incredible range of authorship that includes writings across such genres as philosophy, history, biography, astrology, ritual, science, epistemology, a variety of tantric subjects, and zhentong.

Born into the bloodline of the nomadic Zira family in Dzamtang, it is said that as a child, before he received his formal education, Khenpo Lodrak would wander from his nomad encampment into the nearby forests where he would peel bark from the trees and write on the back of the bark with stones.[16] After his parents discovered what he was doing, they found their son a teacher to instruct him in reading and writing when he was seven years old. At a young age, he learned Tibetan grammar and spelling (*sum rtags*), Indian and Chinese astrology (*rtsis dkar nag*), the details of ritual performance (*cho ga'i phyag len*), and how to perform the arts of dance, maṇḍala drawing, and song (*gar thig dbyangs*).

Khenpo Lodrak entered the Darnga Mountain Retreat when he was twelve years old.[17] As the story is told, he arrived at the mountain retreat (*ri khrod*) with a friend of his who was the same age. Seeing these boys, in order to deter them, the preceptor told them that they could only stay if they memorized the entire litany of practice texts on the sixfold yoga by the next morning. The preceptor handed them each a large body of texts and disappeared. Khenpo Lodrak memorized all of the liturgical texts and amazed his preceptor the next morning, forcing the master to keep his promise and let him stay in retreat.[18]

In a dream the evening before Mati received instructions on the practices of the Kālacakra, oversized stūpas appeared in the four directions of his mind. When his preceptor learned of this, he proceeded to gradually instruct the young Khenpo Lodrak in the common tantra preliminary practices of going to refuge (*skyabs 'gro*) and generating bodhicitta (*sems bskyed*), as well as the uncommon preliminary practices on the generation stage (*bskyed rim*) meditation practices of imagining the connate form of the Kālacakra deity (*lhan skyes*).[19]

When he was thirteen years old, Khenpo Lodrak took the monastic precepts and received his full name.[20] He was instructed in the three isolation practices (*dben pa gsum*) of the Kālacakra before progressing on to the profound path of completion stage practices. As is typical at this point, he was guided through Tāranātha's instruction manual on the completion stage sixfold yoga, *Meaningful to Behold*, which he practiced in retreat for three years.[21] It is said that his yogic experiences deeply enriched his interior life and that at the age of fifteen, after receiving a host of tantric empowerments (*dbang bskur*) on various meditation deities (*yi dam*), he began to have visions in which he would actually encounter these deities and spontaneously compose songs of realization (*nyams mgur*) to them. At this stage of his life, he was described as being like a vase that was seeking to be filled to the brim with the practical instructions (*dmar khrid*) of the magnificent secret Vajrayāna and was regularly requesting esoteric transmissions, empowerments, and instructions.

At the age of eighteen, Khenpo Lodrak went to the Rashuk Mountain Retreat where he began his formal scholastic education with Tsoknyi Gyatso. Khenpo Lodrak spent four years studying the core textbooks (*yig cha*) of the Jonang scholastic curricula, including the major collections of sūtra and tantra along with Bamda Gelek's extensive work on the collected topics in Buddhist logic and epistemology (*bsdus grwa*).[22] Following these studies, Khenpo Lodrak relocated to Tsangwa Monastery, the primary seat (*gdan sa*) of the Jonangpa, where he continued his studies. By this time, it is said that Khenpo Lodrak had become an impressive student who astonished his peers and instructors with his intellectual prowess. During these early years at Tsangwa Monastery, he received many of the essential reading transmissions from the Jonang scriptural tradition (*gzhung lugs*) and he became familiar with the specific tradition upheld at Dzamtang by studying the works of the previous lineages' masters associated with monastery. He also actively sought out transmissions from other traditions, including Shangpa instructions on the inner and outer yogas of Niguma, tantric meditations on Vajrakīlaya and Yamāntaka, and numerous Nyingma instructions on Dzokchen and exorcize rituals, as well as various liturgical instructions from different traditions.

By the time he was thirty, Khenpo Lodrak had deepened his scholastic studies in epistemology (*tshad ma*), the Prajñāparamitā literature (*phar phyin*), progressive stages on the path (*lam rim*), Madhyamaka, Abhidharma, and ethics (*'dul ba*). In parallel, he had excelled in his training in the esoteric arts of the sixfold yoga, the inner and outer sciences of the Kālacakra, and several cycles of the Cakrasaṃvara. However, it was not until he received the full transmission on the *Collected Works* of Dolpopa that he felt as though he was able to comprehend the consummate intent of the sūtras and tantras and realize the definitive view and practice of zhentong.

Having studied for many years, at the age of thirty-nine, Khenpo Lodrak decided to dedicate more time toward contemplation. Though it is understood that he began to assimilate many of the contemplative systems that he had been trained in up to this point in his life, he focused on intensifying his practices of the Kālacakra's sixfold vajrayoga and instructions by the yoginī Niguma. It is said that during this period he would spend hours each day absorbed in meditative stabilization and that he would occasionally come out of meditation only to write.[23]

It is repeated by many who were with him during the latter years of his life that Khenpo Lodrak would meditate and write throughout the day and night with an incomparable tenacity. Many of these works were composed in his room at Tsangwa Monastery where he would often dictate his thoughts to his close disciple Yontan Zangpo (1928–2002), who would transcribe his words verbatim onto a long black slate. Once the slate was full of Khenpo Lodrak's words, Yontan Zangpo would write them down in cursive script on leaves of paper. In addition to the *Great Exposition on Zhentong*, works worth mentioning here include his *History of the Jonang Tradition*, *Presentation of Inner and Outer Philosophical Systems*, *Condensation of Topics on Epistemology*, *Guidance Manual on Practicing the Connate Kālacakra*, *Biographies of the Successive Lives of Dolpopa*, and a *Biography of Padmasambhava*.

During the Cultural Revolution, like many monks in Tibet at that time, Khenpo Lodrak was imprisoned for two years. After being released under the condition that he would not stay at the monastery or wear monk's robes, Khenpo Lodrak took up residence in a small house about twenty minutes away from Tsangwa Monastery, below the Darnga Mountain Retreat where he was introduced to the Kālacakra as a boy. It was here, during his fifty-sixth year, that Khenpo Lodrak passed away.[24]

THE GREAT EXPOSITION ON ZHENTONG

Khenpo Lodrak completed his composition of the *Great Exposition on Zhentong* at Samdrup Norbu Ling in the Dzamtang valley during the year 1965 at age forty-five.[25] This work, though only a few decades old and an infant in comparison to the thousand-year-old tradition of Tibetan Buddhist authorship, has already found its place in the contemporary Jonang scholastic curricula. An advanced Jonang Buddhist Studies College (*jo nang gi bshad grwa*) inside Tibet trains students in a basic curriculum constituting five primary subjects: (1) Epistemology and Logic (*tshad ma*); (2) Prajñāparamitā literature (*phar phyin*); (3) Abhidharma (*mngon pa*); (4) Ethics (*'dul ba*); (5) and Zhentong Madhyamaka (*dbu ma gzhan stong*).[26] These subjects are examined systematically for one to three years, each within the Jonang collegiate educational curricula, culminating with studies in a three-year intensive meditation retreat on the complex cosmological, subtle physiological, and gnosiological systems presented in the *Kālacakra Tantra*.

Within the genre of Jonang zhentong literature, the *Great Exposition on Zhentong* has found its place beside other such classics, including Dolpopa's masterpiece, the *Mountain Dharma: An Ocean of Definitive Meaning* and Tāranātha's *Supreme Vehicle of Madhyamaka* as well as its massive supplementary notes (*zin bris*).[27] Along with these other two, the *Great Exposition on Zhentong* comprises the third major textbook studied within the Zhentong Madhyamaka curriculum at major Jonang monastic universities.

Ground, Path, and Fruition of Zhentong

Paradigmatic of contemplative and philosophical Tibetan treatises, and parallel in structure to Dolpopa's *Mountain Dharma*, the *Great Exposition on Zhentong* is delineated into the threefold schema: (1) ground (*gzhi*), (2) path (*lam*), and (3) fruition (*'bras bu*). Khenpo Lodrak applies this coherent structure systematically to both his discussion on sūtra zhentong in the main body of the text as well as in his addendum discussion on tantra zhentong.[28] For pedagogical reasons, and because of its structure, monks generally begin by studying sūtra zhentong separately from tantra zhentong in preparation for examining Dolpopa's syncretic work that complexly interweaves sūtra and tantra.

Throughout his work, and especially in the section on the ground, Khenpo Lodrak is explicitly synchronizing his presentation with the presentation found in Dolpopa's *Mountain Dharma*. More specifically, he distinguishes ten essential topics to illustrate how buddha-nature resides as a timeless ontological ground; these topics condense and correspond exactly to the fourteen topics that Dolpopa presents in the first section of his *Mountain Dharma*.[29] These ten topics define the seminal technical issues involved in a philosophical articulation of the ground and are considered by the Jonang scholastic tradition to be of essential significance to understanding zhentong thought.[30] This first section, titled *How Buddha-Nature Is the Ground Expanse*, is summarized and further explained according to ten condensed topics:

1. How the universal ground as pristine awareness is the profound actuality of phenomena, the very abiding reality of the ground expanse.

2. How the indivisibility of the expanse and awareness encompass everything stable and wavering.

3. How the very nature that is the existing mode of all Three Precious Jewels is the ultimate actual nature of phenomena.

4. How the very nature of the buddha-nature is exemplified in metaphors.

5. How the very nature of the existing mode is synonymous with the naturally abiding spiritual affinity.

6. How the three patterns of the dimension of phenomena reside.

7. How this very nature resides as the three patterns of what exists.

8. How this very nature is the existing mode of ground and fruition indivisible—nirvāṇa, the absolute dimension of phenomena.

9. How this very nature is the existing mode that subsumes the absolute dimension of phenomena's enlightened qualities.

10. How the intent of this mode was likewise explicated by Nāgārjuna and his heirs.

Khenpo Lodrak elaborates on each of these topics to expand on the ground that Dolpopa introduced. Though the *Great Exposition on Zhentong* opens with a discussion on pristine awareness that is not found among Dolpopa's fourteen topics, Khenpo Lodrak goes on to explain nine of Dolpopa's fourteen topics by citing relevant canonical sources and through juxtaposing a discourse about these topics through rhetorical devices that are based on logic.[31] Once these ten essential topics are discussed, the work discusses a range of issues that are pertinent to understanding zhentong.

In the first section of the work, Khenpo Lodrak discusses the ground or basis for the nature of mind and reality, frequently evoking synonyms that include the "ground expanse" (*gzhi dbyings*), "consummate abiding reality" (*mthar thug gi gnas lugs*), and "basic disposition" (*gshis lugs*). In particular, the ground is synonymous with buddha-nature, the indwelling buddha-nature that is identical to the radiant nature of pristine awareness (*ye shes*)—which is defined to be eternal (*nam yang*), invariable (*mi 'gyur*), enduring (*ther zug*), constant (*rtag*), stable (*brtan*), and everlasting (*g.yung drung*). Not created or destroyed, the ground is effulgently full of enlightened qualities at all times everywhere. This is why it is buddha-nature, indivisible from the fruition of buddhahood. As Khenpo Lodrak elucidates the zhentong view in his introduction to the ground expanse:

> Distorted perceptions of ordinary awareness (*vijñāna, rnam shes*) are at all times relative and are subsumed by what are reputed to be the appearances of what is knowable within the timeless ground. Because the basic disposition (*gshis*) of abiding reality's (*gnas lugs*) original actual nature is ultimately self-manifesting and spontaneous, it is the

> very identity of every aspect within the three realms. This is the essence of the lucid and magnificent vital force (*srog chen*) that is enduring (*ther zug*), everlasting (*g.yung drung*), all-pervasive (*kun khyab*), fearless (*'jig med*), and constant (*rtag*),[32] what is forever without interruptions, free from partialities, and devoid of proliferations—like space.
>
> From within this expanse (dhātu, *dbyings*), the tangible and intangible are self-expressions of the actuality of phenomena (dharmatā, *chos nyid*), the excellent and sublime abiding reality that remains always unimpeded. This is the natural identity of the pure identity that is itself things just as they exist, the common ground (*gzhi gcig*) for the wisdom that goes beyond both saṃsāra and nirvāṇa.[33]

Though the ground resides without alteration or fabrication, Khenpo Lodrak reiterates throughout his treatise that the individual mind-streams of sentient beings stray from their nature and do not recognize their own pristine awareness:

> To explain a little further in-depth, the abiding reality of the ground is the buddha-nature, the ground expanse that encompasses all of saṃsāra and nirvāṇa. While saṃsāra's very ground is the abiding reality within sentient beings, they are unable to recognize this as the actual nature of phenomena. That is, because the distorted perceptions of saṃsāra serve as the basis for the multiple facets of transient deceptive phenomena, the visible and audible qualities of phenomena are artificial. Interdependent co-origination gives rise to the non-deceptive and the multiple variations of perceptual states that perceive differently.
>
> Moreover, because each individual's perceptive state is merely a perception, anyone can transform these as one pleases without feeling helpless. Anyone can experience unbearable suffering and insatiable happiness acutely and thoroughly because their karmic perceptions of both the coarse and ordinary perceive facets of phenomena dissimilarly.[34]

According to the view of zhentong, even while the enlightened qualities of perfection dwell continuously, timelessly, and inherently, there is still the necessity for progressive spiritual effort. That is, it is understood that spiritual progress is matured by engaging in a contemplative process of gradually purifying the inhibiting forces (*sgrib*) that preclude one from realizing his or her intrinsic nature.

The name given to this process is the path—how a meditation practitioner progresses along a particular trajectory of thoughts and actions in a way that is spiritually enhancing. In this section, Khenpo Lodrak identifies the primary fixations inherent in spiritually demeaning ways of living with explanations on how to reverse these detrimental habits in order to traverse in a wholesome manner. Describing moments along this gradual path of meditation, Khenpo Lodrak writes:

> On the path, each bodhisattva and disciple familiarizes themselves with the elegant path according to their own mental aptitude. For whoever traverses the path, in order for them to proceed along favorable conditions that will perceive the actual nature of phenomena and that will correspond with the actual nature of phenomena, vivid perceptions conducive to each individual's own mentality are gradually generated from within the ground expanse. Moreover, the two modes that are to be integrated as they are conducive to individuals are: (1) slightly perceiving the actuality of phenomena's abiding mode and (2) perceiving the path to be adventitiously contrived.[35] By practicing along the progressive path according to what is most conducive, and by fully perceiving what is conducive, a disciple resides within the completely pure levels (*bhūmi, sa*) of enlightenment. By recognizing the treasury of boundless phenomena, the enlightened qualities and the magnificent pristine awareness of the ground expanse, the indivisibility of ground and fruition manifest unusually as natural expressions. In this way, one's own completely perfect consummate abiding reality is regarded as utterly naked, just as it is. This is the level for buddhas alone!
>
> Initially, as one begins to traverse along the path, individuals are inclined toward the expanse of phenomena (dharmadhātu, *chos dbyings*) at various moments during their meditation practice. During these observable processes, what are perceived through gradual meditation are appearances that interfuse with the abiding mode (*gnas tshul*) and the distorted mode (*'khrul tshul*). This perceptive state is threefold: (1) The mere perceptive state due to the meditative mode (*bsgom tshul*) along the path through yoga that is none-other-than the actual abiding mode; (2) The actual nature of the ground, path, and fruition that is ultimate nirvāṇa, self-manifesting pristine awareness; 3) The immense space of never-changing illimitable enlightened qualities. First is how things are, then later through personal experience one enters into certainty regarding what simply exists. In this way, this perceptive state comes about without an object of reference![36]

The natural outcome of traversing the processes of transformation is being an utterly purified buddha being. In the section on fruition, Khenpo Lodrak expounds on the various enlightened dimensions (*sku*), pristine wisdoms (*ye shes*), enlightened qualities (*yon tan*), and activities (*'phrin las*) that are expressed spontaneously while being a buddha:

> Similarly, the residing mode (*bzhugs tshul*) of abiding reality's ground is the existing state of the indivisible ground and fruition. Buddha-nature, that which is one's natural spiritual affinity, is the sublime actual nature of phenomena that occurs during the initial occasion of saṃsāra. To use a metaphor, from the depths of the ocean of the Nāga King to the

> ascended celestial realms, not only all the phenomena of the path and its fruition but also what is definitively real within the basic state that pervades the occasion of saṃsāra's ground as well as the dimension of phenomena's (dharmakāya, *chos sku*) consummate fruition. Once again, metaphorically, just as an incarnation of Brahmā descends below the underground from Brahmā's heavenly abode, likewise it is not only during the occasion of fruition that the phenomenal surface and path reside as abiding reality's elegant actual nature of phenomena.
>
> Like this, without being inclined toward one's spiritual affinity (*gotra*, *rigs*) or the undefiled natural essence of the dimension of phenomena, the very unitary omnipresent undividable nature that pervades every facet of everything remains an undefiled natural existing mode. As for another metaphor, even though the Bhagavān resided on the earth's surface in order to perform the unblemished three secrets for the sake of defected beings, from the timeless and original actuality of phenomena, the abiding reality of unlimited relative phenomena that equals what pervades the three stratums of the world nevertheless resides as innately elegant.[37] This is one's own unblemished and undefiled basic disposition.
>
> Moreover, because incidental fabrications are not merely reduced to vacuous emptiness, the very abiding reality that is the occasion for saṃsāra's ground is always one's unblemished basic disposition. This is the ultimate nature, the nondual dimension of phenomena, the fruition of all buddhas. From time without beginning, this is the absolute dimension of phenomena that is the resultant Mahāmuni.
>
> Residing as the continuum of sentient beings at the time of the ground, this is free from all proliferations at this very instant. Simply as is, this mode is the endowment of supreme yoga. Consequently, the act of its recognition is not similar to an ordinary object of the intellect. Likewise, just as these enlightened dimensions and pristine wisdoms reside within all sentient beings without preference, practitioners along the yogic path—each according to their own mental aptitude—individually recognize, and all experience the singularity of buddhahood.[38]

Khenpo Lodrak presents zhentong according to this coherent structure of ground, path, and fruition because it is understood to be pedagogically effective. If we understand our starting point on the ground, we can more easily and gradually progress along the way toward our destination. The paradox is that the ground is indivisible from its fruit.

Sūtra Zhentong / Tantra Zhentong

Representing the arrangement of the two sources of Indian Buddhist canonical literature from which descriptions of zhentong are cited and derived, the *Great*

Exposition on Zhentong is divided into two sections: (1) sūtra zhentong (*mdo'i gzhan stong*) or exoteric extrinsic emptiness, the philosophical thought of the zhentong tradition that is based on the common or exoteric discourses of the Buddha; and (2) tantra zhentong (*sngags gi gzhan stong*) or esoteric extrinsic emptiness, which refers to the contemplative understanding that is derived from an experience of practicing the six-fold vajrayoga (*rdo rje rnal 'byor yan lag drug pa*) completion stage process of the Kālacakra system, and which more generally derives from Buddhist tantra literature and the *Kālacakra Tantra* in particular.[39]

Distinguishing these two sources for a single zhentong is critically important for Khenpo Lodrak. In fact, at the onset of his work, he sets his intent very clearly by writing, "This composition gradually distinguishes the essential points of the profound meaning of sūtra and mantra [tantra] zhentong according to our own [Jonang] tradition."[40] He goes on to distinguish and contextualize the differences found in the Buddha's teachings:

> Moreover, it is explained like this: All of the eighty-four thousand teachings that were spoken by our teacher are subsumed under two: (1) The causal Pāramitā vehicle; and (2) The resultant Mantra vehicle. As for their profound point, the consummate secret essence falls solely into one single intent.
>
> In this way, with respect to the various faculties and capacities of disciples, there arose various methods for realizing the abiding reality of the three vehicles by means of different practices, according to distinct contexts. The multiple different philosophical systems (*siddhānta*, *grub mtha'*) gradually separated and were thoroughly specified as philosophical systems within their own divisions as they spread throughout the noble land [of India].[41]

Though Khenpo Lodrak accepts that the perfection vehicle (*pāramitāyāna*, *pha rol tu phyin pa'i theg pa*) or causal vehicle (**hetuyāna*, *rgyu'i theg pa*) and the resultant vehicle (**phalayāna*, *'bras bu'i theg pa*) are identical in their destination, they are different in their approaches to the ultimate, and thereby in their presentations of zhentong.[42]

Both the causal and resultant vehicles are understood to progress from the ground through the path to the fruition of complete enlightenment. The causal vehicle's approach toward buddhahood is oriented according to the sūtra (*mdo phyogs*) approach that takes buddha-nature as the causal basis or initial impetus toward buddhahood, while the resultant vehicle's approach is oriented according to the tantra (*sngags phyogs*) approach that recognizes buddhahood to be an ever-present outcome. Corresponding to these distinct approaches to Buddhist practice are two different bodies of Buddhist literature and two lines of transmission from India into Tibet.

Said to have passed orally through the generations as secret teachings (*lkog chos*) until the fourteenth-century efflorescence of the Jonang in central Tibet, sūtra and tantra zhentong were transmitted simultaneously along parallel continuums up to Dolpopa. Synthesizing sūtra and tantra, Dolpopa is credited with having brought these seemingly disparate systems of Indian Buddhist hermeneutical and exegetical thought together, intersecting the Kālacakra transmission lineage with Zhentong Madhyamaka, making secret zhentong more explicit.[43] Interpreting sūtras by means of tantras and vice versa, Dolpopa's interfusion of the technical tantra vocabulary found in the *Kālacakra Tantra* with the philosophical thinking of the Great Madhyamaka consequently redefined the contemplative, intellectual, and literary heritage of the Jonang.

Sūtra Zhentong

The phrase "Great Madhyamaka" (*dbu ma chen po*) varies in meaning according to context and has been applied by a variety of Tibetan scholars, most notably Tsongkhapa Lozang Drakpa (1357–1419), in reference to the Prāsaṅgika-Madhyamaka.[44] However, predating Tsongkhapa, the term is continually reused within Jonang philosophical literature as the name specifying the tradition of zhentong exegesis that is neither Cittamātra nor Prāsaṅgika-Madhyamaka but is synonymous with Zhentong Madhyamaka. In order to clarify this point, Tāranātha makes the distinction between the Common Madhyamaka (*dbu ma phal pa*) or General Madhyamaka (*spyi'i dbu ma*) and the Great Madhyamaka.[45] Defining the General Madhyamaka, Tāranātha's *Essence of Zhentong* reads:

> In Tibet, the General Madhyamaka is known as "rangtong." In both India and Tibet, this system is known to be those who assert that there is no intrinsic essence. The masters of this system are Buddhapālita, Bhāvaviveka, Vimuktasena, and Śāntarakṣita as well as their successors.[46]

While Tāranātha defines the General Madhyamaka as "those who assert that there is no intrinsic essence" (*niḥsvabhāvavādin, ngo bo nyid med par smra ba*), this indefinitely includes both the Prāsaṅgika and Svātantrika approaches to Madhyamaka. In contrast to this General Madhyamaka, Tāranātha goes on to define the Great Madhyamaka:

> In Tibet, the Great Madhyamaka is the Madhyamaka of cognition [only] (*rnam rig gi dbu ma*) and is known as "zhentong." This system is elucidated by the treatises of the majestic Maitreya, Asaṅga, the supreme scholar Vasubandhu, and was greatly clarified by Ārya Nāgārjuna's *Praise to the Ultimate Dimension of Phenomena*.[47]

Consequently, we have two systems of Madhyamaka thought originating in India and taking distinct sets of texts as their doctrinal basis. These are most simply divided into (a) the system of Nāgārjuna according to his *Collection on Reasoning*, and (b) the system of Asaṅga and Maitreya. More specifically, these two exegetical traditions derived from two different Tibetan interpretations of the *Five Maitreya Works* as they were translated from Sanskrit into Tibetan during the late tenth to early eleventh centuries.

Like a string of pearls, the Great Madhyamaka system of zhentong traces its lineal ancestry back through Asaṅga and his half-brother Vasubandhu to Maitreyanātha and his predecessors. With the scholar Brahmin Sajjana, a central figure in the transmission of the *Five Maitreya Works* from Kashmir to Tibet, we find an early division in the methods employed for interpreting these five treatises of Maitreya, the *Uttaratantra* treatise in particular. The differences of interpretation lay with two of Brahmin Sajjana's primary disciples, (1) Lotsāwa Loden Sherab otherwise known as Ngok Lotsāwa (1059–1109) and (2) Tsen Kawoche (b. 1021).[48] Within early Tibetan doxographical literature, this latter system of Tsen Khawoche is referred to as a "contemplative tradition" (*sgom lugs*), while Ngok Lotsāwa's system is known as the "analytic tradition" (*thos bsam gyi lugs*).[49] As these references suggest, the marked distinction between these two traditions is not merely that they accept different sets and interpretations of canonical treatises, but rather that their psychological orientation and methods of transformation are discrete. Articulating a critical tension found in Indian Buddhist archetypes of the individual practitioner—that between the yogin and the scholar—these two traditions encapsulate not only different hermeneutical approaches but dispositions of the Madhyamaka practitioner. In Great Madhyamaka, the contemplative experience is held to be primary while analytical experience is understood to be supportive.[50]

Tantra Zhentong

The Great Madhyamaka elucidates a Buddhist paragdigm about how the relative nature of phenomenal reality is devoid of intrinsic existence or rangtong while the pure, radiant, and continuously effulgent enlightened qualities of ultimate buddhahood are devoid of all superficial obscurations, which is zhentong. This paradigm is not however limited to sūtra sources and presentations but is articulated across a range of Buddhist tantras. Within the Jonang, tantra zhentong is most explicitly revealed in *Kālacakra Tantra*. From its early antecedents up to its contemporary exemplars, the Jonang tradition specializes in this unique tantra, its gnoseological and cosmological thought, and the complex ritual life associated with this esoteric Buddhist literature.

Due largely to its late arrival and reception during the latter transmission and dissemination of Buddhist tantras, the *Kālacakra Tantra* had a profound impact on tantric Buddhist thought and practice in Tibet.[51] As new Tibetan orders emerged during the eleventh through the thirteenth centuries, each sought to align their identity with different aspects of Indic Buddhist thought and praxis, including distinct bodies of yogic and tantric knowledge. While each of these new Sarma orders received and assimilated a complex array of tantras into their newly evolving traditions, each order prioritized and identified with a specific tantra. The Kagyu order aligned with the *Cakrasaṃvara Tantra*, the Sakya order with the *Hevajra Tantra*, the Geluk order with the *Guhyasamāja Tantra*, and the Jonang order with the *Kālacakra Tantra*.

Since there were myriad streams of tantra transmissions occurring and a tremendous cross-fertilization among tantra systems during this formative period, it became incredibly important to synthesize and codify these disparate tantra systems.[52] In the case of the *Kālacakra Tantra*, the Tibetan yogin Kunpang Tukje Tsondru (1243–1313) synthesized seventeen different transmission lineages of the Kālacakra sixfold vajrayoga.[53] This consolidated and recorded existing whispered instructions and oral histories of the tantra for the first time. Kunpangpa's project brought together written and oral instructions from the Tibetan forefathers of the lineage, including those from Yumo Mikyo Dorje (b. 1027), who is claimed to be the earliest author to articulate a view of tantra zhentong.[54] However this history of tantra thought and practice is regarded by the tradition to be normative, and it is not until Dolpopa that the intent of the tantra and the zhentong view was made explicit. As Khenpo Lodrak writes in his *History of the Jonang*:

> The cycle of the Kālacakra teachings—from the time of the kalkī of Shambhala, on through the dissemination of these systems in the noble land of India, until the great Jonangpa master of these teachings [Dolpopa Sherab Gyaltsen] appeared in this world—did nothing more than repeat the sayings of the Rwa and Dro lineages without clarifying our own tradition. Nevertheless, during the latter period of his life, Dolpopa engaged in the intended meaning of the *[Kālacakra] Tantra* and its commentary, the consummation of our [Jonang] tradition.[55]

Keeping with the Great Madhyamaka emphasis on the primacy of contemplative experience, zhentong is a description of an experience of emptiness that is expressed in both sūtra and tantra literature. Though not exclusively limited to Kālacakra practice, within the Jonang context, tantra zhentong refers to an experience that is born directly from the practice of the sixfold vajrayoga completion process of the Kālacakra. The Jonang Kālacakra tradition prioritizes the practice of yoga, the completion stage yoga that is composed of six ancillary phases. This sixfold vajrayoga is: (1) individual withdrawal (*pratyāhāra, so sor sdud pa*), (2) meditative stabilization (*dhyāna, bsam gtan*), (3) harnessing the breath (*prāṇāyāma, srog rtsol*), (4) retention (*dhāraṇā, 'dzin pa*), (5) subsequent mindfulness (*anusmṛti, rjes dran*), and (6) meditative absorption (*samādhi, ting nge 'dzin*).[56]

The word Kālacakra literarlly means "Wheel of Time." Elaborating on the esoteric meaning that the name of the tantra conveys, Bamda Gelek quotes the *Vimalaprabhā* commentary on the root tantra:

> This is how the meaning of Kālacakra is explained:
>
> "Time" (*kāla*) refers to that which is free from the infinitude of

defilement, the wisdom of immutable bliss that realizes the very actuality of all phenomena.

"Wheel" (*cakra*) refers to that which goes completely beyond the limits of the cycle of what can be known within the three worlds. This is wisdom endowed with the very identity of every facet of what can be known without exception and is referred to as "emptiness." This is the image of emptiness: the vajra-dimension. In this way, the enlightened dimension is endowed with every facet of the cycle of what can be known. Time exists due to the gnosis of great immutable bliss: the gnostic dimension.

So, that which is associated with what is known as "time" indicates the single identity of the nature of this twofold enlightened dimension [vajra and gnosis]. Likewise, this is the identity of the indivisibility of bliss and emptiness.

That's why it is called "Wheel of Time."[57]

The phrase in this quote that is being translated here as the "image of emptiness" (*śūnyatā-bimba, stong gzugs*) in reference to the indestructible vajra-dimension is key to the Kālacakra system and critical for understanding tantra zhentong.

Rangtong presentations of emptiness indicate the absence of an intrinsic essence. This refers to both the absence of essence within an egoic self (*gang zag gi bdag nyid*) and the absence of essence within the phenomenal world (*chos kyi bdag nyid*). This emptiness is sometimes specifically named "the emptiness that lacks identity" or "the emptiness of essencelessness" (*ngo bo nyid med pa'i stong pa nyid*). Accordingly, rangtong emptiness is defined as that which is devoid of duality. However, within zhentong contemplative thinking, experience of the ultimate implies an acknowledgment of presence, a constant luminous presence. This presence is known to be synonomous with the image of emptiness that is the natural-born expression of the Kālacakra that emerges for a yogin while practicing the sixfold vajrayoga. That is, according to zhentong tradition, there is something "there" that is not duality.

The abbreviated technical Tibetan term means that there is an image that manifests (*gzugs brnyan*), like a reflection in a mirror, though this term refers to an experience of emptiness that is visceral and somatic, not merely visible or tangible.[58] A point of regular critique is that the image of emptiness is interpreted to be suspended from deep visceral experience. This is not the case. Albeit paradoxical—the term connotes a kind of visual reference, since visual experience is dominant—the danger is to think that the image of emptiness is an external referent (*bāhyārtha, phyi don*) or thing that is sensed objectively. Defining the nature of external referents in the zhentong system, Tāranātha writes in the *Essence of Zhentong*:

In this [zhentong] system, what is not considered to be real is: That which is immaterial, such as the three unconditioned [phenomena]

> and imputed unconditioned [phenomena] as asserted by the Cittamātra system . . . , material forms and so forth that are known to be external referents, the eight types of ordinary awareness, the fifty-one operations of the mind, and in brief—all phenomena outwardly of saṃsāra.[59]

The image of emptiness is not dependent on perception or memory, and therefore not a product of imagination. This is the major point that defines the zhentong view.

The "Three Greats": Mahāmudrā, Dzokchen, and Zhentong

Khenpo Lodrak remarks how the Zhentong Great Madhyamaka tradition of exegesis on buddha-nature arose in sequence with two other systems:

> Here in Tibet, by relying upon different guidance instructions as means for realizing the abiding reality of the Madhyamaka philosophy according to the Mahāyāna, distinct views and practices of Mahāmudrā, Dzokchen, and Madhyamaka arose. In particular, the way for the chariot tradition of the Great Madhyamaka of definitive meaning was eloquently opened by the great Jonangpa master [Dolpopa Sherab Gyaltsen].[60]

Situating the Great Madhyamka tradition alongside Mahāmudrā and Dzokchen, Khenpo Lodrak emphasizes the tantric roots of the Great Madhyamaka, and how the term itself was employed within ancient Tibetan Buddhist doxographical vocabulary.[61] Even though the tradition of Great Madhyamaka associated with the Jonang was not received in Tibet until the later translation period (*phyi dar*) of the Buddhist tantras from India into Tibet, the Dzokchen teachings were received during the early dissemination (*snga dar*) period, and these traditions together are considered the "Three Greats" (*chen po gsum*) of Tibetan Buddhism.[62]

Khenpo Lodrak clearly had an interest in Mahāmudrā and Dzokchen. In a brief guidance text (*khrid yig*), he addressed the distinctions between what he considered to be the four predominant Mahāyāna and Vajrayāna views: (1) zhentong, (2) rangtong, (3) Mahāmudrā, and (4) Dzokchen. In a concise manner, Khenpo Lodrak clarifies points about each view:

> The view of our own [zhentong] tradition is that within the natural lucid radiance of one's own mind, there are coarse and subtle agitations, and there is a gross mentality that fabricates subtle and coarse degrees of laxity. Within the nature of one's own mind, there is an enduring experience of steadiness and stable attention, and there is an infinitely subtle mentality that fabricates these. Pristine awareness is the only unmodified natural flow of freedom; it is the natural manifestation of abiding clear light without fixations, without conceptualizations, and

> without preset references. For the unfortunate, and from the vantage point of those who are less adept, this is difficult to fathom because it lies beyond the domain of what can be expressed through relative thoughts and words.
>
> The view of a rangtong practitioner is that nondual pristine awareness is free from all fixations onto any aspect of what persists as real.
>
> The view of a Mahāmudrā practitioner is that vivid pristine awareness is the mere unmodified cognizance that quells the infinite proliferations of the subject-object complex.
>
> The view of a Dzokchen practitioner is that of primordially pure clear light, naturally manifestating pristine awareness, the radiance of awareness that is the nondual space-awareness that is not corrupted by the qualia of mental fabrications, the forever immutable timeless ground, contemplation of phenomenal reality, the ever-pervasive vast openness, genuine and free from original time, spontaneously arising pristine awareness.[63]

These instructions were given on an occasion when Khenpo Lodrak was making general remarks on the sixfold yoga practices of the Kālacakra and was distinguishing these various views to highlight how reality is regarded from multiple perspectives. The danger with such concise comments is that it's so easy to essentialize these nuanced and profound understandings of the nature of reality. Aware of that danger, and not seeking to decomplexify these views, it's important to note the operative term that Khenpo Lodrak chimes in on is "pristine awareness" (*jñāna*, *ye shes*). This short instruction falls into the subgenre of Tibetan literature that is concerned with making distinctions (*shan 'byed*) about such key terms and concepts. Similar distinctions have been a favorite topic of discussion in Jonang literature since the time of Dolpopa and are considered to be very useful for enhancing one's own understanding of this material and therefore one's own contemplative experience.

Reclaiming Dolpopa's Vision

Inspired by the eclecticsism of Jamgon Kongtrul and Jamyang Khyentse Wangpo, I argue that the early to mid-twentieth century witnessed what surmounted to nothing less than a scholastic renaissance among the Jonangpas in the northeastern cultural domain of Amdo. While myriad sociocultural forces coalesced to create the conditions for this revival, some of the critical factors include: (a) zhentong being elevated and utilized as the philosophical platform for the broader Rimé project; (b) a renewed interest in the yogas of the *Kālacakra Tantra*, particularly by Rimé exemplars; (c) stabilization of the Jonang institutions and monastic colleges in the Dzamtang and Ngawa areas; (d) an intentional exchange with the Geluk scholastic curricula and an appropriation of Geluk-style dialectics for the purpose of presenting zhentong. These forces were coupled with the historical situation that the key intellectuals who inspired this revival lived in Kham and Amdo, under the purview of Qing governance, outside the Ganden Potrang's sphere of influence.

Located on the periphery of Tibet, the Jonangpa spent two and a half centuries rebuilding their institutions and reestablishing their scholastic tradition. By the late nineteenth century, inspired by the creative impulse of Kongtrul and Khyentse, the Jonangpa seized the Rimé vision of ecelecticism as an opportunity to reclaim their own intellectual identity and resituate their identity within the broader intellectual discourse of Tibet. Bamda Gelek and Lozang Chokdrub were two critical Jonang participants in the Rimé historical moment who both in their own ways epitomized this renaissance spirit. There were however numerous other Jonangpa scholars who were instrumental in the reestablishment of the Jonang scholastic tradition in the late nineteenth and early twentieth centuries. Among them were Namnang Dorje from Swe Monastery and Yeshe Gyatso from Drogge Monastery in Amdo Ngawa. Khenpo Lodrak inherited the Rimé vision and, in many ways, his work is the apex of the Jonang participation in this renaissance. For Khenpo Lodrak and his Jonangpa peers however, the task at hand was not merely to legitimate the Jonang but to realign centuries of zhentong philosophical thinking with the pure intent of Dolpopa. This reclaiming of Dolpopa's vision of zhentong is what Tāranātha set out to accomplish in his seventeenth-century writings and what crystallized for Khenpo Lodrak in *The Fearless Lion's Roar* exposition on zhentong.

Notes

1. The codification is an interpretation of two doctrines: emptiness (*śūnyatā, stong pa nyid*) and buddha-nature (*tathāgatagarbha, de bzhin gshegs pa'i snying po*).

2. Ngag dbang, *Rgyu dang 'bras*. See title.

3. See the chapter by Deroche in this volume.

4. Ngag dbang, *Jo nang chos 'byung* 184.

5. Sheehy, "Traversing the Path of Meditation" 171.

6. Sheehy, "Writings of Ngawang Tsoknyi Gyatso" 2.

7. In Tibetan, *Gzhan stong rol mos gad rgyangs*.

8. Blo bzang Mchog grub rgya mtsho's exact dates remain uncertain. We find in his *Collected Works* that he met his own teacher, Kunga Ngedon (1834–1906), at the age of nineteen.

9. See colophon to Tāranātha, *Theg mchog shin tu* 479.

10. Blo bzang Mchog grub rgya mtsho, *Las dang po pa*.

11. Tshogs gnyis Rgya mtsho passed the Kālacakra lineage on to Mkhan po Ngag dbang Blo gros Grags pa.

12. Sheehy, "Writings of Ngawang Tsoknyi Gyatso" 2–3.

13. The titles of these three texts are: (1) *Kun mkhyen jo nang pa chen po'i dgongs pa gzhan stong dbu ma'i tshul legs pa bshad mthar 'dzin gdung 'phrog*; (2) *Kun mkhyen jo nang pa'i bzhes dgongs dbu tshad kyi gzhung spyi dang gung bsgrigs te spyod pa'i spyi don rab gsal snang ba*; (3) *Kun mkhyen chen pos mdzad pa'i grub mtha'i rnam bzhag don gsal gyi 'grel ba phyogs lhung mun sel*. In *Collected Works*. Tshogs gnyis, *Ngag dbang tshogs*.

14. For the full biography of Mkhan po Blo grags, see Mkhan Kun dga' shes rab gsal byed, *Shar 'dzam thang pa*. The publishers of the *Jo nang chos 'byung* also provide a brief

narration of his life written by Btsan lha Ngag dbang tshul khrims. Ngag dbang, *Jo nang chos 'byung* 1–3. In his introduction to the *Jo nang chos 'byung* and *Gzhan stong chen mo*, Kapstein provides a short account of his life based upon the narrative given by the previous publishers of the *Jo nang chos 'byung*, Kapstein. *Contributions to the Study of Jo-nang-pa History* 1–4. Note that he was born in 1920, the year of Iron Monkey (*lcags sprel*).

15. It should be noted that Mi pham Rgya mtsho's famed text on zhentong is titled *The Lion's Roar Proclaiming Zhentong*. See Petit, *Mipham's Beacon of Certainty* 415–427. Mkhan po Blo grags is considered by the Jonang tradition to be the second Mipam.

16. This story was relayed to me orally by Kun dga' Shes rab gsal byed.

17. Kun dga' Shes rab gsal byed, *Shar 'dzam thang pa*, 48. Note that Btsan lha Ngag dbang tshul khrims writes that Mkhan po Blo grags entered the Dar lnga retreat at age nine, Ngag dbang, *Jo nang chos 'byung* 1. The Dar lnga Mountain Retreat (*ri khrod*) is located in Dzamthang, very close to where Mkhan po Blo grags lived, and it remains an active retreat facility for the Jonangpas. The retreat preceptor was 'Dzam ngos Bla ma, a primary disciple of 'Bam mda' Dge legs along with Tshogs gnyis Rgya mtsho.

18. This story was related to me orally while visiting the Dar lnga retreat by a resident monk.

19. The common preliminary practices (*thun mong gi sngon 'gro*) also include the one hundred syllable Vajrasattva recitation (*yig brgya*), maṇḍala offerings, and guru yoga (*bla ma'i rnal 'byor*). Within the Jonang system of Kālacakra practice, the uncommon preliminaries (*thun mong ma yin pa'i sngon 'gro*) are considered to be the generation stage (*bskyed rim*) and the three isolations (*dben pa gsum*).

20. The preceptor here was Ngag dbang Smon lam bzang po. Ngag dbang, *Jo nang chos 'byung*, 3. It is also important to note here that the Jonang succession of transmissions (*brgyud rim*) cites Ngag dbang Smon lam bzang po before Mkhan po Blo grags as his main preceptor for the Kālacakra.

21. Tāranātha, *Zab lam*.

22. 'Bam mda', *Bsdus grwa*. Mkhan Kun dga' shes rab adds that during this time he received several more empowerments, including some from the lineage of Thang stong Rgyal po (1361–1485).

23. Kun dga' Shes rab gsal byed writes that Mati would visit Shambhala on occasion.

24. Among Khenpo Lodro Drakpa' foremost disciples, there is: Ngag dbang Yon tan bzang po (1928–2002), Kun dga' Shes rab gsal byed (b. 1936), Ngag dbang Bsod nams dpal ldan, Ngag dbang 'Jigs med rdo rje, and Ka tog Bla ma rab gsal.

25. The colophon of the *Gzhan stong chen mo* reads that the work began on the fourth day of the fifth month of the Snake Wood year (*shing sbrul*), 1965, and that it was completed on the eighth day of the seventh month of that same year; it was composed at Dpal 'Dzam thang Bsam 'grub Nor bu'i Gling. Ngag dbang, *Rgyud dang 'bras* 508.

26. For a discussion of the core curriculum found within Geluk and Nyingma Tibetan Buddhist studies colleges, see Dreyfus, *Sound of Two Hands* 98–110.

27. For a translation of the *Ri chos*, see Hopkins, *Mountain Doctrine*. Tāranātha's *Theg mchog* is generally referred to as the *Rab byed brgyad* since it is a text discerning eight specific topics on *gzhan stong*: (1) *gnyis min smra ba de dag lta ci smos zhes dbu ma'i rang bzhin ngos bzung ba'i rab tu byed pa ste dang pa'o*, 23; (2) *shes bya'i yul thams cad spyi ldog nas gtan la dbab pa'i rab tu byed pa ste gnyis pa'o*, 29; (3) *sangs rgyas kyi snying po chos kyi dbyings gtan la dbab pa'i rab tu byed pa ste gsum pa'o*, 35; (4) *rnam shes tshogs brgyad sgrub gtan la dbab pa'i rab tu byed pa ste bzhi pa'o*, 42; (5) *chos lnga dang rang bzhin gsum dang rten 'brel gtan la dbab pa'i rab tu byed pa ste lnga pa'o*, 52; (6) *bdag med gnyis gtan la dbab*

pa'i rab tu byed pa ste drug pa'o, 68; (7) *bden pa gnyis gtan la dbab pa'i rab tu dbye pa ste bdun pa'o*, 77; (8) *lam dang 'bras bu gtan la dbab pa'i rab tu byed pa ste brgyad pa'o*, 88. The supplemental notes (*zin bris*) to this masterful work comprise three hundred folios and the last two topics were then commented on by Blo bzang Mchog grub in the *Rab byed phyi ma gnyis gyi 'grel ba*. Tāranātha's *Theg mchog*.

28. For a discussion on the structure of the *Ri chos*, see Hopkins, *Mountain Doctrine* 8–11.

29. These fourteen topics in the *gzhi* section of the *Ri chos*: (1) *dbyings rig dbyer med kyi la thams cad brtan g.yo kun la khyab par bzhugs tshul* [203–211]; (2) *de ltar bzhugs pa de nyid don dam chos nyid kyi dkon mchog gsum ka yin tshul* [211–214]; (3) *yang de nyid bde gshegs snying po yin tshul dpe don mang pos bstan pa* [214–216]; (4) *yang de nyid rang bzhin du gnas pa'i rigs dang don gcig tu bstan pa* [216]; (5) *yang de nyid rgyud sder gsungs pa'i rigs kyi dbye bsdu dang don gcig tu bstan pa* [216–220]; (6) *yang de nyid chos nyid zab mo'i rgyud dang rdo rje'i rigs su bzhugs tshul* [220–225]; (7) *yang de nyid nam mkha' ltar gzhi 'bras ngo bo dbyer med kyi rgyud du bzhugs tshul* [225–229]; (8) *yang de nyid don dam chos sku'i gnas skabs gsum du bzhugs tshul* [229–230]; (9) *yang de nyid de bzhin nyid la sogs pa'i gnas skabs gsum du bzhugs tshul* [230–234]; (10) *yang de nyid nyon mongs pa chen po la sogs pa sngags kyi rigs du marbzhugs tshul* [234–239]; (11) *yang de nyind gzhi 'bras dbyer med kyi myang 'das dang chos sku la sogs par bzhugs tshul* [239–240]; (12) *yang de nyid gzhi 'bras dbyer med kyi chos nyid yongs grub tu bzhugs tshul* [240–241]; (13) *yang de nyin don dam chos sku dang de'i yon tan kun 'dus su bzhugs tshul* [241–252]; (14) *don de ltar 'phags pa klu sgrub yab sras kyang bzhed par bstan pa'o* [252–261].

30. In the *Gzhan stong chen mo*, with these fundamental principles arranged, the second half of this first part moves to address specific philosophical positions at play in the discernment of zhentong as a Buddhist view. Here, Khenpo Lodrak discusses hermeneutical issues involved in interpreting the words of the Buddha, and how philosophical systems fall into the extreme of absolutism (*rtag mtha'*). For a topical outline, see appendix 1 in Sheehy,"The Gzhan stong Chen mo."

31. The corresponding sections are: 1, 2, 3, 4, 8, 9, 12, 13, 14. Sheehy, "The Gzhan stong Chen mo."

32. This is a common reference to the signatures of buddha-nature and is commonly found within the sūtra literature. It is important to note here that I have selected the word "constant" as a translation for the Tibetan term *rtag pa* (*nitya*), which is regularly translated as "permanent." This is a critical technical term in zhentong philosophical thinking and its interpretation has led to variant understandings of zhentong within Tibet. At the end of his *Zab don nyer gcig*, in discussing how this term has been misinterpreted and therefore misunderstood by various Tibetan scholars, Tāranātha assures his readers that if these scholars were to analyze this term properly, they would not be so critical of zhentong. Tāranātha, *Zab don* 221, then continues to explain this term *rtag pa* in the context of its usage within zhentong discourse:

> Furthermore, what is perfect permanence (constancy) is not an insubstantial permanence; this permanence would be the mere opposite of impermanence. This permanence is also not the conditioned permanence that is the permanence of a stream. This is also not the substantial permanence that cannot be known and is asserted by [non-Buddhist] extremists. This is also not a negative permanence that is simply a general truth. Moreover, this is also not asserted

to be likened to an affirmative self-powered permanence. This [permanence] is devoid of fabrications. This is the unchanging expanse that is free from both the negative permanence that is insubstantial and the positive impermanence that is substantial. Even though this is free from the fabrications of permanence and is free from the characteristics of permanence, because this is unchanging, this is the sole permanence.

33. Ngag dbang, *Rgyu dang 'bras* 86.

34. Ngag dbang, *Rgyu dang 'bras* 88.

35. Here it reads, "*gnas tshul chos nyid kyi snang ba bcun tsam dang glo bur bcos ma'i lam gyi snang ba'ang rang 'tsham re 'dres pa'i tshul du de gnyis.*" Ngag dbang, *Rgyu dang 'bras* 88.

36. Ngag dbang, *Rgyu dang 'bras* 88–89.

37. The three secrets (*gsang gsum*) are the concealed states of the (1) body (*sku*), (2) speech (*gsung*), and (3) enlightened mind (*thugs*) of a buddha. The three stratums of the world (*srid pa gsum*) are the subterranean realm of the *nāgās* (*sa 'og gi srid pa*), (2) the terrestrial realm on the surface of the earth where humans live (*sa steng gi srid pa*), and (3) the celestial realm of the devas (*sa bla'i srid pa*).

38. Ngag dbang, *Rgyu dang 'bras* 90.

39. For a record of the sūtra zhentong lineage, see Tāranātha's *Zab mo gzhan stong.* Translated in appendix 2 of Sheehy, "The Gzhan stong Chen mo." For a record of the tantra zhentong lineage, see Tāranātha's *Dus kyi 'khor lo'i brgyud 'debs.* Note that the Sanskrit *ṣaḍ aṅgayoga* is literally "sixfold yoga" while the full phrase in the Tibetan Jonang Kālacakra literature is *rdo rje rnal 'byor ba yan lag drug*, inserting "vajrayoga" into the phrase.

40. Mkhan po Blo grags writes, "*gang de'i rang lugs las brtsams te mdo sngags kyi dbu ma gzhan stong gi zab don gyi gnad rim par phye ba la.*" Ngag dbang, *Rgyu dang 'bras* 40.

41. Ngag dbang, *Rgyu dang 'bras* 40.

42. For a distinction between the causal and resultant vehicles, see Ngag dbang, *Rgyu dang 'bras* 419–424. On this point, Mkhan po Blo grags writes, "*rgyu 'bras theg pa'i mthar thug gi gnas lugs gcig tshul / gnsas skabs slob lam gyi khyad par mi 'dra tshul dang gnyis las.*" Ngag dbang, *Rgyu dang 'bras* 419.

43. Nga dbang, *Jo nang chos 'byung* 97.

44. Most notable is Tsongkhapa, van der Kuijp, *Contributions* 37. The term "Prāsaṅ gika" is a doxographical classification of Madhyamaka that Tibetans retroactively associated with Nāgārjuna.

45. Tāranātha states, "*dbu ma pa la dbu ma phal pa dang dbu ma chen po gnyis*": "There are two systems of Madhyamaka: (1) General Madhyamaka; (2) Great Madhyamaka." Tāranātha, *Gzhan stong snying po* 178. See also Hopkins, *Essence* 55–56.

46. Tāranātha, *Gzhan stong snying po* 178.

47. Tāranātha, *Gzhan stong Snying po* 178. Hopkins, *Essence* 62–63.

48. The *Blue Annals* states, "Though the great lo tsā ba Blo ldan Shes rab and Btsan Kha bo che have heard (their exposition) from the same Sañjana (the text has Sajja-na/ Ch. VI fol. 9b), their methods of exposition of the basic texts show certain differences." Roerich, *Blue Annals* 347. Van der Kuijp notes that "the ultimate source for the two different exegetical traditions that centered on the 'Teachings of Maitreya,' and specifically the *Mahāyānottaratantra*, was Sajjana, a Kashmiri scholar who himself is credited with a commentary on this text." Van der Kuijp, *Contributions* 41. Btsan Kha bo che was also in

Kashmir at the same time as Rwa Lo Rdo rje grags pa and Khyung po Chos kyi brtson 'grus. For an interesting discussion of this meditation tradition, see Mathes, "Pith Instructions."

49. Van der Kuijp makes the point, "It has been variously called '*gzhan-stong dbu-ma chen-po*,' '*rnal-'byor spyod-pa'i dbu-ma*,' '*rnam-(b)rdzun dbu-ma*,' and '*rnam-rig-gi dbu-ma*,' and its pronounced difference . . . seems to stem not only from the fact that it takes a different set of texts as its point of departure, but also—and I think this to be of equal significance—in it implies a different sort of relationship with the religious or mystical experience which Madhyamaka as such attempted to formulate, whether negatively or positively." Then he continues, "the significance of a special kind of psychological disposition which would presuppose this 'Great Madhyamaka' should, I submit, be allotted equal status. This disposition is definitely alluded to in the expression 'meditative school' (*sgom-lugs*) which is employed to describe the essential feature, as opposed to the so-called 'analytical school' (*thos-bsam-gyi lugs*) which denotes its counterpart." Van der Kuijp, *Contributions* 39–40.

50. It should be noted that these claims and associations are largely polemical strategies that by no means define rangtong or zhentong. That is, rangtongpas can value contemplative experience as much as zhentongpas can value scholarship, and vice versa. In fact, however ironically, it was scholarship on zhentong that the Jonangpas sought to revive from the late nineteenth through the twentieth centuries.

51. Sheehy, "Lineage History."

52. Buddhist tantric traditions define authentic transmission (*brgyud*) according to: (1) textual authorization (*lung*) of the tantra, (2) empowerment (*dbang*) of the associated ritual and contemplative practices, and (3) instructions (*khrid*) on the meaning and precise performance of tantric practices.

53. These seventeen sixfold vajrayoga traditions are from: (1) Lotsāwa Gyi jo zla ba'i 'od zer; (2) Lotsāwa Rma dge ba'i blo gros; (3) Khrom Lotsāwa padma 'od zer; (4) Bla ma Nag po mngon shes can; (5) Kha che Paṇchen zla ba dgon po [Kashmiri Paṇḍita Somanātha]; (6) Rwa Lotsāwa chos rab; (7) Tsa mi Lotsāwa sangs rgyas grags; (8) Amoghavajra to Ras chung Rdo rje grags pa; (9–11) Rga lo and Tsa mi; (12–13) Kashmiri Paṇḍita Shakyashri; (14–15) Paṇḍita Vibhūticandra; (16) Paṇḍita Nyi dbang srung ba to Chags Lotsāwa chos rje dpal; (17) Man lung gu ru. Tāranātha, *Rdo rje*, 146–147.

54. Ngag dbang, *Jo nang chos 'byung* 18.

55. Nga dbang *Jo nang chos 'byung* 97.

56. On the sixfold yoga, see Stearns, *Buddha from Dolpo* 104–105.

57. 'Ba' mda' Dge legs rgya mtsho, *Dpal dus kyi 'khor lo'i.*

58. For Dol po pa's usage of this term in zhentong, see Sheehy's chapter in the present volume.

59. Tāranātha, *Gzhan stong snying po* 179–180.

60. Ngag dbang, *Rgyu dang 'bras* 40.

61. Van der Kuijp identifies one of the earliest occurrences of the term *dbu ma chen po* in the *Rnying ma'i rgyud 'bum*. Van der Kuijp, *Contributions* 37. For a discussion on the Great Madhyamaka in the Nyingma tradition, see Dudjom, *Nyingma School* 178–186.

62. The Nyingma tradition originated during the Tibetan imperial period from the eighth to the mid-tenth centuries. This era is known as the "early dissemination" (*snga dar*) or the initial period when tantras were translated from Sanskrit into Tibetan. During this time, the ancient tantras (*rnying rgyud*) were brought to Tibet, arranged, and translated under the direction of the Tibetan king Trisong Deutsen, the Indian abbot Śāntarakṣita, and the Kashmiri master Padmasambhava. The Gsar ma traditions originated during the mid-tenth

century and are comprised of the various cycles of tantras, commentaries, and meditation guidance texts that were translated during this later dissemination (*phyi dar*). On the *chen po gsum*, see van der Kuijp, *Contributions* 37.

63. Ngag dbang, *Khrid yig tshogs* 353–354.

BIBLIOGRAPHY

Tibetan Sources

'Ba' mda' Thub bstan dge legs rgya mtsho. *Bsdus grwa'i spyi don rnam par nges pa chos thams cad kyi mtshan nyid rab tu gsal bar byed pa rin po che'i sgron me*, vol. 1, 1–491. 'Dzam thang.

———. *Dpal dus kyi 'khor lo'i rdzogs rim sbyor ba yan lag drug gi spyi don legs par bshad pa rdo rje bdud rtsi'i chu gter*. In *'Ba' mda' gsung 'bum*, vol. 14, 1–550. 'Dzam thang.

Blo bzang Mchog grub rgya mtsho. *Las dang po pa la nye bar mkho ba'i skal bzang blo gros mig 'byed 'byed*, 1–474. In *'Bras rab 'byams pa blo bzang mthog grub rgya mtsho'i gsung 'bum*, vol. 2.

Khrung go'i bod rig pa dpe skrun khang, 2012.

Btsan Ka bo che. *Gzhan stong gi lta khrid*. In *Jo nang khrid brgya'i brgyud pa'i lo rgyus*. In *Gdams ngag mdzod*, vol. 12, 412–413. Delhi: N. Lungtok and N. Gyaltsan, 1972.

Dol po pa Shes rab rgyal mtshan. *Ri chos nges don rgya mtsho zhes bya ba mthar thug mong ma yin pa'i man ngag*, vol. 3, 189–741. In *Kun mkhyen dol po pa shes rab rgyal mtshan gsung 'bum*. 'Dzam thang.

Kun dga' Shes rab gsal byed. *Shar 'dzam thang pa ngag dbang blo gros grags pa'i rnam thar*. Jonang Publication Series. Mi rigs dpe skrun khang, 2014.

Ngag dbang Blo gros grags pa. *Khrid yig tshogs*, vol. 5, 341–452. In *Blo gros grags pa'i gsung 'bum*, 'Dzam thang.

———. *Jo nang chos 'byung zla ba'i sgron me*. Qinghai: Nationalities Press, 1992.

———. *Phyi nang grub mtha'i rnam bzhag gi bsdus don blo gsal yid kyi rgyan bzang*, vol. 10, 189–295. In *Blo gros grags pa'i gsung 'bum*, 'Dzam thang.

———. *Rgyu dang 'bras bu'i theg pa mchog gi gnas lugs zab mo'i don rnam par nges pa rje jo nang pa chen po'i ring lugs 'jigs med dgong lnga'i nga ro*, vol. 1, 35–516. In *Blo gros grags pa'i gsung 'bum*, 'Dzam thang.

———. *Rgyu dang 'bras bu'i theg pa mchog gi gnas lugs zab mo'i don rnam par nges pa rje jo nang pa chen po'i ring lugs 'jigs med dgong lnga'i nga ro zhes bya ba*. In *Contributions to the Study of Jo-nang-pa History, Iconography and Doctrine: Selected Writings of 'Dzam-thang Mkhan-po Blo-gros-grags-pa*, II. Dharamsala: Library of Tibetan Works and Archives (LTWA), 1993.

Tāranātha. *Dus kyi 'khor lo'i brgyud 'debs*, vol. 2, 177–183. In *Rje btsun tā ra nā tha'i gsung 'bum*. 'Dzam thang.

———. *Gzhan stong dbu ma'i rgyan*, vol. 18, 109–129. In *Rje btsun tā ra nā tha'i gsung 'bum*. 'Dzam thang.

———. *Gzhan stong snying po*, vol. 18, 131–170. In *Rje btsun tā ra nā tha'i gsung 'bum*. 'Dzam thang.

———. *Rdo rje'i rnal 'byor gyi 'khrid yig mthong don ldan gyi lhan thabs 'od brgya 'bar ba*, vol. 4, 123–381. In *Rje btsun tā ra nā tha'i gsung 'bum*. 'Dzam thang.

———. *Theg mchog shin tu rgyas pa'i dbu ma chen po rnam par nges pa'i rnam bshad zin bris*, 85. In *Jo nang je btsun tā ra nā tha'i gsung 'bum dpe bsdur ma*. Beijing: Krung go'i bod rig pa dpe skrun khang, 2008.

———. *Zab lam rdo rje'i rnal 'byor gyi 'khrid yig mthong ba don ldan*, vol. 4, 3–121. In *Rje btsun tā ra nā tha'i gsung 'bum*. 'Dzam thang.

———. *Zab don nyer gcig pa*, vol. 18, 209–222. In *Rje btsun tā ra nā tha'i gsung 'bum*. 'Dzam thang.

———. *Zab mo gzhan stong dbu ma'i brgyud 'debs*, vol. 3, 159–170. In *Kun mkhyen dol po pa shes rab rgyal mtshan gsung 'bum*. 'Dzam thang.

Tshogs gnyis Rgya mtsho. *Ngag dbang tshogs gnyis rgya mtsho gzhan stong phyogs bsgrigs*. Chengdu: Sichuan Nationalities, 2009.

Secondary Sources

Dreyfus, Georges. *The Sound of Two Hands Clapping: The Education of a Tibetan Buddhist Monk*. Berkeley: University of California Press, 2003.

Dudjom, Jikdrel Yeshe. *The Nyingma School of Tibetan Buddhism: Its Fundamentals and History*. Vols. 1–2. Translated by M. Kapstein and G. Dorje. Boston: Wisdom, 1991.

Hopkins, Jeffrey, translator *Mountain Doctrine: Tibet's Fundamental Treatise on Other-Emptiness and the Buddha Matrix*, by Dö-bo-ba Ŝhay-rap-gyel-tsen. Ithaca: Snow Lion, 2006.

———, translator. *The Essence of Other-Emptiness*, by Tāranātha. Ithaca: Snow Lion, 2007.

Kapstein, Matthew. Introduction. In *Contributions to the Study of Jo-nang-pa History, Iconography and Doctrine: Selected Writings of 'Dzam-thang Mkhan-po Blo-gros-grags-pa*. Vols. 1–2. Xylographic Prints from 'Dzam-thang and Rnga-ba, Collected by Dr. Matthew Kapstein and Dr. Gyurme Dorje. Dharamsala: LTWA, 1993.

Mathes, Klaus-Dieter. "The Gzhan stong Model of Reality: Some More Material on Its Origin, Transmission and Interpretation." *Journal of the Internatoinal Association of Buddhist Studies* 34, nos. 1–2 (2011/2012): 187–223.

———. "The Pith Instructions on the Mahāyāna Uttaratantra (Theg chen rgyud bla'i gdams pa): A Missing Link in the Meditation Tradition of the Maitreya Works." In *The Illuminating Mirror: Tibetan Studies in Honour of Per K. Sorensen on the Occasion of his 65th Birthday*, edited by Olaf Czaja and Guntram Hazod. Wiesbaden, 2015.

Pettit, John W. *Mipham's Beacon of Certainty: Illuminating the View of Dzogchen, the Great Perfection*. Boston: Wisdom, 1999.

Roerich, George. *The Blue Annals*. Parts 1–2. Delhi: Motilal Banarsidass, 1996.

Sheehy, Michael R. "Rangjung Dorje's Variegations of Mind: Ordinary Awareness and Pristine Awareness in Tibetan Buddhist Literature." In *Buddhist Thought and Applied Psychological Research*, edited by D. K. Nauriyal, 69–92. Routledge Curzon's Critical Series in Buddhism. London: Routledge Curzon Press, 2005.

———. "The Gzhan stong Chen mo: A Study of Emptiness According to the Modern Tibetan Buddhist Jo nang Scholar 'Dzam thang Mkhan po Ngag dbang Blo gros grags pa (1920–1975)." PhD dissertation, California Institute of Integral Studies, San Francisco, 2007.

———. "A Lineage History of Vajrayoga and Tantric Zhentong from the Jonang Kalachakra Practice Tradition." In *As Long as Space Endures: Essays on the Kalacakra Tantra in Honor of the Dalai Lama*, edited by Edward A. Arnold, 219–235. Ithaca: Snow Lion, 2009.

———. "The Jonangpa after Tāranātha: Auto/biographical Writings on the Transmission of Esoteric Buddhist Knowledge in Seventeenth-Century Tibet." *Bulletin of Tibetology* 45, no. 01 (2009): 9–24.

———. "The Zhentong Madhyamaka Writings of Ngawang Tsoknyi Gyatso (1880–1940)." In *Ngag dbang tshogs gnyis rgya mtsho gzhan stong phyogs bsgrigs*, 1–5. Chengdu: Sichuan Nationalities, 2009.

———. "Traversing the Path of Meditation." In *A Gathering of Brilliant Moons: Practice Advice from the Rimé Masters of Tibet*, edited by Holly Gayley and Josh Schapiro, 171–189. Boston: Wisdom, 2017.

Smith, E. Gene. " 'Jam mgon Kong sprul and the Nonsectarian Movement. In *Among Tibetan Texts: History and Literature of the Himalayan Plateau*, 235–272. Boston: Wisdom, 2001.

Stearns, Cyrus. *The Buddha from Dolpo: A Study of the Life and Thought of the Tibetan Master Dolpopa Sherab Gyaltsen*. Ithaca: Snow Lion, 2010.

van der Kuijp, Leonard W. J. *Contributions to the Development of Tibetan Buddhist Epistemology: From the Eleventh to the Thirteenth Century*. Alt-und Neu-indische Studien, 26. Wiesbaden: F. Steiner, 1983.

Contributors

Marc-Henri Deroche is Associate Professor at Kyōto University (GSAIS, Shishu-Kan), Japan, where he teaches Buddhist studies and cross-cultural philosophy. His doctoral dissertation (École Pratique des Hautes Études, Paris 2011) and a series of articles have investigated the life, works, and legacy of Tibetan author Prajñāraśmi, Terton Sherab Ozer (1518–1584) for the successive revivals of the Nyingma school and the nineteenth-century ecumenical Rimé movement. He is also the coeditor of *Revisiting Tibetan Religion and Philosophy* (2012). His recent research has focused on Dzokchen, including "The *Rdzogs chen* Doctrine of the Three Gnoses" (with Akinori Yasuda, 2015) and a current project on its specific philosophy of vigilance. Having traveled extensively in Tibet and the Himalayas and lived in Kyoto since 2008, his work centers on the philosophical and transcultural significance of the Buddhist paradigm of the development of wisdom according to "listening, reflection, and meditation."

Douglas Duckworth is Associate Professor in the Department of Religion at Temple University. He is the author of *Mipam on Buddha-Nature: The Ground of the Nyingma Tradition* (2008) and *Jamgön Mipam: His Life and Teachings* (2011). He also introduced and translated *Distinguishing the Views and Philosophies: Illuminating Emptiness in a Twentieth-Century Tibetan Buddhist Classic* by Bötrül (2011). He has authored several articles on Buddhist philosophy and serves as coeditor of the *Journal of Buddhist Philosophy.*

Martina Draszczyk, born 1961 in Germany, studied Tibetology and Indology at the University of Hamburg. For many years she acted as an interpreter for Tibetan khenpos at the Karmapa International Buddhist Institute in New Delhi and continued her own training in Buddhist philosophy, epistemology, and meditation with various Tibetan Buddhist teachers. In 2012 she completed her doctoral thesis on *tathāgatagarbha* and Zhentong Madhyamaka at the Department for South Asian, Tibetan and Buddhist Studies of the University of Vienna, Austria. At present she works as a research assistant focusing on Mahāmudrā and various perspectives on buddha-nature at the same department. She also teaches Tibetan Buddhism in the framework of the "Buddhismus Lehrgang" held by the Academy for Buddhism and Christianity in Vienna.

David Higgins received his doctorate from the University of Lausanne, Switzerland, in 2012. He is currently a postdoc research fellow in the Department of South Asian, Tibetan and Buddhist Studies at the University of Vienna, where he is exploring the relationship between Mahāmudrā and Madhyamaka philosophies in Kagyu scholasticism during the postclassical period (15th to 16th c.). His research interests include Indo-Tibetan Buddhist philosophy and epistemology with a particular focus on Kagyu Mahāmudrā and Nyingma Dzokchen doctrinal systems. His doctoral thesis was published under the title *Philosophical Foundations of Classical Rdzogs chen in Tibet: Investigating the Distinction Between Dualistic Mind* (sems) *and Primordial Knowing* (ye shes) (2013). His recent publications include *Mahāmudrā and the Middle Way: Post-Classical Kagyü Discourses on Mind, Emptiness and Buddha Nature*, which he coauthored with Martina Draszczyk.

Matthew T. Kapstein specializes in the history of Buddhist philosophy in India and Tibet, as well as in the cultural history of Tibetan Buddhism more generally. His publications include *The Tibetans* (2006); an edited volume on Sino-Tibetan religious relations, *Buddhism Between Tibet and China* (2009); and a translation of an eleventh-century philosophical allegory in the acclaimed Clay Sanskrit Series, *The Rise of Wisdom Moon* (2009). With Kurtis Schaeffer and Gray Tuttle, he has completed *Sources of Tibetan Traditions* (2013). Kapstein is emeritus Professor of Tibetan Studies at the École Pratique des Hautes Études, Paris, and current Numata Visiting Professor of Buddhist Studies at the University of Chicago.

Yaroslav Komarovski received his PhD from the University of Virginia in 2007 and is Associate Professor of Religious Studies at the University of Nebraska–Lincoln. His research focuses on Madhyamaka and Yogācāra interpretations of the nature of reality and related epistemological, philosophical, and contemplative issues. In particular, he focuses on writings of a seminal Tibetan Buddhist thinker, Shakya Chokden (1428–1507). His major publications include *Tibetan Buddhism and Mystical Experience* (2015) and *Visions of Unity: The Golden Paṇḍita Shakya Chokden's New Interpretation of Yogācāra and Madhyamaka* (2011). His book projects in progress include *Contesting the Ultimate Virtue: Tibetan Buddhist Inquiry into the Virtuous Dimension of Ultimate Reality*, which focuses on Tibetan polemics regarding ultimate reality as a virtue, and *Effulgent Emptiness: Shakya Chokden's Seminal Works on Self- and Other-Emptiness*, an annotated translation of Shakya Chokden's three works on Madhyamaka and Yogācāra.

Klaus-Dieter Mathes is the Head of the Department of South Asian, Tibetan, and Buddhist Studies at the University of Vienna. His current research deals with Tibetan Madhyamaka, Yogācāra, and the interpretations of buddha-nature from the fourteenth to the sixteenth century. He obtained a PhD from Marburg University with a translation and study of the Yogācāra text *Dharmadharmatāvibhāga* (1996). His habilitation thesis was published under the title *A Direct Path to the Buddha Within: Gö Lotsāwa's Mahāmudrā Interpretation of the Ratnagotravibhāga* (2008). Recent publications include *A Fine Blend of Mahāmudrā and Madhyamaka: Maitrīpa's Collection of Texts on Non-conceptual Realization* (Amanasikāra).

Dorje Nyingcha is Associate Professor at the Center for Studies of Ethnic Minorities in Northwest China at Lanzhou University. He began studying Tibetan literature at Northwest Minzu University in Lanzhou where he received his Bachelor of Arts degree in 1995. He received his doctorate in South Asian Studies at Harvard University. His research focuses on biographies and Tibetan Buddhist intellectual history, particularly pre-fourteenth-century intellectual history. His dissertation was on Garungpa Lhai Gyaltsen (1319–1402/3), a student of Dolpopa Sherab Gyaltsen (1292–1361) who became an important scholar and defender of the Jonang tradition in the fourteenth century.

Michael R. Sheehy is Director of Scholarship at the Contemplative Sciences Center and Research Assistant Professor in Tibetan and Buddhist Studies in the Department of Religious Studies at the University of Virginia. He has spent extensive periods collaborating with scholastic and contemplative communities inside Tibet to preserve rare manuscripts in monasteries and private archives across the Tibetan plateau as well as three years training in a Buddhist monastery in the Golok region of far eastern Tibet. His translations and writings give attention to literary and philosophical histories of marginalized traditions of Tibetan Buddhism, specifically the Jonangpa and Shangpa. His current research focus is on meditation manuals and contemplative culture in Tibet. More broadly, his interests abide in the contributions of Buddhism to discourses in the humanities and sciences about contemplative experience, including the use of imagination and visualization, the cultural psychology of meditation, and the dialogue between Buddhism and the sciences.

Dorji Wangchuk is Professor of Tibetan Studies at Universität Hamburg. After completing his studies in a Tibetan Buddhist monastic seminary (*bshad grwa*) in Namdroling monastery in South India, he studied Classical Indology and Tibetology at Universität Hamburg. He wrote his doctoral dissertation on "The Resolve to Become a *Buddha*: A Study of the *Bodhicitta* Concept in Indo-Tibetan Buddhism" and received his PhD from the same university in 2005. Between 1992 and 1996, he taught Tibetan Buddhist monks and nuns in India. Since 1998, he has been teaching and researching at Universität Hamburg in various capacities. He also taught and researched at the University of Copenhagen, McGill University, Renmin University of China, and Tsukuba University. His main teaching and research interests lie in Tibetan Buddhist philosophy, Tibetan Buddhist intellectual history and culture, and Tibetan Buddhist texts and ideas.

Tsering Wangchuk is Assistant Professor and Richard C. Blum Chair in Himalayan Studies in the Department of Theology and Religious Studies at the University of San Francisco. He is the author of *The "Uttaratantra" in the Land of Snows: Tibetan Thinkers Debate the Centrality of the Buddha-Nature Treatise* (2017).

Index

Abhidharma, 2, 110, 119, 123, 206, 217, 224 n. 81, 230 n. 152, 328, 356, 357
Abhidharmakośa, 44 n. 39, 97
Abhisamayālaṃkāra, Ornament of Realization, 4, 5, 11, 99, 117, 126–128, 135 n. 20, 162 n. 27, 166 n. 55, 191 n. 30, 203, 226 n. 103, 224, 251 n. 16 and n. 26, 258, 327, 337
Akṣayamatinirdeśa Sūtra, 3, 104, 105
ālaya (*kun gzhi*), 30, 41 n. 12, 117. See also *ālayavijñāna*
ālayavijñāna (*kun gzhi rnam par shes pa*), 30, 39, 41 n. 12, 60 n. 21, 101–102, 116–118, 128, 133–134 n. 15, 147. See also *ālaya*
Alīkākāravāda, 173–175, 188, 189 n. 5 and n. 12, 331
Amdo, 14, 16, 236, 251, 351, 353–354, 369–370
analytical tradition (*mtshan nyid lugs*), 6
Analysis of Phenomena and Their True Nature. See under *Dharmadharmatāvibhāga*
Analysis of the Jewel Family. See under *Ratnagotravibhāga*
Analysis of the Middle and Extremes. See under *Madhyāntavibhāga*
Analysis of the Three Vows. See under *Distinguishing the Three Vows*
Armor Against Darkness (*Mun pa'i go cha*), 39
Asaṅga, 5, 57, 70, 77, 79, 81, 83, 166 n. 60, 329, 364
Ascertainment of the Three Vows (*Sdom gsum rnam nges*), 14, 237, 238, 246, 251 n. 16 and n. 21. *See also* three vows
Aṣṭasāhasrikā Prajñāpāramitā, 21 n. 51, 126
Ati Yoga, 69, 86
Atiśa, 10, 46 n. 50, 146, 166 n. 60, 342 n. 22
Avataṃsaka Sūtra, 18 n. 24, 79, 164 n. 42, 316 n. 185
awakening mind. See under *bodhicitta*

Bamda Tubten Gelek Gyatso ('Ba' mda' Thub bstan dge legs rgya mtsho), Bamda Gelek, 245, 353–354, 356, 366, 370
Bande Pelyang (Ban de dpal dbyangs), Lotsāwa, 31
Barawa Gyaltsen Pelzang ('Ba' ra ba Rgyal mtshan dpal bzang), 221 n. 38, 249
basis of emptiness (*stong gzhi*), 3, 11, 115, 118, 124, 125, 199, 207, 211, 213, 214, 218
Beacon of Certainty, 16, 23 n. 78, 250 n. 7, 260, 262, 268 n. 2 and n. 8 and n. 15, 269 n. 19 and n. 20 and n. 22, 371 n. 15
Bhavaviveka, 77, 364
Blue Annals, 6, 19 n. 35, 58 n. 1, 110 n. 12, 373 n. 48
Bodhicaryāvatāra, 33, 45 n. 40, 239, 242, 250 n. 11, 258, 261, 269 n. 36, 354
bodhicitta (*byang chub kyi sems*), 31, 32, 34–36, 38, 43 n. 28, 54, 100, 106–107, 145, 177, 180, 186, 193 n. 75, 291, 295 n. 9, 314 n. 159, 356

bodhigarbha (*byang chub snying po*), 8, 29, 32, 33–39, 43 n. 28
bodhimaṇḍa (byang chub snying po), supreme place of awakening, 33–39, 44 n. 37, 45 n. 40
Bodong (bo dong), 247, 252 n. 47
bodhisattva, 14, 33, 38, 55, 85, 119, 134, 159, 177–178, 180, 182–183, 185–188, 191 n. 32, 193 n. 75, 207, 216, 230 n. 148, 237–238, 244, 277, 280, 287, 334, 361
Bon (*bon*), Bonpo, 323, 331, 338, 343 n. 32
Bṛhaṭṭīkā, 8, 21 n. 51, 214, 229 n. 137
Buddhapalita, 77, 129, 130, 328, 337, 342 n. 21, 364
Buton Rinchen Drub (Bu ston Rin chen grub), 10, 66, 83, 96–97, 99, 101, 212, 221 n. 38, 248–249, 253 n. 52, 339, 342 n. 16

Cakrasaṃvara, 69, 86, 357, 366
Candrakīrti, 2, 7, 20 n. 44, 54, 56–57, 59, 61 n. 34, 77, 83, 123–124, 127, 133 n. 7, 138 n. 59, 166 n. 60, 173, 181, 182, 190 n. 28, 193 n. 75, 278, 279, 298, 299 n. 38, 328, 335, 342 n. 21
Catuḥśataka, 242, 252 n. 35
Chodrak Gyatso (Chos grags Rgya mtsho), Seventh Karmapa, 12, 115–116, 119–125, 127, 131, 132 n. 3, 149, 341 n. 11
Chodrak Yeshe (Chos grags Ye shes), Fourth Zhamarpa, 326
Chodrub Sengge (Chos grub Seng ge), 126
Chokle Namgyal (Phyogs las Rnam rgyal), 101–102
Chokle Namgyal (Phyogs las Rnam rgyal), First Karma Trinlepa, 146
Chökyi Jungne (Chos kyi 'Byung gnas), Eighth Situ Paṇchen, 14, 125, 131, 139 n. 68, 200, 339, 352
Chomden Rikpai Raldri (Bcom ldan Rig pa'i ral gri), 9, 53, 58 n. 1, 83
Cittamātra, 20 n. 44, 54, 56–57, 59 n. 13, 61 n. 31, 72, 76–80, 81, 89 n. 24, 90 n. 35, 122, 137 n. 51, 174, 189 n. 12, 198, 204, 205, 213, 214, 228 n. 130, 229 n. 144, 328–329, 331, 338, 354, 364, 368. *See also* Mind-Only
Cittamātra sūtras, 71
Collection of Praises (*Bstod tshogs*), 6, 20 n. 42 173, 243, 337
Collection on Reasoning (*Rigs tshogs*), 77, 173
Collection of Hymns. See under *Collection of Praises*
Compendium of Intentions Sūtra (*Dgongs 'dus pa'i mdo*), 31
Common Madhyamaka (*dbu ma phal pa*), 18 n. 25, 197, 364. *See also* Madhyamaka, Zhentong Madhyamaka, General Madhyamaka, Great Madhyamaka
consciousness, 7, 21 n. 51, 30, 34, 44 n. 37, 56–57, 60 n. 21 and n. 28, 72, 117–118, 121, 123, 128, 130, 133 n. 15, 136 n. 26, 138 n. 59, 147, 178–180, 186, 191 n. 43 and n. 46, 199, 205–206, 220 n. 17 and n. 21, 229 n. 137, 253 n. 48, 259–260, 262–263
contemplative tradition (*sgom lugs*), 6, 9, 340, 352, 357, 365
conventional truth (*kun rdzob bden pa*), 60 n. 28, 100, 118, 148–149, 151, 159–160, 264–267, 292, 314 n. 162. *See also* relative truth

dependent arising, 1, 16, 17 n. 4, 101, 115, 117, 118, 119, 120, 125, 131, 135 n. 23, 148, 158, 240, 261, 267, 284
dependent origination. *See under* dependent arising
Dezhin Shekpa (De bzhin Gshegs pa), Fifth Karmapa, 145
Dharmas of Maitreya. See under *Five Maitreya Works*
Dharmadharmatāvibhāga, Analysis of Phenomena and Their True Nature, 3, 5, 6, 9, 17 n. 16, 18 n. 25, 19 n. 28 and n. 32 and n. 37, 116, 117, 122, 212, 221 n. 39, 221 n. 47 and n. 48 and n. 50, 226 n. 101, 228 n. 126 and n. 130, 337, 342 n. 18
dharmadhātu (*chos dbyings*), 11, 19 n. 40, 100–103, 106, 116, 117, 122, 123, 134 n. 15, 135 n. 20, 137 n. 49, 153–154, 156–157, 159, 161 n. 16, 190 n. 19, 213, 219, 220 n. 16, 276, 293, 295, 337, 361

Dharmadhātustava, Hymn to the Expanse of Reality, 6, 19 n. 40 and n. 41, 20 n. 42, 116, 133 n. 14, 244
dharma-body. See under *dharmakāya*
dharmakāya (*chos sku*), 3, 5, 7, 10, 20 n. 48, 30, 31, 37, 43, 101, 106, 107, 119, 128, 130, 134 n. 15, 147, 150, 153, 154, 156–159, 182–187, 188, 192 n. 54, 193 n. 63 and n. 73 and n. 77, 194 n. 82, 200, 209, 221 n. 29, 226 n. 103 and n. 106 and n. 107, 274, 277, 282, 334, 362
Dharmakīrti, 57, 77, 83, 121, 122–125, 131, 137 n. 44, 138 n. 63, 172, 278, 279, 300 n. 40, 328
Dharmamitra, 81, 83
dharma-sphere. See under *dharmadhātu*
Dignāga, 57, 77, 79, 81, 121–125, 214, 328
Distinguishing the Three Vows (*Sdom gsum rab dbye*), 54, 58 n. 8 and n. 9, 59 n. 10, 246. *See also* three vows
Dolpopa Sherab Gyaltsen (Dol po pa Shes rab rgyal mtshan), Dolpopa, 3, 7–8, 10–17, 18 n. 24, 20 n. 42 and n. 47 and n. 48 and n. 49, 21 n. 50 and n. 51, 22 n. 64, 53–54, 59 n. 14, 60 n. 21, 65–93, 95–102, 107, 109, 125, 127, 128, 130, 132 n.2, 135 n. 24, 140 n. 83, 147, 148, 197–233, 235, 237, 248, 249, 253 n. 48, 263, 269 n. 23, 273, 288, 325, 331, 339, 341, 351, 354–355, 357–359, 364, 366, 368, 369, 370
Dorje Drak Rikzin. *See under* Pema Trinle
Dudjom Rinpoche. *See under* Jikdrel Yeshe Dorje
Dza Patrul Rinpoche. *See under* Patrul Rinpoche
Dzago Geshe. *See under* Lozang Chokdrub Gyatso
Dzamtang (*'dzam thang*), 14, 16, 22 n. 66, 67, 351, 353–357, 369
Dzokchen (*rdzogs chen*), 8, 29–51, 236, 248, 251, 279, 284, 286, 295 n. 9, 296 n. 13, 301 n. 51 and n. 52, 308 n. 113, 310 n. 136, 324, 334, 353, 354, 356, 368–369

early dissemination (*snga dar*), 29, 40 n. 4, 368, 374 n. 62
Eighth Karmapa. *See under* Mikyo Dorje
Eighth Situpa. *See under* Chokyi Jungne
empty form. *See under* image of emptiness
Essence of Zhentong (*Gzhan stong snying po*), 13, 72, 78, 129, 201, 215, 217, 354, 364, 367
Essence Sūtras, 2, 7, 18 n. 24
existential negation. *See under* nonaffirming negation

Fifth Dalai Lama. *See under* Ngawang Lozang Gyatso
Fifth Karmapa. *See under* Dezhin Shekpa
Five Maitreya Works, 4, 7, 9, 74, 77, 99, 203, 243. *See also* Maitreya
four extremes, 15, 236, 288, 315 n. 178
Fourth Council (*Bka' bsdus bzhi pa*), 65–83, 198
Fourth Karmapa. *See under* Rolpai Dorje
Fourth Zhamarpa. *See under* Chodrak Yeshe

Gampopa (Sgam po pa), 145–147, 150, 156, 159, 161 n. 9, 163 n. 39
Gaṇḍavyūha Sūtra, 18 n. 24, 39, 56, 78, 79, 316
Ganden Potrang, 13–15, 237, 251 n. 16, 370
Gangshar Wangpo, Khenpo (Gang shar Dbang po), 16
Garungpa Lhai Gyaltsen (Gha rung pa Lha'i rgyal mtshan), 11, 95–113
Gelong Choshe (Dge slong Chos bshes), 55–56
Geluk (dge lugs), Gelukpa, 1, 13–16, 95, 129, 236, 249, 260, 263, 267, 269 n. 36, 317 n. 187 and n. 188, 323, 325–327, 339, 340, 341 n. 14, 342 n. 21 and n. 22, 346 n. 77, 352–355, 366, 369, 371
General Madhyamaka (*spyi'i dbu ma*), 79, 364. *See also* Madhyamaka, Zhentong Madhyamaka, Great Madhyamaka, Common Madhyamaka
Go Lotsāwa Zhonnu Pel ('Go Lo tsā ba gzhon nu dpal), 6, 17 n. 19, 98, 99, 115, 120, 127, 212, 326, 341 n. 11 and n. 12, 342 n. 22
Gorampa Sonam Sengge (Go rams pa Bsod nams seng ge), 22 n. 64, 236, 246, 250 n. 8, 304 n. 78

great emptiness (*stong pa chen po*), 7, 8, 73, 157, 200, 268
Great Madhyamaka (*dbu ma chen po*), 10, 15, 67, 69, 79–81, 84, 100, 120, 121, 124, 129, 198, 235, 245, 250 n. 6, 323, 331, 364–366, 368, 373 n. 45, 374 n. 49 and n. 61. *See also* Madhyamaka, Zhentong Madhyamaka, General Madhyamaka, Common Madhyamaka
Guhyagarbha Tantra, 31, 34, 38, 311 n.138, 315 n. 174
Guhyasamāja Tantra, 55, 69, 87, 366

Haribhadra, 81, 83, 198, 226 n. 103, 342 n. 21
Hevajra Tantra, 55, 60 n. 18, 146, 160 n. 8, 366
Hymn to the Expanse of Reality. See under *Dharmadhātustava*

image of emptiness (*stong gzugs*), 71–73, 88 n. 14, 367–368
indivisible union, 15, 118, 119, 139. See also *yuganaddha*

Jamgon Kongtrul Lodro Taye ('Jam mgon Kong sprul blo gros mtha' yas), 15–16, 128–131, 140 n. 81 and n. 82 and n. 94, 146, 148–149, 199–201, 219 n. 6, 249, 323–325, 332–333, 336–340, 343 n. 32, 352–353, 369, 370
Jamyang Khyentse Wangpo ('Jam dbyangs Mkhyen brtse'i dbang po), 15–16, 324, 352, 369
Jangter. *See under* Northern Treasure
Jikme Lingpa, 236, 250 n. 12
Jikdrel Yeshe Dorje ('Jigs bral Ye shes rdo rje), 23 n. 76, 236, 251 n. 21
Jñānasārasamuccaya, 242, 252 n. 34 and n. 35
Jonang (*jo nang*), Jonangpa, 3, 9–16, 19 n. 40, 20 n. 46, 53–54, 56–58, 65–93, 95–113, 115, 117, 118, 124, 126–128, 130–132, 132 n. 2, 133 n. 9, 139 n. 70, 147, 148, 160, 197–233, 235, 237, 245, 247, 249, 250 n. 4, 260, 263, 265, 317, 323, 338, 339, 351–377

Kacho Wangpo (Mkha' spyod Dbang po), Second Zharmapa 12, 145–169
Kadam (*bka' gdams*), Kadampa, 1, 8–10, 53–63, 146, 237, 328, 338, 340, 343 n. 30 and n. 35.
Kagyu (*bka' brgyud*), Kagyupa, 11–12, 15, 115–144, 145–169, 199, 200, 201, 249, 323, 324, 326, 338, 339, 341 n. 11, 343 n. 30, 366
Kālacakra Tantra, Kālacakra, 8, 65–93, 97, 197, 198, 218, 284, 314 n. 160, 243 n. 30, 352–354, 356–358, 363–367, 369, 370 n. 11, 371 n. 19 and n. 20, 373 n. 39
Karma Kagyu (*karma bka' brgyud*), 115–144, 145
Karma Trinlepa. *See under* Chokle Namgyal
Kāśyapaparivarta Sūtra, 151, 163 n. 37
Katok Getse Paṇḍita Tsewang Chokdrub. *See under* Tsewang Chokdrub
Katok Monastery (Kaḥ thog dgon), 14, 15, 235, 352
Katok Rikzin Tsewang Norbu. *See under* Tsewang Norbu
Kham, 235, 236, 237, 249
Khenpo Gangshar Wangpo. *See under* Gangshar Wangpo
Khenpo Lodro Drakpa. *See under* Lodro Drakpa
Khyentse Wangpo. *See under* Jamyang Khyentse Wangpo
Kongtrul Lodro Taye. *See under* Jamgon Kongtrul Lodro Taye
Kṛtayuga. *See under* Perfect Eon
kun gzhi ye shes (**ālāyajñāna*), pristine awareness as the substratum, 60 n. 21, 73, 117, 199
Kunga Drolchok (Kun dga' Grol mchog), 9, 12, 21 n. 57 and n. 58, 21–22 n. 59, 22 n. 66, 98, 249, 325, 352–353, 355
Kunpang Tukje Tsondru (Kun spangs Thugs rje brtson 'grus), 97, 366
Kyoton Monlam Tsultrim (Skyo ston Smon lam tshul khrims), 6, 9, 22 n. 60 and n. 63, 53–57, 61 n. 35

Lama Dampa. *See under* Sonam Gyaltsen
Laṅkāvatāra Sūtra, 7, 18 n. 24, 20 n. 44, 55, 56, 59 n. 10, 60 n. 19, 80, 90 n. 35, 101, 115, 122, 128, 130, 151, 258, 268 n. 5

Lelung Zhepai Dorje (Sle lung Bzhad pa'i rdo rje), 14
Lochen Dharmaśrī (Lo chen Dharma shri), 14, 237-238, 246, 251 n. 16 and n. 18 and n. 19 and n. 22 and n. 21 and n. 23, 253 n. 52
Lodro Drakpa (Blo gros Grags pa), Khenpo, 16, 18 n. 24, 20 n. 43, 23 n. 80, 67–68, 70, 77–78, 80, 269 n. 35, 351-377
Lodro Pel (Blo gros Dpal), Lotsāwa, 102
Longchen Rabjam (Klong chen Rab 'byams), Longchen Rabjam Drime Odzer, Longchen Rabjampa, Longchen Drime Ozer, Longchenpa, 15, 16, 38, 96, 235-237, 243, 245-247, 249, 250 n. 3, 252 n. 39, 257, 294, 309 n. 127, 317 n. 187, 331, 339
Lotsāwa Bande Pelyang. *See under* Bande Pelyang
Lotsāwa Lodro Pel *See under* Lodro Pel
Lotsāwa Zu Gawe Dorje. *See under* Zu Gawe Dorje
Lozang Chokdrub Gyatso (Blo bzang Mchog grub rgya mtsho), 16, 353
luminosity, 4, 5, 6, 9, 10, 12, 19 n. 27, 21 n. 53, 22 n. 63, 82, 85, 115, 116, 120, 124–126, 139 n. 79, 147, 150, 157–159, 160 n. 14, 201, 208, 209, 212, 215–217, 284, 286, 304 n. 80, 323, 328, 333, 336

Madhyamaka, 1–5, 7, 11, 15, 19 n. 42, 36, 53, 54, 56–57, 59 n. 13, 61 n. 31 and n. 34, 67, 76–80, 95, 96, 100, 106, 107, 109, 119, 121, 122, 125, 128, 129, 131, 133 n. 7, 140 n. 86, 146, 172, 173, 174, 189 n. 5 and n. 12, 202, 204, 205, 212, 213, 215, 217, 228 n. 130, 236, 240, 245, 247, 248, 257, 259, 260, 262, 264–268, 282, 286, 287, 293, 303 n. 67, 305 n. 86, 311 n. 141 and n. 142, 312 n. 151, 323, 324, 326–329, 331, 337, 338, 339, 341 n. 11, 343 n. 35, 354, 356, 364–365, 368, 373 n. 44 and n. 45, 374 n. 49. *See also* General Madhyamaka, Zhentong Madhyamaka, Great Madhyamaka, Common Madhyamaka
Madhyamakālaṃkara, 56, 57, 60 n. 26 and n. 27, 257, 267, 268 n. 17
Madhyamakāvatāra, 20, 59, 97, 123, 127, 133 n. 7, 139 n. 70, 193, n. 75, 269 n. 26, 298 n. 29, 299 n. 35 and n. 38, 314 n. 162
Madhyāntavibhāga, *Analysis of the Middle and Extremes*, 3, 5, 8, 9, 57, 116, 117, 118, 129, 131, 135 n. 23, 137 n. 52, 190 n. 19, 201, 214–218, 222 n. 47 and n. 50, 259, 299 n. 35, 337, 342 n. 18
Mahāmudrā, 5, 8, 69, 85, 116, 119, 121, 125, 127, 131, 133 n. 3, 145, 146, 148–150, 153, 156, 157, 159, 200, 305 n. 83, 324, 339–340, 341 n. 11, 368–369
Mahāparinirvāṇa Sūtra, 3, 18 n. 24, 41 n. 9, 72, 100–101, 155, 164 n. 44, 296 n. 12, 300 n.45, 308 n. 116
Mahāyānasaṃgraha, 117–119, 126–127, 131, 133 n. 15, 162 n. 21, 189 n. 9, 199, 201
Mahāyānasūtrālaṃkāra, *Ornament of Great Vehicle* Discourses, 4, 5, 122, 123, 190 n. 19, 193 n. 79, 203, 222 n. 47 and n. 48 and n. 49 and n. 50, 239, 262, 337, 342 n. 18
Mahāyānottaratantraśāstropadeśa, 119
Maitreya, 3–9, 58 n. 2, 77, 79, 98, 117, 119, 123, 126, 132 n. 3, 136 n. 35, 149, 164 n. 42, 172, 173, 181, 190 n. 19, 191 n. 30, 198, 199, 202–204, 207, 214, 215, 228 n. 130, 287, 288, 311 n. 139, 327–329, 337, 338, 340, 341 n. 11, 364–365, 373 n. 48. See also *Five Maitreya Works*
Maitrīpa, 5–6, 146, 163 n. 39
Marpa (Mar pa), 146, 163 n. 39, 339, 343 n. 30
Mikyo Dorje (Mi bskyod Rdo rje), Eighth Karmapa, 11–12, 33, 34, 97, 115–119, 126–129, 131, 132 n. 1, 133 n. 7 and n. 12, 135 n. 16 and n. 18 and n. 19 and n. 20, 139 n. 70 and n. 73 and n. 79, 326, 339
Milarepa, 146, 163 n. 39, 339
mind genre (*sems sde*), 31–32, 34, 36, 42 n. 28, 46 n. 51, 312 n.146
Mind-Only, 7, 9, 10, 20 n. 44, 122, 130, 262, 263–264. *See also* Cittamātra
Mindroling (*smin grol gling*), 14, 235–255

Mipam Namgyel Gyatso (Mi pham Rnam rgyal rgya mtsho), 15–16, 23 n. 78, 236, 250 n. 7 and n. 9, 252 n. 29, 257–272, 273–322, 332, 355, 371
momentariness, 11, 119, 120, 230 n. 152
Mountain Dharma, Mountain Dharma: An Ocean of Definitive Meaning (*Ri chos nges don rgya mtsho*), 16, 72, 74–75, 197–198, 210–211, 358

Nāgārjuna, 2, 3, 4, 6, 7, 13, 15, 17 n. 4, 19 n. 40 and n. 41 and n. 42, 20 n. 42, 57, 60 n. 28, 70, 77–79, 83, 122–124, 149, 162 n. 24, 164 n. 41, 166 n. 59, 171–174, 182, 188, 189 n. 5, 192 n. 52 and n. 58, 194 n. 82, 222, 239, 243, 252 n. 27 and n. 37, 257, 287, 288, 300 n. 38, 311 n. 139, 327–329, 335, 337, 338, 359, 364, 373 n. 44
Nāropa, 146, 166 n. 60
Nartang (*snar thang*), 6, 9, 10, 22, 53, 57, 83
nature of mind, 8, 10, 11, 12, 31–33, 35–37, 45, 123–126, 139 n. 79, 158, 199, 200, 226 n. 98, 328, 344 n. 41, 359
negandum. *See under* object of negation
neyārtha (*drang don*), 4, 19 n. 40, 35, 74–75, 150, 212, 247, 253, 310 n. 136, 313 n. 153. *See also* nītārtha
Ngari Paṇchen Pema Wangyel (Mnga' ris Paṇchen padma dbang rgyal), 14, 238
Ngawang Lozang Gyatso, (Ngag dbang Blo bzang rgya mtsho), Fifth Dalai Lama, 13–14, 237, 246, 249–250, 325
Ngawang Tsoknyi Gyatso (Ngag dbang Tshogs gnyis rgya mtsho), 16, 354
Ngok Loden Sherab (Rngog Blo ldan shes rab), 6, 55, 247, 342 n. 16
Niḥvabhāvavāda, 172–174, 181, 189 n. 5 and n. 12, 190 n. 13, 191 n. 32, 328
nirvāṇa, 106–107
nītārtha (*nges don*), 4, 19 n. 40, 74, 150, 212, 253, 310 n. 136, 311 n. 138, 313 n. 153. *See also* neyārtha
nonaffirming negation (*med dgag*), 6, 173, 240–241, 243, 247, 248, 260–262, 268 n. 17, 269 n. 27, 281, 324, 336, 345 n. 54
nonconceptual, 2, 5, 36, 106, 107, 133 n. 9, 135–136 n. 24, 136 n. 29, 161 n. 14, 210, 225 n. 93, 226 n. 103, 242, 244, 245, 251 n. 26, 258–259, 262, 268, 270 n. 43, 332, 333
nonimplicative negation. *See under* nonaffirming negation
Northern Treasure, Jangter, 14, 237
Nubchen Sangye Yeshe (Gnubs chen Sangs rgyas ye shes), 31
Nyawon Kunga Pel (Nya dbon Kun dga' dpal), 96
Nyingma (*rnying ma*), Nyingmapa, 8, 14–16, 17 n. 17, 23 n. 76, 29–51, 235–255, 260, 265, 267, 279, 284, 288, 293, 308 n. 113, 314 n. 160, 317 n. 187, 323, 324, 326, 329, 334, 338–339, 343 n. 30, 352, 355, 356, 371 n. 26, 374 n. 61 and n. 62

object of negation (*dgag bya*), 7, 11, 115, 118, 120, 123, 131, 132, 201, 207, 213, 221 n. 32, 222 n. 54, 224 n. 77, 229 n 137, 241, 261, 270 n. 43, 289
Ornament of Great Vehicle Discourses. See under *Mahāyānasūtrālaṃkāra*
Ornament of Realization. See under *Abhisamayālaṃkāra*

Pakmodrupa (Phag mo Gru pa), 247
Paṇḍita Sajjana. *See under* Sajjana
Pāramitāyāna, 181, 288, 363
Patrul Rinpoche (Dpal sprul Rin po che), 251 n. 16, 353, 354
Pawo Tsuklak Trengwa (Dpa' bo Gtsug lag 'phreng ba), 126
Pema Trinle (Padma 'Phrin las), 237, 251 n. 20
Perfect Eon, Kṛtayuga (*rdzogs ldan*), 8, 65–93
Prajñāpāramitā, Prajñāpāramitā Sūtra, Prajñāpāramitā sūtras, 4–5, 18 n. 21, 24 n. 24, 21 n. 51, 69, 80, 81, 84, 107, 126, 129, 152–154, 156, 159, 238, 286, 293, 303 n.67, 353, 356, 357
pramāṇa, 36, 121–125, 137 n. 44, 206, 278

Pramāṇavārttika, 124, 300 n. 40 and n. 41. *See also* pramāṇa
Pramāṇaviniścaya, 121, 137 n. 44. *See also* pramāṇa
Prāsaṅgika, Prāsaṅgika-Mādhyamika, 16, 109, 128, 140 n. 86, 202, 203–204, 210, 212, 222 n. 49, 236, 240, 243, 245, 248, 270 n. 43, 287–289, 311 n. 140, 312 n. 147, 312 n. 151, 328–329, 331, 333, 337, 338–339, 341 n. 11, 342 n. 21, 343 n. 35, 354, 364, 373 n. 44
Prasannapadā, 127
pristine awareness as the substratum. See under *kun gzhi ye shes*
Profound Inner Principles (*Zab mo nang don*), 116–118, 126, 128, 160, 199–200

quantum entanglement, 1

Rangjung Dorje (Rang byung Rdo rje), Third Karmapa, 12, 96, 99, 115–120, 125, 126–128, 131, 132 n. 1 and n. 3, 135 n. 17 and n. 21 and n. 22 and n. 23, 136 n. 27, 145–149, 155, 159, 160, 160 n. 7, 161 n. 8, 198–201, 218, 220 n. 14 and n. 16, 247, 249, 253 n. 49
rangtong (*rang stong*), 1–16, 18 n. 21, 30, 56, 69, 70, 71, 73–82, 89 n. 20 and n. 23, 99–100, 116, 119–120, 126–127, 129–131, 146–152, 157, 159, 163 n. 38, 171–174, 181–182, 188, 189 n. 5, 191 n. 37, 192 n. 52, 197–198, 203–204, 211–213, 222 n. 54, 238, 240, 246, 260, 263, 265, 267, 269 n. 26, 273, 288, 332–333, 336, 339, 351, 364, 365–369, 374 n. 50
Rangtong Madhyamaka, 79, 338
Ratnagotravibhāga, *Ratnagotravibhāga-vyākhyā*, *Analysis of the Jewel Family*, 3–6, 11, 17 n. 15 and n. 19, 19 n. 27 and n. 28 and n. 29 and n. 37 and n. 38, 30, 35, 39, 40 n. 5, 41 n. 9, 44 n. 37, 97, 99–109, 116, 118–119, 124, 126–128, 130, 132 n. 2, 133 n. 5, 136 n. 32, 140 n. 83, 146–147, 150, 151, 158, 160 n. 7, 164 n. 42, 166 n. 55, 189 n. 11, 193 n. 63, 197–200, 203, 209, 210, 212, 214, 216–218, 219 n. 5, 222 n. 48, 226 n. 105, 228 n. 125, 230 n. 153, 337, 341 n. 11. *See also* Uttaratantra
Ratnaśrī, 14
relative truth (*kun rdzob bden pa*), 5, 7–8, 11, 15, 116, 118, 128, 130, 132, 139 n. 79, 258, 268, 332. *See also* conventional truth
Remdawa Zhonnu Lodro (Red mda' ba Gzhon nu blo gros), Remdawa, 10, 11, 96–97, 100–101, 104, 106–109
Rikral. *See under* Chomden Rikpai Raldri
Rikzin Tsewang Norbu. *See under* Tsewang Norbu
Rimé, 15–16, 249, 323–349, 352–355, 360, 369–370
Rolpai Dorje (Rol pa'i Rdo rje), Fourth Karmapa, 145
Rongton Sheja Kunrik (Rong ston Shes bya kun rig), 200, 339
Rongzom Choki Zangpo (Rong zom Chos kyi bzang po), Rongzompa, 32–37, 235, 250 n. 2, 257, 274, 275–276, 278–279, 287, 289, 291, 293, 294 n. 3, 295 n. 7 and n. 9 and n. 11, 296 n. 13, 297 n. 18, 298 n. 25 and n. 27, 299 n. 36, 300 n. 45 and 46, 301 n. 47 and n. 48 and n. 51 and n. 53 and n. 54 and n. 55 and n. 56, 302 n. 60 and n. 62, 305 n. 84, 308 n. 113 and n. 116 and n. 118, 309 n. 124 and n. 127 and n. 128, 310 n. 133 and n. 134 and n. 135 and n. 136, 311 n. 138, 312 n. 146, 313 n. 157, 314 n. 159 and n. 168, 315 n. 170 and n. 174, 316 n. 185, 317 n. 187

Sajjana, Paṇḍita Sajjana, 6, 9, 10, 21 n. 57, 59 n. 15, 61 n. 35, 77, 98–99, 119–120, 125, 131, 365, 373 n. 48
Sakya Paṇḍita Kunga Gyaltsen (Sa skya Paṇ di ta kun dga' rgyal mtshan), 53, 97, 189 n. 5, 312 n. 146, 342 n. 16
Sakya (*sa skya*), Sakyapa, 1, 12, 22 n. 64, 95, 96, 284, 307 n. 101, 317 n. 187, 323, 324, 326, 328, 338, 339, 342 n. 20, 366

Samādhirāja Sūtra, *Aryasamādhirāja*, 2, 17, n. 3, 30, 41 n. 9, 104, 105, 129, 253 n. 50
Sandhinirmocana Sūtra, 3–4, 7, 11, 18 n.23, 20 n. 44, 80, 104, 107, 129
Sangpu, 96, 237
Śāntarakṣita, 31, 41 n. 11, 57, 181–182, 190 n. 12, 216, 252 n. 34, 339, 342 n. 21, 364, 374 n. 62
Sapan. *See under* Sakya Paṇḍita Kunga
Saraha, 78, 148, 162 n. 24, 163 n. 39
Sarma (*gsar ma*), 288, 289, 329, 334, 365
Sautrāntika, 45, 61 n. 34, 129, 174, 247, 331, 338, 342 n. 21
Sazang Mati Paṇchen (Sa bzang Ma ti pan chen), 53, 102, 127, 132 n. 2, 198, 219 n. 12
Second Zharmapa. *See under* Kacho Wangpo
Seventh Karmapa. *See under* Chodrak Gyatso
Shakya Chokden (Shakya Mchog ldan), 3, 11–12, 16, 116, 125–127, 129–132, 136 n. 31, 139 n. 70, 171–196, 197–233, 325–327, 330, 331, 333, 339, 341 n. 14, 342 n. 20, 343 n. 27, 344 n. 47
Situ Paṇchen. *See under* Chokyi Jungne
sixfold yoga (*ṣaḍaṅgayoga*), sixfold vajrayoga, 8, 71–73, 89 n. 14, 100, 352–353, 356–357, 363, 366–367, 369, 373 n. 39, 374 n. 53 and n. 56
Sonam Gyaltsen (Bsod nams Rgyal mtshan), 96
Śrīmālādevī Sūtra, *Śrīmālādevīsiṃhanāda Sūtra*, *Śrīmālādevīsiṃhanādanirdeśa Sūtra*, 3, 18 n. 24, 41 n. 9, 101, 11 n. 28
Sthiramati, 79, 135 n. 24, 217, 219 n. 142
substratum consciousness. See under *ālayavijñāna*
**sugatagarbha* (*bde bar gshegs pa'i snying po*), 29, 35, 39 n. 3, 42 n. 27, 247–248
sūtra zhentong, 16, 20 n. 43, 358, 362–365, 373 n. 39. *See also* tantra zhentong
Sūtras on the Definitive Meaning, 2, 7, 18 n. 24
svābhāvikakāya, 3, 156, 211, 226 n. 103
Svātantrika, Svātantrika-Madhyamaka, 202–204, 210, 212, 216, 240, 245, 287–289, 311 n. 140, 312 n. 147 and n. 151, 328–329, 333, 337–339, 342 n. 21, 364

tantra zhentong, 16, 353, 358, 362–364, 365–369, 373 n. 39. *See also* sūtra zhentong
Tāranātha (Tā ra nā tha), 3, 10, 11–14, 16, 22 n. 60 and n. 65, 53, 54, 57, 58, 66, 71–72, 77–80, 84, 88 n. 4, 89 n. 24 and n. 29, 97, 125, 129–130, 133, 140 n. 91 and n. 92 and n. 94, 147, 197–233, 249, 250 n. 4, 253 n. 54, 339, 352–365, 358, 364, 367, 370, 370 n. 9, 371 n. 21 and n. 27, 372 n. 32, 373 n. 39 and n. 45 and n. 46, 374 n. 53 and n. 59
tathāgatagarbha (*bde bzhin gshegs pa'i snying po*), Tathāgatagarbha, 2, 3, 29, 30, 35, 42 n. 27, 45 n. 42, 73, 116, 124, 145, 202, 215, 243, 251, 273, 300 n. 42, 303 n. 67, 355, 370 n. 1
Tathāgatagarbha Sūtra, 3, 17 n. 9, 18 n. 24, 41 n. 9, 60 n. 25, 115. *See also* Tathāgatagarbha sutras
Tathāgatagarbha sutras, 3, 17 n. 9, 100, 103–104, 106, 119, 130, 198, 338. *See also Tathāgatagarbha Sūtra*
Teaching of Mountain Hermit. See under *Mountain Dharma*
Terdak Lingpa Gyurme Dorje, 14, 237, 238, 246, 249, 251 n. 18, 253 n. 49
Terse Pema Gyurme Gyatso, 238, 251 n. 16
Third Karmapa. *See under* Rangjung Dorje
three natures. See under *trisvabhāva*
three turnings, 70–71, 95, 96, 98, 103–106. *See also* Wheels of Dharma
three vows, 238, 246. See also *Ascertainment of the Three Vows*, *Distinguishing the Three Vows*
Treasury of Knowledge (*Shes bya kun khyab mdzod*), 128, 131, 146, 160 n. 5, 201, 333
Trengpo Terton Sherab Ozer, Prajñāraśmi, 294 n. 3, 324
trisvabhāva, 2–4, 7–10, 56, 80, 90 n. 34 and n. 35, 116, 131, 147, 198, 200–202, 205, 210, 214–218, 230 n. 152, 252 n. 36, 259, 338

Tsen Kawoche, 6, 9–10, 22 n. 60, 61 n. 35, 77, 79, 98–99, 365
Tsewang Chokdrub (Tshe dbang Mchog grub), 15, 235, 250 n. 5 and n. 6
Tsewang Norbu (Tshe dbang Nor bu), 14–15, 235, 352
Tsongkhapa Lozang Drakpa (Tsong kha pa Blo bzang grags pa), 11, 15, 21 n. 51, 90 n. 41, 129, 229 n. 142, 236, 251 n. 12, 267, 269 n. 25 and n. 26 and n. 38, 270 n. 44, 273, 288, 326, 328, 339, 341 n. 14, 342 n. 22, 345 n. 72, 364, 373
Tukwan Lozang Chokyi Nyima (Thu'u bkwan Blo bzang chos kyi nyi ma), 97
two truths, 15, 16, 89 n. 20, 96, 101, 118, 128, 135 n. 23, 146, 148–149, 162 n. 25, 188, 199, 200, 212, 217, 220 n. 20 amd m/ 21, 223 n. 70, 258–260, 265, 267, 268, 268 n. 8 and n. 43, 327, 343 n. 35, 344 n. 47. *See also* ultimate truth, relative truth, conventional truth

ultimate truth, 2, 5, 8, 11, 15, 20 n. 49, 53, 56, 85, 95, 100, 102, 103, 107, 115, 117, 118, 123, 128, 130, 135 n. 20, 140 n. 79, 148–150, 154, 200, 206, 208, 211, 213–218, 224 n. 85, 225 n. 86 and n. 93, 240, 257–258, 260–262, 265–268, 269 n. 25 and n. 43. *See also* two truths, relative truth, conventional truth
Uttaratantra, 53–58, 58 n. 2, 59 n. 10 and n. 13 and n. 14 and n. 15, 60 n. 17 and n. 25, 61 n. 35, 89 n. 23, 209, 365, 382. See also *Ratnagotravibhāga*

Vaibhāṣika, 128, 129, 174, 247, 338
Vajrayāna, 46 n. 47, 74, 80, 83, 95, 335–337, 356, 368
valid cognition (*tshad 'bras*), 11, 16, 120, 121–122, 174, 206, 275, 277–278, 286, 299 n. 37
Vasubandhu, 8, 19 n.32, 21 n. 51, 53, 57, 70, 77, 79, 81, 83, 116, 198, 214–216, 220 n. 22, 243, 328, 329, 337, 338, 364, 365
Vimalaprabhā, 67, 74, 366
Vimuktisena, 83, 198, 226 n. 103
Vyākhyāyukti, 116

Wheels of Dharma, 4, 60 n. 22. *See also* three turnings

Yeshe De (Ye shes Sde), Zhang, 30, 342 n. 16
Yogācāra, 2–8, 10, 15, 17 n. 5 and n. 15 and n. 17, 20 n. 44, 30, 39, 56–57, 61 n. 34, 77, 89 n. 24, 95, 96, 100, 116–117, 119, 122–125, 129–131, 135 n. 24, 146–147, 172, 173, 181, 189–190 n. 12, 198, 200–202, 213–218, 221 n. 32, 225 n. 93, 226 n. 103, 228 n. 130, 230 n. 152, 240, 247, 248, 252 n. 31 and n. 36, 257–272, 291, 312 n. 147, 328, 342 n. 21, 344 n. 41
yuganaddha (*zung 'jug*), 15, 273–322, 333.
Yumo Mikyo Dorje, 97, 366

Zhalu, 83, 96
Zhang Yeshe De. *See under* Yeshe De
Zhentong Madhyamka (*dbu ma gzhan stong*), 10, 14, 16, 18 n. 24, 65, 67–68, 76–80, 81, 121, 129, 149, 197, 203, 221 n. 32, 267, 339–340, 353–354, 357, 358, 364. *See also* Great Madhyamaka, Common Madhyamaka, General Madhyamaka, Madhyamaka
Zu Gawe Dorje (Gzus Dga' dba'i rdo rje), Lotsāwa, 6
Zur lineage, 236

www.ingramcontent.com/pod-product-compliance
Lightning Source LLC
Chambersburg PA
CBHW020120240426
43673CB00038B/542
9781438477589